Archival Insights into the Evolution of Economics

Series Editor
Robert Leeson
Stanford University
Stanford, CA, USA

This series provides unique insights into economics by providing archival evidence into the evolution of the subject. Each volume provides biographical information about key economists associated with the development of a key school, an overview of key controversies and gives unique insights provided by archival sources.

More information about this series at
http://www.palgrave.com/gp/series/14777

Robert Leeson

Hayek:
A Collaborative
Biography

Part XII: Liberalism in the Classical Tradition,
Austrian versus British

Robert Leeson
Department of Economics
Stanford University
Stanford, CA, USA

and

Notre Dame Australia University
Fremantle, Australia

Archival Insights into the Evolution of Economics
ISBN 978-3-319-74508-4   ISBN 978-3-319-74509-1   (eBook)
https://doi.org/10.1007/978-3-319-74509-1

Library of Congress Control Number: 2018934642

© The Editor(s) (if applicable) and The Author(s) 2018
This work is subject to copyright. All rights are solely and exclusively licensed by the Publisher, whether the whole or part of the material is concerned, specifically the rights of translation, reprinting, reuse of illustrations, recitation, broadcasting, reproduction on microfilms or in any other physical way, and transmission or information storage and retrieval, electronic adaptation, computer software, or by similar or dissimilar methodology now known or hereafter developed.
The use of general descriptive names, registered names, trademarks, service marks, etc. in this publication does not imply, even in the absence of a specific statement, that such names are exempt from the relevant protective laws and regulations and therefore free for general use.
The publisher, the authors and the editors are safe to assume that the advice and information in this book are believed to be true and accurate at the date of publication. Neither the publisher nor the authors or the editors give a warranty, express or implied, with respect to the material contained herein or for any errors or omissions that may have been made. The publisher remains neutral with regard to jurisdictional claims in published maps and institutional affiliations.

Printed on acid-free paper

This Palgrave Macmillan imprint is published by the registered company Springer International Publishing AG part of Springer Nature
The registered company address is: Gewerbestrasse 11, 6330 Cham, Switzerland

Contents

Part I Two Competing Neoclassical Traditions

1 'Austrian Thought and Fascism': 'The Victory of Fascism in a Number of Countries Is Only an Episode in the Long Series of Struggles Over the Problem of Property'   3

2 'Persuade the Intellectuals in the Hopes that Ultimately They Could Be Converted and Transmit My Ideas to the Public at Large'   65

3 Hayek and Aristocratic Influence   103

4 Pigouvian Market Failure   155

Part II Seeing the Utopian 'Theory of the Order as a Whole' to 'Make Politically Possible What Today may be Politically Impossible'

5 Britain, White Supremacism and the 'International Right'   195

6	The 'Free' Market 'Emergency' Demand for 'Fascism'	265
7	'[Italian] Fascism'	305
8	Austrian 'Instincts,' Serfdom, and Spanish and Portuguese 'Fascism'	339
Bibliography		367
Index		407

Dramatis Persona

Austria School founder

- Carl Menger (1840–1921)

Second-generation leaders

- Eugen Böhm Ritter von Bawerk (1851–1914) objected to democracy's 'costly concessions' (presumably, to non-aristocrats);
- Friedrich Freiherr von Wieser (1851–1926) labelled a 'Fascist' because his magnum opus *Gesetz der Macht* (*The Law of Power*) contains 'anti-Semitic statements and an abstract *Führerkult* ... as well as sources indicating the contrary';

Third-generation leaders

- Othmar Spann (1878–1950), the 'Philosopher of Fascism,' introduced Hayek to the Austrian School of Economics and the *Wandervogel*;
- Hans Mayer (1879–1955) is described by Hayek (whose dissertation he supervised) as 'a ferocious Nazi';
- Ludwig 'Elder von' Mises (1881–1973), card-carrying Austro-Fascist and member of the official Fascist social club, aspired to be the intellectual *Führer* of a Nazi-Classical Liberal Pact;

- Joseph Schumpeter (1883–1950) made anti-Semitic remarks and diary notes and was 'unsure whether Hitler would be good or bad for Germany';

Fourth-generation leaders

- Friedrich 'von' Hayek (1899–1992) promoted the deflation that facilitated Hitler's rise to power, created the 'consistent doctrine' of the Mont Pelerin Society (MPS), was awarded the 1974 Nobel Prize for Economic Science for a fraudulent assertion about having predicted the Great Depression, promoted 'Deacon' McCormick's fraud that the founder of the market failure school, A. C. Pigou, was a gunrunner for Stalin despite knowing that 'He may be sometime [*sic*] making things up' and that the crucial evidence was 'pretendedly [*sic*] based on a diary of Pigou';
- Murray Rothbard (1926–1995), 'hate' was his 'muse,' sought to 'accelerate the Climate of Hate in America' through a 'free' market 'outreach' to 'redneck' militia groups, 'Deacon' McCormick promoter, celebrated the first bombing of the World Trade Centre and spotted other building for Al-Qaeda to attack;

Followers—Hayek's 'worst inferior mediocrities'

- Donald McCormick, aka Richard Deacon (1911–1998), *Sunday Times* Foreign Manager, 'free' market fraud, over lunch with Hayek at the Reform Club, displayed Pigou's 1905 diary which 'pretendedly' contained 'evidence' that the inventor of externality analysis was Stalin's agent;
- Harold Benjamin Soref (1916–1993), Conservative M.P., Chairman of the Monday Club Africa and Rhodesia study groups and policy committees, Reform Club member, white supremacist, Standard Bearer at the British Union of Fascists Olympia rally, 'Deacon' McCormick promoter: 'The academic background of the traitors is consistent. It appears to have originated with the pioneering work of Prof. A. C. Pigou ... it would appear that espionage is largely an upper middle class preserve. The working class operators, being merely in it for the money, are less ideologically motivated';

- Hans Sennholz (1922–2007), Professor of Economics, Grove City College, a 'Misean for Life' *Luftwaffe* bomber pilot who rested 'his defense of a free society on revelation ... divinely revealed information';
- William Rees-Mogg, Baron Rees-Mogg (1928–2012), Roman Catholic MPS member, Hayek-promoter, London *Times* editor (1967–1981), must have known that Hayek was a liar;
- Nigel Lawson, Baron Lawson of Blaby (1932–), 'spontaneous order' and privatisation promoter, having overseen the 1986 'Big Bang' deregulation of British financial markets that preceded the Global Financial Crisis, now oversees the climate change 'denialist' Global Warming Policy Foundation;
- Sir Samuel Brittan (1933–), 'spontaneous order' promoter, economics correspondent, *Financial Times*, having uncritically repeated 'von' Hayek's lies, now sits on the Academic Advisory Council of the Global Warming Policy Foundation;
- Leonard Liggio (1933–2014), New York University (NYU) 'Post-Doctoral Fellow,' widely described as, in effect, the bagman of the 'free' market, 'birthright Catholic,' to capture of the state promoted the emulation of the Nazis strategy of creating 'group identity,' is now 'spending eternity with the Master he worshiped';
- Ralph Raico (1936–2016), Professor of History, Buffalo State College, having translated *Liberalism in the Classical Tradition* in which Mises promoted 'Fascists,' 'Germans and Italians,' including 'Ludendorff and Hitler,' insisted that Mises was actually referring to '[Italian] Fascism';
- Arthur Laffer (1938–), economic advisor to Donald Trump, as 'Dr. Laffer' was dismissed by (or obliged to resign from) the University of Chicago for not having a Ph.D.;
- Gary North (1942–), Presuppositionist public stoning theocrat, Mises Institute 'Medal of Freedom' holder, 'Deacon' McCormick promoter;
- Sudha Shenoy (1943–2008), after studying undergraduate economics for five years, was awarded a lower second-class degree and was then listed as 'Dr. Sudha Shenoy' by her employer, the Institute of Economic Affairs, as their 'privatisation' authority to be contacted;
- Kurt Leube (1943–) has no post-secondary qualifications and, according to Hayek, was unable to pass his undergraduate economics units, but as 'Dr. Kurt Leube D.L.E,' 'Abitur/Matura (B.A.) 1954–1963,' 'Economic Philosophy at LSE (UK) 1963–1965,' 'AJD, University

Salzburg, 1971,' 'DLE,' became Professor of Economics, California State University, Hayward/East Bay;
- Llewelyn Rockwell Jr. (1944–), co-founder with Rothbard of the Ludwig von Mises Institute, believed to be the co-author (with Rothbard and North) of the racist and homophobic fund-raising *Ron Paul Newsletters*;
- Mark Skousen (1947–), Mormon missionary, Columbia University Professor, Ludwig von Mises Institute ex-Fellow, founder of 'Freedomfest the world's largest gathering of free minds,' CIA intelligence officer, 'free' market 'wealth building' newsletter salesman, 'Deacon' McCormick promoter: 'It's difficult to say at what point Pigou shifted views and became an underground supporter of revolutionary causes … there is considerable evidence that he had been an underground agent for revolutionary causes much earlier in his career';
- David Gordon (1948–), Mises Institute Senior Fellow, editor of *The Mises Review*, repeats the 'consistent doctrine': Mises' promotion of 'Fascists,' 'Germans and Italians,' including 'Ludendorff and Hitler,' actually related to '[Italian] Fascism';
- Leon Louw (1948–), as 'Dr. Leon Louw,' created a 'CFACT' lobby at the 2011 Durban United Nations Climate Change Conference to 'Debunk Climate Change Propaganda and Provide Balanced Perspective';
- Richard Ebeling (1950–) doubted that John Maynard Keynes could pass any Austrian-examined undergraduate units, earned a living as an NYU 'Post Doctoral Fellow,' sixteen years before being given a Ph.D. by Middlesex Polytechnic/University, proud of the role he played in the privatisation of post-communist Russia (that facilitated the rise of Putin and 'Russia of the Oligarchs'), regarded by the MPS President as unworthy of financial support because he is a 'total fool,' 'Deacon' McCormick promoter': Pigou was both the 'father of modern welfare economics' and part of the 'web of subversion … an important and respected voice of academic reason and reflection' who was calling for deliberate redistribution of wealth and a gradual transformation of the market economy into a socialist planned society … a world-renowned scholar holding up the Soviet Union as a model of a good, caring society (at the very moment that Stalin's Great Purges were sending millions to their execution or to the slave-labour camps of the Gulag). What more legitimate

advocate of socialism and the Soviet Union could be imagined? There was one major problem with Pigou's supposedly disinterested analysis and policy prescriptions: he was a Soviet secret agent. In the interwar years, he served as a recruiter for the Soviet secret police';
- Christopher Monckton (1952–) created (along with 'Dr. Leon Louw') a 'CFACT' lobby at the UN Climate Change Conference, informed by the Clerk of the Parliaments: 'you are not and have never been a Member of the House of Lords';
- Bruce Caldwell (1952–), President of the History of Economics Society, official Hayek biographer, funded by Duke University and the John W. Pope Foundation (which is the sixth largest contributor to what is regarded as the 'Climate Change Counter Movement'), in 'History in the Service of Ideology' (a review of a book in which Mises' card-carrying Austro-Fascist status was revealed) repeats the 'consistent doctrine': although he praised universal 'Fascism,' including 'Germans and Italians,' 'Ludendorff and Hitler,' Mises actually only praised '[Italian] Fascism';
- Matthew White Ridley, 5th Viscount Ridley (1958–), recipient of the 2011 Manhattan Institute Hayek Book Prize, Old Etonian *Times* columnist, having presided over the first run on a British bank since 1866 (Northern Rock), now sits as a member of the Academic Advisory Council of Lawson's Global Warming Policy Foundation;
- Peter Boettke (1960–), Vice-President for Advanced Study and Director of the F. A. Hayek Program for Advanced Study in Philosophy, Politics, and Economics at the Mercatus Center, BB&T Professor for the Study of Capitalism, University Professor of Economics and Philosophy at George Mason University, 'Charles Koch Distinguished Alumnus, The Institute for Humane Studies,' Presuppositionist President of Hayek's MPS, who claims (falsely, it seems) to have held 'visiting professorships at Stanford' and 'completed a post-doc fellowship at Stanford University.'

The 'free' market 'Use of Knowledge in Society'

- 'Deacon' McCormick, Hayek, Skousen, Ebeling, Soref, etc.: externalities were invented by an underground Communist;
- Ebeling and Fox News: National Public Radio is run by Nazis;

- Boettke: 'I love Mises to pieces. His is a story of scientific glory and personal courage in a very dark time in human history. He stood against those forces with the tools of reason embedded in economic science at its finest, and he survived courageously and in doing so provides us with an exemplar of scientific economist, scholar of political economy, and bold and creative social philosophy.'

PART I

Two Competing Neoclassical Traditions

CHAPTER 1

'Austrian Thought and Fascism': 'The Victory of Fascism in a Number of Countries Is Only an Episode in the Long Series of Struggles Over the Problem of Property'

1.1 Hypothesis to Be Tested

Just before the outbreak of World War II, Hayek (1997 [1938], 183) appeared to encourage his readers to focus—not on the Nazi threat (which he referred to as 'fascism') but—on 'the problems which begin when a democracy begins to plan': we may be

> witnessing one of the great tragedies in human history: more and more people being driven by their indignation about the suppression of political and intellectual freedom in some countries [Germany and Austria?] to join the forces which make its ultimate suppression inevitable. It would mean that many of the most active and sincere advocates of intellectual freedom are in effect its worst enemies and far more dangerous than its avowed opponents, because they enlist the support of those who would recoil in horror if they understood the *ultimate consequences*. (emphasis added)

Two years later, Mises (2009 [1978 (1940)], 30) provided some definitive mythology: 'The Austrian School of economics was Austrian in the sense that it emerged from the soil of an Austrian culture that National Socialism would trample down.' And in their 'definitive' 'Friedrich Hayek and His Visits to Chile,' Caldwell and Leonidas Montes (2014a, 3; 2014b; 2015, 263) complained about (unspecified) attempts to 'establish links between Austrian thought and fascism.' The evidence, however, reveals that the Austrian School of Economics is synonymous with both anti-Semitism and the promotion of *political* 'Fascism.'

This *Archival Insights into the Evolution of Economics* (AIEE) series provides a systematic archival examination of the process by which economics is constructed and disseminated. All the major schools will be subject to critical scrutiny; a concluding volume will attempt to synthesise the insights into a unifying general theory of knowledge construction and influence. But two decades as an historian of economic thought was an inadequate preparation for the 2009-planned two-volume *Hayek: A Collaborative Biography*.

Eight years of research later, an unambiguous conclusion emerges: the 'free' market Austrian School of Economics is a not a school of economics—it is a franchised pyramid scheme, a 'bullet train to financial freedom' for frauds, paid sycophants, public stoning theocrats, white supremacists and those with blind faith in the assertions made by socially 'superior' fellow-travellers (Chapters 5 and 8).[1]

To survive, feudalism and neo-feudalism require 'spontaneous' deference to intergenerational entitlements programmes (and the titles by which the government-chosen ones identify themselves). Which school of economics—or any other discipline—embraces ascent into the upper reaches of the income and wealth distribution in return for accepting the self-identifying title of 'worst inferior mediocrities' and 'secondhand dealers':

> what I always come back to is that the whole thing turns on the activities of those intellectuals whom I call the 'secondhand dealers in opinion,' who determine what people think in the long run. If you can persuade them, you ultimately reach the masses of the people. (Hayek 1978, Chapter 2, below)?[2]

After the President of Hayek's Mont Pelerin Society (MPS), Bruno Leoni (1913–1967), was hacked to death by an underworld business associate, Hillsdale College President, George Roche III (1935–2006), emerged as the premier 'free' market fund-raiser and morality-promoter. Roche became a fund-raising liability when his daughter-in-law, Lissa Jackson Roche, was either murdered or committed suicide after confessing to George Roche IV that she had been having sex with his father for nineteen years (Rapoport 2000).

Caldwell—who replaced Roche as the premier 'free' market fund-raiser—may have made a million dollars for himself in a single month on the back of Glenn Beck's Fox News promotion of the *Definitive Edition* of Hayek's (2007 [1944]) *The Road to Serfdom* (Leeson 2015a). Caldwell (2010) then informed readers of *The Washington Post* that 'Hayek himself disdained having his ideas attached to either party.'[3] Yet both the Hayek Archives (which Caldwell seeks to monopolise) and the public record reveal that Hayek was a party political operative for the Conservative Party, the Republican Party and the no-party Operation Condor dictatorships.

This 'free' market influences the public and public policy through a variety of sources including Rupert Murdoch's *Times*, *Sunday Times*, Fox News and *Wall Street Journal* editorial pages; plus inflammatory right-wing radio celebrities such as Rush Limbaugh. The History of Economics Society (HES) is the vehicle through which Austrian 'free' market 'scholars' seek academic credibility. According to Caldwell, 'Friedrich Hayek and His Visits to Chile' was the 'Winner of the Foundation of [sic] Economic Education (FEE) 2015 Best Article Award'[4]: an institution described by Hayek as a 'propaganda' set-up.[5] And at the 2016 Duke University HES conference, it was awarded the 'Craufurd Goodwin Best Article in the History of Economics Prize.'[6] Caldwell is a Past HES President.

Charles Koch's 'academic efforts' have received 'widespread acceptance—in universities like Brown, Dartmouth, and Duke' (Glassman 2011). Goodwin (1988)—the long-time Duke University *History of Political Economy* editor (1969–2009) who in conversation expressed concern about the Austrian colonisation of his community—is the author of 'The Heterogeneity of the Economists' Discourse: Philosopher, Priest, and Hired Gun.' Boettke (2014)—who describes the HES community as 'gullible': they play 'ideological checkers' while he plays 'scholarly chess'—is the 'Charles Koch Distinguished Alumnus, The Institute for Humane Studies.'[7]

Assertions made on behalf of the 'free' market are true because they are made—not by angry callers to right-wing talkback radio but—by 'Dr'-Professors of Economics and 'think' tank Fellows or Senior Fellows (regardless of how those titles were acquired). But economic science rests on evidence—not dressed-up assertions.

1.2 SECOND GENERATION 'AUSTRIAN THOUGHT AND FASCISM'

- Ritter von Bawerk
- 'Freiherr von' Wieser

The academic and senior Federal Reserve economist, J. Herbert Fürth (26 February 1992), reported to his brother-in-law, Gottfried Haberler, that Wieser was anti-Semitic.[8] According to Eugen-Maria Schulak and Herbert Unterköfler (2011, 42), Wieser was labelled a 'Fascist' because his magnum opus *Gesetz der Macht* (*The Law of Power* 1983 [1926]) contains 'anti-Semitic statements and an abstract *Führerkult* ... as well as sources indicating the contrary.'[9]

Wieser (1983 [1926], 226) reflected on the consequences of the 'Great' War: 'When the dynastic keystone dropped out of the monarchical edifice, things were not over and done with. The moral effect spread out across the entire society witnessing this unheard-of event. Shaken was the structure not only of the political but also of the entire social edifice, which fundamentally was held together not by the external resources of power but by forces of the soul. By far the most important disintegrating effect occurred in Russia.'

Four years after Mises (1922, 435) asserted that 'The Lord of Production is the Consumer' ('*Der Herr der Produktion ist der Konsument*'), Hayek (1952 [1926], 555, 567) revealed an attitude that is inconsistent with disinterested scholarship: Wieser

> inspired an admiration coming close to worship among all who came under the spell of his powerful personality. Readers of his work cannot fail to be impressed by his human greatness and universality ... The form of exposition raises this favorite child of the great man [Menger] far above the rank of ordinary scientific literature. Wieser's [1983 (1926)] last book is a fitting demonstration of the general truth that a work which is carried

by a great idea assumes the characteristics of a great piece of art. Having as its architect a *sovereign* master of science, it reaches a towering height above all indispensable detail and becomes related to *artistic creation*. In this last work, where Wieser shakes off the fetters of specialization and disciplinary methods, his unique personality emerges in all its greatness, combining a universal interest in all fields of culture and art, worldly wisdom and experience, detachment from the affairs of the day, *sympathy for the fellow-man*, and freedom from narrow nationalism. In him the civilization of old Austria had found its most perfect expression. (emphasis added)

If 'God' sanctioned the 'entire social edifice' of Wieser's 'monarchical' hierarchy, what would legitimise its replacement? The 'Fascists' that Mises (1985 [1927], 49, 51) praised overthrew democracy in Italy (1922) and then in Spain (1923). Wieser (1983 [1926], 371) praised both: 'In Mussolini, Fascism had a leader of electrifying eloquence, eyes for the future, and determined energy. *The King lent his support to the movement* (emphasis added), which acknowledged its authority, and the army gave its consent. In Spain, the army with its officers was the backbone of the movement. The army had kept in perspective the state as an integral whole, and Primo de Rivera, who took the lead, could feel assured of its following. Mussolini and Primo de Rivera, much as they rely on the military power resources, are nevertheless far from bent on a military dictatorship, let alone a Caesarean rule. They do not want to rise against the idea of democracy, but only against its abuses, and they want to be guided by public opinion, whose following they take as an endorsement. The goal they are striving after would be attained once the old party leadership has been eliminated and the masses had been united under strong national leadership.'

According to Hayek (1978), 'Wieser was much more what one commonly would call an intuitive thinker.'[10] From the Russian Revolution to the collapse of the Soviet Union (1917–1991), fear of Communist expansion dominated world history. Adolf Hitler legitimised the 1945–1989 Russian colonisation of Eastern Europe—of which the 1919 Hungarian Soviet Republic had been a prelude. But referring to Hitler's 1923 Munich *Putsch*, Wieser (1983 [1926], 370)—nine years after the Bolshevik revolution—asserted: 'If Russia and the experiences in Hungary and Munich are disregarded, the upheaval after the World War may be said to have taken place without intervention of dictatorship.

The revolutionary intensity was not high enough for that. To be sure, emergency powers had to be invoked in order to effect the transition to the new order after the collapse of the legitimate governments, but the overwhelming majority everywhere met quickly on the new legal foundation.'

Referring to the 1920 attempted *Putsch* that inspired 'Ludendorff and Hitler,' Wieser (1983 [1926], 370) continued: 'For all that, there were still groups who resisted in words and even in deeds, as exemplified by the Kapp Putsch, not to mention the many people who resign themselves to the new state of affairs only with inner reservations. Little by little the sentiments of the opposition came more united, and the desire for regulating dictator became increasingly more fervent. But, strangely, the reaction against the democratic current did not openly come to the fore in the states directly involved in the upheaval, but in victorious Italy and neutral Spain.'

A legitimate noble title requires a legitimate royal source: a *fons honorum* (the 'fountainhead' or 'source of honor'). Hayek (1978) reflected that the Great War was a 'great break in my recollected history.'[11] It also broke the Habsburg nobility: coats of arms and titles ('Ritter,' 'von,' 'Archduke,' 'Count,' etc.) were abolished on 3 April 1919 by the *Adelsaufhebungsgesetz*, the Law on the Abolition of Nobility. Violators face fines or six months jail. Republics transform 'subjects' into 'citizens': the status of 'German Austrian citizens' equal before the law in all respects was forcibly imposed on Austrian nobles (Gusejnova 2012, 115).

In 'The Cultural Background of Ludwig von Mises,' Erik 'Ritter von' Kuehnelt-Leddihn (n.d.) dated the Austrian *Déluge*:

1908, when the disastrous 'one man-one vote' principle was introduced.

Over a century later, the President of the tax-exempt Mises Institute described the 'free' market 'emergency' war on democracy: 'democracy is a sham that should be opposed by all liberty-loving people … Democracy was always a bad idea, one that encourages mindless majoritarianism, political pandering, theft, redistribution, war, and an entitlement mentality among supposedly noble voters' (Deist 2017).

Referring to contemporary democracy, Hayek (1978) told James Buchanan: 'Even a dictator can say no, but this kind of government cannot say no to any splinter group which it needs to be a majority.'[12] In 1914, Böhm-Bawerk complained: 'We have seen innumerable variations of the vexing game of trying to generate political contentment through material concessions. If formerly the Parliaments were the guardians of thrift, they are today far more like its sworn enemies. Nowadays the political and nationalist parties … are in the habit of cultivating a greed of all kinds of benefits for their co-nationals or constituencies that they regard as a veritable duty, and should the political situation be correspondingly favorable, that is to say correspondingly unfavorable for the Government, then political pressure will produce what is wanted. Often enough, though, because of the carefully calculated rivalry and jealousy between parties, what has been granted to one [group] has also to be conceded to others—from a single costly concession springs a whole bundle of costly concessions' (cited by Ebeling 2010a, 77).

Böhm Bawerk had previously developed Austrian business cycle theory and published *Karl Marx and the Close of His System* (1949 [1896]) and a three-volume *Capital and Interest* (1959 [1888, 1890, 1903]) later translated by Sennholz and republished by Libertarian Press. According to Pepperdine University's George Reisman (2002, 26), Böhm-Bawerk is the 'most important Austrian economist after Ludwig von Mises.' At age 15, Reisman and Raico were recruited 'to hold out through the long libertarian winter of the 1960s and 1970s, thus enabling the breakthrough of Misesian ideas of the 1980s and 1990s' (Hülsmann 2007, 847–848, 896).

1.3 Third Generation 'Austrian Thought and Fascism'

- Spann
- Mayer
- 'Elder von' Mises
- Schumpeter

Mises (1912) developed Böhm-Bawerk's business cycle theory, which Hitler embraced to destroy democracy in Austria and Germany, and which Mises and Hayek used as a knowledge 'front' behind which to promote the deflation that assisted the Nazis rise to power (Leeson 2018a).

Spann was on the moderate anti-Semitic wing: Jews, he argued, should be allowed to live within a corporate ghetto but excluded from society (Wistrich 2012, 237). Schumpeter made anti-Semitic remarks and diary notes, and was 'unsure whether Hitler would be good or bad for Germany' (cited by Swedberg 1992, x–xii). In the Austrian corporate state (*Ständestaat*), Oskar Morgenstern, Hayek's successor as Director of the Austrian Institute of Business Cycle Research, made anti-Semitic comments while presenting himself as the leader of the Austrian School of Economics (Leonard 2010). The support provided by Morgenstern for a 'strong state' would, according to Stephanie Braun, lead to him being 'much misunderstood; for he will be reproached for favoring political fascism for the sake of sound economic policies' (cited by Klausinger 2006, 31, n. 26).

For almost three decades, Sudha Shenoy's non-existent 'The Order of Liberty' biography of Hayek was listed as 'forthcoming' on her cv. The second part of Caldwell's 'definitive' nuanced hagiography will, apparently, be titled 'Hayek: The Philosopher of Liberty.' Boettke (2011, 26) obliges his George Mason University (GMU) graduate students to read Caldwell's (2004) 'celebrated' biography which 'contextualizes (as the title suggests) the development of Hayek's ideas from his student days to his final writings in terms of the intellectual debates he was involved with and the goals he set for his research program in the social sciences. Hayek had a vision, Caldwell identifies it, and then we learn of the trials and tribulations that Hayek faced in seeing that vision through.' When Hayek (1978) arrived at the University of Vienna in 1918, 'somebody put me on to Carl Menger and that caught me definitely.'[13] That somebody was 'Othmar Spann: The Philosopher of Fascism' (Polanyi 1934, 1935)—the dominant influence over Hayek's student days (Leeson 2017, Chapters 5–8).

Wieser retired and 'was succeeded by Mayer, his favorite disciple,' in the year that Hayek (1978) finished his 'first degree.'[14] Mayer—later described by Hayek as 'a ferocious Nazi'—steered 'his protégés through the *habilitation* procedures: Haberler (1927), Morgenstern (1929) and Hayek (1929)' (Klausinger 2014, 198; 2015). Mises (2009 [1978 (1940)], 83) reported that after *Anschluss*,

> Mayer wrote to all members issuing notice that all non-Aryan members were to take leave of the *Nationalökonomische Gesellschaft* [Austrian Economic Association], 'in consideration of the changed circumstances in

German Austria, and in view of the respective laws now also applicable to this state.' This was the last that was heard of the society.

Into the 1950s, Mayer was still recruiting converts such as Karl Socker (1990, 1) to the Austrian School of Economics—Mayer remained a 'fierce supporter of Wieser.'

'Free' Market Believers (FMB) look at Evidence, past (E_{t-1}), present (E_t) and future (E_{t+1}), and see Salvation (*S*); non-FMB do not. In 1926, Mises established the Institute for Business Cycle Research primarily to provide 'academic' employment for Hayek (Hülsmann 2007, 454). The following year, Mises' (1985 [1927], 49, 51) *Liberalism in the Classical Tradition* issued a blunt 'eternal' instruction:

> *It cannot be denied* (emphasis added) that Fascism and similar movements aiming at the establishment of dictatorships are full of the best intentions and that their intervention has, for the moment, saved European civilization. The merit that Fascism has thereby won for itself will live on eternally in history.

The 'similar movements' of 'bloody counteraction' that Mises referred to included the anti-Semitic '*l'Action Française*' plus 'Germans and Italians.' 'Italians' obviously referred to Mussolini's *Il Duce* dictatorship (1922–1943); Mises' (1985 [1927], 44) reference to 'Germans' and 'Ludendorff and Hitler' refers, just as obviously, to the 1923 Ludendorff-Hitler Bavarian *Putsch*—the prelude to the *Führer's* Third Reich (1933–1945).

In a footnote—which they deleted in the Chilean version of their paper—Caldwell and Montes (2014a, 3, n. 8; 2014b, 263, n. 8) provide their 'definitive' statement: 'We might simply point out the other obvious fact that, as a Jew and a Classical Liberal, Mises was *persona non grata* among both the Nazi and Stalinist regimes ... He is as unlikely a candidate for being considered a fascist as he is for being a communist.' Their academically unpublishable paper was published un-refereed in the 'referred,' Rothbard-founded, Boettke-edited *Review of Austrian Economics* and republished in *Estudios Públicos*, the journal of the Chilean *Centro de Estudios Públicos* (Centre for Economic Studies) of which Hayek had been Honorary President.

Boettke (2016a) praised Mises' 'bold and creative social philosophy.' And in *The Last Knight of Liberalism*, Guido Hülsmann (2007,

560, n. 68, 677, n. 149) complained about 'the absurd contention that Mises endorsed Fascism'—before revealing, in a footnote, that Mises was a card-carrying Austro-Fascist. The Austria *Heimwehr* ('Home Defence Guard'), a private military organisation similar to the Nazi SS (*Schutzstaffel*: 'Protective Front'), split into Austro-Fascist and Nazi wings. In September 1933, the Austro-Fascist wing joined the new *Vaterländische Front* ('Fatherland Front'). On 1 March 1934, at the Austrian Chamber of Commerce (*Kammer*) where he worked as a business sector lobbyist, Mises became member number 282632 of the Fatherland Front and member number 406183 of *Werk Neues Leben*, the official Fascist social club. Mises was also the quasi-official theoretician of the Austro-German business sector—many of whom funded the Nazis (Leeson 2018a). The day after *Anschluss*, several Chamber of Commerce

employees greeted each other with 'Heil Hitler.' (Ebeling 2010a, 128)

Mises (1985 [1927], 49–51) declared that Austrian School economists and 'Fascists' were allies but differed in tactics: 'What distinguished liberal from Fascist political tactics is not a difference of opinion regarding the use of armed force to resist armed attackers, but a difference in the fundamental estimation about the role of violence in a struggle for power.' Violence was the 'highest principle' and must lead to 'civil war. The ultimate victor to emerge will be the faction strongest in number … The decisive question, therefore always remains: How does one obtain a majority for one's own party? This however is purely an intellectual matter' (Chapter 2).

1.4 Fourth Generation 'Austrian Thought and Fascism'

- 'von' Hayek
- Rothbard

From the Peterloo Massacre (16 August 1819) to the Law on the Abolition of Nobility (3 April 1919), neo-feudalism retreated before a new spontaneous order: advancing democracy. Unable to openly propose a return to 'rotten boroughs'—where the choice of elected 'representative' typically lay in the visible hand of one person or family—Hayek created 'rotten academics.' His nostalgia related to the Golden Age of 'liberty'—before the 1832 Great Reform Act:

> the present situation, which is only a 150-year event. The beginning of it was 150 years ago. Before that, there was never any serious revolt against the market society, because every farmer knew he had to sell his grain.[15] Things became stationary and our whole thinking in the past 150 years or 200 years has been dominated by a sort of rationalism. (Hayek 1978)[16]

In 1942, Mises wrote a confidential report for the Habsburg Pretender 'on the conditions under which a restoration could be achieved' (Hülsmann 2007, 818).[17] As Hayek was writing *The Road to Serfdom*, the Austrian School philosopher, Erik 'Ritter von' Kuehnelt-Leddihn (pseudonym F. S. Campbell), published *The Menace of the Herd* (1978 [1943]). Austrians embrace monarchy, or anything but democracy (Hoppe 2001), pope and monarch, supported by a 'natural aristocracy' (Rockwell 1994), a 'small, self-perpetuating oligarchy of the ablest and most interested' (Rothbard 1994) or 'dictatorial democracy'[18]—a 'system of really limited democracy' (Hayek 1978).[19]

James Buchanan (1973, 8) complained about rent-seeking: 'Unfortunately, few who have looked carefully at the workings of American democracy would dare predict that the general interest can prevail over divergent special interests. Precisely because they do have special interests, offering them measurable and directly identifiable gains, individuals and groups are willing to invest both time and financial resources in influencing political outcomes.' In 'What Is to Be Done?' a 'Strictly Confidential' conspiracy to use tax-exempt educational funds for 'political arena' purposes, Rothbard (2010 [1961], 8–9)—funded by special interests—declared:

> I think that here we can learn a great deal from Lenin and the Leninists ... the setting forth of what 'revolutionaries' can do to advance their principles ... Our objective is, of course, to advance our principles—to spread libertarian-individualist thought (from now on to be called 'libertarian' for short) among the people and to spread its policies in the political arena. This is our objective, *which must never be lost sight of*. (Rothbard's emphasis)

Leninists correctly calculated that they could never win open franchise elections; and in 1917, they aborted the embryonic Russian democracy. But if what Hayek called 'unlimited democracy' was replaced by a franchise restricted to loyal party members, 'democratic centralism' could guarantee preordained outcomes.

Rothbard (2010 [1961], 8–9) continued:

> We must, then, always aim toward the advancement of libertarian thought, both in its creative development, and its *spread among the intellectuals* and eventually the 'masses.' This is the ultimate essence of our aim, this advancement of the 'hard core' of libertarian thought and libertarian thinkers. The group of totally libertarian thinkers is, in short, the 'hard core' or the 'cadre' ... as individualists and rationalists, as people who want to see individual intellectual excellence and moral principles fostered in society, we favor *intellectual* [emphases added] as opposed to 'progressive,' education.

In the 'free' market, 'intellectual' is code for 'hireling' or invasive 'weed': 'the intellectual, a certain dealer in ideas,' are

> really the worst part. But I think the man who's learned a little science, the little general problems, lacks the humility the real scientist gradually acquires. The typical intellectual believes everything must be explainable, while the scientist knows that a great many things are not, in our present state of knowledge. The good scientist is essentially a humble person. (Hayek 1978)[20]

Hayek (1978) 'believe[d] in democracy as a system of peaceful change of government; but that's all its whole advantage is, no other. It just makes it possible to get rid of what government *we* dislike.'[21] He also described the 'present situation where there is already a lack of the supporting moral beliefs that are required to maintain *our* [emphases added] civilization.'[22]

George Stigler (1911–1991)—who utilised an ideology-driven strategy of knowledge construction and destruction (Leeson 2000, Chapter 3)—devoted his September 1978 MPS Presidential address to the 'hard question: are we a permanent minority?' Could victory be seized from the jaws of defeat by 'the restriction of the franchise to property owners, educated classes, employed persons or some such group'? Stigler's (1978) own attachment to 'free' market ideas grows with the realization of how widely rejected they are. If in fact we seek what many do not wish, will we not be more successful if we take this into account and *contrive* political institutions and policies that allow us to pursue *our* [emphases added] goals?

The following month, James Buchanan asked Hayek about the 'the delusion of democracy'—the franchise being given to 'direct recipients of government largesse, government transfers [and] people who work directly for government ... there's no more overt conflict of interest than the franchise [given] to those groups. Do you agree with me?' Hayek (1978) explained that he preferred his club-based, one-man-one-vote-once electoral college, which he had just tried to persuade General Augusto Pinochet to adopt (Hayek 2013 [1979], 483). A slogan of liberty or 'catchword' was also required: 'the conception of democracy was an artifact which captured public opinion after it had been a speculation of the philosophers. Why shouldn't – as a proper heading – the need for restoring the rule of law become an equally effective catchword, once people become aware of the essential arbitrariness of the present government.'[23]

Milton Friedman (5 March 1951) assured the Federal Reserve Board that James Buchanan was worthy of employment because he was a 'completely and unquestionably loyal to the United States and the American way of life' and held views that were 'fundamentally opposed to those of socialism and communism.'[24] George Mason (1725–1792) is regarded as the father of the United States Bill of Rights. Hayek (1978) explained to Buchanan—later the 'GMU Nobel Laureate' and founder of 'Masonomics'—that he sought to overthrow the Constitution of the United States and replace it by a single sentence written by a dictator-promoting European aristocrat:

> the one phrase in the American Constitution, or rather in the First Amendment, which I think most highly of is the phrase, 'Congress shall make no law....' Now, that's unique, but unfortunately [it goes] only to a particular point. I think the phrase ought to read, 'Congress should make no law authorizing government to take any discriminatory measures of coercion.' I think this would make all the other rights unnecessary and create the sort of conditions which I want to see.

Buchanan asked Hayek 'how would you see this happening?' Hayek explained that the spontaneous order would have to be reconstructed (or contrived): 'I think by several experiments in new amendments in the right direction, which gradually prove to be beneficial, but not enough, until people feel constrained to reconstruct the whole thing.' Hayek assured Buchanan that this would be easily accomplished because 'a constitution is something very changeable and something which has a negative value but *doesn't really concern the people very much* (emphasis added). We might find a new name for it, for constitutional rules.'[25]

According to the libertarian speechwriter, Bruce Bartlett, the average Libertarian Party member, was a

typical 'Star Trek' convention wannabe. (Confessore 2014)[26]

Prometheus, the Journal of the Libertarian Futurist Society, describes its mission: 'imagination is the first step in envisioning a free future – and the peace, prosperity and progress that can take humankind to the stars ... People come to libertarianism through fiction.'[27] In *Law, Legislation and Liberty*, Hayek (1973, 64) implicitly described the personality characteristics of the 'worst inferior mediocrities' that he was recruiting:

> It is not to be denied that to some extent the guiding model of the overall order will always be an utopia, something to which the existing situation will be only a distant approximation and which many people will regard as wholly impractical. Yet it is only by constantly holding up the guiding conception of an internally consistent model which could be realized by the application of the same principles that anything like the effective framework for a functioning spontaneous order will be achieved.

According to 'Hayek's Nobel,'

> Hayek [1974] moves from his specific example to make a more general point, that when dealing with phenomena of 'organized complexity,' often the best we can do is to make pattern predictions, that is, make predictions about some of the general attributes of *the structures that will form themselves* (emphasis added). (Caldwell 2016)

James Buchanan (1973, 12) advised: 'Carefully and constructively, a counter-intelligentsia can be mobilized.' Through fraudulent recommendations, Hayek (1978) created a 'free' market Welfare State for his academically unqualified disciples: 'That I cannot reach the public I am fully aware. I need these intermediaries.'[28] At the 1974 Orwellian-named Institute for Humane Studies 'free' market revivalist meeting, attendees competed with each other over what Friedman described as 'rotten bastard' proposals—the speed with which the non-Austrian Welfare State could be dismantled and the poor, the young, the sick and the old be forced to rely on private charity.[29] Rothbard orchestrated 'free' market economists to chant 'We want externalities' (Blundell 2014, 100, n. 7), and the unifying motto of the anti-Pigouvian 'free' market appears to be: 'We want to evade taxes and receive subsidies.'

The 'training' offered by the feudal 'spontaneous' order created deference to social 'superiors'; later, compulsory universal education weakened neo-feudalism. According to Mises (1985 [1927], 115), compulsory conscription was required in addition to the elimination of the 'spiritual coercion exercised by compulsory education':

> There is, in fact, only one solution: the state, the government, the laws must not in any way concern themselves with schooling or education. Public funds must not be used for such purposes. The rearing and instruction of youth must be left entirely to parents and to private associations and institutions. It is better that a number of boys grow up without formal education than that they enjoy the benefit of schooling only to run the risk, once they have grown up, of being killed or maimed. A healthy illiterate is always better than a literate cripple.

In *Human Action*, Mises (1963, 282; 1966, 282) lobbied for the Warfare State: 'He who in our age opposes armaments and conscription is, perhaps unbeknown to himself, an abettor of those aiming at the enslavement of all.' Hayek (1978) told Leo Rosten: 'To apply the concept of justice, which is an attribute of human action, to a state of affairs, which has not been deliberately brought about by anybody, is just nonsense.' Rosten asked: 'Yes, but can people accept that? They don't seem to be willing to accept that. Under the *training* (emphasis added) of voting, mass education, and so on, we are raised on the assumption that problems can be solved, that we can solve them, and we can solve them fairly.'

Hayek (1978) replied:

That brings us back to things we were discussing much earlier: the revolt against this is an affair of the last 150 years. Even in the nineteenth century, people accepted it all as a matter of course. An economic crisis, a loss of a job, a loss of a person, was as much an act of God as a flood or something else. It's certain developments of thinking, which happened since, which made people so completely dissatisfied with it. On the one hand, that they are no longer willing to accept certain ethical or moral traditions; on the other hand, that they have been explicitly told, 'Why should we obey any rules of conduct, the usefulness or reasonableness of which cannot be demonstrated to us?' Whether man can be made to behave decently, I would even say, so long as he insists that the rules of decency must be explained to him, I am very doubtful. It may not be possible.

Promoting 'human decency,' Hayek (1978) also defended the 'civilisation' of Apartheid from the American 'fashion' of 'human rights':

You see, my problem with all this is the whole role of what I commonly call the intellectuals, which I have long ago defined as the secondhand dealers in ideas. For some reason or other, they are probably more subject to waves of fashion in ideas and more influential in the American sense than they are elsewhere. Certain main concerns can spread here with an incredible speed. Take the conception of human rights. I'm not sure whether it's an invention of the present [Carter] administration or whether it's of an older date, but I suppose if you told an eighteen year old that human rights is a new discovery he wouldn't believe it. He would have thought the United States for 200 years has been committed to human rights, which of course would be absurd. The United States discovered human rights two years ago or five years ago. Suddenly it's the main object and leads to a degree of interference with the policy of other countries which, even if I sympathized with the general aim, I don't think it's in the least justified. People in South Africa have to deal with their own problems, and the idea that you can use external pressure to change people, who after all have built up a civilization of a kind, seems to me morally a very doubtful belief. But it's a dominating belief in the United States now.[30]

'Human decency' means something different to declassed aristocrats than it does to the lower orders. Hayek abandoned his wife and two children to have unrestricted access to his cousin whose cooking and conversation he could barely tolerate. His disciples refer to this 'wonderful love story'; Gerard Radnitzky suggested that it should be made into a film

(Cubitt 2006, 50, 106, 119, 211). And according to the Mises Institute website, *My Years with Ludwig von Mises* is a

> moving account of her life with 'Lu' ... The reader learns that Mises was a warm and gentle husband, in addition to being a great mind ... This is an intimate portrait no Mises admirer can be without ... You owe it to yourself to get to know her and her husband through her work.

Mises met Margit Sereny when he was forty-four, asked her to marry him the following year,

> though he did not sign that 'scrap of paper' as he expressed himself, before he was fifty-eight years old.

In 1925, Margit was a thirty-five-year-old widow with two young children. Mises declined to marry her until after his own widowed mother had died:

> He knew I needed a father for my children; he was aware of the fact that I gave them all the love and affection I was capable of. But children need more than a loving and doting mother. They need guidance and direction for their development, and I, as a mother alone, was well aware that I was not strong enough to give them what they deserved ... Soon after we became engaged, he grew afraid of marriage, the bond it would mean, the change that children would bring to a quiet home, and the responsibilities that might detract him from his work. So it was a stormy relationship, the old problem of Adam and Eve. But we did not live in Paradise - far from it. We never had a fight between us. Lu fought himself, and then made me suffer. (Mises 1984, 1, 18, 19; Hülsmann 2007, 518–522)

In *Socialism*, Mises (1951 [1932], 85, 87, 90) justified his type of behaviour: 'In the life of a genius, however loving, the woman and whatever goes with her occupy only a small place ... Genius does not allow itself to be hindered by any consideration for the comfort of its fellows even of those closest to it.' With respect to women, 'the sexual function,' the urge to 'surrender to a man,' and 'her love for her husband and children consumes her best energies'; anything more was 'a spiritual child of Socialism.'

Mises (1951 [1932], 87, 104, n. 1) reflected: 'Waking and dreaming man's wishes turn upon sex.' His fiancé sometimes 'did not see him for weeks. But I knew very well that he was in town. At least twice daily the telephone rang, and when I answered there was silence at the other end of the line - not a word was spoken. I knew it was Lu ... I was so tormented, so torn to pieces that the children must have felt it.'[31] Margit Mises (1976, 23, 28; 1984, 23, 44) also recalled:

> The one thing about Lu that was as astonishing as it was frightening was his temper. Occasionally he showed terrible outbursts of tantrums. I do not really know what else to call them. I had experienced them in Vienna on various occasions. Suddenly his temper would flare up, mostly about a small, unimportant happening. He would lose control of himself, start to shout and say things, which coming from him, were so unexpected, so unbelievable, that when it happened the first few times I was frightened to death. Whatever I said would enrage him even more. It was impossible to reason with him. So I kept silent or went out of the room. I gradually realized that these outbursts had nothing to do with me. I was just there, I was the outlet which gave him the opportunity to relieve himself.

Mises also relieved himself by feeling Margit's six-year-old daughter: 'I wanted to touch Gitta's hair and think of you.'

According to Rothbard (1973),

> Ludwig Mises's steadfastness and courage in the face of treatment that would have shattered lesser men, was a never-ending wonder to us all. Once the literal toast of both the economics pro-fession and of the world's leaders, Mises was to find, at the very height of his powers, his world shattered and betrayed. For as the world rushed headlong into the fallacies and evils of Keynesianism and statism, Mises's great insights and contributions were neglected and scorned, and the large majority of his eminent and formerly devoted students decided to bend with the new breeze.

Twice, Mises and Hayek have been the 'literal toast' of *some* world leaders and members of the economics profession—by promoting the deflation that facilitated Hitler's rise to power and, later, through the MPS, which became, via its personnel and/or its ideology an arm, in effect, of the State (Leeson 2018b). 'Von' Hayek's (1978) defining trauma was being stripped of his legal aristocratic privileges in 1919 by a 'republic of peasants and workers'[32]; defeat in the American Civil War (1861–1856) was an equivalent trauma for Southern whites—the Klu Klux Klan was a private sector organisation that colonised the ex-Confederate States.

In the nineteenth century, the Supreme Court of the United States focused on issues relating to the balance between the Federal government and the States. The Southern States refused to implement the Reconstruction Amendments (1865–1870): 'No State shall make or enforce any law which shall abridge the privileges or immunities of citizens of the United States; nor shall any State deprive any person of life, liberty, or property, without due process of law; nor deny to any person within its jurisdiction the equal protection of the laws' (14th Amendment); and 'The right of citizens of the United States to vote shall not be denied or abridged by the United States or by any State on account of race, color, or previous condition of servitude' (15th Amendment). States' Rights were—notionally—circumvented: 'The Congress shall have power to enforce this article by appropriate legislation.'

Rothbard was the first person Raico (2013) had met who defended 'a fully voluntary society—nudge, nudge.' The 'free' market is funded by white supremacists and secessionists—Hayek (1978) appeared to pander to these sentiments:

> I think if instead of a Bill of Rights enumerating particular protected rights, you had had a single clause saying that government must never use coercion, except in the enforcement of uniform rules equally applicable to all, you would not have needed the further Bill of Rights, and it would have kept government within the proper limits. It doesn't exclude government rendering services apart from this, but its coercive powers would be limited to the enforcement of uniform rules equally applicable to all.

Rosten asked:

> If we can't get from the economists any reasonably precise guidelines ... If they [politicians] can't get it from the economists, on economic problems – and the core of the problems we've been talking about are surely economic – where do they get their advice?

James Buchanan (1973, 12; 1987)—who expressed 'Faith in the common sense of the common man'—'didn't become acquainted with Mises until I wrote an article on individual choice and voting in the market in 1954. After I had finished the first draft I went back to see what Mises had said in *Human Action* [1949]. I found out, amazingly, that he had come closer to saying what I was trying to say than anybody else.'

The preamble to the US Constitution declares: 'We the People of the United States, in Order to form a more perfect Union, establish Justice, insure domestic Tranquility, provide for the common defence, promote the general Welfare, and secure the Blessings of Liberty to ourselves and our Posterity, do ordain and establish this Constitution for the United States of America.' In *An Essay on Method*, Mises (1962, 93) provided *The Ultimate Foundation of Economic Science*—producer sovereignty: 'the elite' must dominate the 'masses of inferior people' (Chapter 2).

Hayek (1978) replied to Rosten:

> You can *tell the people* (emphasis added) that our present constitutional order forces politicians to do things which are very stupid and which they know are very stupid. I am not personally trying to blame the politicians; I rather blame the institutions which we have created and which force the politicians to behave not only irrationally but I would say almost dishonestly. But they have no choice. So long as they have to buy support from any number of small groups by giving them special privileges, nothing but the present system can emerge. My present aim is really to prevent the recognition of this turning into a complete disgust with democracy in any form, which is a great danger, in my opinion. I want to make clear to the people that it's what I call unlimited democracy which is the danger, where coercion is not limited to the application of uniform rules, but you can take any specific coercive measure if it seems to serve a good purpose. And anything or anybody which will help the politician be elected is by definition a good purpose. I think people can be made to recognize this and to restore general limitations on the governmental powers; but that will be a very slow process, and I rather fear that before we can achieve something like this, we will get something like what [J.L.] Talmon [1962] has called 'totalitarian democracy' – an elective dictatorship with practically unlimited powers. Then it will depend, from country to country, whether they are lucky or unlucky in the kind of person who gets in power. After all, there have been good dictators in the past; it's very unlikely that it will ever arise. But there may be one or two experiments where a dictator restores freedom, individual freedom.

Rosten appeared horrified to discover what he had devoted his career to promoting:

I can hardly think of a program that will be harder to sell to the American people. I'm using 'sell' in the sense of persuade. How can a dictatorship be good?

Hayek replied: 'Oh, it will never be called a dictatorship; it may be a one-party system.' Rosten meekly inquired: 'It may be a kindly system?' Hayek reassured him:

> A kindly system and a one-party system. A dictator says, 'I have 9 percent support among the people.'[33]

The Bill of Rights applied only to the Federal government: the 1965 Voting Rights Act further weakened States' Rights—this time, not just notionally.

After George Wallace was defeated in the 1958 Alabama Gubernatorial Democratic Party primary (by the Klan-backed John Patterson), his aide, Seymore Trammell, recalled him saying, 'Seymore, you know why I lost that governor's race? ... I was outniggered by John Patterson. And I'll tell you here and now, I will never be outniggered again.' When asked why he started using racist messages, Wallace replied,

> You know, I tried to talk about good roads and good schools and all these things that have been part of my career, and nobody listened. And then I began talking about niggers, and they stomped the floor. (cited by Popkin 2012, Chapter 3)

In *I Chose Liberty*, the co-founder of the Ludwig von Mises Institute outlined the 'free' market position:

> My ideological sympathies were and are with those who resisted the federal government's attacks on the freedom of association (not to mention the federalist structure of the Constitution) in the name of racial integration. I never liked Martin Luther King, Jr. I thought he was a fraud and a tool ... Everyone both proponents and opponents, knew exactly what that [1964 Civil Rights] law was: a statist, centralizing measure that fundamentally attacked the rights of property and empowered the state as mind reader: to judge not only our actions, but our motives, and to criminalize them. The good folks who resisted the civil-rights juggernaut were not necessarily ideologically driven. Mostly they resented horrible intrusions into their

communities, the media smears, and the attacks on their fundamental freedoms that civil rights represented. (Rockwell 2010a, 289)

Or as James Buchanan (1973, 6) put it:

George Wallace's reference to the 'brief-case carrying bureaucrats' strikes home to many because of the demonstrable absurdities promulgated everywhere in the name of liberal progress.

According to Boettke (2017), 'Hayek never abandoned economics. He simply returned to his roots.' The von Hayeks co-created the anti-Semitic and proto-Nazi environment that Hitler absorbed when he arrived in Habsburg Vienna. Hayek (1978) 'grew up in an atmosphere which was *governed* (emphasis added) by a very great psychiatrist who was absolutely anti-Freudian: [Julius] Wagner-Jauregg, the man who invented the treatment of syphilis by malaria and so on, a Nobel Prize man.'[34] Konrad Lorenz was also a family friend: 'Oh, yes, I know the whole family. I've seen Lorenz watching ducks when he was three years old.'[35]

Two of the five University of Vienna recipients of the Nobel Prizes for Medicine had Nazi connections: Lorenz (1903–1989) and Wagner-Jauregg (1857–1940). The university website has three links to 'Konrad Lorenz and National Socialism'; plus a link to a 'controversial discussion' about Wagner-Jauregg's involvement with the Nazis. This 'Exculpatory report' states: 'The conviction of the need for population policies was present in all political and social groups.' A list of 'social hygiene' and 'eugenics'-related organisations and associated individuals was provided, including 'Ludwig von Mises, economist and founder of the Institute for Business Cycle Research (now the Austrian Institute for Economic Research), Othmar Spann, philosopher of history and a staunch opponent of Marxism.'[36]

According to Hayek (1978), the composition of Viennese intellectual groups was 'connected with what you might call the race problem, the anti-Semitism. There was a purely non-Jewish group; there was an almost purely Jewish group; and there was a small intermediate group where the two groups mixed.' There was also 'the purely Jewish ones—[Sigmund] Freud and his circle I never had any contact with. They were a different world.'[37] Hayek's (1994, 61) own family was in the 'purely Christian group; but in the university context I entered into the mixed group.'

The phrase 'purely Christian' appears to mean proto-Nazi or anti-Semitic. Hayek's childhood friend, Fürth (20 April 1984), informed Haberler that Hayek's family 'adhered to Nazism long before there was an Adolf Hitler.'[38] Fürth (23 March 1992) also told Paul Samuelson that Hayek's father was the president of a 'highly nationalistic society of "German" physicians' who competed with the politically neutral general Medical Association.[39] Hayek's (1994, 61–62) obsession about his own 'Aryan' ancestry derived from an overheard conversation about his brother Heinrich looking Jewish (Leeson 2017). When Charlotte Cubitt (2006, 51) asked 'whether he felt uncomfortable about Jewish people he replied that he did not like them very much, any more than he liked black people.'

Rosten asked about Mises' (1944, 94–96) description of the *Wandervogel* most of whom had 'one aim only: to get a job as soon as possible with the government. Those who were not killed in the wars and revolutions are today pedantic and timid bureaucrats in the innumerable offices of the German *Zwangswirtschaft*. They are obedient and faithful slaves of Hitler.' Hayek (1978) replied: 'Oh, I saw it happen; it was still quite active immediately after the war. I think it reached the highest point in the early twenties, immediately after the war. In fact, I saw it happen when my youngest brother [Erich] was full time drawn into that circle; but they were still not barbarians yet. It was rather a return to nature. Their main enjoyment was going out for walks into nature and living a primitive life. But it was not yet an outright revolt against civilization, as it later became.'[40]

With respect to 'The Pretence of Knowledge': Hayek's first authorised biographer was the fraud, Shenoy; the third, William Warren Bartley III, was obliged to resign from his full-time University of Pittsburgh Professorship when it was discovered that he was simultaneously employed, full-time, by California State University Hayward/East Bay (CSUH/EB) (Theroux 2015); the fourth, Leube, was removed from his CSUH/EB full professorship when it was discovered that he had none of his claimed educational qualifications; and the fifth used the analogy of a horse's orifice to describe Hayek's lies (Caldwell 2009, 319).[41]

Hayek 'assured' his second authorised biographer that his brother, Heinz, 'had been no Nazi, that he had been somewhat naïve and might even have said silly things now and then, but that he had probably been influenced by his North German wife.' Hayek was 'at pains to point out and was to repeat this many times, that his family could not have Jewish roots' (Cubitt 2006, 51). Dr. Heinrich von Hayek spent the Third Reich injecting chemicals into freshly executed victims of the Nazis. According to one of his colleagues, his victims may not have been dead when his 'experiments' began. He was a *Scharführer* (non-commissioned officer) in the *Sturmabteilung* (SA, Storm Detachment, Assault Division, or Brownshirts), and from 1934 to 1935, *Führer* in the *Kampfring der Deutsch-Österreicher im Reich* (*Hilfsbund*), an organisation of German-Austrians living in Germany that displayed a Swastika in its regalia (Hildebrandt 2013, 2016). When Heinrich was barred from academic employment under German de-Nazification laws, Hayek compared the Holocaust to playing the fiddle in the Viennese Symphony Orchestra: 'It is scarcely easier to justify the prevention of a person from fiddling because he was a Nazi than the prevention because he is a Jew' (*Spectator* 1947; cited by Ebenstein 2003, 390, n. 21)

Hayek's party political influence expanded after his 1974 Nobel Prize. By the time of his second visit to Pinochet's Chile (in 1981), the Thatcher–Reagan revolutions had begun, and the following year, Helmet Kohl became Christian Democratic Union Chancellor of West (and then reunited) Germany (1982–1998). Lorenz Hayek reported that as communism collapsed, his father 'thoroughly enjoyed watching the television pictures from Berlin, Prague, and Bucharest': he 'would beam benignly' while adding 'I told you so' (cited by Cassidy 2000).

The World Trade Center was bombed on 26 February 1993, killing six and injuring hundreds; the 'Blind Sheik,' Omar Abdel-Rahman (apparently an al-Qaeda affiliate who inspired Osama Bin Laden) was sentenced to life imprisonment. Six months after the attack, Rothbard (1993)—Hayek's co-leader of the Austrian School fourth generation—declared: the 'A-rabs' under investigation 'haven't done anything yet. I mean, all they've done so far is not assassinate former President George Bush, and not blow up the UN building or assassinate [US Senator] Al D'Amato.'

At the UN, 'Democracy is a universally recognized ideal and is one of the core values and principles of the United Nations. It provides an environment for the protection and effective realisation of human rights. These values are embodied in the Universal Declaration of Human Rights.'[42] Rothbard (1993) became, in effect, a spotter for al-Qaeda—suggesting targets for future terrorist attacks: 'I must admit I kind of like that bit about blowing up the UN building, preferably with [UN Secretary General] Boutros Boutros-Ghali inside.'

The *Daily Bell* told Rothbard's co-founder of the Mises Institute: 'You have almost singlehandedly led a revolution in thought that has changed the world. How does that make you feel? ... Did you ever dream of this level of success?' Llewelyn Rockwell Jr. (2010b) replied: 'Neither I nor any of my mentors, like Rothbard, nor influences, like Mises, could have imagined such a thing. Of course, reaching minds is what liberty is all about. The default position of the world is despotism. In the sweep of things, liberty is the exception. What makes the exception possible is ideological work, that is, spreading the ideas through every possible means.'

In 'The Future of Liberty Lets Not Give Into Evil,' Rockwell (1997, 92) stated that 'at the Mises Institute, we seek to create a seamless web between academia and popular culture, so as to influence the future in every possible way.' Walter Block (2000, 40), a Mises Institute Senior Fellow, described the Austrian School 'united front' with Neo-Nazis:

> I once ran into some Neo-Nazis at a libertarian conference. Don't ask, they must have sneaked in under our supposedly united front umbrella. I was in a grandiose mood, thinking that I could convert anyone to libertarianism, and said to them, 'Look, we libertarians will give you a better deal than the liberals. We'll let you goosestep. You can exhibit the swastika on your own property. We'll let you march any way you wish on your own property. We'll let you sing Nazi songs. Any Jews that you get on a voluntary basis to go to a concentration camp, fine' ... The problem with Nazism is not its ends, from the libertarian point of view, rather it is with their means. Namely, they engaged in coercion. But, the ends are as just as any others; namely, they do not involve invasions. If you like saluting and swastikas, and racist theories, that too is part and parcel of liberty. Freedom includes the right to salute the Nazi flag, and to embrace doctrines that are personally obnoxious to me. Under the libertarian code, you should not be put in jail for doing that no matter how horrendous this may appear to some. I happen to be Jewish, and my grandmother is probably spinning in her grave as I write this because we lost many relatives in the Nazi concentration camps.

1.5 Fully Funded Epigones

In the 1970s, the rise of the American Religious Right—some of the Presuppostionalist theocratic variety—mirrored the rise of Islamic theocratic fundamentalism: the First Estate (with the self-appointed power to interpret 'God') reemerged as a political and social force. In 1974, the King of Sweden handed a declassed member of the Second Estate the 1974 Nobel Prize for Economics Sciences for a fraudulent assertion about having predicted the Great Depression (Klausinger 2010, 227; 2012, 172, n. 10).[43]

No Swede could receive the Nobel Prize for Economic Sciences during its first five years (1969–1973), and in 1974, the Nobel Selection Committee 'wanted to honor [Gunnar] Myrdal but feared criticism because of his notoriety as an extreme leftist' (Friedman and Friedman 1998, 78). It was 'said at the time that Hayek never expected to win it, and Myrdal never expected to share it' (North 2002). Myrdal was personally obnoxious—and (reportedly) hated by those handing out the Prize. Hayek was 'paired' with Myrdal for reasons of ideological balance—he was an 'equally notorious rightist' (Friedman and Friedman 1998, 78)—plus (reportedly) malice: in the 1930s, Hayek had 'paired' with Gunnar's wife, Alva Myrdal.

The Swedish practical joke had unintended consequences for the 'American Dream.' In 1970 in the USA, about 92% of 30-year-olds had higher pretax inflation-adjusted household earnings than their parents had at the same age. In 2016, for those born in 1980 the 'index of the American dream' has fallen to 50%: only half has as much income as their parents did (Leonhardt 2016). Simultaneously, Pigouvian externalities have risen: dirty air, tainted water, toxic mining and smelter operations cause an estimated 9 million deaths annually, according to The Lancet Commission on Pollution and Health (2017).

According to the Credit Suisse 2017 Global Wealth Report, the richest 1% now owns more than half of all the world's household wealth, while 70% of the world's adults own less than US$10,000.[44] The $10 million tax-exempt gift that Charles Koch gave to American Catholic University (as a reward for its 'ethics')—which represents about 0.001% of the combined assets of the Koch brothers—led to hagiographic celebration in *The Wall Street Journal* (McGurn 2017). In many countries, a $1 donation (0.001% of $10,000) would be too small to qualify for tax-relief.

After the Habsburgs became extinct due to inbreeding, did the House of Lorraine (who acquired their name) acquire legitimacy from 'God' or 'the people'? 'von' Hayek and 'von' Mises continued to address the head of their neo-feudal order as 'His Majesty, Kaiser Otto' and 'Imperial

Highness' (Hülsmann 2007, 818). Otto the Habsburg Pretender declared: 'It isn't bad for a country to have people with a certain tradition, where the father gives the son the same outlook and training' (Watters 2005; Morgan 2011).

Hayek (1978) told James Buchanan: 'I believe there is a chance of making the intellectuals proud of seeing through the delusions of the past. That is my present ambition, you know. It's largely concerned with socialism, but of course socialism and unlimited democracy come very much to the same thing. And I believe – at least I have the illusion – that you can put things in a way in which the intellectuals will be ashamed to believe in what their fathers believed.'[45]

The 'worst inferior mediocrities' that Hayek (2011 [1960], 186) recruited to do his 'bidding' exhibit common characteristics—including being proud of:

- their father's (often crude) prejudices;
- their adolescent age of conversion;
- the role played in their conversion by Ayn Rand's malevolent-romantic fiction; and
- the permanence of their fraternity 'pledge' to their benefactors.

In 'A Classical Liberal Life,' Leonard Liggio (2010, 185–186, 188) reported that his 'progress to classical liberalism began when I was a child ... I was particularly happy with the Republican victory in November, 1946.' After arriving at Georgetown University in 1950, the teenage Liggio (1933–2014) campaigned for Robert Taft to become the 1952 Republican Party nomination: 'I joined Students for Taft and became acquainted with its leaders in New York City, Ralph Raico and George Reisman ... Ralph and George introduced me to Mises.'

Liggio was a

> Catholic, a scholar, and a libertarian. His Catholic faith was his lodestar. Leonard was a 'birthright Catholic,' and from his childhood through to university and graduate work at Georgetown and Fordham and for the rest of his life, Leonard enriched his understanding of his religion and participated in the sacraments of his Church. Ultimately, he was admitted into the Order of the Knights of Malta ... On his deathbed, he received the Last Rites of the Catholic Church. I trust that my friend Leonard is spending eternity with the Master he worshiped. (Raico 2014)

In 'How I Became a Liberal,' Alejandro Chafuen (2010, 82–83)—the author of *Christians for Freedom: Late Scholastic Economics* (1986)—reported: 'When I look back into my history to find the reasons I fell in love with liberty, I have to start with my blood heritage and upbringing.' His grandfather 'graduated from the University of Vienna, and his proud Genovese and cultured upbringing helped him view with contempt the barbaric motives and customs of the socialist hordes.' His grandmother was 'brought up' in the 'culturally rich Veneto region of the Austrian-Hungarian empire. She was a woman of faith until the end. Antonio looked up to culture but down on all earthly powers.' His father

> was influenced by an Anglo-Saxon notion of liberty, and my mother Lydia, influenced by an 'Austrian-Hungarian' virtue-based approach … I cherish the gentle and humble demeanor of both Hayek and [Benjamin] Rogge, but it was Leonard Read and Sennholz who were to have the biggest influence on my road to liberty. When I met them, as a late teenager, I had read all the books, or at least 90 percent, of the books published and disseminated by FEE.

The Heartland Institute policy 'expert' and GMU graduate, Steven Horwitz (2011), 'became a libertarian at age 16 … I took an Introduction to Economics class and was totally hooked. The economic way of thinking just made total sense to me. The more Economics I took, and the more Austrian stuff I read, the more I became convinced that being an economist is what I wanted to do.' When asked 'What did you find then in Austrian economics that you didn't find in mainstream textbooks?' Horwitz answered: 'Given that I was an Austrian before I took any economics, it's hard to answer that question!'

In 'How I Became a Libertarian and an Austrian Economist,' the Heartland Institute policy 'expert,' Ebeling (2016), described his first encounter with 'liberty':

> When I was about seventeen, and living in Hollywood, I met two men who introduced me to the works of Ayn Rand. I ran into them at a restaurant called 'Hody's' that was at the corner of Hollywood and Vine. Drawing me into a conversation, they asked if I had ever heard of Ayn Rand. I replied that I had heard of the Rand Corporation, but was an 'Ayn'? They handed me a copy of Ayn Rand's Capitalism: the Unknown Ideal, and told me to read it and come back in three days. I did, and we met.

In 1968, Ebeling visited the *Goddess of the Market*: 'Ayn Rand was dressed in a red denim railway man's-like outfit with a train conductor's cap, and her husband, Frank O'Conner [sic], was in a Nehru suit with beads. I have no idea of the meaning or reason for either one.'

In 'How I Became Almost a Libertarian,' Jeremy Shearmur (2010, 333–334, 339) revealed insightfulness usually lacking in his comrades: 'the early death of my father led to my becoming psychologically resistant to arbitrary male authority, and thus gave me a psychological predisposition toward libertarianism ... I also find Mises and Rothbard better as cheerleaders than as sources of really telling scholarship.'

In *Create Your Own Economy: The Path to Prosperity in a Disordered World*, GMU's Tyler Cowen (2009) stated that he was an 'upper-middle-class white male who all his life felt like he belonged to the dominant group in American society. Suddenly I was faced with the suggestion that I could be part of a minority, and a very beleaguered minority at that ... I have since become comfortable with my affiliation with autism, and indeed proud of it, but it's not a thought I was ready for at the time.'

In *I Chose Liberty*, Cowen (2010, 92–93) reported that when he was 'about thirteen, I decided I wanted to read all of the good books in the public library ... I found Ayn Rand; my grandmother also recommended her to me. *Capitalism: The Unknown Ideal* had a big influence on me, as did *Atlas Shrugged*. Hayek and Rothbard followed shortly thereafter.' Also at age 13, 'my father brought me up to FEE. I met Leonard Read, an unforgettable experience, still the most charismatic speaker I have seen. I learned some Austrian economics there.'

Leube (2004)—who promotes himself as the guardian of 'von' Hayek's role as both the 'protector of science' and defender of the hereditary aristocratic order—claims that Hayek—while still living in Chicago—invited him—while still a teenager, living in Austria—to make a 'ten day' visit: 'we discovered that we are actually related. So I call him my Uncle.' Hayek, 'my good old teacher and friend,' was born in Vienna—

> where else? Of course, all great economists are coming from Austria. That is just the way it is. Even Milton Friedman claims nowadays that he was born under Austro-Hungarian auspices.

Since 1974, how many billions of dollars has the taxpayer provided to 'free' market Professors of Economics at the Citadel Military College, the University of Carolina at Greensboro, Auburn University, University of Nevada, Los Vegas (UNLV), CSUH/EB, GMU, etc.? From a scientific perspective, their 'knowledge' is un-trustworthy; but their promotional self-interest, however, generates positive externalities—by illuminating cult dynamics.

The 'Fascists' that Mises (1985 [1927], 49, 51)—a card-carrying Austro-Fascist and member of the official 'Fascist' social club—praised included 'Germans and Italians,' 'Ludendorff and Hitler'; and Hayek (1978; 1994, 95) was a party political operative who described himself as 'rather malicious … I don't keep my mouth shut.' He sneered at everyone, spread the rumour that opponents suffered from erectile dysfunction, and self-censored comments about John Kenneth Galbraith: 'I won't use the exact phrase, which would be libelous and which I don't want to be recorded.'[46]

Cult members tend to display multiple forms of illiteracy—and defer to those with 'The Pretence of Knowledge.' 'It is written' in The Holy Gospel of Friedrich von Hayek According To St. Bruce:

- 'Hayek had throughout his career been known for keeping his disagreements with opponents on a professional level' and it was 'characteristic' of him 'not to lash out at his critics' (Caldwell 2004, 147; 2007, 22; 2016, 11; Caldwell and Montes 2014a, 17; 2014b; 2015, 275);
- 'Hayek himself disdained having his ideas attached to either party' (Caldwell 2010); and
- Mises only promoted '[Italian] Fascism' (Caldwell 2008).

Hayek V (1978; 1994, 37–40) was very specific: 'The earliest paternal ancestor of whom more than the bare name is known is my great-great-grandfather.' This pre-von Hayek 'served one of the great aristocratic landowners'; von Hayek I developed two textile factories; von Hayek II was a public servant; von Hayek III was a 'bit of a young naval dandy' and became a schoolmaster'; and von Hayek IV was a doctor for the Ministry of Health with an 'unsatisfied ambition' to 'become a university professor.'[47] But The Holy Gospel of Friedrich von Hayek According To St. Kurt 'knows' differently: 'going back into the 1600s,' Hayek's family were 'always Professors' (Leube 2004).

According to Alfred Regnery (2008, 318), MPS co-founder, John Davenport, was a 'scion of the family who had founded Yale University [in 1701] and a committed free marketer.' In 'A Life Among Austrians,' George Koether (2000, 5) reported intergenerational deference: in 'many ways,' Mises was 'still attached to the old world: he had a color picture of the Emperor Franz Josef II hanging on the wall' of his New York rent-controlled apartment. At the 'age of 14,' Cowen 'met Walter Grinder, whom a friend of my father's (George Koether) had introduced to my father and me. Walter was a huge influence on me. From him I learned how it was possible to dedicate one's life to ideas ... Richard Fink was a key influence. I met him when I was 15, through Walter Grinder.' Cowen 'learned a great deal' from Block, Ebeling, Joseph Salerno and Donald Lavoie; 'plus I attended NYU [New York University] Austrian seminars regularly. I also had early contact with the Institute for Humane Studies [IHS]. I remain grateful that so many of the people at these institutions were willing to spend their time with a young kid.'

Cowen 'followed' Fink to GMU where 'Rich' had 'built up the Center for the Study of Market Processes. I learned more from Rich than is possible to say, not just about economics, but also about institution building, strategy, personalities, and many other matters ... I am Director of the Mercatus Center at George Mason University, which is the re-named Center for the Study of Market Processes, although it is now much larger, so I am following in Rich's footsteps very directly.' The academic fraud, Shenoy, who was employed by the Center for the Study of Market Processes, obtained lifetime tenure at the University of Newcastle, Australia, not through the market process but through the 'free' market: special pleading by Hayek and the National Tertiary Education Union (of which she was a voluntary member). Her father was an MPS member.

According to North, 'When people curse their parents, it unquestionably is a capital Crime. The integrity of the family must be maintained by the threat of death' (cited by Olson 1998). North (2010, 240) reported: 'To give you some idea of how conservative dad was, when the U.S. Government suggested that employees drive with their lights on out of respect to the anniversary of Martin Luther King's assassination, dad drove home that evening with his lights off, risking a ticket and a collision.' North's 'main academic interest in 1958 was anti-Communism.' At age 14, he had been taken to 'hear the anti-Communist Australian physician Fred Schwarz ... My parents were conservative Republicans.'

The Mises Institute 'Distinguished Fellow,' Hans-Herman Hoppe (1995, 36), regards Rothbard as his

> closest and dearest fatherly friend. I loved him like a son loves his father, and it makes me happy to know that Murray looked upon me as one of his favorite sons. My ten years with Murray were the highlight of my own life, and the memories of our association will forever remain my most precious personal treasure.

Hoppe also told his UNLV students that because they don't have children and 'live riskier lifestyles,' 'homosexuals tend to plan less for the future than heterosexuals.' John Maynard Keynes's wife, Lydia, had miscarriages—but Hoppe insisted that Keynes' 'spend it now' philosophy was influenced 'by his homosexuality.' After a formal complaint, Hoppe (in his next lecture) elaborated: 'Italians tend to eat more spaghetti than Germans, and Germans tend to eat more sauerkraut than Italians. It is not universally true, he said, but it is generally true' (Lake 2005).

In Hoppe's (2017) retelling:

> A cry-baby student complained, and the university's affirmative action commissar immediately, as if he had only waited for this opportunity, initiated official proceedings against me, threatening severe punitive measures if I were not to instantly and publicly recant and apologize. 'Intransigent' as I was, I refused to do so. And I am certain that it was only this steadfast refusal of mine to beg for forgiveness that, after a full year of administrative harassment, I ultimately emerged victorious from this battle with the thought police, and the university administration suffered an embarrassing defeat. A year later I resigned from my position and left UNLV and the US for good.

The 'free' market has polluted scientific discourse through sycophantic-client departments of economics. Their ideology-driven psycho-babble invites a negative-sum game counter-examination.

F. E. Smith, 1st Earl of Birkenhead (1872–1930), described British interwar coal owners as the 'most stupid body of men I have ever encountered' (cited by Johnson 2009, Chapter 4). The 1926 General Strike radicalised Keynes (1936, 116), who found a use for coal mines:

> If the Treasury were to fill old bottles with banknotes, bury them at suitable depths in disused coalmines which are then filled up to the surface

with town rubbish, and leave it to private enterprise on well-tried principles of laissez-faire to dig the notes up again ... there need be no more unemployment.

Fellowships have academic status because—outside the 'free' market—they are competition based; but at GMU, Fink 'arranged a fellowship' for the unemployed Boettke (2010a, 61, 62), who became 'completely enamoured' of his benefactor. Most students aspire to become scholars by displaying (to non-fellow-ideologues) their ability to critically evaluate evidence, and in the competitive market, the quantity of available jobs—for genuine academics or tennis or basketball professionals—is limited. But the Koch brothers have a combined coal- and oil-derived net worth of almost $100 billion and their demand for additional members of the 'academic community of libertarian scholars'—to evaluate whether they should have full-cost pricing (that is, externality taxes) imposed upon them—is effectively infinite. Such demand creates its own supply.

When Charles Koch first 'started trying to do anything, to have a magazine or a seminar, we'd be lucky if we could get half a dozen professors or scholars there'—but now has what he calls 'cadres of freedom advocates.' According to Kim Dennis, President of the Searle Freedom Trust,

> 'Often people who make a lot of money feel like their philanthropy is a way of compensating for their business success. But Charles is not "giving back." He is supporting the things that made his business success possible.' It's all of a piece. (cited by Glassman 2011)

The 'free' market is presented as an attack on 'special interest groups'—yet the GMU Hayek-Koch-Fink 'Structure of Social Change Liberty Guide' is marketed to such groups:

> Citizen activist or implementation groups are needed in the final stage to take the policy ideas from the think tanks and translate them into proposals that citizens can understand and act upon. These groups are also able to build diverse coalitions of individual citizens and special interest groups needed to press for the implementation of policy change.

Is any aspect of the 'free' market unrelated to fund-raising? Fink (1996) continued:

We at the Koch Foundation find that the Structure of Social Change model helps us to understand the distinct roles of universities, think tanks, and activist groups in the transformation of ideas into action. We invite you to consider whether Hayek's model, on which ours is based, is useful in your philanthropy. Though I have confined my examples to the realm of public policy, the model clearly has much broader social relevance.

In 'Creating Your Path to a Policy Career,' the tax-exempt IHS describes itself a 'unique organisation that assists undergraduate and graduate students who have a special interest in individual liberty. Each year IHS awards more than $600,000 in scholarships and sponsors the attendance of hundreds of students at its summer seminars.'[48] The 'guiding idea' of Hayek's (1979) 'development' was the 'discovery' that the 'price system is really essential as a *guide* (Hayek's emphasis) to enable people to fit into an order.' On cost–benefit grounds, how do the taxpayers of Virginia evaluate the GMU Hayek-Koch-Fink 'knowledge' assembly line that they fund? As a 'note-digging' escalator to the upper reaches of the wealth and income distribution for 'chanting' Randian adolescents orchestrated by a self-described 'cheerleader'? Boettke (2015) motivates his GMU students and others by explaining that he lives in a 'different world than the 99%' and 'I'd like to make more money.'

In 'Charles Rowley on the State of Macroeconomics,' Boettke (2010b) stated that 'Rowley has never shied away from speaking truth to power. This is a very admirable trait.' Rowley described Rich Fink as a 'third-rate political hack' and a 'man who is very appropriately named.' Rowley declined an invitation from Heritage President, Edwin Feulner, to serve on the host committee of the MPS golden anniversary conference because 'large subsidies from corporations' had led to 'extravagant junketing' and 'Too many meeting are now dominated by wealthy individuals, foundation executives and the like' (cited by MacLean 2017, 207–209). In 2016, Boettke was elected MPS President.

Dr. Hendrik Frensch Verwoerd (1901–1966) described Apartheid as 'a policy of good neighborliness.'[49] In *The Wall Street Journal*, Horwitz (2014), the Ball State University 'Schnatter Distinguished Professor of Free Enterprise,' described oil companies as just good 'neighbors':

> When one thinks of progressives' long list of capitalist villains, the oil industry is probably near the top. It stands accused of the worst forms of self-interested and antisocial behavior, exploiting workers and consumers

alike. What tells a different story is how oil companies behaved during a major natural disaster affecting their employees and customers ... we too easily forget that these firms are part of their communities. The people who work for Walmart in New Orleans or for Imperial Oil in Fort McMurray have every reason to want to see their fellow citizens treated well. The peaceful exchanges that make up the free market are built on mutual benefit. As companies engage in peaceful commerce with their friends and neighbors, they begin to inculcate what the economist Deirdre McCloskey calls the 'bourgeois virtues,' which go vividly on display when disaster strikes. Many Albertans, as they return to their homes now that the fires have subsided, are glad today that they lived near those supposedly evil oil companies.

What got Horwitz (2011) 'started in Austrian economics was its defense of the market,' and according to Boettke (2017), 'The market economy based on property, prices, and profit-and-loss solves the knowledge problem by alerting individuals to profit opportunities by guiding them in decisions through relative price adjustments and disciplining them through the penalty of loss.' This penalty hit the Center for Independent Education when Charles Koch decided it was a 'sunk cost. He stopped his funding stream, and allowed the market to run its course' (Glassman 2011).

The uninformative 'Kochtopus' label was invented by ejected courtiers. Koch largesse is distributed in a contestable-type market—one word of dissent from a GMU economist and the Mercatus Centre could be relocated to the Citadel Military College. A 'rising tide lifts all boats' is a 'trickle down' cliché—but a pulled plug sinks all rotten ships. Boettke (2015), the Director of the F. A. Hayek for Advanced Study in Philosophy, Politics, and Economics, lives in a 'different world than the 99%' and 'I'd like to make more money.' Loss aversion may explain the absence of dissent: Boettke is, presumably, fearful of the post-Koch sinkhole.

According to the inspirer of the Hayek-Koch-Fink 'knowledge' assembly line: 'To do the bidding of others is for the employed the condition of achieving his purpose' (Hayek 2011 [1960], 186). According to James Glassman (2011), 'For decades, [Charles] Koch has supported such university-based programs quietly, seeking little or no credit and drawing little attention.' But David Koch told Brian Doherty (2007, 409): 'If we're going to give a lot of money, we'll make darn sure they spend it in a way that goes along with our interest. And if they make a wrong turn and start doing things we don't agree with, we withdraw funding. We do exert that kind of control.' Boettke (2010c) dutifully reported:

> We receive financial support from a multiplicity of sources, the Koch Foundation being one among the many ... We also are at a state university so we receive tax payer support as well in the interest of full disclosure. I have met many of our donors through the years and they are wonderful individuals who care passionately about liberty and economic education and economic scholarship. Both Charles and David Koch are the same way. They care passionately about the cause of economic and political liberty and they have generously provided significant funds to support numerous efforts. I have had many conversations with Charles over the years, including about research priorities for a free society. He has never once tried to influence what I was working on, or the way I was working on it.

In *Liberalism in the Classical Tradition*, Mises (1985 [1927], 49, 51, 153) insisted: 'If modern civilization were unable to defend itself against the attacks of hirelings, then it could not, in any case, remain in existence much longer': Fascist 'intervention has, for the moment, saved European civilization.' To GMU's James Buchanan, Hayek (1974; 1978; 1994, 83–86) expressed his general contempt of 'secondhand dealers'[50]; and in terms of 'pattern prediction,' he connected erectile dysfunction to 'someone who could write to any subject where he was given instruction' and 'make a case for a brief that was presented to him.'[51]

In 1979, the teenage Boettke had a religious experience at the hands of a 'Misean for Life' *Luftwaffe* bomber pilot who rested 'his defense of a free society on revelation ... divinely revealed information' (Robbins 2010): 'Within a *very short period, I was a convert* (emphasis added) to the principles of the private-property order and saw government as more the source of problems than the solution to them. Sennholz pointed me in the direction of the Austrian School of economics, and I decided to become a professional economist. But everyone at Grove City was exposed to Sennholz's wonderful lectures in classes and a few times every year in our morning church obligation. His lectures sang to me from the first time I heard them, and unlike many of my classmates, I loved the tune. So much so, in fact, that I decided to become an academic economist' (Boettke 2010a, 58). But who pays the piper?

Referring to Keynes, Ebeling (2010b)—who took eight years to pass his undergraduate degree—asked his fellow Austrians:

> Would any of us give much of a passing grade to any student who argued like this on an economic exam?

Ebeling has named successive dogs after a card-carrying Austro-Fascist ('Ludwig von Mises III, etc.), and Boettke (2010d) 'tells *all* (emphasis added)' of his students to 'love Mises to pieces.' In 2011, the Misean-motivated Anders Behring Breivik killed eight people by detonating a car bomb in Oslo and then shot dead 69 participants of a Workers' Youth League summer camp (Tietze 2015). Would a student who didn't 'love' a 'Ludendorff and Hitler' promoter be allowed to obtain a GMU degree?

Boettke's (2010a, 59) father

> often said to me, 'I was not put on this earth to praise you, but to raise you … The cream will rise to the top.'

Winston Churchill warned about Fascism and the 'sink into the abyss of a new Dark Age made more sinister, and perhaps more protracted, by the lights of perverted science.'[52] In the 'free' market, 'liberty' and 'property' are best protected by 'Fascists' (Mises) and Operation Condor dictators (Hayek), and 'science' is used for non-standard purposes. Although Mises repeatedly plagiarised the phrase 'consumer sovereignty' from Frank A. Fetter (Leeson 2015b, Chapter 7), 'it is written' in The Holy Gospel of Ludwig von Mises According To St. Peter: 'His is a story of scientific glory' (Boettke 2016a).

Boettke (2010a, 60; 2012)—who describes his 'depression'—failed as a tennis and basketball professional and has, knowingly or otherwise, devoted his life to preserving 'born-with-a-silver-spoon-in-the-mouth' intergenerational entitlements:

> I am a very unhappy person because I have very high scientific aspirations and because I believe the endowment from Mises and Hayek is so great, the fact that I edited the Review of Austrian Economics and not the American Economic Review, to me is a failure, like I failed, because I have the silver spoon in my mouth which is Mises and Hayek and I can't get these ideas out. I must be the worst communicator ever. I don't believe

in the barrier of entry so it's all of my own failure. One of my colleagues asked me, 'Pete when are you ever going to be happy.' And I answered 'I will be happy when I am the Ludwig von Mises – Professor at the F.A. Hayek Centre for Advanced Studies at Princeton University. Then I will be happy.' He looked at me and said 'oh my god, you're going to be sad your whole live [*sic*].'

Referring to 'a resurrection of truth,' Mises (1944, 115) stated:

> The aim of the popularization of economic studies is not to make every man an economist ... It is a war of ideas. Public opinion will determine victory and defeat.

According to Boettke (2001, 198), 'Markets are like weeds. They are impossible to stamp out.' Using the analogy of an official licence issued by the Roman Catholic Church, Liggio (27 May 1985) promised James Buchanan that the 'imprimatur of George Mason University' will churn-out 'crop after crop' of invasive weeds, or hirelings (cited by Maclean 2017, 188).[53] According to Jane Mayer (2010, 2016), Liggio (who was employed by the Koch-funded, IHS, 1974–1998) wrote 'National Socialist Political Strategy: Social Change in a Modern Industrial Society with an Authoritarian Tradition' which described the Nazis' successful creation of a youth movement as key to their capture of the state. Like the Nazis, libertarians, Liggio suggested, should organise university students to create 'group identity.'

Keynes is (possibly apocryphally) attributed with the phrase: 'When the facts change, I change my mind. What do you do, sir?' In 'Reflections on Becoming an Austrian Economist and Libertarian and Staying One,' Boettke (2010a, 62) 'became convinced' that he 'could do Austrian economics for a living' by 'drinking beer, playing pool and talking about economics and libertarianism.' Grinder and Liggio were 'very influential on me, both in terms of their suggestions of research projects one could explore and the way one should interact with interested students to build an academic community of libertarian scholars.' In a future edition of AIEE, Boettke should write 'An Open Letter to the Taxpayers of Virginia,' justifying 'ideological orgies' and dismissive proclamations about the 'non-concept' of education (Leeson 2018b).[54]

According to sciencecorruption.com, it is 'apparent' that Boettke's GMU colleague, Walter E. Williams 'wrote pro-corporate material extensively for the tobacco industry, and probably for a range of other problem industries as well.' His 'value' to the 'tobacco industry was largely because he was African-American and therefore had considerable clout among some minority groups—especially in the Black Press ... Payments for network services were laundered through a couple of channels linked to GMU's Center for the Study of Public Choice and its director Robert Tollison,' but 'most' payments went directly to Williams 'or passed through the laundry service offered by the George Mason Foundation.'[55]

Boettke (2012)—North's fellow Presuppositionist—describes himself as a middle-aged 'cheerleader.' In

'When A Man Like Walter Williams Calls You To Duty, You Report'—
Fred Boettke

Boettke (2016b) reported: 'My father was not very political, he did though hold strong principles ... he became familiar with the ideas of Walter E. Williams, and came to respect Walter's common-sense as well as Walter's intellectual courage.' Without a college education, how did Fred Boettke encounter Williams? Presumably, via Limbaugh's inflammatory far-right radio show to which Williams (2010, 132–133) was a regular contributor.

In *Up from the Projects*, Williams (2010, 43, 127) described gate-crashing a white's only dance—which stopped the dancing. In 1978, he was invited to attend MPS meetings—in which after-dinner dancing was a regular feature. In his history of the London School of Economics (LSE), Ralf Dahrendorf (1995, plate 17, between 268 and 269) reproduced a photograph of academics dancing (a regular lunchtime activity). Hayek described Sir Arthur Lewis, his LSE colleagues and the winner of the 1979 Nobel Prize for Economic Sciences, as an 'unusually able West Indian negro'; when asked what his

> attitude to black people was ... he said that he did not like 'dancing Negroes.' He had watched a Nobel laureate doing so which had made him see the 'the animal beneath the facade of apparent civilization.' (Cubitt 2006, 23)

The 1975 Hillsdale College MPS meeting was devoted to 'von' Hayek: 'Few other scholars, if any, have adorned the social sciences in our time as Hayek has done,' as Arthur Shenfield asserted in the brochure.[56] According to an article in William Buckley's Jr. *National Review*, the climax of this tax-exempt meeting was Roche III toasting Elizabeth II accompanied by

> a mood of sheer bliss ... as if an Invisible Hand had prankishly arranged a sneak preview of Utopia ... Such fellowship is of course much enhanced in the vicinity of the bar, which was open three times a day ... What we could not expect was the pampering and elegant food that attended us from beginning to end ... One fellow disappeared into the service regions with a bottle of champagne for the staffers, and almost immediately a fresh bottle appeared on his table. It was magic ... Clearly, unseen benefactors had picked up the tab; otherwise Hillsdale's budget would have rocketed into federal orbit ... It was lovely. (Wheeler 1975)

But in 1975, there was a threat—Buchanan noted to MPS Secretary Ralph Harris that if Thomas Sowell were 'elected' to the MPS, this would be a 'first' because 'Sowell is, as you perhaps know, a black' (cited by Schmelzer 2010, 34).

Hayek (1976, 189, n. 25) may have been horrified—the following year, in *Law, Legislation and Liberty, Volume 2: The Mirage of Social Justice*, he explained that in 1940, he was offered the opportunity of sending his children to relative safety, which obliged him to consider the 'relative attractiveness of social orders as different as those of the USA, Argentina and Sweden ...' For himself, with a developed (aristocratic) personality, 'formed skills and tastes, a certain reputation and with affiliations with classes of particular inclinations,' the Old World was optimal; but 'for the sake of my children who still had to develop their personalities, then, I felt that the very absence in the USA of sharp social distinctions which would favour me in the Old World should make me decide for them in the former (I should perhaps add that this was based on the tacit assumption that my children would there be based with a white not with a coloured family.)'

Sowell (1930–) and Williams (1936–) are the same age as Hayek's children, Christine (1929–) and Lorenz (1934–2004). Williams (2010, 33, 83) reflected about 'the father I never had'—Hayek was one of the 'great philosophers' who inspired him; and 'some of the most important things' that Sowell (2002, 126–127) learnt at the University of Chicago did not seem at all important at first. One of those things whose relevance I did not see immediately was an essay by Friedrich Hayek [1945] entitled 'The Use of Knowledge in Society.'

Bartley, the initiator of *The Collected Works of F. A. Hayek* project, identified unjust parental beatings as a crucial step in his development (Leeson 2013, Chapter 9). The 'free' market appears to be a 'Stockholm Syndrome' magnet for those with 'disciple'-obsessed parents; but had Hayek not been invited to Stockholm in December 1974, the Austrian School of Economics would probably be little more than a lobby group for the tobacco industry and the Koch brothers.

According to Rockwell (1991):

> children have what economists call a 'high time preference' ... The punishing of children must take this into account. One good whack on the bottom can have an effect ... street criminals, as economist Murray N. Rothbard points out, have the time preference of depraved infants.

In 'free' market mythology, both inflation and *The Road to Serfdom* are slippery slopes that will deliver unpleasant 'whacks,' while deflation (that facilitated Hitler's rise to power) was a beneficial upfront 'whack.'

In Chile, Hayek (1981) stated that

> democracy needs 'a good cleaning' by strong government.

Hayek and Hitler sought to create *irreversible* versions of the past. Hitler's method was to 'cleanse the nation of its enemies' (cited by Heiden 1944, 312), and the 'Model Constitution' that Hayek (2013 [1979], 483) sent to Pinochet 'would of course make all socialist measures for redistribution impossible'—and could, therefore, only be imposed when socialists were unable to effectively object. Hayek (1981) supported the kleptocrat Pinochet (1973–1990), the coordinator of the Argentine 'Dirty War' (1976–1981), General Jorge Rafael Videla and other 'transitional' dictators:

> When a government is broken, and there are no recognized rules, it is necessary to create rules to say what can be done and what cannot be done. In such circumstances it is practically inevitable for someone to have almost absolute powers. Absolute powers that they *should* (emphasis added)

precisely use to avoid and limit any absolute power in the future. It may seem a contradiction that precisely I say this, as I plead for limiting government's powers in people's lives and maintain that many of our problems are born, just out of the excess of government. But, however, when I refer to this dictatorial power, I am only talking for a transitional period. As a means for establishing a stable democracy and liberty, free of impurities. Only in this way I can justify, advise it.

But after 'cleansing' by Hitler, Pinochet and Videla, socialists won elections in Germany, Chile and Argentina.[57] The father of the Socialist Party's Chilean President (2006–2010; 2014–), Michele Bachelet, had been detained by Pinochet and effectively tortured to death; and the Brazilian Democratic Labor Party's President (2011–2016), Dilma Rousseff, broke down during a ceremony marking the release of a report by Brazil's National Truth Commission which documented the Junta's (1964–1985) forced disappearances, killings, torture and sexual violence—of which she had been a victim (Taylor 2014). Clearly, the permanent (largely imaginary) threats faced by the 'free' market require the permanent credible threat of a 'Fascist' coup.

Two concepts of civilisation revolve around the extent of power—should it be separated or concentrated? Liberalism in the non-Austrian classical tradition is fearful of power concentrated in the hands of government, labour unions or corporations. Red Terrorists sought to monopolise power to liquidate enemies and competitors as a prelude to utopia (the 'withering away of the State'); and behind the 'slogan of liberty,' White Terror promoters seek to concentrate power in the hands of a 'dictatorial democracy' where henchmen would liquidate enemies, and follow orders from their social superiors, 'guided' by the 'utopia' of the 'spontaneous' order (Hayek 1973, 64; 1978[58]).

What contractual or epistemological status does eternity have in the 'free' market? 'It cannot be denied that Fascism and similar movements aiming at the establishment of dictatorships are full of the best intentions and that their intervention has, for the moment, saved European civilization. The merit that Fascism has thereby won for itself will live on eternally in history' (Mises 1985 [1927], 49, 51). The delusional Lieutenant Mises misjudged Corporal Hitler; and 'Lieutenant' Hayek's 'should' was lost on General Leopoldo Galtieri (who he met in Argentina as a member of the Military Junta) who succeeded Videla as President of the Junta and who used his 'absolute power' to invade the Falkland Islands.

Mises (1944, 108) flip-flopped on Hitler and complained about those who

> never take into account the possibility that the almighty government of their utopia could aim at ends of which they themselves entirely disapprove. They always tacitly assume that the dictator will do exactly what they themselves want him to do … The most enthusiastic supporters of Marxism, Nazism, and Fascism were the intellectuals, not the boors.

And in a letter to the London *Times* on 'Holding the Falklands, Britain justified in attack on Argentina,' Hayek (17 February 1983) insisted that:

> Argentina ought perhaps to be reminded that no rule of international law would forbid to retort to another military attack on what for 150 years has been under the jurisdiction of Britain by some counter-attack on the geographical source of such bellicose action. That might well be a more effective protection than turning the Falklands into a fortress. An aggressor has no right to demand that hostile action be confined to the region he chooses.[59]

Jon Anderson (1998) had

> dinner at the elegant Sheraton Hotel in Santiago with a close friend of the Pinochet family. She was a slender, attractive widow of about fifty, whose late husband had been a military officer. When I asked her if he had participated in the coup, she replied emphatically, 'Oh yes! He was very active. He even dealt with the prisoners.' She grimaced theatrically. I realized that what she meant was that he had been involved in the roundup of leftist suspects and their subsequent torture and execution. I tried to get her to be more specific. 'You're talking about los fusilamientos—the firing squads?' I asked tentatively. She nodded. 'But my husband liked to do things correctamente, and he always secured the help of lawyers.' She was referring to the lawyers who served as prosecutors in the martial-law 'war tribunals' set up to try the thousands of people detained following the coup. Even so, I ventured, that kind of duty must have been difficult for him. She nodded, but explained that the area they lived in had been a stronghold of leftist terrorists. 'It was a war,' she said. 'It was either you or them. (emphases in original)'

The 'correctamente' firing squads began on the morning of Pinochet's coup, and the disappearances continued long after Hayek's first visit:

The fact was that most of the horrible things took place during the earliest period of the first year, even the first three months. The coup itself first and then the assembling of people in the stadium and so on. I kept track of the disappearances in Chile and they were ever declining numbers and reached zero somewhere around '78. Meanwhile, I withheld any collaboration by me with the Chilean government for something like five years until those disappearances were zero. (Harberger 2016)

Democracy in post-'Fascist' Portugal (1974), the resulting retreat from Empire in Angola and Mozambique, plus the death of Franco (1975) were perceived as existential threats to the 'International Right' (Teacher 2018a, b). In 1977, Hayek initially planned to visit Nicaragua (then 'owned' by the 1927–1979 Somoza dynasty), plus Chile, Argentine, Brazil; but ended up visiting Portugal and Spain in addition to the three Operation Condor countries (Caldwell and Montes 2014a, 20, n. 64, n. 66; 2014b; 2015, 278, n. 64, n. 66).

The 2014 report by Brazil's National Truth Commission which documented the Junta's human rights abuses also noted that the USA had spent 'years teaching the torture techniques to the Brazilian military during that period' (Taylor 2014). In Argentina, about 30,000 'impurities' disappeared, and in 'cleansed' Chile, 3197 were murdered, 20,000 were officially exiled and their passports marked with an 'L,' and about 180,000 fled into exile (Wright and Oñate 2005, 57; Montes 2015, 7). Hayek was contemptuous of what he dismissed as Amnesty International's 'bunch of leftists' who publicised evidence about Pinochet's human rights abuses (Farrant and McPhail 2017), and he was equally *blasé* in Argentina, where Videla confirmed the aspiration to

> go to a liberal market economy… In order to become more efficient, society needed to be disciplined. (cited by Klor et al. 2017, 3)

Had the planned 'free' market 'Fascist' coups of the 1970s actually taken place and succeeded, Britain could have joined Operation Condor (Teacher 2018a, b). And had the British neoclassical economist, A. C. Pigou, still been alive, Hayek (1992 [1945], 223), Ebeling, Skousen, Harold Soref M. P., etc., could have testified against him and he, too, may have been subject to 'free' market justice: 'Neither legal scruples nor a false humanitarianism should prevent the meeting out of full justice … shooting in cold blood.'

Hayek had a sophisticated criminal mind—but his blue blood, white-collar crimes are easy to detect. Had he been 'Fred Hayek' in Alf Garnett's East End or in New Jersey Archie Bunker land, he would have been excoriated by Murdoch's tabloids as a 'Welfare Cheat'—but because he was defending intergenerational entitlement programmes, he is 'Our Father' to the 'free' market Welfare State.

Because he was a neo-feudal icon, 'Friedrich von Hayek' largely evaded detection; and when caught (e.g. taking the 'free' market exit after a hit-and-run accident), he perjured his way out of the consequences by telling the apprehending officer that he was 'Dr. von Hayek,' 'Nobel Peace Prize' recipient (Leeson 2018a). As he neared the end of his life, Naval Lieutenant Donald McCormick (aka Richard Deacon) sold at auction the archival material that revealed him to be a fraud, while the for-general-consumption-posthumous interviews in which 'Lieutenant' Hayek apparently gloated are being suppressed by his fund-raising disciples (Leeson 2015b, Chapter 2).

1.6   Volume Overview

1.6.1   Part One

The 'free' market 'Use of Knowledge in Society' is promoted by (apparently) highly accredited 'academics': employed by the University of Chicago, New York University, George Mason University, Citadel Military College, the University of Carolina at Greensboro, California State University Hayward/East Bay, etc. They have, they assert, PhDs and 'completed post-doc fellowships at Stanford,' NYU, etc.; and the Institute of Economic Affairs (IEA) offered their employee, 'Dr. Sudha Shenoy,' as an advisor to the press and clients on privatisation issues. Chapter 2 examines whether those who promote the 'free' market actually have the high-status credentials that underpins their policy 'expert' advocacy.

Hayek's life was largely defined by his interactions with six exclusive clubs; he also legitimised three others. The first and last of the six were noble: the House of Habsburg intergeneration entitlement programme which—until April 1919—allowed him, legally, to attach the prefix 'von' to his name; plus the post-nominal Companion of Honour which the House of Windsor conferred on him almost two-thirds of a century later. Two he co-created: the *Geistkreis* and the MPS; another was, supposedly, merit based: the Nobel laureates. The sixth was his Reform Club 'home.' The seventh was the IEA and its dozens of offshoots, and the eighth, the far-right Monday Club, which during Hayek's lifetime, was on the verge of expulsion from the Conservative Party. The ninth was the 'Spooks Club' or 'Jackdaw Network' which he promoted after an encounter over lunch at the Reform with 'Deacon' McCormick, the right-wing fraud. Chapter 3 examines these clubs.

Nobel Prizes create a non-hereditary nobility—should the 1974 Nobel Prize for Economic Science have been awarded to a secular-religion-promoting fraud whose 'children's' academic entitlements are assisting the process of re-feudalisation? Should the oil-, coal- and tobacco-funded Professors think tank 'Fellows' who promote this religion be accorded policy 'expert' status? Should this religion be taught in economics departments? Markets—and the framework and full-cost pricing (Pigouvian externality taxes) within which they can provide the socially optimal result—require a more thorough and dispassionate examination than 'free' market advocates are either willing or able to provide. Chapter 4 examines the process by which the 'free' market sought to dismiss externalities as a Russian hoax transmitted by Pigou on Stalin's behalf.

1.6.2 Part Two

Public universities employ two types of 'academics': those who forgo monetary income in pursuit of what economists call 'psychic income' (making unexpected discoveries, etc.), and rent-seekers who see the taxpayer as a cash cow to be milked (by extracting a non-universal basic income) while doing 'the bidding' of their real employers—the tobacco industry and the carbon lobby.[60]

Austrian economic 'theory' is unlike any other 'theory' the AIEE editor has ever encountered. As GMU's Lawrence White (2008) unintentionally revealed, it is a respectable front behind which to promote the deflation that facilitated Hitler's rise to power. According to Hayek (1978; 1994, 86), economics is a species of personal knowledge—and becomes socially accepted by recruiting 'spreaders ... secondhand dealers in ideas' who

> have to play a very important role and are very effective. But, of course, in my particular span of life I had the misfortune that the intellectuals

were completely conquered by socialism. So I had no intermediaries, or hardly any, because they were prejudiced against my ideas by a dominating philosophy.[61]

Keynes 'knew *his own* (emphasis added) economics and was intelligent enough to construct a theory.' In contrast, William Beveridge—the author of *Unemployment: A Problem of Industry* (1909), *Full Employment in a Free Society* (1944), and co-author of *Tariffs: the Case Examined* (1931)—'knew no economics whatsoever ... He was a marvelous expositor. He had the gift of making it lead to *any bridge you gave him* (emphasis added).'

Hayek (1999 [1977], 132) explained that the 'free' market 'bridge' led to an imaginary 'spontaneous' Utopia: 'I have often had occasion to explain, but may never have stated in writing that I strongly believe that the chief task of the economic theorist or political philosopher should be to operate on public opinion to make politically possible what today may be political impossible.' The year before receiving the Nobel Prize for Economic Sciences, Hayek (1973, 61–62) explained how 'free' market science could assist:

> What helpful insights science can provide for the guidance of policy consists in an understanding of the general nature of the spontaneous order, and not in any knowledge of the particulars of a concrete situation, which it does not and cannot possess ... The only theory which in this field can lay claim to scientific status is a theory of the order as a whole.

Certain personality types have 'instincts' that make them vulnerable to bogus Bilgewater 'Dukes,' Romanov 'Princesses' and Habsburg 'vons' and 'Counts'—an aristocratic placebo effect. In addition to the opinion editors of Murdoch's *Wall Street Journal*, climate change scepticism has been coordinated by four journalists, Sir Samuel Brittan (*The Financial Times*), Nigel, The Lord Lawson of Blaby PC (*The Financial Times, The Sunday Telegraph* and the *Spectator*), The 3rd Viscount Monckton of Brenchley (former editor of the Roman Catholic *The Universe*), The (zoology-trained) 5th Viscount Ridley of Blagdon (*The Times*); plus a 'think' tank activist, 'Dr.' Leon Louw, and economists who have been orchestrated by Rothbard to chant 'We want externalities' and assert that externalities are a Soviet hoax. According to 'von' Mises, 'Fascist' had 'saved European civilization,' and 'von' Hayek sought to save the 'civilization' of Apartheid from the American 'fashion' of 'human rights.' Chapter 5 examines the links between 'free' market, the far-right and white supremacist regimes.

According to Liggio (2010, 188), 'Classical Liberalism lost a giant with Murray's death.' Rothbard described the interwar emergency that Fascism had *solved*; and Hayek, his fellow fourth generation Austrian School leader, saw similar merits in Pinochet's and Videla's Juntas. Chapter 6 documents the permanent emergency that motivates Austrian School economists and philosophers and which drives them to embrace military dictatorships and the extra-parliamentary right.

'Free' market economists embrace the form or pose of scholarship, while also promoting crude caricatures and outright fraud: National Public Radio is run by 'Nazis'; and externalities invented by an underground Communist. Some of this 'knowledge' appears to have been inspired by the satirical television show, Monty Python's Flying Circus, and some had been derived from official government white supremacist propaganda (Rhodesia and Apartheid South Africa). 'Free' market funding is provided by the Gaddafi family, the Liechtenstein tax haven, the tobacco industry and the carbon lobby. And the best defence of 'economic liberalism' is, they believe, provided by political 'Fascists' and tax-evading billionaire populists. Mises' promotion of the Warfare State has been rectified by deletion, and his promotion of all 'Fascists,' 'German and Italian,' including 'Ludendorff and Hitler,' has been rectified by insertion: '[Italian].' Chapter 7 examines these 'free' market rectifications.

In Europe, 'Fascism,' as defined and praised by Mises, overthrew democracy in Italy (1922), Spain (1923), Portugal (1926), Germany (1933), Austrian (1934) and Spain (1936–1939); and in Latin America, similar outcomes occurred in what became known as the Operation Condor countries: Paraguay (1954), Brazil (1964), Bolivia (1971), Uruguay (1973), Chile (1973) and Argentina (1976). In 1940, Mises had not wished to leave neutral Switzerland when escaping 'Fascists': he apparently preferred to live in 'Fascist' Portugal rather than the USA.

In 1960, Prime Minister Verwoerd, created the Republic of South African, refused to accept black ambassadors from Commonwealth states and blocked non-white sportsmen from representing 'their' country.' In 1961, Verwoerd appointed Balthazar Johannes Vorster—who had been interned during World War II as a Nazi sympathiser—as Minister of Justice. In 1962, Hayek appeared to have considered Apartheid South

Africa as his post-Chicago retirement home, while simultaneously trying to persuade Portugal's Dr. António de Oliveira Salazar, to supplement his 'God, Fatherland, and Family' 'Fascist' dictatorship with *The Constitution of Liberty*. And in 1977, Hayek sent Pinochet a copy of his *Law, Legislation and Liberty* 'Model Constitution.' Hayek and Mises encountered 'instinctive' sycophancy; and Hayek related the defence of the neo-feudal 'spontaneous' order to an 'artistic creation'—yet economists don't *expect* to encounter 'artistic creations' masquerading as scholarship. Chapter 8 examines what lies behind the 'slogan of liberty.'

NOTES

1. The presumption of innocence prevails: 'free' market promoters should be placed in the final category until *evidence* relegates them into one or more of the preceding categories.
2. Friedrich Hayek, interviewed by James Buchanan 28 October 1978 (Centre for Oral History Research, University of California, Los Angeles, http://oralhistory.library.ucla.edu/).
3. 'Even though Hayek himself disdained having his ideas attached to either party, he nonetheless provided arguments about the dangers of the unbridled growth of government' (Caldwell 2010).
4. http://public.econ.duke.edu/~bjc18/Caldwell_Vita2010-2016.pdf. Accessed 22 October 2017.
5. Hayek (28 August 1975) to Arthur Seldon. Hayek Archives Box 27.6.
6. http://historyofeconomics.org/awards-and-honors/best-article-prize/.
7. https://www.peter-boettke.com/curriculum-vita/. Accessed 30 October 2017.
8. Fürth Archives Hoover Institution Box 6. Fürth was Professor of Economics at Lincoln University, the Catholic University, Washington, the American University, Washington, International University of Luxembourg, Lecturer at the Foreign Service Institute, economic specialist with the Federal Reserve Board, Chief of the Eastern European and Near Eastern Section, the Western European and Commonwealth Section and the International Financial Operations Section; and Associate Adviser, Adviser and Associate Economist, and Consultant to the Federal Open Market Committee.
9. With Hayek, Fürth co-founded the *Geistkreis* from which 'girls' were excluded: 'the women, who were excluded from the *Geistkreis*–Stephanie Browne, Helene Lieser, and Ilse Minz–were all members of the Mises seminar but not of the Geistkreis.' Hayek (1978) also sought to exclude his childhood friend: 'Well, [Furth] wasn't really an economist. He

learned a lot of economics by that association [the *Geistkreis*], but he was not primarily interested in economics. He finally made use of this when he had to go to the United States to get a position as an economist, but in Vienna he was not an economist.' Axel Leijonhufvud asked: 'He went to the Federal Reserve Board once he came here?' Hayek replied: 'Well, no, I think he began with a teaching post at one of the Negro universities in Washington.' Friedrich Hayek, interviewed by Axel Leijonhufvud date unspecified 1978 (Centre for Oral History Research, University of California, Los Angeles, http://oralhistory.library.ucla.edu/).

10. Friedrich Hayek, interviewed by James Buchanan 28 October 1978 (Centre for Oral History Research, University of California, Los Angeles, http://oralhistory.library.ucla.edu/).
11. Friedrich Hayek, interviewed by Robert Chitester date unspecified 1978 (Centre for Oral History Research, University of California, Los Angeles, http://oralhistory.library.ucla.edu/).
12. Friedrich Hayek, interviewed by James Buchanan 28 October 1978 (Centre for Oral History Research, University of California, Los Angeles, http://oralhistory.library.ucla.edu/).
13. Friedrich Hayek, interviewed by Leo Rosten 15 November 1978 (Centre for Oral History Research, University of California, Los Angeles, http://oralhistory.library.ucla.edu/).
14. Friedrich Hayek, interviewed by Earlene Craver date unspecified 1978 (Centre for Oral History Research, University of California, Los Angeles, http://oralhistory.library.ucla.edu/).
15. Friedrich Hayek, interviewed by Leo Rosten 15 November 1978 (Centre for Oral History Research, University of California, Los Angeles, http://oralhistory.library.ucla.edu/).
16. Friedrich Hayek, interviewed by Axel Leijonhufvud date unspecified 1978 (Centre for Oral History Research, University of California, Los Angeles, http://oralhistory.library.ucla.edu/).
17. 'Mises wrote that there was no contradiction between national self-determination and a monarchical regime, provided that the monarchy was established by a free referendum.'
18. Friedrich Hayek interviewed by Leo Rosten 15 November 1978 (Centre for Oral History Research, University of California, Los Angeles, http://oralhistory.library.ucla.edu/).
19. Friedrich Hayek, interviewed by Jack High date unspecified 1978 (Centre for Oral History Research, University of California, Los Angeles, http://oralhistory.library.ucla.edu/).
20. Friedrich Hayek interviewed by Robert Bork 4 November 1978 (Centre for Oral History Research, University of California, Los Angeles, http://oralhistory.library.ucla.edu/).

21. Friedrich Hayek, interviewed by Leo Rosten 15 November 1978 (Centre for Oral History Research, University of California, Los Angeles, http://oralhistory.library.ucla.edu/).
22. Friedrich Hayek, interviewed by Robert Chitester date unspecified 1978 (Centre for Oral History Research, University of California, Los Angeles, http://oralhistory.library.ucla.edu/).
23. Friedrich Hayek, interviewed by James Buchanan 28 October 1978 (Centre for Oral History Research, University of California, Los Angeles, http://oralhistory.library.ucla.edu/).
24. Friedman Archives Box 22.9.
25. Friedrich Hayek, interviewed by James Buchanan 28 October 1978 (Centre for Oral History Research, University of California, Los Angeles, http://oralhistory.library.ucla.edu/).
26. The present writer detected a similar cult-like atmosphere while delivering a seminar to the GMU Ph.D. program.
27. http://www.lfs.org/index.htm.
28. Friedrich Hayek, interviewed by Robert Chitester date unspecified 1978 (Centre for Oral History Research, University of California, Los Angeles, http://oralhistory.library.ucla.edu/).
29. Conversation with David Henderson (7 July 2011), who attended the 1974 revivalist conference and heard Friedman make the remark.
30. Friedrich Hayek, interviewed by Robert Chitester date unspecified 1978 (Centre for Oral History Research, University of California, Los Angeles, http://oralhistory.library.ucla.edu/).
31. Margit Mises (1984, 20–21) attributed Mises' behaviour to shyness: 'He wanted to hear my voice.'
32. Friedrich Hayek, interviewed by Robert Chitester date unspecified 1978 (Centre for Oral History Research, University of California, Los Angeles, http://oralhistory.library.ucla.edu/).
33. Friedrich Hayek, interviewed by Leo Rosten 15 November 1978 (Centre for Oral History Research, University of California, Los Angeles, http://oralhistory.library.ucla.edu/).
34. Friedrich Hayek, interviewed by Leo Rosten 15 November 1978 (Centre for Oral History Research, University of California, Los Angeles, http://oralhistory.library.ucla.edu/).
35. Friedrich Hayek, interviewed by Earlene Craver date unspecified 1978 (Centre for Oral History Research, University of California, Los Angeles, http://oralhistory.library.ucla.edu/).
36. http://www.univie.ac.at/archiv/tour/21.htm.
37. Friedrich Hayek, interviewed by Earlene Craver date unspecified 1978 (Centre for Oral History Research, University of California, Los Angeles, http://oralhistory.library.ucla.edu/).

38. Fürth Archives. Hoover Institution Box 5.
39. Fürth Archives. Hoover Institution Box 6.
40. Friedrich Hayek interviewed by Leo Rosten 15 November 1978 (Centre for Oral History Research, University of California, Los Angeles, http://oralhistory.library.ucla.edu/).
41. 'So much for going to the horse's mouth for clarification!' (Caldwell 2009, 319).
42. http://www.un.org/en/sections/issues-depth/democracy/.
43. Referring to the 1929 American crash, Hansjörg Klausinger (2010, 227; 2012, 172, n. 10), the editor of *Business Cycles*, the seventh volume of Hayek's *Collected Works*, confirmed: 'there is no textual evidence for Hayek predicting it as a concrete event in time and place': we lack 'convincing evidence of a prediction that conformed to what Robbins (2012 [1931], 172–173) suggested in his foreword.'
44. http://publications.credit-suisse.com/tasks/render/file/index.cfm?fileid=168E2808-9ED4-5A5E-19E43EA2A731A4ED.
45. Friedrich Hayek, interviewed by James Buchanan 28 October 1978 (Centre for Oral History Research, University of California, Los Angeles, http://oralhistory.library.ucla.edu/).
46. Friedrich Hayek, interviewed by Robert Chitester date unspecified 1978 (Centre for Oral History Research, University of California, Los Angeles, http://oralhistory.library.ucla.edu/).
47. Friedrich Hayek, interviewed by Robert Chitester date unspecified 1978 (Centre for Oral History Research, University of California, Los Angeles, http://oralhistory.library.ucla.edu/).
48. http://www.learnliberty.org/wp-content/uploads/2014/08/CreatingYourPathToAPolicyCareer.pdf.
49. https://www.youtube.com/watch?v=vPCln9czoys.
50. Friedrich Hayek, interviewed by James Buchanan 28 October 1978 (Centre for Oral History Research, University of California, Los Angeles, http://oralhistory.library.ucla.edu/).
51. In this instance, Hayek was referring to William Beveridge (Chapter 2, below).
52. https://www.winstonchurchill.org/resources/speeches/1940-the-finest-hour/their-finest-hour/.
53. Liggio 'foresaw "crop after crop" of advocates.'
54. Boettke should also take that opportunity to correct any errors of fact or interpretation.
55. http://sciencecorruption.com/ATN187/00298.html.
56. Davenport Archives Box 38.5.

57. In 1983, the Radical Civic Union's Raúl Ricardo Alfonsín won the first post-dictatorship election. The Radical Civic Union is a member of the Socialist International.
58. Friedrich Hayek interviewed by Leo Rosten 15 November 1978 (Centre for Oral History Research, University of California, Los Angeles, http://oralhistory.library.ucla.edu/).
59. https://www.margaretthatcher.org/document/117186.
60. The reader must decide into which of these two categories each individual 'free' market advocate falls.
61. Friedrich Hayek, interviewed by Robert Chitester date unspecified 1978 (Centre for Oral History Research, University of California, Los Angeles, http://oralhistory.library.ucla.edu/).

REFERENCES

Archival Insights into the Evolution of Economics (and Related Projects)

Farrant, A., & McPhail, E. (2017). Hayek, Thatcher, and the Muddle of the Middle. In R. Leeson (Ed.), *Hayek: A Collaborative Biography Part IX: The Divine Right of the 'Free' Market*. Basingstoke, UK: Palgrave Macmillan.

Leeson, R. (2000). Inflation, Disinflation and the Natural Rate of Unemployment: A Dynamic Framework for Policy Analysis. *The Australian Economy in the 1990s* (pp. 124–175). Sydney: Reserve Bank of Australia.

Leeson, R. (Ed.). (2013). *Hayek: A Collaborative Biography Part I Influences from Mises to Bartley*. Basingstoke, UK: Palgrave Macmillan.

Leeson, R. (Ed.). (2015a). *Hayek: A Collaborative Biography Part III Fraud, Fascism and Free Market Religion*. Basingstoke, UK: Palgrave Macmillan.

Leeson, R. (Ed.). (2015b). *Hayek: A Collaborative Biography Part II Austria, America and the Rise of Hitler, 1899–1933*. Basingstoke, UK: Palgrave Macmillan.

Leeson, R. (2017). *Hayek: A Collaborative Biography Part VII 'Market Free Play with an Audience': Hayek's Encounters with Fifty Knowledge Communities*. Basingstoke, UK: Palgrave Macmillan.

Leeson, R. (2018a). *Hayek: A Collaborative Biography Part VIII: The Constitution of Liberty: 'Shooting in Cold Blood' Hayek's Plan for the Future of Democracy*. Basingstoke, UK: Palgrave Macmillan.

Leeson, R. (2018b). *Hayek: A Collaborative Biography Part XI: Orwellian Rectifiers, Mises' 'Evil Seed' of Christianity and the 'Free' Market Welfare State*. Basingstoke, UK: Palgrave Macmillan.

Teacher, D. (2018a). 'Neutral Academic Data' and the International Right. In R. Leeson (Ed.), *Hayek: A Collaborative Biography Part XIII 'Fascism' and*

Liberalism in the (Austrian) Classical Tradition. Basingstoke, UK: Palgrave Macmillan.
Teacher, D. (2018b). Private Club and Secret Service Armageddon. In R. Leeson (Ed.), *Hayek: A Collaborative Biography Part XIII 'Fascism' and Liberalism in the (Austrian) Classical Tradition*. Basingstoke, UK: Palgrave Macmillan.
Theroux, D. (2015). Hayek and Me. In R. Leeson (Ed.), *Hayek: A Collaborative Biography Part V Hayek's Great Society of Free Men*. Basingstoke, UK: Palgrave Macmillan.
Tietze, T. (2015). Anders Breivik, Fascism and the Neoliberal Inheritance. In R. Leeson (Ed.), *Hayek: A Collaborative Biography Part VI Good Dictators, Sovereign Producers and Hayek's 'Ruthless Consistency'*. Basingstoke, UK: Palgrave Macmillan.

Other References

Anderson, J. L. (1998, October 19). The Dictator. *The New Yorker*. http://www.newyorker.com/magazine/1998/10/19/the-dictator-2.
Beveridge, W. (1909). *Unemployment: A Problem of Industry*. London: Longman, Green.
Beveridge, W. (1931). *Tariffs: The Case Examined*. London: Longmans, Green.
Beveridge, W. (1944). *Full Employment in a Free Society*. London: Allen and Unwin.
Block, W. (2000). Libertarianism vs Objectivism; A Response to Peter Schwartz. *Reason Papers, 26*, 39–62. http://www.reasonpapers.com/pdf/26/rp_26_4.pdf.
Blundell, J. (2014). IHS and the Rebirth of Austrian Economics: Some Reflections on 1974–1976. *Quarterly Journal of Austrian Economics, 17*(1), 92–107. https://mises.org/library/ihs-and-rebirth-austrian-economics-some-reflections-1974%E2%80%931976.
Boettke, P. J. (2001). *Calculation and Coordination Essays on Socialism and Transitional Political Economy*. London: Routledge.
Boettke, P. J. (2010a). Reflections on Becoming an Austrian Economist and Libertarian and Staying One. In W. Block (Ed.), *I Chose Liberty: Autobiographies of Contemporary Libertarians*. Auburn, AL: Ludwig von Mises Institute.
Boettke, P. J. (2010b, January 12). Charles Rowley on the State of Macroeconomics. *Coordination Problem*. http://www.coordinationproblem.org/2010/01/charles-rowley-on-the-state-of-macroeconomics.html.
Boettke, P. J. (2010c, December 12). EXCLUSIVE INTERVIEW Peter Boettke on the Rise of Austrian Economics, Its Academic Inroads and Why the Market Should Decide by Anthony Wile. *Daily Bell*. http://www.thedailybell.com/exclusive-interviews/anthony-wile-peter-boettke-on-the-rise-of-austrian-economics-its-academic-inroads-and-why-the-market-should-decide/.

Boettke, P. J. (2010d, October 3). EXCLUSIVE INTERVIEW Steve Horwitz on GMU, the Mises Controversy and the Promise of Austrian Economics in the 21st Century by Anthony Wile. *Daily Bell.* http://www.thedailybell.com/exclusive-interviews/anthony-wile-steve-horwitz-on-gmu-the-mises-controversy-and-the-promise-of-austrian-economics-in-the-21st-century/.

Boettke, P. J. (2011). Teaching Austrian Economics to Graduate Students. *Journal of Economics and Finance Education, 10*(2), 19–30. http://www.economics-finance.org/jefe/econ/special-issue/Special%20Issue%20AE%20003%20Boettke-Abstract.pdf.

Boettke, P. J. (2012). Interview with Peter Boettke. *Rationality Unlimited.* https://rationalityunlimited.wordpress.com/2012/04/02/interview-with-peter-boettke/.

Boettke, P. J. (2014, June 7). Robert Leeson, Hayek and the Underpants Gnome. *Coordination Problem.* http://www.coordinationproblem.org/2014/06/robert-leeson-hayek-and-the-underpants-gnomes.html.

Boettke, P. J. (2015, January 25). The Transformative Rise of Austrian Economics. *The Daily Bell.* http://www.thedailybell.com/exclusive-interviews/anthony-wile-peter-boettke-the-transformative-rise-of-austrian-economics/.

Boettke, P. J. (2016a, October 17). Ludwig von Mises, the Academic. *The Freeman.* https://fee.org/articles/ludwig-von-mises-the-academic/.

Boettke, P. J. (2016b, March 30). 'When A Man Like Walter Williams Calls You To Duty, You Report'—Fred Boettke. *Coordination Problem.* http://www.coordinationproblem.org/2016/03/31/.

Boettke, P. J. (2017, September 17). Hayek's Epistemic Liberalism. *Online Library of Liberty.* http://oll.libertyfund.org/pages/lm-hayek.

Böhm Bawerk, E. (1949 [1896]). *Karl Marx and the Close of His System.* New York: Augustus M. Kelley.

Böhm-Bawerk, E. (1959). *Capital and Interest* (3 Vols., H. Sennholz, Trans.). South Holland, IL: Libertarian Press.

Buchanan, J. (1973, Fall). Prospects for America's Third Century. *Atlantic Economic Journal, 1,* 3–13. https://link.springer.com/article/10.1007/BF02299808.

Buchanan, J. (1987). An Interview with Laureate James Buchanan. *Austrian Economics Newsletter, 9*(1). http://mises.org/journals/aen/aen9_1_1.asp.

Caldwell, B. (2004). *Hayek's Challenge: An Intellectual Biography of F.A. Hayek.* Chicago: University of Chicago Press.

Caldwell, B. (2007). Introduction and Editorial Notes. In F. A. Hayek (Ed.), *The Road to Serfdom Texts and Documents: The Definitive Edition. The Collected Works of F.A. Hayek.* Chicago: University of Chicago Press.

Caldwell, B. (2008). Book Review: History in the Service of Ideology: A Review Essay of Jörg Guido Hülsmann. *Mises: The Last Knight of Liberalism*. *History of Economic Ideas*, *16*(3), 143–148.

Caldwell, B. (2009). A Skirmish in the Popper Wars: Hutchison versus Caldwell on Hayek, Popper, Mises, and Methodology. *Journal of Economic Methodology*, *16*(3), 315–324. http://www.tandfonline.com/doi/pdf/10.1080/13501780903129306.

Caldwell, B. (2010). The Secret Behind the Hot Sales of 'The Road to Serfdom' by Free-Market Economist F. A. Hayek. *The Washington Post*. http://voices.washingtonpost.com/shortstack/2010/02/the_secret_behind_the_hot_sale.html\.

Caldwell, B. (2016). Hayek's Nobel. In P. Boettke & V. Storr (Eds.), *Revisiting Hayek's Political Economy*. Bingley, UK: Emerald.

Caldwell, B., & Montes, L. (2014a, August). *Friedrich Hayek and His Visits to Chile* (CHOPE Working Paper No. 2014-12).

Caldwell, B., & Montes, L. (2014b). Friedrich Hayek and His Visits to Chile. *Review of Austrian Economics* (First Online: 26 September 2014).

Caldwell, B., & Montes, L. (2015, September). Friedrich Hayek and His Visits to Chile. *Review of Austrian Economics*, *28*(3), 261–309.

Cassidy, J. (2000, June 30). The Hayek Century. *Hoover Digest* (3). http://www.hoover.org/research/hayek-century.

Chafuen, A. (2010). How I Became a Liberal. In W. Block (Ed.), *I Chose Liberty: Autobiographies of Contemporary Libertarians*. Auburn, AL: Ludwig von Mises Institute.

Confessore, N. (2014, May 17). Quixotic '80 Campaign Gave Birth to Kochs' Powerful Network. *New York Times*. https://www.nytimes.com/2014/05/18/us/politics/quixotic-80-campaign-gave-birth-to-kochs-powerful-network.html.

Cowen, T. (2009). *Create Your Own Economy: The Path to Prosperity in a Disordered World*. New York: Dutton.

Cowen, T. (2010). A Short Intellectual Autobiography. In W. Block (Ed.), *I Chose Liberty: Autobiographies of Contemporary Libertarians*. Auburn, AL: Ludwig von Mises Institute.

Cubitt, C. (2006). *A Life of August von Hayek*. Bedford, UK: Authors on Line.

Dahrendorf, R. (1995). *LSE: A History of the London School of Economics and Political Science, 1895–1995*. Oxford: Oxford University Press.

Deist, J. (2017, February 17). Democracy, the God That's Failing. *Mises Wire*. https://mises.org/blog/democracy-god-thats-failing.

Doherty, B. (2007). *Radicals for Capitalism: A Freewheeling History of the Modern. American Libertarian Movement*. New York: Public Affairs.

Ebeling, R. M. (2010a). *Political Economy, Public Policy and Monetary Economics: Ludwig Von Mises and the Austrian Tradition*. New York: Routledge.

Ebeling, R. M. (2010b, January 12). Charles Rowley on the State of Macroeconomics. *Coordination Problem*. http://www.coordinationproblem. org/2010/01/charles-rowley-on-the-state-of-macroeconomics.html.
Ebeling, R. M. (2016, May 2). How I Became a Libertarian and an Austrian Economist. *Future of Freedom Foundation*. https://www.fff.org/explore-freedom/article/became-libertarian-austrian-economist/.
Ebenstein, A. (2003). *Friedrich Hayek: A Biography*. Chicago: University of Chicago Press.
Fink, R. (1996). From Ideas to Action: The Role of Universities, Think Tanks, and Activist Groups. *Philanthropy Magazine, 10*(1). http://www.learnliberty.org/wp-content/uploads/2014/08/CreatingYourPathToAPolicyCareer.pdf.
Friedman, M. F., & Friedman, R. D. (1998). *Two Lucky People: Memoirs*. Chicago: University of Chicago Press.
Glassman, J. K. (2011, Fall). Market-Based Man. *Philanthropy Roundtable*. http://www.philanthropyroundtable.org/topic/excellence_in_philanthropy/market_based_man.
Goodwin, C. (1988). The Heterogeneity of the Economists' Discourse: Philosopher, Priest, and Hired Gun. In A. Klamer, D. N. McCloskey, & R. M. Solow (Eds.), *The Consequences of Economic Rhetoric*. Cambridge: Cambridge University Press.
Gusejnova, D. (2012). Nobel Continent: German Speaking Nobles as Theorists of European Identity in the Inter-War Period. In M. Hewitson & M. D'Auria (Eds.), *Europe in Crisis: Intellectuals and the European Idea* (pp. 1917–1957). New York, US: Berghahn.
Harberger, A. C. (2016). *Sense and Economics: An Oral History with Arnold Harberger*. Interviews Conducted by Paul Burnett in 2015 and 2016 Oral History Center. California: The Bancroft Library, University of California, Berkeley. http://digitalassets.lib.berkeley.edu/roho/ucb/text/harberger_arnold_2016.pdf.
Hayek, F. A. (1952 [1926]). Hayek on Wieser. In H. W. Spiegel (Ed.), *The Development of Economic Thought*. New York: Wiley.
Hayek, F. A. (1973). *Law, Legislation and Liberty Volume 1: Rules and Order*. Chicago: University of Chicago Press.
Hayek, F. A. (1974). The Pretence of Knowledge. *Nobel Lecture*. https://www.nobelprize.org/nobel_prizes/economic-sciences/laureates/1974/hayek-lecture.html.
Hayek, F. A. (1976). *Law, Legislation and Liberty Volume 2: The Mirage of Social Justice*. Chicago: University of Chicago Press.
Hayek, F. A. (1978). *Oral History Interviews*. Los Angeles: Centre for Oral History Research, University of California. http://oralhistory.library.ucla.edu/.
Hayek, F. A. (1979, December 5). A Period of Muddle-Heads. *Newsweek*.

Hayek, F. A. (1981, April 12). Extracts from an Interview Friedrich von Hayek. *El Mercurio.* http://www.economicthought.net/blog/wp-content/uploads/2011/12/LibertyCleanOfImpuritiesInterviewWithFVonHayekChile1981.pdf.

Hayek, F. A. (1983, February). Interview with F. A. Hayek. *Cato Policy Report.* http://www.cato.org/policy-report/february-1982/interview-fa-hayek.

Hayek, F. A. (1992). *The Fortunes of Liberalism Essays on Austrian Economics and the Ideal of Freedom. The Collected Works of F.A. Hayek* (P. Klein, Ed.). Chicago: University of Chicago Press.

Hayek, F. A. (1994). *Hayek on Hayek an Autobiographical Dialogue.* Supplement to *The Collected Works of F.A. Hayek* (S. Kresge & L. Wenar, Eds.). Chicago: University of Chicago Press.

Hayek, F. A. (1997). *Socialism and War: Essays, Documents, Reviews. The Collected Works of F.A. Hayek* (B. Caldwell, Ed.). Indianapolis: Liberty Fund.

Hayek, F. A. (1999). *Good Money Part 1 The New World. The Collected Works of F.A. Hayek* (S. Kresge, Ed.). Chicago: University of Chicago Press.

Hayek, F. A. (2007 [1944]). *The Road to Serfdom: The Definitive Edition. The Collected Works of F.A. Hayek* (B. Caldwell, Ed.). Chicago: University of Chicago Press.

Hayek, F. A. (2011 [1960]). *The Constitution of Liberty. The Definitive Edition. The Collected Works of F.A. Hayek* (R. Hamowy, Ed.). Chicago: University of Chicago Press.

Hayek, F. A. (2013). *Law, Legislation and Liberty.* London: Routledge.

Heiden, K. (1944). *Der Fuehrer* (R. Manheim, Trans.). Boston: Houghton Mifflin.

Hildebrandt, S. (2013, July). Wolfgang Bargmann (1906–1978) and Heinrich von Hayek (1900–1969): Careers in Anatomy Continuing Through German National Socialism to Postwar Leadership. *Annals of Anatomy Anatomischer Anzeiger, 195*(4), 283–295. http://www.sciencedirect.com/science/article/pii/S0940960213000782.

Hildebrandt, S. (2016). *The Anatomy of Murder Ethical Transgressions and Anatomical Science During the Third Reich.* New York: Berghahn.

Hoppe, H.-H. (1995). In L. H. Rockwell, Jr. (Ed.), *Murray Rothbard: In Memorandum.* Auburn, AL: Ludwig von Mises Institute.

Hoppe, H.-H. (2001). *Democracy the God That Failed: The Economics and Politics of Monarchy, Democracy and Natural Order.* New Brunswick: Transaction Publishers.

Hoppe, H.-H. (2017, October 7). Coming of Age with Murray. Mises Institute's 35th Anniversary Celebration in New York City. https://mises.org/library/coming-age-murray-0.

Horwitz, S. (2011, April 29). New Spanish Volume of Interviews with Austrians Steven Horwitz. *Coordination Problem.* http://www.coordinationproblem.org/2011/04/new-spanish-volume-of-interviews-with-austrians.html.

Horwitz, S. (2014, June 12). In Natural Disasters, Companies Operate Like Neighbours. *Wall Street Journal.* https://www.wsj.com/articles/in-natural-disasters-companies-operate-like-neighbors-1465338881, https://dailytimes.com.pk/76210/in-natural-disasters-companies-operate-like-neighbours/.

Hülsmann, J. G. (2007). *Mises: The Last Knight of Liberalism.* Auburn, AL: Ludwig von Mises Institute.

Johnson, P. (2009). *Churchill.* New York: Viking.

Keynes, J. M. (1936). *The General Theory of Employment, Interest and Money.* London: Macmillan.

Klausinger, H. (2006). From Mises to Morgenstern: Austrian Economics During the Ständestaat. *Quarterly Journal of Austrian Economics, 9*(3), 25–43.

Klausinger, H. (2010). Hayek on Practical Business Cycle Research: A Note. In H. Hagemann, T. Nishizawa, & Y. Ikeda (Eds.), *Austrian Economics in Transition: From Carl Menger to Friedrich Hayek* (pp. 218–234). Basingstoke, UK: Palgrave Macmillan.

Klausinger, H. (2012). Editorial Notes. In F. A. Hayek (Ed.), *Business Cycles. The Collected Works of F.A. Hayek.* Chicago: University of Chicago Press.

Klausinger, H. (2014). Academic Anti-semitism and the Austrian School: Vienna 1918–1945. *Atlantic Economic Journal, 42,* 191–204.

Klausinger, H. (2015, June). Hans Mayer, Last Knight of the Austrian School, Vienna Branch. *History of Political Economy, 47*(2), 271–305.

Klor, E. F., Saiegh, S., & Satyanath, S. (2017). *Cronyism in State Violence: Evidence from Labor Repression During Argentina's Last Dictatorship.* Mimeo. http://pages.ucsd.edu/~ssaiegh/paper_KSS.pdf.

Koether, G. (2000). A Life Among Austrians. *Austrian Economics Newsletter, 20*(3). https://mises.org/system/tdf/aen20_3_1_0.pdf?file=1&type=document.

Kuehnelt-Leddihn, E. (pseudonym Campbell, F. S.). (1978 [1943]). *The Menace of the Herd: Or, Procrustes at Large (Studies in Conservative Philosophy).* New York: Gordon Press.

Lake, R. (2005, February 5). Lecture Causes Dispute. *Los Vegan Review Journal.* https://web.archive.org/web/20050209040615/http://www.reviewjournal.com/lvrj_home/2005/Feb-05-Sat-2005/news/25808494.html.

Leonard, R. (2010). *Von Neumann, Morgenstern, and the Creation of Game Theory: From Chess to the Social Sciences.* Cambridge: Cambridge University Press.

Leonhardt, D. (2016, December 8). The American Dream, Quantified at Last. *New York Times.* https://www.nytimes.com/2016/12/08/opinion/the-american-dream-quantified-at-last.html.

Leube, K. R. (2004, February 10). Friedrich A. Hayek: His Life and Work. Auditorio Friedrich A. Hayek, Universidad Francisco Marroquín, Guatemala. http://www.newmedia.ufm.edu/gsm/index.php/Leubehayek.

Liggio, L. (2010). A Classical Liberal Life. In W. Block (Ed.), *I Chose Liberty: Autobiographies of Contemporary Libertarians.* Auburn, AL: Ludwig von Mises Institute.

MacLean, N. (2017). *Democracy in Chains: The Deep History of the Radical Right's Stealth Plan for America.* New York: Viking/Penguin Random House.
Mayer, J. (2010, August 30). Covert Operations: The Billionaire Brothers Who are Waging a War Against Obama. *New Yorker.* https://www.newyorker.com/magazine/2010/08/30/covert-operations.
Mayer, J. (2016). *Dark Money: The Hidden History of the Billionaires Behind the Rise of the Radical Right.* New York: Penguin.
McGurn, W. (2017, October 2). The Morality of Charles Koch. *Wall Street Journal.* https://www.wsj.com/articles/the-morality-of-charles-koch-1506983981.
Mises, L. (1912). *Theorie des Geldes und der Umlaufsmittel.* Munich: Duncker and Humblot.
Mises, L. (1922). *Die Gemeinwirtschaft: Untersuchungen über den Sozialismus.* Jena: Gustav Fischer Verlag. http://docs.mises.de/Mises/Mises_Gemeinwirtschaft.pdf.
Mises, L. (1944). *Bureaucracy.* New Haven: Yale University Press.
Mises, L. (1949). *Human Action: A Treatise on Economics* (1st ed.). New Haven: Yale University Press.
Mises, L. (1951 [1932]). *Socialism: An Economic and Sociological Analysis* (J. Kahane, Trans.). New Haven: Yale University Press.
Mises, L. (1962). *The Ultimate Foundation of Economic Science: An Essay on Method.* New York: Van Nostrand.
Mises, L. (1963). *Human Action: A Treatise on Economics* (2nd ed.). New Haven: Yale University Press.
Mises, L. (1966). *Human Action: A Treatise on Economics* (3rd ed.). Chicago: Henry Regnery.
Mises, L. (1985 [1927]). *Liberalism in the Classical Tradition* (R. Raico, Trans.). Auburn, AL: Mises Institute.
Mises, L. (2009 [1978 (1940)]). *Memoirs.* Auburn, AL: Ludwig von Mises Institute.
Mises, M. (1976). *My Years with Ludwig von Mises.* New York: Arlington House.
Mises, M. (1984). *My Years with Ludwig von Mises* (2nd ed.). Cedar Falls, IA: Center for Futures Education.
Montes, L. (2015). *Friedman's Two Visits to Chile in Context.* http://jepson.richmond.edu/conferences/summer-institute/papers2015/LMontesSIPaper.pdf.
Morgan, L. (2011, July 18). End of a Royal Dynasty as Otto von Habsburg is Laid to Rest... with His Heart Buried in a Crypt 85 Miles Away. *MailOnline.*
North, G. K. (2002, January 21). Mises on Money. *Lewrockwell.com.* https://archive.lewrockwell.com/north/north83.html.
North, G. K. (2010). It All Began with Fred Schwartz. In W. Block (Ed.), *I Chose Liberty: Autobiographies of Contemporary Libertarians.* Auburn, AL: Ludwig von Mises Institute.
Olson, W. (1998, November). Reasonable Doubts: Invitation to a Stoning Getting Cozy with Theocrats. *Reason.* http://reason.com/archives/1998/11/01/invitation-to-a-stoning.

Polanyi, K. (1934). Othmar Spann: The Philosopher of Fascism. *New Britain*, 3(53), 6–7.
Polanyi, K. (1935). The Essence of Fascism. In D. Lewis, K. Polanyi, & J. Kitchen (Eds.), *Christianity and the Social Revolution*. London: Gollancz.
Popkin, S. (2012). *The Candidate: What It Takes to Win—And Hold—The White House*. Oxford: Oxford University Press.
Raico, R. (2013, February 20). An Interview with Ralph Raico. Mises Institute. https://mises.org/library/interview-ralph-raico-0.
Raico, R. (2014, October, 16). Leonard Liggio, RIP. *lewrockwell.com*. https://www.lewrockwell.com/lrc-blog/515224/.
Rapoport, R. (2000). *Hillsdale: Greek Tragedy in America's Heartland*. Oakland, CA: RDR Books.
Regnery, A. S. (2008). *Upstream: The Ascendance of American Conservatism*. New York: Threshold.
Reisman, G. (2002, March 16). Eugen von Böhm-Bawerk's 'Value, Cost, and Marginal Utility'. Austrian Scholars' Conference of the Ludwig von Mises Institute, Auburn, AL. https://www.capitalism.net/articles/Reisman%20Full.pdf.
Robbins, J. (2010). The Sine Qua Non of Enduring Freedom. *The Trinity Review* (295). http://www.trinityfoundation.org/PDF/The%20Trinity%20Review%2000295%20SineQuaNonEnduringFreedom.pdf.
Robbins, L. (2012 [1931]). Foreword. In F. A. Hayek (Ed.), *Business Cycles Part I. The Collected Works of F.A. Hayek* (H. Klausinger, Ed.). Chicago: University of Chicago Press.
Rockwell, L. (1994, December). The Cognitive State. *Rothbard Rockwell Report*, 18–19. http://www.unz.org/Pub/RothbardRockwellReport-1994dec-00018.
Rockwell, L. H., Jr. (1991, March 10). COLUMN RIGHT: It's Safe Streets Versus Urban Terror: In the '50s, Rampant Crime Didn't Exist Because Offenders Feared What the Police Would Do. *Los Angeles Times*.
Rockwell, L. H., Jr. (1997). The Future of Liberty Lets Not Give Into Evil. *Vital Speeches of the Day*, 64(3), 88–91. https://www.econbiz.de/Record/the-future-of-liberty-lets-not-give-into-evil-llewelyn-h-rockwell-jr-founder-and-president-of-the-ludwig-von-mises-institute/10005980503.
Rockwell, L. H., Jr. (2010a). Libertarianism and the Old Right. In W. Block (Ed.), *I Chose Liberty: Autobiographies of Contemporary Libertarians*. Auburn, AL: Ludwig von Mises Institute.
Rockwell, L. H., Jr. (2010b, February 21). EXCLUSIVE INTERVIEW Lew Rockwell on von Mises, Ron Paul, Free Markets and the Future of Freedom By Anthony Wile. *Daily Bell*.
Rothbard, M. N. (1973, October, 20). Ludwig von Mises 1881–1973. *Human Events*, 7.
Rothbard, M. N. (1993, August). Who Are the Terrorists? *Rothbard Rockwell Report*, 4(8). http://www.unz.org/Pub/RothbardRockwellReport-1993aug-00001.

Rothbard, M. N. (1994). Nation by Consent. Decomposing the National State. *Journal of Libertarian Studies*, *11*(1), 1–10. https://mises.org/library/uk-nation-consent.

Rothbard, M. N. (2010). *Strictly Confidential: The Private Volker Fund Memos of Murray N. Rothbard* (D. Gordon, Ed.). Auburn, AL: Ludwig von Mises Institute.

Schmelzer, M. (2010). *Freiheit für Wechselkurse und Kapital: Die Ursprünge neoliberaler Währungspolitik und die Mont Pélerin Society*. Marburg, Germany: Metropolitis.

Schulak, E. M., & Unterköfler, H. (2011). *The Austrian School of Economics: A History of Its Ideas, Ambassadors, and Institutions* (A. Oost-Zinner, Trans.). Auburn, AL: Ludwig von Mises Institute.

Shearmur, J. (2010). How I Became Almost a Libertarian. In W. Block (Ed.), *I Chose Liberty: Autobiographies of Contemporary Libertarians*. Auburn, AL: Ludwig von Mises Institute.

Socker, K. (1990). The State of Economics Today in Austria an Interview with Karl Socker. *Austrian Economics Newsletter*, 1–4. https://mises.org/library/state-economics-austria-today-interview-karl-socher.

Sowell, T. (2002). *A Personal Odyssey*. New York: Simon and Schuster.

Stigler, G. J. (1978). Why Have the Socialists Been Winning? Mont Pelerin Society 1978 General Meeting, Hong Kong, September 3–9.

Swedberg, R. (1992). *Schumpeter: A Biography*. Princeton: Princeton University Press.

Taylor, A. (2014, December 12). Brazil's Torture Report Brings President Dilma Rousseff to Tears. *Sydney Morning Herald*. http://www.smh.com.au/world/brazils-torture-report-brings-president-dilma-rousseff-to-tears-20141211-125fzz.html.

Watters, S. (2005, June 28). Von Habsburg on Presidents, Monarchs, Dictators. *Women's Wear Daily*. http://www.wwd.com/eye/people/von-habsburg-on-presidents-monarchs-dictators.

Wheeler, T. (1975, 26 September). Mont Pelerin Society: Microeconomics, Macrofellowship. *National Review*.

White, L. H. (2008). Did Hayek and Robbins Deepen the Great Depression? *Journal of Money, Credit and Banking*, *40*, 751–768.

Wieser, F. (1983 [1926]). *The Law of Power*. University of Nebraska–Lincoln: Bureau of Business Research.

Williams, W. (2010). *Up from the Projects: An Autobiography*. Stanford, CA: Hoover Press.

Wistrich, R. S. (2012). *Who's Who in Nazi Germany*. New York: Routledge.

Wright, T. C., & Oñate, R. (2005). Chilean Diaspora. In C. R. Ember, M. Ember, & I. Skoggard (Eds.), *Encyclopedia of Diasporas: Immigrant and Refugee Cultures Around the World* (Vol. II, pp. 57–65). New York: Springer. https://mises.org/system/tdf/qjae5_3_4.pdf?file=1&type=document.

CHAPTER 2

'Persuade the Intellectuals in the Hopes that Ultimately They Could Be Converted and Transmit My Ideas to the Public at Large'

Caldwell and Montes (2014a, 52; 2014b; 2015a, 305) assert that they 'have presented *evidence* [emphasis added] that Hayek's ideas were little known in Chile in the 1970s. As such, it is very unlikely that they played a role in the creation of the 1980 Chilean Constitution. It also does not seem that those who invoked his name to defend their own positions correctly represented Hayek's actual views.' In the Chilean version of their paper, this was narrowed down to 'Pedro Ibáñez and Carlos Cáceres, who knew Hayek, did not necessarily correctly interpret his ideas' (2015b, 127).[1]

On the unexamined surface of 'liberty': the 'priests and hired guns' (Goodwin 1988) of the 'free' market project the appearance of being highly credentialed and evidence-respecting. Beneath the surface, however: the inventor of the Laffer Curve was dismissed (or obliged to resign) from the University of Chicago after it was discovered that 'Dr. Art Laffer' was in reality 'Mr. Laffer' (Stigler wrote the recommendation suggesting the cut); in an IEA press release on privatisation, their employee, 'Dr Sudha Shenoy,' was listed as the authority to be contacted[2]; in order to 'Debunk Climate Change Propaganda and Provide Balanced Perspective,' 'Dr Leon Louw' and 'Lord Monckton' created a 'CFACT' lobby at the 2011 Durban United Nations Climate Change conference[3]; 'Dr. Kurt Leube D.L.E,' CSUH/EB Professor of Economics, has no post-secondary qualifications and, according to

© The Author(s) 2018
R. Leeson, *Hayek: A Collaborative Biography*,
Archival Insights into the Evolution of Economics,
https://doi.org/10.1007/978-3-319-74509-1_2

Hayek, was unable to pass his undergraduate economics units; Ebeling earned a living as an NYU 'Post Doctoral Fellow,' sixteen years before obtaining a Ph.D.; and Boettke (2009a)—who had one (unsuccessful) opportunity to obtain a non-Austrian educational qualification and was obliged to retake first-year college at Grove City—claims (falsely, it seems) to have 'completed a post-doc fellowship at Stanford' (Leeson 2018b, Chapter 4).

According to his GMU cv, Boettke obtained a 'B.A. in Economics, Grove City College, May 1983,' an M.A. in 1987, a Ph.D. in 1989 and was a GMU 'Visiting Assistant Professor of Economics, 1987–1988.'[4] Boettke (2011, 19) also asserts that he has been 'teaching college economics since 1985, and during the past quarter of a century of teaching 20 of those years has been spent teaching Ph.D students.' Boettke (2012) described himself as a middle-aged 'cheerleader'—in 1991, did he—an untenured, freshly minted graduate of a low-status institution—teach NYU Ph.D. students?

The Mises Institute *Scholars Edition* of *Human Action* (1998) deleted Mises' (1963, 282; 1966, 282) lobbying for the Warfare State. The required readings for Boettke's (2011, 25) 'Austrian Theory of the Market Process I' consists of 'Mises's [?] *Human Action*; Hayek's [1948] *Individualism and Economic Order*; Rothbard's [2001 (1962)] *Man, Economy, and State*; and [Israel] Kirzner's [1978] *Competition and Entrepreneurship* … You are expected to not just read these works, but to master these texts in the same way that you were expected to master [Boettke's emphases] the texts of Mas-Colell in microeconomics or David Romer in macroeconomics.' Boettke was addressing 'advanced students of economics whose goal is to become a scholar in the fields of economics and political economy.' Yet it appears that at GMU, Boettke offers not a training in economics but a career path for followers: 'If you want to be an Austrian economist, then you need have to know these works by Mises, Hayek, Rothbard, and Kirzner.' The taxpayer would object to funding students to uncritically 'master' Adolf Hitler's work—do they wish to fund students to 'master' the study of Hitler's enablers (Mises and Hayek) together with a spotter for Al-Qaeda (Rothbard)?

In the *Review of Austrian Economics* version of their paper, Caldwell and Montes (2014a, 17; 2014b; 2015a, 275) report further 'evidence': 'Hayek had throughout his career been known for keeping his disagreements with opponents on a professional level'—a false assertion repeated in the first instalment of Caldwell's (2004, 147) 'definitive' biography and in a chapter for a GMU volume edited by Boettke and Virgil Storr (Caldwell 2016, 11). According to David O'Mahony (a self-described 'friend'), Hayek's 'sense of humour was delightfully impish, as, for example, when he used to turn off his hearing aid with obvious relish rather than endure a pompous speaker. He was always courteous and polite.'[5] And according to an editorial in the *Austrian Economics Newsletter* (1993, 2), Hayek had a 'general reluctance to engage in direct confrontation with his colleagues.'

Hitler (1941 [1925], 955) referred to 'old impotent State structures,' and Hayek (1994, 95, 85) implied that the founder of the British Welfare State suffered from erectile dysfunction—quoting Beveridge's future wife: 'He isn't man enough; he isn't man enough. I know.' Hayek—who wrote *Essays on the impotent price structure of Britain and monopoly in the labour market* (1984)—told Nadim Shehadi: 'I personally believe that Beveridge was completely incapable of any sexuality' (cited by Dahrendorf 1995, 156).

Those who came of age during the 'Great' War became known as the 'lost generation'; the first generation of Keynesian tended to come of age during the Austrian-promoted Great Depression. In *The Daily Telegraph*, Hayek (1976a [30 September 1975]) used contemptuous ('doctrinaires') and Nazi-style ('plague') language to denigrate the 'lost generation' of Keynesians whose 'quack medicine' will 'survive among those blind doctrinaires who have always been convinced that they have the key to salvation, another plague like Marxism, with which it indeed has much in common.' Hayek (1994, 95)—who described himself as 'rather malicious ... I don't keep my mouth shut'—told Cubitt (2006, 5) that he and his fellow European émigrés sat in the 'sardonic corner' of the LSE Common Room making 'malicious' comments about the competence of their English colleagues.

In one sense, 'Hayek' was a Randian hero—the Archives reveal that he had a visceral dislike of Jews, non-whites and many of his fellow libertarians. In public, Hayek (1976b, 87) referred to the similarities between himself and the 'majority of my contemporary libertarian economists'; but in private, when Raico invited him to join the Board of Advisors of the Center for Libertarian Studies (CLS), Hayek (23 November 1975) agreed on one condition—that he would not be placed in the company of those whose views he 'intensely' disliked.[6]

Characteristically, when Hayek (8 August 1948) sought a publishing outlet for 'Intellectuals and Socialism,' he asked John Davenport to deposit his fee in a New York bank rather than remit it to him not in England where he was planning what Lionel Robbins called a 'bootleg' divorce.[7] In 'The Intellectuals and Socialism,' Hayek (1949, 427, 437) expressed contempt for the 'inferior ... mediocrities' that he was recruiting. Referring to 'the nature of intellectual work,' Hayek (1978a) calculated: 'Of course, scientists are pretty bad, but they're not as bad as what I call the *intellectual*, a certain dealer in ideas, you know. They are really the worst part. But I think the man who's learned a little science, the little general problems, lacks the humility the *real* [emphases added] scientist gradually acquires.'[8]

Having promoted deflation to deal with 'mighty' labour unions, Hayek (2007 [1944], Chapter 10; 1949) then needed to recruit 'the worst part' and assist them to 'Get on Top':

> What we lack is a liberal Utopia, a program which seems neither a mere defense of things as they are nor a diluted kind of socialism, but a truly liberal radicalism which does not spare the susceptibilities of the mighty (including the [labour] trade unions), which is not too severely practical, and which does not confine itself to what appears today as politically possible. We need *intellectual* [emphasis added] leaders who are willing to work for an ideal, however small may be the prospects of its early realization.

In *Law, Legislation and Liberty*, Hayek (1973, 64) reiterated the faith-based religious foundation of 'free' market 'knowledge':

> It is not to be denied that to some extent the guiding model of the overall order will always be an utopia, something to which the existing situation will be only a distant approximation and which many people will regard as wholly impractical. Yet it is only by constantly holding up the guiding conception of an internally consistent model which could be realized by the application of the same principles that anything like the effective framework for a functioning spontaneous order will be achieved.

Hayek (1978a) told James Buchanan that this spontaneous order would have to be reconstructed (Chapter 1, above) and (using his dissembling word, 'curious') explained to Robert Chitester that

> I am in a curious conflict because I have very strong positive feelings on the need of an 'un-understood' moral tradition, but all the factual assertions of religion, which are crude because they all believe in ghosts of some

kind, have become completely unintelligible to me. I can never sympathize with it, still less explain it.⁹

For Mises, the crucial factors in his friendship were Hayek's 'integrity' and appreciation for 'free' markets. Hayek (12 January 1941) assured Mises that he need have no fear about him becoming 'converted' to Keynesianism (cited by Hülsmann 2007, 701). For Hayek, however, his own status and income out-trumped ideology: a position perfectly consistent with Austrian perceptions about *Human Action* (Mises 1949). With respect to ideology, Hayek (1978a) described the problem:

> The good scientist is essentially a humble person. But you already have the great difference in that respect between, say, the scientist and the engineer. The engineer is the typical rationalist, and he dislikes anything which he cannot explain and which he can't see how it works. What I now call constructivism I used to call the engineering attitude of mind, because the word is very frequently used. They want to direct the economy as an engineer directs an enterprise. The whole idea of planning is essentially an engineering approach to the economic world.¹⁰

Three decades before, in *Individualism and Economic Order* 'Socialist Calculation I. The Nature and History of the Problem,' Hayek (1948, 121) also reflected: 'The increasing preoccupation of the modern world with problems of an engineering character tends to blind people to the totally different character of the economic problem and is probably the main cause why the nature of the latter was less and less understood.' In 1948, while marketing *The Road to Serfdom* in America, Hayek delivered a Mises-organised lecture on 'Why I am not a Keynesian.'¹¹ Two years later, Hayek became the American sales agent for the engineering-derived Keynesian Phillips Machine¹² and recruited Fritz Machlup as a sub-agent.¹³

The British Classical Liberal, Richard Cobden (1804–1865), welcomed the advance of democracy as an assault on the intergenerational privileges of 'aristocratic plunderers' (Edsall 1986, 52–53). Cubitt (2006, 122, 10) reported that her employer, 'von' Hayek, was one of these plunderers.

The incompetence of those who administered the neo-feudal 'spontaneous' order was revealed by the half-million casualties pointlessly inflicted during the Battle of Passchendaele (July–November 1917). A century later, ascribed status was further undermined when an

'Untouchable' was elected the 14th President of the world's largest democracy, India (Najarjuly 2017). Mises (1985 [1927], 43) asserted that the 'statesmen representative of democracy soon rendered it everywhere ridiculous. Those of the old regime had displayed a certain aristocratic dignity, at least in their outward demeanor. The new ones, who replaced them, made themselves contemptible by their behavior. Nothing has done more harm to democracy in Germany and Austria than the hollow arrogance and impudent vanity with which the Social-Democratic leaders who rose to power after the collapse of the empire conducted themselves.'

One of those politicians was Wilhelm Miklas (1872–1956) who rose from low ascribed status to become President of the Austrian Republic. Mises (2009 [1978 (1940)], 80) sneered at his educational background:

> Miklas, who had been a secondary school history teacher, once participated in a discussion on the 'most favored nation' clause with me and Professor Richard Reisch, the then president of the National Bank. In the course of the discussion I mentioned the [1871] Peace of Frankfurt. Miklas inquired as to when and between which countries this treaty had been signed.

According to Boettke (2011, 21–22), both Hayek and Mises 'objected to being labeled, though they were both proud of their educational and intellectual heritage in Vienna.' The classically educated Hayek (1994, 84) concluded Department of Economics meetings with a call-to-action against the LSE Director who had recruited him: '*Beveridge delendus est*' ('Beveridge should be destroyed'). But: 'It turned out that the LSE economists, and even Lionel Robbins, had not had a classical education … I found out that not one of them understood what I was saying. It's a famous phrase, a story from, I believe, Cicero … I assumed this to be popular knowledge …'

At the LSE, Hermann Finer (1945)—who presumably heard Hayek making racist and anti-Semitic remarks—detected his 'thoroughly Hitlerian contempt for the democratic man.' Mises shared this contempt. In private celebration of *Atlas Shrugged*, Mises (2007a [1958], 11) told Ayn Rand: 'You have the courage to tell the masses what no politician told them: you are inferior and all the improvements in your conditions which you simply take for granted you owe to the effort of men who are better than you.' With respect to intergenerational inferiority, in 1943, Mises informed a correspondent that he did 'not believe that a member of the Hitler youth or of the equivalent groups in Italy, Hungary or so on can ever turn toward honest work and non-predatory jobs. *Beasts cannot be domesticated within one or two generations* [emphasis added]' (cited by Hülsmann 2007, 817). But according to Ebeling (Society for the History of Economics, SHOE 20 December 2015): 'Mises wrote in several of his writings on the biological and historical wrong-headedness of the racial and racist theories of his time, and always argued that the hallmark of a liberal democracy was an impartial rule of law with equal civil rights and economic liberty for all in society.'

Referring to 'Ludendorff and Hitler' and other 'Fascists,' Mises (1985 [1927], 44) concluded: 'Many arguments can be urged for and against these doctrines, depending on one's religious and philosophical convictions, about which any agreement is scarcely to be expected. This is not the place to present and discuss the arguments pro and con, for they are not conclusive.'

Newspapers reports of the 1923 Ludendorff and Hitler Bavarian *Putsch* stated that as a prelude to a march on Berlin, 'Hitlerites stormed through the town and invaded first class restaurants and hotels in search of Jews and profiteers' (Walsh 1968, 289). Two years later, Hitler (1939 [1925], 518) asserted in *Mein Kampf*: 'At the beginning of the war, or even during the war, if 12,000 or 15,000 of these Jews who were corrupting the nation had been forced to submit to poison gas ... then the millions of sacrifices made at the front would not have been in vain.'

In 'The Role of Doctrines in Human History,' Mises (1990 [1949/1950], 301–302) distinguished between 'esoteric teaching'—for 'advanced spirits'—and 'exoteric' teaching—for 'helpless ... credulous ... narrow-minded dullards':

> All doctrines are taught and accepted at least in two different, nay, conflicting varieties ... Catholicism [for example] had a different meaning for Cardinal Newman and for the hosts of the credulous ... The same dualism can be stated with all social, economic, and political doctrines ... An unbridgeable gulf separates the esoteric teaching from the exoteric one.

Hayek (1997 [1949], 224) insisted that there was a crucial distinction between the '*real* [emphasis added] scholar or expert and the practical man of affairs' and non-propertied intellectuals, who were a 'fairly new phenomenon of history' and whose low ascribed status deprived them of what Hayek regarded as a central qualification: 'experience of the working of the economic system which the administration of property gives.' According to Mises (1990 [1949/1950], 301–302): 'Between the philosophers and scholars who contrive new ideas and build up elaborate systems of thought and the narrow-minded dullards whose poor intellect cannot grasp but the simplest things there are many gradual transitions ... Only a small elite has the ability to absorb more refined chains of thought. Most people are simply helpless when faced with the more subtle problems of implication or valid inference.'

In 'Liberty's Heritage,' John Hospers (1978, 12, 14) cited Rose Wilder Lane: 'My attachment to these United States is wholly, entirely, absolutely The Revolution, the real world Revolution, which men began here and which has, so to speak, a foothold on earth here. If reactionaries succeed in destroying the revolutionary structure of social and political human life here, I care no more about this continent than about any other.' As a 'free' market promoter, she did not 'think that any honesty is involved in paying taxes. Taxation is plain armed robbery; tax-collectors are armed robbers. I will save my property from them in any way that I think I can get away with.' She took

> advantage of every legality that any attorney can find in the tax 'laws' so called, and regulations. I have no scruples about this whatever, anything that I want to do with *my* [Lane's emphasis] money, and that I can in any way slip under any legality so that the robbers won't find it and rob me of some of it, I do. They make the legalities, trying to be smart about who gets how much of my property; and to keep as much as possible of my own, I'll outsmart them if I can.

Lane (5 July 1947) told Mises that as an American she was 'of course' 'fundamentally' opposed to democracy and to 'anyone advocating or defending democracy, which in theory and practice is the basis of socialism.' It was 'precisely democracy' that was 'destroying the American political structure, American law, and the American economy' (cited by Hülsmann 2007, 859). The tax-evading Hayek (1978a) partially agreed:

> of course socialism and unlimited democracy come very much to the same thing ... a modern kind of democracy, which I call unlimited democracy,

is probably more subject to the influence of special interests than any former form of government was. Even a dictator can say no, but this kind of government cannot say no to any splinter group which it needs to be a majority.[14] I'm afraid so long as we retain the present form of unlimited democracy, all we can hope for is to slow down the process, but we can't reverse it. I am pessimistic enough to be convinced that unless we change our constitutional structure, we are going to be driven on against people's wishes deeper and deeper into government control.[15]

Mises was FEE's *'spiritus rector'*—literally: *'Führer'* or 'ruler' (Hülsmann 2007, 884). As populism provides opportunities for a would-be *Führer*, so the slogan of 'consumer sovereignty' protects tobacco producers from the intended consequences of their product (addiction). In *Human Action*, Mises (1998 [1949], 24) explained what truth meant to him: 'Granted that science cannot give us truth—and who knows what truth really means—at any rate it is certain that it works in leading us to success.' In *An Essay on Method*, Mises (1962, 93) provided *The Ultimate Foundation of Economic Science*—producer sovereignty ('the elite' must dominate the 'masses of inferior people'):

> If the small minority of enlightened citizens who are able to conceive sound principles of political management do not succeed in winning the support of their fellow citizens and converting them to the endorsement of policies that bring and preserve prosperity, the cause of mankind and civilization is hopeless. There is no other means to safeguard a propitious development of human affairs than to make the masses of inferior people adopt the ideas of the elite. This has to be achieved by convincing them. It cannot be accomplished by a despotic regime that instead of enlightening the masses beats them into submission. In the long run the ideas of the majority, however detrimental they may be, will carry on. The future of mankind depends on the ability of the elite to influence public opinion in the right direction.

Ebeling (2014) complained about those who 'arrogantly believe they know better how other people should live and interact with their fellow men, and who want to manipulate the outcomes of human life more to their own liking.' Mises (1966, 723–724) was an interventionist—a totalitarian all-round 'knowledge' planner—who would decide what that 'right direction' would be. He distrusted the operation of the market 'unhampered' by him and his fellow ideologues and was imitating what he described as intervention by another elite—the government:

as soon as the outcome brought about by the operation of the unhampered market differs from what the authorities consider 'socially' desirable, the government interferes. That means the market is free as long as it does precisely what the government wants it to do. It is 'free' to do what the authorities consider to be the 'right' things, but not to do what they consider the 'wrong' things; the decision concerning what is right and what is wrong rests with the government. Thus the doctrine and the practice of interventionism ultimately tend to abandon what originally distinguished them from outright socialism and to adopt entirely the principles of totalitarian all-round planning.[16]

The threat to Mises' (2007b [1957], 66–67) 'liberty' came from an 'intolerant majority': 'There is virtually only one factor that has the power to make people unfree—tyrannical public opinion. The struggle for freedom is ultimately not resistance to autocrats or oligarchs but resistance to the despotism of public opinion. It is not the struggle of the many against the few but of minorities—sometimes of a minority of but one man—against the majority. The worst and most dangerous form of absolutist rule is that of an intolerant majority. Such is the conclusion arrived at by Tocqueville and John Stuart Mill.' Friedman's (2017 [1991]) conclusion about Mises and his followers is expressed in 'Say "No" to Intolerance.'

In *The Constitution of Liberty*, Hayek (2011 [1960], 186) asserted that the less-free find freedom through servitude: 'To do the bidding of others is for the employed the condition of achieving his purpose.' With respect to *The Road to Serfdom*, Hayek (1978a)

> was never quite happy with the title, which I really adopted for sound. The idea came from [Alexis de] Tocqueville, who speaks about the road to servitude; I would like to have chosen that title, but it doesn't sound good. So I changed 'servitude' into 'serfdom,' for merely phonetic reasons.[17]

De Tocqueville's (1835–1840, Book 2, Chapter 2) comparison of democracy with the supposed merits of an aristocratic-based hierarchy appears to describe the foundations of Mises' (1998 [1949]) *Human Action*: 'Aristocracy had made a chain of all the members of the community, from the peasant to the king: democracy breaks that chain, and severs every link of it. As social conditions become more equal, the number of persons increases who, although they are neither rich enough nor powerful enough to exercise any great influence over their fellow-creatures, have nevertheless acquired or retained sufficient education and fortune to satisfy their own wants. They owe nothing to any man, they expect nothing from any man; they acquire the habit of always considering themselves as standing alone, and they are apt to imagine that their whole destiny is in their own hands. Thus not only does democracy make every man forget his ancestors, but it hides his descendants, and separates his contemporaries from him; it throws him back forever upon himself alone, and threatens in the end to confine him entirely within the solitude of his own heart.'

The 'guiding idea' of Hayek's (1979) 'development' was the 'discovery' that the 'price system is really essential as a *guide* [Hayek's emphasis] to enable people to fit into an order.' Using his dissembling word, Hayek (1978a) described the British spontaneous order: 'the curious thing is that in the countryside of southwest England, the class distinctions are very sharp, but they're not resented. [laughter] They're still accepted as part of the natural order.'[18]

Wieser (1983 [1926], 293) described the 'spontaneous submission to the protection of the mighty one' in 'old Austria' and the 'Prussian part of Poland.'[19] In Austria and Prussia, the 'spontaneous' neo-feudal order that emerged after the 1848 revolution had been consciously (intelligently) designed: a 'glaringly unequal' electoral systems. Prussia had a three-class tax-based franchise for elections to the Lower House of the State Parliament: in this public, oral (that is, not secret), males-only ballot, a first (highest tax)-class vote was worth 17.5 times the value of a third (lowest tax)-class vote (Dwyer 2001, 132; Ponting 1998; Taylor 1955, Chapter 5). Extension of the franchise and equal-weighted votes came during the Weimar Republic.

Neoclassical theory predicts that incumbents will seek to deter entry to protect their privileged position; Hayek (1992 [1944], 208) promoted 'an affirmative attitude towards democracy without any superstitious deference to all its dogmatic applications, particularly without condoning the oppression of minorities any more than that of majorities.' Nobles and employers may have been the minorities he and Mises had in mind: until 1907, of 253 seats in the Lower House of the Habsburg Parliament, 85 were elected by 5000 nobles, and 21 by the 500 members of the Chambers of Commerce (Bark 2007, 18, 21; Ponting 1998; Hülsmann 2007, 187–188, 851, n26). This corporate-style state could be described as a weak version of Galbraith's (1952) countervailing power.

The *Economist* correctly noted that 'The great achievement of parliamentary democracy is that it takes potentially violent political conflicts and civilises them'[20]; before falsely asserted that 'Mises and Hayek were among the 20th century's most principled and pugnacious opponents of fascism, as well as articulate advocates of liberal democracy.'[21] Hayek (1978a) told Rosten: 'I believe in democracy as a system of peaceful change of government; but that's all its whole advantage is, no other. It just makes it possible to get rid of what government *we* [emphasis added] dislike.'[22]

The Mises Institute President provided a translation from the Austrian: 'democracy is a sham that should be opposed by all liberty-loving people … Democracy was always a bad idea, one that encourages mindless majoritarianism, political pandering, theft, redistribution, war, and an entitlement mentality among supposedly noble voters' (Deist 2017). For 'exoteric' purposes, Mises (1985 [1927], 44–45) nuanced his promotion of 'Ludendorff and Hitler': 'The only consideration that can be decisive is one that bases itself on the fundamental argument in favor of democracy.' Ludendorff ran for President in March 1925 (and received 1.1% of the vote). During the Great Depression—which Hayek and Mises sought to deepen—Hitler ran for President and obtained 36.8% of the vote (the Communist Party obtained 10.2%). Who else but Hitler could Hayek and Mises have supported in the 1932 German elections (Leeson 2018a)? Who else but 'neo-fascists' could Rothbard—one of 'Mises's most brilliant students' (Hülsmann 2007, 1022–1023)—have supported in the 1994 Italian elections (Chapter 6, below)?

Hayek described Pinochet's Junta as judicious—staffed by 'educated, reasonable, and insightful men - men who honestly hope that the country can be returned to a democratic order soon' (cited by Farrant et al. 2012, 518). After promoting General 'Ludendorff and Hitler,' Mises (1985 [1927], 44–45) nuanced his promotion of democracy: '*To be sure, it should not and need not be denied* [emphasis added] that there is one situation in which the temptation to deviate from the democratic principles of liberalism becomes very great indeed.' Mises described an emergency situation in which democracy produced policies of which he disapproved: 'If judicious men see their nation, or all the nations of the world, on the road to destruction, and if they find it impossible to induce their fellow citizens to heed their counsel, they may be inclined to think it only fair and just to resort to any means whatever, in so far as it is feasible and will lead to the desired goal, in order to save everyone from disaster. Then the idea of a dictatorship of the elite, of a government by the minority maintained in power by force and ruling in the interests of all, may arise and find supporters. But force is, never a means of overcoming these difficulties. The tyranny of a minority can never endure unless it succeeds in convincing the majority of the necessity or, at any rate, of the utility, of its rule. But then the minority no longer needs force to maintain itself in power.'

In 'Deception of Government Intervention,' Mises (1964) told *Christian Economics* readers: 'The intellectual and moral faculties of man can thrive only where people associate with one another peacefully. Peace is the origin of all human things, not - as Heraclitus said - war. But as human nature is, peace can be established and preserved only by a power fit and ready to crush all peacebreakers.' Referring to those with whom he sought to form a Nazi-Austrian School Pact, Mises (1985 [1927], 48–49, 51) also asserted: 'As soon as the first flush of anger had passed, their policy took a more moderate course and will probably become even more so with the passage of time. This moderation is the result of the fact that traditional liberal views still continue to have an unconscious influence on the Fascists.'

In inter-war 'Europe of the Dictators,' the democratic centre—what Hayek (1978a) denigrated as republics of 'peasants and workers'— looked likely to be squeezed out of existence.[23] Stalin used his producer sovereignty to prevent national Communist Parties collaborating with social democrats to stop the Nazis; while Mises' 'biggest academic' project in 1931–1932 was the second edition of *Sozialismus* (Hülsmann 2007, 653).

The unemployment-inducing deflation that Mises and Hayek promoted undermined labour unions: revenue (union dues) fall and outgoings (unemployment benefits) increase. Twenty-three months before Hitler came to power, Mises (2006 [28 February 1931], 158, 166-7) expressed outrage to the Association of German Industry: the other trade unions—'labor unions'—were aiming for 'pseudo-economic democracy ... If this system were carried out, it would disorganize the entire production apparatus and thus destroy *our* [emphasis added] civilization.' Mises offered an evangelical assault: 'The labor unions use force to attain their goals. Only union members, who ask the established union wage rate and who work according to union-prescribed methods, are permitted to work in industrial undertakings. Should an employer refuse to accept union conditions, there are work stoppages. Workers who would like to work, in spite of the reproach heaped on such an undertaking by the union, are forced by acts of violence to give up any such plan. This tactic on the part of the labor unions presupposes, of course, that the government at least acquiesces in their behavior. If the government were to proceed against those who molest persons willing to work and those who destroy machines and industrial equipment in enterprises that want to hire strikebreakers, as it normally does against the other perpetrators of violence, the situation would be very different. However, the characteristic feature of modern governments is that they have capitulated to the labor unions.'

Bartley (a homosexual who reportedly died of AIDS-related cancer) talked openly about his 'Last Tango in Vienna' biographical conclusion: Hayek's sexual activity with his cousin and second wife (but not, presumably, his first wife) resembled his own. Hayek (1978a) cut Robert Bork short when he began to ask about 'sexual permissiveness' and 'depravity':

> Well, I think America is in a very early stage of the process. You see, it comes with a restriction of economic freedom, which only then has effects on the mental or intellectual freedom. In a way, American development is probably a generation behind the one which gave me the illustrations–the German development. The American degree of restrictions of freedom is perhaps comparable to what it was in Germany in the 1880s or 1890s under Bismarck, when he began to interfere with the economic affairs. Only ultimately, under Hitler, did the government have the power which American government very nearly has. It doesn't use it yet to interfere with intellectual freedom. In fact, perhaps the danger to intellectual freedom in the United States comes not from government so much as from the [labour] trade unions.[24]

To defend Mises' promotion of 'Fascists,' his translator, Raico (2012, 250, 275, 274), referred to the 'position of mainstream of Italian economics, which included Vilfredo Pareto and Maffeo Pantaleoni.' Pareto 'endorsed the Fascist takeover, and, a year before his death, permitted Mussolini to appoint him to the Senate.' Pareto suggested that the 'author of an article in the socialist paper *Avanti!* endorsing the strikers' violence should be taken care of by General Bava Beccaris, who had just supervised a massacre of violently protesting socialists in Milan.' Pareto explained:

To lack the courage needed to defend oneself, to abandon any resistance, to submit to the generosity of the victor, even more, to carry cowardice to the point of assisting him and facilitating his victory, is the characteristic of the feeble and degenerate man. Such an individual merits nothing but scorn, and for the good of society it is useful that he should disappear as quickly as possible.

After returning from his 1977 tour of the Operation Condor countries, Hayek (1978a) explained to James Buchanan how to force labour unions to 'give in'—'you just had to raise your finger' (Leeson 2018, Chapter 2). And Esteban Klor, Sebastian Saiegh and Shanker Satyanath (2017) described how 'free' market cronyism (that Hayek supported in Videla's Argentina) determined who would disappear:

> Strikes at the firm level can be deterred by credibly signaling that a firm is able and willing to use its ties to the regime to access the state's repressive apparatus in response to labor activism … Only the disappearance of a union representative in a firm provides a credible signal of a connected firm's ability and willingness to access the repressive apparatus of the state. The resort to disappearances by connected firms may thus be driven by the incentive of credibly deterring future strikes.

This research

> may also serve to strengthen scholars' perceptions of the pervasiveness of cronyism. This would be justified because we have showed that even in a prominent case where political actors claimed to be motivated by the goal of attacking rent-seeking, the deployment of violence by these very actors followed the logic of cronyism. In light of the evidence presented here it would also make good sense to treat justifications for human rights violations based on high-minded goals with a greater degree of skepticism.

Hayek (1949, 432–433) declared: 'what we lack is a liberal Utopia.' Hayek's second authorised biographer reported that when caught in the 'cheating matter'—stealing, or double-dipping, from 'educational charities' to maintain his aristocratic lifestyle—Hayek 'just laughed, said he did not mind in the least, that all his professional considerations had been based on financial considerations.' When Walter Morris complained to Cubitt about being 'deceived [,] Hayek laughed, and told me that he had wanted to have nothing to do with this but did not mind being told about it as an anecdote' (Cubitt 2006, 122, 10). Hayek's fifth authorised biographer owes a

> special debt to Mrs. Dorothy Morris of the Morris Foundation, Little Rock, who provided me with the 'seed money' for the project … Walter Morris was instrumental in the creation of the *Collected Works* [of F. A. Hayek] project, and the Morris Foundation has been constant in its support throughout the years. I first sought financial support for the project at the Mont Pelerin meeting. (Caldwell 2007, x)

Adam Smith famously declared: 'People of the same trade seldom meet together, even for merriment and diversion, but the conversation ends in a conspiracy against the public, or in some contrivance to raise prices.' Two trade unions emerged from the Third Estate—for labour and employers, respectively. 'Von' Mises (1909–1938; 1945–1973) and 'von' Hayek (1947/1950–1992) were paid Second Estate lobbyists for employer trade unions.

Many leading 'free' market economists embrace 'Fascism' (Chapter 1); in contrast, German labour unions resisted: only 1.34% of those elected to industrial councils represented the Nazis (Kummer 1932, 14).[25] Wilhelm Keppler recalled Hitler announcing that when he achieved power, he would abolish labour unions and political parties—although Turner (1985, 243) doubts that he makes such a statement (at least in public). But in power, Hitler abolished all non-Nazi political parties and all labour unions—union leaders were taken into 'protective custody,' and workers were obliged to join the National Socialist Union. Hitler received a 0.03% levy on wages and salaries of employees of the German Trade Association (Davidson 1966, 192–193, 230, 204; Shirer 1960, 252–253; Bullock 1991, 133). Austrian-promoted deflation had been 'one of the strongest agents working towards the Republic's downfall' (Stolper 1967, 116–119).

The post-communist 'reconstruction' that facilitated the rise of 'Putin of the Oligarchs' (Haiduk 2015) had been 'informed' by 'von' Mises' blind faith in 'private charity.' Ebeling (2014b; 1997) was 'frequently in the Soviet Union during its last years, doing consulting work on market reform and privatization'—where he 'lectured on privatization' and 'consulted with the Lithuanian government, the City of Moscow and the Russian Parliament.' Ebeling's only qualifications were an eight-year undergraduate degree from California State College (later University), an M.A. from the Austrian program at Rutgers University and the Hillsdale College Ludwig von Mises Professorship of Economics. He was, presumably, one of Rothbard's 'We want externalities' chanters (Blundell 2014, 100, n. 7). Mont Pelerin Society (MPS) President, James Buchanan (14 April 1986), regarded Ebeling as unworthy of financial support from the 'free' market Welfare State because he is a 'total fool.'[26]

According to Ebeling (2015a), 'In spite of the pervasiveness of the [non-Austrian] Welfare State in our modern society and the tax burden that is imposed to fund it, it is worth remembering that Americans' generosity and benevolence still stands as a beacon for the world. In 2013, Americans donated nearly $420 billion to charitable causes, and this was a nearly 13% increase over the 2012 level of voluntary philanthropy in the United States. But a culture of self-responsibility and benevolence can be and is undermined by a paternalistic state, in which the government not only takes away the income and wealth through which individuals can express and reflect their values and beliefs, but weakens the very idea that such decisions and judgments should be in private rather than political hands.' But in 2015, 'Charitable giving' accounted for 2.1% of gross domestic product, and the majority of tax-deductible charitable dollars went to religion (32%), education (15%), human services (12%), grant-making foundations (11%) and health (8%).[27]

As Adam Smith famously declared: 'it is not from the benevolence of the butcher, the brewer, or the baker that we expect our dinner, but from their regard to their own interest.' The 'free' market is funded by the 'educational' charities associated with Richard Mellon Scaife (Teacher 2018a). His mother, Sarah Cordelia Mellon, was the niece of Andrew Mellon, the deflation-promoting Treasury Secretary (1921–1932) who, according to President Herbert Hoover (1952, 29–32), was responsible for his one-term status:

> Two schools of thought quickly developed within our administration discussions. First was the 'leave it alone liquidationists' headed by Secretary of the Treasury Mellon, who felt that government must keep its hands off and let the slump liquidate itself. Mr. Mellon had only one formula: 'Liquidate labor, liquidate stocks, liquidate the farmers, liquidate real estate.' He insisted that, when the people get an inflation brainstorm, the only way to get it out of their blood is to let it collapse. He held that even a panic was not altogether a bad thing. He said: 'It will purge the

rottenness out of the system. High costs of living and high living will come down. People will work harder, live a more moral life. Values will be adjusted, and enterprising people will pick up the wrecks from less competent people.'[28]

In 1932—with 23.53% Great Depression unemployment—17,000 'Great' War veterans and their families demanded early cash-payment redemption of their 1924 service certificates. The Army Chief of Staff, General Douglas MacArthur, used six tanks to remove the 'Bonus Expeditionary Force' and demolish their Washington camp. 'Lt. Col. Richard M. Ebeling, PhD' (2013) was outraged at

> pictures of 'anti-austerity' demonstrations in many European countries. The cries are all the same: 'Please don't take away my government job, don't take away my government pension, don't take away my government health care, my government-guaranteed wage and work conditions, my government mandated month's vacation, my government provided... everything.'

Referring to 'pediacracy,' David Brooks (2017) noted that over the 'past generation, members of the college-educated class have become amazingly good at making sure their children retain their privileged status. They have also become devastatingly good at making sure the children of other classes have limited chances to join their ranks ... As soon as they get money, they turn it into investments in their kids ... Upper-middle-class parents have the means to spend two to three times more time with their preschool children than less affluent parents. Since 1996, education expenditures among the affluent have increased by almost 300%, while education spending among every other group is basically flat ... We in the educated class have created barriers to mobility that are more devastating for being invisible.'

In 'Austrian Economics and the Public Mind,' the *Financial Times* journalist Michael Prowse (2014 [1996]) explained to the Mises Institute 'Scholars' Conference at Auburn University how he became an Austrian: 'simply moving from England to the U.S. six years ago.' The 'free market/libertarian case is presented with far greater vigor here than in the U.K. My *faith* [emphasis added] in markets as a ladder of personal opportunity has been strengthened because here in the U.S. the link between wealth and social class seems less pronounced than in Europe.

It is striking how often U.S. supporters of liberty and free markets come from relatively humble backgrounds.'

Some who benefit from government-assisted upward social mobility seek to kick away the ladder for future generations. How did Ebeling become the acknowledged 'Grand Old Man' of the 'free' market? The taxpayer may have devoted hundreds of thousands of dollars in an attempt to provide him with an education (primary and secondary school, California State College, The State University of Rutgers, Middlesex Polytechnic/University), and before his employment at the government-funded Citadel Military College, he had been employed at Rutgers.

Sennholz—a 'Misean for Life' *Luftwaffe* bomber pilot—was 'almost alone among eminent free enterprise economists' in resting 'his defense of a free society on revelation … divinely revealed information' (John Robbins 2010). Referring to a card-carrying Austro-Fascist and promoter of 'Ludendorff and Hitler,' Sennholz would announce to his Grove City College students: 'next week we will discuss the master's work' (cited by Boettke 2009b). Boettke told Doherty (2007, 423–424) that Sennholz didn't 'reach you with the technical aspects, but with the ideological aspects. Sennholz explained the welfare state as this giant circle with all of our hands in our neighbors' pockets. This was 15 years ago and I can still remember it. How many people with one lecture 15 years ago can make you still remember that lecture? … Sennholz could get you hyped up on your ability to walk through fire for *the truth* [emphasis added].'

Ebeling's (2017) mission is to replace 'pocket-picking political plunderers' with 'Private benevolence.' In 'Austrian Economics on the Rise,' Ebeling (1974) described the tax-exempt Austrian revivalist conference at which attendees competed with each other over what Friedman described as 'rotten bastard' proposals: the speed with which non-Austrian (i.e. non-aristocratic, non-tax-exempt and non-academic) 'entitlements' could be eliminated—forcing wounded veterans, the sick, the elderly, the young, the poor and the famine-stricken to seek private charity.[29] As Bettina Greaves (1998) put it, publicly funded 'care for the sick and elderly,' etc., is 'contrary to freedom and contrary to capitalism, and they produce undesirable consequences for society in the long run. They impede the ability of people to cooperate in their own material betterment.'

In 'A World Without the Welfare State,' Ebeling (2015a) asserted: 'The [non-Austrian] Welfare State makes us all poorer in character and independence.' Referring to 'healthy self-correcting market rebalancing and readjustment,' Ebeling (2013) insisted:

> a degree of price 'deflation' is always likely to be part of the recovery period of the business cycle ... Nobody has a crystal ball to read the shape-of-things-to-come. The reason for this is that nothing is predetermined or foreordained. History is the product of human action, and human action is the result of ideas put into motion. That is why we should never 'give up' or think there is no hope or chance. Ideas do have consequences – for good or evil. Our responsibility is to be voices of reason and sound thinking in defense of liberty.

In *Deflation and Liberty*, Hülsmann (2008a, 7, 14–15) also insisted: 'We should not be afraid of deflation. We should love it as much as our liberties'—Rothbard was 'The outstanding modern theoretician of deflation.' Hülsmann asked: 'what is actually wrong with deflating the money supply, from an economic point of view? This question will be at center stage here, which can fortunately build on Rothbard's analysis of deflation, which demonstrated in particular the beneficial role that deflation can have in speeding up the readjustment of the productive structure after a financial crisis. But no economist seems to have been interested in further pursuing the sober analysis of the impact of deflation on the market process, and of its social and political consequences. The truth is that deflation has become the scapegoat of the economics profession. It is not analyzed, but derided. One hundred years of pro-inflation propaganda have created a quasi-total agreement on the issue.' 'It's evilness' is regarded by economists as 'beyond dispute.'

When *in*flationary expectations become embedded in the system, A. W. H. Phillips' macroeconomic model became 'unstable' (Leeson 1994a, b, 1997). When *de*flation (or price falls) becomes expected, quantities will adjust: demanders will (wherever possible) delay expenditures to take advantage of a lower future price, while suppliers will attempt to sell their current inventory to avoid having to sell later. As the downturn deepens, firms will delay production plans—debt deflation will drive many out of business.

According to Ebeling (2014a:)

It was precisely the Austrian economists, such as Ludwig von Mises and Friedrich A. Hayek, who argued that economic depressions do not just 'happen' due to some inherent irrationality in investor psychology.

In the *New York Times*, Sylvia Nasar (1992) reported that Hayek was 'respected for early contributions to monetary theory.' But as Lawrence White (2008) revealed, monetary theory was—for Mises and Hayek—a respectable front behind which to promote the deflation that deepened the Great Depression and which assisted Hitler's rise to power.

Deflation directly benefits the purchasing power of the cashed-up donors who appear to have purchased the Austrian School of Economics and their 'free' market. Deflation also assaults labour trade union power: real wages—and thus unemployment—will inevitably and indiscriminately rise. In *A Critique of Interventionism*, Mises (2011 [1929], 15–16) made an *ex cathedra* assertion: 'In the capitalist social order unemployment is merely a transition and frictional phenomenon. Various conditions that impede the free flow of labor from place to place, from country to country, may render the equalization of wage rates more difficult. They may also lead to differences in compensation of the various types of labor. But with freedom for entrepreneurs and capitalists they could *never* [emphasis added] lead to large-scale and permanent unemployment. Workers seeking employment could always find work by adjusting their wage demands to market conditions. If the market determination of wage rates had not been disrupted, the effects of the World War and the destructive economic policies of the last decades would have led to a decline in wage rates, but not to unemployment. The scope and duration of unemployment, interpreted today as proof of the failure of capitalism, results from the fact that labor unions and unemployment compensation are keeping wage rates higher than the unhampered market would set them.'

Two decades later, Mises expressed 'fear' that some MPS members were 'themselves becoming inadvertently infected by the virus of intervention—minimum wages, social insurance, contra-cyclical fiscal policy, etc.:

> But what would you do,' it was put to him, 'if you were in the position of our French colleague, Jacques Rueff?' who was present and at the time responsible for the fiscal administration of Monaco. 'Suppose there were

widespread unemployment and hence famine and revolutionary discontent in the principality. Would you advise the government to limit its activities to police action for the maintenance of order and the protection of private property?' Mises was intransigent. He responded: 'If the policies of non-intervention prevailed—free trade, freely fluctuating wage rates, no form of social insurance, etc.—there would be no acute unemployment. Private charity would suffice to prevent the absolute destitution of restricted hard core of unemployables. (Peterson 2009, 9)

Richard Vedder (1999) reiterated this message: 'As I became interested in macroeconomics, I realized that unemployment is a key factor in sorting out the theoretical issues. That's when I read Hutt, as well as Hayek, and the early writings of Edwin Cannan, Lord Beveridge, and Lionel Robbins. They all pointed to the fact that markets are the way to deal with labor problems.'

According to Hülsmann (2008a, 14–15, n. 6):

> The main engines of the propaganda have been the state universities of the West, as well as an exaggerated faith in the authority of monetary 'experts' in the service of the IMF, the World Bank, the Federal Reserve, and other government agencies charged with the technical details of spreading inflation. Is it really necessary to point out the *non sequitur* implied in granting expert status in matters monetary to the employees of these organizations? An obvious parallel is the case of the economists on the payroll of labor unions who, because 'labor' unions pay them, are considered to be experts in labor economics. Clearly, if one called labor unions 'associations for the destruction of the labor market'—which most of them are by any objective standard—the expertise of their employees would stand in a more sober light.

Machlup (1980) described the 'knowledge' dissemination process (through which 'free' market economists assisted Hitler's rise) as 'not the right recipe' because it 'did not satisfy people.' During the 1930s, 'most of us Austrians' explained 'widespread unemployment' by

> disparity between labor cost and commodity prices–but this was not enough, especially not at a time when the quantity of money had fallen so badly. So this was why all the Austrian attempts, even Hayek's Austrian business-cycle theory, did not satisfy people. In the midst of the greatest contraction of money circulation, of incomes, of employment and so on, our recommendations were to let the economy be shaken down and have everything that's wrong liquidated, and let all the structural distortions be

repaired. Well, at that moment, in 1933, this was not the right recipe. At that moment, in the United States, with unemployment of 25 per cent it was more important to put a few, more people to work and, in these circumstances, every microeconomic argument was lost. Capital theory was no longer mentioned. This sort of economic theory is quite difficult–and why study and grapple with anything that wasn't directly applicable to the immediate problem, the problem of putting people to work? Pure theory was rejected, as irrelevant.

When asked by *Austrian Economics Newsletter*, 'Given the subsequent problems that occurred once the banking system started collapsing in the United States in the early thirties, do you feel that Professor Hayek's analysis of what brought on the depression was correct?' Machlup (1980) replied: 'Yes, I do, absolutely. I have always accepted it. The stable price level during the early twenties was the beginning of our downfall; this was a period of particularly fast growth of total output and, to keep price levels from falling, one had to create a good deal of money which was all fed into investment and this high rate of investment turned out to be unsustainable in the long run.' And when asked to provide a recommendation for Hayek's Nobel Prize, Machlup (1974) repeated the fraud about his having predicted the Great Depression.

Machlup (13 December 1946) asked Mises for advice about a forthcoming talk to the US Chamber of Commerce: he had to both 'practical and political.' Labour unions began as a self-help 'spontaneous' order (Jackson 2015)—but Machlup felt he had no choice but to insist that monopoly wages are the only purpose of labour unions and that strong labour unions mean 'unemployment and inflation and lead to an authoritarian state. Can an honest man avoid such statements?' He asked if there were any alternatives before, somewhat sheepishly, stating that since he assumed that it was 'politically unthinkable' to outlaw labour unions should the government resort to wage controls? Mises replied that he should tell the Chamber of Commerce: first, 'liberate yourself from false ideas. *Study economics* [emphasis in original].' Then go on to 'convince' others. Mises claimed that he rejected any outlawing or limitation of the liberty of association. No 'liberties' should be abolished, only coercion (cited by Hülsmann 2007, 861).

With respect to the enemy of the 'free' market 'order,' Hayek (1978a) was 'most concerned, because it's the most dangerous thing at the moment, with the power of the [labour] trade unions in Great Britain. While people are very much aware that things can't go on as they are, nobody is still convinced that this power of the trade unions to enforce wages which they regard as just is not a justified thing.[30] They can use force to prevent people from doing the work they would like.'[31] Pinochet, the strongest agent working towards the Chilean Republic's downfall, sought to abolish all political parties and trade unions (Barros 2004, 188): Hayek was pleased that his dictatorship had avoided '[labour] trade union privileges of any kind' (cited by Farrant et al. 2012, 522).

One month after Pinochet seized power, Hayek (1978b [1973], 109) told an IEA audience: 'Today it is rarely understood that the limitations of all coercion to the enforcement of general rules of just conduct was the fundamental principle of classical liberalism, or, I would almost say, its definition of liberty.' The original 'Chicago Boy,' Arnold Harberger (2016), contrasted his Allende-era (1970–1973) visits to the former Chilean Christian Democratic President (1964–1970), Eduardo Frei, with his Pinochet-era (1973–1990) visits: 'I used to visit Eduardo Frei in the Allende period. I made a point of visiting him basically every time I went to Chile. And the DINA, which was the intelligence agency of Pinochet government, they were watching all the time because he was at that point in opposition.'

What does 'liberty' look and sound like? Hayek (3 August 1978) told readers of the London *Times* that he had 'not been able to find a single person even in much maligned Chile who did not agree that personal freedom was much greater under Pinochet than it had been under Allende.' 3197 Chileans were murdered, 20,000 were officially exiled and their passports marked with an 'L,' and about 180,000 fled into exile—about 2% of the population (Wright and Oñate 2005, 57; Montes 2015, 7).

King Louis XV's official chief mistress (1745–1751), Madame de Pompadour, is attributed with the phrase 'Après nous, le déluge.' The Hayeks had been recruited into the Habsburg intergeneration entitlement program in 1789. Four years later, the *Ancien Regime* symbolically 'shook' when the former Louis XVI—renamed by his former subjects *Citoyen Louis Capet* (Citizen Louis Capet)—was guillotined. The 'Great' War between the dynasties further undermined intergenerational entitlements and ended neo-feudalism in Europe. Arthur Koestler (1950, 19) described some of those affected by the deluge: 'Those who refused to admit that they had become déclassé, who clung to the empty shell of gentility, joined the Nazis and found comfort in blaming their fate on Versailles and the Jews.' Liggio (1979) attributed Mises with the phrase 'to turn the flood one must change the mentality of the intellectuals. Then the masses would follow.'

By April 1938, it had become clear that not only did the Nazis suppress political and intellectual freedom but were also bent on world domination. The Great Depression—which Hayek and Mises had sought to deepen—discredited the 'free' market and made government planning respectable. Mises (1985 [1927], 51) left an eternal instruction: 'It cannot be denied that Fascism and similar movements aiming at the establishment of dictatorships are full of the best intentions and that their intervention has, for the moment, saved European civilization. The merit that Fascism has thereby won for itself will live on eternally in history.' Hayek (1997 [1938], 183) did not dissent from his 'master's' edict and encouraged his readers to focus not on Nazi human rights abuses but on 'the problems which begin when a democracy begins to plan' (Chapter 1). Those who objected to Nazi concentration camps were a threat to Hayek's 'liberty.'

Mises (1985 [1927], 48) noted that 'The militaristic and nationalistic enemies of the Third International felt themselves cheated by liberalism. Liberalism, they thought, stayed their hand when they desired to strike a blow against the revolutionary parties while it was still possible to do so. If liberalism had not hindered them, they would, so they believe, have bloodily nipped the revolutionary movements in the bud. Revolutionary ideas had been able to take root and flourish only because of the tolerance they had been accorded by their opponents, whose will power had been *enfeebled* by a regard for liberal principles that, as events subsequently proved, was *overscrupulous* [emphases added] ... They had had, even though reluctantly, to exclude murder and assassination from the list of measures to be resorted to in political struggles.'

Harberger (2016) 'accompanied [U.S. Treasury Secretary and later Secretary of State, and MPS member, George] Shultz on his 1974 visit to Pinochet and heard him lecture about various and sundry things, including human rights':

> The fact was that most of the horrible things took place during the earliest period of the first year, even the first three months. The coup itself first and then the assembling of people in the stadium and so on. I kept track of the disappearances in Chile and they were ever declining numbers and reached zero somewhere around '78. Meanwhile, I withheld any collaboration by me with the Chilean government for something like five years until those disappearances were zero.

Hayek's (1992a [1945], 223) 'Plan for the Future of Germany' began with a description of what became Pinochet's 'Plan for the Future of Chile': 'Neither legal scruples nor a false humanitarianism should prevent the meeting out of full justice ... shooting in cold blood.' But Hayek's family were proto-Nazis and later card-carrying Nazis (Chapter 1). Referring to Pinochet et al., Reisman (2006) stated: 'Life and liberty are positively helped by the death and disappearance of such mortal enemies' as 'Communists and Nazis.' Fellow Austrians, Caldwell and Montes (2014a, 50, 52; 2014b; 2015a, 304), refer to what they describe as the 'uncomfortable question of why Hayek chose to remain silent about the human rights abuses that took place under [Pinochet's] junta, a question about which we can only offer conjectures.'

In the non-Chilean version of their paper, Caldwell and Montes (2014a, 18; 2014b; 2015a) made 17 references to human rights. For their Chilean audience, Section 9—'Why Didn't Hayek Condemn Pinochet's Human Rights Abuses?'—was deleted and only four references to human rights were retained: three to 'los abusos de DD.HH' ('human rights abuses') plus 'Of course, it was revulsion over human rights abuses that caused so many people to advise him not to visit Chile'—which they translated by replacing 'revulsion' with 'tema,' 'subject' or 'theme' (Caldwell and Montes 2015b, 95).[32]

In the non-Chilean version, Caldwell and Montes (2014a, 11; 2014b; 2015a, 270) provided their human rights credentials: 'The Junta Militar imposed harsh political repression. Congress was closed on September 21, 1973, and the systematic persecution of communists, socialists, and indeed anyone linked to the left, was initiated. The first three months after the coup were particularly violent, but human rights abuses extended throughout the entire period in which the military regime was in power (official figures put the final death toll at 3197). The murders and torture are both a stigma and a wound for Chilean republican history that still mark and pain its citizens.' For their Chilean audience (2015b), this section was deleted—as were all references to 'torture' ('tortura').[33]

Mises (1985 [1927], 48) did not object to the eugenics-style 'unscrupulous methods' pursued by Hitler et al.: 'The fundamental idea of these movements—which, from the name of the most grandiose and tightly disciplined among them, the Italian, may, in general, be designated as Fascist—consists in the proposal to make use of the same unscrupulous methods in the struggle against the Third International as the latter employs against its opponents. The Third International seeks to exterminate its adversaries and their ideas in the same way that the hygienist strives to exterminate a pestilential bacillus; it considers itself in no way bound by the terms of any compact that it may conclude with opponents, and it deems any crime, any lie, and any calumny permissible in carrying on its struggle. The Fascists, at least in principle, profess the same intentions.'

Mises (1990 [1949/1950], 297, 302) explained: 'To make social doctrines work the support of public opinion is needed. Those scores of millions who ride on the railroads and listen to the broadcast without any idea of how railways have to be constructed and operated and how the radio works, have to grasp the incomparably more difficult problems of social cooperation, if society has to operate satisfactorily. Thus the great bulk of the low-browed, the masses who do not like to think and to reflect, the inert people who are slow in grasping new complicated ideas *have to decide* [emphasis added]. Their doctrinal convictions, how crude and naive they may be, fix the course of events. The state of society is not the outcome of those theories which have the support of the small group of advanced spirits, but the result of the doctrines which the masses of laymen consider as sound ones.'

Liggio (1979) attributed Mises with the phrase 'to turn the flood one must change the mentality of the intellectuals. Then the masses would follow.'

Hayek (1978a) told James Buchanan:

what I always come back to is that the whole thing turns on the activities of those intellectuals whom I call the 'secondhand dealers in opinion,' who determine what people think in the long run. If you can persuade them, you ultimately reach the masses of the people.[34]

Mises (1990 [1949/1950], 297, 302) referred to the power of 'secondary' sources of 'popular doctrines': 'As the study of doctrines is not a goal for itself, it has to pay no less attention to the popular doctrines than to the doctrines of the philosophical authors and their books. Of course, the popular doctrines are derived from the logically elaborated and refined theories of the scholars and scientists. They are secondary, not primary. But as the application of social doctrines necessitates their endorsement by public opinion and as public opinion mostly turns towards the popular version of a doctrine, the study of the latter is no less important than that of the perfect conception. For history a *popular slogan* [emphasis added] may sometimes vouchsafe more information than the ideas formulated by scholars. There are popular and generally accepted beliefs which are so contradictory and manifestly indefensible that no serious thinker ever dared to represent them systematically. But if such a belief provokes action it is for historical research no less important than any other doctrine applied in practice. History has not to limit its endeavors either to sound doctrines or to doctrines neatly expounded in scholarly writings; it has to study all doctrines which determine human action.'

The year before Mises' (1985 [1927]) *Liberalism in the Classical Tradition*, 'von' Wieser (1983 [1926], 38, 45) expressed similar sentiments: 'traces of true leadership may be perceived only when the despot rallies the masses in order to have them fight and work for himself. When despotic leadership thus turns into *lordly leadership* [emphasis in original], the function of leading the way is performed more efficaciously; compliance with the commands imposed by the lord on his subject is already genuine following ... Every truly active following by the masses must be borne by spiritual and moral forces - how else could a sense for law and ethics, true culture, and *a strong sense of liberty* [emphasis added] endure with the populace.'

According to 'Ritter von' Kuehnelt-Leddihn (1992), with the 'exception of Fritz Machlup, the original Austrian school consisted of members of the nobility': Hayek 'descended from a family ennobled at the end of the eighteenth century by the Holy Roman Emperor.' Machlup's (1980) 'first major teacher was Friedrich von Wieser' who was 'quite old. In 1920–1921, my first year at the University, he gave the big lecture on economic theory. Well, he never knew me. I was one of the very few people who attended the lectures regularly. I found the lectures pretty hard to take. They were terribly dull, and it was hard to keep one's mind on the subject. There was nothing wrong with the contents of his lectures, just with the delivery, He read from a manuscript. At the end of the year I felt I hadn't learned enough and I came back as an auditor for the second year, because I took my studies very seriously. So I studied for two years with Wieser.'

In contrast, 'von' Hayek (1978a) recalled that 'von' Wieser 'was a most impressive teacher, a very distinguished man whom I came to admire very much, I think it's the only instance where, as very young men do, I fell for a particular teacher. He was the great admired figure, sort of a grandfather figure of the two generations between us. He was a very kindly man who usually, I would say, floated high above the students as a sort of God ... he was for a long time my ideal in the field, from whom I got my main general introduction to economics.'[35]

Charles Brunie (26 February 1986), Chair of Oppenheimer Capital Corp, nominated 'Princess of Spain, Gerarda de Orleans-Borbon of Sanlucar de Barrameda, Spain' for MPS membership.[36] Prince Nikolas von Liechtenstein was nominated in 1990, as were Gerarda Orléans-Borbón and Álvaro Antonio Fernando Carlos Felipe de Orleans y Sajonia-Coburgo-Gotha, Prince of the non-existent Royal House of France, the 6th Duke of Galliera.[37] James Buchanan (1992, 130) met his first 'Princess' through a 'luxurious' MPS meeting. Ebeling (2014a) complained about 'those in Washington' who 'show the arbitrary arrogance of bygone kings and princes who asserted the right to change the rules at any time and in any way as they deemed fit.'

Alongside the Philip Morris tobacco lobbyist, Roy Marden, Ebeling was nominated for MPS membership by Carolina de Bolivar, director of Mexico's Ludwig von Mises Cultural Institute and supporter of Vicente Fox, the President of Coca-Cola México, who became President of Mexico: 'Many of our members and friends are now in the new Congress or working with the transition for Fox' (de Bolivar cited by Utley 2000). Thomas Hazlett asked:

> So if a businessman says to you, 'What can I do?' from the state down, your suggestion is to send a check to the IEA or a reasonable facsimile.

Hayek replied: 'Oh, yes. Of course, do the same thing here' (Chapter 1).[38] Half a century before, Wieser (1983 [1926], 257, 363) had described 'The Modern Plutocracy': 'The Law of Small Numbers found in the economy a field of application of equally great effect as it once had in the victory of arms. While the multitude of the weak was pressed down, out of the bourgeois middle class there arose to dizzying heights the elite of the capitalists, joining the rulers of earlier times and exceeding them still in wealth and finally even in social influence. The great economic rulers had won under the slogan of liberty, which opened for them the road to unchecked activity. They demanded ever more impetuously the green light for themselves, but the uninhibited unfolding of their energies meant coercion for all the weak who stepped into their way. Could the liberals still talk about freedom?' Wieser (1926, 354) capitalised 'Slogan of Liberty' ('*Losung der Freiheit*').

Notes

1. 'Pedro Ibáñez y Carlos Cáceres, quienes conocían a Hayek, no necesariamente interpretaron sus ideas.'
2. MPS Archives Box 2.7.
3. http://www.cfact.org/2011/11/16/946/.
4. https://www.peter-boettke.com/curriculum-vita/. Accessed 25 October 2017.
5. http://libertystory.net/LSTHINKHAYEKLIFE.htm.
6. CLS Archives Box 1.1.
7. Davenport Archives Box 3.24.
8. Friedrich Hayek interviewed by Robert Bork 4 November 1978 (Centre for Oral History Research, University of California, Los Angeles, http://oralhistory.library.ucla.edu/).
9. Friedrich Hayek, interviewed by Robert Chitester date unspecified 1978 (Centre for Oral History Research, University of California, Los Angeles, http://oralhistory.library.ucla.edu/).
10. Friedrich Hayek interviewed by Robert Bork 4 November 1978 (Centre for Oral History Research, University of California, Los Angeles, http://oralhistory.library.ucla.edu/).
11. Hayek Archives Box 38.24.
12. The Phillips Machine (MONIAC) is on display in a variety of places, including the Science Museum, London, and the University of Leeds.
13. Machlup suggested that the Harvard Keynesian, Seymour Harris, might be interested in the purchase. Hayek Archives Box 36.17.
14. Friedrich Hayek, interviewed by James Buchanan 28 October 1978 (Centre for Oral History Research, University of California, Los Angeles, http://oralhistory.library.ucla.edu/).
15. Friedrich Hayek, interviewed by Thomas Hazlett 12 November 1978 (Centre for Oral History Research, University of California, Los Angeles, http://oralhistory.library.ucla.edu/).
16. This section has been deleted from *The Scholars' Edition* (1998).
17. Friedrich Hayek, interviewed by Leo Rosten 15 November 1978 (Centre for Oral History Research, University of California, Los Angeles, http://oralhistory.library.ucla.edu/).
18. Friedrich Hayek, interviewed by Leo Rosten 15 November 1978 (Centre for Oral History Research, University of California, Los Angeles, http://oralhistory.library.ucla.edu/).
19. Wieser also referred to 'European Turkey' and 'western Russia.'
20. https://www.economist.com/news/britain/21725268-and-if-you-dont-agree-you-can-get-stuffed-british-politics-has-become-dangerously-bad-tempered.

21. https://www.economist.com/blogs/democracyinamerica/2011/08/ fishing-fascists.
22. Friedrich Hayek, interviewed by Leo Rosten 15 November 1978 (Centre for Oral History Research, University of California, Los Angeles, http://oralhistory.library.ucla.edu/).
23. Friedrich Hayek, interviewed by Robert Chitester date unspecified 1978 (Centre for Oral History Research, University of California, Los Angeles, http://oralhistory.library.ucla.edu/).
24. Before being cut-off, Bork had asked: 'I suppose a lot of people would say that, in fact, in some sense freedom was increasing in America, because we certainly now have much more freedom for racial minorities … There is much more freedom in the area of sexual permissiveness. There is much more freedom–if you want to call these things freedom–in the area of things that may be said or written or shown on film or shown on the stage. Now, I suppose the latter could be evidences of depravity rather than freedom, but I take it you think -' Friedrich Hayek interviewed by Robert Bork 4 November 1978 (Centre for Oral History Research, University of California, Los Angeles, http://oralhistory.library.ucla.edu/).
25. 5.28% represented the communists.
26. To Feulner. MPS Archives Box 82.
27. https://www.nptrust.org/philanthropic-resources/charitable-giving-statistics/.
28. Lawrence White (2008) doubts that Hoover was accurately portraying Mellon's views.
29. Conversation with David Henderson (7 July 2011), who attended the 1974 revivalist conference and heard Friedman make the remark.
30. Friedrich Hayek, interviewed by James Buchanan 28 October 1978 (Centre for Oral History Research, University of California, Los Angeles, http://oralhistory.library.ucla.edu/).
31. Friedrich Hayek, interviewed by Leo Rosten 15 November 1978 (Centre for Oral History Research, University of California, Los Angeles, http://oralhistory.library.ucla.edu/).
32. 'Evidentemente el tema de los derechos humanos en Chile era la motivación de quienes le aconsejaban no viajar a Chile.'
33. With respect to the 'morals' of the academic market, it is conventional to alert an editor if a submitted essay has already been published. Caldwell and Montes (2015b) refer to the English-language version of their paper as if it were almost unrelated to the Chilean version.
34. Friedrich Hayek, interviewed by James Buchanan 28 October 1978 (Centre for Oral History Research, University of California, Los Angeles, http://oralhistory.library.ucla.edu/).

35. Friedrich Hayek, interviewed by Earlene Craver date unspecified 1978 (Centre for Oral History Research, University of California, Los Angeles, http://oralhistory.library.ucla.edu/).
36. MPS Archives Box 82.
37. MPS Archives Box 93.
38. Friedrich Hayek, interviewed by Thomas Hazlett 12 November 1978 (Centre for Oral History Research, University of California, Los Angeles, http://oralhistory.library.ucla.edu/).

References

Archival Insights into the Evolution of Economics (and Related Projects)

Farrant, A., McPhail, E., & Berger, S. (2012). Preventing the "Abuses" of Democracy: Hayek, the "Military Usurper" and Transitional Dictatorship in Chile? *American Journal of Economics and Sociology, 71*(3), 513–538.

Haiduk, K. (2015). Hayek and Coase Travel East: Privatization and the Experience of Post-socialist Economic Transformation. In R. Leeson (Ed.), *Hayek: A Collaborative Biography Part VI Good Dictators, Sovereign Producers and Hayek's 'Ruthless Consistency'*. Basingstoke, UK: Palgrave Macmillan.

Jackson, B. (2015). Hayek, Hutt and the Trade Unions. In R. Leeson (Ed.), *Hayek: A Collaborative Biography: Part V Hayek's Great Society of Free Men*. Basingstoke, UK: Palgrave Macmillan.

Leeson, R. (1994, November). A.W.H. Phillips, Inflationary Expectations and the Operating Characteristics of the Macroeconomy. *Economic Journal, 104*(427), 1420–1421.

Leeson, R. (Ed.). (2013). *Hayek: A Collaborative Biography Part I Influences From Mises to Bartley*. Basingstoke, UK: Palgrave Macmillan.

Leeson, R. (2018). *Hayek: A Collaborative Biography Part XI Orwellian Rectifiers, Mises' 'Evil Seed' of Christianity and the 'Free' Market Welfare State*. Basingstoke, England: Palgrave Macmillan.

Other Reference

Bark, D. L. (2007). *Americans and Europeans Dancing in the Dark on Our Differences and Affinities, Our Interests, and Our Habits of Life*. Stanford, CA: Hoover Institution Press.

Barros, R. (2004). *Constitutionalism and Dictatorship. Pinochet, the Junta, and the 1980 Constitution*. Cambridge: Cambridge University Press.

Blundell, J. (2014). IHS and the Rebirth of Austrian Economics: Some Reflections on 1974–1976. *Quarterly Journal of Austrian Economics, 17*(1),

92–107. https://mises.org/library/ihs-and-rebirth-austrian-economics-some-reflections-1974%E2%80%931976.
Boettke, P. J. (2009a, August 4). Setting the Record Straight. *Coordination Problem.* http://austrianeconomists.typepad.com/weblog/2009/08/setting-the-record-straight-on-austropunkism-and-the-sociology-of-the-austrian-school-of-economics.html.
Boettke, P. J. (2009b August 19). *Human Action: The Treatise in Economics.* FEE, https://fee.org/articles/human-action-the-treatise-in-economics/.
Boettke, P. J. (2011). Teaching Austrian Economics to Graduate Students. *Journal of Economics and Finance Education, 10*(2), 19–30. http://www.economics-finance.org/jefe/econ/special-issue/Special%20Issue%20AE%20003%20Boettke-Abstract.pdf.
Boettke, P. J. (2012). Interview with Peter Boettke. Rationality Unlimited. https://rationalityunlimited.wordpress.com/2012/04/02/interview-with-peter-boettke/.
Brooks, D. (2017, July 11). How We Are Ruining America. *New York Times.* https://www.nytimes.com/2017/07/11/opinion/how-we-are-ruining-america.html.
Buchanan, J. (1986, October 26). Why Governments 'Got Out of Hand.' *The New York Times.*
Buchanan, J. (1992). I Did Not Call Him 'Fritz': Personal Recollections of Professor F. A. v. Hayek. *Constitutional Political Economy, 3*(2), 129–135.
Bullock, A. (1991). *Hitler: A Study in Tyranny.* New York: Harper Perennial.
Caldwell, B. (2004). *Hayek's Challenge: An Intellectual Biography of F.A. Hayek.* Chicago: University of Chicago Press.
Caldwell, B. (2007). Introduction and Editorial Notes. In F. A. Hayek (Ed.), *The Road to Serfdom Texts and Documents: The Definitive Edition. The Collected Works of F.A. Hayek.* Chicago: University of Chicago Press.
Caldwell, B. (2016). Hayek's Nobel. In P. Boettke & V. Storr (Eds.), *Revisiting Hayek's Political Economy.* Bingley, UK: Emerald.
Caldwell, B., & Montes, L. (2014a, August). *Friedrich Hayek and His Visits to Chile* (CHOPE Working Paper No. 2014–12).
Caldwell, B., & Montes, L. (2014b). Friedrich Hayek and His Visits to Chile. *Review of Austrian Economics* (First Online: 26 September 2014).
Caldwell, B., & Montes, L. (2015a, September). Friedrich Hayek and His Visits to Chile. *Review of Austrian Economics, 28*(3), 261–309.
Caldwell, B., & Montes, L. (2015b). Friedrich Hayek y Sus Dos Visitas a Chile. *Estudios Públicos,* No. 137 (Verano): 87–132. https://www.cepchile.cl/cep/site/artic/20160304/asocfile/20160304101209/rev137_BCaldwell-LMontes.pdf.
Cubitt, C. (2006). *A Life of August von Hayek.* Bedford, UK: Authors on Line.
Dahrendorf, R. (1995). *LSE: A History of the London School of Economics and Political Science, 1895–1995.* Oxford: Oxford University Press.

Davidson, E. (1966). *The Trials of the Germans: An Account of the Twenty-two Defendants Before the International Military Tribunal at Nuremberg.* London: Macmillan.
Deist, J. (2017, February 17). Democracy, the God That's Failing. *Mises Wire.* https://mises.org/blog/democracy-god-thats-failing.
Doherty, B. (2007). *Radicals for Capitalism: A Freewheeling History of the Modern. American Libertarian Movement.* New York: Public Affairs.
De Tocqueville, A. (1835–1840). *Democracy in America.* London: Saunders and Otley.
Dwyer, P. G. (2001). *Modern Prussian History, 1830–1947.* London: Longman.
Ebeling, R. M. (1974, October). Austrian Economics on the Rise. *Libertarian Forum.* http://mises.org/daily/4174.
Ebeling, R. M. (1997, August). The Free Market and the Interventionist State. *Imprimus, 26*(8) (MPS Archives Box 122).
Ebeling, R. M. (2013, June 15). Richard Ebeling on Higher Interest Rates, Collectivism and the Coming Collapse. *Daily Bell.* http://www.thedailybell.com/gold-silver/anthony-wile-richard-ebeling-on-higher-interest-rates-collectivism-and-the-coming-collapse/.
Ebeling, R. M. (2014a, February 16). EXCLUSIVE INTERVIEW, Gold & Silver. Richard Ebeling on Austrian Economics, Economic Freedom and the Trends of the Future. *Daily Bell.* http://www.thedailybell.com/gold-silver/anthony-wile-richard-ebeling-on-austrian-economics-economic-freedom-and-the-trends-of-the-future/.
Ebeling, R. M. (2014b, June 16). The Rise and Fall of Classical Liberalism. *Free Market Liberalism.* https://rebeling.liberty.me/the-rise-and-fall-of-classical-liberalism-by-richard-ebeling/.
Ebeling, R. M. (2015, March 25). A World Without the Welfare State. *Future of Freedom Foundation.* https://www.fff.org/explore-freedom/article/world-without-welfare-state/.
Ebeling, R. M. (2017, March 20). Trump's Budgetary Blueprint Retains America's Welfare State. *Heartland Institute.* https://www.heartland.org/news-opinion/news/trumps-budgetary-blueprint-retains-americas-welfare-state.
Edsall, N. (1986). *Richard Cobden Independent Radical.* Cambridge, MA: Harvard University Press.
Finer, H. (1945). *The Road to Reaction.* Chicago: Quadrangle Books.
Friedman, M. F. (2017 [1991]). Say 'No' to Intolerance. In R. Leeson & C. Palm (Eds.), *Milton Friedman on Freedom.* Stanford, CA: Hoover Press.
Galbraith, J. K. (1952). *American Capitalism: The Concept of Countervailing Power.* Boston: Houghton Mifflin.
Goodwin, C. (1988). The Heterogeneity of the Economists' Discourse: Philosopher, Priest, and Hired Gun. In A. Klamer, D. N. McCloskey, & R. M. Solow (Eds.), *The Consequences of Economic Rhetoric.* Cambridge: Cambridge University Press.

Harberger, A. C. (2016). Sense and Economics: An Oral History with Arnold Harberger. Interviews Conducted by Paul Burnett in 2015 and 2016 Oral History Center, The Bancroft Library, University of California, Berkeley, California. http://digitalassets.lib.berkeley.edu/roho/ucb/text/harberger_arnold_2016.pdf.

Hayek, F. A. (1948). *Individualism and Economic Order.* Chicago: University of Chicago Press.

Hayek, F. A. (1949). The Intellectuals and Socialism. *University of Chicago Law Review, 16*(3), 417–433.

Hayek, F. A. (1973). *Law, Legislation and Liberty Volume 1: Rules and Order.* Chicago: University of Chicago Press.

Hayek, F. A. (1976a, February 23). Politicians Can't Be Trusted with Money. American Institute for Economic Research Reports (Hayek Archives Box 109.1).

Hayek, F. A. (1976b, March 18). Institutions May Fail, But Democracy Survives. *US News and World Report* (Hayek Archives Box 109.4).

Hayek, F. A. (1978a). Oral History Interviews. Centre for Oral History Research, University of California, Los Angeles. http://oralhistory.library.ucla.edu/.

Hayek, F. A. (1978b). *New Studies in Philosophy, Politics, Economics and the History of Ideas.* London: Routledge & Kegan Paul.

Hayek, F. A. (1979, December 5). A Period of Muddle-Heads. *Newsweek.*

Hayek, F. A. (1984). *1980s Unemployment and the Unions: The Distortion of Relative Prices by Monopoly in the Labour Market. Essays on the Impotent Price Structure of Britain and Monopoly in the Labour Market.* London: Institute of Economic Affairs.

Hayek, F. A. (1992). *The Fortunes of Liberalism Essays on Austrian Economics and the Ideal of Freedom. The Collected Works of F.A. Hayek* (P. Klein, Ed.). Chicago: University of Chicago Press.

Hayek, F. A. (1994). *Hayek on Hayek an Autobiographical Dialogue.* Supplement to *The Collected Works of F.A. Hayek* (S. Kresge & L. Wenar, Eds.). Chicago: University of Chicago Press.

Hayek, F. A. (1997). *Socialism and War: Essays, Documents, Reviews. The Collected Works of F.A. Hayek* (B. Caldwell, Ed.). Indianapolis: Liberty Fund.

Hayek, F. A. (2007 [1944]). *The Road to Serfdom: The Definitive Edition. The Collected Works of F.A. Hayek* (B. Caldwell, Ed.). Chicago: University of Chicago Press.

Hayek, F. A. (2011 [1960]). *The Constitution of Liberty. The Definitive Edition. The Collected Works of F.A. Hayek* (R. Hamowy, Ed.). Chicago: University of Chicago Press.

Hitler, A. (1939 [1925]). *Mein Kampf* (J. Murphy, Trans.). London: Hurst and Blackett.

Hitler, A. (1941 [1925]). *Mein Kampf.* New York: Raynal and Hitchcock.

Hospers, J. (1978, April). Liberty's Heritage. *Libertarian Review*, pp. 11–14. http://www.unz.org/Pub/LibertarianRev-1978apr-00011.

Hoover, H. (1952). *The Memoirs of Herbert Hoover, Vol. 3: The Great Depression 1929–1941*. New York: Macmillan.

Hülsmann, J. G. (2007). *Mises: The Last Knight of Liberalism*. Auburn, AL: Ludwig von Mises Institute.

Hülsmann, J. G. (2008). *Deflation and Liberty*. Auburn, AL: Ludwig von Mises Institute.

Kirzner, I. (1978). *Competition and Entrepreneurship*. Chicago: University of Chicago Press.

Klor, E. F., Saiegh, S., & Satyanath, S. (2017). Cronyism in State Violence: Evidence from Labor Repression During Argentina's Last Dictatorship. Mimeo. http://pages.ucsd.edu/~ssaiegh/paper_KSS.pdf.

Koestler, A. (1950). Arthur Koestler. In R. Crossman (Ed.), *Communism: The God That Failed*. New York: Harper and Row.

Kuehnelt-Leddihn, E. R. (1992). The Road from Serfdom. *National Review*, 44(8), 32.

Kummer, F. (1932). German Trade-Unions and Their 1931 Congress. *Monthly Labor Review* 01,34(1).

Leeson, R. (1994a, May). A.W.H. Phillips, M.B.E. (Military Division). *Economic Journal*, 104(424), 605–618.

Leeson, R. (1994b, November). A.W.H. Phillips, Inflationary Expectations and the Operating Characteristics of the Macroeconomy. *Economic Journal*, 104(427), 1420–1421.

Leeson, R. (1997, February). The Trade-off Interpretation of Phillips' Dynamic Stabilisation Exercise. *Economica*, 64(253), 155–173.

Leeson, R. (2018). *Hayek: A Collaborative Biography Part VIII the Constitution of Liberty: 'Shooting in Cold Blood' Hayek's Plan for the Future of Democracy*. Basingstoke, UK: Palgrave Macmillan.

Liggio, L. (1979). *Mont Pelerin: 1947–1978, the Road to Libertarianism*. Libertarianism.org. https://www.libertarianism.org/publications/essays/mont-pelerin-1947-1978-road-libertarianism.

Machlup, F. (1974, December). Hayek's Contribution to Economics. *Swedish Journal of Economics*, 76, 498–531.

Machlup, F. (1980). An Interview with Fritz Machlup. *Austrian Economics Newsletter*, 3(1). https://mises.org/library/interview-fritz-machlup.

Mises, L. (1949). *Human Action: A Treatise on Economics*. New Haven: Yale University Press. First edition.

Mises, L. (1950, May 4). Middle-of-the-Road Policy Leads to Socialism. *Commercial and Financial Chronicle*.

Mises, L. (1962). *The Ultimate Foundation of Economic Science an Essay on Method*. New York: Van Nostrand.

Mises, L. (1963). *Human Action: A Treatise on Economics* (2nd ed.). New Haven: Yale University Press.
Mises, L. (1964, February 4). Deception of Government Intervention. *Christian Economics*. https://history.fee.org/publications/deception-of-government-intervention/.
Mises, L. (1966). *Human Action: A Treatise on Economics*. Chicago: Henry Regnery. Third edition.
Mises, L. (1985 [1927]). *Liberalism in the Classical Tradition* (R. Raico, Trans.). Auburn, AL: Mises Institute.
Mises, L. (1990). *Money, Method and the Market Process*. Auburn, AL: The Ludwig von Mises Institute; Norwell; MA: Kluwer Academic Publishers. Selected by Margit von Mises and Edited with an Introduction by Richard M. Ebeling.
Mises, L. (1998 [1949]). *Human Action: A Treatise on Economics the Scholars Edition*. Auburn, AL: Ludwig von Mises Institute.
Mises. L. (2006). *The Causes of the Economic Crisis and Other Essays Before and After the Great Depression* (P. Greaves, Ed.). Auburn Alabama: Ludwig von Mises Institute.
Mises, L. (2007a [1958]). Mises and Rothbard Letters to Ayn Rand. *Journal of Libertarian Studies, 21*(4), 11–16.
Mises, L. (2007b [1957]). *Theory and History an Interpretation of Social and Economic Evolution*. Auburn, AL: Ludwig von Mises Institute.
Mises, L. (2009 [1978 (1940)]). *Memoirs*. Auburn, AL: Ludwig von Mises Institute.
Mises, L. (2011 [1929]). *A Critique of Interventionism*. Auburn, AL: Ludwig von Mises Institute.
Montes, L. (2015). *Friedman's Two Visits to Chile in Context*. http://jepson.richmond.edu/conferences/summer-institute/papers2015/LMontesSIPaper.pdf.
Najarjuly, N. (2017, July 20). India Picks Ram Nath Kovind, of Caste Once Called 'Untouchables,' as President. *New York Times*.
Nasar, S. (1992, March 24). Friedrich von Hayek Dies at 92; An Early Free-Market Economist. *New York Times*. http://www.nytimes.com/1992/03/24/world/friedrich-von-hayek-dies-at-92-an-early-free-market-economist.html.
Peterson, W. H. (2009). *Mises in America*. Auburn, AL: Ludwig von Mises Institute.
Prowse, M. (2014 [1996]). Austrian Economics and the Public Mind. *Austrian Economics Newsletter*, 16(1). https://mises.org/library/austrian-economics-and-public-mind.
Ponting, C. (1998). *Progress and Barbarism: The World in the Twentieth Century*. New York: Random House.
Raico, R. (2012). *Classical Liberalism and the Austrian School*. Auburn, AL: Ludwig von Mises Institute.

Robbins, J. (2010). The *Sine Qua Non* of Enduring Freedom. *The Trinity Review*, 295. http://www.trinityfoundation.org/PDF/The%20Trinity%20Review%2000295%20SineQuaNonEnduringFreedom.pdf.

Rothbard, M. N. (2001 [1962]). *Man, Economy and State, with Power and Market: Scholars' Edition*. Auburn, AL: Ludwig von Mises Institute.

Reisman, G. (2006, December 16). General Augusto Pinochet Is Dead. *Mises Wire*. https://mises.org/blog/general-augusto-pinochet-dead.

Shirer, W. L. (1960). *Rise and Fall of the Third Reich*. London: Secker and Warburg.

Stolper, G. (1967). *The German Economy from 1870 to the Present Day*. New York: Harcourt, Brace & World.

Taylor, A. J. P. (1955). *Bismarck the Man and the Statesman*. London: Hamish Hamilton.

Teacher, D. (2018). 'Neutral Academic Data' and the International Right. In R. Leeson (Ed.), *Hayek: A Collaborative Biography Part XIII 'Fascism' and Liberalism in the (Austrian) Classical Tradition*. Basingstoke, UK: Palgrave Macmillan.

Turner, H. A. (1985). *German Big Business and the Rise of Hitler*. New York: Oxford University Press.

Vedder, R. (1999). A Passion for Economics: An Interview with Richard K. Vedder. *Austrian Economics Newsletter*, 19(1). https://mises.org/library/passion-economics-interview-richard-k-vedder.

Walsh, M. C. (1968). *Prologue A Documentary History of Europe 1848–1960*. Melbourne, Australia: Cassell.

White, L. H. (2008). Did Hayek and Robbins Deepen the Great Depression? *Journal of Money, Credit and Banking*, 40, 751–768.

Wieser, F. (1983 [1926]). *The Law of Power*. University of Nebraska–Lincoln: Bureau of Business Research.

Wright, T. C., & Oñate, R. (2005). Chilean Diaspora. In C. R. Ember, M. Ember, & I. Skoggard (Eds.), *Encyclopedia of Diasporas: Immigrant and Refugee Cultures Around the World* (Vol. II, pp. 57–65). New York: Springer. https://mises.org/system/tdf/qjae5_3_4.pdf?file=1&type=document.

Wieser, F. (1983 [1926]). *The Law of Power*. University of Nebraska–Lincoln: Bureau of Business Research.

CHAPTER 3

Hayek and Aristocratic Influence

SUMMARY

Hayek's life was largely defined by his interactions with six exclusive clubs; he also legitimised three others. The first and last of the six were noble: the House of Habsburg intergeneration entitlement programme which—until April 1919—allowed him, legally, to attach the prefix 'von' to his name; plus the post-nominal Companion of Honour which the House of Windsor conferred on him almost two-thirds of a century later. Two he co-created: the *Geistkreis* and the Mont Pelerin Society; another was, supposedly, merit-based: the Nobel laureates. The sixth was his Reform Club 'home.' The seventh was the Institute of Economic Affairs and its dozens of offshoots; and the eighth, the far-right Monday Club, which during Hayek's lifetime, was on the verge of expulsion from the Conservative Party. The ninth was the 'Spooks Club' or 'Jackdaw Network' which he promoted after an encounter over lunch at the Reform with Donald McCormick (aka Richard Deacon), the *Sunday Times* Foreign Manager and far-right fraud.

3.1 HAYEK'S CLUBS

Hayek (1978a) reflected on 'the whole traditional concept of aristocracy, of which I have a certain conception – I have moved, to some extent, in aristocratic circles, and I like their style of life.'[1] His life was largely defined by his interactions with six exclusive clubs; he also legitimised three others.

© The Author(s) 2018
R. Leeson, *Hayek: A Collaborative Biography*,
Archival Insights into the Evolution of Economics,
https://doi.org/10.1007/978-3-319-74509-1_3

The first and last of the six were noble: the House of Habsburg intergeneration entitlement programme which—until April 1919—allowed him, legally, to attach the prefix 'von' to his name; plus the post-nominal Companion of Honour which the House of Windsor conferred on him almost two-thirds of a century later. Two he co-created: the *Geistkreis* (1921–1938) and the Mont Pelerin Society (1947–); another was, supposedly, merit-based: the Nobel laureates (1974–). The sixth was his Reform Club 'home' (1931–1992). The seventh was the IEA and its dozens of offshoots; and the eighth, the far-right Monday Club, which during Hayek's lifetime, was on the verge of expulsion from the Conservative Party. The ninth was the 'Spooks Club' or 'Jackdaw Network' which he promoted after an encounter over lunch (24 October 1984) at the Reform with Donald McCormick (aka Richard Deacon), the right-wing fraud and biographer of two Reform Club Prime Ministers, David Lloyd George (1963) and William Ewart Gladstone (1965), and the author of *British Connection Russia's Manipulation of British Individuals and Institutions* (1979) and *The Cambridge Apostles a History of Cambridge University's Elite Intellectual Secret Society* (1985).

For Hayek (1978a; 1994, 78), 'the one indulgence I granted myself was the membership of the Reform Club, which became very important to me and now is the only 'home' I have known for close to forty years.' His association with the Club began in October 1931, a month after he arrived at the LSE: 'at once I became in a sense British, because that was a natural attitude for me, which I discovered later. It was like stepping into a warm bath where the atmosphere is the same as your body.'[2] In 1982, Hayek told his appointed biographer, Cubitt (2006, 88), that if his second wife pre-deceased him, he would return to live in England—presumably at the Reform. In October 1984, when Queen Elizabeth II ennobled him as her Companion of Honour, he travelled to Buckingham Palace (and back) from the Reform, where he was later rewarded with a black-tie dinner (9 July 1985).[3] In 1989, he expressed sadness at the thought that he may not see the Club again.[4] In 1991, he was too ill to travel to Washington to receive the Presidential Medal of Freedom from President George W. H. Bush—but he died a Reform Club member.

According to the second General Editor of *The Collected Works of F.A. Hayek*: 'In manners and temperament Hayek felt entirely at home in England. Or rather he felt entirely at home in the England which still preserved much of the character of the nineteenth century. In such figures as Henry Thornton [1760–1815] and Sir Leslie Stephen

[1832–1904], and even more so in Lord Acton [1834–1902], he recognised kindred spirits ... Sharing the sport of mountaineering gave him an appreciation of the character of Sir Leslie Stephen' (Kresge 1994, 14). According to Cubitt (2006, 163), Hayek stated that he had known Stephen and had met his daughter, Virginia Woolf.[5]

Hayek also 'met a descendant of Henry Thornton, E.M. Forster, as a fellow member of the Reform Club' (Kresge 1994, 14). Forster and the Soviet spy, Guy Burgess, appeared in 'Deacon' McCormick's (1979, 56–57) *British Connection*: from his 'sanctuary at Kings,' Cambridge, Forster allegedly declared that:

> no political creed except communism offered the intelligent man any hope ... and that if he had to choose between betraying his country and betraying his friend, he hoped he 'would have the guts to betray his country.'

When Anthony Blunt invoked Forster's logic in defence of his own treachery, the Oxford Regius Professor of Modern History, Hugh Trevor-Roper, was led to 'explode: Be damned to his conscience' (cited by Boyle 1982, 495).

Referring to Edmund Burke (1729–1797), the *Collected Works* General Editor continued: 'Not so surprisingly, perhaps, that Hayek would realise the necessity of the social institutions of manners and morals, law and language, for the evolution of civilisation. He later described himself as a Burkean Whig ... [After his divorce] He did what other outcasts have done before him. He went to America and wrote a constitution of liberty' (Kresge 1994, 14, 23).

Enlightenment philosophers sought to reconstruct society along 'rational' (as opposed to 'superstitious') grounds. In *Reflections on the Revolution in France*, Burke (1790) defended 'the aristocratic concepts of paternalism, loyalty, chivalry, the hereditary principle' and irrational prejudice. It was preferable to depend on the 'general bank and capital of nations and of ages' than on intellect. Previously, according to Burke, English statesmen had wisely 'preferred this positive, recorded, hereditary title to all which can be dear to the man and the citizen, to that vague speculative right, which exposed their sure inheritance to be scrambled for and torn to pieces by every wild litigious spirit.'

Within months of arriving in England, 'von' Hayek began investigating Thornton's history and seeking a portrait[6]; in 1938, he wrote to the Cambridge Regius Professor of Modern History, George Macaulay

Trevelyan, asking about the existence of Thornton's letters.[7] Hayek (1939) edited and wrote an introduction to Thornton's *Enquiry into the nature and effects of the paper credit of Great Britain, 1802*.

The Trevelyan family were part of the extended Booth family, which included Macaulays, Hobhouses, Meinertzhagens, Fletchers and two lines of Potters (Beatrice Potter married Sidney Webb with whom she co-founded the LSE).[8] Charles Booth's (1889, 1891) *Life and Labour of the People of London* influenced the development of what became known as the 'Welfare State.' Thirty members of the extended Booth family were Reform Club members (Woodbridge 1978, 22).

Booths were to the Reform Club what Cecils and their Houses—Cecil House, Burghley House, Salisbury House and Hotel Cecil—were to the Tories. William Cecil (1520–1598) founded the Cecil dynasty which produced two Prime Ministers. His life illustrated the process of feudal advancement: rising from a minor Welsh noble family (that had fought on Henry VII's winning side at the 1485 Battle of Bosworth) to the most powerful non-royal in England and Wales. The intermediate steps consisted of: a young MP (1543), Princess Elizabeth's surveyor of estates (1550), Queen Elizabeth's Principal Secretary (1558), royal revenue raiser, Master of the Court of Wards and Liveries (1561) and 1st Baron Burghley (1571), from where he controlled the House of Lords.

Thomas Babington Macaulay (1853) noted that when the Divine Right of Kings ruled, 'Office was the shortest road to boundless wealth.' In his four decades at the pinnacle of Elizabethan politics, Cecil acquired a personal fortune that was inherited by his heirs. The 'spymaster,' Sir Francis Walsingham, preceded him as Lord Privy Seal; he was succeeded by his son, Robert Cecil, who was elevated to Baron Cecil (1603), Viscount Cranborne (1604) and Earl of Salisbury (1605).

One Cecil, the 7th Marquess of Salisbury, was leader of the Conservatives in the House of Lords immediately before hereditary peers were expelled (1999). This almost-hereditary leader's position had been held by his grandfather (the 5th Marquess), his great-grandfather (the 4th Marquess) and great-great-grandfather (the 3rd Marquess).

Most, if not all, male Cecils and Salisburys have been Old Etonians. But not all Old Etonian politicians have been Tory loyalists: Hugh Dalton, the 5th Earl of Rosebery, Wogan Phillips, William Forbes-Sempill (the 19th Baron Sempill) and Burgess all 'crossed the chapel' (to the Labour and Liberal and Communist Parties and Japanese and Soviet Empires, respectively).

In September 1979, Blunt instructed his lawyer, Michael Rubinstein, to contact Andrew Boyle's publishers, Hutchinson, to obtain an advance copy of *The Fourth Man* (1979, 1982). The satirical magazine, *Private Eye* (8 November 1979), picked up the story and declared that 'the Blunt truth is that 'Maurice' = Sir Anthony Blunt' (cited by Penrose and Freeman 1987, 533; Boyle 1982, 488). Boyle's book was published on Guy Fawkes Day. Ten days later, Prime Minister Thatcher (15 November 1979) informed the House of Commons that in April 1964, Blunt had admitted passing information to the Russians between 1940 and 1945.[9] Blunt became the first person since the 1916 trial and execution of Sir Roger Casement to be stripped of his knighthood. The Old Etonian, Lord Home, who was the Prime Minister when Blunt's treachery was first revealed, denied having been informed (Boyle 1982, 491–492).

Through G. M. Trevelyan, in 1934 Burgess obtained a temporary academic position at Cambridge; but one of his referees, the Cambridge economist, Dennis Robertson, declined to support his application for an Assistant Master's job at Eton. Trevelyan subsequently helped Burgess obtain employment at the BBC. After Neville Chamberlain signed the Munich agreement with Adolf Hitler, Harold Nicholson (23 November 1938) recorded in his diary: 'I got to the Reform to have a talk with Guy Burgess who is in a state about the BBC. He tells me that a technical talk by Admiral Richmond about our strategic position in the Mediterranean (which had been definitely announced) was cancelled as a result of a telephone message from Horace Wilson to the Director General. This has incensed him, and he wants to resign and publish why. I urged him to do nothing of the sort.' Burgess did resign from the BBC and was appointed to the War Office as a 'propaganda expert' (Boyle 1982, 120, 158, 180–181, 183).

In 1945, Nicholson provided an insight into the process by which 'Second Estate' titles are created. Over dinner at the Reform, Burgess informed him 'that (on what authority I don't know, but I suspect Hector McNeil) that [Ernest] Bevin has turned me down for Chairman of the British Council, and that in some way my peerage was involved in that appointment, so this too has disappeared' (cited by Boyle 1982, 302).

Over dinner at the Reform, Burgess would handover lengthy 'Top Secret' dispatches intended only for the eyes of the Foreign Secretary. On what may have been his last journeys out of London, he went to Eton for tea with the headmaster, Sir Robert Birley, to report that the

Salisbury family had requested him to complete the biography of 'one of his great heroes, the Third Marquess of Salisbury' (Boyle 1982, 398–400).

In 1951, Burgess and Donald Maclean disappeared; and they later reappeared in Moscow. The search for the Third Man began—Kim Philby was the major suspect. The Old Etonian Nicholas Elliott, head of MI6 in Beirut and Allied-occupied Vienna (coincidentally, the setting for the 1949 'Third Man' movie), confronted (but did not detain) Philby— who immediately escaped to Moscow. Although dogged by his failure to apprehend Philby, Elliott rose to become director of the MI6 'club' (Hastings 1994). Many concluded that in future, the British 'old boy's network' was unsuited for the exercise of power.

Elliott's (1993) autobiography was—somewhat unimaginatively— named after a children's game: *With My Little Eye: Observations Along the Way*. In *With My Little Eye: The Memoirs of a Spy-Hunter*, 'Deacon' McCormick (1982, 106) asserted that in 1953, he wrote: 'it can be expected that both men will eventually turn up in Moscow'—but, he claimed, his long-deceased editor, the Old Etonian Ian Fleming, deleted these prophetic words and replaced them: 'it is now almost certain that Burgess and Maclean are dead and intelligence circles believe that Maclean was murdered shortly after he left this country.'

In 1934, the 19th Baron Sempill inherited both his title and Craigievar Castle. In 1940, Prime Minister Winston Churchill's security adviser, Lord Swinton, reported the 'official knowledge that Lord Sempill is at the moment in a serious financial situation.' The Directorate of Military Intelligence discovered that since 1922, the Japanese had been paying Sempill for classified military intelligence. Six days after the attack on Pearl Harbor, further evidence of Sempill's treachery was discovered (Lashmar and Mullins 1998).

According to the National Archives, Sempill

> was associated with a number of Fascist or semi-Fascist individuals and organisations, including 'Action,' 'The Link,' and the 'Constitutional Reform Association.'[10]

Having trained their bomber pilots, Sempill provided the Japanese with the classified military information from Churchill's August 1941 Atlantic Charter meeting with President Franklin Delano Roosevelt aboard *HMS Prince of Wales*. Three days after the attack on Pearl Harbor, the *Prince of*

Wales and *HMS Repulse* were sunk by the Japanese: 840 sailors were lost, 513 in *Repulse* and 327 in *Prince of Wales*.

The 'old boy's network' looked after their own: the 19th Baron Sempill was allowed to retire from public office and remain a peer (Lashmar and Mullins 1998); the National Gallery commissioned drawings of him (1946 and 1950).[11] Craigievar Castle and one of his titles were inherited, after a sex change operation, by his sister and later brother, Sir Ewan Forbes of Craigievar, 11th Baronet of Craigievar.

Elliott's father, the Old Etonian Sir Claude Aurelius Elliott (1888–1973), Head Master and Provost of Eton, was President of the Alpine Club, and Chairman of the Himalayan Committee when the 1953 British Mount Everest expedition succeeded in reaching the summit. News of the expedition's success was released on the morning of Elizabeth II's coronation. Related to Leslie Steven, Elliott almost certainly climbed mountains with A. C. Pigou (Young 1951), and in retirement lived in Pigou's Lake District cottage, which he had first visited at the start of the twentieth century (Russell 1975).

Elliott rejected Burgess' application for a teaching post at Eton (Boyle 1982, 456). Six years after Elliott's death, and a decade after his son's retirement as head of MI6, Blunt was publically revealed to have been the Fourth Man (Boyle 1979, 1982), and Pigou was fraudulently accused of being the Fifth (McCormick 1979; Hayek 1994).

Between 1924 and 1955, the Conservatives were led by two Old Harrovians, Stanley Baldwin (1924–1937) and Churchill (1940–1955), plus an Old Rugbeian, Neville Chamberlain (1937–1940). Three Old Etonians followed: Anthony Eden (1955–1957), Harold Macmillan (1957–1963) and Alec Douglas-Home (1963–1965). Between 1965 and the leadership of the Old Etonian David Cameron (2005–2016), the Conservatives experimented with five non-Etonian leaders (four with low ascribed status). One, Michael Howard, was a Reform Club member; another, Margaret Thatcher, 'crossed the Mall' from the (Tory) Carlton Club to the Reform to borrow ideas that were in many ways antithetical to the traditions of her Party.

Both Cameron and the Old Etonian Mayor of London, Boris Johnson (2008–2016) and Foreign Secretary (2016–), re-embraced 'one nation conservatism': the idea that the upper classes have paternalistic obligations to those below them. This post-1832 Tory strategy originated with Benjamin Disraeli, who's *Sybil* (1845)—published in the same year as Friedrich Engels' (1845) *Condition of the Working Class in England*.

Disraeli's novel began in a London Club and from there explored the *Two Nations*.

Nation states emerged and strengthened as Habsburg feudal power waned. To maintain their 'blue' blood, members of the ruling Houses of Europe usually married cousins. Isabella I of Castile's grandson became Charles V, Holy Roman Emperor; for dynastic purposes, her daughter, Catherine of Aragon, married Henry VIII. Isabella, who was responsible for the final *Reconquista* of the Iberian Peninsular, funded Christopher Columbus' voyages (1492–1503) to the Americas, which fuelled the growing rivalry between Europe's sea-faring nations.

New legends of earlier colonisation emerged: the Welsh/British Tudors needed to establish a presence in the Americas to assert their own prior claim. If Henry VIII was a King-Emperor, not just a King, he may no longer be subject to the authority of the Pope and could thus become 'free' to remarry. The Welsh Prince Madoc emerged as the 'discoverer' of America three centuries before Columbus. 'Deacon' McCormick's (1967) *Madoc and the Discovery of America: Some New Light on an Old Controversy* provided fraudulent assertions about Madoc and the origins of the Mormon religion (Kimberley 2015).

The founder of the Cecil dynasty was closely involved with the execution of Mary, Queen of Scots, on the basis of the possibly fraudulent Casket letters. 'Deacon' McCormick (1967, 1968), utilised 'knowledge' about Walsingham, *John Dee: Scientist, Geographer, Astrologer and Secret Agent to Elizabeth I* and the Madoc myth for fraudulent commercial purposes. 'Deacon' McCormick's claim that Ian Fleming gleaned '007' from the secret signature of Elizabethan magician–spy John Dee was also a hoax (Spence 2015). In Burgess, Philby and Maclean, Malcolm Muggeridge detected the James Bond syndrome: 'his boozy amours, his tough postures, his intelligence expertise, are directly related to the same characteristics in Fleming's heroes' (cited by Boyle 1982, 502). At least in part, 'Deacon' McCormick (1993) owed his career in journalism to Fleming whose biography he wrote; he aspired to possess many of these Bond-like attributes (Leeson 2015).

During the Reformation, Henry founded the Anglican Church to facilitate his divorce from Catherine of Aragon (he fathered Elizabeth I with his second wife, Anne Boleyn). The Church of England is sometimes referred to as the 'Conservative Party at prayer,' while the Reform Club was the Liberal Party in Parliament. Twelve out of sixteen of Earl Russell's (1846–1852) cabinet were Reform members; a dozen members served in Earl Rosebery's (1884–1885) cabinet (Woodbridge 1978, 34; Crook 1973, 16).

Hayek (1994, 80, 98, 135) typically worked at home before lunching at the Reform Club or the LSE. His wartime evenings, which he spent dining in the Combinations Room and at High Table, King's College, Cambridge, were 'particularly congenial, and it completed the process of thorough absorption in English life, which from the beginning, I had found very easy.'[12] His 'new company' included a free trade ally and market failure opponent, Pigou, plus their common macroeconomic adversary, Keynes.

At the Reform, three journalists, Oscar Hobson, J. A. Spender and Robbins' father-in-law, A. G. Gardiner, met daily in the Smoking Room (Ashley 1978; Howson 2011, 109). Hobson was the first financial journalist to be knighted: he was successively financial editor of the *Guardian* and city editor of the *News Chronicle* (1920–1959). It seems likely that Hayek joined the 'high priests of laissez faire'—or 'George Schwartz's Tobacco Parliament'—who met frequently in the Smoking Room (Burlingham and Billis 2005, 140). Like Hayek, Graham Hutton was a regular lunch-taker at the Reform, and later—with Schwartz—sat on the IEA Advisory Board. Coincidentally, Hutton began working for the *Economist* in 1933, around the same time as Douglas Jay, whose son, Peter, was economics editor of *The Times* during Hayek's period of peak influence (Dudley Edwards 1995).

Before his divorce, Hayek entertained guests, such as Friedman, at his family home.[13] After Christmas 1949, he never lived in England again: the Reform and its bed 'chambers' became even more central to his London existence. Visitors were invited to join him for meals at the Reform, including breakfast.[14] Just before Mrs. Thatcher's first general election victory, Hayek and Sir Keith Joseph had a 'STRICTLY PRIVATE AND CONFIDENTIAL' lunch at the Reform (26 April 1979).[15]

3.2 Entitlement History

The Enlightenment facilitated the Road from Serfdom to Democracy—aided and abetted by the consequences of the Industrial Revolution. Social stratification was transformed: at the upper end, 'Lords,' 'Sirs' and 'vons' began to lose their inherited privileges; at the lower end, serfs and slaves were replaced by what Hayek (1978a) denigrated as 'peasants and workers.'[16] Initially, social mobility—both upward and downward—increased; but after the 1970s, the opportunities for mobility lessened (Leonhardt 2016).

In 1789, Hayek's (1994, 37, 39) paternal family acquired a 'von' from Kaiser Josef II: Josef Hayek (1750–1830) had served 'one of the great aristocratic landowners of Moravia,' became a secretary and then steward of the estate, before 'almost accidentally' developing two new textile factories. Hayek was equally attentive to the maternal history, yet devoted only two paragraphs to them: the 'von Jurascheks – although from a "younger" family and ennobled over a generation later – were definitely upper-class bourgeoisie and wealthier by far. My grandfather Franz von Juraschek had been a university professor and later a top ranking civil servant, with a scholarly background and international reputation as a statistician.'

At the University of Vienna, Hayek (1978a) benefited from his maternal family connections to both sides of the second generation Austrian School, Ritter von Böhm Bawerk and 'von' Wieser: 'I happened to know [Böhm Bawerk] as a friend of my grandfather and a former colleague at [the University] of Innsbruck, and as a mountaineering companion of my grandfather's.[17] Personally I ultimately became very friendly with [Wieser]; he asked me many times to his house. How far that was because he was a contemporary and friend of my grandfather's, I don't know.'[18]

In 1789, serfdom was formally abolished in France: elsewhere, feudalism was further undermined by Napoleon's armies. Varieties of serfdom survived in Austria until 1848 and in Russia until 1861. In Britain, the end came much earlier: beginning with the 1381 Peasants Revolt. Three generations separated von Hayek I from von Hayek V[19]; within the Austrian School of Economics, Hayek and 'Ritter von' Kuehnelt-Leddihn were part of the pre-1806 Habsburg-ennobled cohort: 'hereditary knight[s] of the Holy Roman Empire.'[20]

1789–1919—the period in which Hayek's paternal family were legally entitled to attach 'von' to their name—corresponds to a recognisable episode of world history. Louis XV's mistress is attributed with the prophetic words '*après nous, le Déluge*': the Great War, the 1917 Bolshevik revolution, and their aftermaths, were the *Déluge*. In the 1970s, an equivalent sense of impending Armageddon descended on private clubs and secret services (Teacher 2018a, b).

The Communist Manifesto (2011 [1848]) famously declared: 'A spectre is haunting Europe - the spectre of communism. All the powers of old Europe have entered into a holy alliance to exorcise this spectre: Pope and Tsar, Metternich and Guizot, French Radicals and German police-spies.' Karl Marx was rather proud of having married Jenny von Westphalen, whose paternal grandfather, Baron Christian von Westphalen, had played an important role in elevating the military status of Prussia during the 1756–1763 Seven Years' War (Berlin 1978, 59).[21] His *Communist Manifesto* co-author, Friedrich Engels, was a fourth-generation textile mill owner with different social aspirations: what he observed in Manchester inspired *The Condition of the Working Class in England* (1845).

On a *Road to Serfdom* promotional tour, 'von' Hayek's (1978a) aristocratic representation of 'liberty' impressed Americans: 'I began with a tone of profound conviction, not knowing how I would end the sentence, and it turned out that the American public is an exceedingly grateful and easy public ... I didn't know in the end what I had said, but evidently it was a very successful lecture ... what I did in America was a very corrupting experience. You become an actor, and I didn't know I had it in me. But given the opportunity to play with an audience, I began enjoying it [laughter].'[22]

In his *Historical Setting of the Austrian School of Economics*—published by Arlington House, named after the property confiscated by the Union from the Confederate General, Robert E. Lee—Mises (2003 [1969], 19) claimed that:

> When the German professors attached the epithet 'Austrian' to the theories of Menger and his two earliest followers and continuators, they meant it in a pejorative sense. After the battle of Königgrätz [1866] the qualification of a thing as Austrian always had such a coloration in Berlin, that 'headquarters of *Geist*,' as Herbert Spencer sneeringly called it.

In 1820, Thomas Tooke presented a free trade petition to Parliament; in Parliament, Disraeli (20 February 1846) referred to 'the disciples of the school of Manchester' to denigrate the promoters of laissez-faire— especially Cobden and John Bright, Reform Club members, and founders of the Manchester-based Anti-Corn Law League. In a letter to Henry Drummond, Disraeli (19 November 1848) described himself as a 'wretched correspondent – in the matter of letter writing, being of the Manchester school & caring only for the imports' (Chaloner 1962, 137; Monypenny 1912, 363; Disraeli and Gunn 2004, 482).

Caldwell (2010) informed readers of *The Washington Post*: 'Hayek himself disdained having his ideas attached to either party.' The Hayek Archives—which Caldwell seeks to monopolise—reveal that the MPS courted a variety of British Conservative Party politicians—including Enoch Powell,[23] Sir Keith Joseph, Reginald Maudling,[24] Geoffrey Howe,[25] David Howell,[26] William Proudfoot,[27] Russell Lewis (Conservative Political Centre),[28] Rhodes Boyson,[29] John Biffen and Sir Peter Agnew.[30] In 1973, Agnew, a devout Christian, received the Shah of Iran's Order of Homayoun (Order of the Lion and the Sun), was President of 'Archduke' Otto 'von' Habsburg's European Documentation and Information Centre and received the *Orden del Mérito Civil* (Order of Civic Merit) from General Francisco Franco. He was nominated for MPS membership in the same year as Habsburg nominated Jean Violet (Teacher 2018a, b).[31]

Boyson was born the son of a cotton-spinner in a Lancashire mill town (Daily Express Obituary 2012). In 1967, he joined the Conservative Party because of his 'research into the cotton industry and the Manchester school of liberal economic philosophy. Here was a body of men who believed that a free enterprise economy was not only efficient but brought moral growth to all men … Cobden had a moral view of society and believed that free enterprise would not only bring prosperity but social harmony at home and peace abroad within a system of universal free trade' (Eccleshall 1990).

The neo-feudal century began after the 1815 Battle of Waterloo. In 1819, at St. Peter's Field, Manchester, the British cavalry charged a demonstration demanding the reform of Parliamentary representation. The Peterloo Massacre resulted in the deaths of fifteen demonstrators and, indirectly, the foundation of the *Manchester Guardian* (1821). Hayek's (1978a) American 'stunt' failed to impress those who lived in the area most closely associated with the textile factories of the British industrial revolution: 'Soon after I came back [from America] I was asked to give a lecture to some public group at Manchester, and I tried to do my American stunt. With the stolid north English citizens not moving a muscle in their faces, I very nearly broke down because I could not be guided by their expression. It's the sort of lecturing you can do with the American audience but not the British audience.'[32]

3.3 Hayek and Early Reform Club History

According to G. M. Trevelyan, anyone attempting to write about the nineteenth century would have to be familiar with 'this great Club' (cited by Burlingham and Billis 2005, 8). The same is almost (but not quite) true of the twentieth century. As the Liberal Party declined, so too did the influence of the Reform,[33] but it retained political and social significance.

The 1832 Great Reform Act spawned 'registration societies' to enlist the newly enfranchised voters (Dudley Edwards 1995, 10–11). According to its website, the Reform Club was founded in 1836 to 'counter the machinations of the Tory Carlton Club,' which had been founded four years before.[34] Sir Robert Peel's 1934 Tamworth Manifesto laid the foundations of the Conservative Party, which would, henceforth, 'reform to survive': the Reform Act was 'a final and irrevocable settlement of a great constitutional question.' Simultaneously, the Liberal Party emerged from the Whigs. In 1841, Peel formed a Government—but a split emerged over the Corn Laws. The free trade Peelites, including Gladstone, President of the Board of Trade, 'crossed the floor' to form the Liberal Party (Gash 1972).

Disraeli and Edward Smith-Stanley (14th Earl of Derby) led the Protectionist Conservatives—what remained after the Peelites left. Manchester School 'Little Englanders' wished to be free of the financial burden of the colonies; from the 1870s, the Conservatives embraced the 'New Imperialism.' In 1876, Disraeli made Victoria Empress of India; she ennobled him as 1st Earl of Beaconsfield.

On the surface, the two parties also differed with respect to social reform and personal behaviour. Some libertine Tories pursued conspicuous 'drunk-as-a-lord' haughtiness; Gladstonian finance remains a byword for parsimonious. Gladstone (1990, clxxxvi) pursued prostitutes to 'rescue' them, while the future Edward VII's sexual encounters undermined the image of bourgeois respectability that Queen Victoria sought to project for her dynasty (Ridley 2012, 57).

Between 1852 and 1894, Disraeli and Gladstone alternated in office (as Prime Minister and Chancellor of the Exchequer). Gladstone was the first Liberal Party Prime Minister (1868–1874), and Lloyd George may have been the last (1916–1922). His coalition was 'brought down' after a meeting at the Carlton Club (McCormick 1975, 11).

'Deacon' McCormick was relatively well known as a dubious and sensationalist author. In *The Private Life of Mr. Gladstone*, 'Deacon' McCormick (1965, 28, 76–77, 171, 183) reported an unsourced account of Gladstone putting 'a half-starved girl who looked more like ten than the fifteen years she actually admitted to ... on his knee and solemnly, but in a simple language and without embellishment, told her the true story of Christmas.' The girl wanted to change her name to Gladstone but said 'him being in the Government it wud ave dun him no good at all.' The 'secret clue' behind Gladstone's 'strange passion for reforming women' could be found in the 'Gladstone Diaries' and also in the 'letters and diaries of various social workers.'

In Reform circles, 'Deacon' McCormick may not have *The Pursuit of Reason: The Economist 1843* been highly regarded. Owen Dudley Edwards (1969, 390, 391), the brother of Ruth Dudley Edwards, Reform Club member and author of *–1993* (1995), described *The Private Life of Mr. Gladstone* as in many ways 'exceedingly bad'; the author had ascribed to 'his audience an ignorance equal to his own.' 'Deacon' McCormick had 'examined certain manuscripts, although not apparently, the Gladstone diaries preserved at Lambeth, on whose significance he dwells lovingly.'

'Deacon' McCormick's (1963, 18, 27, 29, 30, 31, 324–334) *The Mask of Merlin A Critical Biography of David Lloyd George* reveals the same pattern. Chapter 2 of 'Deacon' McCormick's *Temple of Love* (1962) was entitled 'Strength Through Bundling'; Chapter 2 of *The Mask of Merlin* ('Bible and Bundling') contained sensational revelations about the teenage sex life and religious ecstasy of the future Prime Minister. According to 'Deacon' McCormick, religion was 'the natural outlet in the emotions of a passionate race.' During the Welsh revival, some of these religious ceremonies 'invariably ended up in sexual orgies.'

The biographer inserted himself into the narrative: 'I was eight years old when I first heard him speak and that is still an unforgettable experience.' Later, he had been 'given extracts from letters written' by 'Moses Roberts of Caernarvon' (who 'seems to have been a close crony of Lloyd George in his early teens') which revealed that the two of them 'were sorely tempted by two Irish girls' with whom they enjoyed '*caru gwely,*' which 'means literally courting in bed or bundling.' After being deeply moved by a sermon on sin which ended in a 'paroxysm of ecstasy,' the teenage Lloyd George supposedly confessed to Roberts that 'From this day I am ready to go out and preach to the world like that man. I know exactly what my message is.'

'Deacon' McCormick's sources included direct conversations with people many of whom—including Lloyd George—had been dead for decades; unpublished correspondence; plus private and unpublished diaries from Admiral Gaunt and Vivian Phillips, which were 'not available for general inspection.'

'Deacon' McCormick (1963, 278–289) sensationally alleged that there had been an unnoticed spy in the Berghof, Hitler's headquarters in Obersalzberg in the Bavarian Alps: 'Working as a secretary in the archives of the Berghof was a young woman, Helga Stultz, who was an informer for the American intelligence ... Back to Washington went this report from Helga: "I have overheard a conversation between Hitler and [Dr Robert] Ley. They discussed the visit of the Duke of Windsor. Ley said he was keeping in close touch with the ex-English Prime Minister, Lloyd George, through the Arbeitsfront [German Labour Front]".'

Stultz then relayed a verbatim account from the *Führer*:

> Hitler was very excited. 'You must find a way of letting Lloyd George know that in my opinion the only hope of an understanding with Britain would be if he returned to power and the ex-King [Edward VIII] came back to the throne. That cannot happen unless there is a war. But, though the British don't want to fight and have no stomach for it, I believe they may blunder into war. If that happens, they will collapse within a year. We should have new rulers to deal with and I am certain Lloyd George would give us back our colonies without any fuss. He promised me he would agree to this.'

'Deacon' McCormick (1963, 289, 295) reported that wartime Nazi intelligence

> diaries reveal that 'An attempt is to be made to set down the agent Lehrer with a wireless operator on the coast of South Wales in order to establish better communications with the Welsh nationalists.'

Stultz reported back to Washington that 'Lloyd George's name is often mentioned here in a favourable context.'

This account captivated Paul Addison (1971, 364, 362, 379) who reported that in 'September 1936 Lloyd George made his celebrated visit to Hitler'—adding, with citations to 'MacCormick [*sic*]': 'Was Lloyd George's career running parallel with that of Petain or Quisling?' Less impressed was John Grigg (1973, 305, 54n), a London *Times* columnist and author of *The Young Lloyd George* (1973), *Lloyd George:*

The People's Champion (1978) and *Lloyd George: From Peace To War 1912–1916* (1983): 'the author's technique is slapdash, and his allegations and innuendoes should be treated as critically as he has tried to treat Lloyd George.'

Grigg hinted at fraud. Referring to one of 'Deacon' McCormick's sources—a thesis on 'Nonconformity's Battle in Wales' by Reverend Thomas Charles Williams—Grigg noted that 'The thesis is not listed in the British Museum catalogue, there is no copy of it in the National Library of Wales, nor any reference to it in H.L. William's biography of Thomas Charles Williams … McCormick's evidence would suffer from being third-hand even if it were less dubious on other grounds.' Grigg also implicitly noted 'Deacon' McCormick's ability to address his market: 'His book, however, is not without interest.'

'Deacon' McCormick (1985, 200) listed Charles Buller (1806–1848) as one of the *Cambridge Apostles*. Hayek (16 February 1982) informed William Thomas that there was an unidentified bronze bust of Buller in the Reform which he had been able to identify by its broken boxer's nose when, forty-odd years before, he had started collecting the letters and diaries of John Stuart Mill.[35] 'Deacon' McCormick also shared an interest in spiritualism with another Reform Club member, Sir Arthur Conan Doyle, who he had conjured-up to support his claim to have discovered *The Identity of Jack the Ripper* (1970a, 224). In *The Master Book of Spies: the World of Espionage, Master Spies, Tortures, Interrogations, Spy Equipment, Escapes, Codes & How You can Become a Spy* and *Who's Who in Spy Fiction*, 'Deacon' McCormick (1973, 105; 1977, 66) asserted that Conan Doyle had 'brought in Sherlock Holmes to resolve what a baffled secret service could not cope with.'

3.4 Hayek and Later Reform Club History

Reform Club members have typically been associated with Whigs, Liberals and their causes: free trade, the expansion of the franchise, Catholic emancipation, the supremacy of Parliament over the Divine Right of Kings, etc. However, in 1913, the Liberal Government's failure to extend the franchise to women led to the smashing of Reform Club windows (Burlingham and Billis 2005, 216; Woodbridge 1978, 93–94). In 1928—almost a century after the passage of the Great Reform Act—British women received the vote on equal terms with men.

In 1981, women were allowed to apply for Reform Club membership—'long before any of the other traditional clubs,' as their website boasts.[36] There was resistance: as one Club Chairman put it

> It is often said that women are not 'clubbable.' (cited by Burlingham and Billis 2005, 227)

If not clubbable, women played other roles at the Reform: 'it was the practise of members to leave the club in the evening saying a clear good night to the porter to establish an alibi and then, having found a suitable lady companion, to return with her through those other [unlocked] back doors and up to the chambers' (Burlingham and Billis 2005, 225).

Reformed Characters: the Reform Club in History and Literature is, in part, a celebration of 'characters,' some raffish. Woodrow (later Lord) Wyatt, the author of the Cold War *The Peril in Our Midst* (1956) who had 'close links to British intelligence' (Lashmar and Oliver 1998, 111). The four-time married Woodrow (later Lord) Wyatt provided a story about two telephone calls he received at the Club. The first was to have dinner plus 'entertainment. I've got a girl for you … a half-Hawaiian nurse redolent with sensual Pacific beauty.' Wyatt insisted that the girl had to 'dance bare-breasted for a tired soldier from the front.' The second call was from the now-pregnant nurse, saying 'My fiancé won't like it' (Burlingham and Billis 2005, 220).

A portrait and a marble bust of Gladstone adorn the Reform. In July 1974, *Penthouse* 'gentleman's' magazine negotiated a 'fashion shoot' in the Club—described in the Club history as 'ANIMATED BUST'—along with the reflection that 'Who can doubt that for Mr. Gladstone's ghost in particular these visions must have had a deep sociological interest' (Burlingham and Billis 2005, 28, 218–220).

In 1977, 'von' Hayek—as he was known in Club circles—wrote to the Secretary complaining about the presence of ladies in the library. According to Cubitt (2006, 32, 77, n. 38), as a child, Hayek 'discovered that he could read by studying the torn-up newspaper people used for lavatory paper in those days.' As an adult, Hayek found inspiration 'more often in the lavatory than one would have thought'; it was the presence of ladies in the lavatories (or having to share them) that made women (as servants or members) so inconvenient to him.

In 1972, John Vaizey proposed that women be admitted as members. Robbins supported Vaizey but warned that there were 'many dinosaurs about' (Howson 2011, 896); possibly coincidentally, Harold Soref M. P. resigned from the Reform in 1973.[37] Directly or indirectly, in 1913 Sylvia Pankhurst may have been responsible for the smashed windows. 'Deacon' McCormick (1979, 8, 52) asserted that she was the 'first British woman to establish relations with the Comintern,' was an important member of the Communist Party of Great Britain and was associated with a 'summer school for left wing politics at Derwentwater where Pigou was an occasional speaker.' In his review of 'Deacon' McCormick's *British Connection*, Soref (1979) stated: 'In his last television utterance, Herbert Marcuse disclosed that his major allies and agents for world revolution were Women's Lib.' Marcuse was associated with Marxist-orientated Frankfurt Institute for Social Sciences: a favourable reference to the Frankfurt Institute was 'more than [Hayek] could endure' (Cubitt 2006, 31).[38]

When in 1981 the vote to admit women came, Hayek denied having very strong views; he was merely looking forward to the 'sociological' study the debate would provide.[39] In Hayek's 'overseas members' category, the vote was 30–25 in favour.[40] The final outcome he had 'not been glad' about (Cubitt 2006, 77).

There are similarities between the Habsburg *fin de siècle* and the British 'winter of discontent': the first became a failed state (1918–1919); the second appeared to be failing (1978–1979). Hayek told Cubitt (2006, 15) that of the two Empires he had watched decline, 'England's downfall had been the more painful to him.' In 1919, the *Déluge* washed away the legal basis of Habsburg inherited titles and privileges: 'The tradition died very largely; it died particularly in my native town Vienna, which was one of the great cultural and political centers of Europe but became the capital of a republic of peasants and workers afterwards. While, curiously enough, this is the same as we're now watching in England, the intellectual activity survives this decay for some time. The economic decline [in Austria] already was fairly dreadful, [as was] cultural decline' (Hayek 1978a).[41]

Hayek's fellow Austrian, Hitler, unintentionally created the foundations for German economic success: after the fall of the Third Reich, Imperial pretensions were renounced and replaced by an export-based, social market economy (Vanberg 2013; Goldschmidt and Hesse 2013; Filip 2018). Equally abruptly, a similar export-based (as opposed to

Empire-based) strategy dominated policymaking in defeated Japan. The British Empire, according to Adam Smith (1986 [1776], 324), had been founded 'for the sole purpose of raising up a people of customers ... a project altogether unfit for a nation of shopkeepers; but extremely fit for a nation whose government is influenced by shopkeepers.'

But Empires breed inherited privileges, which can easily become caste-like incubuses. Such influences were detectable at the Reform. When the newsagent chain owner, W. H. Smith, attempted to join, he was

> blackballed as a presumptuous 'tradesman.'

In the 1970s, one member complained that the wrong types were being admitted: the Club, he complained, had become 'full of sock salesmen' (Burlingham and Billis 2005, 206, 218; Woodbridge 1978, 82–83).

Members stayed in 'chambers' on the third floor. According to the 1985 *Architects Journal*, above them lay the 'spartan and perilous world of servants, attic accommodation ... all routes of escape (escape that for the poor servants in the attic) are fireproof.' As a result, in the late 1970s, a servant was burnt to death: 'the fire was so intense it proved impossible to open his door.' When a few books were placed in the Servant's Hall, the attic dwellers stated that they would use them 'to be better fitted to discharge the duties of our station with credit to ourselves and increased satisfaction to our employers' (cited by Burlingham and Billis 2005, 225, 238–239).

A Reform Club kitchen porter was not so docile: he was tried and executed for the murder of Christine Granville, a wartime Special Operations Executive agent (Burlingham and Billis 2005, 241). 'Deacon' McCormick (1970a, 222, 223, 228) solved *The Identity of Jack the Ripper* via a witness who referred to seeing 'a Russian ... with a dark moustache.' Evidence was then provided which suggested that Granville's death may have been 'in some way manipulated by someone in the underworld of espionage': 'Teddy Knight' told 'Deacon' McCormick (1993, 143–147, 154) that he saw Granville the night before she was murdered in a West End nightclub 'talking to a well dressed Russian woman.'

Anthony Sampson's (1962) *Anatomy of Britain* revealed the extensive, but previously subterranean, family connections between the Conservative Party and the Dukes of Devonshire and Marlborough. Britain, Sampson concluded, was stuck in an old world of complacent assumptions of superiority. This British reluctance to adapt to post-Imperial splendour was, in a sense, symbolised by 'von' Hayek and his 'natural' or 'spontaneous' order: acquired (and, therefore, subsequently inherited) feudal titles and privileges offered a superior avenue for social advancement compared to low-status manufacturing or commerce.

Hayek (1978b [1968], 183–184) asserted: 'The fact is, that, though the existence of a spontaneous order not made for a particular purpose cannot be properly said to have a purpose, it may yet be highly conducive to the achievement of many different individual purposes not known as a whole to any single person, or relatively small group of persons. Indeed, rational action is possible only in a fairly orderly world.'

Rosten (1908–1997), an LSE graduate and Anglophone, asked Hayek about 'the depth of the class distinction [in England], which is just beginning to disappear, has created degrees of bitterness which I've never found in the United States. There is a hatred.' Hayek (1978a) responded: 'My impression of England may be wrong in the sense that I only really know the south. All you are speaking about is the north of England, where I think this feeling prevails. But if you live in London—Right now my relations are mainly in the southwest of England, where my children live, and I don't find any of this sharp resentment. And the curious thing is that in the countryside of southwest England, the class distinctions are very sharp, but they're not resented. [laughter] They're still accepted as part of the natural order.'[42]

In *Reformed Characters: The Reform Club in History and Literature*, Hayek is described as 'a natural Reformer' (Burlingham and Billis 2005, 143). The Conservatives regarded themselves as the 'natural' party of government; in the 1920s, Churchill sneered at Labour as 'not fit to govern' (Seaman 1966, 132). After Churchill's defeat, the newly elected Labour Government began to implement the 1942 Beveridge Report Welfare State proposals. 'Deacon' McCormick (1976a, 181, 191) opposed 'the Welfare State (to be found in its most bountiful and easily exploitable form in the United Kingdom)' because it had created 'mass affluence.' The 'advent of the Welfare State in Europe since World War II has paved the way to a new and fruitful ground for the con-trickster as well as the truly idle person.' According to 'Deacon' McCormick (1970b, 28), the Labour Minister responsible for constructing the National Health Service, Aneurin Bevan, 'was saved from complete failure by his native Welsh cunning and his fondness for power.'

Beveridge, later Baron Beveridge, Liberal leader in the House of Lords, wrote much of his 1942 Report at the Reform (Woodbridge 1978, 156); his 'ablest research assistant' was Harold Wilson (cited by Foot 1968, 37). Other Liberals contributed to the expansion of the role of the State. In January 1885, Joseph Chamberlain, a Cabinet Minister in Gladstone's Third Government, asked rhetorically: 'what ransom will property pay for the security of property it enjoys?' The word 'ransom' suggests brigandage, rather than justice, and nine days later was replaced with 'insurance.' Chamberlain explained that he was proposing that 'the community as a whole, cooperating for the benefit of all,' could improve the lot of the poor (Marsh 1994, 186).

The 1832 Great Reform Act was followed by a Second (1867) and a Third (1884). The passage of the 1867 Reform Bill, combined with increased industrial disputation, encouraged Marx to declare to Engels: 'Things are moving forward, and in the next revolution, which is perhaps nearer than it seems, we (i.e. you and I) have this powerful machine in our hands' (cited by McLellan 1976, 378). Yet the expansion of the franchise did not disadvantage the Tories: with the exception of two minority Liberal Governments (1892–1895), they were in office from 1885 to 1905: under the 3rd Marquess of Salisbury (Robert Gascoyne-Cecil, Lord Robert Cecil and Viscount Cranborne), and then his Old Etonian nephew, Lord and Baron of Hailes, Arthur Balfour.

Gladstone's conversion to Irish Home Rule led Joseph Chamberlain and 61 Liberals (including two Reform members, John Bright and Sir George Otto Trevelyan, G. M. Trevelyan's father) to cross the floor to form the Liberal Unionists. In September 1903, Chamberlain resigned from the Conservative and Unionist Government and toured the country speaking against free trade; a campaign promoted by the Tariff Reform League. A single British Empire trading block ('Imperial Preference') protected by high tariff walls could, they argued, counteract the growing power of the USA and Germany—and also fund the Welfare State.

The Liberal Government's 1911 National Insurance Act, a pre-Beveridge version of the British Welfare State, was modelled, in part, on Chancellor Otto von Bismarck's Second Reich (state-funded old-age pensions, accident insurance, medical care and unemployment insurance). After visiting Germany, Chancellor Lloyd George stated, in his intentionally provocative 1909 'People's Budget' Speech, that the British should aim to be: 'putting ourselves in this field on a level with

Germany; we should not emulate them only in armaments' (cited by Beveridge 1953, 80).

The extension of the franchise and the rise of Labour encouraged Lloyd George to propose an increase in the progressive income tax; plus a land tax, which would have adversely affected Conservative Party landowners. The Tories preferred raising revenue through tariffs. The House of Lords vetoed the budget (30 November 1909) in violation of a constitutional convention.

In the January 1910 General Election, the Liberals proposed to reduce the power of the hereditary Lords. In the resulting hung Parliament, the Lords accepted the budget (the land tax having been dropped). These constitution tensions continued until a second 1910 General Election. After the June 1911 coronation of George V, Parliament returned to constitutional discussions. The proposed Parliament Act was resisted by 'diehards' and the 'No-Surrender Committee,' led by Lord Halsbury, the 4th Marquess of Salisbury, plus the 'King and Country' party, which including the newly elected Tory M. P., Leo Amery (Faber 2005, 68–69).

The Lords surrendered after George V threatened to dilute their status by creating sufficient Liberal peers to overcome their Conservative majority. The resulting 1911 Parliament Act confirmed the supremacy of the House of Commons in fiscal matters: the right of the Lords to veto money bills was completely removed, and the Lord's right of veto over other public bills was replaced with a maximum delay of two years.[43] The December 1910 General Election was the last to be held prior to the 1914–1918 *Déluge* that created an unstable 'interwar' environment that undermined the nascent democratic institutions of those Continental European countries with more-entrenched hereditary privileges.

The 1958 Life Peerages Act weakened the hereditary dominance of the upper house and also allowed for the creation of female peers. The 1963 Peerage Act further severed the link between birth and feudal status. This allowed Anthony Wedgewood Benn to renounce the title which he inherited on the death of his father, the 2nd Viscount Stansgate[44]; he also requested that 'Wedgewood' be dropped.

In 1980, 'Tony Benn' proposed the abolition of the House of Lords. Almost a generation later, the Labour Government's 1999 House of Lords Act expelled all but 92 hereditary peers. The 7th Marquess of Salisbury voluntarily left the House of Lords in protest at new rules concerning the declaration of financial interests—for the first time since the sixteenth century, no member of the Cecil family sat in the British Parliament.

Blunt informed Burgess that Maclean's interrogation would begin on Monday 28 May 1951. Burgess hired a car and visited the Reform Club to make various phone calls; Blunt arranged to collect him from the Reform at 6 pm. But Burgess didn't turn up; after dinner, Blunt left the Reform saying 'I feel I must go now and look for him' (Boyle 1982, 401–402, 413). One call was to Goronwy Rees (1972, 214)—which Burgess didn't pay for (Rees' number was posted on the members' noticeboard and when the date was noticed by a journalist, his house was besieged in the hope of uncovering the secrets of Burgess' treachery).

Unlike Burgess, Harold Laski, the Jewish, Manchester-born son of a cotton merchant and Labour Party Chairman during the 1945 Hayek-influenced 'Gestapo' election, was beyond the pale. Laski—described by Hayek (1994, 82) as 'a pathological liar'—had to withdraw his Reform application because of the 'outcry it caused' (Burlingham and Billis 2005, 215, 132). Laski applied for membership at the same time as Hayek, when the Club 'badly needed members' (Woodbridge 1978, 86).

The 1901 Taff Vale Railway Co v Amalgamated Society of Railway Servants left labour unions liable for damages caused by industrial action; it also increased their determination to gain electoral representation. The 1903 Lib–Lab Pact, negotiated between Herbert Gladstone (the Old Etonian Liberal Chief Whip) and Ramsey MacDonald (Secretary of the Labour Representation Committee and illegitimate son of a farm labourer) facilitated the return of 29 Labour MPs at the 1906 election. The ensuing 1906 Trade Disputes Act prevented labour unions from being sued for damages incurred during a strike. In a letter to *The Times* ('Trade Union Immunity Under the Law'), Hayek (21 July 1977) asked: 'When will the British public at last learn to understand that there is no salvation for Britain until the special privileges granted to the trade unions by the Trade Disputes Act of 1906 are revoked?'[45]

In the early twentieth century, Liberals and Conservatives were relatively socially homogenous. Labour represented the newly enfranchised working classes and their intellectual sympathisers: in the 1920s, they replaced the Liberals as the alternative to the Conservatives. This had consequences at the Reform: 'In the old days when Lloyd George came into the coffee room, everybody stood up until he sat down.' Subsequent Liberal Party leaders were less revered: in 1963, when Jo Grimond lunched there, 'few people recognised him and nobody stood up' (Burlingham and Billis 2005, 46). The Old Etonian Grimond was married to Laura Miranda Bonham Carter, Asquith's granddaughter.

The 3rd Marquess of Salisbury was the last Prime Minister to remain in the House of Lords throughout his term of office. In 1963, Alec Douglas-Home, 14th Earl of Home, became the last member of the House of Lords to be appointed Prime Minister and the last Conservative leader to 'emerge' through the 'customary processes' of consultation with Tory 'grandees.' Before contesting a by-election, he was obliged to disclaim his peerage and become a commoner (an option that had only just become available through the 1958 Peerage Act). His successor, Edward Heath, was the first Conservative leader to be elected by ballot (1965). Both Heath and his successor, Mrs. Thatcher, underwent radical vocal transformations—presumably to disguise their social backgrounds, and also, perhaps, in the hope of adding to their electoral appeal among the deferential sections of the working classes.

According to Geoffrey Wood (2006, 145), the Heath Government (1970–1974) initiated the 'greatest peacetime inflation since the reign of Henry the Eighth.'[46] The 1926–1927 miners' strike radicalised Keynes (1936); the 1973–1974 miners' strike exacerbated class conflict and resulted in a third twentieth-century election on the theme 'Who Governs Britain?' The hung Parliament led Prime Minister Heath to offer the Liberals a coalition with their leader, Jeremy Thorpe, as Home Secretary. Talks collapsed and Labour took office (March 1974). A second general election on 10 October 1974—the day after the announcement of Hayek's Nobel Prize—resulted in a Labour Government with a three-seat majority.

By 1977, the Labour Government needed Liberal support to stay in office (the fourth Lib–Lab pact). Hayek (24 March 1977) complained in *The Times*:

> May one who has devoted a large part of his life to the study of the history and the principles of liberalism point out that a party that keeps a socialist government in power has lost all title to the name 'Liberal.' Certainly no liberal can in future vote 'Liberal.'[47]

The post-1929 deflation that Hayek and Mises promoted fatally undermined democracy in Germany and Austria, and the MPS-initiated stagflation of the 1970s could have produced similar outcomes. On 9–11,

1973, Pinochet overthrew the democratically elected government of Chile; Reagan approved Pinochet's September 1976 terrorist attack on Washington that killed Orlando Letelier and an American citizen, Ronni Karpen Moffitt (Leeson 2018a). The month before, Reagan had won 45.9% of the primary vote in the strongest challenge to a sitting President (Gerald Ford) since 1912.

Between February 1975 and May 1976, two British leaders (Heath and Thorpe) were deposed and a third, Wilson, resigned on his 60th birthday and 'spoke darkly' to journalists Barrie Penrose and Roger Courtiour

> of two military coups which he said had been planned to overthrow his government in the late 1960s and in the mid 1970s,' Penrose writes. 'Both were said to involve high-ranking elements in the British army, eager to see the back of Labour governments.' 'Both involved a member of the Royal Family - Prince Louis Mountbatten.' Lord Mountbatten would be installed as an interim prime minister following the military coup, Wilson believed. (Wheeler 2006)

Penrose and Courtiour secretly taped the conversations—but evidence is required before a conspiracy against Wilson becomes more than speculation. There is, however, no doubt that some Hayekians engaged coup-friendly elements in the upper reaches of the British military (Leeson 2018a).

Hayek's party political influence has previously been taken to be a post-1979 phenomenon. But of the 1975–1976 replacements: Thatcher was an overt Hayekian; Jo Grimond was a regular contributor to Fisher's IEA and attended the 1984 MPS meeting; and Hayek (1977) celebrated the policies of the New Labour Prime Minister, James Callaghan, as 'the greatest victory of all I think we have had' (Chapter 5).

In the general election of 3 May 1979, the Liberals lost two seats—including Thorpe's. The Old Etonian Thorpe had written to a male model and former stable boy, Norman Scott, thanking him for his letter which 'arrived all by itself at my breakfast table at the Reform.' Thorpe promised to take Scott on a holiday: 'Bunnies can (and will) go to France' (cited by Burlingham and Billis 2005, 188). Five days after the election, Thorpe stood trial at the Old Bailey charged with Scott's attempted murder.[48]

3.5 Hayek's Intersecting Clubs

In 1931, Robbins had been a Reform member for only two years (Howson 2011, 170); shortly afterwards, he nominated Hayek, who was seconded by the financial journalist, Oscar Hobson, and supported by four LSE colleagues, Schwartz, Hutton, Arnold Plant and Frank Paish; plus Jacques Kahane, George Paish, Sam Chaloner, Frederick Phillips and John F. Huntington.[49]

Hayek and his first family lived in Hampstead Garden Suburb, close to at least four LSE colleagues: Robbins, Plant, Schwartz and Frank Paish. Hayek's clubs intersected: at the 1947 foundation MPS meeting, Robbins wrote the Society Statement of Aims; Hobson, Plant and Schwartz were proposed foundation members; Hutton was 'elected' in 1957 and became Chairman of the 1968 British MPS Organising Committee. Hutton also played an important role at the IEA and authored the IEA pamphlet, *All Capitalists Now* (1960). In 1984, he joined Hayek for an IEA dinner after his ennoblement at Buckingham Palace.[50]

One of James Buchanan's (1965) most insightful contributions was his *Economica* essay on 'An Economic Theory of Clubs.' Hayek's clubs provided new and sometimes glamorous experiences. Friedman dated the beginning of his 'active involvement in the political process' to the founding MPS meeting: a 'young, naïve provincial American' who, like George Stigler, was on his first trip outside the USA (Friedman and Friedman 1998, 159). Buchanan (1992, 130) met his first 'Princess' through a 'luxurious' MPS meeting. Through the Society, Friedman, Stigler and Buchanan would, presumably, have met the Habsburg Pretender—all three, together with four fellow members, Maurice Allais, Ronald Coase, Gary Becker and Vernon Smith, probably met their first legitimate King and Queen in Stockholm (1976, 1982, 1986, 1988, 1991, 1992 and 2002, respectively).

After winning the 1974 Nobel Prize for Economic Sciences, Hayek (1978a) objected to the currency devaluation caused by four ennoblements in the first decade: Jan Tinbergen (1969), Wassily Leontief (1973), Myrdal (1974) and Sir Arthur Lewis (1979). Thomas Hazlett reminded Hayek of Myrdal's complaint that he had 'certainly never been much troubled by epistemological worries.' Hayek (1992 [1977]) responded: 'it is certainly a rather extreme case combined with an intellectual arrogance that, even among economists, is rare. Myrdal has been in opposition on these issues even before Keynes came out. His book on monetary doctrines and values and so on dates from the late 1920s. He has his own peculiar view on this subject which I think is wrong. His book couldn't even be reproduced now. I don't think he has ever been a good economist.'

According to Hayek (1978a), Leontief was engaged in 'agitation for planning ... I don't think he ever understood any economics.'[51] Peter Bauer (17 August 1975) replied to a letter (which is not in the Hayek Archives) sympathising with Hayek's 'feelings' about being bracketed with Myrdal: Myrdal's and Tinbergen's Nobel Prizes tell a 'lot' about the state of economics.[52]

Shortly afterwards, the value of the Prize was—from Hayek's perspective—further diluted by the Keynesian econometrician, Lawrence Klein (1980), and Sir Richard Stone (1984), who developed the national income accounts.[53] When the University of Michigan considered promoting Klein from part-time lecturer to full professor, William A. Patton (11 February 1955), an accountant and son-to-be MPS member, insisted that Hayek be allowed to respond 'candidly.' In case Hayek was unaware of the ideological dimension, Patton reminded him that Klein was 'completely' in the 'wrong camp.'

The University of Michigan formally invited Hayek to assess Klein, although Hayek's written reply (if he made one) has not apparently survived.[54] Klein (1986, 26) had worked under Arthur Burns at the National Bureau of Economic Research on 'savings behaviour, especially with respect to the Pigou effect'; but in 'the McCarthy era I left Michigan for the peace and academic freedom of Oxford.' Patton's campaign succeeded (Leeson 2017). Shenfield (1988) shared Hayek's animosities: 'I doubt if it will be long before the names of Myrdal, Leontieff [*sic*], Klein, and Stone sink without trace in the worlds of scholarship and informed economic discussion. Or take Veblen. Here was a bad economist if ever there was one.'

3.6 THE ROAD TO DIVORCE

Coronations were eagerly anticipated at the Reform and elsewhere. One historian recalled that when Queen Victoria was close to death, members of Gentlemen's Clubs

> waited around anxiously throughout the day ... In their clubs, however, the politicians were deep in solemn discussion ... There was conversation,

but it was 'muffled,' in the words of one clubman, 'as though the talkers were talking under their breath' ... The American writer Henry James walked down Pall Mall from the Reform and sensed real fear among the people around him, who were dazed by the news.

Another writer reflected that in 1952, he was 'lucky enough to watch the coronation proceeding from my club in Pall Mall (how *happy* [emphasis in original] the Queen looked. It cheered the heart to see her). Drinks flowed, many toasts were drunk ...' (cited by Burlingham and Billis 2005, 245, 246).

Hayek became a Reform Club member on 9 January 1935, shortly after he began to push his wife for a divorce.[55] The following year, George V's son, Edward VIII, became unacceptable as King-Emperor. During the Reformation, the Church of England had been constructed to facilitate a royal divorce, but the twice-divorced Pennsylvanian Bessie Wallis Simpson, nee Warfield, would not be allowed to become Queen Wallis I. The in-bred Houses of Europe favoured marriages between cousins: the Habsburg Archduke Franz Ferdinand's marriage to the lesser-status Countess Sophie Chotek von Chotkowa was only accepted on a morganatic (non-inherited privilege) basis because 'although the Chotek blood was undeniably blue, it was not tinged with the necessary purple' (Brook-Shepherd 2003, 17–18, 20; Taylor 1964, 85, 249; 1974, 1). But a similar arrangement was not acceptable in Britain: Edward had become obsessed with a 'social climber.'

The Britain press initially cooperated in the suppression of information. In November 1936, Edward received a letter from his own Private Secretary informing him that 'The silence of the British Press on the subject of Your Majesty's friendship with Mrs Simpson is not going to be maintained.' There were two alternatives: Mrs. Simpson should leave the country or a general election would be called in which the King would be resented because of the damage he was doing to 'the Crown, the corner-stone on which the whole Empire rests.' Edward discussed the matter with his friend, Walter Monckton, later 1st Viscount Monckton of Brenchley, who later relayed the devastating news that Mrs. Simpson would be 'simply the Duchess of Windsor,' without the prefix 'Her Royal Highness' (Simpson 1956, 244, 298).

In addition to Monckton, Edward was supported by Mosley, Lloyd George and the Beaverbrook and Northcliffe/Rothermere media empires (Blake 1985; Simpson 1956, 257). Rothermere (21 June 1927) published a *Daily Mail* editorial entitled 'Hungary's Place in the Sun' in which he supported the restoration of the territory lost in the 1920 Peace Treaty of Trianon. Attempts were made to make him King of Hungary (László and Rady 2004, 196, 202–203).

In late 1917, the last Romanov Emperor, Nicholas II, who had been forced to abdicated, referred to 'Bolshevik scoundrels' in his diary: his last entry may have been 'Lord, save Russia.'[56] In his forced 1936 abdication speech, Edward informed his ex-subjects that 'you must believe me when I tell you that I have found it impossible to carry the heavy burden of responsibility and to discharge my duties as King as I would wish to do without the help and support of the woman I love … I now quit altogether public affairs and I lay down my burden. It may be some time before I return to my native land, but I shall always follow the fortunes of the British race and Empire with profound interest, and if at any time in the future I can be found of service to his majesty in a private station, I shall not fail' (cited by Mosley and Le Vien 1981, 121; Pugh 2005, 385). Edward departed immediately for Austria. After the divorce proceedings were completed, he and his bride honeymooned in Castle Wasserloenburg, Austria. Coincidentally, Mises' stepdaughter, Gitta Sereny (2001 [1995], 9), performed for them in Vienna (as Shakespeare's Juliet).

Irritated by the 'royal back-seat driver,' George VI instructed the phone operator at Buckingham Palace not to automatically put through calls from his departed brother and sent Monckton to 'Austria to explain the new facts of life' to the ex-King (Morton 2015, Chapter 7). In Austria, Edward was informed by Alfonso VIII, the last Bourbon King of Spain (reigned 1886–1931), that as a new member of the 'former monarchs' club, he should expect to be somewhat declassed when it came to seating arrangements at social occasions. But Edward was personally reassured by Hitler, who told him he was 'against' Bolshevism. During a pre-Anschluss visit to Hitler, Edward told his wife to look at a map of Germany: 'look quickly at Austria. Frontier's gone.' When he and 'Fruity' Metcalfe learnt of the declaration of war against Germany, Edward declared 'I am afraid in the end this may open the way for world communism' (Simpson 1956, 299, 300, 308, 306, 319).

The phoney war ended in May 1940. A memorandum (7 July 1940) from an informant inside occupied Czechoslovakia to Sir Alexander

Cadogan, permanent secretary at the Foreign Office stated: 'A new source in close touch with Von Neurath's [the German protector of Bohemia's] entourage in Prague has reported that the Germans expect assistance from the Duke and Duchess of Windsor, the latter desiring at any price to become Queen. The Germans have been negotiating with her since June 27. The status quo in England expect an understanding to form an anti-Russian alliance. The Germans propose to form an opposition government with the Duke of Windsor, having first changed public opinion by propaganda. The Germans think King George [VI] will abdicate during the attack on London' (Boggan 1996). Edward was informed that if he returned to Britain without an invitation, his allowance would be cut. He spent almost all the next thirty-six years in exile; in 1972, his body was returned to England for burial (Mosley and Le Vien 1981; Panton 2011, 162).

While Edward was rejecting the dynastic appeal of cousins, Hayek was embracing their romantic appeal. Hayek (1994, 98, 126) explained 'I should never have wished to leave England, especially if I could have continued to live at Cambridge... English ways of life seemed so naturally to accord with all my instincts and dispositions that, if it had not been for very special circumstances, I should never have wished to leave the country again.'

Hayek's disciples referred to this 'wonderful love story' with his cousin and second wife; Gerard Radnitzky suggested that it should be made into a film. Cubitt (2006, 50, 106, 119, 211) noticed that Hayek and his second wife were only 'at peace' with each other when they reminisced about the 'shared time of their early' childhood lives. Helene told Cubitt that she would have married him in 1923—had he proposed. Instead, in March 1923, Hayek went to America, and so she married Hans Warhanek. According to Cubitt, on his immediate return, Hayek 'reproached' Helene for marrying and urged her to obtain a divorce, despite the fact that she had just given birth to a son, Max (3 April 1924). On 4 August 1926, Hayek (1978a), on the 'rebound,' married a secretary in the *Abrechnungsamt*, the civil service Office of Accounts in which he worked, Helen ('Hella') Berta Maria 'von' Fritsch, because she bore some 'superficial' resemblance to Helene.[57]

Initially (1931–1939), Hayek (1994, 78) and his first family lived in rented accommodation (Constable Close and 15 Turner Close, Hampstead Garden Suburb); in 1939, Hayek sold his book collection to the Bank for International Settlements at Basle to 'raise the down payment for the house I then bought.' Husbands and wives usually buy house together: Hayek (1994, 136) reiterated that 8 Turner Close, 'I bought.'

This may just be a reflection of the status of wives in the 1930s, but there is an alternative explanation. Hayek described an idyllic arrangement: he, Robbins, Plant, Schwartz and Frank Paish 'just walked into each other's houses at any time of day or evening. For instance, we would not formally entertain each other, but whenever one of us had guests, it was a matter of course that the others would come in after dinner from next door' (cited by Ebenstein 2003, 82). Ebeling (2001) recounted an alternative picture: 'Ludwig M. Lachmann once told me that dinner at Hayek's home in London in the late 1930s was an awkward and embarrassing affair. By this time, Hayek and his first wife were not speaking to each other. At the dinner table, Lachmann carried on conversations with the two of them, but they said not a word to each other.'

Hayek told Cubitt (2006, 64, 67) that Helene had been his 'first love': during his first marriage, he had secretly visited her. Apparently looking for sympathy, Hayek added: Hella had 'refused to sleep with him for a whole year.' Hella hoped that the 'Iron Curtain would descend on Vienna' and Helene, and thus save her marriage. When Hayek left, she initially went into denial and then appeared to threaten suicide: the 'children would be left helpless.'

To Helene, Hella was a 'non-person': she had 'dreamed that she, Hayek and Hella had been sitting at a table, and that there had suddenly been a flash, that Hella had gone and the chair where she was sitting had been empty.' After Hayek left, Hella 'pleaded' with Helene that she 'loved her husband and wanted him to stay with her.' Starting, presumably, in 1934, two letters from Helene would arrive simultaneously: one for Hayek, the other for Hella (in which she was, apparently, reminded that she was unwanted by her husband and should, therefore, return to Vienna). Hayek may have intended that 8 Turner Close was to be—not for his first wife (and children)—but for his second.[58] For Hayek's son, Laurence, the onset of War brought relief: the 'dreaded letters from Austria no longer arrived.' Hayek and Helene kept in touch 'via a neutral country': for Hella, Laurence and his sister, Christine, the reappearance of the letters reawakened the 'fear of Helene Warhanek' (Cubitt 2006, 287, 382, 387).

After Hitler's suicide (30 April 1945), VE Day was celebrated, coincidentally, on Hayek's 46th birthday (8 May 1945). Between March and May 1945, Hayek (1994, 103) was on a *Road to Serfdom* promotional tour of the USA seeking funding for his post-divorce life as a 'free' man: 'practically all my contacts that led to later visits and finally made my move to Chicago possible were made during this trip.' According to his fifth official biographer, Hayek got his Andy Warhol moment: '15 minutes of fame' (Caldwell 2007, 20). Thirty-four years later, Hayek later sent Mrs. Thatcher a telegram thanking her for the 'best' 80th birthday present anyone could have given him.[59] On his 86th birthday, *The Times* published a celebratory article by Mises' stepdaughter, Gitta Sereny (1985), entitled 'The Sage of the Free Thinking World.'

Hayek's (1978a) father had a thwarted ambition to have the 'title of professor': the 'tradition in our family made us feel that a university professor was the sum of achievement, the maximum you could hope for, but even that wasn't very likely.'[60] His father's 'unsatisfied ambition' gave Hayek the 'idea that there was nothing higher in life than becoming a university professor.'[61] To get 'just a foot in the university' it was necessary to 'find what was called a *Habilitations-Vater*, a man who would sponsor you… unless one of them liked you, well there was just no possibility.'[62] Hayek also reflected: 'There was a period when the possession of a professorship gratified me.'[63] In 1934, after eight years of marriage and three years as a professor, Hayek pushed Hella for a divorce.[64] Simultaneously, a civil war erupted in both Austria and Germany. In the Night of the Long Knives (30 June–2 July 1934), Hitler disposed of various rivals. On 30 June 1934, the German Nazis killed the last Chancellor of the Weimar Republic (1919–1933), Kurt von Schleicher; on 25 July 1934, the Austrian Nazis killed the last Chancellor of the First Austrian Republic (1919–1934), Englebert Dollfuss.[65]

Hayek (1978a) studied economics as 'part of the law degree; so I did a regular law degree, although only the first part in the normal way. Thus, I have a very good education in the history of law. But then I discovered that I could claim veterans' privileges, and so I did the second part in modern law in a rush and forgot most of modern Austrian law. I was later again interested. In fact, in 1939, or rather in 1940, I was just negotiating with the Inner Temple people to read for a barrister there when I had to move to Cambridge.'[66] Under Paragraph 83 of the 1811 Habsburg Civil Code, 'weighty considerations' could be considered grounds for remarriage (Silverman 1984, 87–88, 691–702). As Hayek pressured Hella for a divorce, he may have attempted to have her certified as insane: a pseudoscientific graphological (handwriting) analysis by Dr. Erika Smekal-Hubert concluded that Hella was 'deeply inhibited, was slightly psychopathic, quarrelsome, and was likely to have sudden emotional outbursts. She was a wayward, autistic person, who should live alone and was neither a good wife nor a good mother. The one for Hayek was couched in the most agreeable, even enthusiastic terms' (Cubitt 2006, 141).

In *The Constitution of Liberty*, Hayek (2011 [1960], 64) described

'inner' or 'metaphysical' (or sometimes 'subjective') freedom

as 'the extent to which a person is guided in his actions by his own considered will by his reason or lasting conviction rather than by momentary impulse of circumstance.' Hayek (1978a) had an 'inner need' to marry Helene: 'I know I've done wrong in enforcing divorce. Well, it's a curious story, I married on the rebound when the girl I had loved, a cousin, married somebody else. She is now my present wife. But for twenty-five years I was married to the girl whom I married on the rebound, who was a very good wife to me, but I wasn't happy in that marriage. She refused to give me a divorce, and finally I enforced it. I'm sure that was wrong, and yet I have done it. It was just an inner need to do it … I would probably do it again.'[67] For at least a quarter of a century, Hayek (1994, 116) described his depression as 'inner trembling' (see also Cubitt 2006, 236).

Hayek (11 June 1961) recorded his year of 'misery' for posterity: his depression was, he wrote, sparked by having to give up smoking on 11 May 1960, exactly two months before Hella's death. Not smoking, he wrote, proved hard for another 'two' months. Then general discomfort gave way to other more 'definite' symptoms, which appeared to be unrelated to the cessation of smoking: tiredness, sudden attacks of exhaustion, loss of appetite, poor sleep, weight loss, plus 'depressions.'[68]

Hayek's (11 June 1961) condition deteriorated during March and April 1961; while he was at the University of Virginia, his depression took 'suicidal' forms.[69] Hayek (5 June 1961; 22 July 1961) informed the William Volker Charities Fund that he had been suffering from 'acute' depression and 'extreme' dejection and panic about his future, which had resulted in a year of 'enforced' rest.[70]

For the last 15 years of his life, Hayek employed—but neglected to pay—his secretary, soiled-bed nurse, cook and chauffeur, who was 'almost permanently in debt until about three years before Hayek's death.' When Cubitt (2006, 10) asked him if he minded having to 'beg' from libertarian charities to pay for her services, he 'just laughed, said he did not mind in the least, that all his professional considerations had been based on financial considerations.' The financial negotiations of the divorce, which were protracted and acrimonious, appear to have begun when their daughter, Christine Maria Felicitas Hayek (1929–), was eighteen and her brother, Lorenz (Laurence) Joseph Heinrich Hayek (1934–2004), thirteen. Hayek (7 February 1948) wrote to a potential donor that the period for which he felt 'morally' obliged to stay with his first family was approaching its end: he now wished to seriously consider the sufficiently attractive position in the USA that he had been offered three years before. The reason Hayek (1994, 126) accepted the Chicago position 'was in the first instance solely that it offered the financial possibility of that divorce and remarriage.' Lunch at the Reform (2 May 1949) with Nef helped facilitate the divorce.[71] It led to Hayek's 'abdication' from the LSE and his instalment as Professor of Social and Moral Science at the University of Chicago's Committee on Social Thought.

After leaving the USA in 1924, Hayek did not return for over two decades. He then made three visits in rapid succession (1945, 1946 and 1947), followed by surreptitious migration (27 December 1949). In 1945, Harold Luhnow, President of the Volker Fund, pressed Hayek (1994, 126–127) to write an American version of *The Road to Serfdom*. Hayek recalled that he estimated that it would cost $30,000 over three years adding that he would need an American university appointment. Luhnow told Hayek 'Money is yours,' and Hayek claimed that within three weeks he had received offers from three USA universities. Yet the American version of *The Road to Serfdom* was never produced (which Hayek attributed to Henry Simon's death).

In the early 1930s, Hayek's fraud about having predicted the Great Depression appears to have been uncovered at the University of Chicago (Leeson 2018b). In early 1948, after being rejected (i.e. not even formally considered) by the University of Chicago Department of Economics, Hayek began to persuade *Road to Serfdom* donors to finance his planned post-divorce life. Hayek (9 May 1948) explained to Luhnow that his relationship with his cousin had been the 'dominating' factor of the greater part of his life: by the mid-1930s, his first marriage had become 'purely formal.' Hayek informed Luhnow that although between 1931 and 1939 he met Helene only two or three times a year, she became his partner in all of his 'intellectual' work. The motive for migrating to America was to preserve his 'working' capacity.[72]

Yet according to Cubitt (2006, 13, 76, 92, 164, 211), Hayek could not tolerate Helene's intellectual interests: when they visited art galleries on their delayed honeymoon, 'he had deliberately walked away from her whenever she had wanted to draw his attention to a painting.' Hayek was in the habit of leaving the table 'half way through a sentence of hers'; 'he always shook his head before she had even finished her sentence.' They 'bickered most of the time, Mrs Hayek disputing almost everything her husband said.' Hayek had, she said, 'destroyed her creativity by disregarding her interests. He laughed at her, which I thought very unkind and even cruel.'

Catholics, as Henry VIII discovered, were not generally permitted to divorce: Hayek planned to become, in effect, a bigamist.[73] Hayek's pocket diary records the road to divorce. Action came immediately after Christmas 1949: he reminded himself to telephone Popper (27 December); to write to Nef on arrival at the Hotel Commodore (29 December); and then meet Nef in the Hotel lobby (31 December). Nef (5 January 1950) thanked Hayek for the 'private' assurance he had given in New York that he would join 'us.' Nef (6 September 1950) then congratulated Hayek and his new wife on their 'happiness.'[74]

Hayek apparently informed his family seven weeks after his abrupt departure: Christine (6 February), Hella (16 February) and Lorenz (11 May). Hayek kept his mother informed: 'Telegr. Mama' (16 February), 'BRIEF MAMA' (11 May).[75] Mises' mother 'had the attitude of a general and a will of iron, showing little warmth or affection for anyone' (Mises 1984, 23–25); Hayek paid for his mother—known in the family as *Eisentante*, the 'iron aunt,' because she was free of the 'female evil of hysteria'—to turn up at 8 Turner Close to take control of the situation (Cubitt 2006, 64, 77).

Hayek (1994, 153) drew an unusual analogy between his mother and his experiences as a Great War airplane artillery spotter: 'Once the Italian practically caught us. One in front, firing through the propeller. When they started firing, my pilot, a Czech, spiralled down. I unbelted myself, climbed on the rail. My pilot succeeded in correcting the spin just above the ground. It was exciting… I lack nerves. I believe this is a thing I inherited from my mother.' His family were further infuriated by this unannounced and intrusive arrival of the 'iron aunt.' When, against Hayek's wishes, his mother broadcast the news about the marriage,

Hayek rebuked her for spoiling Helene's 'new found happiness' (Cubitt 2006, 127).

International trade diminished the prohibitions of the Roman Catholic Church. Hayek's lawyer discovered that—with minimal residency—a divorce could be obtained in Arkansas (Cubitt 2006, 66). In March 1950, 'F.A. VON HAYEK' was appointed Visiting Professor of Finance at the University of Arkansas, at a salary of $7500 per year (he signed himself as 'von' Hayek).[76] In a sense, it was a double divorce: he resigned from the LSE in February 1950.

Hayek, who had to establish residency in America to get a divorce, informed Luhnow (11 March 1950) that although he had resigned from the LSE, he could not—on legal advice—sign his Chicago contract until July 1950 to avoid a challenge to the genuineness of his domicile in Arkansas. Nef had co-founder the Committee on Social Thought in 1941 with Knight and Robert Hutchins. Hayek (13 July 1950), whose contact was dated 1 July 1950, apologised to President Hutchins for his delay in accepting: Hella had used the rumour that he had already accepted the position in Chicago in a manner little short of 'blackmail' to question his divorce-induced residency status. Hayek was now, happily, a 'free' man—although Hella had 'extorted' a divorce settlement from him.

Hayek's fellow MPS member, Reform Club supporter, and former LSE colleague, Frank Paish, was one of Hella's executors. At Probate, her effects amounted to £14,291, 1 shilling and 10 pence, which at the prevailing exchange rate (£1 = US$2.80) equated to a little over $40,000.[77] Between 1944 and 1947, Hayek's (1944) *The Road to Serfdom* sold 100,000 English-language copies, earning £30,000, the equivalent of $84,000 (Ebenstein 2003, 209). At the time of Hella's death, Hayek's University of Chicago annual salary was $17,000, plus $1000 European travel allowance and 7.5% employer superannuation contribution.[78]

3.7 The Nobel Consequences of Rule XXX?

Hayek (1978a) knew Bertrand, the 3rd Earl Russell, 'fairly well. In the final years of the war, he was back in Cambridge, and while I was still in Cambridge I saw him.'[79] In 1938, Bertrand Russell (1985, 459–461), the winner of the 1950 Nobel Prize for Literature, taught at the University of Chicago: he found the city 'beastly' and the weather 'vile.'

President Hutchins was, he thought, attempting to force 'neo Thomism on the faculty.' Russell was as aristocratic as Hayek; his Reform Club grandfather had also promoted the 1832 Great Reform Act. But Russell, a divorced atheist, was unable to take a job at the City College of New York because 'earnest Christian taxpayers objected... if I appeared anywhere in public. I should probably have been lynched by a Catholic mob, with full approval of the police.' In court, Russell (1985, 461) was accused of being 'lecherous, libidinous, lustful, venerous, erotomaniac, aphrodisiac, irreverent, narrow-minded, untruthful, and bereft of moral fiber' (see also Weidlich 2000). Popper (10 March 1950) worried that something similar might happen to the atheist, Hayek, who he hoped would be secure with his Chicago contract, because they may react badly to his divorce.[80] With understatement, the *Collected Works* General Editor noted that Hayek 'never felt entirely at home in Chicago' (Kresge 1994, 29).

Hayek (1994, 83, 78, 95) believed that during his first decade in England, he and Robbins 'worked beautifully together,' until 'I'm afraid he fell under Keynes' influence,' and acquired 'corrupt' attitudes through government service. Yet Robbins was the 'most loyal friend of anyone you could meet'; Robbins and his wife 'became *our* (emphasis added) closest friends.' Hayek reinforced this to Cubitt (2006, 63): Robbins had been a 'family friend.'[81] Robbins' loyalty to Hella outtrumped his loyalty to Hayek and their intellectual causes.

In 1971, the Nobel Selection Committee invited Machlup— Hayek's close friend, fellow Austrian School economist and founding MPS member—to write an 'appraisal' of Hayek's worthiness for a Nobel Prize—which he completed in September 1971.[82] Robbins' (1971) *Autobiography* was published simultaneously. The rupture with Robbins—plus other aspects of Hayek's behaviour—may have led to him being expelled, or forced to resign, from the Reform: this may have had adverse implications for the 1971–1974 Nobel Prize decision-making process.

Hayek, who may have defrauded an insurance company, was an income tax-evader: in Germany, he failed to declare both his US social security payments and his 'Moonie Nobel Prize.'[83] When he was caught, he feared that his property would be impounded. Hayek stole or double-dipped from libertarian think tanks and charities: when his *Collected Works* donor, Walter Morris, found out, he became 'angry.' Hayek had 'not thought fit to tell' Morris and appeared to instruct his secretary to do likewise (Cubitt 2006, 35–36, 177, 264, 288). The year before Hayek left the LSE, his Hampstead neighbour and fellow London University academic, C. E. M. Joad, had been convicted of a minor financial irregularity: the 'Train Ticket Scandal.' Joad's chances of a peerage evaporated, and he was 'forced to leave' the Reform (Burlingham and Billis 2005, 213).

Hayek's 'very special circumstances' led to him being shunned by his LSE colleagues: Popper (circa 1950) told him that his name was 'nearly taboo' in the School (Popper's emphasis).[84] Since Hayek had become a Reform Club member courtesy of his LSE colleagues, he would presumably have been shunned at the Reform also—and could have been expelled. A fifty-member petition was ordinarily required; but during the planning and after the execution of the divorce, Hayek's seconder, Oscar (1948, 1952) and then Sir Oscar Hobson (1956) was Club Chairman. Twelve out of eighteen Committee members had to approve the expulsion—against which there was no appeal (Woodbridge 1978, 15, 89–90, 165).

Rule XXX specifies that 'ungentlemanly' conduct was inconsistent with Reform Club membership (Woodbridge 1978, 94, 165). Hayek was 'cut to the quick' when the editor of *Encounter*, Melvin Lasky, suggested that it was 'caddish' to desert one's wife (Cubitt 2006, 65). Had Hayek ventured inside the Reform before the 'shun' was lifted, he may have been insulted: 'honour' may have obliged him to resign. Such a response was almost expected: Joseph Chamberlain resigned from the Reform when his two brothers were blackballed; he left the Liberal Party shortly afterwards (Burlingham and Billis 2005, 200–201; Woodbridge 1978, 89–90).

In 1961, Robbins (1971, 117, 154, 234) resigned from the Reform and 'crossed the building' to join the Athenaeum after overhearing a disparaging remark—which he thought was directed at him—about the quantity theory of money. Robbins also later reflected: 'I had become the slave of theoretical constructions which, if not intrinsically invalid as regards logical consistency were inappropriate to the total situation which had then developed and which therefore misled my judgement': he confessed that he would 'willingly' see his 1934 *Great Depression* 'forgotten.'

The 1963 Robbins Report on higher education embraced social inclusion: the 'Robbins principle' made university places 'available to all who were qualified for them by ability and attainment.' It also repudiated the climate that Robbins and Hayek had created at the LSE: 'in the graduate school there are no ultimate authorities, no orthodoxies to which the pupil must subscribe' (Thompson 2012). This led to what Robbins described as a 'not inconsiderable degree of hostility from some of the senior members.' In 1969, he resigned and rejoined the Reform after demanding—and receiving—a written apology from an Athenaeum club member who had described him in 'most uncomplimentary terms' (Howson 2011, 895).

Behind his back, Hayek made similar remarks about Robbins. In an interview for the *Cato Policy Report*, Hayek (1983) reinforced his 'disdain' for policy advisors: 'You can either be an economist or a policy advisor.' Referring to Robbins, Hayek added: 'I have seen in some of my closest friends and sympathizers — I won't mention any names — who completely agreed with me, how a few years in government corrupted them intellectually and made them unable to think straight.' For posthumous biographical purposes, Hayek (1994, 78) was specific: during his first decade in England, he and Robbins 'worked beautifully together,' until 'I'm afraid he fell under Keynes' influence,' and acquired 'corrupt' attitudes through government service.

Hayek had conflicts with four Presidents of the Royal Economic Society: Pigou (1937–1940), Beveridge (1940–1945), Keynes (1945–1946) and Robbins (1954–1956). However, Keynes and Hayek were, personally, on friendly terms (despite being intellectual opponents). Keynes (28 April 1941) invited Hayek to fill a vacancy on the Council of the Royal Economic Society;[85] and was dead by the time of Hayek's divorce. And only in 1984 did Hayek come to believe that President Pigou had—in 1939—tried to recruit him as a Soviet spy.

But the Hayek-Beveridge dispute was personal. Hayek (1994, 84) concluded LSE departmental meetings with '*Beveridge delundus est*' ('Thus I believe that we must destroy Beveridge'). The Royal Economic Society initially resembled a gentleman's club: those who continuing membership would bring 'dishonour' could be dealt with (Coats 1968, 360). Robbins, Hayek's Reform Club nominator, could have used his position as President of the Royal Economic Society to 'destroy' Hayek.

Friedman stayed with Robbins during a 1952 visit to the LSE (Leeson 2003, Chapter 15). Friedman (1995) reflected that Hayek 'got very involved in the British scene, but his first wife was more or less left on her own to take care of the kids... my feeling is she was not very happy... as I gathered from Robbins at the time, he sort of left her in the lurch in London, never having really struck down real roots... All I know is that Robbins thought he had treated her in an absolutely unacceptable manner... by the standards of that time, and more importantly... the standards of Lionel Robbins... I believe that he would think that a provocation would have to be very, very great indeed to justify such behaviour. And I share his view.'

But Robbins had an unusual personality characteristic. Hayek told Cubitt (2006, 5) that he and his fellow Europeans émigrés sat in the 'sardonic corner' of the LSE Common Room making 'malicious' comments about the competence of their English colleagues. Kingsley Martin described the LSE in the 1920s: 'war raged between the Socialists and the advocates of *laissez-faire*' (cited by Dahrendorf 1995, 188). But Robbins (1971, 73–74, 124) recalled a more harmonious atmosphere: 'How agreeable at teatime in the Common Room to listen to friendly badinage between [Richard] Tawney and [Theodore] Gregory on the merits and demerits of the free enterprise system.'

In a lecture on 'The Origins and Effects of Our Morals: A Problem for Science,' Hayek (1984 [1983], Chapter 17) declared that:

> Man will have to recognise that it is neither his inborn instincts nor his intelligence on which his future chiefly depends. It is his faith in traditional morals, which I fear have been progressively crumbling for the last few generations, a process which is gaining alarming speed. But its authority has already been gravely weakened, and this has been done chiefly by the supercilious conceit of the so-called intellectuals, those 'dupes of their own sophistry' as Adam Smith called them, who conceived that they could invent a better moral which they thought would more fully gratify their desires.

In particular, Hayek singled out 'their anti-property and anti-family doctrines.'

According to a Caldwell-chosen editor of *The Collected Works of F.A. Hayek*: 'One of the themes in Hayek's works on political philosophy is the importance of the Rule of Law that gives security and certainty to people in their person and property' (Ebeling 2014). Hayek (1946) had been given the privilege of writing the fiftieth anniversary review of the LSE for *Economica*—but after directing his lawyer to go jurisdiction shopping to facilitate the abandonment of his wife and children, Robbins (June 1950) explained to MPS members that he had 'behaved in such a way that I find it impossible to reconcile with the conception of his character and his standards which I have cherished through twenty years of friendship. As far as I am concerned the man I know is dead and I should find it almost intolerably painful to have to meet his successor' (Howson 2011, 664, 704–706; Cockett 1995, 28, 116, 120; Hartwell 1995, 40–41). Robbins was particularly enraged by the inadequacy of the financial arrangements of what he described as a 'bootleg divorce' (Cubitt 2006, 64, 67); such was the friction that Hayek (10 November 1950) was forced to explain to Machlup that it would be very difficult for him to ask Robbins to contribute an essay for Mises' *Festschrift*.[86]

Robbins severed contact with Hayek and the MPS—he worried about the prospect of 'damage to causes with which Hayek had been associated' (Cubitt 2006, 67). But Hayek (1994, 95) noticed that Robbins had 'one extremely likeable habit. He's the most loyal friend of anyone you could meet.' If he were asked his memories of 'close friends… it would be honest but it would not be true. Much embellished.' The death of Hayek's first wife in 1960 appeared to have enabled Robbins (1971, 128) to state that his association with Hayek 'was an especially happy one.' Had the first Mrs. Hayek enjoyed a normal life expectancy, or had Robbins not forgiven Hayek and referred to the scandal in his 1971 autobiography, the Nobel Prize Selection Committee *may* have looked elsewhere for a balance to Myrdal in 1974.

Instead, Robbins (27 September 1960) wrote to Hayek (presumably c/o the Reform Club) saying that he had passed a 'vaguely familiar but unidentifiable figure' at the Reform the previous evening, who had later been identified by Kahane (Howson 2011, 846–847).[87] This led to reconciliation—encouraged by Machlup—at his son Lorenz's wedding (15 July 1961), captured in photographic (and rectified) form in *The Collected Works of F.A. Hayek* (1994, plate 27): 'A friendship was resumed after the interval of the Chicago years.' Shortly after the reconciliation, in a review of 'Hayek on Liberty' in *Economica*, the LSE journal, Robbins (1961, 81) praised Hayek's 'moral ardour.'

NOTES

1. Friedrich Hayek, interviewed by Robert Chitester date unspecified 1978 (Centre for Oral History Research, University of California, Los Angeles, http://oralhistory.library.ucla.edu/).
2. Friedrich Hayek, interviewed by Robert Chitester date unspecified 1978 (Centre for Oral History Research, University of California, Los Angeles, http://oralhistory.library.ucla.edu/).
3. From the Reform Club Chairman to Hayek (21 January 1985). Hayek Archives Box 45.21.
4. To Russell Burlingham (20 January 1989). Hayek Archives Box 96.2.
5. Since Hayek was fourteen when Stephen died, this seems unlikely. Either Hayek was confused or exaggerating; or Cubitt misremembered.

6. Hayek (2 May 1932) to Mrs. P. M. Thornton. Hayek Archives Box 70.9.
7. Trevelyan (14 January 1938) to Hayek. Hayek Archives Box 70.9.
8. The other Potter line produced Beatrix Potter.
9. http://hansard.millbanksystems.com/commons/1979/nov/21/mr-anthony-blunt.
10. http://discovery.nationalarchives.gov.uk/SearchUI/details/C11050182?uri=C11050182-william-francis-forbes-sempill-alias-lord-details&descriptiontype=Full.
11. http://www.npg.org.uk/collections/search/person.php?LinkID=mp11737.
12. Before Hayek (1994, 82) obtained dining rights at King's, evenings were spent dancing at the wartime home of the LSE historian, Lancelot Beales. However, Hayek didn't remember his wife, or any other female, being present (Robbins 1971, 166).
13. Friedman (23 May 1947) to Hayek. Hayek Archives Box 73.40.
14. To Edwin Feulner (27 February 1980). Hayek Archives Box 24.22.
15. Hayek Archives Box 45.21.
16. Friedrich Hayek, interviewed by Robert Chitester date unspecified 1978 (Centre for Oral History Research, University of California, Los Angeles, http://oralhistory.library.ucla.edu/).
17. Friedrich Hayek, interviewed by James Buchanan 28 October 1978 (Centre for Oral History Research, University of California, Los Angeles, http://oralhistory.library.ucla.edu/).
18. Friedrich Hayek, interviewed by Armen Alchian 11 November 1978 (Centre for Oral History Research, University of California, Los Angeles, http://oralhistory.library.ucla.edu/).
19. Heinrich II, Gustav III and August IV.
20. http://www.lewrockwell.com/blog/lewrw/archives/022221.html.
21. Jenny von Westphalen was descended from the House of Stuart on her mother's side.
22. Friedrich Hayek, interviewed by Robert Chitester date unspecified 1978 (Centre for Oral History Research, University of California, Los Angeles, http://oralhistory.library.ucla.edu/).
23. Powell was elected in 1969 and resigned in 1980. MPS Archives Boxes 66 and 44.2.
24. Jewkes (25 January 1960) to Hunold. MPS Archives Box 41.6.
25. MPS Archives Box 66.
26. MPS Archives Box 45.5.
27. MPS Archives Box 52.2.
28. MPS Archives Box 53.3.
29. MPS Archives Box 66.
30. MPS Archives Box 41.11.
31. MPS Archives Box 55.5.

32. Friedrich Hayek, interviewed by Robert Chitester date unspecified 1978 (Centre for Oral History Research, University of California, Los Angeles, http://oralhistory.library.ucla.edu/).
33. In 1940, shortly after the fall of France, an 'Under-Secretaries Plot' was hatched at the Reform to sweep out of government all the remaining old guard of the 1930s (Faber 2005, 369–371).
34. http://www.reformclub.com/.
35. Hayek Archives Box 52.43.
36. http://www.reformclub.com/home/about/history.
37. Soref had been a member since 1950. No Club-based explanation for his departure has, apparently, survived. I am grateful to Simon Blundell, Reform Club Librarian, for this information.
38. Hayek (1994, 85) and Robbins (1971, 139–141) successfully opposed Beveridge's attempt to relocate the Frankfurt Institute to the LSE as part of a rescue operation of eminent scholars from Nazi persecution. Decades later, Hayek remained 'full of venom about the Frankfurt Institute and its possible move to the LSE' (Dahrendorf 1995, 291).
39. Hayek Archives Box 74.30.
40. Hayek Archives Box 45.21.
41. Friedrich Hayek, interviewed by Robert Chitester date unspecified 1978 (Centre for Oral History Research, University of California, Los Angeles, http://oralhistory.library.ucla.edu/).
42. Friedrich Hayek, interviewed by Leo Rosten 15 November 1978 (Centre for Oral History Research, University of California, Los Angeles, http://oralhistory.library.ucla.edu/).
43. The maximum term of a Parliament was also reduced from seven years to five.
44. He inherited the Benn Baronetcy of The Old Knoll from his grandfather, Sir John Benn, and became the 2nd Viscount Stansgate on the death of his father (his elder brother was killed in World War II).
45. http://www.margaretthatcher.org/document/114630.
46. In 1973, price inflation was 9.8%; it fell to 8.66% in 1982. In between, in only one year (1978) was inflation in single digits (Wood 2006, 142, Table 1).
47. https://www.margaretthatcher.org/document/114626.
48. Thorpe's wife figured marginally in Bartley's (1989, 11, n. 11) incomplete biography of Popper.
49. I am grateful to Simon Blundell, Reform Club Librarian, for this information.
50. Hayek Archives Boxes 74.30, 46.25 and 76.20.
51. Referring to economic planning, Hayek (1978a) stated 'It had died down very much, but when two years ago in this country this planning bill of Senator [Hubert] Humphrey's and the agitation of Leontief and these people came forward, I was amazed that people were again swallowing what I

thought had been definitely refuted.' Friedrich Hayek, interviewed by Jack High date unspecified 1978 (Centre for Oral History Research, University of California, Los Angeles, http://oralhistory.library.ucla.edu/).
52. Hayek Archives Box 11.33.
53. Stone was rewarded as a 'pioneer and the driving force in respect of both the theoretical underpinning and the practical application of different systems for national accounts. These formed the basis both of the economic analysis of the prevailing lack of balance in Britain and for the economic political recommendations.' James Meade and Stone 'were in charge of collecting, processing and systematizing all the enormous statistical material which Keynes required for his analysis of the imbalances in the British national economy. In this research environment—with all the stimulus provided by the prevailing tight economic situation and under the great personal influence given by Keynes himself in regard to ideas and encouragement—the analytical technique was born which is covered by the designation "national" or "social accounts." The experiments with systematic processing of the overwhelmingly rich material of budget statistics, caused Keynes to exclaim, "We are in a new era of joy through statistics".' http://www.nobelprize.org/nobel_prizes/economic-sciences/laureates/1984/press.html.
54. Hayek Archives Box 67.6.
55. I am grateful to Simon Blundell, Reform Club Librarian, for this information.
56. http://www.alexanderpalace.org/palace/ndiaries1917.html.
57. Friedrich Hayek, interviewed by Armen Alchian 11 November 1978 (Centre for Oral History Research, University of California, Los Angeles, http://oralhistory.library.ucla.edu/). Letter to Harold Luhnow. Hayek Archives Box 58.16.
58. According to Cubitt (2006, 211, 290), Helene informed her that she had been the 'victim of ups and downs, believing that at one time divorce was possible, and at other times it was not.' Helene showed Cubitt some letters dating from 1937 to convince her that she had 'not persuaded Hayek to leave his first wife.' This is of course not inconsistent with other 'up' letters in which she did.
59. http://www.margaretthatcher.org/document/112178.
Hayek Archives Box 101.26.
60. Friedrich Hayek, interviewed by Earlene Craver date unspecified 1978 (Centre for Oral History Research, University of California, Los Angeles, http://oralhistory.library.ucla.edu/).
61. Friedrich Hayek, interviewed by Robert Chitester date unspecified 1978 (Centre for Oral History Research, University of California, Los Angeles, http://oralhistory.library.ucla.edu/).

62. Friedrich Hayek, interviewed by Earlene Craver date unspecified 1978 (Centre for Oral History Research, University of California, Los Angeles, http://oralhistory.library.ucla.edu/).
63. Friedrich Hayek, interviewed by Robert Chitester date unspecified 1978 (Centre for Oral History Research, University of California, Los Angeles, http://oralhistory.library.ucla.edu/).
64. Hayek (6 March 1950) to Karl Popper. Popper Archives Box 305.14.
65. Mussolini declared that 'The independence of Austria, for which he [Dollfuss] has fallen, is a principle that has been defended and will be defended by Italy even more strenuously.' The Italian army mobilised on the Austrian border. The Fascist civil war within Austria (Austro-Fascists versus Nazis) could have led to an international war between Fascists (Italy versus Germany). Hitler backed down, and *Anschluss* was delayed until 1938 (Shepley 2013).
66. Friedrich Hayek interviewed by Robert Bork 4 November 1978 (Centre for Oral History Research, University of California, Los Angeles, http://oralhistory.library.ucla.edu/).
67. Friedrich Hayek, interviewed by Armen Alchian 11 November 1978 (Centre for Oral History Research, University of California, Los Angeles, http://oralhistory.library.ucla.edu/).
68. Hayek Archives Box 119.2.
69. Hayek Archives Box 119.2.
70. Hayek Archives Box 58.19.
71. The proposed date was 20 April 1949.
72. To Harold Luhnow. Hayek Archives Box 58.16.
73. Helene denied the bigamy accusation, telling Cubitt (2006, 92) they had 'married only after Hella von Hayek had died.' Ebenstein (2003, 169) reports: 'Hayek's divorce was granted on July 13, 1950, in the chancery court of Washington County, Arkansas. He then married Helene Bitterlich in Vienna before returning to Chicago for the autumn term.'
74. Hayek Archives Box 122.4.
75. Hayek Archives Box 122.4.
76. Hayek Archives Box 54.29. In 1940, Mises declined a job offer from the University of California Los Angeles because they could only offer an annual salary of $4000 (Hülsmann 2007, 748).
77. http://wiz.ancestry.com.au/wiz/RecordImage/?recordId=167107261904.
78. Hayek Archives Box 58.19.
79. Friedrich Hayek, interviewed by Leo Rosten 15 November 1978 (Centre for Oral History Research, University of California, Los Angeles, http://oralhistory.library.ucla.edu/).
80. Hayek Archives Box 44.1.

81. According to Cubitt (2006, 63) Hayek had two 'intimates,' Popper, who 'had reason to be grateful to him' and Robbins. Hayek's only friend was Walter Magg who died in 1917.
82. Machlup (19 November 1974) to Hayek. Hayek Archives Box 36.18.
83. According to 'consumer sovereignty' promoters, compulsory restraints are 'seatbelts on the Road to Serfdom.' In 1979, three years after it became compulsory in West Germany for drivers to wear seatbelts, Hayek wrote-off his car in the Black Forest. He was saved from injury by his seatbelt, while his wife (who had not been restrained) suffered serious injuries. Helene complained that Hayek had made a statement to the police about an imaginary on-coming car which had caused the crash: Hayek was so angry that he threatened to leave her. Helene refused to be driven by her husband again: 'neither the car nor the driver was, as far as I know, ever discovered' (Cubitt 2006, 35–36).
84. Hayek Archives Box 44.1.
85. Hayek Archives Box 30.19.
86. Hayek Archives Box 36.17.
87. Hayek Archives Box 46.25.

REFERENCES

Archival Insights into the Evolution of Economics (and Related Projects)

Addison, P. (1971). Lloyd George and compromise peace in the Second World War. In A. J. P. Taylor (Ed.), *Lloyd George: Twelve Essays* (pp. 361–384). London: Hamilton.

Ashley, M. (1978). Preface. In Woodbridge, G. 1978. *The Reform Club 1836-1978 A History from the Club's Records*. Privately printed for members of the Reform Club in association with Clearwater Publishing Company. New York.

Berlin, I. (1978). *Karl Marx: His life and environment*. Oxford: Oxford University Press.

Blake, R. (1985). *The Conservative Party from Peel to Thatcher*. London: Fontana.

Boggan, S. (1996, December 4). Britain's would-be Nazi Queen. *The Independent*. http://www.independent.co.uk/news/britains-would-be-nazi-queen-1312830.html.

Brook-Shepherd, G. (2003). *Uncrowned Emperor: The Life and Times of Otto Von Habsburg*. London: Hambledon and London.

Filip, B. (2018). Hayek and Popper on Piecemeal Engineering and Ordo-Liberalism. In R. Leeson (Ed.), *Hayek: A Collaborative Biography Part XIV: Liberalism in the Classical Tradition: Orwell, Popper, Humboldt and Polanyi*. Basingstoke, UK: Palgrave Macmillan.

Goldschmidt, N., & Hesse, J.-O. (2013). Eucken, Hayek, and The Road to Serfdom. In R. Leeson (Ed.), *Hayek: A Collaborative Biography Part II Influences, from Mises to Bartley*. Basingstoke, UK: Palgrave Macmillan.
Leeson, R. (2003). *Ideology and the International Economy: The Decline and Fall of Bretton Woods*. Basingstoke, UK: Palgrave Macmillan.
Leeson, R. (Ed.). (2013). *Hayek: A Collaborative Biography Part I Influences from Mises to Bartley*. Basingstoke, UK: Palgrave Macmillan.
Leeson, R. (2017). *Hayek: A Collaborative Biography Part VII 'Market Free Play with an Audience': Hayek's Encounters with Fifty Knowledge Communities*. Basingstoke, UK: Palgrave Macmillan.
Leeson, R. (2018a). *Hayek: A Collaborative Biography Part VIII: The Constitution of Liberty: 'Shooting in Cold Blood' Hayek's Plan for the Future of Democracy*. Basingstoke, UK: Palgrave Macmillan.
Leeson, R. (2018b). *Hayek: A Collaborative Biography Part XV: Chicago and the 1974 Nobel Prize for Economic Sciences*. Basingstoke, UK: Palgrave Macmillan.
Kimberley, H. (2015). 'Deacon' McCormick and the Madoc Myth. In R. Leeson (Ed.), *Hayek: A Collaborative Biography Part III Fraud, Fascism and Free Market Religion*. Basingstoke, UK: Palgrave Macmillan.
Teacher, D. (2018a). 'Neutral Academic Data' and the International Right. In R. Leeson (Ed.), *Hayek: A Collaborative Biography Part XIII 'Fascism' and Liberalism in the (Austrian) Classical Tradition*. Basingstoke, UK: Palgrave Macmillan.
Teacher, D. (2018b). Private Club and Secret Service Armageddon. In R. Leeson (Ed.), *Hayek: A Collaborative Biography Part XIII 'Fascism' and Liberalism in the (Austrian) Classical Tradition*. Basingstoke, UK: Palgrave Macmillan.
Vanberg, V. (2013). Hayek in Freiburg. In R. Leeson (Ed.), *Hayek: A Collaborative Biography Part I Influences, from Mises to Bartley*. Basingstoke, UK: Palgrave Macmillan.

Other References

Bartley, W. W., III. (1989). Rehearsing a Revolution—Karl Popper: A Life. Mimeo.
Beveridge, W. (1953). *Power and Influence*. London: Beechhurst.
Booth, C. (1889). *Life and Labour of the People of London* (Vol. 1). London: Macmillan.
Booth, C. (1891). *Life and Labour of the People of London* (Vol. 2). London: Macmillan.
Boyle, A. (1979). *The Fourth Man the Definitive Account of Kim Philby, Guy Burgess, and Who Recruited Them to Spy for Russia*. New York: Bantum.
Boyle, A. (1982). *The Climate of Treason* (2nd ed.). London: Hutchison.
Buchanan, J. (1965). An Economic Theory of Clubs. *Economica, 32*(125), 1–14 (New Series).

Buchanan, J. (1992). I Did Not Call Him 'Fritz': Personal Recollections of Professor F. A. v. Hayek. *Constitutional Political Economy*, *3*(2), 129–135.
Burke, E. (1790). *Reflections on the Revolution in France*. London: J. Dodsley.
Burlingham, R., & Billis, R. (2005). *Reformed Characters: The Reform Club in History and Literature*. London: Reform Club.
Caldwell, B. (2007). Introduction and Editorial Notes. In F. A. Hayek (Ed.), *The Road to Serfdom Texts and Documents: The Definitive Edition. The Collected Works of F.A. Hayek*. Chicago: University of Chicago Press.
Caldwell, B. (2010). The Secret Behind the Hot Sales of *'The Road to Serfdom'* by Free-Market Economist F. A. Hayek. *The Washington Post*. http://voices.washingtonpost.com/shortstack/2010/02/the_secret_behind_the_hot_sale.html.
Chaloner, W. H. (1962). In C. F. Charter (Ed.), *The Birth of Modern Manchester. In Manchester and its Region a Survey Prepared by the British Association*. Manchester: Manchester University Press.
Coats, A. W. (1968). The Origins and Early Development of the Royal Economic Society. *Economic Journal*, *78*, 349–371.
Cockett, R. (1995). *Thinking the Unthinkable Think Tanks and the Economic Counter-Revolution, 1931–1983*. London: Harper Collins.
Crook, J. M. (1973). *The Reform*. London: The Reform Club.
Cubitt, C. (2006). *A Life of August von Hayek*. Bedford, UK: Authors OnLine.
Dahrendorf, R. (1995). *LSE: A History of the London School of Economics and Political Science, 1895–1995*. Oxford: Oxford University Press.
Daily Express Obituary. (2012, September 1). Blunt Tory Rhodes Boyson Devoted to Education. *Daily Express*. http://www.express.co.uk/expressyourself/343295/Blunt-Tory-Rhodes-Boyson-devoted-to-education.
Disraeli, B. (1845). *Sybil the Two Nations* (3 Vols.). London: Henry Colburn.
Disraeli, B., & Gunn, J. A. W. (2004). *Benjamin Disraeli Letters: 1852–1856*. Toronto: University of Toronto Press.
Dudley Edwards, O. (1969, March). Review of *The Private Life of Mr. Gladstone*, by Richard Deacon. *Irish Historical Studies*, *XVI*(63), 389–392.
Dudley Edwards, R. (1995). *The Pursuit of Reason: The Economist 1843–1993*. London: Hamish Hamilton.
Ebeling, R. M. (2001). F.A. Hayek a Biography. Review of Friedrich Hayek: A Biography by Alan Ebenstein. *Mises Daily*. https://mises.org/daily/638/FA-Hayek-A-Biography.
Ebeling, R. M. (2014, February 16). EXCLUSIVE INTERVIEW, Gold & Silver. Richard Ebeling on Austrian Economics, Economic Freedom and the Trends of the Future. *Daily Bell*. http://www.thedailybell.com/gold-silver/anthony-wile-richard-ebeling-on-austrian-economics-economic-freedom-and-the-trends-of-the-future/.
Ebenstein, A. (2003). *Friedrich Hayek: A Biography*. Chicago: University of Chicago Press.

Eccleshall, R. (1990). *English Conservatism Since the Restoration: An Introduction and Anthology*. London: Unwin Hyman.
Elliott, N. (1993). *With My Little Eye: Observations Along the Way*. London: Michael Russell.
Engels, F. (1969 [1845]). *The Condition of the Working Class in England*. London: Panther.
Faber, D. (2005). *Speaking for England: Leo, Julian and John Amery, the Tragedy of a Political Family*. London: Free Press.
Foot, P. (1968). *The Politics of Harold Wilson*. UK: Penguin.
Friedman, M. (1995). Interview with Alan Ebenstein. Mimeo.
Friedman, M. F., & Friedman, R. D. (1998). *Two Lucky People: Memoirs*. Chicago: University of Chicago Press.
Gash, N. (1972). *Sir Robert Peel: The Life of Sir Robert Peel After 1830*. New Jersey: Rowman and Littlefield.
Gladstone, W. E. (1990). *The Gladstone Diaries: Volume 10: January 1881–June 1883* (H. C. G. Mathew, Ed.). Oxford: Oxford University Press.
Grigg, J. (1973). *The Young Lloyd George*. Berkeley: University of California Press.
Grigg, J. (1978). *Lloyd George: The People's Champion*. London: Methuen.
Grigg, J. (1983). *Lloyd George: From Peace To War 1912–1916*. London: Eyre.
Hartwell, R. M. (1995). *A History of the Mont Pelerin Society*. Indianapolis: Liberty Fund.
Hastings, S. (1994, April 19). Obituary: Nicholas Elliott. *The Independent*. http://www.independent.co.uk/news/people/obituary-nicholas-elliott-1370833.html.
Hayek, F. A. (1939 [1802]). Introduction. In H. Thornton (Ed.), *Enquiry into the Nature and Effects of the Paper Credit of Great Britain, 1802*. London: George Allen and Unwin. Edited with an introduction by F.A. Hayek. http://oll.libertyfund.org/titles/thornton-an-enquiry-into-the-nature-and-effects-of-the-paper-credit-of-great-britain.
Hayek, F. A. (1944). *The Road to Serfdom*. London: Routledge.
Hayek, F. A. (1946, February). The London School of Economics 1895–1945. *Economica, XIII*, 1–31 (New Series).
Hayek, F. A. (1977, September). An Interview with Friedrich Hayek, by Richard Ebeling. *Libertarian Review*, 10–18 (Hayek Archives Box 109.14).
Hayek, F. A. (1978a). *Oral History Interviews*. Centre for Oral History Research, University of California, Los Angeles. http://oralhistory.library.ucla.edu/.
Hayek, F. A. (1978b). *New Studies in Philosophy, Politics, Economics and the History of Ideas*. London: Routledge & Kegan Paul.
Hayek, F. A. (1983, February). Interview with F.A. Hayek. *Cato Policy Report*. http://www.cato.org/policy-report/february-1982/interview-fa-hayek.
Hayek, F. A. (1984). *The Essence of Hayek* (C. Nishiyama & K. R. Leube, Eds.). Stanford, CA: Hoover Institution Press.

Hayek, F. A. (1992 [1977], July). The Road from Serfdom. *Reason.* http://reason.com/archives/1992/07/01/the-road-from-serfdom/5.
Hayek, F. A. (1994). *Hayek on Hayek an Autobiographical Dialogue.* Supplement to *The Collected Works of F.A. Hayek* (S. Kresge & L. Wenar, Eds.). Chicago: University of Chicago Press.
Hayek, F. A. (2011 [1960]). *The Constitution of Liberty. The Definitive Edition. The Collected Works of F.A. Hayek* (R. Hamowy, Ed.). Chicago: University of Chicago Press.
Howson, S. (2011). *Lionel Robbins.* Cambridge: Cambridge University Press.
Hülsmann, J. G. (2007). *Mises: The Last Knight of Liberalism.* Auburn, AL: Ludwig von Mises Institute.
Keynes, J. M. (1936). *The General Theory of Employment, Interest and Money.* London: Macmillan.
Klein, L. (1986). Lawrence R. Klein. In W. Breit & R. W. Spencer (Eds.), *Lives of the Laureates Seven Nobel Laureates.* Cambridge, MA: MIT Press.
Kresge, S. (1994). Introduction. In F. A. Hayek (Ed.), *Hayek on Hayek an Autobiographical Dialogue.* Supplement to *The Collected Works of F.A. Hayek* (S. Kresge & L. Wenar, Eds.). Chicago: University of Chicago Press.
Lashmar, P., & Mullins, A. (1998, August 24). Churchill Protected Scottish Peer Suspected of Spying for Japan Second World War: Government Papers Show Prominent Aristocrat was Believed to be Leaking Naval Secrets to Tokyo. *The Independent.* http://www.independent.co.uk/news/churchill-protected-scottish-peer-suspected-of-spying-for-japan-1173730.html.
László, P., & Rady, M. (Eds.). (2004). *British–Hungarian Relations Since 1848.* London: Hungarian Cultural Centre, School of Slavonic and East European Studies, University of London.
Leonhardt, D. (2016, December 8). The American Dream, Quantified at Last. *New York Times.* https://www.nytimes.com/2016/12/08/opinion/the-american-dream-quantified-at-last.html.
Macaulay, T. B. (1853). *The History of England from the Accession of James II.* Philadelphia: Porter and Coates.
Marsh, P. T. (1994). *Joseph Chamberlain: Entrepreneur in Politics.* New Haven: Yale University Press.
McCormick, D. (1962). *Temple of Love.* London: Jarrolds.
McCormick, D. (1963). *The Mask of Merlin: A Critical Biography of David Lloyd George.* London: Macdonald.
McCormick, D. (1965). *The Private Life of Mr. Gladstone.* London: Frederick Muller.
McCormick, D. (1967). *Madoc and the Discovery of America: Some New Light on an Old Controversy.* London: Frederick Muller.
McCormick, D. (1968). *John Dee: Scientist, Geographer, Astrologer and Secret Agent to Elizabeth I.* London: Frederick Muller.
McCormick, D. (1970a). *The Identity of Jack the Ripper* (2nd ed.). London: John Long.

McCormick, D. (1970b). *Murder by Perfection: Maundy Gregory, the Man Behind Two Unsolved Mysteries*. London: John Long.
McCormick, D. (pseudonym: Deacon, R.). (1973). *The Master Book of Spies: The World of Espionage, Master Spies, Tortures, Interrogations, Spy Equipment, Escapes, Codes & How You Can Become a Spy*. London: Hodder Causton.
McCormick, D. (1975). *The Hell-Fire Club: The Story of the Amorous Knights of Wycombe*. London: Sphere.
McCormick, D. (1976). *Taken for a Ride: The History of Cons and Con-men*. London: Hardwood Smart.
McCormick, D. (1977). *Who's Who in Spy Fiction*. London: Hamish Hamilton.
McCormick, D. (pseudonym: Deacon, R.) (1979). *The British Connection Russia's Manipulation of British Individuals and Institutions*. London: Hamish Hamilton.
McCormick, D. (pseudonym: Deacon, R.) (1982). *With My Little Eye: The Memoirs of a Spy-Hunter*. London: Frederick Muller.
McCormick, D. (pseudonym: Deacon, R.) (1985). *The Cambridge Apostles: a History of Cambridge University's Elite Intellectual Secret Society*. London: Royce.
McCormick, D. (1993). *17F—The Life of Ian Fleming*. London: Peter Owen.
McLellan, D. (1976). *Karl Marx His Life and Thought*. St. Albans, England: Granada.
Mises, L. (2003 [1969]). *The Historical Setting of the Austrian School of Economics*. Auburn, AL: Ludwig von Mises Institute.
Mises, M. (1984). *My Years with Ludwig von Mises* (2nd ed.). Cedar Falls, IA: Center for Futures Education.
Monypenny, W. F. (1912). *The Life of Benjamin Disraeli, Earl of Beaconsfield Volume II 1837–1846*. London: The Times Publishing Company.
Morton, A. (2015). *17 Carnations: The Windsors, the Nazis and the Cover-Up*. London: Michael O'Mara.
Mosley, D., & Le Vien, J. (1981). *The Duchess of Windsor*. London: Stein and Day.
Panton, J. (2011). *Historical Dictionary of the British Monarchy*. Plymouth, UK: Scarecrow.
Penrose, B., & Freeman, S. (1987). *Conspiracy of Silence: the Secret Life of Anthony Blunt*. London: Vintage.
Pugh, M. (2005). *Hurrah For The Blackshirts!: Fascists and Fascism in Britain Between the Wars*. London: Pimlico.
Rees, G. (1972). *Chapter of Accidents*. New York: The Library Press.
Ridley, J. (2012). *Bertie: A Life of Edward VII*. London: Chatto and Windus.
Robbins, L. (1961, February). Hayek on Liberty. *Economica*, 28(109): 66–81.
Robbins, L. (1971). *Autobiography of an Economist*. London: Macmillan.
Russell, B. (1985). *Autobiography*. London: Unwin.
Russell, S. (1975). In Memoriam Sir Claude Elliott 1888–1973. *Alpine Journal*, 295–298. https://www.alpinejournal.org.uk/Contents/Contents_1975_files/AJ%201975%20294-304%20In%20Memoriam.pdf.

Sampson, A. (1962). *Anatomy of Britain*. London: Hodder & Stoughton.
Seaman, L. C. B. (1966). *Post-Victorian Britain 1902–1951*. London: Methuen & Co.
Sereny, G. (1985, May 9). The Sage of the Free Thinking World. *The Times*.
Sereny, G. (2001). *The Healing Wound Experiences and Reflection on Germany, 1938–2000*. London: Allen Lane and Penguin.
Shenfield, A. (1988 [1968]). *On the State of Bad Economics*. London: Libertarian Alliance. http://www.libertarian.co.uk/lapubs/econn/econn012.pdf.
Shepley, N. (2013). *Hitler, Chamberlain and Munich: The End Of The Twenty Year Truce*. UK: Andrews.
Silverman, P. (1984). Law and Economics in Interwar Vienna Kelsen, Mises and the Regeneration of Austrian Liberalism. Department of History, Faculty of the Division of the Social Sciences, University of Chicago PhD.
Simpson, B. W. (1956). *The Heart Has Its Reasons The Memoirs of the Duchess of Windsor*. London: Michael Joseph.
Smith, A. (1986). *The Essential Adam Smith* (R. Heilbroner, Ed.). New York: W. W. Norton.
Soref, H. (1979, September). Disgrace Abounding. *Review of The British Connection*. *Tory Challenge*, 9–10.
Spence, R. B. (2015). Donald McCormick: 2 + 2 = 5. In Leeson, R. (Ed.) *Hayek: A Collaborative Biography Part III Fraud, Fascism and Free Market Religion*. Basingstoke, England: Palgrave Macmillan.
Taylor, A. J. P. (1964). *The Habsburg Monarchy 1809–1918: A History of the Austrian Empire and Austria Hungary*. UK: Peregrine.
Taylor, A. J. P. (1974). *The First World War: An Illustrated History*. England: Penguin.
Thompson, D. W. (2012). Widening Participation from an Historical Perspective: Increasing our Understanding of Higher Education and Social Justice. In T. N. Basit & S. Tomlinson (Eds.), *Social Inclusion and Higher Education*. Bristol: Policy Press.
Wheeler, B. (2006, March 9). Wilson 'Plot': The Secret Tapes. *BBC News*. http://news.bbc.co.uk/2/hi/uk_news/politics/4789060.stm.
Weidlich, T. (2000). *Appointment Denied: The Inquisition of Bertrand Russell*. New York: Prometheus Books.
Wood, G. (2006, January). 364 Economists on Economic Policy. *Econ Journal Watch*, 3(1), 137–147.
Woodbridge, G. (1978). *The Reform Club 1836–1978: A History from the Club's Records*. Privately Printed for Members of the Reform Club in Association with Clearwater Publishing Company, New York.
Wyatt, W. (1956). *The Peril in Our Midst*. London: Phoenix House.
Young, G. W. (1951). *Mountains with a Difference*. London: Eyre and Spottiswoode.

CHAPTER 4

Pigouvian Market Failure

Summary

Nobel Prizes create a non-hereditary nobility—should the 1974 Nobel Prize for Economic Science have been awarded to a secular-religion-promoting fraud whose 'children's' academic entitlements are assisting the process of re-feudalisation? Should the oil-, coal- and tobacco-funded Professors and think tank 'Fellows' who promote this religion be accorded policy 'expert' status? Should this religion be taught in economics departments? Markets—and the framework and full-cost pricing (Pigouvian externality taxes) within which they can provide the socially optimal result—require a more thorough and dispassionate examination than 'free' market advocates are either willing or able to provide. This chapter examines the process by which the 'free' market sought to dismiss externalities as a Russian hoax transmitted by A. C. Pigou on Stalin's behalf.

4.1 London and Cambridge 'Opinion'

Hayek (1978a) arrived in London on 22 September 1931 to begin a one-year visiting professorship at the LSE[1]: 'it was really from the first moment arriving there that I found myself for the first time in a *moral* (emphasis added) atmosphere which was completely congenial to me and which I could absorb overnight.'[2] Hayek was introduced to the Reform Club on the evening of the general election (27 October 1931), taken as a guest by Robbins, to watch 'our' hopes for the old Liberal Party 'collapse.'[3]

© The Author(s) 2018
R. Leeson, *Hayek: A Collaborative Biography*,
Archival Insights into the Evolution of Economics,
https://doi.org/10.1007/978-3-319-74509-1_4

The Thomas Tooke Professorship of Economic Science and Statistics was revived for him on 1 August 1932.[4] This was quite an honour for a thirty-three year old whose only academic position had been as an unsalaried lecturer.[5] Between 1919 and 1982, it was held by only two people, Hayek (1932–1950) and A. W. H. Phillips (1958–1967), and held in abeyance at all other times.[6]

Three days before his arrival, Britain had been forced to abandon the Gold Standard (Titcomb 2015). Hayek (1978a) reflected: 'I can't really defend the gold standard, because I think it rests—its effectiveness rested—in part on a superstition, and the idea that gold money as such is good is just wrong. The gold standard was good because it prevented a certain arbitrariness of government in its policy; but merely preventing even worse is not good enough, particularly if it depends on people holding certain beliefs which are no longer held.'[7]

In the 'free' market, policy outcomes are perceived as a battle between superstitions: Hayek (1978a) was

> frankly trying to destroy the superstitious belief in our particular conception of democracy which we have now, which is certainly ultimately ideologically determined, but which has created without our knowing it an omnipotent government with really completely unlimited powers, and to recover the old tradition, which was only defeated by the modern superstitious democracy, that government needs limitations. For 200 years the building of constitutions aimed at limiting government. Now suddenly we have arrived at the idea where government, because it is supposedly democratic, needs no other limitations. What I want to make clear is that we must reimpose limitations on governmental power.[8]

Hayek (1978a) promoted reverence towards alternative superstitions:

> I am in a curious conflict because I have very strong positive feelings on the need of an 'un-understood' moral tradition, but all the factual assertions of religion, which are crude because they all believe in ghosts of some kind, have become completely unintelligible to me. I can never sympathize with it, still less explain it.[9]

In Weimar Germany, Hayek promoted deflation plus government inaction—which facilitated Hitler's rise to power. Afterwards, Hayek (2012 [1933], 176) continued to promote deflation to overcome price and wage rigidities:

There can be little question that these rigidities tend to delay the process of adaptation and that this will cause a 'secondary' deflation which at first will intensify the depression but ultimately will help to overcome these rigidities.

Three years after the Wall Street crash, Keynes, Pigou, Josiah Stamp, D. H. Macgregor, Walter Layton and Arthur Salter published a letter in *The Times* advocating spending as a remedy for the Great Depression (17 October 1932); in response, 'von' Hayek and three Reform and LSE colleagues, Robbins, Plant and Gregory, promoted the stock market as a remedy—adding: 'No one thinks that deflation in itself is desirable' (19 October 1932).[10] With respect to the 'moral atmosphere,' the exchange involved four Reform Club members who later joined the British Second Estate as Lords: Robbins on one side, Layton, Salter and Stamp on the other. Other LSE/Reform Club members who later became Lords included Beveridge, Geoffrey Crowther, Nicholas Kaldor and Thomas Balogh (Woodbridge 1978, 21).

In Cambridge in 1931, Hayek was regarded as an incomprehensible 'nut' after providing unconvincing arguments to an audience including Richard Kahn and Joan Robinson (Kahn cited by Samuelson 2009). Joan Robinson (1972, 2–3) recalled: 'While the controversy about public works was developing, Professor Robbins sent to Vienna for a member of the Austrian school to provide a counter-attraction to Keynes. I very well remember Hayek's visit to Cambridge on his way to the London School. He expounded his theory ... The general tendency seemed to show that the slump was caused by consumption.'

Kahn (1984, 181–182) asked: 'Is it your view that if I went out tomorrow and bought a new overcoat that would increase unemployment?' Turning to a backboard full of triangles, Hayek replies 'Yes ... but it would take a very long mathematical argument to explain why.' As the Pigou story unfolded, Bartley, Hayek's third official biographer, sent— and Hayek received—a copy of the relevant pages of Kahn's account (11 September 1984).[11]

Robinson (1972, 2–3) devoted her Richard T. Ely American Economic Association Lecture to an extrapolation from Hayek's performance: 'This pitiful state of confusion' was a reflection of 'the first crisis of economic theory.' After the publication of *The General Theory*, Hayek became increasingly marginalised within the economics profession and, according to Coase, 'lost support' at the LSE (cited by Ebenstein 2003, 73).

During 1937–1938, Galbraith (1981, 86) attended Hayek's LSE seminars, which were devoted to explaining to Hayek 'why he was wrong'; Hayek was obliged to listen in 'compelled silence.' Hayek (1994, 92) responded by reporting a problematic, if not fictitious, conversation in which Keynes allegedly stated that Kahn and Robinson were 'just fools.'

A month after Hitler came to power, the Reichstag Fire provided the excuse for an unrestrained assault on labour unions and associated political parties. Marinus van der Lubbe, a young Communist with learning difficulties, confessed under torture and was guillotined (10 January 1934).[12] Two days after the Reichstag Fire, 'von' Hayek (1933, 122, 124, 128), in his inaugural professorial lecture on 'The Trend of Economic Thinking,' contrasted Pigou's 'social enthusiasm' with the 'wonder' associated with the movement of 'heavenly bodies ... today it is regarded almost as a sign of moral depravity if the economists finds anything to marvel at in his science; i.e. he finds an unsuspected order in things which arouses his wonder.' The economy was a mysterious 'organism'—but interventionist economists had focused on the 'unsatisfactory aspects of economics life, rather than what was owed to the working of the system.' As a result, 'the non economist ... is always likely to feel injured if the economist implies that there are inter-relations between things which he does not see ... When we begin to understand their working, we discover again and again that necessary functions are discharged by spontaneous institutions. If we try to run the system by deliberate regulation, we should have to invent such institutions, and yet at first we did not even understand them when we saw them.' There is '*sense - Sinn* - in the phenomena; that they perform a necessary function it is an animistic, anthropomorphic interpretation of phenomena, the main characteristic of which is that they are not willed by any mind.'

The 1960 'Coase versus Pigou' evening at Aaron Director's house in Chicago was the 'most exciting intellectual event' of Stigler's (1988, 75) life. Coase attempted to persuade twenty Chicago economists (including Director, Stigler, Friedman, Harberger, Gregg Lewis, Lloyd Mints, Reuben Kessel, Martin Bailey and John McGee) that Pigouvian externalities need not restrain 'free' markets in the absence of transaction costs. According to Stigler, during the course of the evening, the vote changed from 20 for Pigou to 21 for Coase. This effectively partitioned economics into two epochs: After Coase (A.C.) and 'Before Coase' (B.C.).

Hayek didn't attend the 'Coase versus Pigou' evening but had an equivalent 'Eureka!' experience culminating in lunch at the Reform

Club (24 October 1984). Shortly after the publication of *The British Connection*, Margaret Thatcher (21 November 1979) addressed the House of Commons about the Fourth Man: 'I thought it right to confirm that Professor Blunt had indeed been a Soviet agent and to give the House the salient facts ... Professor Blunt has said that during his period in the Security Service from 1940–1945 he regularly passed to Russian intelligence anything that came his way which would be of interest to them ... There is no doubt that British interests were seriously damaged by his activities.'[13]

Hayek (1978a) told Chitester

> You see, I'm very interested in politics; in fact, in a way I take part. I now am very much engaged in strengthening Mrs. Thatcher's back in her fight against the [labour] unions. But I would *refuse* to take any sort of political position or political responsibility. I write articles; I've even achieved recently the dignity of an article on the lead page of the London *Times* on that particular subject. I'm represented in England as the inspirer of Mrs. Thatcher, whom I've only met twice in my life on social occasions. I enjoy this, but on the principle that I will not ask, *under any circumstances* [emphases added], what is politically possible now. I concentrate on what I think is right and should be done if you can convince the public. If you can't, well it's so much the worse, but that's not my affair.[14]

Yet Cubitt (2006, 48) reported that 'Hayek was active in the political scene in Germany, too, despite having claimed that he never interfered in the affairs of state of any country other than his own.' Otto the Habsburg Pretender was 'another politician he wished to further.'

Hayek (16 March 1983) mendaciously informed readers of *The Times*

> Since you describe me as one 'of Mrs. Margaret Thatcher's economic advisers' (March 10) I may be allowed to say that, while I have the greatest admiration for her principles and proud when told, that they resemble mine, I am too much aware of my limited knowledge of political possibilities to presume to advise her on particular decisions.[15]

Hayek (28 August 1979) wrote a 'Personal and Confidential' letter to Thatcher advising her to hold a referendum to limit the power of labour trade unions—which was 'now' politically and constitutionally possible (presumably because of the 1975 referendum on membership of the European Economic Community).

Mrs. Thatcher's (17 September 1979) diary reveals that they had a 'confidential' meeting;[16] Cubitt (2006, 39) reported that when they met, Hayek felt that Thatcher was expecting 'him to pass on some secret advice, but that he had none to give her.' Hayek (11 June 1981) later explained in a 'confidential' letter to John Burton that the Prime Minister made him feel rather a 'fool': when he revealed the purpose of his visit—the 'urgency' of drastic labour trade union reform and to obtain authorisation for it through a 'referendum'—she already knew about his proposal. Hayek suspected that two 'wet' Cabinet Ministers, James Prior and Sir Ian Gilmore, were the 'chief' obstacles to be overcome.[17]

Caldwell (2010a) informed readers of *The Washington Post* that 'Hayek himself disdained having his ideas attached to either party.' Yet the public evidence plus the Hayek Archives (of which Caldwell is the 'free' market monopolist) reveals that Hayek was a party political operative who advised which of Mrs. Thatcher's Cabinet Minister—including Prior—must be sacked (Leeson 2017).

Simultaneously, Hayek had two disappointments: Friedman had 'taken his place' as the leading libertarian (Cubitt 2006, 167); and Thatcher and Ronald Reagan's policies were 'modest in their ambitions' (cited by Forbes 1989, 44). Mrs. Thatcher stated: 'Professor Blunt has admitted that he was recruited for Russian intelligence when he was at Cambridge before the war … To us today it seems extraordinary that a man who had made no secret of his Marxist beliefs could have been accepted for secret work in any part of the public service, let alone the Security Service.'[18] Professor Pigou made no secret of his market failure beliefs: Hayek's planned op-ed piece for *The Times* may have led to a further revelation in the House of Commons about Pigou being the Fifth Man—followed by a single issue referendum on trade unions.

4.2 Free Trade and the Reform Club

Ceteris paribus, tariffs reduce, and free trade increases, the real wage: tariffs, therefore, encourage the formation of aggressive trade unions to counteract the fall. Tariffs also lead to international tensions; Manchesterism was always associated with liberal optimism about international peace. 'Imperial Preference' advocates competed for influence with free trade imperialists.

All Liberal Prime Ministers have been Reform Club members; Sir Henry Campbell-Bannerman was elected leader at the Reform

(Burlingham and Billis 2005, 106–107). In December 1905, Edward VII invited him to become the first Liberal Prime Minister of the twentieth century. There is an intimate connection between the Reform Club, free trade and the *Economist* (Dudley Edwards 1995): Campbell-Bannerman declared that the free trade cause was a fight 'against those powers, privileges, injustices, and monopolies which are unalterably opposed to the triumph of democratic principles.' Taxes were 'the plaything of the tariff reformer' (cited by McLean 1974, 362).

In 1906, the Conservative split over free trade led to a Liberal landslide. According to Noel Annan (1991, 23), Pigou was 'at home in the post-1906 Liberal Party.' In contrast, Hayek (1978b, 130) reflected that the 1905–1908 Campbell-Bannerman Government should perhaps 'be regarded as the last liberal government of the old type, while under his successor, H. H. Asquith [1908–1916], new experiments in social policy were undertaken which were only doubtfully compatible with the older liberal principles.'

In 1909, to pay for the 'New Liberal' welfare expenditure (plus the mounting costs of the pre-war arms race), the Chancellor of the Exchequer, Lloyd George, proclaimed, in language that President Lyndon Johnson echoed half a century later: 'This is a war Budget. It is for raising money to wage implacable warfare against poverty and squalidness.' The 'new' expenditures were largely to be paid for taxes on the 'old' aristocracy: death duties were increased, and taxes were raised on luxuries, alcohol and tobacco and upper level income. The House of Lords Conservative Unionist opposition, which included many large landowners, rejected the budget. Prior to New Labour (1997–2010), all British Labour Government (1924, 1929, 1945, 1964 and 1974), to a greater or lesser extent, have taken office accompanied by similar perceptions about the threats to 'liberty' and 'property.'

Hayek (1995 [1952], 229) contributed to this perception: in 1928, immediately prior to Ramsay MacDonald becoming Labour Prime Minister, Keynes and Lloyd George converted

> the British Liberal Party to the semi-socialist program expounded in the 'Liberal Yellow Book.'

In 1906, Pigou and his free trade associates prevailed—but the Great Depression revived the Protectionist cause. Keynes' 1930–1931 advocacy of tariffs caused a 'sensation' in Britain (JMK XX, 489); Joan Robinson (1962, 64, 84) referred to this 'great outcry against Keynes' treachery towards Free Trade.'

Keynes first met the thirty-two-year-old Robbins in September 1930, on the Committee of Economists of the Economic Advisory Council. Robbins made a passionate defence of free trade in the face of what he must have regarded as Cambridge vacillations by Keynes and, to a lesser extent, Pigou. According to Robbins (1971, 152), Keynes 'read aloud a letter to the Secretary commenting adversely on my emotional state ... It was intimated ... that my presence was no longer desired at the final meeting of the Committee ... All this was unspeakably painful and anxious while it lasted.'

A few weeks before the 1929 general election, Dalton (1986, 53, 63, 100) noted in his diary that he was working to secure Robbins' return to the LSE as a 'Junior Professor.' In August 1929, Robbins informed Dalton that the newly elected Labour Government was 'the most popular government since the war.' After Robbins became a professor, Dalton (21 October 1929) noted that he had made a 'very good start.' Robbins (30 March 1930) and Colin Clark predicted to Dalton that 'trade will begin to improve this summer.'

Robbins' mood changed drastically after being appointed to the Committee of Economists. After dinner at the Reform Club with Robbins, Dalton (1986, 122–124) recorded that Pigou had declined to join Robbins in writing a Minority Report on the grounds that it would be 'ungentlemanly.' Pigou suspected that Robbins was looking for fame: 'If you want to make a row outside can't you find some other way of doing it?' Robbins threatened to refer the matter to the Prime Minister, the Cabinet and the Chancellor of the Exchequer, and then 'left the room. Pigou buried his head in his hands.' Robbins' behaviour was witnessed by his fellow Reform Club member and Committee of Economists co-member, Josiah Stamp.

In May 1931, Beveridge (1931) and a group of LSE economists, including Robbins, Plant, George Schwartz and John Hicks, restated the free trade cause in *Tariffs: the Case Examined*. In the previous few months, Plant (Cassell Professor of Commerce) and Schwartz (lecturer in Commerce) had been recruited to the LSE and Hicks had been promoted to lecturer (Howson 2011, 170; Robbins 1971, 126; Hayek 1946, 23–24). The free trade connection may have played a significant part in Beveridge's decision to recruit Hayek to the LSE.

When Dalton (1986, 165) returned to teach at the LSE, Robbins and his wife came to stay with his family. Dalton (January 1932) reflected: 'His intellectual development is a disappointment. He will do much distinguished work in economic theory. But he has stiffened in an old fashioned laissez-faire attitude of approach to current problems. He is bemused by modern Viennese theory and by the *personality* (emphasis added) of Hayek in particular.' Dalton was Parliamentary Under-Secretary at the Foreign Office in MacDonald's Labour Government (1929–1931).

According to his Nobel Peace Prize biography, Phillip Noel-Baker 'participated in the formation, the administration, and the legislative deliberations of the two great international political organisations of the twentieth century - the League of Nations and the United Nations.' During the Peace Conference, he was principal assistant to Robert Cecil, 1st Viscount Cecil of Chelwood, on the committee which drafted the League of Nations Covenant. He also contributed to the League's prisoner-of-war and refugee work. Between 1929 and 1931, he was a member of the British delegation to the Assembly of the League, before becoming assistant to Arthur Henderson, the chairman of the Disarmament Conference.[19]

In 1984, Hayek was led to believe that in Geneva in September 1930, there had been the 'sensational theft of the keys of Foreign Office dispatch-boxes from Mr. Philip Noel-Baker, who was then Parliamentary Secretary to the British Foreign Secretary Arthur Henderson, in Ramsey MacDonald's 1929–1931 Labour Government ... At first there were attempts to deny the incident had ever occurred, and certainly the episode of the theft of the keys was hushed up.' The mystery was, allegedly, partly solved by 'Deacon' McCormick's (1979, 115–116) father-in-law:

> But a pertinacious *Daily Mail* correspondent in Geneva, the late H. Challinor James, refused to be browbeaten not only by threats, but by pressures brought to bear on his employees. However, on 2 October 1930, the *Daily Mail* published a report which stated '... the first step was to find out if the hand of Moscow had been at again been at work against Britain ...'[20]

This appears to be a dubious reconstruction—other newspapers (19 September 1930) reported that a revolver-wielding 'cat burglar' broke into Noel-Baker's bedroom and stole his keys: 'their disappearance suggests that the theft was the work of someone operating on behalf of a foreign power ... the last occasion that despatch box keys were stolen occurred in Russia in 1908.'[21]

Nevertheless, Challinor James's son-in-law—allegedly—completed the solution of the mystery: Pigou facilitated the theft by providing the Soviets with the not-very-mysterious information about where Noel-Baker 'kept his keys'—in his 'trousers' pocket.' According to 'Deacon' McCormick (1979, 116), the imaginary 'Roger' explained that

'Noel-Baker never guessed that it was one of his greatest friends who let him down.'

4.3 A 1905 Diary?

The British Embassy in Bonn (22 May 1984) telephoned Hayek to inform him that Mrs. Thatcher wished to honour him: a letter from the Prime Minister to Professor 'von' Hayek confirming the award was sent (25 May 1984). A further letter to 'von' Hayek confirmed that he would have an 'unaccompanied' audience with the Queen (22 June 1984). Signing himself 'von' Hayek (2 July 1984) acknowledged the letter from Windsor Castle and confirmed that he would be 'free' to meet the Queen on that date. Mrs. Thatcher (18 October 1984) informed him:

> I cannot tell you how delighted I am with the leather bound edition you have sent me of 'The Road to Serfdom';

adding in her own hand 'It means so much to me. I remember well the days when I first read it.'[22] According to John Blundell (2008, 30), Mrs. Thatcher read *Road to Serfdom* as an undergraduate (1943–1947), during which time she was President of the Oxford University Conservative Association (1946). Given her time constraints, she probably read the official Conservative election manifesto version. Sherman had the impression that she had not read Hayek prior to 1974 (Young 1989, 22).

The MPS had been courting the Duke of Edinburgh at least since 1968 on the grounds that a visit by him to their Society 'would be appreciated by our American members.'[23] In his *Evening Standard* column Paul Johnson (9 December 1976) asked 'Who's afraid of the formidable Fritz?'[24] Johnson reported that Hayek (1978c) and the Duke of Edinburgh (1978) would both contribute to an IEA publication, *The Coming confrontation: Will the Open Society Survive to 1989?* Johnson stated that 'we can all add "Hear, hear!"' to the Duke's essay on the choice between collectivism and freedom. In a letter to *The Times Literary Supplement* (14 January 1978), Hayek appeared to doubt Johnson's reliability as a historian and commentator.[25] However, Johnson, Sir Keith Joseph and 19 others were on Hayek's 'PRIVATE AND CONFIDENTIAL' list for lunch at the Reform Club (26 April 1979).[26]

The Duke of Edinburgh, 'who, as usual, was talking about high taxation as a major disincentive,' told Tony Benn (1996 [11 July 1969], 212 [23 February 1968], 181; [5 July 1977], 423): 'Well, if you go to the East End, they waive their little flags and are very keen on the monarchy.' The Queen should attend Cabinet meetings:

> In Saudi Arabia, you know, King Khalid holds court every day. People come and say 'Your Majesty I haven't got a telephone' and he raises it with his ministers. That's what the monarchy should be like.

The Duke (1978) published 'Intellectual Dissent and the Reversal of Trends' in the IEA *The Coming Confrontation*. In *Approaching 1984*, 'Deacon' McCormick (1980a, 24, 49, 57, 105) reported that the Duke had been converted to a *Road to Serfdom*-style prediction of a 'Big Brother' State. This would happen by 2000, 'unless we were all eternally vigilant. Yet the ridiculous thing is that he had to risk breaking the rules to make such a speech.' A 'healthy Western democracy' was contrasted with what would have 'happened under either Stalin or Hitler ... But perhaps the last word should be with the Duke of Edinburgh, speaking in October 1977 ...'

The Private Secretary to Queen Elisabeth, the Queen Mother, declined the offer of a complimentary copy of Hayek's (1960) *Constitution of Liberty* on the grounds that the author was not 'personally known' to her.[27] This may have led Hayek to believe that the Queen Mother or the Queen 'opposed his receiving an honour' (Cubitt 2006, 138). However, on 25 October 1984, Hayek was taken the short journey to Buckingham Palace to be 'received' by the Queen[28]; to receive a badge, inscribed '*IN ACTION FAITHFUL AND IN HONOUR CLEAR*'; and to be enlisted into the Order of the Companion of Honour.[29] Hayek told *The Times*: 'I was amazed by her. That ease and skill, as if she'd known me all my life' (Sereny 1985). He was impressed by the Queen's knowledge of his work and family and told his daughter-in-law that after a twenty-minute audience, he was 'absolutely besotted' with her. Afterwards, when Hayek was returned to the Reform Club, he reflected: 'I've just had the happiest day of my life' (cited by Ebenstein 2003, 305). He had wished to become 'Sir Friedrich' or, better still, 'Sir Fredrick' (Cubitt 2006, 29); but now, at least, had a Windsor post-nominal 'CH' to compensate him for the 1919 loss of his Habsburg 'von' prefix.

In Germany and Austria, the 1917 overthrow of the Romanovs was a prelude to the 1919 overthrow of the Hohenzollerns and Habsburgs; in Britain, it was a prelude to George V's transformation of the House of Saxe-Coburg Gotha into the House of Windsor (July 1917), and the creation of the Companion of Honour (June 1917). The Honour was presumably designed to create an achievement-based avenue for social advancement: one of the first members was the Principal of Sheffield Technical School, William Ripper.

In his review of *The Fatal Conceit*, Dallas University's Samuel Bostaph (1989, 16) gushed about the 'life-enhancing characteristics of the rules framework ... such a view grafted to the corpus of Hayek's manifesto allows the conclusion that the customs and traditions that promote free-market capitalism are not only necessary to support modern civilisation, they are also good.' 'Deacon' McCormick's fraudulent *British Connection* had been withdrawn by the publishers after four days— Hayek told him that he planned to use 'the standing offer to print an article of mine on the chief page of *The Times* for an essay on the Vanished Book!' (Leeson 2013, 187). Hayek (11 November 1983; 10 January 1984) complained to *The Times* that they had published an article under his name that he 'never' wrote.[30] Cubitt (2006, 111) reported that according to Shenoy, the LSE political philosopher, John Gray, was distributing advance copies of *The Fatal Conceit*. Hayek believed that he may have given permission to Gray to publicise *The Fatal Conceit* and that this had led to an unauthorised essay in *The Salisbury Review* which *The Times* had reprinted. In compensation, Hayek negotiated with *The Times's* editor, Charles Douglas-Home, a 'claim' for 'space' if he should ever feel the 'urge' to write.[31]

'Deacon' McCormick (28 September 1984) explained why he was 'delighted' that Hayek had contacted him:

> though not an economist, I am not only a fervent admirer of what you preach, but probably in my enthusiasm for your code and rules that I almost go beyond it. I believe (1) that we awakened too late to the insidious, if seemingly plausible doctrines of Keynes, and that he spelt the doom of 19th century Radical Liberal free trade, free market economics, even ruining the Liberal Party of any credence in the process; (2) that my motto is 'Less than enough is a means to an end.' This is not meant to be reactionary, but simply that today people are abnormally greedy because they have been conditioned to be greedy. (cited by Leeson 2013, 191–192)

The Reform Club dress code requires the wearing of a jacket and tie. 'Deacon' McCormick (1973, 23) advised that to make a commercial deal for 'the proverbial song,' it was necessary to dress appropriately: 'put on an old pair of seaboots, a sweater and a pair of baggy trousers ... and then casually inquire ...' 'Deacon' McCormick did not attend university but would have seen academics on television. His readings about Pigou presumably including Harry Johnson's (1960, 150) report of Pigou living 'up to his reputation for sartorial economy, appearing at the Marshall Library in the fifties one day proudly wearing a suit bought before the First World War.' Leube, who claims to have accompanied Hayek to the Reform Club lunch, described 'Deacon' McCormick as 'not an impressive person - he was shabbily dressed.' Leube has a personal cobbler and a personal tailor.[32]

In 'A Classical Liberal Life,' Liggio (2010, 186, 193) reported that as an undergraduate at Georgetown University, he 'benefited from top refugee teachers: Tibor Kerekes had been Otto von Habsburg's tutor.' In 2004, Otto's father, Charles I, was beatified by Pope John Paul II as 'Blessed Karl of Austria,' and 'Count' Leube (2004) claimed that he and Hayek were 'actually related. So I call him my Uncle.' At IHS, Liggio—a 'birthright Catholic' (Raico 2014)—funded Ebeling and the academic fraud, Sudha Shenoy (the daughter of an MPS Board member).

According to Mises (1985 [1927], 115): 'There is, in fact, only one solution: the state, the government, the laws must not in any way concern themselves with schooling or education. Public funds must not be used for such purposes.' Rothbard's (2010 [1961], 7) mission was to 'rechannel educational funds from various blind alleys into which they have fallen'—he was a 'giant' of 'Classical Liberalism' (Liggio 2010, 188). Possibly inspired by 'Deacon' McCormick's non-existent diary, Leube (with Hayek's assistance) obtained tens of thousands dollars from Liggio to write about the (apparently non-existent) Böhm-Bawerk diary. When asked about the product, Liggio (email to Leeson, 19 July 2011) refused to answer the question and, instead, simply repeated what was already apparent: nothing on Böhm-Bawerk resulted from this funding. Liggio declined to reply to follow-up email from Leeson, 20 July 2011 ('You gave funds to Kurt Leube for such an essay: it never got written?') which necessitated a telephone call in which Liggio, somewhat evasively, explained that tax-exempt funds—when spent to promote the 'free' market—remain unaccounted for.

James Buchanan asked Hayek: 'Given this reading of the history of the last century, and given this destruction of these moral values, which we did not really understand why we hold, how can we expect something analogous to that to be restored? Or how can we hope that can be restored?' Hayek (1978a)—a serial liar—replied:

> Well, I wish I knew. My present concern is to make people see the error. But that's an intellectual task, and how you can undo this effect– Well, I have an idea the thing is on the whole effective via its effect on the teaching profession … I don't think it's hopeless that we might train another generation of teachers who do not hold these views, who again return to the rather traditional conceptions that *honesty and similar things are the governing conceptions* (emphasis added). If you persuade the teaching profession, I think you would get a new generation brought up in quite a different view.

Buchanan asked: 'And you don't see a necessity for something like a religion, or a return to religion, to instill these moral principles?' Hayek—who 'didn't believe a word' of Christianity—[33] replied:

> Well, it depends so much on what one means by religion. You might call every belief in moral principles, which are not rationally justified, a religious belief. In the wide sense, yes, one has to be religious. Whether it really needs to be associated with a belief in supernatural spiritual forces, I am not sure. It may be. It's by no means impossible that to the great majority of people nothing short of such a belief will do.[34]

In November 1962, George Wallace became Governor of Alabama with 96% of the vote—from the end of Reconstruction to the 1965 Voting Rights Act, most blacks had been disenfranchised throughout the South. Standing on the spot where Jefferson Davis had been sworn-in as President of the Confederate States of America 102 years before, Wallace famously proclaimed:

> In the name of the greatest people that have ever trod this earth, I draw the line in the dust and toss the gauntlet before the feet of tyranny, and I say segregation now, segregation tomorrow, segregation forever.

In neoclassical economics, an individual's real wage reflects (marginal) productivity which in turn reflects human capital. On 11 June 1963, Governor Wallace 'stood in the schoolhouse door' (the University of

Alabama's Forder Auditorium) to prevent non-whites having access to human capital formation and thus upward social mobility.

Republican Party strategist, Lee Atwater, described the strategy through which Nixon and Reagan won the White House:

> As to the whole Southern strategy that Harry Dent and others put together in 1968, opposition to the Voting Rights Act would have been a central part of keeping the South. Now [Reagan] doesn't have to do that. All you have to do to keep the South is for Reagan to run in place on the issues he's campaigned on since 1964 ... and that's fiscal conservatism, balancing the budget, cut taxes, you know, the whole cluster... You start out in 1954 by saying, 'Nigger, nigger, nigger.' By 1968 you can't say 'nigger' - that hurts you. Backfires. So you say stuff like forced busing, states' rights and all that stuff. You're getting so abstract now [that] you're talking about cutting taxes, and all these things you're talking about are totally economic things and a byproduct of them is [that] blacks get hurt worse than whites. And subconsciously maybe that is part of it. I'm not saying that. But I'm saying that if it is getting that abstract, and that coded, that we are doing away with the racial problem one way or the other. You follow me - because obviously sitting around saying, 'We want to cut this,' is much more abstract than even the busing thing, and a hell of a lot more abstract than 'Nigger, nigger.' (cited by Lamis 1990, 26; Giroux 2010)

In the 1968 Presidential election, Wallace received 9901,118 votes (13.5% of the total). Rothbard's (1992, 6) 'Outreach to the Redneck' sought to mobilise this constituency for the 'free' market: in Louisiana, former Klansman 'David Duke picked up 55% of the white vote; he lost in the runoff because the fear campaign brought out a massive outpouring of black voters.' The

> anti-Duke hysteria ... resorted to questioning the sincerity of Duke's conversion to Christianity - even challenging him to name his 'official church.'

'Ron Paul' (in his fund-raising 'Newsletter' believed to have been written by Rothbard, Rockwell and North) stated: 'even in my little town of Lake Jackson, Texas, I've urged everyone in my family to know how to use a gun in self defense ... for the animals are coming' (cited by Leeson 2017, Chapter 12). According to Hayek, 'animals' were an expression of 'a spontaneous order' (Caldwell 2005); and Hayek said that he did not like 'dancing Negroes'! He had watched a Nobel laureate doing so, which had made him see the 'the animal beneath the facade of apparent civilization.' (Cubitt 2006, 23–24)

James Buchanan's (1973, 7) 'America's Third Century' battle-plan detected

a revolt against the oppression of taxes imposed by governments at all levels, taxes that are increasingly seen to support unproductive and essentially parasitic members of society. George Wallace exploited this attitude successfully and expressed it in his slogan, 'send them a message.' It was in recognition of the strength of this attitude that Richard Nixon patterned his major electoral [1972] victory, and it was this that offered the origin for his second-term theme of budgetary restriction.

Buchanan's (1973, 12) 'counter-intelligentsia' must be 'small at first, and its ideas must be developed so as to command respect even by those who are our ideological enemies.'

'Von' Hayek (1978a) noted that 'The robber baron was a very honored and honorable person, but he was certainly not an honest person in the ordinary sense. The whole traditional concept of aristocracy, of which I have a certain conception—I have moved, to some extent, in aristocratic circles, and I like their style of life. But I know that in the strict commercial sense, they are not necessarily honest.'[35] Leube claims to be descended from a fourteenth-century Habsburg Count, to have lost count of the number of castles he owns, and to be constantly short of cash or 'ready money.' In compensation, 'Dr.' Leube was provided with a green card, and after CSUH/EB abruptly changed his title from 'Professor' to 'Emeritus Professor,' the taxpayers of California made him their pensioner-for-life.

During the September 1984 MPS meeting, Hayek led a 'pilgrimage' to the Old Oast House, Malting Lane, Cambridge, the wartime home where he wrote *The Road to Serfdom*. Hayek told the pilgrimage organisers that the house could easily hold over a hundred people because there had been no problem accommodating a large cocktail party to 'empty' the 'barrel' of sherry he had brought back from Gibraltar in September 1944.[36] Hayek (1994, 95) reflected about his time doing a social survey of Gibraltar for the Colonial Office: 'don't tempt me to tell you anecdotes about this; it would be endless.' In 1946, 'Deacon' McCormick was editor of the *Gibraltar Chronicle*; his *Wicked Village* was a supposedly autobiographical account of the (actual) purchase of house in a (mythical) village called 'Codiham'—later acknowledged to be The Oast House, Liptraps Lane, High Brooms, just outside Tunbridge Wells (1960, 7, 8; 1993, 17).

In 1984, 'Deacon' McCormick's stories about Pigou reminded Hayek of his trips over the mountains into Carinthia to see his cousin and longed-for second wife. For Helene, 'her beloved Carinthia' was 'where she belonged.' In 1933, Hayek suggested to his first wife that they should visit Helene; Hella refused, and so in 1934, Hayek went alone to Austria. Shortly after his son Laurence's birth (15 July 1934), Hayek 'suddenly turned up' in Carinthia and suggested to Helene the divorce which he had first proposed in 1924, but which took until 1950 to finalise (Cubitt 2006, 46, 285).

According to *The British Connection* (1979, 81–82, 84, 121), 'There are, perhaps, two types of the perfect secret agent—the sublimely unobtrusive and cautious, of which Pigou was over a very long period the archetype, and the outrageous exhibitionist moving noisily around in the highest circles, drawing attention to himself by his conduct and comments, but for that reason never being suspected. Burgess was to a large extent the latter type.' In contrast, Pigou had

> an unerring nose for recruits to the cause ... at his best as a recruiter of agents according to the very few who knew of his talent and zest for what he confidentially called 'picking out the Marxist plums.'

As a University of Vienna student, Hayek (1994, 54; 1978a) was introduced to the Austrian School through Spann who 'soon ceased to be interested in technical economics and was developing what he called a universalist social philosophy. But he, being a young and enthusiastic man, for a very short time had a constant influence on all these young people. Well, he was resorting to taking us to a midsummer celebration up in the woods, where we jumped over fires and—It's so funny [laughter].'[37] According to 'Deacon' McCormick (1979, 82; 1980a, 10, 28), Pigou—who passed recruits over to an Austrian for processing:

> looked for two qualities in his recruits – first, a commitment to what he would have always called by the euphemism of 'universal socialism' rather than communism: second by testing the potential recruit through mountaineering.

'Roger' explained:

> It is quite true that he invariably suggested a mountaineer as a recruit ... he had 'a thing' about mountaineers: he felt that in time of war or crisis they could get across borders more easily than others ... It was very rare that Pigou recruited anyone as a Soviet agent unless, by his standards, he passed both these tests.

Pigou 'would put forward names, initiate an occasional recruit, but he never personally engaged them. It was always left to other here to make the final approach. His link was directly to the Soviet network here in Switzerland.'

Recruits were handed over to 'Comintern personnel ... An important figure in this sphere was Arnold Deutsch, an Austrian Comintern agent,' with a postgraduate qualification from the University of London. It was Deutsch who had probably instructed Burgess and Philby 'to leave the party and go underground ... Burgess occasionally went on rock-climbing expeditions with Pigou in Wales.' According to 'Deacon' McCormick, Philby specialised in 'discarding wives ... Quite often he would slip across the border into France, ostensibly for brief relaxation, but nobody seems to recall exactly what he did or where he went on these occasions. He may well have met his Soviet courier in St Jean de Luz.'

Otto Bauer's (1919) *Der Weg zum Sozialismus* (The Road to Socialism) was published in Vienna during Hayek's student days. From his first letter in *The Times* (1925) on the necessity of translating Mises' (1922) *Sozialismus* into English, through *Collectivist Economic Planning Critical Studies on the Possibilities of Socialism* (1935), through *The Road to Serfdom* (1944), addressed to 'The Socialists of All Parties,' to *The Fatal Conceit: The Errors of Socialism* (1988) and beyond, Hayek was the 'most famous opponent of socialism in all its forms' (Friedman and Friedman 1998, 78). Hayek believed that Pigou tried to recruit him as a 'Marxist plum' because of his ability to get across borders, and then took him mountain climbing in the Lake District to ascertain whether he was committed to 'universal socialism.' Hayek told 'Deacon' McCormick that he had been 'subject by [Pigou] to exactly the tests which you described ... Also, characteristically, he dropped me as suddenly when he discovered that my political views made me wholly unsuitable for the purposes he evidently had in mind ... I am at last more or less persuaded that you must be right' (cited by Leeson 2013, 191).

A. J. P. Taylor (1979) correctly detected that 'Deacon' McCormick was a ridiculous fantasist: 'I add my own crumb of disinformation: Pigou's [Lake District] house at Buttermere is clearly the original for that described by John Buchan in *The Thirty Nine Steps*.' Austrians regard Keynes as 'bitchy' (Caldwell 1995, 28); Lord Chalfont (16 August 1979) informed 'Deacon' McCormick that he would be used as source material for his forthcoming *Star Wars: suicide or survival?* (Jones 1985) and that Taylor was just 'bitchy.'[38]

Pigou (1942) was a mountain enthusiast (Kahn 1984, 125; Austin Robinson 1968, 94; Plumptre 1975, 250); his obituary appeared in the *Alpine Journal*. Pigou (1921, 508) reviewed Keynes' (1921) *Treatise on Probability* in the context of the 'Mummery crack on the Grepon.' (A. F. Mummery and J. A. Hobson's (1889) *The Physiology of Industry* became part of Keynes' (1936) attack on Pigou.[39]) In his June 1939 Presidential Address to the Royal Economic Society, Pigou (1939, 220) referred to 'The mountaineer, who year after year has followed a supreme guide, risks becoming imbued with the spirit of a follower, unapt himself to lead.'[40] According to Robbins (1971, 134–135), 'only Hayek, who shared his passion for great heights, knew him at all well.'[41] Hayek was informed that Pigou had twin passions: 'communist economics and mountain climbing' ('Deacon' McCormick 1979, 8, 184–195).

Mountains and their Clubs were important to Hayek: he signed a letter to Sir Frederic Bartlett as 'F.A. v. Hayek F.B.A. & Alpine Club.'[42] Citing Sir Leslie Stephen's book on mountaineering—presumably, *The Playground of Europe* (1871)—Hayek (1994, 136) reflected that he 'knew the mountaineering literature, and that helped me fit into the English atmosphere ... But it was only when I looked at a certain book by Richard Deacon, which is a pseudonym, that it occurred to me why Pigou suddenly got interested in me. Deacon suggests that Pigou was interested in people who could cross frontiers. I had forgotten about the fact that in 1939 I wanted to visit Austria and I didn't want to be suspected of having any special privileges with the Germans. In fact I was visiting my present wife. Very soon after that, Pigou got interested in me, and the contrast of his sudden interest in me and then suddenly dropping me—after he had asked me to come up to the Lake District and stay with him, and climb with him—fits in so perfectly with the Deacon story. But as late as July or August of 1939, I went to Austria very much in the awareness that I could risk it, even though it was likely that war might break out at any moment. I knew those mountains [in Carinthia] so well that I could just walk out.'

Pigou (1905) published *Principles and Methods of Industrial Peace* as he—allegedly—sent Stalin messages in code: 'The Pigou diary of 1905 was based on a 9-cell key in which the letters of the alphabet are disposed in groups of 3. The entries cited are for 21 and 24 August. [Deacon Papers]' ('Deacon' McCormick 1979, 263, Chapter 1, n. 6; 1989, 177, Chapter 5, n. 6). However, Chapter 10, 'Cupid's Paperchase,' in *Love in Code, or, How to Keep Your Secrets*, indicates that 'Deacon' McCormick (1980b, 14–15, 44–47, 65, 100, 129, 167, acknowledgments) was as much a Trickster inviting discovery as a serious Cold War fraud: 'one of the most remarkable documents of romantic love in code is a collection of diary jottings and minute sketches from 1905, hitherto unpublished. An absolute gem of its kind, it traces the fortunes of two young lovers, Hugh and Cecily,' whose incestuous relationship produced children. Their code was identical to another 'nine-cell diagram' used elsewhere in the book.

Pigou—allegedly—kept a record of his treason in a pocket diary; Hugh and Cecily communicated in a 'small pocket diary.' The two pages razored out of Pigou's diary and the reproduced 'page from Hugh's diary' both cover the dates 4 May and 8 May (1980b, 24, 114, 115, 116). Pigou's 1905 diary and Hugh's 1905 diary are one and the same. At the Reform Club lunch, Hayek had an additional reason for noticing the razored out pages: 8 May was his birthday.

For 'Deacon' McCormick (1980b, 33–34) 'roger' meant sex: Senator William Byrd of Westover kept a diary in which he recorded his sexual conquest in parks: 'picked up two women ... rogered her three times to her great satisfaction.' 'Deacon' McCormick told Hayek he couldn't disclose 'Roger's' identity, 'because he could be at risk from the KGB,' but he could instead provide 'photocopies of the Pigou diaries in code' (Leeson 2013, 192).

'Deacon' McCormick informed Hayek that

> I cannot disclose the identity of my informant 'ROGER' as yet, mainly because he could be at risk from the KGB.

'Deacon' McCormick was more forthcoming with other evidence: 'I can let you have photocopies of the Pigou diaries in code.' Lunch on October 24th would be 'splendid.' Hayek recorded in his diary (24 October) '12.50 McCormick 3.30' and (25 October) 'Queen.'[43]

William 'Bill' Deedes (23 August 1983), the editor of *The Daily Telegraph* (1974–1986), offered Hayek £350 to write a leader page article on Orwell and 1984; Hayek (5 September 1983) declined on the grounds that he was trying to finish what became known as *The Fatal Conceit: The Errors of Socialism* (1988). Hayek (4 October 1984) was still intensely busy and wrote to Jacques Schatz withdrawing his offer to write a book Preface on the grounds that he had to 'firmly' resist 'all distractions.'[44] On the same day, however, Hayek (4 October 1984) replied to 'Deacon' McCormick: 'I will now only explain that my chief aim is to do an essay on the sort of suppression of information which the withdrawal of your book illustrates, and my picking out Pigou as an examply [*sic*] is merely due to me knowing a good deal about him which made the story at first incredible and then quite plausible' (cited by Leeson 2013, 193).

'Deacon' McCormick (10 October 1984) replied that in *The British Connection* he had 'tried to show that people can also be manipulated by the USSR without knowing it. I do not put Pigou in quite the same category as Blunt, or Philby, but he was an agent of influence, directly or indirectly, over very many years, and what was important was to show how this started in pre-revolutionary days.' Hayek (15 October 1984) replied: 'What you say about Pigou agrees very much with my impression of the man, who would wish to help a fascinating experiment, but not directly harm his country harm. Nevertheless it is historically important because representative of intellectual, particularly *Cambridge opinion* (emphasis added) of the time.'

After the Reform Club lunch, 'Deacon' McCormick (27 October 1984) wrote to Hayek: 'I was so glad that we were able to cover so much ground in so short a time. If I can help further in any way, or send you any information, or copies of notes, documents etc., do please let me know. It is, as you say, the suppression of information which creates more dangers and problems than it prevents, and it is one reason why the KGB finds it easier to plant disinformation in such a psychological climate. When information is suppressed, false information can so easily be fed into the vacuum, and thus exploited among those eager for information, but not getting it' (cited by Leeson 2013, 193).

Newly discovered archival material is scholarly gold. In 1984, the University of Chicago Press published volume 2 of Noel Annan's *Leslie Steven The Godless Victorian*. A third of a century earlier, Hayek (25

November 1951) had written to Annan about his *Leslie Stephen: His Thought and Character in Relation to His Time* (1952) asking about a notebook, which may have contained evidence that Stephen had been using demand and supply curves at a very early stage. Hayek added that he was only interested in the diary if it had not been seen by other economists, such as Kahn. Annan—later a severe critic of 'Deacon' McCormick - replied from King's College, Cambridge that he had not seen the notebook, and indicated that a lot of material had perished in wartime air raids.[45]

Hayek (8 January 1954) applied for libertarian funding associated with the newly discovered diary-letters which John Stuart Mill wrote during the journey through Southern Europe. Hayek (1951, 239) also unearthed Mills' correspondence with an Englishman named 'Noel,' and wrote to Philip Noel-Baker—later a severe critic of 'Deacon' McCormick—seeking further information.[46]

For the 100th anniversary of the birth of the Austrian School, Hayek (1992 [1973], n. 104) inspected Alfred Marshall's notes on Menger's (1871) *Principles of Economics* (*Grundsätze der Volkswirtschaftslehre*) and concluded that 'they seem to me to be written in Marshall's handwriting of an early date.' Hayek wrote to John Robson, the editor of the *Mill News Letter*, about a letter he discovered as he was surreptitiously emptying his desk at the LSE, before departing for the U.S., stating that apart from the handwriting there can be no doubt that it is an autograph of J. S. Mill.[47] The signature 'A.C. Pigou' appears on the 1905 diary: shortly afterwards, in *The Mask of Treachery: Spies, Lies, Buggery and Betrayal: The First Documented Dossier on Anthony Blunt's Cambridge Spy Ring*, Costello (1988, 176, 646–547, n. 13) reported that the signature of 'Sir [*sic*] Arthur Pigou ... appears genuine to those who know it ... Deacon also told me that corroboration for his contention that Pigou – who sponsored Keynes at the beginning of his career – was a longtime secret supporter of the Soviet Union came from the noted economist Professor F.A. von Hayek.'

The 1905 diary 'revealed' that Pigou was gun-running for Stalin ('Deacon' McCormick 1979, 4). In only one sense is the diary genuine: it is a genuine 1905 diary, which recorded significant dates (the beginning of the fox-hunting season, the shooting seasons for Grouse, Partridge and Pheasant, birthdays for King Edward VII and Queen Alexandra, etc.). There is also what appears to be an authentic ballpoint entry (in handwriting that doesn't match Pigou's) referring to a village in Braintree, Essex, almost mid-point between Cambridge and Frinton-on-Sea (where 'Deacon' McCormick took holidays): 'Steeple Bumpstead No books 686A A 1398.14.10.'[48]

Hayek's diary records a visit from his third official biographer on Remembrance Sunday (11 November 1984).[49] The transcript record that Bartley asked Hayek 'What about these documents?' to which Hayek replied: 'The only relevant document he has, is supposed to have is the 1905 [*sic*].' Bartley responded: 'That's the one I was going to ask you about. That refers to Stalin.' Hayek replied: 'At that time – well that exists' (cited by Leeson 2013, 195).

In 1984, there must have been an additional apprehension about bogus diaries. In February 1983, when the fake Hitler diaries were first presented, it was a 'moment of almost religious solemnity … The diaries cast a spell over the room' (Harris 1986, 138; Weinberg 2015). In *The Last Days of Hitler*, Trevor-Roper (1947) established his reputation by, using the alias 'Major Oughton,' interviewing the last people to have been present in the bunker with Hitler. Trevor-Roper (publically) and Hayek (privately) embraced the Hitler diary fraud. Trevor-Roper's reputation suffered an almost irreversible decline; Cubitt (2006, 96) reflected that Hayek's embrace of the Hitler fraud 'must have been a mortifying experience.'

According to the author of *Selling Hitler*, Rupert Murdoch 'ruled his Empire in a manner not dissimilar to that which Hitler employed to run the Third Reich.' In April 1983, Murdoch wanted to bid for the serial rights for the Hitler diaries: the editor of *The Times*, Douglas-Home, phoned Trevor-Roper and asked him to fly to Zurich that afternoon to confirm their authenticity—which he duly did. Douglas-Home and Murdoch then flew to Zurich the following day. Douglas-Home told Gitta Sereny of *The Sunday Times* that it was the 'greatest historical find of the twentieth century.' Sereny asked if *The Times* were running them—to which Douglas-Home responded 'no you are.' When the holocaust denier, David Irving, exposed the diaries as fakes, Douglas-Home replied 'I have smelt them. I'm a minor historian and we know about the smell of old documents. They certainly smelt.' When Trevor-Roper expressed doubts, Douglas-Home advised him not to 'burn his boats' at the forthcoming press conference. Instead, Trevor-Roper confessed to the press that there was 'such a thing as a perfect forgery' (Harris 1986, 258–263, 302, 307, 320, 322).[50]

Trevor-Roper was one of Mrs. Thatcher's speech-writers: in 1979, she ennobled him as Lord Dacre. In 1982, when she asked: 'When can we expect another book from you? Lord Dacre replied: 'Well, Prime Minister, I have one on the stocks'; to which Mrs. Thatcher retorted: 'On the stocks? On the stocks? A fat lot of good that is! In the shops, that is where we need it!' (Hunt 2010).

Trevor-Roper (1976) had recently completed a study of a fraudulent naval officer: *A Hidden Life: the Enigma of Sir Roger Backhouse*. In August 1973, Trevor-Roper (1976, 4, 116–117) took possession (at Basel airport) of Backhouse's memoirs: 'One of the mysteries concerning Backhouse surrounds the Chinese diary, the diary of Ching-shan, which, he tells us, he discovered in 1900, during the Boxer Rising ... Victor Purcell, in his authoritative book on *The Boxer Rising* [1963] ... concluded that the diary was forged.' Referring to Backhouse's assertion that he was in possession of the 'diary of the all-powerful Grand Eunuch of the Empress dowager, who had ruled her court for forty years, Li Lien-ying,' Trevor-Roper concluded that the diary was 'non-existent.'

Naval Lieutenant 'Deacon' McCormick was aware of Pigou's involvement in the anti-tariff cause, prior to the 1906 general election: he took notes from the J. Saltmarsh and L. P. Wilkinson (1960) memoir ('During Jo Chamberlain's campaign Pigou went on tour, giving free trade lectures and pamphleteering'[51]). The *British Connection* (1979, 82, 121) stated that 'Pigou never allowed himself to be dragged into the public political arena; his only concession to this had been in the pre-1914 era when he addressed a few meetings on a free trade platform.' In *Protective Preferential Import Duties*, Pigou (1906, 37, n. 1, 47, n. 1) referred to Chamberlain's speech of 4 November 1905. Yet all Pigou apparently recorded in his 1905 diary were coded messages to Stalin. Pigou also took mountaineering holidays—but there is no mention of these either.

'Deacon' McCormick (1976b, 58) reflected: 'it would seem that there were some medieval fakers at work in the fifteenth century.' In *The Master Book of Spies*, he asked: 'Are the letters on the following pages written by the same person? Or could they be forged?' (1973, 179). In *Taken for a Ride the History of Cons and Con-men*, 'Deacon' McCormick (1976a, 174) stated that a 'splendidly impressive concocted document ... drawn up on government paper, was duly handed over.' 'Deacon' McCormick must have acquired a copy of Pigou's signature on Board of Trade notepaper (circa 1918) and, as promised, showed Hayek the concocted Pigou diary.[52]

The younger man's signature differs from the 1958 signature on his will: the signature in the diary looks, to the amateur eye, like a forgery.

Elementary reasoning suggests that the diary that Hayek inspected and validated over lunch at the Reform Club could not have belonged to Pigou and was, instead, a malicious hoax. In *The Fourth Man*, Andrew Boyle (1979, 22) noted that 'Soviet agents in British Establishment guises would be the last people to leave diaries or other incriminating notes lying around ...' Why would Pigou sign his diary? This is unusual behaviour for non-spies; why would Pigou sign a record of treacherous activities? The signature contradicts *The British Connection* in which a spy supposedly told 'Deacon' McCormick (1979, 64): 'I do not think that he [Pigou] could ever have been prosecuted. You see, it was all in his head.'

In September 1984, Hayek spent several days in Cambridge for the MPS fortieth celebration of *The Road to Serfdom*. Pigou (1944, 219), presumably at Keynes' request, reviewed *The Road to Serfdom* in the *Economic Journal*: 'whether we agree with Professor Hayek or not, few who read through this earnest and admirably written plea will fail to be interested and stimulated by his treatment of it, and fewer still will close the book without a feeling of respect for and sympathy with the author.'

Hayek was *not* dropped by Pigou—diary entries such as 4.30 Pigou Tea (1 November 1934)[53] were followed by See Pigou (18 May 1945) and Tea and Pigou lecture (13 May 1949).[54] Pigou (7 July 1944) wrote to Hayek, from his mountain climbing home in the Lake District, informing him that 'his section' had proposed Hayek's elevation as Fellow of the British Academy (F.B.A): 'Congratulations! ... you ought to have belonged to it years ago.'[55] This, too, became a poignant memory for Hayek (24 January 1982) who recalled that five years later (autumn 1949) he had been offered the position of Secretary of the British Academy: a 'great' honour which he probably would have 'jumped on' had he not had to keep his divorce plans secret from his first family. Later, he rather regretted not having taken the honour because it would have finally 'naturalised' him.[56]

While in Cambridge in 1984, Hayek could also have made inquiries about, or better still, obtained a copy of Pigou's will, which stated that the 'remainder of the contents of my rooms at Cambridge at the time of my death ... [are] to be used or disposed of in such a manner as the said Provost and Scholars [of King's College] may direct.'[57] If Pigou had kept a diary, it seems likely that it would have been destroyed shortly after his death. The probability that 'Deacon' McCormick was able to obtain the 1905 diary seems—from a non-Austrian perspective—to be arbitrarily close to zero. Hayek told his third appointed biographer that 'Deacon' McCormick 'may be sometime [*sic*] making things up'—but promoted the fraud anyway (cited by Leeson 2013, 195).

Walter Monckton (1891–1965) 'converted' Churchill to 'black propaganda' and served thrice as Director General: of the Press and Censorship Bureau (1939), the Ministry of Information (1940) and British Propaganda and Information Service in Egypt (1942–1945) (Montgomery Hyde 1991, 110). He (and his male descendants) were rewarded in perpetuity (Viscount Monckton of Brenchley). In July 1941, he was 'sent on a propaganda mission to the Soviet Union in an effort to smooth relations between the two mutually suspicious and hostile allies' (Axelrod 2007, 570). Conveniently dead, Monckton must have been considered as a candidate for exposure as a Soviet agent in 'Deacon' McCormick's (1979) fraud-based *The British Connection Russia's Manipulation of British Individuals and Institutions*.

Warren Nutter (15 July 1961) confided to Friedman that 'the obvious danger' of creating a political 'rallying point' for 'free' market ideologues 'is that of slipping from scholarship to propaganda' (cited by MacLean 2017, 95). According to Hayek (1978a), 'Government work corrupts. I have observed in some of my best friends, who as a result of the war got tied up in government work, and they've ever since been statesmen rather than scholars.'[58] Caldwell (2010b, 2) reports that in 1939, the British Ministry of Information 'failed to ask for his assistance. Instead of working for the government as a propagandist, Hayek would begin writing' *The Road to Serfdom*. In that brilliant piece of propaganda, Hayek (2007 [1944], v) protested:

> When a professional student of social affairs writes a political book, his first duty is plainly to say so. This is a political book ... But, whatever the name, the essential point remains that all I shall have to say is derived from certain ultimate values. I hope I have adequately discharged in the book itself a second and no less important duty: to make it clear beyond doubt what these ultimate values are on which the whole argument depends. There is, however, one thing I would like to add to this. Though this is a political book, I am as certain as anybody can be that the beliefs set out in it are not determined by my personal interests.

In for posthumous consumption oral history interviews, Hayek explained what these 'ultimate values' were: fraud. *The Road to Serfdom* (1944), he explained, had been written for personal interests: to allow the 'old aristocracy' to resume their ascribed status and to drive the 'new aristocracy'—labour trade unionists and elected politicians—back down the road back to serfdom (Leeson 2015, Chapter 3).

The 'Great' War undermined European dynastic intergenerational entitlement programmes. The Habsburg-born, Austrian–educated Koestler (1950, 19) described some of the affected: 'Those who refused to admit that they had become déclassé, who clung to the empty shell of gentility, joined the Nazis and found comfort in blaming their fate on Versailles and the Jews. Many did not even have that consolation; they lived on pointlessly, like a great black swarm of tired winter flies crawling over the dim windows of Europe, members of a class displaced by history.'

As *The Wall Street Journal* reported: 'In Tough Times, Religion Can Offer a Sturdy Shelter Many recent studies have shown that religious observance can strengthen resilience to stress and illness' (Konner 2017). Together with two other malevolently mentally ill individuals—Rand and Rothbard—'von' Hayek and 'von' Mises fabricated the 'free' market religion: it remains a magnet for homosexuals seeking to be free of legal and social discrimination and theocrats who seek to publically stone them to death.

According to a fair-mined observer (who observed Hayek and his disciples at close quarters) the Austrian School of Economics is a cult:

> There was a great difference in focus between Hayek (the Austrians) and Chicago as a whole. I really respect and revere those guys. I am not one of them, but I think I once said that if somebody wants to approach economics as a religion, the Austrian approach is about as good as you can get. They approach it from the angle of philosophy: They derived the principles of free market economics from what they saw as 'the nature of man' and other fundamental principles. (Harberger 1999)

At University of Chicago, 'most of us' read Hayek's (1944) *The Road to Serfdom*,

> without necessarily becoming religious fanatics on the subject, I think most people were on the side of that message … if we became convinced of the virtues of market economics, it was by studying the functioning of market economics rather than by becoming co-religionists, so to speak. (Harberger 2016)

Harberger is a 'somewhat reluctant' MPS member 'because I'm not as doctrinaire as those guys. I do look at economics in a more instrumental way rather than an ideological way ... let's say there was a big tent with a bunch of very narrow churches inside. [laughter]'

In the interest of social mobility, David Brooks (2017) queried the 'pediacracy' by which 'upper-middle-class Americans' have 'put cultivating successful children at the center of life.' Hayek promoted what Kevin Phillips (1974), the co-author of Richard Nixon's 1968 'southern strategy,' described as 'mediacracy'—whereby the mass media have effective control over the voting public and thus political outcomes. Hayek (1978a) needed 'intellectuals, by which I don't mean the original thinkers but what I once called the secondhand dealers in ideas.[59] That I cannot reach the public I am fully aware. I need these intermediaries.'[60]

Nobel Prizes create a non-hereditary nobility—but should the 1974 Nobel Prize for Economic Science have been awarded to a secular-religion-promoting fraud whose 'children's' academic entitlements are assisting the process of re-feudalisation? Should the oil-, coal- and tobacco-funded Professors and think tank 'Fellows' who promote this religion be accorded policy 'expert' status? Should this religion be taught in economics departments? Markets—and the framework and full-cost pricing (Pigouvian externality taxes) within which they can provide the socially optimal result—require a more thorough and dispassionate examination than 'free' market advocates are either willing or able to provide.

Notes

1. Statement by the LSE Director, 13 March 1950. Hayek Archives Box 35.13.
2. Friedrich Hayek, interviewed by Robert Chitester date unspecified 1978 (Centre for Oral History Research, University of California, Los Angeles, http://oralhistory.library.ucla.edu/).
3. Hayek Archives Box 45.21. Correspondence 28 January 1985.
4. Statement by the LSE Director 13 March 1950. Hayek Archives Box 35.13.
5. 'When I finally achieved it [*Privatdozent*], what I got from student fees just served to pay my taxi, which I had to take once a week from my office to give a lecture at the university. That's all I got from the university.' Friedrich Hayek, interviewed by Earlene Craver date unspecified 1978 (Centre for Oral History Research, University of California, Los Angeles, http://oralhistory.library.ucla.edu/).

6. The previous holders were James Thorold Rogers (1859–1890), Francis Ysidro Edgeworth (1890–1891), William Cunningham (1891–1897), William Albert Samuel Hewins (1897–1904), Charles Stewart Loch (1904–1908) and Edmund John Urwick (1908–1919). After a post-Phillips abeyance, the chair was held by Denis Sargan, Tony Atkinson and Peter Robinson.
7. Friedrich Hayek, interviewed by Jack High date unspecified 1978 (Centre for Oral History Research, University of California, Los Angeles, http://oralhistory.library.ucla.edu/).
8. Friedrich Hayek, interviewed by Robert Bork 4 November 1978 (Centre for Oral History Research, University of California, Los Angeles, http://oralhistory.library.ucla.edu/).
9. Friedrich Hayek, interviewed by Robert Chitester date unspecified 1978 (Centre for Oral History Research, University of California, Los Angeles, http://oralhistory.library.ucla.edu/).
10. Gregory joined the Reform in 1932. I am grateful to Simon Blundell, Reform Club Librarian, for this information.
11. Hayek Archives Boxes 120.3 and 126.1.
12. On 6 December 2007, the Attorney General of Germany nullified the verdict and posthumously pardoned van der Lubbe.
13. http://www.margaretthatcher.org/speeches/displaydocument.asp?docid=104175.
14. Friedrich Hayek, interviewed by Robert Chitester date unspecified 1978 (Centre for Oral History Research, University of California, Los Angeles, http://oralhistory.library.ucla.edu/).
15. https://www.margaretthatcher.org/document/114511.
16. On the same day, Mrs. Thatcher's engagement diary records a 9 a.m. meeting with Laurens van der Post, who spent three and a half years in a Japanese prisoner-of-war camp with Hayek's successor as Tooke Professor, A. W. H. Phillips (Leeson 1994).
17. Hayek Papers Box 93.15.
18. http://www.margaretthatcher.org/speeches/displaydocument.asp?docid=104175.
19. http://www.nobelprize.org/nobel_prizes/peace/laureates/1959/noel-baker-bio.html.
20. 'Deacon' McCormick's third wife was Eileen Dee Challinor James.
21. 'Serious Theft.' *Brisbane Courier*, 19 September 1930. http://trove.nla.gov.au/ndp/del/article/21584668.
22. Hayek Archives Box 101.26.
23. Harris to Hayek 28 March 1968. Hayek Archives Box 74.30.
24. Hayek Archives Box 74.30.
25. Hayek Archives Box 107.2.
26. Hayek Archives Box 45.21.

27. Hayek Archives Box 18.26.
28. Popper (21 June 1984) to Hayek. Popper had been made a Companion of Honour in 1982. Hayek Archives Box 44.2.
29. This Order consists of the sovereign, plus no more than 65 Companions. Membership of the Order became spontaneously available on the death of an existing companion.
30. Hayek Archives Box 101.29.
31. Hayek Archives Box 107.2.
32. Conversation with Leube, 27 June 2009.
33. Friedrich Hayek, interviewed by Robert Chitester date unspecified 1978 (Centre for Oral History Research, University of California, Los Angeles, http://oralhistory.library.ucla.edu/).
34. Friedrich Hayek, interviewed by James Buchanan 28 October 1978 (Centre for Oral History Research, University of California, Los Angeles, http://oralhistory.library.ucla.edu/).
35. Friedrich Hayek, interviewed by Robert Chitester date unspecified 1978 (Centre for Oral History Research, University of California, Los Angeles, http://oralhistory.library.ucla.edu/).
36. Hayek Archives Box 89.9.
37. Friedrich Hayek, interviewed by Earlene Craver date unspecified 1978 (Centre for Oral History Research, University of California, Los Angeles, http://oralhistory.library.ucla.edu/).
38. 'Deacon' McCormick Archives. Sayer Collection. British Connection file.
39. Mummery was killed in 1895 attempting to climb the Himalayan mountain, Nanga Parbat. In *The General Theory*, Mummery was allocated the role of soldier in the 'brave army of heretics,' a courageous fighter 'against the ranks of orthodoxy' who had 'a sublime disregard for intellectual authority,' and who regarded excess saving as responsible for the under employment of capital and labour in recessions. According to Keynes (1936, 365, 369, 371), Mummery and Hobson, were 'aware that interest was nothing whatever except payment for the use of money.' Keynes (29 July 1935)—who was 'normally buoyant' (Kahn 1974, 369)—wrote to Kahn in a mood of semi-despair about the 'very angry' draft of his book which had alienated most of those who had seen it. Kahn acted immediately. The following day Keynes' spirits were revived, writing to Kahn: 'Thanks very much for taking so much trouble about the Mummery ... *The Physiology of Industry* is a wonderful book' (JMK, XIII, 634).
40. Pigou discussed both the 'Marshallian dictatorship' and economic reform in mountaineering terms. The struggle against 'evils too plain to be ignored' was difficult; but 'difficulties, which deter the weak, are a spur and stimulus to the strong. To display them, not to conceal them, is the way to win worthy recruits. Neither by the timidity that waits at a

distance, nor by the wild rush of undisciplined ardour is the summit of great mountains attained. First we must understand our task and prepare for it; and then, in the glow of sunrise, *by united effort* (emphasis added), we shall at last, perhaps, achieve' (1912, 488). Academic economists often suffered the same fate as bookish mountaineering texts: 'unintended comedy' (1935, 12); but *The General Theory* was a 'new way of tackling an unclimbed mountain'; an intellectual difficulty was a 'lion in the path,' to be looked boldly in the eye (1950, 62, 64).

41. Kaldor, Kahn, Joan Robinson and Piero Sraffa had regular Sunday walks from Cambridge to Granchester which became part of 'university folklore.' They also shared summer holidays in the Alps or in the Scandinavian mountains and formed a 'war circus' or 'secret seminar' (Targetti 1992, 13). All also walked or climbed with Pigou in the Lake District. On one occasion, Kaldor ate Pigou's entire weekly butter ration over tea; Sraffa had to save up his marmalade ration to provide compensation (Thirlwall 1987, 78).
42. Hayek Archives Box 11.30.
43. Hayek Archives Box 123.7.
44. Hayek Archives Box 48.13.
45. Hayek Archives Box 10.19.
46. Hayek Archives Box 17.37.
47. Hayek Archives Box 46.30.
48. 'Deacon' McCormick Archives. Sayer Collection. British Connection file. The first British patent for the ballpoint pen was filed on 15 June 1938.
49. Hayek Archives Box 123.7.
50. In *The Sunday Times* in 1977, Trevor-Roper reviewed Irving's book—stating that 'no praise can be too high for his [Irving's] indefatigable, scholarly industry.' Trevor-Roper added that Irving 'seizes on a small, but dubious particle of "evidence"; builds upon it, by private interpretation, a large general conclusion; and then overlooks or re-interprets the more substantial evidence and probability against it. Since this defective method is invariably used to excuse Hitler or the Nazis and to damage their opponents, we may reasonably speak of a consistent bias, unconsciously distorting the evidence ... When a historian relies mainly on primary sources, which we cannot easily check, he challenges our confidence and forces us to ask critical questions. How reliable is his historical method? How sound is his judgment? We ask these questions particularly of a man like Mr. Irving, who makes a virtue of—almost a profession—of using arcane sources to affront established opinions ... He may read his manuscript diaries correctly. But we can never be quite sure, and when he is at most original, we are likely to be least sure' (cited by Evans 2002, 16, 46–47, 110).

51. 'Deacon' McCormick Archives. Sayer Collection. British Connection file.
52. 'Deacon' McCormick Archives. Sayer Collection. British Connection file.
53. Hayek Archives Box 121.7.
54. Hayek Archives Box 127.3.
55. Hayek Archives Box 8.9.
56. To Jacquetta Hawkes. Hayek Archives Box 44.8.
57. A copy of the will can be found in the 'Deacon' McCormick Archives. Sayer Collection. British Connection file.
58. Friedrich Hayek, interviewed by Robert Chitester date unspecified 1978 (Centre for Oral History Research, University of California, Los Angeles, http://oralhistory.library.ucla.edu/).
59. Friedrich Hayek, interviewed by Leo Rosten 15 November 1978 (Centre for Oral History Research, University of California, Los Angeles, http://oralhistory.library.ucla.edu/).
60. Friedrich Hayek, interviewed by Robert Chitester date unspecified 1978 (Centre for Oral History Research, University of California, Los Angeles, http://oralhistory.library.ucla.edu/).

REFERENCES

Archival Insights into the Evolution of Economics (and Related Projects)

Leeson, R. (1994, May). A.W.H. Phillips, M.B.E. (Military Division). *Economic Journal, 104*(424), 605–618.

Leeson, R. (Ed.). (2013). *Hayek: A Collaborative Biography Part I Influences from Mises to Bartley*. Basingstoke, UK: Palgrave Macmillan.

Leeson, R. (Ed.). (2015). *Hayek: A Collaborative Biography Part III Fraud, Fascism and Free Market Religion*. Basingstoke, UK: Palgrave Macmillan.

Leeson, R. (2017). *Hayek: A Collaborative Biography Part VII 'Market Free Play with an Audience': Hayek's Encounters with Fifty Knowledge Communities*. Basingstoke, UK: Palgrave Macmillan.

Weinberg, G. L. (2015). The Hitler Diary Fraud. In R. Leeson (Ed.), *Hayek: A Collaborative Biography Part III Fraud, Fascism and Free Market Religion*. Basingstoke, UK: Palgrave Macmillan.

Other References

Annan, N. (1991). *Our Age: The Generation That Made Post-war Britain*. London: Fontana.

Axelrod, A. (2007). *Encyclopedia of World War II* (Vol. 1). New York: Infobase.

Bauer, O. (1919). *Der Weg zum Sozialismus*. Vienna: Ignaz Brand.

Benn, T. (1996). *The Benn Diaries*. London: Arrow.

Beveridge, W. (1931). *Tariffs: The Case Examined.* London: Longmans, Green.
Blundell, J. (2008). *Margaret Thatcher: A Portrait of the Iron Lady.* New York: Algora.
Bostaph, S. (1989, Spring–Summer). Review of Hayek's The Fatal Conceit. *Austrian Economics Newsletter*, 13–16. https://mises.org/library/subjective-value-theory-and-government-intervention-labor-market-full-edition-vol-10-no-3.
Boyle, A. (1979). *The Fourth Man the Definitive Account of Kim Philby, Guy Burgess, and Who Recruited Them to Spy for Russia.* New York: Bantum.
Brooks, D. (2017, July 11). How We Are Ruining America. *New York Times.* https://www.nytimes.com/2017/07/11/opinion/how-we-are-ruining-america.html.
Buchanan, J. (1973). Prospects for America's Third Century. *Atlantic Economic Journal, 1,* 3–13. https://link.springer.com/article/10.1007/BF02299808.
Burlingham, R., & Billis, R. (2005). *Reformed Characters: The Reform Club in History and Literature.* London: Reform Club.
Caldwell, B. (1995). Editorial Notes. In B. Caldwell, (Ed.), *Contra Keynes and Cambridge. The Collected Works of F.A. Hayek.* Chicago: University of Chicago Press.
Caldwell, B. (2005, January). Interview: Hayek for the 21st Century. *Reason.* http://public.econ.duke.edu/~bjc18/Publications_Frameset.htm.
Caldwell, B. (2010a). The Secret Behind the Hot Sales of '*The Road to Serfdom*' by Free-Market Economist F.A. Hayek. *The Washington Post.* http://voices.washingtonpost.com/shortstack/2010/02/the_secret_behind_the_hot_sale.html.
Caldwell, B. (2010b). Introduction. In F. A. Hayek (Ed.), *Studies on the Abuse and Decline of Reason. Texts and Documents. The Collected Works of F.A. Hayek.* London: Routledge.
Costello, J. (1988). *The Mask of Treachery: Spies, Lies, Buggery and Betrayal: The First Documented Dossier on Anthony Blunt's Cambridge Spy Ring.* New York: William Morrow.
Cubitt, C. (2006). *A Life of August von Hayek.* Bedford, UK: Authors OnLine.
Dalton, H. (1986). *The Political Diaries of Hugh Dalton, 1918–1940, 1945–1960* (B. Pimlott, Ed.). London: Cape.
Dudley Edwards, R. (1995). *The Pursuit of Reason: The Economist 1843–1993.* London: Hamish Hamilton.
Duke of Edinburgh. (1978). Intellectual Dissent and the Reversal of Trends. In Chaloner, W. H. (Ed.) *The Coming Confrontation: Will the Open Society Survive to 1989?* London: Institute of Economic Affairs.
Ebenstein, A. (2003). *Friedrich Hayek: A Biography.* Chicago: University of Chicago Press.
Evans, R. J. (2002). *Telling Lies About Hitler: The Holocaust, History and the David Irving Trial.* London: Verso.
Forbes. (1989, May 15). Interview of F. A. Hayek. *Forbes.*

Friedman, M. F., & Friedman, R. D. (1998). *Two Lucky People: Memoirs*. Chicago: University of Chicago Press.
Galbraith, J. K. (1981). *A Life in Our Time*. Boston: Houghton Mifflin.
Giroux, S. S. (2010). *Between Race and Reason: Violence, Intellectual Responsibility, and the University to Come*. Stanford, CA: Stanford University Press.
Harberger, A. C. (1999, March). Interview with Arnold Harberger. An Interview with the Dean of the 'Chicago Boys.' *The Region*. The Federal Reserve Bank of Minneapolis. https://www.minneapolisfed.org/publications/the-region/interview-with-arnold-harberger.
Harberger, A. C. (2016). Sense and Economics: An Oral History with Arnold Harberger. Interviews Conducted by Paul Burnett in 2015 and 2016 Oral History Center. California: The Bancroft Library, University of California, Berkeley. http://digitalassets.lib.berkeley.edu/roho/ucb/text/harberger_arnold_2016.pdf.
Harris, R. (1986). *Selling Hitler*. London: Faber and Faber.
Hayek, F. A. (1933, May). The Trend of Economic Thinking. *Economica, 40*, 121–137.
Hayek, F. A. (1935). *Collectivist Economic Planning Critical Studies on the Possibilities of Socialism*. London: Routledge & Kegan Paul.
Hayek, F. A. (1944). *The Road to Serfdom*. London: Routledge.
Hayek, F. A. (1946, February). The London School of Economics 1895–1945. *Economica, XIII*, 1–31 (New Series).
Hayek, F. A. (1951). *John Stuart Mill and Harriet Taylor*. London: Routledge.
Hayek, F. A. (1952 [1926]). Hayek on Wieser. In H. W. Spiegel (Ed.), *The Development of Economic Thought*. New York: Wiley.
Hayek, F. A. (1960). *The Constitution of Liberty*. Chicago: University of Chicago Press.
Hayek, F. A. (1978a). *Oral History Interviews*. Los Angeles: Centre for Oral History Research, University of California. http://oralhistory.library.ucla.edu/.
Hayek, F. A. (1978b). *New Studies in Philosophy, Politics, Economics and the History of Ideas*. London: Routledge & Kegan Paul.
Hayek, F. A. (1978c). Will the Democratic Ideal Prevail? In W. H. Chaloner (Ed.), *The Coming Confrontation: Will the Open Society Survive to 1989?* (pp. 61–73). London: Institute of Economic Affairs.
Hayek, F. A. (1979, December 5). A Period of Muddle-Heads. *Newsweek*.
Hayek, F. A. (1988). *The Fatal Conceit: The Errors of Socialism. The Collected Works of F.A. Hayek* (W. W. Bartley III, Ed.). Chicago: University of Chicago Press.
Hayek, F. A. (1992). *The Fortunes of Liberalism Essays on Austrian Economics and the Ideal of Freedom. The Collected Works of F.A. Hayek* (P. Klein, Ed.). Chicago: University of Chicago Press.
Hayek, F. A. (1994). *Hayek on Hayek an Autobiographical Dialogue*. Supplement to *The Collected Works of F.A. Hayek* (S. Kresge & L. Wenar, Eds.). Chicago: University of Chicago Press.

Hayek, F. A. (1995). *Contra Keynes and Cambridge. The Collected Works of F.A. Hayek* (B. Caldwell, Ed.). Chicago: University of Chicago Press.
Hayek, F. A. (2007 [1944]). *The Road to Serfdom: The Definitive Edition. The Collected Works of F.A. Hayek* (B. Caldwell, Ed.). Chicago: University of Chicago Press.
Hayek, F. A. (2012). *Business Cycles Part II. The Collected Works of F.A. Hayek* (H. Klausinger, Ed.). Chicago: University of Chicago Press.
Howson, S. (2011). *Lionel Robbins*. Cambridge: Cambridge University Press.
Hunt, T. (2010, July 10). Hugh Trevor-Roper the Biography Review. *Daily Telegraph*. http://www.telegraph.co.uk/culture/books/bookreviews/7879092/Hugh-Trevor-Roper-the-Biography-review.html.
Johnson, H. G. (1960). A. C. Pigou 1877–1959. *Canadian Journal of Economics and Political Science, 26,* 150–155.
Jones, A.G. (1985). *Star Wars: Suicide or Survival?* London: Wei denfeld & Nicolson.
Kahn, R. F. (1974). On Re-reading Keynes. *Proceedings of the British Academy* (pp. 361–391).
Kahn, R. F. (1984). *The Making of Keynes' General Theory*. Cambridge: Cambridge University Press.
Keynes, J. M. (1921). *Treatise on Probability*. London: Macmillan.
Keynes, J. M. (1936). *The General Theory of Employment, Interest and Money*. London: Macmillan.
Koestler, A. (1950). Arthur Koestler. In R. Crossman (Ed.), *Communism: The God That Failed*. New York: Harper & Row.
Konner, M. (2017, July 1). In Tough Times, Religion Can Offer a Sturdy Shelter. *Wall Street Journal*. https://www.wsj.com/articles/in-tough-times-religion-can-offer-a-sturdy-shelter-1498829765.
Lamis, A. P. (1990). *The Two-Party South*. Oxford: Oxford University Press.
Leube, K. R. (2004, February 10). Friedrich A. Hayek: His Life and Work. Auditorio Friedrich A. Hayek, Universidad Francisco Marroquín, Guatemala. http://www.newmedia.ufm.edu/gsm/index.php/Leubehayek.
Liggio, L. (2010). A Classical Liberal Life. In W. Block (Ed.), *I Chose Liberty: Autobiographies of Contemporary Libertarians*. Auburn, AL: Ludwig von Mises Institute.
MacLean, N. (2017). *Democracy in Chains. The Deep History of the Radical Right's Stealth Plan for America*. New York: Viking/Penguin Random House.
McCormick, D. (1960). *The Wicked Village*. London: Jarrolds.
McCormick, D. (pseudonym: Deacon, R.) (1973). *The Master Book of Spies: The World of Espionage, Master Spies, Tortures, Interrogations, Spy Equipment, Escapes, Codes & How You Can Become a Spy*. London: Hodder Causton.
McCormick, D. (1976a). *Taken for a Ride: The History of Cons and Con-men*. London: Hardwood Smart.

McCormick, D. (1976b). *A Biography of William Caxton: The First English Editor, Printer, Merchant, and Translator.* London: Frederick Mueller.
McCormick, D. (pseudonym: Deacon, R.) (1979). *The British Connection Russia's Manipulation of British Individuals and Institutions.* London: Hamish Hamilton.
McCormick, D. (pseudonym: Deacon, R.) (1980a). *Approaching 1984.* London: David & Charles.
McCormick, D. (1980b). *Love in Code, or, How to Keep Your Secrets.* London: Eyre Metheun.
McCormick, D. (pseudonym: Deacon, R.) (1989). *Super Spy: The Man Who Infiltrated the Kremlin and the Gestapo.* London: Macdonald.
McCormick, D. (1993). *17F—The Life of Ian Fleming.* London: Peter Owen.
McLean, J. J. (1974). *Campbell-Bannerman: The New Imperialism and the Struggle for Leadership Within the Liberal Party, 1892–1906.* Ann Arbor, MI: University Microfilms International.
Menger, C. (1871). *Grundsätze der Volkswirtschaftslehre.* Wien: Erster allgemeiner Teil.
Mises, L. (1922). *Die Gemeinwirtschaft: Untersuchungen über den Sozialismus.* Jena: Gustav Fischer Verlag. http://docs.mises.de/Mises/Mises_Gemeinwirtschaft.pdf.
Mises, L. (1985 [1927]). *Liberalism in the Classical Tradition* (R. Raico, Trans.). Auburn, AL: Ludwig von Mises Institute.
Montgomery Hyde, H. (1991). *Walter Monckton.* London: Sinclair-Stevenson.
Mummery, A. F., & Hobson, J. A. (1889). *The Physiology of Industry: Being an Exposure of Certain Fallacies in Existing Theories of Economics.* London: John Murray.
Phillips, K. (1974). *Mediacracy: American Parties and Politics in the Communications Age.* New York: Doubleday.
Pigou, A. C. (1905). *Principles and Methods of Industrial Peace.* London: Macmillan.
Pigou, A. C. (1906). *Protective Preferential Import Duties.* London: Macmillan.
Pigou, A. C. (1912). *Wealth and Welfare.* London: Macmillan.
Pigou, A. C. (1921). Review of Keynes' *Treatise on Probability. Economic Journal, 31,* 507–512.
Pigou, A. C. (1935). *Economics in Practice: Six Lectures on Current Issues.* London: Macmillan.
Pigou, A. C. (1939). Presidential Address. *Economic Journal, XLIV*(194), 215–221.
Pigou, A. C. (1942). Night Life on High Hills. *Alpine Journal,* 246–255.
Pigou, A. C. (1944). Review *Road to Serfdom. Economic Journal, 54,* 217–219.
Pigou, A. C. (1950). *Keynes's 'General Theory': A Retrospective View.* London: Macmillan.

Plumptre, A. (1975). Maynard Keynes as a Teacher. In M. Keynes, (Ed.), *Essays on John Maynard Keynes*. Cambridge: Cambridge University Press.
Raico, R. (2014, October 16). Leonard Liggio, RIP. lewrockwell.com. https://www.lewrockwell.com/lrc-blog/515224/.
Robbins, L. (1971). *Autobiography of an Economist*. London: Macmillan.
Robinson, A. (1968). Arthur Cecil Pigou. *International Encyclopaedia of the Social Sciences, 12*. New York: Macmillan.
Robinson, J. (1962). *Economic Philosophy*. Chicago: Aldine.
Robinson, J. (1972). The Second Crisis of Economic Theory. *American Economic Review, 62*(1), 1–10.
Rothbard, M. N. (1992, January). Right-Wing Populism: A Strategy for the Paleo Movement. *Rothbard Rockwell Report*, 5–14. http://rothbard.altervista.org/articles/right-wing-populism.pdf.
Rothbard, M. N. (2010). *Strictly Confidential: The Private Volker Fund Memos of Murray N. Rothbard* (D. Gordon, Ed.). Auburn, AL: Ludwig von Mises Institute.
Saltmarsh, J., & Wilkinson, L. P. (1960). *Arthur Cecil Pigou 1877–1959. A Memoir Prepared by the Direction of the Council of King's College Cambridge*. Cambridge: University Press Printed for King's College.
Samuelson, P. A. (2009). A Few Remembrances of Friedrich von Hayek (1899–1992). *Journal of Economic Behavior and Organization, 69*, 1–4.
Sereny, G. (1985, May 9). The Sage of the Free Thinking World. *The Times*.
Stigler, G. J. (1988). *Memoirs of an Unregulated Economist*. New York: Basic Books.
Targetti, F. (1992). *Nicholas Kaldor: The Economics and Politics of Capitalism as a Dynamic System*. Oxford: Clarendon Press.
Taylor, A. J. P. (1979, July 22). Reds Under Beds. *Observer*.
Thirlwall, A. (1987). *Nicholas Kaldor*. Brighton: Wheatsheaf Press.
Titcomb, J. (2015, January 7). How the Bank of England Abandoned the Gold Standard. *Daily Telegraph*. http://www.telegraph.co.uk/finance/commodities/11330611/How-the-Bank-of-England-abandoned-the-gold-standard.html.
Trevor-Roper, H. (1947). *The Last Days of Hitler*. New York: Macmillan.
Trevor-Roper, H. (1976). *A Hidden Life: The Enigma of Sir Roger Backhouse*. London: Macmillan.
Woodbridge, G. (1978). *The Reform Club 1836–1978. A History from the Club's Records*. Privately Printed for Members of the Reform Club in Association with Clearwater Publishing Company, New York.
Young, H. (1989). *One of Us*. London: Macmillan.

PART II

Seeing the Utopian 'Theory of the Order as a Whole' to 'Make Politically Possible What Today may be Politically Impossible'

CHAPTER 5

Britain, White Supremacism and the 'International Right'

SUMMARY

Having declared that 'what we lack is a liberal Utopia,' 'von' Hayek insisted that 'It is not to be denied that to some extent the guiding model of the overall order will always be an utopia.' Certain personality types have 'instincts' that make them vulnerable to bogus Bilgewater 'Dukes,' Romanov 'Princesses' and Habsburg 'vons' and 'Counts'—an aristocratic placebo effect. In addition to the opinion editors of Rupert Murdoch's *Wall Street Journal*, climate change scepticism has been coordinated by four journalists: Sir Samuel Brittan (*The Financial Times*), Nigel, The Lord Lawson of Blaby PC (*The Financial Times, The Sunday Telegraph* and the *Spectator*), The 3rd Viscount Monckton (former editor of the Roman Catholic *The Universe*), The (zoology-trained) 5th Viscount Ridley (*The Times*); plus a 'think' tank activist, 'Dr.' Leon Louw, and economists who have been orchestrated by Murray Rothbard to chant 'We want externalities' and assert that externalities are a Soviet hoax. According to 'von' Mises, 'Fascist' had 'saved European civilization,' and 'von' Hayek sought to save the 'civilization' of Apartheid from the American 'fashion' of 'human rights.' Their 'free' market is promoted by frauds, paid sycophants, public stoning theocrats, white supremacists and those with blind faith in the assertions made by socially 'superior' fellow-travellers. According to the 'Charles Koch Distinguished Alumnus' and President of Hayek's Mont Pelerin Society, the 'institutional framework' determines 'what we can learn, how we will learn, and who will learn.' This chapter examines the links between 'free' market, the far-right and white supremacist regimes.

In 1923, the British *Fascisti* was founded by Rotha Lintorn-Orman and Leopold Ernest Stratford George Canning (4th Baron Garvagh): members included three Brigadier-Generals (Sir Ormonde de l'Épée Winter, Julian Tindale-Biscoe and Roland Erskine-Tulloch), two Admirals (Sir Edmund Robert Fremantle and Sir Reginald Godfrey Otway Tupper), a Rear-Admiral (William Ernest Russell Martin), two Major-Generals (James Spens and Thomas David Pilcher), and two Lieutenant Colonels (Daniel Burges and Edward Southwell Russell, 26th Baron de Clifford). Aristocratic members included Dorothy, Viscountess Downe, Lady Sydenham of Combe, Baroness Zouche, Nesta Webster, George William James Chandos Brudenell-Bruce (6th Marquess of Ailesbury), Algernon William Stephen Temple-Gore-Langton (5th Earl Temple of Stowe), Sir Michael William Selby Bruce (11th Baronet) and Sir Arthur Henry Hardinge.

The British *Fascisti* was an 'extreme right-wing group with a disproportionate number of generals and admirals, and dedicated to unrelenting struggle against the powers of evil represented by bolshevism' (Skidelsky 1975, 291). Four Conservative MPs were also British *Fascisti* members: Colonel Sir Charles Rosdew Forbes-Leith, 1st Baronet (Torquay 1910–1923), Sir Patrick Joseph Henry Hannon (Birmingham Moseley 1921–1950), Lord Ernest Hamilton (North Tyrone 1895–1892) and John Baker White (Canterbury 1945–1953). Other members included the manager and captain of the English national cricket team, Sir Frederick Charles Toone and Arthur Edward Robert Gilligan (Benewick 1969; Griffiths 1983; Thurlow 2006; Pugh 2005; Dorril 2006). In 1975, Gilligan became a founder member of the National Association for Freedom (NAFF) while White became NAFF Chair in Kent. Just before the 1979 British General Election, Hayek and John Tyndall attended a Reform Club Political Committee Dinner (26 April 1979),[1] and the following year, John Tyndall organised one of Hayek's lectures.[2]

According to *Fascism in Britain: From Oswald Mosley's Blackshirts to the National Front*, after John Tyndall had been sentenced to six months prison for making explosives (the 'weedkiller' label had been replaced by 'Jew killer'), some of his associates went underground, naming themselves Column 88, after the post-1934 Austrian Nazi group (Thurlow 2006, 237). Research, however—which Hayek, Ebeling, Skousen, Soref, et al. failed to undertake with respect to the transparently fraudulent assertion that the founder of the market failure school, Pigou, was one of Stalin's agents—reveals that the second John Tyndall was associated with

NAFF, and not, apparently, the National Front, British National Party and League of Empire Loyalists.

After his Nobel Prize, Hayek was relentlessly promoted by *The Daily Telegraph*, *The Sunday Telegraph* and the London *Times*, under the editorship of the Roman Catholic William Rees-Mogg (1967–1981) and the Old Etonian, Charles Douglas-Hume (1982–1985), and especially under Murdoch's ownership (1981–). The *Times* had earlier (1912–1919, 1923–1941) been edited by the Old Etonian, Geoffrey Dawson (1874–1944)—appointed by the paper's owner, Lord Northcliffe. After Northcliffe's death, Dawson returned as editor under the ownership of John Jacob Astor V (of the 'Cliveden set'). Dawson, a member of the Anglo-German Fellowship, used his editorship to support the Baldwin/Chamberlain Conservative Party governments (1936–1940) and their policy of appeasing Hitler—any mention of Nazi anti-Semitism was prohibited. Three months before Hitler came to power, *The Times* published a letter from four LSE economics, Gregory, 'von' Hayek, Plant and Robbins (1932), insisting that Britain follow the same austerity policies that had intensified the Great Depression in Germany.

Hayek (1992a [1963], 29–30) described his LSE colleagues, Edwin Cannan and Gregory, as Mises' 'kindred spirits.' Before Hayek (1978a) arrived in 1931, the LSE 'was half-Austrian already. [laughter]'[3] What was the missing half?

According to Mises (1993 [1964], 36), Cannan (1861–1935) was 'the *last* [emphasis added] in the long line of eminent British economists.' The crucial distinction between *Edwin Cannan: Liberal Doyen* (Ebenstein 1997) and *Mises: The Last Knight of Liberalism* (Hülsmann 2007, 677, n149) is that only one was a card-carrying Fascist (and member of the official Fascist social club) and only one promoted Fascist violence to achieve Austrian School ends. According to Mises (1985 [1927], 47–48), a business sector lobbyist: 'The militaristic and nationalistic enemies of the Third International felt themselves cheated by liberalism' because of the exclusion of 'murder and assassination from the list of measures to be resorted to in political struggles.'

According to Mises (1985 [1927], 49, 51): 'It cannot be denied that Fascism and similar movements aiming at the establishment of dictatorships are full of the best intentions and that their intervention has, for the moment, saved European civilization. The merit that Fascism has thereby won for itself will live on eternally in history.' A generation later,

Hayek's (1973, 3) *Law, Legislation and Liberty* asserted: 'It can hardly be denied that, since this type of democracy has come to be accepted, we have been moving away from that ideal of individual liberty of which it had been regarded as the surest safeguard, and are now drifting towards a system which nobody wanted. Signs are not wanting, however, that unlimited democracy is riding for a fall and that it will go down, not with a bang, but with a whimper.'

According to Hayek (1973, 3): 'It is already becoming clear that many of the expectations that have been raised can be met only by taking the powers out of the hands of democratic assemblies and entrusting them to the established coalitions of organized interests and their hired experts.' A few weeks before the announcement of his Nobel Prize, Hayek told Seigen Tanaka (1974):

> It may be said that effective and rational economic policies can be implemented only by a superior leader of the philosopher-statesman type under powerful autocracy. And I do not mean a communist-dictatorship but rather a powerful regime following democratic principles.

Hayek was determined that Operation Condor dictators—who administered crony-based coalitions of organised interests with 'experts' hired from the business elite (Filip 2018)—would not feel 'cheated' just because they led bloodthirsty Juntas that fitted Mises' (1985 [1927]) definition of 'Fascism.' Moreover, in protecting 'property,' 'Fascists' protected the intellectual foundations and the defining qualification of liberty-promoters: 'experience of the working of the economic system which the administration of property gives' (Hayek 1997 [1949], 224).

In the 1932 German elections, who else but Hitler could Hayek and Mises supported (Leeson 2018a)? In 1934, Soref–Hayek's fellow Reform Club member and fellow 'Deacon' McCormick promoter and later Conservative Monday Club M.P. (Ormskirk 1970–1974)—was a standard bearer at the British Union of Fascists Olympia rally. Five years previously—and the year after Cannan's (1928) deflation-promoting *An Economist's Protest*—Hayek (1995 [1929], 68)—while praising Cannan's 'fanatical conceptual clarity' and his 'kinship' with Mises' 'crusade'— noted that he and the British-Austrians had failed to realise the necessary next step: 'Cannan by no means develops *economic* liberalism to its *ultimate* [emphases added] consequences with the same ruthless consistency as Mises.' According to Caldwell (1995, 70, n. 67), this was an apparent reference to *Liberalism in the Classical Tradition*, in which Mises (1985 [1927], 19, 51) stated:

> The program of [Austrian] liberalism, therefore, if condensed into a single word, would have to read: *property* [Mises' emphasis] ... All the other demands of liberalism result from this fundamental demand ... The victory of Fascism in a number of countries is only an episode in the long series of struggles over the problem of property.

Mises' aspired to provide intellectual leadership:

> The great danger threatening domestic policy from the side of Fascism lies in its *complete* faith in the decisive power of violence. In order to assure success, one must be imbued with the will to victory and always proceed violently. This is its highest principle ... The suppression of all opposition by sheer violence is a most unsuitable way to win adherents to one's cause. Resort to naked force—that is, without justification in terms of *intellectual arguments accepted by public opinion*—merely gains new friends for those whom one is thereby trying to combat. In a battle between force and an idea, the latter always prevails. (emphases added)[4]

Hayek (1978a)

> just learned he [Mises] was usually right in his conclusions, but I was not completely satisfied with his argument. That, I think, followed me right through my life. I was always influenced by Mises's answers, but not fully satisfied by his arguments. It became very largely an attempt to improve the argument, which I realized led to correct conclusions. But the question of why it hadn't persuaded most other people became important to me; so I became anxious to put it in a more effective form.[5]

The Reformation created a competition for Princes and public opinion—the astronomer, Giordano Bruno (1548–1600), concluded that the universe could have no celestial body at its 'center' was tried for heresy by the Roman Inquisition and burned at stake. The absolutist Charles de Ganahl Koch (1935–) has ruled over his section of the 'free' market almost as long as the absolutist Sun King, Louis XIV, ruled over Roman Catholic France (1643–1715).

Hayek (1978a) told Thomas Hazlett: 'I'm sure you can't operate any other way. You have to persuade the intellectuals, because they are the makers of public opinion. It's not the people who really understand things; it's the people who pick up what is fashionable opinion. You have to make the fashionable opinion among the intellectuals before journalism and the schools and so on will spread it among the people at large.'[6] In 2016, the Charles Koch Foundation provided $10 million for the GMU Law School to be renamed the 'Antonin Scalia Law School' and to fund the 'F.A. Hayek Law, Legislation, and Liberty Scholarship.'[7] When Justice Scalia (1936–2016) died, Senate Republicans insisted that they would not consider any Supreme Court nominee put forth by President Barack Obama. On 16 March 2016, Merrick Garland was formally nominated to the vacant post of Associate Justice on the Supreme Court—but for the remaining 293 days of Obama's presidency, Senate Republicans refused to allow him to be considered.

Some 'free' market advocates are public stoning theocrats, while others want to end the separation of Church and State. The *Catholic Herald* celebrated Trump's 2017 nomination for the Supreme Court: Neil 'Gorsuch is good news for religious and social conservatives - and for those who value the separation of powers.'[8] But according to *The Wall Street Journal's* William McGurn, there is no genuine separation of powers. After Gigot stated: 'if you want any Supreme Court justice by Donald Trump approved, nominee approved you really have to do it this year,' McGurn replied:

> Shouting Merrick Garland, and so forth. It's especially important for Republicans because the court, and especially the Supreme Court, that's a Democratic legislature. That's where they go because they can't get votes in state legislatures and so forth. It's very important to get jurors who are Constitutionalists and not people who want to make up the law and institute it.[9]

Senator Joe McCarthy's 'first important blow' against supposed communists in the US State Department was reported the following day in only two newspapers—one of which was the *Chicago Tribune* (Buckley and Bozell 1954, 160, n. 50–51). The *Tribune* produced what Herbert Simon (1991, 121) regarded as a 'thick stream of bile' in its battle to save what it regarded as the American way of life against the New Deal. According to Rexford Tugwell (1972, 169), the *Tribune* continued to print stories that were 'straight Hoover. It might have been culled from the Memoirs.' The *Tribune* fanned anti-communist flames, and the Illinois State Senate established a committee to investigate subversive influences in the educational system (Schlesinger 1960, 88, 94, 529, 604, 607; Stigler 1988, 157; Ickes 1953, 368, 376).

McCarthy received financial backing from the *Tribune's* publisher, Colonel Robert McCormick (Revere 1959, 115). According to the *Chicago Tribune's* John Kass (2017), during her confirmation hearings for the US Court of Appeals for the Seventh Circuit, Amy Coney Barrett was asked in effect:

> Are you now, or have you ever been, a Christian? 'Do you consider yourself an orthodox Catholic?' cooed [Dick] Durbin in that oily voice of his. It got worse with [Diane] Feinstein. 'When you read your speeches, the conclusion one draws is that the dogma lives loudly within you,' said Feinstein, the ranking Democrat on the Judiciary Committee. 'And that's of concern when you come to big issues that large numbers of people have fought for for years in this country' ... This is about abortion.

After Barrett was placed on Trump's short list for the US Supreme Court, *Wall Street Journal* editor, Gigot (25 November 2017), reflected about Durbin: 'That was a stunning question at a confirmation hearing. And basically said, if you are too Orthodox in your religious belief, maybe you don't have the ability to serve on the nation's highest court.'

Addressing *The Wall Street Journal's* deputy editor, Dan Henninger, Gigot (5 May 2012), stated: 'Dan, we'll put it on the table, we are all Catholics here, grew up with Catholic social teaching'; to which Henninger replied: 'Right.'[10] At a Catholic University of America conference on 'Good Profit,' sponsored by the university's Busch School of Business and Economics (and the Napa Institute), chairman and co-founder, Timothy Busch, told Charles Koch that he was 'the refounder of America' (Roberts 2017). McGurn (2017) appeared to salivate in his *Wall Street Journal* op-ed piece on 'The Morality of Charles Koch'—the $10 million gift to the Busch School of Business and Economics was a reward for its 'ethics.'

According to the author of *Selling Hitler*, Rupert Murdoch 'ruled his Empire in a manner not dissimilar to that which Hitler employed to run the Third Reich' (Harris 1986, 263). Murdoch journalists suffer from what is described as 'PMT - Pre Murdoch Tension': the certainty that *someone* will be fired during the course of a Murdoch visit. During the 2016 Presidential election, *The Wall Street Journal's* editorial features editor, Mark Lasswell, was sent on leave (and then sacked) after 'Gigot blocked Lasswell from publishing op-eds critical of Trump's business practices and which raised questions about his alleged ties to Mafia figures.' There has been a 'shift, also, at the highest levels of the organization, as the paper's owner Rupert Murdoch went from Trump sceptic to ally over the course of the election.' McGurn was one of the 'Trump-sympathetic writers' (Gray 2017).

Mises rectified his Austro-Fascist membership and the Hayek's Nazi memberships—has *The Wall Street Journal* ever published any adverse evidence about either 'free' market hero? Why has virtually all the evidence that might have impaired fund-raising has been suppressed until the publication of *Archival Insights into the Evolution of Economics*?

Doherty's (2007) sympathetic *Radicals for Capitalism* reported a dissenter: 'It could seem almost comic, this sudden injection of enormous wealth into a small movement, this bizarre gravitational shifting as Planet Koch adjusted everyone's orbits.'[11] And *Enemy of the State* reflected on those who 'follow the mood and movements of their benefactor like flowers in the field, their faces turned towards the sun' (Raimondo 2000, 239). In 'Hayek's Epistemic Liberalism,' the 'Charles Koch Distinguished Alumnus, The Institute for Humane Studies' explained:

> Economic actors in the private sector as well as the public sector face a *knowledge problem* [emphasis in original], and the *institutional framework* [emphasis added] in each respective arena of social interaction provides answers to what we can learn, how we will learn, and who will learn. (Boettke 2017)

After the Nazis came to power, Stalin flip-flopped and encouraged a Popular Front; as—from the safety of neutral Manhattan—did Mises (2009 [1978 (1940)], 118):

> Leaders of the Social Democratic Party who had fled to London, Paris, and Prague now openly refused any support of Austria in her fight against Hitler. They felt there was no difference between Austrian 'fascism' and that of the Nazis, and that it was not the charge of the western democracies to interfere in the struggle between the two fascist groups.

In the January 1932 Preface to the second German edition of *Socialism*, Mises (1951 [1932], 17, 24) stated:

The incompatible success of Marxism is due to the prospect it offers of fulfilling those dream-aspirations and dreams of *vengeance* which have been so deeply embedded in human soul from time immemorial. It promises a Paradise on earth, a land of Hearts' Desire full of happiness and enjoyment, and - sweeter still to the loser's in life's game - *humiliation of all who are stronger and better than the multitude* [emphases added]. Logic and reasoning, which might show the absurdity of such dreams of bliss and revenge, are to be thrust aside ... I know only too well how hopeless it seems to convince impassioned supporters of the Socialistic Idea by logical demonstration that their views are preposterous and absurd. I know only too well that they do not want to hear, to see, or above all to think, and that they are open to no argument.[12]

What does the 'free' market sound like? Hayek (1975) told an American Enterprise Institute audience that his opponents (in this instance, Keynesians) had 'forfeited their right to be heard.' Two years earlier, Pinochet decided that his opponents (those promoting socialist measures for redistribution) had also forfeited their right to be heard: 3197 Chileans were murdered, 20,000 were officially exiled and their passport was marked with an 'L' and about 180,000 fled into exile (Montes 2015, 7; Wright and Oñate 2005). Hayek was contemptuous of what he dismissed as Amnesty International's 'bunch of leftists' who provided evidence about the Junta's human rights abuses (Farrant and McPhail 2017).

Fifty years after Mises' (1985 [1927]) *Liberalism in the Classical Tradition*, Hayek (2013 [1979], 483) sent his 'Model Constitution' to Pinochet: 'A constitution like the one here proposed would of course make all socialist measures for redistribution impossible.' In Chile, Hayek (1981) also stated that

democracy needs 'a good cleaning' by strong governments ... when I refer to this dictatorial power, I am talking of a transitional period, solely. As a means of establishing a stable democracy and liberty, clean of impurities. This is the only way I can justify it - and recommend it.

Hayek's (1944) *Road to Serfdom* played an important but surreptitious—and possibly illegal—role in the Conservative Party's 1945 election propaganda (Shearmur 2006, 310). It also influences Churchill's 1945 'gestapo' election speeches (Lane 2013). According to *Fortune's* John Chamberlain (1982, 85), Mitch Davenport left *Fortune* to become speech-writer for the 1940 Republican Party Presidential candidate, Wendell Willkie: 'Mitch's intellectual romance with Willkie made a long and amusing story.' Aaron Director interrupted the Metropolitan Club lunch of a third *Fortune* journalist, John Davenport (1981, 3), to ask whether he would ask Willkie (1892–1944), the prospective 1944 Republican Party Presidential candidate, to write the Foreword to *The Road to Serfdom* (1944). In 1940, Willkie had won 10 states to President Roosevelt's 38—thus out-performing Hoover (1932) and Alf Landon (1936); Willkie's popular vote (22,348,480) set a then-record for the Republican Party. But in 1944, Wendell Willkie was too busy, and Director 'ran into' Chamberlain (1982, 125; 1944) 'on the street' and invited him to write the Foreword to the American Edition—which he did.

In a 1986 preliminary report on his History of the MPS, R. M. Hartwell reported that 7% of members were politicians, 2% were government officials and 25% were businessmen.[13] Hayek told the 1959 MPS meeting that they had recruited men of 'action.' In addition to exerting influence in Italy (via President Luigi Einaudi, 1948–1955), Germany (via Chancellor Ludwig Erhard, 1963–1966) and France (via the economic adviser, Jacques Rueff), 'our representative' sat on Eisenhower's Council of Economic Advisers—presumably a reference to Karl Brandt (CEA 1958–1961), a founding Society member.[14]

MPS CEA Chairs have included Arthur Burns (1953–1956), Paul McCracken (1969–1971), Greenspan (1974–1970) and Beryl Sprinkel (1985–1989); several other members have served on the CEA. Other served elsewhere—including Secretary of State Shultz, President of the Czech Republic Václav Klaus, Sri Lankan Prime Minister Ranil Wickremasinghe, British Foreign Secretary Sir Geoffrey Howe, New Zealand Finance Minister Ruth Richardson, Antonio Martino, Silvio Berlusconi's Minister of Foreign Affairs (1994), Carlos Cáceres, Pinochet's Central Bank President (1982–1983), Finance Minister (1983–1984) and Minister of the Interior and Public Security (1988–1990) (Leeson 2018b).

Caldwell may have made for himself more than a million dollars in *Definitive Edition* royalties in a single month after the unrelenting promotion of Hayek's (2007 [1944]) *Road to Serfdom* by Murdoch's Fox News conspiracy theorist, Glenn Beck. As the 'free' market monopolist of the Hayek Archives and the fifth official (and 'definitive') biographer, Caldwell (2010a) then informed readers of *The Washington Post*: 'Hayek himself disdained having his ideas attached to either party.'

Wayne Brough, a GMU graduate and employee of FreedomWorks (a Koch Foundation offshoot) and 'Tea Party-friendly activist group,' told *The New York Times* his group's goal is to 'eventually fill Congress with Hayekians.' And Caldwell 'said he hoped that we were experiencing, partly through [Paul] Ryan's ascendancy' in the Republican Party, 'the first stage of a slow but steady embrace of Hayek's philosophy' (Davidson 2012).

Both the Hayek Archives and the public record reveal that Hayek was a party political operative—for the Conservative Party, the Republican Party and Franz-Josef Strauss' Christian Social Union—a coalition partner with the Christian Democratic Union. *The Daily Telegraph's* Peter Utley (13 January 1981), for example, thanked Hayek for agreeing to address the Conservative Party Research Department.[15] What else is revealed by Hayek's for-posthumous-consumption oral history interviews that Austrians are suppressing (Leeson 2015, Chapter 2)? Or the Hitler postcards with which the Hayek family communicated and which have, apparently, been stolen from Hayek's Archives and sold on the 'free' market?[16]

On 11 February 1975, Margaret Thatcher became Opposition Leader. In summer 1975, John Ranelagh (1992, ix) (and Michael Jones) prepared a paper on the occasion of her 'only visit' to the Conservative Research Department. Interrupting the presentation, she

> reached into her briefcase and took out a book. It was Friedrich von Hayek's *Constitution of Liberty* ... she held the book up for all of us to see. 'This' she said sternly, 'is what we believe' and banged Hayek down on the table.

In 'A Period of Muddle-Heads,' Hayek (1979) told *Newsweek* readers that he had 'no doubt' that Thatcher's 'ideas are right.'[17]

Hayek (1992b [1977]) described the MPS achievement: a 'consistent doctrine and some international circles of communication.' In 'An Intellectual History' of GMU Law, School Dean, Henry Manne (1993), explained that the 'entire curriculum is permeated with a distinctive intellectual flavor, emphasized and developed by almost every professor. Without this consistent approach by almost an entire faculty, it would not be possible to develop the depth and sophistication of learning that characterizes George Mason.' But referring to the Austrian revival, Hayek told Ebeling (1975): 'you never know why the truth is ultimately recognized, but to me it seems that's what happened.'

John Blundell (2014, 98, n. 5) noted the attraction of Apartheid for 'free' market advocates: 'South Africa (RSA) was a very attractive spot for would be emigrants. Among Austrian economists one thinks of [William] Hutt and Lachmann as well as Kirzner.' In 2002, at the London MPS meeting which he organised, Blundell discovered that Hayek's LSE colleague, Plant, spent 'most of the 1920s at the University of Cape Town,' and the 'Manne family, as in Henry Manne of Law and Economics fame, had moved UK to RSA to USA.'

At the University of Rochester, Manne (1928–2015) created the Economics Institute for Law Professors, in which, 'for the first time, law professors were offered intensive instruction in microeconomics with the aim of incorporating economics into legal analysis and theory.' The Economics Institute (renamed as 'Law & Economics Center') moved to the University of Miami where Manne 'began the John M. Olin Fellows Program in Law and Economics, which provided generous scholarships for professional economists to earn a law degree. That program (and its subsequent iterations) has gone on to produce dozens of professors of law and economics, as well as leading lawyers and influential government officials.' The creation of Law & Economics Center (which subsequently moved to Emory University and then to GMU) was one of the

> foundational events in the Law and Economics Movement. Of particular importance to the development of US jurisprudence, its offerings were expanded to include economics courses for federal judges. At its peak a third of the federal bench and four members of the Supreme Court had attended at least one of its programs, and every major law school in the country today counts at least one law and economics scholar among its faculty. Nearly every legal field has been influenced by its scholarship and teaching.[18]

One young legal scholar reported that he 'drooled' when offered a 'thousand dollar honorarium to write a paper': 'It was very helpful.' Manne described his mission as 'really like sales work, calling on people face-to-face, offering your product and seeing if you could interest them. I grew up in sales, so I really did like it.' He was

> not asking for charity ... Corporations had a long-range interest in what went on in universities, and if they didn't begin tending to it, it was going to jump up and bite them. (cited by Teles 2008, 111, 117)

Hayek's (1978a) 'concern' was to 'persuade the intellectuals in the hopes that ultimately they could be converted and transmit my ideas to the public at large.'[19] Does GMU recruit (persuade/convert?) disinterested scholars through open competition or desperadoes through the 'free' market? After multiple failures, a 'friend' arranged for the taxpayers of Virginia to provide Boettke with lifetime employment (K. Evans 2010). Euphemistically, perhaps, Manne sought to recruit to GMU those he described as feeling 'underappreciated' at other schools (cited by Teles 2008, 116, 117). According to McLean (2017, 185), 'white men' were targeted for recruitment.

In 1960, Prime Minister Dr. Hendrik Frensch Verwoerd created the Republic of South African, refused to accept black ambassadors from Commonwealth states and blocked non-white sportsmen from representing 'their' country. In 1961, Verwoerd appointed Balthazar Johannes Vorster—who had been interned during World War II as a Nazi sympathiser—as Minister of Justice. In 1962, Hayek appeared to be considering Apartheid South Africa as his post-Chicago home (Leeson 2015, Chapter 3). Rothbard's (1992, 6) 'Outreach to the Redneck' included the former Klansman, David Duke, while the Apartheid 'Outreach' had a preference for 'black and Libertarian or Conservative' MPS members—including Thomas Sowell and GMU's Walter Williams (Chapters 6 and 7).

Hayek told the 1984 MPS meeting:

> We have to recognize that we owe *our* [emphasis added] civilization to beliefs which I have sometimes have offended some people by calling 'superstitions' and which I now prefer to call 'symbolic truths' ... We must return to a world in which not only reason, but reason and morals, as equal partners, must govern our lives, where the truth of morals is simply one moral tradition, that of the Christian west, which has created morals in modern civilization. (cited by Leeson 2013, Chapter 9)

Hayek (1978a) also defended the 'civilisation' of Apartheid from the American 'fashion' of 'human rights,'[20] while Verwoerd, the 'Architect of Apartheid,' described his system as 'a policy of good neighborliness' (Chapter 1). Speaking to Parliament in 1964 as Minister for Coloured Affairs, P. W. Botha (the last Prime Minister, 1978–1984, and the first Executive State President, 1984–1989) stated: 'I am one of those who believe that there is no permanent home for even a section of the Bantu in the white area of South Africa and the destiny of South Africa depends on this essential point. If the principle of permanent residence for the black man in the area of the white is accepted then it is the beginning of the end of civilisation as we know it in this country' (cited by McGreal 2006).

Rothbard was the first person Raico (2013) had met who defended 'a fully voluntary society—nudge, nudge.' In *Freeman*, John Davenport (1985) was more open—'The Anti-Apartheid Threat' sought to 'strike down all customs and laws making for the separation of the races' and to 'bludgeon South Africa into changing her racial ways.' Bantustans, he asserted, had merit: there were 'some three million Coloureds, product of early mixed marriages, who most closely resemble our American blacks, and finally seventeen million Bantu speaking a variety of tongues who retain strong tribal affiliations. Perhaps half of these live in the increasingly autonomous homelands; the other half in close association with whites in the country's urban areas.'

The KwaZulu Bantustan was established by the Apartheid government which was led (until its abolition along with Apartheid) by one of the John Davenport's (1985) authorities: 'In a powerful article in *The Wall Street Journal*, Chief of the Zulus, Mangosuthu Gatsha Buthelezi, warned against this disinvestment policy. The cutting edge for social change, he argued, has been the presence of American corporations. Anything which decreases U.S. investment in South Africa, now running to two and a half billion dollars, must drag down the living standards of blacks no less than whites.' Another of Davenport's authorities was an unnamed Chief of a Shona tribe who allegedly told him: 'If you take nothing else back to your country, tell your people that these men (the so-called nationalist leaders do not represent my people.'[21]

John Davenport (23 August 1985) assured Pat Buchanan that the abolition of Apartheid would be a mistake: he was convinced that as long as there is 'any' South Africa to 'argue' about, it will 'need segregation of the races and tribes as well as minority rule.' One-man-one-vote would reduce South Africa to a 'rock' at the Cape of Good Hope.[22] With respect to his other 'free' market cause—defending white rule in Rhodesia–Davenport (7 December 1976) told the incoming Secretary of State, Cyrus Vance, that it was time to 'stop penalizing our friends while rewarding our enemies.'[23] Although Balthazar Johannes Vorster (South African Prime Minister, 1966–1978 and President, 1978–1979) had been interned during the war as a Nazi sympathiser, Davenport (1985) assured President Reagan that South Africa had fought 'shoulder-to-shoulder' (against the Austro-Germans) during two world wars.[24]

Democracy in post-'Fascist' Portugal (1974), the resulting retreat from Empire in Angola and Mozambique, plus the death of Franco (1975) were perceived as existential threats to the 'International Right' (Teacher 2018a, b). In what appears to be a transcript of a radio broadcast on 'The Role of the White Man in Southern Africa,' John Davenport—describing himself as a 'scholar'—advocated 'against the sudden application of panaceas like majority rule.' Individualism led 'almost inevitably to the concept of one-man-one-vote democracy.' This was especially inappropriate in Africa—what was needed was the 'reconciliation of individuality and community [Davenport's emphasis].'[25]

Although South Africa was close to a Police State, John Davenport gave lectures in the USA on 'The Need to Limit Government and Free the Market'—'anything with the word Liberty in it is good.'[26] But in writing 'The Keynesian Vacuum,' Davenport was obliged to ask George Pearson (27 July 1977) for readings and was provided with a reference to Rothbard plus Institute for Humane Studies publications by the public stoning theocrat, North, and the academic fraud, Shenoy.[27]

In *Economica*, Pigou (1954, 74) issued a 'warning to those who take their opinions from newspapers!'[28] Hayek (1978a) noted the 'corrupting' influences that journalists were exposed to: 'it's a necessity to pretend to be competent on every subject, some of which they really do not understand. They are under that necessity, I regret; I'm sorry for them. But to pretend to understand all the things you write about, and habitually to write about things you do not understand, is a very corrupting thing.'[29] Hayek could have been referring to Rees-Mogg (2011), who was perfectly equipped for his role as Hayek's intermediary:

> I had the basic qualities not of a good historian, but of a good journalist – I had trenchant opinions: I wrote with vigour at short notice on any subject: I was manifestly clever, without being particularly consistent, accurate or profound.

One of these opinions was that Keynes' rejection of moral rules led him to reject the gold standard 'which provided an automatic control of monetary inflation.' One former colleague at *The Times* observed that Rees-Mogg had the enthusiasms of an economically uneducated man: 'Hard as it may be to believe today, he discovered Europe and for a while saw that as a panacea. He discovered incomes policy and got all excited. He discovered the gold standard and the same thing happened.

Peter Jay (then economics editor of *The Times*) told him about monetarism and he fell for that' (*Independent* 1993). Hayek could also have been referring to John Davenport, who combined lucidity with ideology and incompetence.

Hayek (1978a) was contemptuous of journalists—including, presumably, those such as John Davenport (1904–1987) who he recruited to the MPS—because of 'a certain attribute which is common to journalists of judging opinions by their likely appeal to the public.'[30] In her Ely Lecture to the American Economic Association, 'The Second Crisis of Economic Theory,' Joan Robinson (1972, 1) stated:

> In 1932, Professor (now Lord) Robbins published the famous essay in which he describes economics as the subject that deals with the allocation of scarce means between alternative uses. No doubt this was the expression of a long tradition but the date of publication was unlucky. By the time the book came out there were three million workers unemployed in Great Britain and the statistical measure of GNP in U.S.A. had recently fallen to half its former level. It was just a coincidence that the book appeared when means for any end at all had rarely been less scarce.

Joan Robinson (1903–1983) was married to Austin Robinson (1897–1993), the editor of the Royal Economic Society's *Economic Journal*. In 'An English Summer' (reflections on a visit to wartime Britain), John Davenport received an 'invitation' from

> Lionel Robbins, a middle-aged economist and husband of the equally famous Joan Robinson ... It was then explained to be how the Mss. for his famous [Theory of] *General Theory of Employment, Interest and Money* was practically dragged out of his [Keynes'] library page by page in the mid-Thirties. Keynes apparently was for further tinkering and perfecting his remarkable these [sic] but his students and fellow academicians had the percipience that it was, so to speak, 'Now or never.'

John Davenport was under the impression that what became known as Keynesianism had influenced interwar America: 'In the event the General Theory appeared in 1936, in time to profoundly influence the spending policies of the New Deal. Had it appeared in, say, 1938 when the clouds of World War II were gathering and when the trickling war orders were reviving the American economy, the master work might have proved a dud.'[31]

John Davenport had what appears to be unrestricted access to all the world's most influential players. Keynes, for example, told him Churchill had called him into talk because he was suspicious of his 'Treasury experts.' As Chancellor of the Exchequer, Churchill had felt himself to be 'baffled and unsure.'

In '"Coming Clean" on Southern Africa,' John Davenport repeated the official propaganda that legitimised Apartheid: the 'internal race problem' consisted of 'giving more home rule and responsibility to the three to five million blacks who have been lured away from their homelands into South Africa's urban areas where they live [sic] close proximity to whites.' Davenport insisted that Americans be 'mighty careful that our perverse Utopianism does not end by allowing the Soviets to turn the Cape of Good Hope into Cape Gulag!'[32]

Together with two other MPS members—John Chamberlain and William Rickenbacker—John Davenport appeared to coordinate the campaign to defend the Southern African white regimes—Davenport even circulated a leaflet: 'PROTECT THE AMERICAN INTEREST IN SOUTH AFRICA.' This was part of a wider propaganda campaign. In 'PROPOSED CORPORATE AD CAMPAIGN,' Davenport sought to lobby 'Chairmen and Presidents of FORTUNE's 500 corporations whom we want to persuade that the job of educating the public can [Davenport's emphasis] be done and that Chase [Bank?] is willing to take a leadership role in telling their story – the story of American business performance, products, profits and motivations.'[33]

During a visit to Salisbury, John Davenport (28 September 1976) published a letter in the *Rhodesian Herald* insisting that sanctions must be lifted because it had 'never been put to a vote of the American people. Recent opinion polls in the US indicate that Americans favor treating Rhodesia as we would treat any other independent nation.' In 'An Honest Policy Towards Rhodesia,' Davenport equated the 'right' that followed the 1965 Unilateral Declaration of Independence to that which attached to the 1776 American version.[34] In 'Southern Africa in Transition,' Davenport reminded his (radio?) audience that the 'early settlers' had 'dropped anchor off Table Mountain at about the same time that American Pilgrims anchored off Plymouth Rock.' America should help blacks and whites to 'develop their own homelands'— Apartheid.[35] The whites of Southern African were 'the Lost Tribe'—and as a Georgian, President Carter should know all about the 'difficulties in achieving harmony in racial relations.'[36] Rhodesia was a 'Moral Issue'— its choice of government was 'strictly Rhodesia's business.'[37]

Rickenbacker (8 May 1977) suggested that John Davenport cooperates with the American-Rhodesian Association's 'Hands Off Africa' crusade which asserted that if Rhodesia fell—because of '**RACIAL BIAS**'—this would 'leave the free world isolated within a Soviet-controlled crescent [bold in original].' Davenport responded with 'Proposal for a Monthly Letter on Rhodesia,' to replace the closed Washington Rhodesia Information Office.[38] Citing Davenport, John Chamberlain (1977) told readers of the *New Haven Register* that the Transkei Bantustan had 'recently achieved its independence from South Africa,' and 'follows the free enterprise philosophy.'

John Davenport sent telexes (no dates—but presumably late 1970s) to both P. K. Botha (then South African Minister of Foreign Affairs) and Ian Smith (Rhodesian Prime Minister) telling them that 'public opinion here' is 'swinging' (to Botha) or 'running' (to Smith) 'strongly in your favor.'[39] Davenport (21 July 1985) insisted to Pat Buchanan that Reagan must veto Anti-Apartheid Act legislation because the 'whole' Anti-Apartheid movement is 'simply generating <u>terrorism</u> [Davenport's emphasis].' If the South African government was unsuccessful in maintaining law and order, 'we lose the whole ball game to the Soviets.'[40]

John Davenport (16 July 1986) told Senator Jesse Helms that sanctions would 'benefit no one but the Soviet Union,' and 'amid the inevitable ensuing anarchy, the toll of black lives will be unconscionable.' But Congressman Jack Kemp (17 October 1985)—who told Davenport that he had quit football to take up politics after reading Hayek's (1960) *Constitution of Liberty*—also told him: 'As Americans, we care deeply about human rights ... we oppose the denial of God-given rights whenever and wherever it may occur.'[41]

Reagan's veto of the 1986 Comprehensive Anti-Apartheid Bill was overridden by the Senate (78–21) and the House (313–83)—the first foreign policy veto overridden in the twentieth century. Ostensibly, the 'free' market concern related to the Soviet 'menace'—but in an internal *Fortune* memo referring to 'the Negro and the race problem,' John Davenport (27 June 1963) promoted 'states' rights.'[42] He had been informed by 'Voting Rights and Legal Wrongs'—a campaign against the 1965 Voting Rights Act by the Virginia Commission on Constitutional Government.[43]

In a circular letter, John Davenport (23 July 1968) defended 'free association'—that is, both segregation and Apartheid—because 'Negro and white relations should be left wholly voluntary.' Referring to the

5 BRITAIN, WHITE SUPREMACISM AND THE 'INTERNATIONAL RIGHT' 213

'necessity of order to preserve voluntarism and liberty,' Davenport stated: 'The breakdown of order ... goes far beyond the Negro problem.' The 'reign of ethical relativity,' he suggested, may be the

> product of one further development – the breakdown or the gradual disappearance of religion. We live in a secular age where homage is paid to all kinds of giddy rational abstractions, - Democracy, One-Man One-Vote, Equality, and of course Freedom from all and for all, with diminishing signs of homage to the one abstraction, or rather concretion, which could act as a <u>ground</u> [Davenport's emphasis] for values and purpose, whether called God, the Creator, the Universal Mind or what have you. Yet without such ground I wonder whether values and purpose can survive, and I speak as one who sometimes finds Christianity a pretty distant light-house.[44]

In 1806, Thomas Jefferson proposed that the 'free' international slave trade be criminalising—asking Congress to 'withdraw the citizens of the United States from all further participation in those violations of human rights ... which the morality, the reputation, and the best of our country have long been eager to proscribe' (Chapter 4). In his Inaugural Address, President John F. Kennedy also explicitly addressed human rights: 'We dare not forget today that we are the heirs of that first revolution. Let the word go forth from this time and place, to friend and foe alike, that the torch has been passed to a new generation of Americans–born in this century, tempered by war, disciplined by a hard and bitter peace, proud of our ancient heritage–and unwilling to witness or permit the slow undoing of those human rights to which this nation has always been committed, and to which we are committed today at home and around the world.' Americans would 'pay any price, bear any burden, meet any hardship, support any friend, oppose any foe to assure the survival and the success of liberty.'[45]

Geoffrey Robinson (representing some of those seeking to highlight the 2009 death of Russian lawyer Sergei Magnitsky in a Moscow prison) described the 2012 US Magnitsky Act (a bipartisan bill which sought to punish the Russian officials responsible for Magnitsky's death) as one of the 'most important new developments in human rights' which provides a 'way of getting at the Auschwitz train drivers, the apparatchiks, the people who make a little bit of money from human rights abuses and generally keep under the radar.'[46]

Hayek's MPS (1947–) and the North Atlantic Treaty Organisation (1949–) were defining Cold War institutions. As Hayek was defending the 'civilisation' of Apartheid from American 'fashion' of 'human rights' (Chapter 1), Moss (1978, 116) sought to persuade Americans that they needed a military alliance with South Africa: 'As a first step in implementing this needed policy change, the arms embargo should be dropped and serious consideration should be given to the formation of a South Atlantic Treaty Organization.'

The Monday Club had been established in 1961 to support white supremacism in South Africa and Rhodesia, and was later expelled from the Conservative Party. In 'Disgrace Abounding,' his review of *The British Connection* in the Monday Club journal, *Tory Challenge*, Soref (1979, 9–10) stated that 'Deacon' McCormick had undertaken 'monumental research to produce this essential reading of our bad times … The academic background of the traitors is consistent. It appears to have originated with the pioneering work of Professor A.C. Pigou … it would appear that espionage is largely an upper middle class preserve. The working class operators, being merely in it for the money, are less ideologically motivated.'

Soref (1979) concluded: 'Whether communism is allowed to dominate Southern Africa is now a matter for the British government … the only beneficiaries of present events appear to be the Soviet [*sic*]. The West betrayed the Shah [of Iran] creating the oil crisis. Further Communist penetration can only lead to the Russians and their allies taking the strategic minerals of Southern Africa, leading to mass unemployment and economic decay in the West.'

Soref (20 September 1979) informed 'Deacon' McCormick that his *Tory Challenge* review would be distributed at the 1979 Conservative Party Conference: *The British Connection* was a masterly project; Soref, who was amazed that he was not more bitter about its suppression, promised that he was at 'Deacon' McCormick's 'disposal.'[47]

The Conservatives had won the May 1979 election, and Nigel Lawson became Financial Secretary to the Treasury (1979–1981). Soref—Chairman of the Monday Club Africa and Rhodesia study groups and policy committees and co-author with Julian Amery, John Biggs-Davidson, Stephen Hastings and Patrick Wall of *Rhodesia and the Threat to the West* (1976)—was a member of the Reform Club, a white supremacist and a 'former Blackshirt' (Anson 2010; Janner and Taylor 2008, 146; Dorril 2006, 632). The British Union of Fascists website (not necessarily a reliable source) is more specific: before becoming a Conservative MP, the Jewish Soref was a Standard Bearer at the British Union of Fascists Olympia rally.[48]

Hayek's planned post-Nobel book, *What is Wrong With Economics*, contained an appendix on John Stuart 'Mill's Muddle' (Caldwell 2016, 13). Hayek's 'The Muddle of the Middle' was an Annual Dinner 'Guest of Honour' lecture to the Monday Club (Farrant and McPhail 2017). In 'Monday Club still on Reich Track,' *The Times* (2 June 2006), in a report of the Monday Club's Annual General Meeting, quoted its chairman, Merlin Charles Sainthill Hanbury-Tracy, 7th Baron Sudeley, as stating: 'True though the fact may be that some races are superior to other … Hitler did well to get everyone back to work' (Rifkind 2006).

According to Rothbard (1994, 7), the third, and 'of course the most dreaded by the Western media,' constituent of the Freedom Alliance is the National Alliance:

> a renamed and reconstituted 'neo-fascist' party that, until its current leader Gianfranco Fini took it over in 1991, was known for four decades as the Italian Social Movement. The dynamic young Fini changed its name and modified its 'neo-fascist' ideology, changing its nostalgic devotion to the fascist corporate state into a kind of moderate free-market party, strong in central and southern Italy.

The Italian Social Movement (*Movimento Sociale Italiano*, MSI) had been formed in 1946 by supporters of the former dictator, Mussolini. In May 1968, General Giovanni De Lorenzo (1907–1973) was elected as a monarchist MP, joining the far-right MSI in 1971. In April 1967, De Lorenzo (previously Head of *Servizio per le Informazioni e la Sicurezza Militare*, SIFAR, and Commandant of the Carabinieri) had been dismissed as Chief of the Army General Staff for having spied on the Italian Government. Giulio Andreotti (later *Democrazia Cristiana*, DC, Prime Minister 1972–1973, 1976–1979, 1989–1992) was entrusted with the destruction of the voluminous files De Lorenzo had compiled on prominent Italian public figures, but it later transpired that, prior to their destruction, the files had been copied and given to Licio Gelli, Grand Master of the P2 masonic lodge (Teacher 2018a).

According to John Cornwell (1999, 2003), on the eve of the 1952 local elections in Rome, in which again the Communist and Socialist parties threatened to win, Pius XII, declaring that the war against communism was a holy war, excommunicated members of the Communist Party. He also asked the Jesuit, Father Riccardo Lombardi, to speak with de Gasperi to encourage the Christian Democrats to consider a political alliance with the Rightist parties, monarchist and neofascist—including the Italian Social Movement. He promoted a domino theory: if 'the Communists win in Rome, in Italy, it will cast a shadow on the entire world: France would become Communist, and then Spain and then all of Europe.'

Following the 1963 elections, in which the Communists gained 25% of the vote, De Lorenzo used his unprecedented powers to launch a vast anti-communist operation which started with the training of the 'gladiators' the same year. Simultaneously, with some twenty top Carabinieri commanders, De Lorenzo finalised Plan Solo, a *coup d'état* scheduled for summer 1964. Opposition to the coup would be minimised by a wave of preventive arrests based on the files that De Lorenzo had built up on 157,000 people since 1959 (Bull 2012, 4). The coup was cancelled at the last moment as the result of a pact between the Socialists and the DC, but De Lorenzo continued planning for a later coup.

In 1964, under De Lorenzo's guidance, SIFAR funded the creation of the Alberto Pollio Institute which, the following year, organised the now infamous conference which marked the ideological birth of the strategy of tension. Held in the Parco dei Principi hotel (3–5 May 1965), the conference was attended by the elite of the Italian military and the extreme-right, including Europe's most notorious fascist terrorist, Stefano Delle Chiaie, a key actor in the *stragi* which rocked Italy throughout the 1970s. Delle Chiaie's group *Avanguardia Nazionale* (AN, 'National Vanguard') had been founded in 1959 with funding from prominent industrialist and banker Carlo Pesenti, a future backer of the Cercle complex. AN had been preparing for a strategy of tension since the spring of 1964 when the Italian neo-fascist militants had followed courses in terrorism and psychological warfare. In Rome on 6 October 1975, AN attempted to assassinate Bernard Leighton and his wife—reportedly as a 'favour to Pinochet who had direct contacts with and the full support of Delle Chiaie' (Bull 2012, 39; Ravelli and Bull 2018).

In January 1970, Ian Greig's 'Subversion Committee' organised a Monday Club seminar on subversion—the panel included Greig, G. K. Young, Charles Lyons (Confederation of British Industry) and Sir Robert Thompson (Brian Crozier's Institute for the Study of Conflict).

Young and Greig's preoccupation with subversion was shared by the main speaker: General De Lorenzo. In the February 1974 election, Young was the unsuccessful Conservative Party candidate for Brent East; and Greig (1979) was the author of 'Iran and the lengthening Soviet shadow.'

De Lorenzo had been invited by Young, who was an expert on Italian Fascist policing methods. Posted to Rome just after the war, Young had dismantled the German and Italian intelligence networks for MI6 in close cooperation with his Office of Strategic Services counter-intelligence (OSS X-2) counterpart (1945–1947), James Jesus Angleton, later the legendary (and notorious) chief of CIA counter-intelligence from 1954 until his dismissal in December 1974, and thereafter a powerful focus of opposition to restriction of the CIA until his death in 1987.

De Lorenzo was a major figure in the Italian strategy of tension, particularly during his time as head of the Carabinieri (October 1962–January 1966). His speech to the Monday Club came midway between the beginning of this strategy of tension (April 1969) and the Borghese coup (December 1970); at the time of his visit, De Lorenzo was also a key figure in an anti-communist resistance network within the Carabinieri and the secret services codenamed *Rosa dei Venti* (which had been set up after the failure of Plan Solo)—it was a major component in the Italian *Gladio* network and was later implicated in a further coup planned for the spring of 1973 (Teacher 2018a).

Winston Churchill's (1874–1965) grandfather was John Winston Spencer-Churchill, 7th Duke of Marlborough; his grandson, Winston Churchill (1940–2010), was Monday Club Conservative MP, and a member of NAFF's 'informal action committee' (Crozier 1993, 118). He became the general coordinator appointed by Thatcher for the government's attack on the Campaign for Nuclear Disarmament (1979–1990). Churchill was the son of Randolph Churchill (1911–1968)—an SAS founding member and lifelong intimate of Colonel Sir Archibald David Stirling (1915–1990) who founded 'Great Britain 75,' one of three right-wing private militias that planned to take over the government in the event of civil unrest. The other two were Major-General Sir Walter Walker's Civil Assistance and G. K. Young's Unison. Walker had been commander of Britain's counter-insurgency campaign in Borneo, and the Monday Club's Young had been MI6 Deputy Chief and 'coup-master' (Teacher 2018a).

On 30 January 1972, soldiers of the 1st Battalion, Parachute Regiment shot 26 unarmed civilians during a peaceful protest march by the Northern Ireland Civil Rights Association. Following a 12-year inquiry, the Saville Report (made public in 2010) concluded that the shootings were both 'unjustified' and 'unjustifiable': all of those shot were unarmed, none posed a serious threat, no bombs were thrown and soldiers 'knowingly put forward false accounts' to justify their firing. Conservative Prime Minister David Cameron then made a formal apology on behalf of the UK.

In the 1970s, Churchill had 'strongly defended the Army in Ulster,' and 'demanded the return of the death penalty for terrorism.' This had impressed Thatcher, and in November 1976 she appointed him a front bench defence spokesman. But in November 1978, she had sacked him 'with great personal sadness' for voting against sanctions on Rhodesia (*Daily Telegraph* 2010).

Habsburg was the Vice President of Paneuropean Union, a movement for European Union that had been founded in 1923 by Comte Richard Coudenhove Kalergi. Dr. Joseph Retinger's European Movement (EM), however, was the main component in the CIA's campaign to infiltrate and control the wave of political sentiment favourable to European Union in the immediate post-war period (Teacher 2018a). EM had been co-founded by Winston Churchill's son-in-law, Duncan Sandys (1908–1987), who in May 1935 had devoted his maiden House of Commons speech to promoting *Anschluss*: 'The setting up of a Danubian Economic Federation, or possibly a union with Hungary under a restored Hapsburg monarchy, would be the most satisfactory solution to the problem; but, failing this, even a union with Germany would undoubtedly be preferable to the indefinite prolongation of the present dangerous state of uncertainty.' He also promoted German rearmament: 'Quite apart from the fact that Germany has already taken the law into her own hands, I do not consider that the repeal of the disarmament provisions of the various Peace Treaties would, in actual fact, lead to an increase in arms. On the contrary, I believe that the announcement of the German rearmament programme brings new hope of a general limitation of arms by all countries.'[49]

Hayek told Cubitt (2006, 15) that of the two Empires he had watched decline, 'England's downfall had been the more painful to him.' In 1935, Sandys insisted that Hitler could be tolerated if he promised to exclude the British Empire from his expansion plans: 'In the course of the Berlin conversations, the German Chancellor informed our

Ministers that Germany would not return to Geneva unless all imputations as to her unworthiness to administer Colonial mandates were removed. As long as this is purely a matter of honour, surely a concession of this kind would be in accordance with that spirit of conciliation which we are trying to promote. At the same time, Germany should be clearly asked, once her honour is satisfied, to make a categorical declaration freely renouncing all actual territorial claims and ambitions in the Colonial field. This is the one and only question which is of direct and vital interest to Great Britain and to the British Empire. If Germany once again becomes a Colonial Power, not only will her interests clash with ours in that field, but she will also inevitably be drawn into rivalry with us as a naval Power. Surely, then, it is the first elementary duty of British statesmanship to see to it that the great energies, ambitions and enthusiasms of the new Germany are directed into channels where they will not clash with the essential interests of Great Britain. Therefore, I cannot too strongly urge His Majesty's Government, in directing our foreign policy, to lend a sympathetic ear to Germany's legitimate claims and aspirations in other fields, provided that they can obtain real satisfaction on what to us is the vital issue, namely, the Colonial and naval question.'[50]

Sandys was Secretary of State for Commonwealth Relations (1960–1964), Secretary of State for the Colonies (1962–1964) and an active member of the Monday Club. In 1966, Edward Heath sacked him from the Shadow Cabinet because of his strong support for Ian Smith's 1965 Rhodesian Unilateral Declaration of Independence. Sandys presumably attended Hayek 'Guest of Honour' Monday Club annual dinner address on 'The Muddle of the Middle.'

In 1979, the Old Etonian Adam Ridley—Count Alexander Konstantinovich Benckendorff's grandson—became Thatcher's Director of the Conservative Research Department and played a leading part in promoting privatisation.[51] As Sir Adam Ridley, he moved into insurance and merchant banking: director of Hambros (1985–1997) and non-executive director of Morgan Stanley (2006–2013).

In 1979, Selsdon Group members were invited to the Carlton Club to hear Hayek's 'Muddle of the Middle' 'Guest of Honour' lecture at the Monday Club annual dinner. At the launch of the Selsdon Group, the Old Etonian Nicholas Ridley (19 September 1973) embraced what he believed to be Abraham Lincoln's philosophy: 'You cannot bring about prosperity by discouraging thrift. You cannot strengthen the weak by weakening the strong. You cannot help the wage earner by pulling down the wage payer. You cannot further the brotherhood of man by encouraging class hatred. You cannot help the poor by destroying the rich. You cannot establish sound security on borrowed money. You cannot keep out of trouble by spending more than you earn. You cannot build character and courage by taking away a man's initiative and independence. You cannot help men permanently by doing for them what they could and should do for themselves.' At the 1992 Republican National Convention, ex-President Reagan also embraced Lincoln's 'American Charter.' In reality, these were the words of an evangelical preacher and anti-strike organiser, W. J. H. Boetcker (Steers 2007, 91–92).

In the London *Times*, Simon Jenkins reported that Mrs. Thatcher became Conservative leader through

> the 'peasants' revolt' of the dispossessed right-wing.[52]

The 1978 Ridley Report outlined the strategy that would be pursued against the miners in 1984–1985. As Secretary of State for Transport (1983–1986), Ridley prepared for the miners' strike by stock-piling coal, thus enabling a much longer resistance than in 1973–1974. In 1988, Ridley also persuaded her government to introduce a Poll Tax. In 1381, the Poll Tax had initiated the Peasants' Revolt: on 31 March 1990, two 'feeder' marches met in London to protest against the Poll Tax, after having followed the routes of the two armies taken in 1381. On 14 July 1990, Ridley was forced to resign as Secretary of State for Trade and Industry after being interviewed in the *Spectator* by Dominic Lawson (Nigel Lawson's son and brother-in-law of The 3rd Viscount Monckton), in which he described the proposed European and Monetary Union as 'a German racket designed to take over the whole of Europe ... I'm not against giving up sovereignty in principle, but not to this lot. You might just as well give it to Adolf Hitler, frankly' (Lawson 2011; Morgan 2001, 492; Turner 2000, 132; Dorey 1995, 131; Arblaster 1984, 346; Jenkins 2006).

The Ridleys of Blagdon, Northumberland, were 'a good example of a gentry dynasty': their landed wealth originated from the purchase of estates confiscated from the Jacobite rebels after the 1715 uprising. Matthew Ridley (1716–1778) became Governor of the Newcastle-upon-Tyne Company of Merchant Adventurers and four times Mayor of (and five times Member of Parliament for) Newcastle. By 1815, 'the head of the family had for many years been a Baronet and an M.P.': they owned coal mines, farms and other businesses (McCord and Purdue 2011, 111).

Nicholas Ridley was the second son of Matthew White Ridley (The 3rd Viscount Ridley) and the grandson of the Matthew White Ridley (The 2nd Viscount Ridley and Chairman of the Tariff Reform League). He objected to Heath's U-Turn against the sentiments formulated at the Selsdon Park Hotel prior to the 1970 election. There were also differences in ascribed status between Heath and his detractors. At Eton, Jo Grimond had Anthony Fisher as his fag; Grimond was later a regular contributor to Fisher's IEA and attended the 1984 MPS meeting. Hayek was the inspiration behind Sir Keith Joseph's Centre for Policy Studies, set up in the aftermath of the 1973-1974 miners' strike. In *The Future of Liberalism: The Inaugural Eighty Club Lecture*, Grimond (1980), who in 1976 returned as caretaker Liberal leader after Jeremy Thorpe's resignation, declared that 'Much of what Mrs Thatcher and Sir Keith Joseph say and do is in the mainstream of liberal philosophy.'

At Eton, Tam Dalyell was Ridley's fag. Possibly apocryphally, Ridley reportedly stated that 'at Eton, I wish I had beaten him more!' (Barberis 2005, 8, 193; Galbraith 2000, 24). Dalyell—Labour M.P. and 'Father' of the House of Commons and later a promoter of the Austrian School fraud, 'Deacon' McCormick—complained that Prime Minister Tony Blair had been 'unduly influenced by a cabal of Jewish advisers' including Peter Mandelson, Lord Levy (Blair's personal envoy on the Middle East) and Jack Straw (the Foreign Secretary). Dalyell told *The Daily Telegraph*: 'I am not going to be labelled anti-Semitic. My children worked on a kibbutz. But the time has come for candour.' According to Dalyell, Blair was also indirectly influenced by Jews in the Bush administration, including Richard Perle (a Pentagon adviser), Paul Wolfowitz (deputy defence secretary) and Ari Fleischer (the President's press secretary) (Brown and Hastings 2003).[53]

In *My Style of Government: The Thatcher Years*, Ridley (1991, 110–111, 115) explained that Prime Minister Thatcher was a 'good chemist, but she has never been a country person, who understood and felt deeply about these things as I did.' Ridley initiated legislation to oblige 'local authorities and others to remove litter.' Throughout this campaign, Ridley indulged inconspicuous 'fag-in-the mouth' consumption, presumably in protest against what the Austrian Leon Louw regards as 'a kind of hysteria, a peculiar semi-religious fundamentalist Puritanism ... a vicious assault' on choice: 'The anti-tobacco fanatics ... the nicotine Nazis will not stop until there is full prohibition.'[54] Nicholas Ridley, Baron Ridley of Liddesdale (1929–1993), died of lung cancer, aged 64.

According to Hayek (2011 [1960], 186), 'To do the bidding of others is for the employed the condition of achieving his purpose.' And according an *American Journal of Public Health* article on 'Tobacco Industry Efforts to Undermine Policy-Relevant Research,' Thomas DiLorenzo, Professor of Economics at GMU and the Joseph A. Sellinger, SJ School of Business and Management, Loyola University, Maryland, had 'worked on a number of tobacco industry projects, including a Philip Morris and RJ Reynolds–funded project at the Independent Institute (a tobacco industry–funded think tank).' In 1995, GMU's James Bennett 'billed RJ Reynolds $150,000 for work he and DiLorenzo were doing on a book titled CancerScam: The Diversion of Federal Cancer Funds to Politics'—which

> conformed to Philip Morris' action plan by 'elevating the issue of public funding (primarily federal) to conduct anti-tobacco ... research' and accusing government agencies and health charities of diverting funding away from 'the common goal of finding a cure for cancer.' (Landman and Glanz 2009)

Robert Tollison and Richard E. Wagner were recruited to GMU and published *Smoking and the State* (1988, 1992) as Boettke studied for a GMU Ph.D. (1983–1989).[55] According to the Tobacco Institute, their book had been 'commissioned' by the Institute to 'rebut' Pigouvian externalities—'the "social costs" claims' made by anti-smokers.[56] Bennett and Lorenzo's 1990 book proposal provided the conclusion that their research would independently produce: 'debunking' what they described as the 'rhetoric' of the health charities by 'exposing' the reality of their operations and aims so as to 'discredit' them in the 'minds of the public ... op-eds and articles for the media will then be prepared based of these studies.'[57] In 'The Case for Ordinary Economics,' Boettke (2017) and Stefanie Haeffele-Balch informed *USA Today* readers: 'Limiting the influence of special interests and tying budgets to performance are just some ways to hold politicians accountable and ensure better policy outcomes.' Boettke, who succeeded Wagner as Director of the GMU graduate programme, is (or rather, was) a policy 'expert' at the Heartland Institute, and is also on the list of what sciencecorruption.com calls the 'cash-for-comments network' of the tobacco lobby: 'each op-ed now earned the economists $3,000. Presentations made to conferences earned them $5,000.'[58]

In 'Friedrich Hayek Y Sus Dos Visitas A Chile,' Caldwell and Montes (2015) asserted: 'It has even been suggested that he [Hayek] suffered from depression (Kresge and Wenar 1994, 130–131).'[59] The 'suggestion'—which was not a suggestion—came not from Stephen Kresge and Leif Wenar but from Hayek (1994, 130–131) who, in the supplementary volume to *The Collected Works of F.A. Hayek*, referred not only to his 'depression'—from which he had been 'suffering for almost two years'—but also to an earlier 'severe depression which lasted exactly a year' (1960–1961). The Hayek Archives—which Caldwell seeks to control—provide more detail.

After the premature death of his first wife, Hayek lost about a decade to mental illness (1960–1961, 1969–1974, 1985–). Friedman (22 July 1969) suggested to Ralph Harris that the Caracas MPS meeting should 'do something about Hayek'—such as a dinner in his honour.[60] From the IEA, Harris (16 September 1970) offered to supply Hayek with the name of a doctor who had treated him for depression[61]; Popper (3 May 1974) told him that there was 'no need' to be depressed.[62] Hayek (28 January 1971) declined to recommend anyone to Leland Yeager to fill one or two academic openings for Hayekians at the University of Virginia because there were hardly any trained economists with 'any' interest in the problems he had been working on for the last two decades.[63]

In 'The Pit of State Control,' 'von' Hayek told the *St Andrew's Citizen*: '[Labour] Trade union mentality has come to govern the whole country. Basic elements of liberty are being engulfed by collectivism' (cited by Taylor 1976). Three years earlier, 'von' Hayek—gripped by suicidal depression—polled last as Chancellor of the University of St Andrews, behind the Old Etonian, Baron Ballantrae, the last British-born Governor General of New Zealand, and Sir Thomas Malcolm Knox, a Hegel scholar.[64]

The patron of the Selsdon Group, Richard Law, 1st Baron Coleraine, had earlier written a *Road to Serfdom* pastiche, *Return from Utopia* (1950); but when the Selsdon Group formulated their 1973 manifesto to 'secure that free market conditions prevail to the greatest possible extent,' Hayek was not mentioned.[65] This may have reflected Hayek's diminished public profile, but within the Conservative Party he continued to exert influence and was one of the first Selsdon Group speakers.[66]

In Zurich in 1919–1920, Hayek (1994, 64) worked in the laboratory of the brain anatomist, Constantin von Monakow, 'tracing fibre bundles through the different parts of the human brain.' von Monakow and

S. Kitabayashi (1919) had just published 'Schizophrenie und Plexus chorioidei' in *Schweizer Archiv für Neurologie und Psychiatrie* (Swiss Archives of Neurology and Psychiatry—a journal von Monakow had founded in 1917).

In 1991, he told his second wife to put him—not in a nursing home—but into

> a lunatic asylum, yet their doctor said he was in perfect physical shape. His hallucinatory experiences exhausted him … Sometimes he would see things in vivid shapes, green meadows, writing on the wall, and even perceived sounds. No matter how strongly Mrs. Hayek would deny the reality of these apparitions he would insist that he had seen and heard them. On one such occasion he was so distressed because she would not believe him that he clutched my hand and said that the presence of persons and their singing had lasted for nine hours. (Cubitt 2006, 355–356)

Hayek's mental illness manifested itself in obsessive self-interest and extreme mood swings: he was being 'looked after by a psychiatrist and a neurologist' (Cubitt 2006, 168). Hayek (1978a) explained that 'it would sound so frightfully egotistic in speaking about myself–why I feel I think in a different manner. But then, of course, I found a good many instances of this in real life.'[67]

After his second prolonged bout of suicidal depression (1969–1974), Hayek always carried a razor blade with which to slash his wrist; he wanted to know 'where "the poison", that is arsenic, could be obtained.' During his third bout (1985–), the second Mrs. Hayek instructed Cubitt (2006, 89, 111, 168, 174, 188, 284, 317, 328) not to let her husband near the parapet of their balcony. When asked 'What did Hayek think about subject *x*?' his fellow Austrian-LSE economist (1933–1948), Lachmann (1906–1990), would routinely reply: 'Which Hayek?' (cited by Caldwell 2006, 112). Cubitt noted that Hayek became 'upset' after reading an article on schizophrenia, and 'wondered whether he thought it was referring to himself or Mrs. Hayek.' The 1974 Nobel Prize exacerbated this personality split: Grinder detected 'almost two different people' (Ebenstein 2003, 264).

Mises' mental illness manifested itself in the same mood swings that Hayek exhibited. In the year he embraced 'Fascists,' including 'Ludendorff and Hitler,' Mises told Margit (1984, 24, 44, 63, 169–170): 'I cannot live any more without you'; and in New York,

Very often he would say: 'If it were not for you, I would not want to live any more.'

She interpreted Mises' 'attacks' on her as 'really a sign of depression, a hidden dissatisfaction and the sign of a great, great need for love.' At other times, the *Führer* of the 'Tribe of Mises' saw himself as God-like, able to solo-generate perfect knowledge: he

> specially objected to listening to [broadcast] commentators. 'I can do my thinking alone,' was his reaction.

Hayek (1992b [1977]) described the MPS achievement: a 'consistent doctrine and some international circles of communication.' After both Mises and Hayek were safely dead, James Buchanan (1992, 130) felt emboldened to mention how this 'consistency' was maintained: there was 'too much deference accorded to Hayek, and especially to Ludwig von Mises who seemed to demand sycophancy.'

Margit Mises (1984, 24, 44, 63, 169–170) interpreted her fiancé's 'attacks' on her as 'really a sign of depression, a hidden dissatisfaction and the sign of a great, great need for love.' At GMU, Boettke 'often' instructs his students to

> 'love Mises to pieces,' by which he means never lose sight of why you entered the discipline in the first place. (A. Evans 2010, 79)

Hayek (28 August 1975) told Arthur Seldon that FEE was a 'propaganda' set-up.[68] In FEE's *Freeman*, Boettke (2016a) illustrates what passes for disinterested scholarship at GMU ('Masonomics'): 'His [Mises] is a story of scientific glory and personal courage in a very dark time in human history. He stood against those forces with the tools of reason embedded in economic science at its finest, and he survived courageously and in doing so provides us with an exemplar of scientific economist, scholar of political economy, and bold and creative social philosophy.'

Boettke (2010, 64) imitates Rothbard: 'When I first started teaching (and even today), I would listen to tapes of Rothbard lectures and try to imitate his ability to combine theory, history, and jokes to convey the principles of economics to those who are *innocent* [emphasis added] of its teachings.' Rothbard (1973) was a fund-raising sycophant:

> For those of us who have loved as well as revered Ludwig von Mises, words cannot express our great sense of loss: of this gracious, brilliant and wonderful man; this man of unblemished integrity; this courageous and lifelong fighter for human freedom; this all-encompas-sing scholar; this noble inspiration to us all. And above all this gentle and charm-ing friend, this man who brought to the rest of us the living embodiment of the culture and the charm of pre-World War I Vienna.
>
> And always there as an inspiration and as a constant star. For what a life this man lived! Ludwig Mises died soon after his 92nd birthday, and until near the end he led his life very much in the world, pouring forth a mighty stream of great and immortal works, a fountainhead of energy and productivity as he taught continually at a university until the age of 87, as he flew tirelessly around the world to give papers and lectures on behalf of the free market and of sound economic science—a mighty structure of coherence and logic to which he contributed so much of his own creation.
>
> But oh, Mises, now you are gone, and we have lost our guide, our Nestor, our friend. How will we carry on without you? But we have to carry on, because anything less would be a shameful be-trayal of all that you have taught us, by the example of your noble life as much as by your immortal works. Bless you, Ludwig von Mises, and our deepest love goes with you.

Rothbard (1973) combined sycophancy with lies:

> Readers of Mises's majestic, formidable and uncompromising works must have been often surprised to meet him in person. Perhaps they had formed the image of Ludwig Mises as cold, severe, austere, the logical scholar repelled by lesser mortals, bitter at the follies around him and at the long trail of wrongs and insults that he had suffered. They couldn't have been more wrong; for what they met was a mind of genius blended harmoniously with a personality of great sweetness and benevolence. Not once has any of us heard a harsh or bitter word escape from Mises' lips. Un-failingly gentle and courteous, Ludwig Mises was always there to encourage even the slightest signs of productivity or intelligence in his friends and students; always there for warmth as well as for the mastery of logic and reason that his works have long proclaimed him.

Mises transmitted his perfect knowledge in return for sycophancy. But if sycophants deviated—by, for example, recommending the use of the price mechanism for foreign exchange—they became excommunicated devils. Machlup went to extraordinary lengths to find employment for

Mises—but at the 1965 Stresa MPS meeting, Machlup said some 'pleasant, conventional words' to Margit Mises (1984, 145–146):

> When Lu saw this, he pulled me away from Machlup. 'I don't want you to talk to him,' he said. 'I don't want you ever to talk to him again.' He was so excited that I became frightened, gave Machlup a sign, and stayed behind with Lu. We went to our room, and I saw that Lu was really unhappy about Machlup. 'He was in my seminar in Vienna,' Lu said, 'he understands everything.'

A few days before the announcement of Hayek's Nobel Prize, John Chamberlain (1974) reported that Hayek, Mises, Rothbard and Friedman had been 'trying to warn the world of Keynesian delusions ever since World War II.' But: 'It is too much to hope' that the British Labour Party Prime Minister (1964–1970, 1974–1976), 'Harold Wilson will ever listen to the Mont Pelerin gospel.'

Less than two years later, Callaghan, the next British Prime Minister (1976–1979), apparently influenced by his son-in-law (the economics editor of *The Times*, Peter Jay) 'seemed,' according to the *Economist*, to 'kill off Keynesian demand management' at the 1976 Labour Party Conference: 'We used to think that you could spend your way out of a recession and increase employment by cutting taxes and boosting government spending. I tell you in all candour that that option no longer exists, and in so far as it ever did exist, it only worked on each occasion since the war by injecting a bigger dose of inflation into the economy, followed by a higher level of unemployment as the next step.'[69]

Another two years later, Hayek (1997 [1978], 185, n. 65) celebrated the 'fundamental truth' contained in the opening paragraphs of the final communiqué of the 1977 Downing Street 'summit' meeting of political leaders from the left—Callaghan (Prime Minister, 1976–1979), Carter (Democratic Party President, 1977–1981) and Helmut Schmidt (Social Democratic Chancellor of West Germany, 1974–1982)—and the right—Giscard d'Estaing (French President, 1974–1981), Takeo Fukuda (Liberal Democratic Party Prime Minister of Japan, 1976–1978) and Andreotti (Christian Democrat Prime Minister of Italy, 1976–1979):

> The first few lines said: 'Inflation is not a remedy for unemployment, but is one of its major causes.'

Hayek (1977) told Ebeling that this Communique was 'the greatest victory of the anti-Keynesians ... the greatest victory of all I think we have had ... You know, Keynesian economics seems to be dead.' Indeed, according to Hayek, the 'London-Summit' was *plus royaliste que le roi*—they put it 'too strongly because, unfortunately, in the short run inflation can in most situations reduce unemployment.'

The following year, when Rosten asked: 'Are you impressed, as you get older, as I get older, by the unbelievable intensity with which people maintain their beliefs, and the difficulty of getting people to change their minds in the face of the most extraordinarily powerful evidence?'; Hayek (1978a)—who was consumed by 'free' market fantasy—replied: 'Well, one has to be if one has preached this thing for fifty years without succeeding in persuading. [laughter]' To which Rosten objected: 'You mean you still are the voice in the wilderness? Well, you can hardly say that.'[70]

When asked: 'What do you consider to be the main lesson one can extract from an analysis of the Great Depression?' Hayek (2009 [1979], 14) replied: 'I think that the artificial expansion of the boom led to the depression. Then authorities made things worse by a process of deliberate contraction. It is very clear to me that the monetary authorities caused the 1929 Crash and they are also responsible for subsequent cycles ... They made a great mistake before and after the crisis.'

On 9 October 1974, the Nobel Prize press release announced that 'von' Hayek and Myrdal were to be rewarded for their 'pioneering work in the theory of money and economic fluctuations and for their penetrating analysis of the interdependence of economic, social and institutional phenomena.'[71] The institution most responsible for the economic and social consequences of the world-wide inflation of 1970 was the US Federal Reserve. When asked *what* caused this inflation, Friedman would snap back: 'Arthur Burns,' the anti-Keynesian recruit to Hayek's MPS who presided over (1970–1978) the Federal Reserve (Leeson 2003).

On 15 October 1974, Hayek informed readers of *The Daily Telegraph*: 'The responsibility for current world-wide inflation, I am sorry to say, rests wholly and squarely with the economists, or at least with that great majority of my fellow economists who have embraced the teachings of Lord Keynes. What we are experiencing are simply the economic consequences of Lord Keynes ... We have in fact been led into a frightful position.' Keynes, however, opposed inflation—he promoted a once-and-for-all increase in the price level to assist the process of reducing both the real wage and unemployment (Leeson 1999).

'Free' market economists denigrate opponents by using sexually charged language: 'scabrous,' 'camp followers,' etc. (Caldwell 2004, 257; Mises 1960 [1948], 55). In contrast—they falsely assert—it was 'characteristic' of Hayek not to lash out at his critics (Caldwell 2007, 22). Hayek (1994, 78, 85, 95), however, repeatedly gossiped about William Beveridge's alleged erectile dysfunction: Beveridge's partner

> burst out, 'He isn't man enough; he isn't man enough. I know' … My stories about [Harold] Laski and Beveridge can be rather malicious.

Caldwell (2010b) insisted that non-Hayekians 'could perhaps learn something from him: a little Austrian politesse is a nice prophylactic against stridency.' His source was Hayek (1978b [1976], 235) who described himself as displaying 'politeness to a fault' because he 'hardly ever attributed to opponents anything beyond intellectual error.'[72] Using a word that the Nazis used to justify the liquidation of the Jews and other 'enemies of the State,' Hayek (1978b [1975], 200)—a few pages earlier—insisted that Keynes became the 'inflationist or at least rabid anti-deflationist of the 1930s.'

Mises (2000 [1944], 128) insisted that 'The fall in prices and wage rates is the preliminary step toward recovery and future real prosperity,' and Rothbard's 'In Defense of Deflation' explained:

> Deflation would bring about the necessary 'smashing' of downwardly rigid wages and prices, so the appropriate resource allocations could occur to help bring about sound long-term economic activity. (cited by Ebeling 1975)

Hayek (1978b [1974], 193) stated: 'We must face the fact that in the present situation merely to stop the inflation or even to slow down its rate will produce substantial unemployment. *Certainly nobody wishes this* [emphasis added], but we can no longer avoid it and all attempts to postpone it will only increase its ultimate size.'

The interwar deflation that Hayek and Mises promoted created the unemployment that assisted Hitler's rise to power; the MPS-initiated stagflation of the 1970s helped produce the Thatcher-Reagan move to the political right; and the 'Great Recession' (2007–2009) that followed the Randian- and Austrian-promoted deregulation of the financial system, also fuelled populists forces.

Before *The Road to Serfdom* (1944), Hayek's major contribution to world history (1929–1933) had been—from a democratic perspective—the dysfunctional promotion of the deflationary manipulation of the price mechanism: falling general prices, rising real wages and thus increased unemployment. As Hitler was gaining electoral momentum, Hayek (1975, 5) regarded deflation-induced 'allocative corrections' and the removal of 'distorted relative prices'—that is, eliminating rigidities in wages—as 'desirable': at the 'beginning of the Great Depression … I believed that a process of deflation of some short duration might break the rigidity of wages which I thought was incompatible with a *functioning* [emphasis added] economy.'

Hayek's (16 October 1974) *Daily Telegraph* solution 'can be achieved only by that steady restructuring of the use of all resources in adapting to changing real conditions which the debauching of the monetary medium prevents and only a *properly functioning* [emphasis added] market can bring about.' He also cautioned 'We are probably approaching a critical test of democracy about the outcome of which one must feel apprehensive.' Four years later, Hayek (1978a) elaborated to Rosten: 'So I rather fear that we shall have a return to some sort of dictatorial democracy, I would say, where democracy merely serves to authorize the actions of a dictator. And if the system is going to break down, it will be a very long period before real democracy can reemerge.'

Hayek (1978a) described the origins of the threat to the spontaneous order: 'The beginning of it was 150 years ago. Before that, there was never any serious revolt against the market society, because every farmer knew he had to sell his grain.' Rosten asked: 'Can you have a *functioning* [emphasis added] society without some higher dedication, fear, faith?' Hayek (1978a) replied that ancient 'Greek democracy' was 'essentially irreligious for all practical purposes … This brings us back to something which we discussed very much earlier. There is still the strong innate need to know that one serves common, concrete purposes with one's fellows. Now, this clearly is the thing which in a really great society is unachievable. You cannot really know. Whether people can learn this is still part of the emancipation from the feelings of the small face-to-face group, which we have not yet achieved. But we must achieve this if we are to maintain a large, great society of free men. It may be that our first attempt will break down.'[73]

After his 1974 Nobel Prize for Economic Sciences, Hayek exerted a major influence not only on the Reagan administration and the Pinochet regime but also on the Conservative Party: his 'free' market vision inspired the 1986 British Big Bang deregulation of the financial sector, overseen by Nigel Lawson. In *Free Agent: The Unseen War 1941–1991*, Crozier (1993, 106) described Lawson as one of his collaborators; but Crozier is not mentioned in Lawson's *The View From No. 11. Memoirs of a Tory Radical*. Lawson (1992, 4) acknowledges having been the undergraduate president of the Strasbourg Club, 'which was devoted to the then unfashionable cause of European union'—but made no mention of Habsburg or the Cercle Pinay (Teacher 2018a).[74]

The upper Habsburg Estates were primarily focused on maintaining the 'privileges of their aristocratic members ... the nobles regarded the Austrian people as an extension of their own peasantry, their only function to keep the nobility in luxury' (Taylor 1964, 14, 188–189). Mises lived with his mother until he was fifty-three: 'The only explanation I could find was that his mother's household was running smoothly - their two maids had been with them for about twenty years - and Lu could come and go whenever it pleased him and could concentrate on his work without being disturbed' (Margit Mises 1984, 25). Hayek (1978a) 'moved, to some extent, in aristocratic circles, and I like their style of life.'[75] Hayek's (1994, 39, 78) maternal grandparents 'kept at least three servants'; during the 'Great' War, Hayek shared an 'Italian servant girl' who had 'been quite willing to sit on his lap' (Cubitt 2006, 46, 76, 240).

The 1901 British census reported that 31.6% of females over the age of 10 were in paid employment: there were 1,690,686 female domestic servants (40.5% of the adult female working population).[76] Hayek's style of life was challenged by 'the servant problem': as the *Economist* (17 December 2011) noted, 'By the early 20th century, the rich were getting the uncomfortable sense that the foundations of the social order were shifting.'[77] Between 1910 and 1923, the proportion of the Viennese workforce employed as domestic servants fell from 9.3 to 6.3% (Kirk 1996, 14, Table 0.2).

Nigel Lawson (1932–), the grandson of a Latvian merchant, had been born into a 'comfortable' Jewish 'Hampstead household, complete with nanny, cook and parlourmaid.' Between 1931 and 1949, Hayek (1994, 78) lived in Hampstead Garden Suburb: 'We were of course still running the house with the help of a regular maid. These were usually Austrian girls.' With his second wife, he had a *'bedienerin'* or 'servant' (Cubitt 2006, 46, 76, 240).

Had *Unternehmen Seelöwe* (Operation Sea Lion) succeeded, *Einsatzgruppen* death squads under Dr. Franz Six would have established the Nazi New Order and liquidated Britain's Jewish population: Dr. Heinrich von Hayek could have been provided with a fresh supply of victims to experiment on. Samuel Brittan (1977; 1988; 2005, 300–315)—the author of *The Economic Consequences of Democracy, A Restatement of Economic Liberalism* and 'Hayek's Contribution'—and his brother, Leon (Thatcher's Home Secretary, 1983–1985), were children of Lithuanian Jews who had migrated to Britain just before the Holocaust.

Two years after being knighted 'for services to economic journalism,' Sir Samuel Brittan (1995, 105, 113) noted that 'remarkably,' Hayek was—like many others 'of Austrian origin'—a 'subject for life-and-time hagiography' and 'I enjoy a good wallow as much as anyone else.' Hayek 'came to see economics as part of a much wider study of spontaneous social order.'

In 1992, Nigel Lawson (1992, 13) became Baron Lawson of Blaby and praised Hayek's 'spontaneous order': he was grateful to Thatcher because she was

> thankfully free of that middle-class guilt that had made most leading politicians, of both parties, who had received expensive private education, ashamed of quality, embarrassed by capital and tolerant of the excesses of organized labour. Margaret instinctively realized the need to regain the moral as well as the practical initiative from collectivism. In this she as strongly fortified by the practical writings of the economist and philosopher Friedrich Hayek ... Hayek's development of the concept of a spontaneous natural order provided a strong philosophical underpinning for the market, not least by demonstrating that our understanding of the nature of society and the economy is too partial to admit economic management by the state.

Hayek (1978a) described this spontaneous natural order: 'the curious thing is that in the countryside of southwest England, the class distinctions are very sharp, but they're not resented. [laughter] They're still accepted as part of the natural order.'[78]

Faith-based deregulation could only lead to a (2007–2009) Big Bang—'recessionary forces of typhoon proportions ... financial and economic meltdowns' (Leeson 2005). A. W. H. Phillips provided the building blocks which—when expanded to include banks—can mitigate if not avoid the economic cycle (Leeson 2011). But the MPS-initiated stagflation of the 1970s discredited economic orthodoxy—the Thatcher-Reagan policy response facilitated one component of re-feudalisation: growing income and wealth inequality and a shrinking middle class. To his credit, the MPS President, Deepak Lal (2009), came close to issuing a Society *mea culpa*: 'complacency' about financial sector deregulation had preceded the Global Financial Crisis. But according to Hayek (1978a), social scientists should aspire to hold a position within a faith-based 'knowledge' disseminating hierarchy and acquire 'a profound respect for the existence of other orderly structures in the world, which they admit they cannot fully understand and interpret.'[79]

Nigel Lawson (1992, 626, 628), Thatcher's Chancellor of the Exchequer (1983–1989) who oversaw the 1986 'Big Bang,' tolerated the excesses of organised capital and asserted that capital strikes and thus the business cycle were, in effect, acts of God: 'by acting in the imprudent way they did,' banks

> inflicted terrible damage on their own profit-and-loss accounts and balance sheets. The 'authorities' cannot fine-tune bank lending. That is one of the reasons why the economic cycle cannot be avoided.

Harberger (2016) described MPS meetings: 'thank God less so today than at the beginning, you had a whole claque of gold bugs that would be getting up and making half-hour speeches about the beauties of the gold standard and why it was always wrong to go off the gold standard and how we have to go back. And that just drove everybody nuts, Friedman and me in particular. [laughter]' As Hayek was embracing 'Deacon' McCormick's 'Spooks Club,' 'Jackdaw Network' and a fraudulent 1905 diary (24 October 1984), Friedman (2 October 1984) complained to the journalist-editor of the *Mont Pelerin Society Newsletter* about their account of his presentation to the Vancouver MPS meeting which reported that he favoured a return to the gold standard. Somewhat diplomatically, Friedman reported that this was 'erroneous.'[80]

The editor of *Grant's Interest Rate Observer*, James Grant (1996), illustrated the quality of Austrian business cycle thinking: Alan Greenspan's colleague

> Alan Blinder was particularly cocky about this after he left the Fed. He would say: 'If we had only gotten this right in 1990, we wouldn't have had a recession.' Imagine. If they can get the right funds rate, well never

have another downturn. Wow. That's pretty good! How did the Soviet state ever come to grief? It didn't have the right interest rate! Again, once you accept the principles of the Clairvoyance Standard–that the central bank, knowing the future, should act to improve it before it happens–then you can argue about who is the clearer clairvoyant. The method itself is unsound.

Grant offered a cyclical explanation for Truth:

> In the boom cycle, people are not so much interested in a message that says: a bust is simply a necessary part of the business cycle. In a false prosperity, good economic ideas are marginalized. That's why Austrians should prepare right now to offer the best explanation when the tide turns, as it always does. Who knows? Maybe well find ways to make the bust intellectually profitable. In time, Austrian economics could be again seen as the mainstream theory. It should be.

In 2003, Auburn University's Professor of Economics, Roger Garrison (2003), was the first 'Hayek Visiting Fellow' at the LSE. In his 'Hayek Lecture,' it 'was easy to come down on the side of Hayek. The economy is sent into recession not by some ill-fated attempt by workers to save more but by an ill-advised attempt of the central bank to stimulate more growth than savers are willing to finance. Further, the central bank's attempts to reignite the boom after the bust has come is more likely to postpone a genuine recovery than to hasten it. If Keynes won the day against Hayek, it was because of the political popularity of his policy prescriptions and not because of the cogency of his theorizing.'

Garrison then received an email from Prime Minister Blair's economic advisor, Derek Scott (LSE alumni), who had listened to the lecture from the balcony:

> He was clearly taken by the Hayekian ideas, describing the lecture as 'a breath of fresh air.' 'I only wish that more people looked at the world through similar eyes,' he wrote ... he invited me to pay a visit to No. 10 Downing Street.

Toby Baxendale (2011), who was invited along with Garrison to 10 Downing Street, introduced a reprint of *Hayek's Prices and Production* with an agenda: 'This volume reminds us of a time when Austrian theory sat at the top of the table of debate, and offers us the way to return there ... An old Polish soldier who had settled in London after World War II exposed me to the teachings of Hayek when I was sixteen years old. He had fought the Nazi machine as a member of the Royal Air Force.' This had led him to establish an 'Austrian Hedge Fund that applies our methodology to exchange rate determination and indeed to credit spreads ... The point is that although the cause and effect of an increase in Austrian Money Supply and the associated effect on its purchasing power parity is certain, when it will happen depends on the subjective valuations of people. So we apply no mathematical tools to help us predict when the effect will be seen, we trade the position as and when it becomes apparent visually.'

Herbert Hoover (1952, 29–32) blamed his one-term status on the advice given to him by his Treasury Secretary, Andrew Mellon: 'liquidate labor, liquidate stocks, liquidate farmers, liquidate real estate... it will purge the rottenness out of the system. High costs of living and high living will come down. People will work harder, live a more moral life. Values will be adjusted, and enterprising people will pick up from less competent people' (Chapter 2). Over coffee in the Prime Minister's residence, Garrison (2003) advised about the USA: 'Some needed liquidation has taken place; more liquidation is undoubtedly in order.' Baxendale concurred:

> What struck me during the visit at No. 10—and I hope it struck Mr. Scott, too—is that the story as told by an academic economist and as told by a real live entrepreneur/businessman were in perfect harmony. I've become aware over the years that this is a characteristic of Austrian economics that cannot be matched by other schools of macroeconomic thought. Hayek's ideas ring true in the financial and business community in ways that the 'rational expectations' of new classicism or the 'menu costs' of new Keynesianism do not. (Garrison 2003)

After returning to the USA, Scott and Baxendale had breakfast which, in Garrison's (2003) judgment, 'evidenced a continuing interest in Hayekian ideas and their implications for policy prescription and institutional reform ... I hope that in Austrian circles the year 2003 will be remembered as the year that Hayekian economics returned to LSE ... Other Hayek Visiting Fellows in the years ahead and possibly an ongoing Hayek program can turn the 2003 visit into the start of something grand.'

According to John Allison, the CEO of the Cato Institute, 'put balls and chains on good people, and bad things happen' (cited by Martin 2009). But as those who were jailed as a result of their involvement in Watergate discovered: regulation imposes private costs. The IEA hosted a 1987 conference on 'The Costs of Regulation' without addressing the social costs of deregulation.[81]

In 'Austrian Economics and the Public Mind,' the journalist Michael Prowse (2014 [1996]) explained to the Mises Institute 'Scholars' Conference at Auburn University that 'over the years,' he had 'managed to publish quite a few articles and columns on Austrian and Classical Liberal themes in the London Financial Times':

> Last fall, I smuggled in a piece on Austrian business cycle theory in the form of an imaginary conversation on the U.S. economic outlook between Keynes and Mises. You will be pleased to hear that it ended with Keynes describing Mises as a 'genius' and declaring 'you never know, I might become an Austrian.'

Prowse summarised his journalistic mission: Austrians 'tend to be opposed to intervention, period. They understand that the goal of public policy should be to maintain free entry to all markets–that this is the precondition for competition to work its magic. I am certain the public would find this clear policy stance appealing–if it understood the underlying rationale … I believe that Mises, were he still alive, would be immensely gratified by the extent to which market capitalism has become the watchword and catchword of our day. That it has become so, of course, in large measure reflects his efforts.'

In London, Garrison (2003) attended the IEA's 'Hayek Memorial Lecture,' which was delivered 'this year by Bill Emmott, editor-in-chief of *The Economist*.' The following year, in his Mansion House speech to the City of London annual dinner, the Labour Party Chancellor of the Exchequer (1997–2007), Gordon Brown, stated that 'in budget after budget I want us to do even more to encourage the risk takers' (cited by Kirkup 2008). Four years before Lehman Brothers disappeared, Dr. Brown opened their London headquarters and told their bankers: 'I would like to pay tribute to the contribution you and your company make to the prosperity of Britain … During its 150 year history, Lehman Brothers has always been an innovator, financing new ideas and inventions before many others even began to realize their potential.'[82]

Almost three decades after Prime Minister Callaghan embraced Hayek-style economics at the Labour Party conference, Brown told a Confederation of British Industry audience: 'I believe 2005 will go down in history as ... an important economic moment ... My vision is of a Britain made for globalisation – the location of choice and the place for business to be ... Britain is well placed to become world leaders in some of the worlds' fastest growing, most wealth creating sectors ... my first and foremost commitment is to maintain economic stability: stability yesterday, today and tomorrow ... at every point I want to work with you and listen to your concerns so that just as we are meeting the stability challenge, we can meet all long term challenges by making the reforms you need and the modernisation you require and the country requires for economic success.'

Brown continued: 'We all agree that at the heart of the modern enterprise challenge is minimising regulatory concerns ... Whenever I go to the USA and talk to businessmen and women there, they express exactly the same frustrations about regulation and the same hopes about reducing burdens. And I know that you feel that what we need is real delivery – and I want to underline this by a better understanding of risk and indeed implementing a modern risk based approach to regulation so that the culture change we all agree upon can be advanced ... In the old regulatory model – and for more than one hundred years – the implicit principle from health and safety to the administration of tax and financial services has been, irrespective of known risks or past results, 100% inspection whether it be premises, procedures or practices. So regulation came to mean that government routinely and continuously inspected everyone and everything, demanded information from all of us on a blanket basis, required forms to be filled in for all issues subject to regulation and inspection – the only barrier to complete coverage usually being a lack of resources. This approach, followed for more than a century of regulation by governments of all parties is outdated. The better, and in my opinion the correct, modern model of regulation – the risk based approach - is based on trust in the responsible company, the engaged employee and the educated consumer, leading government to focus its attention where it should: no inspection without justification, no form filling without justification, and no information requirements without justification, not just a light touch but a limited touch. The new model of regulation can be applied not just to regulation of environment, health and safety and social standards but is being applied to other areas vital to the success of British business: to the regulation of financial services and indeed to the administration of tax. And more than that, we should not only apply the concept of risk to the enforcement of regulation, but also to the design and indeed to the decision as to whether to regulate at all.'

Brown promised new legislation: 'we will make this risk based approach a statutory duty of the regulators. And driving further the risk based approach in financial services, I will publish at the Pre Budget Report 10 new simplification and deregulatory measures which will cut demands for information, forms and reporting requirements including cutting by 15% disclosures of change of control and up to 20 FSA consultations each year. So we will abolish this requirement and reduce the burdens placed upon you - the first of a series of regulatory requirements which by working together we can abolish in the interests of the British economy.' This was Brown's 'radical commitment to minimise regulation' and to maximise flexibility and to 'reach out and to take our rightful place in the world. A vision of Britain as the place to be. Let us together make Globalisation work for Britain to the benefit of all - for British companies, the British economy and the British people.'[83]

Two years later, in his Mansion House speech, Brown congratulated his audience 'on these remarkable achievements, an era that history will record as the beginning of a new golden age for the City of London ... I believe it will be said of this age, the first decades of the 21st century, that out of the greatest restructuring of the global economy, perhaps even greater than the industrial revolution, a new world order was created.'

In 2009, the Governor of the Bank of England, Mervyn King, described the regulatory environment as being 'like a church' whose congregation 'ignores its sermons ... Warnings are unlikely to be effective when people are being asked to change behaviour which seems to them to be highly profitable ... So it's not entirely clear how the Bank will be able to discharge its new statutory responsibility if we can do no more than issue sermons or organise burials ... Blaming individuals is no substitute for acknowledging the failure of the system.'[84]

In June 2007, Brown replaced Blair as Prime Minister, and Alistair Darling replaced Brown as Chancellor. The Labour government's (1997–2010) faith in a new British Empire based on financial services lasted another four months—until Britain returned to the era preceding the 'New Imperialism' of the 1870s, when the 1st Earl Russell was Prime Minister and Gladstone Chancellor. In September 2007, under the chairmanship of Ridley's nephew, the Old Etonian, Matthew White Ridley, The 5th Viscount Ridley, Northern Rock became the first British bank since Overend, Gurney & Company (10 May 1866) to suffer a bank run.[85] His Old Etonian father, Matthew White Ridley, The 4th Viscount Ridley, had also been chairman of Northern Rock (1987–1992) and had sat on the board for 30 years.

Shortly before Northern Rock failed and was nationalised, The 5th Viscount Ridley (2006) stated: 'Government is a very dangerous toy. It is used to fight wars, impose ideologies and enrich rulers. True, nowadays, our leaders do not enrich themselves (at least not on the scale of the Sun King), but they enrich their clients: they preside over vast and insatiable parasitic bureaucracies that grow by Parkinson's Law and live off true wealth creators such as traders and inventors. Sure, it is possible to have too little government. Only, that has not been the world's problem for millennia. After the century of Mao, Hitler and Stalin, can anybody really say that the risk of too little government is greater than the risk of too much? The dangerous idea we all need to learn is that the more we limit the growth of government, the better off we will all be.'

As President, Reagan (27 March 1984) informed Eamonn Butler of the Adam Smith Institute that 'von' Hayek played 'an absolutely essential role in preparing the ground for the resurgent conservative movement in America.'[86] Hayek sought to overthrow the constitution of the USA (Chapter 1); and (like Nixon), Reagan succeeded in undermining that constitution. Rep. Lee H. Hamilton (D-Ind.), the chairman of the House committee on the Iran-contra scandal stated that 'Congress will probably consider impeaching President Reagan if it discovers that Reagan knew about the diversion of profits from his secret arms sales to Iran' (McManus 1987).

In 1964 in Neshoba County, Mississippi, Klansman Cecil Ray Price organised the murder and disappearance of three voter registration activists, James Chaney, Andrew Goodman and Michael Schwerner. Because the State of Mississippi refused to prosecute the killers for murder (a state crime), the Federal government charged 18 individuals with conspiring to deprive the three activists of their civil rights (by murder).

In 1980, Republican candidate Reagan informed a Neshoba County Fair audience:

> I believe in state's rights; I believe in people doing as much as they can for themselves at the community level and at the private level. And I believe

that we've distorted the balance of our government today by giving powers that were never intended in the constitution to that federal establishment. And if I do get the job I'm looking for, I'm going to devote myself to trying to reorder those priorities and to restore to the states and local communities those functions which properly belong there. (cited by Myers 2007)

John Farrell (2017) documented Nixon's treason: on 22 October 1968, ordering John Haldeman to 'monkey wrench' President Lyndon Johnson's efforts to strike a peace deal in Vietnam—an 'October surprise' that would have reflected credit on the Democrats. William Casey was Reagan's 1980 campaign manager and first CIA Director (1981–1987), and may also have committed treason by ensuring that the American hostages held in Iran would not be released until Reagan's first day as President (Teacher 2018b).

In 1978, Casey and Fisher founded the Manhattan Institute for Policy Research. According to SouceWatch, the Institute sought and received funding from tobacco companies: an R. J. Reynolds memo reveals that the Manhattan Institute was targeted as an independent third party to help reduce the public's perception of danger associated with exposure to second-hand smoke.[87]

In 1981, *The Times* was acquired by Murdoch's News International in controversial circumstances. In 1986, Murdoch sacked 6000 Fleet Street production employees and relocated his four main titles, *The Times*, *The Sunday Times*, the *Sun* and the *News of the World*, to a new plant in Wapping. Murdoch's defeat of the Fleet Street unions transformed industrial relations in Britain.

In a Manhattan Institute third annual Walter B. Wriston Lecture in Public Policy, Murdoch (1990) described 'The War on Technology' in Hayekian terms: 'we were encouraged by Mrs. Thatcher's victory in the miners' strike and by signs that authorities were prepared to protect private property from the actions of massed pickets ... The war between new technology and outmoded social institutions continues. At stake is the very idea of human progress ... The great truth, which being an immigrant perhaps I can see more clearly than the average citizen, is this: Modernization is Americanization. It is the American way of organizing society that is prevailing in the world ... The decision to rely on market forces is the essence of modernization. Yet technological change often provokes atavistic, authoritarian responses. The real danger of the present technological revolution is that we may be panicked by future shock into regressive schemes of regulation ... The immediate result of our victory was greater freedom and flexibility, and higher profits, for News Corp. But the Battle of Wapping also ushered in a silver age of British newspaper journalism.'[88]

Ridley's (2010) *The Rational Optimist: How Prosperity Evolves* was awarded the $50,000 2011 Hayek Book Prize by the Manhattan Institute. In his acceptance speech, The 5th Viscount Ridley (2011) declared: 'As Hayek understood, it is human collaboration that is necessary for society to work ... the key feature of trade is that it enables us to work for each other not just for ourselves; that attempts at self-sufficiency are the true form of selfishness as well as the quick road to poverty; and that authoritarian, top-down rule is not the source of order or progress.' In 2013, Ridley, a columnist for the London *Times*, was elected as a Conservative hereditary peer in the House of Lords. Alongside Sir Samuel Brittan, Ian Plimer, MPS President Lal and IEA's Alan Peacock, Ridley sits on the 'Academic Advisory Council' of what is regarded as the 'UK's most prominent source of climate-change denial'—Nigel Lawson's Global Warming Policy Foundation (Johnson 2014).

Friedman and Stigler calculated that a draw was all that was required for a paradigmatic challenger to obtain their objectives (Leeson 2000, Chapter 3). Doubts—about the medical evidence regarding the harm caused by tobacco and the causes and consequences of climate change—are all that are required to establish a draw against the relevant scientific community. By any objective standard, the populist opinions of The 3rd Viscount Monckton of Brenchley (a classics major with a diploma in journalism) have little or no epistemological validity compared to, for example, the Review on Climate Change and Policy Response to Climate Change for the Federal, State and Territory Governments of Australia (2007–2008) and Ross Garnaut's 2011 independent update provided for the incoming Liberal Government.

Certain personality types have 'instincts' that make them vulnerable to bogus Bilgewater 'Dukes,' Romanov 'Princesses' and Habsburg 'vons' and 'Counts'—an aristocratic placebo effect. In addition to the opinion editors of Murdoch's *Wall Street Journal*, climate change scepticism has been coordinated by four journalists: Samuel Brittan (*The Financial Times*), Nigel, The Lord Lawson of Blaby PC (*The Financial Times, The Sunday Telegraph* and the *Spectator*), The 3rd Viscount Monckton (a former editor of the Roman Catholic *The Universe*) and The (zoology-trained) 5th Viscount Ridley (*The Times*). Monckton 'displayed a Nazi swastika next to a quote from Professor Garnaut' and compared statements made by Hitler to Garnaut's suggestion that 'people should accept the mainstream science of climate change':

> That again is a fascist point of view, that you merely accept authority without question. Heil Hitler, on we go.[89]

In *The Wall Street Journal*, Ridley (2014) declared:

> Almost every environmental scare of the past half-century proved exaggerated, including the population 'bomb,' pesticides, acid rain, then ozone hole, falling sperm counts, GM [Genetically Modified] crops and killer bees. In every case institutions gained a lot of funding from the care and then quietly converged on the view the problem was much more moderate than the extreme voices had argued. Global warming is no different.

According to Donald Trump (6 November 2012),

> The concept of global warming was created by and for the Chinese in order to make U.S. manufacturing non-competitive.[90]

Trump (23 January 2016) also stated:

> They say I have the most loyal people — did you ever see that? Where I could stand in the middle of 5th Avenue and shoot somebody, and I wouldn't lose any voters. It's like incredible.[91]

It took almost eight decades for Hayek's fraud about having predicted the Great Depression to be reported (Klausinger 2012, 172, n. 10; 2010, 227); Hayek's for-posthumous-consumption oral history interviews are being suppressed, presumably for fund-raising purposes (Leeson 2015, Chapter 2); and for three decades, the 'free' market (i.e. monopolised) Hayek Archives have kept their secrets. Hayek (1978a)—who must have been amazed at the sycophancy of those who kept him financially and emotionally afloat—told Rosten: 'Our society is built on the fact that we serve people whom we do not know.'[92]

The 'free' market is promoted by frauds, paid sycophants, public stoning theocrats, white supremacists and those with blind faith in the assertions made by socially 'superior' fellow-travellers. At *The Financial Times*, Samuel Brittan (1995, 20, 113) reported that Hayek has 'suffered from both sycophantic admirers and scoffers, unwilling to make the effort to see what he was getting at ... Hayek soon dropped the von in front of his name, although sneering critics often insisted on re-inserting it.'

But Hayek (1994, 37) referred to

> the minor title of nobility (the 'von') which the family *still bears*. (emphasis added)

The Times (17 December 1931) reported that 'von Hayek' had been appointed to the University of London Tooke Professorship; at the LSE Hayek was known as '*von* Hayek'; he wore his family coat of arms on his signet ring (Ebenstein 2003, 75, 298). In Frederic Benham's (1932, v) *British Monetary Policy*, his LSE colleague, 'Professor von Hayek,' was thanked. *The Times* (19 October 1932) published a letter from 'von' Hayek (and three LSE colleagues, T. E. Gregory, Arnold Plant and Lionel Robbins) on 'Spending and Saving Public Works from Rates.' Over half a century later—with Hayek's approval—the shield of his coat of arms was reproduced on the cover of *The Fatal Conceit: The Errors of Socialism* (1988) (Cubitt 2006, 274).[93] Hayek (1994, 107) explained: 'you are only prohibited from calling yourself von in Austria ... I was a law abiding citizen and completely stopped using the title von.'

In his publications, Hayek repeatedly added the illegal 'von' to his name—including symbolically, his *Economica* essay on 'The Maintenance of Capital' (1935). Yet, in a letter to *The Times*, Hayek (14 November 1981) professed deep indignation that 'von' had been attached to his name: perhaps even Labour MPs could be 'shamed' into not answering arguments by reference to 'descent.' After British naturalisation in 1938, he did not, he claimed, generally use it himself in that form.[94] However, in and out of Austria, professionally and personally, Hayek repeatedly attached 'von' to his name,[95] and the Freiburg doorplate from where he sent the 'descent' letter to *The Times* was labelled 'Prof. Dr. Friedrich A. von Hayek' (Ebenstein 2003, 317).

Hayek's (1978a) 'principle' was 'that I will not ask, under any circumstances, what is politically possible now. I concentrate on what I think is right and should be done if you can convince the public. If you can't, well it's so much the worse, but that's not my affair.'[96] *The Times* didn't publish the 'descent' letter presumably because at least some employees knew that Hayek was lying. At the University of Salzburg, where he worked from 1969 to 1977, his notepaper was headed 'PROF. F. A. von HAYEK'—and on this notepaper, Hayek (8 October 1977) had written to Rees-Mogg making a calculation about what was politically possible: in order to win electoral support from 'rank and file' labour union members, Hayek insisted that *The Times* push Mrs. Thatcher to obtain a 'mandate' to strip labour unions of their privileges.[97]

Referring to 'Deacon' McCormick's (1979) transparent fraud, Hayek (19 May 1984) told Bartley that 'it is almost incredible that such an account (pretendedly [*sic*] based on a diary of Pigou) should have remained so unnoticed ... some masterpiece of suppression must have been done.' Hayek had an automatic publishing outlet: 'I am playing with the idea of using the standing offer to print an article of mine on the chief page of The Times for an essay on the Vanished Book!' Bartley (4 July 1984) informed Hayek that he had made 'no real progress with the Pigou story: [John] Hicks says it must certainly be false; Graham Hutton says everyone knows it to be true' (cited by Leeson 2013, Chapter 9).

Three months later, Hayek had lunch at the Reform Club with 'Deacon' McCormick and pressed-ahead with his plan to write for either *The Times* or the Cold War magazine, *Encounter*. Had ill-health not intervened, he would, no doubt, have used *The Times* to celebrate Ronald Coase's 1991 Nobel Prize for Economic Sciences. According to 'free' market economists: negative externalities don't exist; and if they did, 'The Coase Theorem' reveals that they should be left to the 'free' market; and besides, 'we want externalities' (Chapter 8).

Having been stripped of the legal right to use his Habsburg 'von,' Hayek aspired to become a House of Windsor Baronet: 'Sir Friedrich' or, better still, 'Sir Fredrick' (Cubitt 2006, 29). Hayek (1994, 37, 107, 137) provided a misleading explanation for his British 'von': it was

> inevitably on my birth certificate. So that when I got naturalised in England and for that purpose submitted the birth certificate, when I received the certificate of naturalisation, my English name suddenly became 'von Hayek.' Now it was a moment when I was very anxious to go on an English passport for a holiday to Europe, so instead of invoking the bureaucracy to change this I put up with this ... in 1939 I wanted to visit Austria and didn't want to be suspected of having any special privileges with the Germans. In fact I was visiting my present wife.[98]

Mises provided an equally implausible justification:

> After he left Vienna, he added the 'von' back in. In America, he dropped the 'von' in his private life, but continued to use it in his writings, so that bibliographers would know he was the same man. (Greaves 1998)

In 2009, Monckton began his testimony to a US congressional energy and commerce committee hearing with

> I bring fraternal greetings from the Mother of Parliaments to the Congress of your athletic democracy and I pray that God's blessings may rest upon your councils.

When queried, he insisted: 'I am The Viscount Monckton of Brenchley (as my passport shows), a member of the Upper House but without the right to sit or vote, and I have never pretended otherwise' (cited by Kamen 2009).

David Beamish (18 July 2011), the Clerk of the Parliaments, wrote to Monckton:

> My predecessor, Sir Michael Pownall, wrote to you on 21 July 2010, and again on 30 July 2010, asking that you cease claiming to be a Member of the House of Lords, either directly or by implication. It has been drawn to my attention that you continue to make such claims. In particular, I have listened to your recent interview with Mr Adam Spencer on Australian radio. In response to the direct question, whether or not you were a Member of the House of Lords, you said 'Yes, but without the right to sit or vote.' You later repeated, 'I am a Member of the House.' I must repeat my predecessor's statement that you are not and have never been a Member of the House of Lords.[99]

Monckton claimed he had 'investigated scientific fraud' and had advised 'institutions on climate change': the leading proposals on reducing emissions of carbon dioxide—'a harmless and beneficial trace gas'—would 'threaten' the lives of poor people, 'gravely ... diminish liberty,' maybe 'render ... unlawful the pursuit of happiness' and lead to 'fiscal incontinence':

> The ice sheets of Greenland and Antarctica are thickening. The Sahara is greening. There is no 'climate crisis,' he said. So the 'correct policy ... is

not to cap or tax carbon dioxide emissions. It is to have the courage to do nothing.' (cited by Kamen 2009)

Leon Louw (2011), a policy 'expert' at the Heartland Institute, told *The Daily Bell*: 'The book that had the greatest influence on me was Mises' book, *Human Action*. That was the book that converted me and clinched the deal. I am an extreme Austrian myself; my colleagues are Austrian, as are all people who work full-time for the [South African Free Market] Foundation.'[100] Louw, a Committee member of the 'Association for Rational Inquiry into Claims of the Paranormal,' explained that he 'became converted to capitalism mainly by the literature of Ayn Rand and [the Cold War science fiction writer] Robert Heinlein.' When asked: 'Is the Foundation based on Austrian economics? Are you a supporter of Austrian economics?' Louw (2011) replied: 'Yes, yes, yes. We are all very much Austrian ... We often get involved in orthodox battles for think tanks such as the assault on liberty in the name of climate change ... We might, for example, defend people who run pyramid schemes or people who deal drugs or prostitution or whatever.'[101]

Louw claims to have a UNISA Bachelor of Law[102]; also, elsewhere, a UNISA BA (African Studies).[103] He also asserts that 'sustainable development' is 'voodoo science' (cited by Driessen 2005, 68–69). In order to 'Debunk Climate Change Propaganda and Provide Balanced Perspective,' 'Dr Leon Louw' and 'Lord Monckton' created a 'CFACT' lobby at the 2011 Durban United Nations Climate Change conference.[104] According to his Heartland Institute policy 'expert' website, 'Christopher Monckton, Third Viscount Monckton of Brenchley, was Special Advisor to British Prime Minister Margaret Thatcher from 1982 to 1986.' On Labour Day, 2012, 'Lord Monckton addressed an enthusiastic crowd of 100,000 West Virginia mineworkers and their families on a mountain-top, the only venue large enough.' And in Australia, he was invited to give a 'personal briefing to Tony Abbott, at the time leader of the Opposition and subsequently prime minister.'[105]

In 1984, Abbott (1957–) entered St Patrick's Seminary as a trainee priest; before becoming a journalist for *The Catholic Weekly*. In 2017, after being dumped as Prime Minister by his own Liberal Party, Abbott told Nigel Lawson's Global Warming Policy Foundation that 'at least so far it is climate change policy that is doing harm; climate change itself is probably doing good – or at least more good than harm.' Climate change policy was analogous to 'primitive people' who 'once killed goats to appease the volcano gods':

Beware the pronouncement, 'the science is settled,' Mr Abbott said, according to a speech posted on the think tank's website. 'It's the spirit of the Inquisition, the thought-police down the ages.'[106]

Monckton was recruited to Sir Keith Joseph's Centre for Policy Studies by Alfred Sherman (1919–2006), who was described in his obituary as

> an impossible man. Mean-spirited, spiteful, envious and resentful, he never had a good word to say about anyone else's intellect and overvalued his own. He had moved to the political Right from the millenarian Marxist Left, without abandoning its sectarian habits of mind. He thought that a firing-squad was too good for anyone who disagreed with him.

Sherman helped to persuade Mrs. Thatcher

> that far from being a banal suburbanite, she was at the frontline of economic thinking, alongside Hayek, Friedman and Von Mises ... At a Tory conference Peregrine Worsthorne once offered Sherman a lift. As they walked to the car, Alfred was denouncing the working classes. To a man, they were idle, shiftless, useless: too demoralised by welfare and socialism to be any good for anything. They arrived at the car, which had a very flat tyre. Neither of them had a clue what to do. Fortunately, a passing member of the working class observed their plight and changed the tyre. He departed. Perry waited for a change of tone: in vain. Sherman merely continued: 'As I was saying, absolutely no good, the whole lot of them.' (Anderson 2006)[107]

Sherman's contempt mirrored 'von' Mises' (2007 [1958], 11) who told Ayn Rand: 'You have the courage to tell the masses what no politician told them: you are inferior and all the improvements in your conditions which you simply take for granted you owe to the effort of men who are better than you.'

Sherman was as committed to the 'free' market as Hayek: one of his *Daily Telegraph* colleagues recalled:

> His dishonesty over money was a standing joke, every Friday being marked by a huge and improved expenses claim, which the Editor, Bill Deedes, let through out of tolerance and for amusement. A claim of £2 for the cloakroom at the Reform Club which does not now, and did not then, charge for its cloakroom, merely illustrates a comic and brazen rapacity. (Pearse 2006)

Monckton asserts: 'it was I who—on the prime minister's behalf—kept a weather eye on the official science advisers to the government, from the chief scientific adviser downward' (Ward 2010). John Gummer, Conservative Party Chairman (1983–1985), stated that Monckton was a 'bag carrier in Mrs. Thatcher's office. And the idea that he advised her on climate change is laughable' (cited by Readfearn 2011).

Notes

1. Hayek Archives Box 45.21.
2. Hayek Archives Box 20.13.
3. Friedrich Hayek, interviewed by Jack High date unspecified 1978 (Centre for Oral History Research, University of California, Los Angeles, http://oralhistory.library.ucla.edu/).
4. Mises (1985 [1927], 19) defined property as the 'private ownership of the means of production (for in regard to commodities ready for consumption, private ownership is a matter of course and is not disputed even by the socialists and communists).'
5. Friedrich Hayek, interviewed by Earlene Craver date unspecified 1978 (Centre for Oral History Research, University of California, Los Angeles, http://oralhistory.library.ucla.edu/).
6. Friedrich Hayek, interviewed by Thomas Hazlett 12 November 1978 (Centre for Oral History Research, University of California, Los Angeles, http://oralhistory.library.ucla.edu/).
7. https://www.law.gmu.edu/news/2016/scalia_school_of_law_announcement.
8. http://www.catholicherald.co.uk/commentandblogs/2017/02/01/why-neil-gorsuch-is-an-outstanding-supreme-court-nomination/.
9. http://www.foxnews.com/transcript/2017/11/25/can-republicans-deliver-on-christmas-tax-cut.html.
10. http://www.foxnews.com/transcript/2012/05/07/bin-laden-bragging-rights-should-president-obama-claim-credit.html.
11. In his hagiographic introduction to *Strictly Confidential: The Private Volker Fund Memos of Murray N. Rothbard*, Doherty (2010, ix) declared: 'When it comes to modern American libertarianism, Rothbard was the Man. That I was not able to meet him and get his fresh words into my book [2009] is my greatest regret associated with it.'
12. Mises added: 'But new generations grow up with clear eyes and open minds. And they will approach things from a disinterested, unprejudiced perspective. It is for them that this book is written.'

13. Davenport Archives Box 24.3.
14. Davenport Archives Box 23.9.
15. Hayek Archives Box 97.20.
16. They were, presumably, stolen before the Archives arrived at the Hoover Institution.
17. Hayek Archives Box 109.39.
18. https://www.law.uchicago.edu/news/henry-g-manne-52-1928-2015.
19. Friedrich Hayek, interviewed by Robert Chitester date unspecified 1978 (Centre for Oral History Research, University of California, Los Angeles, http://oralhistory.library.ucla.edu/).
20. Friedrich Hayek, interviewed by Robert Chitester date unspecified 1978 (Centre for Oral History Research, University of California, Los Angeles, http://oralhistory.library.ucla.edu/).
21. As cited by 'Dr. Nelson Adams' (9 March 1977) to Secretary of State Cyrus Vance. Davenport Archives Box 5.36.
22. Davenport Archives Box 1.7.
23. Davenport Archives Box 5.36.
24. Davenport Archives Box 1.7.
25. Davenport Archives Box 17.6.
26. Davenport Archives Box 16.10, 16.4.
27. Davenport Archives Box 32.3.
28. Pigou (1954) was reviewing an autobiography in which the author, Beveridge (1953), admitted to writing leading articles in the *Morning Post* on subjects 'of which I am colossally ignorant ... I wrote about three quarters of one column in just over the hour.'
29. Friedrich Hayek, interviewed by Robert Chitester date unspecified 1978 (Centre for Oral History Research, University of California, Los Angeles, http://oralhistory.library.ucla.edu/).
30. Friedrich Hayek, interviewed by Robert Chitester date unspecified 1978 (Centre for Oral History Research, University of California, Los Angeles, http://oralhistory.library.ucla.edu/).
31. Davenport Archives Box 15.19.
32. Davenport Archives Box 15.13.
33. Davenport Archives Box 16.34.
34. Davenport Archives Box 9.5.
35. Davenport Archives Box 10.5.
36. Davenport Archives Box 11.1.
37. Davenport Archives Box 16.44.
38. Davenport Archives Box 9.7.
39. Davenport Archives Box 9.6.
40. Davenport Archives Box 1.7.

41. Davenport Archives Box 1.7.
42. Davenport Archives Box 9.8.
43. Davenport Archives Box 31.1.
44. Davenport Archives Box 23.7.
45. https://www.jfklibrary.org/Asset-Viewer/BqXIEM9F4024ntFl7SVAjA.aspx.
46. https://www.humanrights.gov.au/news/stories/international-human-rights-lawyer-geoffrey-robertson-speaks-fate-assange.
47. 'Deacon' McCormick Papers. Sayer Collection. British Connection folder.
48. http://www.oswaldmosley.com/british-union.htm.
49. http://hansard.millbanksystems.com/commons/1935/may/02/foreign-office#S5CV0301P0_19350502_HOC_285.
50. http://hansard.millbanksystems.com/commons/1935/may/02/foreign-office#S5CV0301P0_19350502_HOC_285.
51. Count Alexander Konstantinovich Benckendorff (1849–1917) was one of the three aristocrats who signed the 1905 Treaty of Björk, a secret mutual defence accord between Kaiser Wilhelm II and Tsar Nicholas II of Russia—which illustrated, in a foreign policy context, how incompetent the Divine Right of Kings had become.
52. http://www.margaretthatcher.org/document/107869.
53. Dalyell stated 'There is rather more to the matter than meets the eye. MI5 has been circulating a so-called gay story … The story was commented on in Oldfield's biography by Richard Deacon.' http://hansard.millbanksystems.com/commons/1987/may/06/northern-ireland-police#S6CV0115P0_19870506_HOC_397.
54. http://www.desmogblog.com/leon-louw.
55. http://econfaculty.gmu.edu/pboettke/cv.html. Accessed 4 November 2017.
56. https://www.industrydocumentslibrary.ucsf.edu/tobacco/docs/#id=yqxm0123.
57. https://www.industrydocumentslibrary.ucsf.edu/tobacco/docs/#id=lgkc0081.
58. It's not clear whether or not any of Boettke's op-ed pieces (if written) were published. http://sciencecorruption.com/ATN166/01477.html.
59. 'Por una serie de razones, Hayek no estaba contento. Su estado de ánimo afectó su trabajo intelectual. Incluso se ha sugerido que sufrió una depresión (Kresge y Wenar 1994, 130–131).'
60. Hayek Archives Box 154.1.
61. Hayek Archives Box 19.19.
62. Hayek Archives Box 44.1.

63. Hayek Archives Box 55.22.
64. Ballantrae, 3261 votes, Knox, 1924 votes, 'von' Hayek, 990 votes. Hayek Archives Box 55.13.
65. http://www.selsdongroup.co.uk/manifesto.pdf.
66. Anthony Flew (4 December 1973) to Hayek. Hayek Archives Box 19.24.
67. Friedrich Hayek, interviewed by James Buchanan 28 October 1978 (Centre for Oral History Research, University of California, Los Angeles, http://oralhistory.library.ucla.edu/).
68. http://www.margaretthatcher.org/document/114609. Hayek Papers Box 27.6.
69. http://www.economist.com/blogs/buttonwood/2013/09/economic-policy.
70. Friedrich Hayek, interviewed by Leo Rosten 15 November 1978 (Centre for Oral History Research, University of California, Los Angeles, http://oralhistory.library.ucla.edu/).
71. http://www.nobelprize.org/nobel_prizes/economic-sciences/laureates/1974/press.html.
72. Hayek was citing Schumpeter (1946, 269). Hayek (1973, 161, n. 18) had repeated the quote three years earlier—adding that he was also motivated by 'profound conviction.'
73. Friedrich Hayek, interviewed by Leo Rosten 15 November 1978 (Centre for Oral History Research, University of California, Los Angeles, http://oralhistory.library.ucla.edu/).
74. Mrs. Thatcher's presence at a 'Bilderberg meeting in Turkey in 1975' is mentioned in passing without elaboration (Lawson 1992, 47).
75. Friedrich Hayek, interviewed by Robert Chitester date unspecified 1978 (Centre for Oral History Research, University of California, Los Angeles, http://oralhistory.library.ucla.edu/).
76. http://www.nationalarchives.gov.uk/pathways/census/living/making/women.htm.
77. http://www.economist.com/node/21541717.
78. Friedrich Hayek, interviewed by Leo Rosten 15 November 1978 (Centre for Oral History Research, University of California, Los Angeles, http://oralhistory.library.ucla.edu/).
79. Friedrich Hayek, interviewed by Robert Chitester date unspecified 1978 (Centre for Oral History Research, University of California, Los Angeles, http://oralhistory.library.ucla.edu/).
80. MPS Archives Box 47.2.
81. IEA Archives Box 1.4.
82. http://www.telegraph.co.uk/news/newstopics/politics/2969215/Gordon-Browns-curse-did-the-prime-minister-kill-Lehman-Bros.html.

83. http://www.cbi.org.uk/ndbs/press.nsf/0363c1f07c6ca12a 8025671c00381cc7/ee59d1c32ce4ec12802570c70041152c?OpenDocument.
84. http://news.bbc.co.uk/2/hi/business/8106209.stm.
85. http://www.economist.com/node/9832838.
86. Hayek Archives Box 24.72.
87. http://www.sourcewatch.org/index.php?title=Manhattan_Institute_for_Policy_Research.
88. http://www.city-journal.org/article01.php?aid=1631.
89. http://www.abc.net.au/news/2011-06-22/monckton-compares-garnaut-to-hitler/2767930.
90. https://twitter.com/realdonaldtrump/status/265895292191248385?lang=en.
91. http://time.com/4191598/donald-trump-says-he-could-shoot-somebody-and-not-lose-voters/.
92. Friedrich Hayek, interviewed by Leo Rosten 15 November 1978 (Centre for Oral History Research, University of California, Los Angeles, http://oralhistory.library.ucla.edu/).
93. Hayek (20 October 1987) to Bartley. Hayek Papers Box 126.4.
94. Hayek Papers Box 170. https://www.margaretthatcher.org/document/117176.
95. Hayek Papers Box 12.19.
96. Friedrich Hayek, interviewed by Robert Chitester date unspecified 1978 (Centre for Oral History Research, University of California, Los Angeles, http://oralhistory.library.ucla.edu/).
97. https://www.margaretthatcher.org/document/117129.
98. Hayek told his second authorised biographer that this had been a 'clerical error' (Cubitt 2006, 29).
99. http://www.parliament.uk/business/news/2011/july/letter-to-viscount-monckton/.
100. http://heartland.org/leon-louw.
101. https://www.thedailybell.com/3266/Staff-Report-Leon-Louw-on-Sinking-South-Africa-and-How-Free-Market-Thinking-Can-Help-Recover-Prosperity.
102. http://www.whoswho.co.za/leon-louw-3162.
103. http://www.myvirtualpaper.com/doc/brookepattrick/water_sewage_and_effluent_september2011/2011090201/5.html#4.
104. http://www.cfact.org/2011/11/16/946/.
105. https://www.heartland.org/about-us/who-we-are/lord-christopher-monckton.

106. http://thenewdaily.com.au/news/national/2017/10/10/tony-abbott-climate-change-goat/.
107. http://www.margaretthatcher.org/document/110865.

REFERENCES

Archival Insights into the Evolution of Economics (and Related Projects)

Farrant, A., & McPhail, E. (2017). Hayek, Thatcher, and the Muddle of the Middle. In R. Leeson (Ed.), *Hayek: A Collaborative Biography Part IX: The Divine Right of the 'Free' Market*. Basingstoke, UK: Palgrave Macmillan.

Filip, B. (2018). Hayek on Limited Democracy, Dictatorships and the Free-Market Economy: An Interview in Argentina in 1977. In R. Leeson (Ed.), *Hayek: A Collaborative Biography Part XIII: 'Fascism' and Liberalism in the (Austrian) Classical Tradition*. Basingstoke, UK: Palgrave Macmillan.

Leeson, R. (1999). Keynes and the Keynesian Phillips Curve. *History of Political Economy, 31*(3), 494–509.

Leeson, R. (2000). Inflation, Disinflation and the Natural Rate of Unemployment: A Dynamic Framework for Policy Analysis. *The Australian Economy in the 1990s* (pp. 124–175). Sydney: Reserve Bank of Australia.

Leeson, R. (2003). *Ideology and the International Economy: The Decline and Fall of Bretton Woods*. Basingstoke, UK: Palgrave Macmillan.

Leeson, R. (2005, August 19). Assessing the Effect of Taxes on the Economy: Deflate Housing Bubble with Targeted Taxes. *San Francisco Chronicle*. http://www.sfgate.com/default/article/Assessing-the-Effect-of-Taxes-on-the-Economy-2646541.php.

Leeson, R. (2011, December). The MONIAC Updated for the Era of Permanent Financial Crises. *Economia Politica, 4*(4), 103–130.

Leeson, R. (Ed.). (2013). *Hayek: A Collaborative Biography Part I Influences from Mises to Bartley*. Basingstoke, UK: Palgrave Macmillan.

Leeson, R. (Ed.). (2015). *Hayek: A Collaborative Biography Part III Fraud, Fascism and Free Market Religion*. Basingstoke, UK: Palgrave Macmillan.

Leeson, R. (2018a). *Hayek: A Collaborative Biography Part VIII the Constitution of Liberty: 'Shooting in Cold Blood' Hayek's Plan for the Future of Democracy*. Basingstoke, UK: Palgrave Macmillan.

Leeson, R. (2018b). *Hayek: A Collaborative Biography Part XI: Orwellian Rectifiers, Mises' 'Evil Seed' of Christianity and the 'Free' Market Welfare State*. Basingstoke, UK: Palgrave Macmillan.

Ravelli, G., & Bull, A. C. (2018). The Pinochet regime and the transnationalization of Italian Neo-fascism. In R. Leeson (Ed.), *Hayek: A Collaborative*

Biography Part XIII: 'Fascism' and Liberalism in the (Austrian) Classical Tradition. Basingstoke, England: Palgrave Macmillan.

Teacher, D. (2018a). 'Neutral Academic Data' and the International Right. In R. Leeson (Ed.), *Hayek: A Collaborative Biography Part XIII 'Fascism' and Liberalism in the (Austrian) Classical Tradition*. Basingstoke, UK: Palgrave Macmillan.

Teacher, D. (2018b). Private Club and Secret Service Armageddon. In R. Leeson (Ed.), *Hayek: A Collaborative Biography Part XIII 'Fascism' and Liberalism in the (Austrian) Classical Tradition*. Basingstoke, UK: Palgrave Macmillan.

Other References

Amery, J., Biggs-Davidson, J., Hastings, S., Soref, H., & Wall, P. (1976). *Rhodesia and the Threat to the West*. London: Monday Club.

Anderson, B. (2006, August 31). Obituary Sir Alfred Sherman. *The Times*. https://www.margaretthatcher.org/document/110865.

Anson, D. (2010). *The Sad Old State of Cloud Cuckoo Land—British Jews, the Right, and Islamophobia*. http://daphneanson.blogspot.com.au/2010/12/sad-old-state-of-cloud-cuckoo-land.html.

Arblaster, A. (1984). *The Rise and Decline of Western Liberalism*. Oxford: Basil Blackwell.

Barberis, P. (2005). *Liberal Lion: Jo Grimond: A Political Life*. London: I.B. Taurus.

Baxendale, T. (2011, January 9). The Rediscovery of Hayek's Masterpieces. *Mises Daily*. https://mises.org/library/rediscovery-hayeks-masterpieces.

Benewick, R. (1969). *A Study of British Fascism: Political Violence and Public Order*. London: Allan Lane.

Benham, F. (1932). *British Monetary Policy*. London: P.S. King & Son.

Beveridge, W. (1953). *Power and Influence*. London: Beechhurst.

Blundell, J. (2014). IHS and the Rebirth of Austrian Economics: Some Reflections on 1974–1976. *Quarterly Journal of Austrian Economics, 17*(1), 92–107. https://mises.org/library/ihs-and-rebirth-austrian-economics-some-reflections-1974%E2%80%931976.

Boettke, P. J. (2010). Reflections on Becoming an Austrian Economist and Libertarian and Staying One. In W. Block (Ed.), *I Chose Liberty: Autobiographies of Contemporary Libertarians*. Auburn, AL: Ludwig von Mises Institute.

Boettke, P. J. (2016, October 17). Ludwig von Mises, the Academic. *The Freeman*. https://fee.org/articles/ludwig-von-mises-the-academic/.

Boettke, P. J. (2017, September 17). Hayek's Epistemic Liberalism. *Online Library of Liberty*. http://oll.libertyfund.org/pages/lm-hayek.

Brittan, S. (1977). *The Economic Consequences of Democracy*. London: Temple Smith.
Brittan, S. (1988). *A Restatement of Economic Liberalism*. London: Macmillan.
Brittan, S. (1995). *Capitalism with a Human Face*. Cambridge, MA: Harvard University Press.
Brittan, S. (2005). *Against the Flow Reflections of an Individualist*. London: Atlantic Books.
Brown, C., & Hastings, C. (2003, May 4). Fury as Dalyell Attacks Blair's 'Jewish Cabal.' *The Daily Telegraph*. http://web.archive.org/web/20071115200404/http://www.telegraph.co.uk/news/main.jhtml?xml=/news/2003/05/04/ndaly04.xml&sSheet=/portal/2003/05/04/ixportaltop.html.
Buchanan, J. (1992). I Did Not Call Him 'Fritz': Personal Recollections of Professor F. A. v. Hayek. *Constitutional Political Economy, 3*(2), 129–135.
Buckley, W. F., Jr., & Bozell, L. B. (1954). *McCarthy and His Enemies the Record and Its Meaning*. Chicago: Henry Regnery.
Bull, A. C. (2012). *Italian Neofascism: The Strategy of Tension and the Politics of Nonreconciliation*. Oxford: Berghahn.
Caldwell, B. (1995). Editorial Notes. In B. Caldwell (Ed.), *Contra Keynes and Cambridge. The Collected Works of F.A. Hayek*. Chicago: University of Chicago Press.
Caldwell, B. (2004). *Hayek's Challenge: An Intellectual Biography of F.A. Hayek*. Chicago: University of Chicago Press.
Caldwell, B. (2006). Popper and Hayek: Who Influenced Whom? In I. Jarvie, K. Milford, & D. W. Miller (Eds.), *Karl Popper: A Centenary Assessment* (Vol. I, pp. 111–124). Burlington: Ashgate.
Caldwell, B. (2007). Introduction and Editorial Notes. In F. A. Hayek (Ed.), *The Road to Serfdom Texts and Documents: The Definitive Edition. The Collected Works of F.A. Hayek*. Chicago: University of Chicago Press.
Caldwell, B. (2010a). The Secret Behind the Hot Sales of 'The Road to Serfdom' by Free-Market Economist F.A. Hayek. *The Washington Post*. http://voices.washingtonpost.com/shortstack/2010/02/the_secret_behind_the_hot_sale.html.
Caldwell, B. (2010b, September). Review of P. Mirowski & D. Phehwe (Eds.), *The Road from Mont Pelerin: The Making of the Neoliberal Thought Collective*. EH.NET. http://eh.net/book_reviews/the-road-from-mont-plerin-the-making-of-the-neoliberal-thought-collective/.
Caldwell, B. (2016). Hayek's Nobel. In P. Boettke & V. Storr (Eds.), *Revisiting Hayek's Political Economy*. Bingley, UK: Emerald.
Caldwell, B., & Montes, L. (2015). Friedrich Hayek y Sus Dos Visitas a Chile. *Estudios Públicos*, No. 137 (Verano), 87–132. https://www.cepchile.cl/

cep/site/artic/20160304/asocfile/20160304101209/rev137_BCaldwell-LMontes.pdf.
Cannan, E. (1928). *An Economist's Protest*. London: P.S. King & Son.
Chamberlain, J. (1944). Foreword. In F. A. Hayek (Ed.), *The Road to Serfdom*. Chicago: University of Chicago Press.
Chamberlain, J. (1974, September 28). May We Borrow the Crystal Ball? *Chicago Tribune*. http://archives.chicagotribune.com/1974/09/28/page/34/article/may-we-borrow-the-crystal-ball.
Chamberlain, J. (1977, April 19). Africa: Why Not Peace. *New Haven Register* (Davenport Archives Box 9.5).
Chamberlain, J. (1982). *A Life With the Printed Word*. Chicago: Regnery Gateway.
Cornwell, J. (1999). *Hitler's Pope the Secret History of Pius XII*. New York: Viking.
Cornwell, J. (2003, October 29). Hitler's Pope. Pope Pius XII Helped Hitler Destroy German Catholic Political Opposition. *Vanity Fair*. http://www.vanityfair.com/style/1999/10/pope-pius-xii-199910.
Crozier, B. (1993). *Free Agent the Unseen War 1941–1991*. London: HarperCollins.
Cubitt, C. (2006). *A Life of August von Hayek*. Bedford, UK: Authors OnLine.
Davenport, J. (1981, July). Reflections on Mont Pelerin. *The Mont Pelerin Society Newsletter*.
Davenport, J. (1985, August 1). The Anti-apartheid Threat. *The Freeman*. https://fee.org/articles/the-anti-apartheid-threat/.
Davidson, A. (2012, August 21). Prime Time for Paul Ryan's Guru (The One Who's Not Ayn Rand). *New York Times*. http://www.nytimes.com/2012/08/26/magazine/prime-time-for-paul-ryans-guru-the-one-thats-not-ayn-rand.html.
Doherty, B. (2007). *Radicals for Capitalism: A Freewheeling History of the Modern American Libertarian Movement*. New York: Public Affairs.
Doherty, B. (2010). *Strictly Confidential: The Private Volker Fund Memos of Murray N. Rothbard* (D. Gordon, Ed.). Auburn, AL: Ludwig von Mises Institute.
Dorey, P. (1995). *Conservative Party and the Trade Unions*. London: Routledge.
Dorril, S. (2006). *Black Shirt: Sir Oswald Mosley and British Fascism*. London: Viking.
Driessen, P. (2005). *Eco-imperialism Green Power, Black Death*. New Delhi: Liberty Institute.
Ebeling, R. M. (1975, July). The Second Austrian Conference. *Libertarian Forum*, Vol. VII, No. 7, pp. 4–8. http://rothbard.altervista.org/articles/libertarian-forum/lf-7-7.pdf.

Ebenstein, A. (1997). *Edwin Cannan: Liberal Doyen.* London: Routledge (Foreword by Arthur Seldon).
Ebenstein, A. (2003). *Friedrich Hayek: A Biography.* Chicago: University of Chicago Press.
Evans, A. (2010). The Parallels Between Sports Coaching and Graduate Teaching: Coach Boettke as Exemplar. *The Journal of Private Enterprise,* 26(1), 73–83.
Evans, K. (2010, August 28). Spreading Hayek, Spurning Keynes. Professor Leads an Austrian Revival. *Wall Street Journal.*
Farrell, J. (2017). *Richard Nixon: The Life.* New York: Doubleday.
Galbraith, R. (2000). *Inside Out: The Biography of Tam Dalyell: The Man They Can't Gag.* New York: Mainstream.
Garrison, R. (2003). LSE'S First Hayek Visiting Fellow. *Austrian Economics Newsletter (Fall).* https://mises.org/system/tdf/aen23_3_1_0.pdf?file=1&type=document.
Grant, J. (1996). The Trouble with Prosperity: An Interview with James Grant. *Austrian Economics Newsletter,* 16(4).
Gray, R. (2017, February 10). Conflict over Trump Forces Out an Opinion Editor at *The Wall Street Journal. The Atlantic.* https://www.theatlantic.com/politics/archive/2017/02/conflict-over-trump-forces-out-an-opinion-editor-at-the-wall-street-journal/516318/.
Greaves, B. (1998). Mises's Bibliographer: An Interview with Bettina Bien Greaves. *Austrian Economics Newsletter,* 18(4) (Winter). https://mises.org/library/misess-bibliographer-interview-bettina-bien-greaves.
Greig, I. (1979). Iran and the Lengthening Soviet Shadow. *Atlantic Community Quarterly,* 17(1), 66–72.
Griffiths, R. (1983). *Fellow Travellers of the Right British Enthusiasts for Nazi Germany, 1933–39.* Oxford: Oxford University Press.
Grimond, J. (1980). *The Future of Liberalism: The Inaugural Eighty Club Lecture.* London: Association of Liberal Lawyers.
Harberger, A. C. (2016). Sense and Economics: An Oral History with Arnold Harberger. Interviews Conducted by Paul Burnett in 2015 and 2016 Oral History Center, The Bancroft Library, University of California, Berkeley, California. http://digitalassets.lib.berkeley.edu/roho/ucb/text/harberger_arnold_2016.pdf.
Harris, R. (1986). *Selling Hitler.* London: Faber and Faber.
Hayek, F. A. (1935, August). The Maintenance of Capital. *Economica,* 2, 241–276 (New Series).
Hayek, F. A. (1944). *The Road to Serfdom.* London: Routledge.
Hayek, F. A. (1960). *The Constitution of Liberty.* Chicago: University of Chicago Press.

Hayek, F. A. (1973). *Law, Legislation and Liberty Volume 1. Rules and Order.* Chicago: University of Chicago Press.

Hayek, F. A. (1975). *A Discussion with Friedrich von Hayek.* Washington, DC: American Enterprise Institute. https://www.aei.org/wp-content/uploads/2017/03/Discussion-with-Friedrich-von-Hayek-text.pdf.

Hayek, F. A. (1977, September). An Interview with Friedrich Hayek, by Richard Ebeling. *Libertarian Review,* 10–18 (Hayek Archives Box 109.14).

Hayek, F. A. (1978a). *Oral History Interviews.* Centre for Oral History Research, University of California, Los Angeles. http://oralhistory.library.ucla.edu/.

Hayek, F. A. (1978b). *New Studies in Philosophy, Politics, Economics and the History of Ideas.* London: Routledge & Kegan Paul.

Hayek, F. A. (1979, December 5). A Period of Muddle-Heads. *Newsweek.*

Hayek, F. A. (1981, April 12). Extracts from an Interview Friedrich von Hayek. *El Mercurio.* http://www.economicthought.net/blog/wp-content/uploads/2011/12/LibertyCleanOfImpuritiesInterviewWithFVonHayekChile1981.pdf.

Hayek, F. A. (1992a). *The Fortunes of Liberalism Essays on Austrian Economics and the Ideal of Freedom. The Collected Works of F.A. Hayek* (P. Klein, Ed.). Chicago: University of Chicago Press.

Hayek, F. A. (1992b [1977], July). The Road from Serfdom. *Reason.* http://reason.com/archives/1992/07/01/the-road-from-serfdom/5.

Hayek, F. A. (1994). *Hayek on Hayek an Autobiographical Dialogue.* Supplement to *The Collected Works of F.A. Hayek* (S. Kresge & L. Wenar, Eds.). Chicago: University of Chicago Press.

Hayek, F. A. (1995). *Contra Keynes and Cambridge. The Collected Works of F.A. Hayek* (B. Caldwell, Ed.). Chicago: University of Chicago Press.

Hayek, F. A. (1997). *Socialism and War: Essays, Documents, Reviews. The Collected Works of F.A. Hayek* (B. Caldwell, Ed.). Indianapolis: Liberty Fund.

Hayek, F. A. (2007 [1944]). *The Road to Serfdom: The Definitive Edition. The Collected Works of F.A. Hayek* (B. Caldwell, Ed.). Chicago: University of Chicago Press.

Hayek, F. A. (2009 [1979]). A Conversation with Professor Friedrich A. Hayek. In D. Pizano (Ed.), *Conversations with Great Economists.* Mexico: Jorge Pinto Books.

Hayek, F. A. (2011 [1960]). *The Constitution of Liberty. The Definitive Edition. The Collected Works of F.A. Hayek* (R. Hamowy, Ed.). Chicago: University of Chicago Press.

Hayek, F. A. (2013). *Law, Legislation and Liberty.* London: Routledge.

Hoover, H. (1952). *The Memoirs of Herbert Hoover, Vol. 3: The Great Depression 1929–1941.* New York: Macmillan.

Hülsmann, J. G. (2007). *Mises: The Last Knight of Liberalism.* Auburn, AL: Ludwig von Mises Institute.

Ickes, H. L. (1953). *The Secret Diary of Harold L. Ickes: The First Thousand Days*. New York: Simon & Schuster.

Janner, G., & Taylor, D. (2008). *Jewish Parliamentarians*. London: Vallentine Mitchell.

Jenkins, S. (2006). *Thatcher and Sons: A Revolution in Three Acts*. London, UK: Penguin.

Johnson, I. (2014, May 11). Academic Claims That the Former Chancellor's Foundation Complained to His Employer. *Independent*. https://web.archive.org/web/20140511082724/http://www.independent.co.uk/environment/climate-change/nigel-lawsons-climatechange-denial-charity-intimidated-environmental-expert-9350069.html.

Kamen, A. (2009, March 16). On Warming, a Cold Splash From Across the Pond. *Washington Post*. http://www.washingtonpost.com/wp-dyn/content/article/2009/03/15/AR2009031501855.html.

Kass, J. (2017, September 12). Durbin, Democrats Reveal Their Bigotry in Questioning of Judicial Nominee from Notre Dame. *Chicago Tribune*. http://www.chicagotribune.com/news/columnists/kass/ct-federal-judge-catholic-kass-met-0913-20170912-column.html.

Kirk, T. (1996). *Nazism and the Working Class in Austria: Industrial Unrest and Political Dissent in the National Community*. Cambridge: Cambridge University Press.

Kirkup, J. (2008, September 16). Gordon Brown's Curse: Did the Prime Minister Kill Lehman Bros? *Telegraph*. http://www.telegraph.co.uk/news/newstopics/politics/2969215/Gordon-Browns-curse-did-the-primeminister-kill-Lehman-Bros.html.

Klausinger, H. (2010). Hayek on Practical Business Cycle Research: A Note. In H. Hagemann, T. Nishizawa, & Y. Ikeda (Eds.), *Austrian Economics in Transition: From Carl Menger to Friedrich Hayek* (pp. 218–234). Basingstoke, UK: Palgrave Macmillan.

Klausinger, H. (2012). Editorial Notes. In F. A. Hayek (Ed.), *Business Cycles. The Collected Works of F.A. Hayek*. Chicago: University of Chicago Press.

Kresge, S. (1994). Introduction. In F. A. Hayek (Ed.), *Hayek on Hayek an Autobiographical Dialogue*. Supplement to *The Collected Works of F.A. Hayek* (S. Kresge & L. Wenar, Eds.). Chicago: University of Chicago Press.

Lal, D. (2009). *The Mont Pelerin Society: A MANDATE RENEWED*. MPS Presidential Address. http://www.econ.ucla.edu/lal/MPS%20Presidential%20Address%203.5.09.pdf.

Landman, A., & Glanz, S. A. (2009, January). Tobacco Industry Efforts to Undermine Policy-Relevant Research. *American Journal of Public Health*, 99(1), 45–58.

Lane, M. (2013). The Genesis and Reception of The Road to Serfdom. In R. Leeson (Ed.), *Hayek: A Collaborative Biography Part I Influences From Mises to Bartley*. Basingstoke, England: Palgrave Macmillan

Lawson, D. (2011, September 24). Ridley Was Right It May Have Cost Him His Job, but He Was Correct to be Concerned About Our Loss of Sovereignty. *The Spectator.* http://www.spectator.co.uk/features/7256363/ridley-was-right/.

Lawson, N. (1992). *The View from No. 11. Memoirs of a Tory Radical.* London: Bantam.

Louw, L. (2011, November 20). Leon Louw on Sinking South Africa—And How Free-Market Thinking Can Help Recover Prosperity. *Daily Bell.* http://www.thedailybell.com/exclusive-interviews/anthony-wile-leon-louw-on-sinking-south-africa-and-how-free-market-thinking-can-help-recover-prosperity/.

Manne, H. G. (1993). *An Intellectual History of the George Mason University School of Law.* GMU Law and Economics Center. https://www.law.gmu.edu/about/history.

MacLean, N. (2017). *Democracy in Chains. The Deep History of the Radical Right's Stealth Plan for America.* New York: Viking/Penguin Random House.

McCord, N., & Purdue, W. A. (2011). *British History 1815–1914.* Oxford: Oxford University Press.

McCormick, D. (pseudonym: Deacon, R.) (1979). *The British Connection Russia's Manipulation of British Individuals and Institutions.* London: Hamish Hamilton.

McGreal, C. (2006, February 7). Brothers in Arms—Israel's Secret Pact with Pretoria. *Guardian.* https://www.theguardian.com/world/2006/feb/07/southafrica.israel.

McGurn, W. (2017, October 2). The Morality of Charles Koch. *Wall Street Journal.* https://www.wsj.com/articles/the-morality-of-charles-koch-1506983981.

McManus, D. (1987, June 15). Reagan Impeachment Held Possible: It's Likely if He Knew of Profits Diversion, Hamilton Says. *Los Angeles Times.* http://articles.latimes.com/1987-06-15/news/mn-4220_1_president-reagan.

Mises, L. (1951 [1932]). *Socialism: An Economic and Sociological Analysis* (J. Kahane, Trans.). New Haven: Yale University Press.

Mises, L. (1960). *Planning for Freedom and Twelve Other Essays and Addresses.* South Holland, IL: Libertarian Press.

Mises, L. (1985 [1927]). *Liberalism in the Classical Tradition* (R. Raico, Trans.). Auburn, AL: Mises Institute.

Mises, L. (1993 [1964]). Indefatigable Leader. Remarks by Ludwig von Mises on the Occasion of Henry Hazlitt's 70th birthday, on November 28, 1964. In Sennholz, H. (Ed.), *The Wisdom of Henry Hazlitt.* New York: The Foundation for Economic Education, Inc. http://www.mises.ch/library/Hazlitt_Wisdom_of_HH.pdf.

Mises, L. 2000. *Selected Writings of Ludwig von Mises, Vol. 3: The Political Economy of International Reform and Reconstruction.* Indianapolis: Liberty Fund.

http://oll.libertyfund.org/titles/mises-selected-writings-of-ludwig-von-mises-vol-3-the-political-economy-of-international-reform-and-reconstruction.

Mises, L. (2007 [1958]). Mises and Rothbard Letters to Ayn Rand. *Journal of Libertarian Studies, 21*(4), 11–16.

Mises, L. (2009 [1978 (1940)]). *Memoirs*. Auburn, AL: Ludwig von Mises Institute.

Mises, M. (1984). *My Years with Ludwig von Mises* (2nd ed.). Cedar Falls, IA: Center for Futures Education.

Montes, L. (2015). *Friedman's Two Visits to Chile in Context*. http://jepson.richmond.edu/conferences/summer-institute/papers2015/LMontesSIPaper.pdf.

Morgan, K. O. (2001). *Britain Since 1945: The People's Peace*. Oxford: Oxford University Press.

Moss, R. (1978, Summer). On Standing Up to the Russians in Africa. *Policy Review*, 97–116. http://www.unz.org/Pub/PolicyRev-1978q3-00097.

Murdoch, R. (1990). The War on Technology. *City Journal* Manhattan Institute Third Annual Walter B. Wriston Lecture in Public Policy. http://www.city-journal.org/article01.php?aid=1631.

Myers, D. B. (2007, January 24). Recording of Reagan's Fair Speech Found. *Neshoba Democrat*. http://www.neshobademocrat.com/Content/NEWS/News/Article/Recording-of-Reagan-s-Fair-speech-found/2/297/13920.

Pearse, E. (2006, September 4). Sir Alfred Sherman. *Independent*. http://www.independent.co.uk/news/obituaries/sir-alfred-sherman-414683.html.

Pigou, A. C. (1954, February). Beveridge. Power and Influence (Book Review). *Economica, 21*(81), 73–76 (New Series).

Prowse, M. (2014 [1996]). Austrian Economics and the Public Mind. *Austrian Economics Newsletter, 16*(1). https://mises.org/library/austrian-economics-and-public-mind.

Pugh, M. (2005). *Hurrah for The Blackshirts!: Fascists and Fascism in Britain Between the Wars*. London: Pimlico.

Raico, R. (2013, February 20). *An Interview with Ralph Raico*. Mises Institute. https://mises.org/library/interview-ralph-raico-0.

Ranelagh, J. (1992). *Thatcher's People*. London: Harper Collins.

Raimondo, J. (2000). *An Enemy of the State: The Life of Murray N. Rothbard*. New York: Prometheus Books.

Readfearn, G. (2011, May 6). *Australia Prepares to Swallow Monckton Yet Again*. ABC. http://www.abc.net.au/unleashed/1816194.html.

Rees-Mogg, W. (2011). *Memoirs*. New York: HarperCollins.

Revere, R. H. (1959). *Senator Joe McCarthy*. London: Methuen.

Ridley, N. (1991). *My Style of Government: The Thatcher Years*. London: Hutchinson.

Ridley, M. W. (2006). *Government is the Problem Not the Solution*. Edge The World Question Centre. http://edge.org/q2006/q06_11.html.

Ridley, M. W. (2010). *The Rational Optimist: How Prosperity Evolves*. New York: HarperCollins.
Ridley, M. W. (2011). *Hayek Award Acceptance Speech*. Manhattan Institute. http://www.manhattan-institute.org/video/index.htm?c=092611MI.
Ridley, M. W. (2014, March 27). Climate Forecast: Muting the Alarm Even While It Exaggerates the Amount of Warming, the IPCC is Becoming More Cautious About Its Effects. *Wall Street Journal*. http://online.wsj.com/news/articles/SB10001424052702303725404579460973643962840.
Rifkind, H. (2006, June 2). People: Monday Club Still on Reich Track. *The Times*.
Roberts, T. (2017, October 11). Koch, Turkson Speak at Catholic University's 'Good Profit' Conference. *National Catholic Reporter*. https://www.ncronline.org/news/people/koch-turkson-speak-catholic-universitys-good-profit-conference.
Robinson, J. (1972). The Second Crisis of Economic Theory. *American Economic Review*, 62(1), 1–10.
Rothbard, M. N. (1973, October 20). Ludwig von Mises 1881–1973. *Human Events*, 7.
Rothbard, M. N. (1992, January). Right-Wing Populism: A Strategy for the Paleo Movement. *Rothbard Rockwell Report*, 5–14. http://rothbard.altervista.org/articles/right-wing-populism.pdf.
Rothbard, M. N. (1994, July). Revolution in Italy! *Rothbard-Rockwell Report*, 5(7), 1–10. http://www.unz.org/Pub/RothbardRockwellReport-1994jul-00001.
Schlesinger, A. M. (1960). *The Politics of Upheaval*. Boston: Houghton Mifflin Harcourt.
Schumpeter, J. (1946, June). Review: F. A. Hayek, The Road to Serfdom. *Journal of Political Economy*, 54, 269–270.
Shearmur, J. (2006). Hayek, The Road to Serfdom, and the British Conservatives. *Journal of the History of Economic Thought*, 28, 309–314.
Simon, H. (1991). *Models of My Life*. New York: Basic Books and Sloan Foundation Series.
Skidelsky, R. (1975). *Oswald Mosley*. London: Macmillan.
Soref, H. (1979, September). Disgrace Abounding. Review of *The British Connection*. *Tory Challenge*, 9–10.
Steers, E. (2007). *Lincoln Legends: Myths, Hoaxes, and Confabulations Associated with Our Greatest President*. Lexington: University of Kentucky Press.
Stigler, G. J. (1988). *Memoirs of an Unregulated Economist*. New York: Basic Books.
Tanaka, S. (1974, May 17). What Will Happen to the World as Keynesian Economic Theories Are Disproved? Views of Professor Hayek, a World-Famous Authority on Inflation Sought. *Shuukan Post* (Hayek Archives Box 52.28).

Taylor, A. J. P. (1964). *The Habsburg Monarchy 1809–1918: A History of the Austrian Empire and Austria Hungary*. UK: Peregrine.
Taylor, B. (1976, August 28). The Pit of State Control. *St Andrew's Citizen* (MPS Archives Box 48.4).
Teles, S. M. (2008). *The Rise of the Conservative Legal Movement: The Battle for Control of the Law*. Princeton: Princeton University Press.
Thurlow, R. C. (2006). *Fascism in Britain: From Oswald Mosley's Blackshirts to the National Front*. London: I.B. Tauris.
Tollison, R., & Wagner, R. E. (1988). *Smoking and the State*. Lexington, MA: DC Health.
Tollison, R., & Wagner, R. E. (1992). *The Economics of Smoking*. Boston: Kluwer Academic Publishing.
Tugwell, R. (1972). *In Search of Roosevelt*. Cambridge, MA: Harvard University Press.
Turner, J. (2000). *The Tories and Europe*. Manchester: Manchester University Press.
von Monakow, C., & Kitabayashi, S. (1919). Schizophrenie und Plexus Chorioidei. *Schweizer Archiv für Neurologie und Psychiatrie 5*, 378–392.
Ward, B. (2010, June 22). Thatcher Becomes Latest Recruit in Monckton's Climate Sceptic Campaign Monckton's Use of Britain's Former PM Illustrates That Climate Denialism Is About Politics, Not Science. *Guardian*. http://www.theguardian.com/environment/2010/jun/22/thatcher-climate-sceptic-monckton.
Wright, T. C., & Oñate, R. (2005). Chilean Diaspora. In C. R. Ember, M. Ember, & I. Skoggard (Eds.), *Encyclopedia of Diasporas: Immigrant and Refugee Cultures Around the World Volume II* (pp. 57–65). New York: Springer. https://mises.org/system/tdf/qjae5_3_4.pdf?file=1&type=document.

CHAPTER 6

The 'Free' Market 'Emergency' Demand for 'Fascism'

Summary

The political 'Fascists' that Mises believed had 'saved European civilization' included 'Ludendorff and Hitler.' Mises was a card-carrying Austro-Fascist and member of the official Fascist social club; Rothbard described the interwar emergency that Fascism had *solved*; and Hayek, his fellow fourth-generation Austrian School leader, saw similar merits in the Operation Condor dictatorships that targeted dissidents for liquidation. This chapter documents the permanent emergency that motivates Austrian School economists and philosophers and which drives them to embrace military dictatorships and the extra-parliamentary right.

6.1 'Democracy Needs a "Good Cleaning" by Strong Government'

According to the Fox News 'expert,' Dinesh D'Souza (2017), Franco and Pinochet were 'authoritarian without being fascists or Nazis.' And in 'From Democracy to Dictatorship,' a summary of Hayek's (2013 [1973–1979]) *Law, Legislation and Liberty*, the MPS President stated: 'Fortunate will be those who then get an authoritarian Franco, Salazar or Pinochet rather than their alternatives' (Shenfield 1980, 565). Yet all three dictators fitted Mises' (1985 [1927], 49) definition of a 'Fascist.'

According to the Mises Institute 'Rothbard Medal of Freedom' holder:

Mises served as the lone Marine who led the initial assaults against the statists' machine gun nests in academia. He did it from outside academia's walls. The University of Vienna never hired its most distinguished economics graduate. Hayek was part of the second wave: Mises's early disciples, who began volunteering for duty in the early 1920's. These included Lionel Robbins, Wilhelm Röpke, and several world-famous economists who by 1940 had left 'military service' to become part of the 'diplomatic corps,' seeking a cease-fire with the enemy. For this, they were rewarded well by the enemy: major publishing houses, academic tenure, and the honorary presidency of at least one regional economics association. Yet at age 85, Mises was still tossing grenades at the enemy's bunkers. (Hayek also remained on duty in the field, but he was always more of a sniper.) (North 2002)

The USA suffered 418,500 military and civilian deaths during World War II.[1] Mises received offers from 'smaller schools such as the University of Rochester, but would not settle for second-rate institutions' (Hülsmann 2007, 846–847). As the Third Reich fell (to whose rise he had contributed so much), the sixty-three-year-old Mises received a Visiting Professorship at an Ivy League University, NYU, which Lawrence Fertig, an NYU trustee, arranged. Rothbard (1973) gushed:

> But shamefully neglected though he was, coming to America to a second-rate post and deprived of the opportunity to *gather* the best students, Ludwig Mises never once complained or wavered. He simply hewed to his great purpose, to carve out and elaborate the mighty struc-ture of economics and social science that *he alone had had the genius to see as a coherent whole*; and to stand four-square for the individualism and the freedom that he realized was required if the human race was to survive and pros-per. He was indeed a constant star that could not be deflected one iota from the body of truth which he was the first to see and to present to those who would only listen. (emphases added)

Gathered sycophants were moths to Mises' flame:

> And despite the odds, slowly but surely some of us began to gather around him, to learn and listen and derive sus-tenance from the *glow* (emphasis added) of his person and his work. And in the last few years, as the ideas of liberty and the free market have begun to revive

with increasing swiftness in America, his name and his ideas began to strike chords in us all and his greatness to become known to a new generation.

Optimistic as he always was, I am confident that Mises was heart-ened by these signs of a new awaken-ing of freedom and of the sound economics which he had carved out and which was for so long forgotten. We could not, alas, recapture the spirit and the breadth and the eru-dition; the ineffable grace of Old Vienna. But I feverently hope that we were able to sweeten his days by at least a little.

There are two sub-chapters devoted to 'Fascism' (one on 'The Argument of Fascism') in Chapter 1 ('The Foundations of Liberal Policy') of Mises' (1985 [1927], 19, 42–51) *Liberalism in the Classical Tradition*, which, according to Hülsmann (2007, 556), 'remains one of the most important manifestos of *political* (emphasis added) liberalism.' In a footnote to their non-Chilean version of 'Friedrich Hayek and His Visits to Chile,' Caldwell and Montes (2014a, 3, n. 8; 2014b n. 8; 2015b, 263, n. 8) complain about (unspecified) attempts to 'establish links between Austrian thought and fascism':

> The fascism charge regarding Mises is based on a couple of sentences taken his book *Liberalism in the Classical Tradition* ... Mises regarded the emergence of fascism in the 1920s as a reaction to 'the frank espousal [by the communists] of a policy of annihilating opponents and then murders committed in the pursuance of it' and in this context praised fascism as 'an emergency makeshift' that 'has, for the moment, saved European civilisation' (Mises 1985 [1962], 47, 51). He was offering a comment on a pressing issue of the day.[2]

Referring to Mises, Hayek (1978) reflected: 'Being for ten years [1921–1931] in close contact with a man with whose conclusions on the whole you agree but whose arguments were not always perfectly convincing to you, was a great stimulus.'[3] The British *Fascisti* was established in 1923. Six years later, Hayek (1995 [1929], 68), while praising Edwin Cannan's 'fanatical conceptual clarity' and his 'kinship' with Mises' 'crusade,' noted that British-Austrians had failed to realise necessary consequences of the whole system of Classical Liberal thought: 'Cannan by no means develops economic liberalism to its ultimate consequences with the same ruthless consistency as Mises.' According to Caldwell (1995, 70, n. 67), the third general editor of *The Collected Works of F.A. Hayek*, Hayek was probably referring to *Liberalism in the Classical Tradition* in which Mises (1985 [1927], 49, 51) insisted that:

> The program of [Austrian] liberalism, therefore, if condensed into a single word, would have to read: *property* (Mises' emphasis) that is, private ownership of the means of production (for in regard to commodities ready for consumption, private ownership is a matter of course and is not disputed even by the socialists and communists). All the other demands of liberalism result from this fundamental demand … The victory of Fascism in a number of countries is only an episode in the long series of struggles over the problem of property.

In his January 1932 Preface to the second German edition of *Sozialismus*, Mises (1951 [1932], 20) declared that this long struggle was the problem of 'our epoch':

> The problem which here confronts us is the socialisation of ownership in the means production, i.e. the very problem over which a worldwide and bitter struggle has been waged now for a century, the problem κατ ἐξοχήν [by far] of our epoch.

Referring to 'the great fight between Capitalism and Socialism,' Mises (1951 [1932], 514–515) concluded *Sozialismus* by reference to the pressing issue—not 'of the day' but—again—of the 'epoch':

> Everyone carries a part of society on his shoulders; no one is relieved of his share of responsibility by others. And no one can find a safe way out for himself if society is sweeping toward destruction. Therefore, everyone, in his own interests, must thrust himself vigorously into the intellectual battle. None can stand aside with unconcern; the interest of everyone hangs on the result. Whether he chooses or not, every man is drawn into the great historical struggle, the decisive battle into which our epoch has plunged us.

Mises (1951 [1932], 508) also expressed 'Hitlerian contempt for the democratic man': 'It is true that the masses do not think … Of itself the mass psyche has never produced anything but mass crime, devastation and destruction.' In the July 1932 German Federal election, the Nazis emerged as the largest party in the Reichstag. In September 1932, Mises informed Hayek (1995 [1976], 145–146) and others that 'after twelve months Hitler would be in power.' In October 1932, Hayek promoted a share price-driven response to the Great Depression: 'Under modern conditions the security markets are an indispensable part of the mechanism of investment. A rise in the value of old securities is an indispensable preliminary to the flotation of new issues' (Gregory, von Hayek, Plant and Robbins 1932). Hitler became Chancellor on 30 January 1933.

Hayek then reinvented himself as a *Road to Serfdom* political theorist. According to its Statement of Aims, the MPS was born amid an ongoing emergency:

> The central values of civilization are in danger. Over large stretches of the Earth's surface the essential conditions of human dignity and freedom have already disappeared. In others they are under constant menace from the development of current tendencies of policy. The position of the individual and the voluntary group are progressively undermined by extensions of arbitrary power. Even that most precious possession of Western Man, freedom of thought and expression, is threatened by the spread of creeds which, claiming the privilege of tolerance when in the position of a minority, seek only to establish a position of power in which they can suppress and obliterate all views but their own.[4]

Emergency papers followed on 'The Present Political Crisis' (Michael Polanyi 1947), 'The Proletarianized Society' (Wilhelm Röpke 1949), 'The Demand for Social Security' (K. F. Maier 1949) and 'Soviet Expansion in the under-developed world' (Louis Baudin 1956). In 'The Grave Diggers of Western Freedom,' Jean-Pierre Hamilius (1976, 143, 161, 164), the MPS Secretary, declared that 'anti-capitalist intellectuals' were not only 'destroying capitalism' but also 'advancing on their road of their own elimination … Lets Defend Capitalism.'

In the MPS-circulated 'The Position of Business in Public Affairs,' one employer trade union described a linguistic and religious emergency:

> 'Main Street' is no longer by itself able to rescue free enterprise. The self-made individuals of former years are dying and retiring. Their successors are often brain-washed … The great backdrop to the drama of public affairs is that an economy basically demand order. The Commies (and some leftist-liberals) know this quite coldly. As it is said, 'If men will not be ruled by God, they will be ruled by tyrants,' and disbelieving in God, the Commies know that tyranny will be accepted as the price of order; this

is why they promote disorder everywhere. They are busy using our facile optimism about America and about 'human progress' to prepare the grave of freedom. They create disorder and disruption in the meaning of our words and in our patterns of government.

They had 'mobilized a force of 10,000 business firms, associations and individuals from every State in the Union including Alaska and Hawaii, to mount a conclusive counter-attack against the Communist-laborite juggernaut. JOIN THESE PATRIOTS AND FIGHT GOON TACTICS BY ORGANISATION (capitals in original).' In 'America's war-to-the-death with Marxism,' they had 'fought to reduce high income-tax brackets (greatest waste of free enterprise capital).'[5]

In the *New York Times* celebration of his Nobel Prize, James Buchanan's (1986) wrote that democracy could not hold the

> Leviathan-like proclivities of government in check ... Western societies face a task of reconstruction; basic political institutions must be re-examined and rebuilt so as to keep governments as well as citizens within limits of toleration ... Public choice theory offers an analytical setting that allows us to discuss genuine reconstruction in our constitution that may be made without major social costs.

Mises (1985 [1927], 49) reported that 'Many people approve of the methods of Fascism, even though its economic program is altogether anti-liberal and its policy completely interventionist, because it is far from practicing the senseless and unrestrained destructionism that has stamped the Communists as the archenemies of civilization. Still others, in full knowledge of the evil that Fascist economic policy brings with it, view Fascism, in comparison with Bolshevism and Sovietism, as at least the lesser evil. For the majority of its public and secret supporters and admirers, however, its appeal consists precisely in the violence of its methods.'

Rothbard (2016 [1974], Chapter 41) didn't object to a vigilante 'pornography of violence' (in a 'just cause') and appeared to define 'fascist ideology' as 'self-defence by victims of crime':

> *Death Wish* is a superb movie, the best hero-and-vengeance picture since Dirty Harry. [Charles] Bronson, an architect whose young family has been destroyed by muggers, drops his namby-pamby left-liberalism, and begins to pack a gun, defending himself brilliantly and uncompromisingly against a series of muggers who infest New York City. Yet he

never kills the innocent, or commits excesses. Naturally, even though he is only defending himself against assault, the police, who have failed to go after the muggers and who acknowledge the fall in the crime rate due to Bronson's activities, devote their resources to pursuing him instead of the criminals who terrorize New York. It is a great and heroic picture, a picture demonstrating one man's successful fight for justice. As might be expected, *Death Wish* has been subjected to hysterical attacks by the left-liberal critics who acknowledge the power and technical qualities of the picture, which they proceed to denounce for its 'fascist ideology' (self-defense by victims against crime) and its 'pornography of violence' (in a just cause) … Don't miss Death Wish; it says more about 'the urban problem' than a dozen 'message' documentaries, and it helps bring back heroism to the movies.

In 'free' market circles, Rothbard was known as 'Robhard' (Skousen 2000). According to Liggio (2010, 188), 'Classical Liberalism lost a giant with Murray's death.' Liggio was a 'birthright Catholic' who 'promoted our ideals, much as an Italian Christian Democratic politician might operate, but needless to say without the financial corruption' (Raico 2014). But when asked to account for tens if not hundreds of thousands of tax-exempt dollars that he had distributed to finance what appears to be fraud, Liggio offered merely evasive platitudes (Chapter 4).

Rothbard (1994a, 5), Hayek's co-leader of the fourth generation of the Austrian School of Economics, complained about an 'unfortunate blindness' which 'underscores' one of the 'major problems of nineteenth century classical liberalism': modern libertarians 'like' to call themselves:

> 'classical liberals,' heirs of nineteenth century free-market liberalism.

This 'homage' was generally true, but when applied to liberalism in Europe, especially in the 'Catholic countries of Europe,' it 'glosses' over 'two *major and grievous* (emphasis added) errors' of classical liberalism. The first was its opposition to Christianity in general, and to the 'Catholic Church in particular,' and the second was its 'overweening centralism,' in the name of:

> 'efficiency,' and its willingness to ride roughshod over the rights and liberties of separate and particular regions and 'nations.' In short, in several crucial ways, classical liberals weren't 'paleo' enough, and were mired in the early stages of cultural Leftism.

Two years after being en-Nobeled by the King of Sweden, Hayek (1976b) told FEE (Australia) that he was 'personally convinced that even the supposedly advanced form socialism, such as in Sweden, eventually *must* lead to the same total state control … ultimately they will be forced to become totalitarian.' Hayek had the 'impression' that Australia was 'treading the same path that all the Western nations are treading.' The 'system of unlimited democracy' Hayek asserted, in the 'long run, creates a society which is not governable … I *do believe* that our present form of government in the Western World has an *inherent* self-destructive tendency and is *not likely* to last very long.'[6] 'Present trends,' Hayek (1976a) told the Economic Society of Australia and New Zealand, 'make it seem *likely* that … existing political institutions will break down under stresses which they cannot bear (emphases added)' (see also Champion 2015).

Two years later, Hayek (1978) re-declared this permanent emergency: 'of course socialism and unlimited democracy come very much to the same thing … a modern kind of democracy, which I call unlimited democracy, is probably more subject to the influence of special interests than any former form of government was. Even a dictator can say no, but this kind of government cannot say no to any splinter group which it needs to be a majority.'[7] 'I'm afraid so long as we retain the present form of unlimited democracy, all we can hope for is to slow down the process, but we can't reverse it. I am pessimistic enough to be convinced that unless we change our constitutional structure, we are going to be driven on against people's wishes deeper and deeper into government control.'[8]

Rothbard (1994a, 3) identified 1948 as an emergency—when the Communists looked likely win the Italian elections, the CIA and the US poured 'millions in dollars and propaganda into stopping the Communists and installing the Christian Democrats.' Hayek (1977) identified another emergency: 'I'm frightfully alarmed about Italy because Italy may start developments on the European continent, which are dreadfully alarming. Assuming that a sort of civil war comes there between the Communists and the others, the Russians may intervene and we cannot know what that may lead to.'

Rothbard (1994a, 3, 4) asserted that 1994 was also an emergency: with the Center collapsing, and the Right 'seemingly nonexistent,' 'everyone' believed that the Communists, 'refurbished and renamed' as a 'Social Democratic' Democratic Party of the Left, would win power in the March 1994 Italian elections. Because single-winner districts had replaced proportional representation, the 'ex' Communists faced the electorate as leaders of a Progressive Alliance, which included a small hard-line Communist Party (the 'Communists Refounded'). Thus, nearly a half-century after communists had been 'turned back at the pass,' it looked very much that they would now, 'suitably cleaned up, buttoned down, and renamed, finally come to power in Italy.'

Hence Rothbard's support of the National Alliance,

> the so-called 'neofascists.'

In 'Civilization at Risk' (1976) and in 'Socialism By Default,' John Davenport (1949) declared emergencies: 'Without admitting it – maybe without knowing it – the Truman administration is giving the US another push towards socialism.' Referring to 'socialism, communism, planning, or state capitalism,' Mises (1950) insisted: 'All these terms signify the same thing.'[9] Reisman (2001, 12) provided Austrian 'emergency' logic: 'it is not accidental that socialism is totalitarian. You might imagine that a socialist is democratically elected. But if he wants to establish socialism, the first thing he has to do is steal all the property in the country. On the way, he will meet resistance, because otherwise, people will be totally wiped out. Then he must make a choice. Because anyone seriously bent on establishing socialism must proceed as an armed robber prepared to commit murder. In other words, it takes the communists to establish socialism. A social democrat won't have the stomach for it.'

Rothbard (1994a, 8) described the interwar emergency that Fascism had *solved*: it was a 'largely successful attempt to defend and conserve existing institutions: the family, the Church, the nation, and private property, from the wave of revolutionary destructionism.' Rothbard introduced his discussion of 'neo-fascists' with: 'Fast forward to the present day and we now have a National Alliance' and 'The Heroic Paleos: the Northern League.'

According to Hülsmann (2008, 188–189), the same emergency continued into the twenty-first century: it is 'widely known' that the (non-Austrian) Welfare State:

> has been a major factor in the decline of the family ... It is among other things because they recognize the family's effectiveness in establishing social norms that Christians seek to protect it. And it is precisely for the same reason that advocates of moral license seek to undermine it. The welfare state has been their preferred tool in the past thirty years.

In both *Christian Century* and *Christian Economics*, Mises (1961a, b) declared that the (non-Austrian) Welfare State was an emergency—the 'Antithesis' of 'Liberty': 'What separates the Communists from the advocates of the Welfare State is not the ultimate goal of their endeavours, but the method by means of which they want to attain a goal that is common to both of them.'

As editor of *Private Practice*, Rockwell (1974, 21) sought to avert an emergency: governments should restrict their activities to 'external defense, internal security and courts of law … In medicine especially, men must be free to innovate, to dream, to challenge, to experiment, to create. End this, with the deadening hand of Washington, and all the American people will suffer, now and in the future.' Alongside him at *Private Practice* were M. Stanton Evans (senior editor), George Roche III (contributing editor) and William Rickenbacker (finance editor).[10]

The MPS is/was a clearing house for 'free' market funding. From Emory University, Helmut Schoeck (11 May 1960) sought 'honorarium' funding for authors who would derive preconceived conclusions about the 'intrusion' of public agencies into the 'free' market for medicine. Schoeck also wanted a list of authors that 'we shall need' to derive this conclusion.[11] Hayek (1962) provided a glowing Preface for the result: *Financing Medical Care: An Appraisal of Foreign Programs*.

According to Boettke (2001, 267; 2015), 'Wealthier is healthier'; 'I live in a different world than the 99%' and 'I'd like to make more money.' As Angus Deaton (2017) points out, the 'free' market is expensive. The USA 'spends 18% of GDP on health care yet has one of the lowest life expectancies of any rich country. If spending were reduced to 12% of GDP, in line with France, Germany, or Switzerland, a trillion dollars—$8000 for every family—could be transferred out of unproductive activities and could supplement median earnings, the stagnation of which owes much to rising health-care costs.'

In *The Freeman*, Jarret Wollstein (1992a), director of the International Society for Individual Liberty and the founder of the National Liberty Speakers Agency, declared:

> National health insurance has destroyed quality health care and freedom of choice in countries throughout the world. To avoid that disaster in America, it is urgent that all lovers of liberty marshal their facts and raise their voices. We need to counter the relentless, socialist propaganda for government takeover of medicine now filling our schools, media, and public forums.

One of Wollstein's (1992b) authorities was 'Dr. Francis A. Davis' who 'estimated in the March 1991 issue of *Private Practice* that government regulations have already increased the cost of medical care by up to 50 percent!' According to Davis (1974, 4), the Chairman and Publisher of Private Practice, he was fighting 'this battle against the destruction of our profession.' And when Arthur Kemp became Director of the American Medical Association's Economic Research Department, Albert Hunold (25 March 1960) reminded him that this was a 'most' important job because of the Welfare State 'tendencies' in the USA.[12]

Deaton (2017) described who benefits from the 'free' market: 'Much of that trillion dollars goes to enrich the owners and executives of drugs companies, device manufacturers and relentlessly consolidating hospitals. This rent-seeking is supported by an army of lobbyists: there are more than twice as many lobbyists for the pharmaceutical and health-products industry than there are Congressmen. All of this works to keep prices high, to force the government to buy any drug approved by the Food and Drug Administration, and to fend off the creation of an evaluative agency like Britain's NICE. Perhaps the most egregious case today is America's opioid epidemic, which in 2015 killed 16,000 people from overdoses of prescription drugs, in essence legalised heroin sold as painkillers. The producers of these drugs have made billions of dollars in profits.'

As Charles Koch (1978, 30) perceptively noted:

> The majority of businessmen today are not supporters of free enterprise capitalism. Instead they prefer 'political capitalism,' a system in which government guarantees business profits while business itself faces both less competition *and* more security for itself. (Koch's emphasis)

Pfizer, one of the world's largest pharmaceutical companies, funded the Centre for Libertarian Studies (Leeson 2018b). A large number of pharmaceutical companies, including Roche Laboratories, Merck Sharp and Dohme (later Merck & Co., Inc.), Eli Lilly and Company, Ayerst Laboratories and USV Pharmaceuticals paid for advertising space in *Private Practice* (a glossy magazine which was circulated for 'free').

According to 'free' market logic, the prospect of the USA embracing the health care systems that almost all other Organisation for Economic Cooperation and Development countries have embraced for decades is an emergency—an irreversible stepping-stone on the road to communism which must, therefore, be stopped:

One of Ludwig von Mises's keenest insights was on the cumulative tendency of government intervention. The government, in its wisdom, perceives a problem (and Lord knows, there are always problems!). The government then intervenes to 'solve' that problem. But lo and behold! instead of solving the initial problem, the intervention creates two or three further problems, which the government feels it must intervene to heal, and so on toward socialism. No industry provides a more dramatic illustration of this malignant process than medical care. We stand at the seemingly inexorable brink of fully socialized medicine, or what is euphemistically called 'national health insurance ... socialized medicine could easily bring us to the vaunted medical status of the Soviet Union: everyone has the right to free medical care, but there is, in effect, no medicine and no care. (Rothbard 2007 [1995], Chapter 20)

A *Wall Street Journal* (27 July 1965) editorial on 'The Cult of Compulsion'—a celebration of John Davenport's (1965) *The US Economy*—concurred: 'The fact is that for every benefit there is a coercion. Medicare, whatever else may be said of it, is naked compulsion.' Unemployment benefits are also an emergency—'a huge menace to economic recovery in certain times and places,' according to the *Austrian Economics Newsletter*. Morgan Reynolds (2003), a Mises Institute Adjunct Scholar, concurred: 'Oh, certainly. In the 1920s, unemployment benefits nearly destroyed the entire British economy, and later led to the appearance that the Keynesian theory was being validated.' Reynolds was 'chief economist at the U.S. Department of Labor, 2001–2002,' and had 'retired as a professor of economics at Texas A&M University.'[13]

When Charles Koch first 'started trying to do anything, to have a magazine or a seminar, we'd be lucky if we could get half a dozen professors or scholars there'—but now has what he calls 'cadres of freedom advocates.' According to Kim Dennis, President of the Searle Freedom Trust,

> 'Often people who make a lot of money feel like their philanthropy is a way of compensating for their business success. But Charles is not "giving back." He is supporting the things that made his business success possible.' It's all of a piece. (cited by Glassman 2011)

Invoking 'the fate of humanity,' the 'Charles Koch Distinguished Alumnus, The Institute for Humane Studies,' declared a permanent emergency: 'an almost spiritual admission and admonition. I truly believe that the teaching of economics is a higher calling for which we have been enlisted ... The fate of civilization is intimately tied to our ability to communicate the basic teachings of our discipline' (Boettke 2011, 23–24). Mathew 22.14 cites Jesus: 'many are called, but few are chosen.' Boettke (2011, 21) sought to rectify the bible: 'Just to be clear, what we are trying to *pull off* (emphasis added) is no less of an accomplishment than what happened with the Keynesian revolution mid twentieth century. We want to place an Austrian inspired economist in every university and college in the US within the next 30 years, and clusters of centers for research and education in 20 or more schools, with half of those being in graduate programs and at least 1 or 2 in elite PhD programs.' Boettke (2012) 'will be happy when I am the Ludwig von Mises Professor at the F.A. Hayek Centre for Advanced Studies at Princeton University. Then I will be happy.'

The Cold War was an ongoing emergency. It appears to have increased economists' tolerance of inflation and to have a thrust a misinterpretation of A. W. H. Phillips' stabilisation model centre stage (Leeson 1997a, b, 1998). The founder of *The Freeman* didn't 'see how you can say a person's body belongs to the state' (Chamberlain 1987). In 1953, FEE (citing H. B. Liddell Hart) declared an emergency: once conscription is 'adopted in peacetime, it will be hard to resist the extension of the principle to all other aspects of life. We ought to think carefully, and to think ahead, before taking a decisive step towards totalitarianism.'[14] FEE's '*spiritus rector*,' Mises (1963, 282; 1966, 282), declared an equal and opposite emergency: 'He who in our age opposes armaments and conscription is, perhaps unbeknown to himself, an abettor of those aiming at the enslavement of all.' This was John Davenport's (1958) 'new intellectual synthesis' which 'taking the full measure of the enemy without the gates, will cleave to the principle of the free society at home.'

Boettke's (2011, 22) 'message to graduate students is to learn from Mises and Hayek in the way that they approached their research and teaching in economics and political economy.' As Mises (1985 [1927]) sought to become the *Führer* of a 'Fascist'-Austrian School Pact, so Rothbard (1994a) appeared to have similar aspirations: in a 'remarkable feat deployed at the last minute,' Silvio Berlusconi started from 'scratch,' creating a new political party, *Forza Italia* (Go, Italy) in January 1994, 'sweeping' to victory only two months later in the March 1994 elections.

Rothbard (1994a) praised Berlusconi as a 'Dynamic media billionaire.' A quarter of a century later, another populist television 'star'—with the backing of Murdoch's Fox News and the use of inflammatory chants plus the slogan, 'I Am Your Voice!'—was elected President of the USA. Rothbard (1994a, 4)—who motivated Austrian economists by orchestrating them to chant: 'We Want Externalities!' (Blundel 2014, 100, n. 7)—asked: how did Berlusconi had done do it: with 'money of course, with bold use of his TV networks and media empire,' assisted by 'bright young marketing and managerial experts' from his conglomerate, Fininvest. Roberto Lasagna, his campaign manager and party organiser, was the Italian head of the 'famed ad agency,' Saatchi & Saatchi. *Forza Italia* is a popular Italian 'chant' at national soccer matches: Berlusconi owns Milan A. C., one of the 'best' soccer teams in Europe. But *Forza Italia* could not have won the 1994 Italian elections 'alone'; instead, Berlusconi 'shrewdly' put together a tripartite coalition of the 'Right, the Freedom Alliance.'

The Northern League was Rothbard's (1994a, 9) 'personal favorite' among the three members of the Freedom Alliance: 'about one thing we can be confident: the Freedom Alliance is tough-minded and hard-nosed.' The Northern League is 'separatist, bitterly critical of southern welfare parasites and Roman centralism, is staunchly free-market in economics (its leaders have read and admire Ludwig von Mises), is staunchly bourgeois in social makeup, and favors immigration restrictions against welfare moochers from the south and elsewhere.' The 'biggest clash' is between the Northern League's regional separatism and the National Alliance's 'devotion to the centralized Roman State.' Otherwise, many of the discussions and debates within the National Alliance 'sound' like a more hostile version of 'discussions' within the John Randolph Club.

With the entry of Pat Buchanan into the 1992 presidential race, Rothbard (1992a) ranted (in his Presidential Address to the John Randolph Club): 'The radical right is back, all over the place, feistier than ever and getting stronger ... We shall break the clock of social democracy. We shall break the clock of the Great Society. We shall break the clock of the welfare state. We shall break the clock of the New Deal. We shall break the clock of Woodrow Wilson's New Freedom and perpetual war. We *shall* (Rothbard's emphasis) repeal the twentieth century.'

Rothbard (1926–1995) was a populist without popular support. In his obituary, Buckley (1995) described him as huffing and puffing in the little cloister whose walls he labored so strenuously to contract, leaving him, in the end, not as the father of a swelling movement that 'rous [ed] the masses from their slumber,' as he once stated his ambition, but with about as many disciples as David Koresh had in his little redoubt in Waco.

Rothbard sought to rectify this isolation by forming the John Randolph Club with the Rockford Institute which founded in 1976, by MPS member John A. Howard and run by Pastor John Neuhaus and his Center for Religion and Society with former (and future) Defence Secretary Donald Rumsfeld on the Board.[15] Leopold Tyrmand had founded the Rockford Institute's *Chronicles of Culture* magazine as a conservative alternative to *The New York Review of Books*; his successor, Thomas Fleming, shortened the magazine's name to *Chronicles*, redirected its focus 'from cultural critique to ideological war,' and recruited Samuel Francis as a columnist and 'collaborator' (Frum 2003).

Francis advocated 'uninhibited racial nationalism': protecting the interests of the 'Euro-American cultural core'—a 'nationalist ethic may often require government action.' *Chronicles* 'championed the Southern Confederacy of the 1860s and the anti-civil rights resistance of the 1960s' and advocated a variety of populist causes: industrial protection, restrictions on non-white immigration, minimum-wage laws, and attacks on corporations that moved operations offshore (Frum 2003).

Francis declared that 'The civilization that we as whites created in Europe and America could not have developed apart from the genetic endowments of the creating people.' After being sacked from the Moonies' *Washington Times* (following a speech at the 1994 conference of the white supremacist American Renaissance organisation), he became editor-in-chief of the Citizens' Informer, the newspaper of the Council of Conservative Citizens, the 'successor group to the White Citizens' Councils of the segregated South' (Frum 2003).

With a circulation of 17,000, *Chronicles* was:

> tilted toward a white, European tradition, called nativism among scholars, and ... was 'insensitive to the classic language of anti-Semitism.'

One of Fleming's lead editorials argued that:

unchecked immigration from third world nations threatened to undermine the essentially European character of the United States. 'One doesn't wish to be unkind,' the article said, 'but cultural pluralism is not the most attractive legacy we can leave to our children.' (Bernstein 1989)

On Reagan's inauguration day, *The Wall Street Journal* published Tyrmand's (20 January 1981) 'The Conservative Ideas in Reagan's Victory' which asserted that 'Von Mises devoted his life to proving that capitalism and free enterprise are sources of humanity and virtue (which makes him an ancestor of supply-side macroeconomics), and that any form of collectivism and statism must end in totalitarian oppression.'

The Republican Party 'Southern Strategy' peeled-away low ascribed status Democrats from their traditional party affiliation. The elitism of the Right is contempt-based; while the elitism of the Left tends to be somewhat patronising. The 'presuppositions of Harvey Road' (Keynes' childhood home) found a shrill elitist echo across the Atlantic.

While running for the White House in 2008, Barack Obama stated: 'You go into these small towns in Pennsylvania and, like a lot of small towns in the Midwest, the jobs have been gone now for 25 years and nothing's replaced them. And they fell through the Clinton administration, and the Bush administration, and each successive administration has said that somehow these communities are gonna regenerate and they have not. And it's not surprising then they get bitter, they cling to guns or religion or antipathy toward people who aren't like them or anti-immigrant sentiment or anti-trade sentiment as a way to explain their frustrations' (cited by Ross 2015). And while running for the White House in 2016, Hilary Clinton stated: 'You know, to just be grossly generalistic, you could put half of Trump's supporters into what I call the basket of deplorables. Right? The racist, sexist, homophobic, xenophobic, Islamaphobic — you name it. And unfortunately there are people like that. And he has lifted them up' (cited by Chozick 2016).

In 'Right-Wing Populism: A Strategy for the Paleo Movement,' Rothbard (1992b, 6) sought an 'Outreach to the Redneck'—including the former Klansman, David Duke, who 'picked up 55% of the white vote' in Louisiana and only lost the run-off because the 'fear campaign brought out a massive outpouring of black voters.' In 'A New Strategy for Liberty,' Rothbard (1994b) believed that he had solved the 'coordination problem' between Austrian economists and 'Redneck' militia groups:

A second necessary task is informational: we can't hope to provide any guidance to this marvellous new movement until we, and the various parts of the movement, find out what is going on. To help, we will feature a monthly report on 'The Masses in Motion.' After the movement finds itself and discovers its dimensions, there will be other tasks: to help the movement find more coherence, and fulfil its magnificent potential for overthrowing the malignant elites that rule over us.

Rothbard (1994c) explained that 'the least' Austrians could do 'is accelerate the Climate of Hate in America, and hope for the best.'

The *Los Angeles Times* reported that President Trump instructed police recruits: 'Please don't be too nice. Like when you guys put somebody in the car and you're protecting their head, you know the way you put their hand so they don't hit their head and they've just killed somebody … you can take that hand away.' With respect to 'thugs being thrown into the back of a paddy wagon,' he instructed: be 'rough' with the 'animals' (cited by Demick and Lee 2017).

In the *Los Angeles Times*, Rockwell (1991) was equally inflammatory: 'As recently as the 1950s--when street crime was not rampant in America--the police always operated on this principle: No matter the vagaries of the court system, a mugger or rapist knew he faced a trouncing--proportionate to the offense and the offender--in the back of the paddy wagon, and maybe even a repeat performance at the station house. As a result, criminals were terrified of the cops, and our streets were safe.'

According to Trump: 'For years and years,' laws have been made to 'protect the criminal. Totally protect the criminal, not the officers. You do something wrong, you're in more jeopardy than they are. These laws are stacked against you. We're changing those laws … They butchered those little girls. They kidnap. They extort. They rape, and they rob. They prey on children. They shouldn't be here.'[16] According to Rockwell (1991): 'The result is city terrorism, though we are seldom shown videos of old people being mugged, women being raped, gangs shooting drivers at random or store clerks having their throats slit.'

Brian Crozier's 6I was the 'Politbureau' of an anti-communist 'Sixth International' (Teacher 2018a, b) and after the collapse of *that* form of producer sovereignty (1917–1991), Rothbard (1994a, 11) hoped to form his own 'International'—devoted to a producer sovereignty over which *he* could exert influence: 'We can see, rising out of the mist, out of this ferment, a new Nationalist International, a Right-wing International, a Fifth International, an international of disparate and sovereign nationalities, each free and independent, each on its own land. Contrary to popular notions, there is nothing at all contradictory about a nationalist international, a free and genuine comity of sovereign nations.'

Like Mises (1985 [1927]), Rothbard (1994a, 8) promoted *political* 'Fascism' to defend Austrian *economic* liberalism: 'The militant Fascist movement succeeded in saving Italy from two monstrous evils: revolutionary Communism and revolutionary anarcho-syndicalism. This preservation and defense was its great achievement. Was Fascism perfect? Obviously not.' But initially, *Il Duce* (like Pinochet) promoted Austrian economic liberalism: in its 'early' years, under the supervision of Mussolini's 'free-market' Minister of Finance, Albert di Stefano, the 'Fascists succeeded in cutting the budget, slashing taxes, and privatizing much of State industry.'

Rothbard (1994b, 4) praised Antonio Martino, the MPS President (1988–1990), Foreign Minister in the 'new' Italy, and Berlusconi's 'Economic Guru' and 'long-time close adviser.' Martino's strategy resembled that which facilitated the rise of Putin's Russia of the Oligarchs: government expenditures will be curbed by 'massive' privatisation—including schools and national health insurance. Moreover, under the influence of the MPS, Forza Italia will cut into the 'gigantic parasitic bureaucracy' that has been 'strangling' economic and social life' in Italy. Although Martino was Friedman's former student and a former Heritage Foundation Fellow he is 'far friendlier to the Austro-libertarian minority' within MPS than are most other members of the Society's 'moderate free-market power elite' associated with Friedman and Heritage's Edwin Feulner.

In *I Chose Liberty*, Chafuen (2010, 83)—MPS member, Fisher's Atlas Network beneficiary, and author of *Christians for Freedom: Late Scholastic Economics* (1986)—described the interwar emergency: his maternal grandfather 'graduated from the University of Vienna, and his proud Genovese and cultured upbringing helped him view with contempt the barbaric motives and customs of the socialist hordes,' and his mother was

> influenced by an 'Austrian-Hungarian' virtue-based approach.

Chafuen (2010, 85) 'first fell in love with liberty; I then fell in love with God. Soon thereafter, I learned that they were the same thing, the true Liberty. Following liberty has been a challenging and rewarding journey. I hope it never ends.' The Austrian emergency also never ends.

In Europe, 'Fascism,' as defined and praised by Mises (1985 [1927]), overthrew democracy in Italy (1922), Spain (1923), Portugal (1926), Germany (1933), Austrian (1934) and Spain (1936); and in Latin America, similar operations occurred in what became known as the Operation Condor countries: Paraguay (1954), Brazil (1964), Bolivia (1971), Uruguay (1973), Chile (1973) and Argentina (1976). Alois Hudal (1885–1963), a Roman Catholic titular bishop who was head of the Austrian-German congregation of Santa Maria dell'Anima in Rome, was one of the links between the two episodes. In his 1937 book, *Die Grundlagen des Nationalsozialismus* (*The Foundations of National Socialism*), Hudal praised Hitler; and when it was published sent a copy to Hitler dedicated to 'The Siegfried of German Greatness.' He later established 'ratlines' to Latin America and elsewhere—escape routes for Nazi war criminals (Steinacher 2011).

The MPS President declared a permanent emergency: 'Latin America is well known for its endemic political instability, coups d'etat, widespread underdevelopment, monetary instability, disproportionate foreign debts, corruption, violence, and recently, the implausible scenario of oil-rich countries going broke. Today, most Latin American countries are regressing to standards of living of earlier decades. To varying degrees their economies are being deliberately sabotaged by terrorists, obviously well supported by the Marxist international movement and aimed ultimately at the United States.' It was land reform that inevitably led to 'violence' (Ayau 1984).

According to Rothbard (1994a, 4), the 'Austrolibertarian wing' of the MPS is centred in Spain and Latin America. MPS member, Ronald Hamowy (2003), described their influence: 'As is customary, the Mt. Pelerin meetings were held in one of the most expensive hotels in the city as befitted the fact that almost all attendees were either think-tank executives traveling on expense accounts, South American latifundia owners, for whom hundred-dollar bills were small change, or the officers of the Society itself, a self-perpetuating oligarchy who, thanks to its members' dues, traveled around the world in first-class accommodations.' Chafuen (2010, 84) described the 'Dirty War' (1974–1983) emergency in which 30,000 (impurities) 'disappeared': 'With support from the military and friendly segments of the civil society, Argentines were able to prevent a Communist takeover of the country. The military, not without fault or sin, provided some space to liberals who, from a different angle, shared their same determination to stop left-wing terror.'

Chafuen's (2010, 84) inspiration was a 'Misean for Life' *Luftwaffe* bomber pilot: 'I recall that the number of young liberals in the country could be counted with both hands, with fingers to spare. I was able to recommend that all of them be given the same scholarship that I received, thanks to Hans Sennholz via Benegas Lynch, to study at Grove City College in Pennsylvania ... I, as well as other young Argentines, returned from Grove City to teach at the best Argentine universities.' Sennholz 'almost alone among eminent free enterprise economists, rests his defense of a free society on revelation ... divinely revealed information' (John Robbins 2010).

Pinochet fitted Mises' definition of a political 'Fascist.' In addition to describing the interwar 'emergency' that led Mises to embrace 'Fascism,' Caldwell and Montes (2014a, 51; 2014b, 2015a, 304) report that 'the 1970s was an ideologically fraught time'—hence Hayek's support of Pinochet's Junta and its 'economic liberalization.'

One week after the announcement of his Nobel Prize for Economic Sciences, Hayek (16 October 1974) declared an emergency in *The Daily Telegraph*: what is likely to 'drive us further on this perilous road will be the panicky reaction of politicians every time a slowing down of inflation leads to a substantial rise of unemployment.' Although Austrian-promoted deflation had led to the Austrian-led Third Reich, Hayek focused on inflation—a 'process we must avoid at any price. It can be tolerated only by those who wish to destroy the market order and to replace it by a Communist or some totalitarian system.'

In Face the Press, Hayek (22 June 1975a) provided a salesman's choice: 'It's not a question of what the country is willing to tolerate. The longer you have inflation, the more greater unemployment becomes inevitable. We will have no choice. It's all the matter that government can't avoid the unemployment which is caused by the previous misdirection of labor, which the inflation has produced.' And in *Full Employment at Any Price?* Hayek (1975b) referred to the inflation of the 1970s (which had been induced by Arthur Burns, Chair of Nixon's Federal Reserve and a recruit to Hayek's MPS) as 'the present crisis.' Hence Hayek's support of Mrs. Thatcher—who appears to have been the beneficiary of the 'unscrupulous methods' of the anti-democratic right, including *The Daily Telegraph* columnist, Robert Moss.

Austrian 'knowledge' has a common structure—the aspirations of sovereignty-seeking producers. David John Marotta, for example, derived his understanding of the world from his father, 'George Marotta, who I consider a financial Rembrandt. I grew up amongst my father's work at the Hoover Institution alongside Milton Friedman, Edward Teller, Thomas Sowell, and other great research fellows there. We have developed our own principles of freedom investing to guide many of our strategic investment decisions.' Hayek's policy influence expanded noticeably after the 1974 Nobel Prize; but according to David John Marotta: 'By the 1980's his ideas finally found favor and rose to policy under Ronald Reagan in the United States, under Margaret Thatcher in Great Brittan, and then under Kurt Waldheim was reimported back into Austria.'[17] Austrian President Waldheim (1986–1992) had been a member of the National Socialist German Students' League, a division of the Nazi Party, and had lied about his wartime awareness of—and possible involvement with—war crimes.

For Austrians, the Chilean Socialist Party's Salvador Allende was observationally equivalent to the British Labour Party's Michael Foot. Moss (1973, 205, iv) wanted it to be known that

> the course that Allende's government steered led inevitably to a violent confrontation ... The chief reason while Chile matters to the outside world ... is that in Chile, a Marxist strategy for the conquest of political power from within a democratic system came dangerously close to success. The lesson, and the warning, can hardly be neglected by those countries that could one day find themselves confronted by a similar set of circumstances. It is profoundly to be hoped that Chile's tragedy, resulting in the temporary death of democracy, will not be repeated. But it must not be forgotten who was primarily responsible for it ... there must be no confusion about where the responsibility lies. It lies with Dr Allende and his fellow-Marxists, who pursued their plans for the seizure of total power to the point where the opposition despaired of restraining them by constitutional means.

After Foot won the first round of the Parliamentary Labour Party leadership election (25 March 1976), *Free Nation*, the journal of The National Association for Freedom (NAFF), published, under Moss' editorship, an unsigned lead article headed 'Affront to the Queen' in which it was argued that the Head of State should refuse to see Foot and therefore prevent him becoming Prime Minister if he was elected leader of the Labour Party.[18] In 1976, James Callaghan beat Foot and became Hayek-influenced; was defeated by the Hayekian Thatcher in 1979; and succeeded by Foot in 1980. As Hayek's LSE colleague, Tawney, put it, English socialism 'owed more to Methodism than to Marxism' (cited by Perkins 1989, 49). On 9 June 1983, Thatcher won a second term; and Foot resigned as Labour leader. In the absence of any non-Austrian knowledge, we should presume that in 1976 had Allende been defeated in his fifth contested Presidential election he, too, would have accepted the result.

Murdoch's publishing business model combines two forms of pornography: page one outrage plus page three nudity (with miniskirts replacing nudity on Fox News). According to the salacious *News of the World* and other Murdoch papers, Foot—codename 'Boot'—met his KGB handlers at the Gay Hussar, a Soho restaurant—a libel which resulted in substantial damages being paid. Foot's lawyer said that Times Newspapers' 'unsuccessful attempt to prevent Mr. Murdoch from appearing in court had prompted the company's decision to reach a settlement.' Foot added that if Murdoch 'owns newspapers which can make accusations of this nature, he should appear in court when they are raised' (Williams 1995).

Hayek met Reagan in the White House and formed a low opinion of his intelligence (Cubitt 2006, 144). Reagan celebrated Pinochet's 1976 terrorist attack on Washington which killed an American citizen in addition to the Chilean former diplomat, Letelier (Leeson 2018a). Rothbard was a spotter for Al-Qaeda in their efforts to bomb targets in New York (Chapter 1); and for the World Trade Center celebration of the 100th anniversary of Mises' birth, Reagan (on the 40th anniversary of the bombing of Pearl Harbor) sent a telegram to Rothbard et al.: as a 'wise and kindly mentor,' Mises was

> quick to encourage all those who sought to understand the meaning of freedom ... von Mises ... rekindled the flames of liberty in new generations of thinkers ... we owe an incalculable debt to this dean of the Austrian school of economics for expanding our knowledge and inspiring a new vision of liberty in our age.[19]

The Archives reveal that Hayek proposed to choreograph an election stunt for Reagan—despite what he alleged was his 'strict' rule not to take part in current political activities of a country of which he was not a citizen (17 June 1979).[20] Ten days earlier, Hayek (7 June 1980) had suggested to the Hoover Institution's Director, Glenn Campbell, that during his next visit he would like Reagan to be cross-examined before the press by Hoover economists, including himself: this would have allowed Reagan to show his confidence and to demonstrate that he was taken seriously by economists. Hayek sought a specific role in winning the 1980 election: he wanted to tell the media his 'joke' that since Reagan was twelve years his junior, he was clearly good for an unconstitutional third term.[21] Of the 74 members of the Reagan 1980–1981 Task Forces, 22 were MPS members (Peterson 1996).

Policy advocates often co-align on multiple fronts: market failure deniers (and climate change deniers in particular) are often proponents of 'free' market 'liberty' for the financial sector. Hayek referred to the Greens as the new barbarians in our midst[22]; and informed a correspondent that had he been a younger man, he would have concentrated on exposing Greens, instead of focusing almost exclusively on exposing Reds.[23]

Rothbard's (1994c) 'Climate of Hate' was directed at Pigou, environmentalists, government employees, non-whites and the poor. In 1991, the Soviet Union collapsed and the anti-Pigovian, Coase (who had been repeatedly nominated by Hayek) was awarded the Nobel Prize for Economic Sciences. But Pigovians continued to exert influence: in 1992, the United Nations Framework Convention on Climate Change aimed to 'stabilize greenhouse gas concentrations in the atmosphere at a level that would prevent dangerous anthropogenic interference with the climate system.' According to Rothbard (1992a), this was the work of a 'few left-wing hysterics': 'most real scientists have a very different view of such environmental questions.'

For Austrians like Reisman (2005 [1990]), environmentalism is an 'emergency':

> These intellectual toxins can be seen bobbing up and down in the 'intellectual mainstream,' just as raw sewage can be seen floating in a dirty river. Indeed, they fill the intellectual mainstream. Virtually, every college and university in the Western world is a philosophical cesspool of these doctrines, in which intellectually helpless students are immersed for several years and then turned loose to contaminate the rest of society. These irrationalist doctrines, and others like them, *are the philosophical substance of contemporary liberal arts education.* Clearly, the most urgent task

confronting the Western world, and the new intellectuals who must lead it, is *a philosophical and intellectual cleanup*. Without it, Western civilization simply cannot survive. It will be killed by the poison of environmentalism. (Reisman's emphases)

Reisman (2001) reflected:

> What's at issue here is a philosophical problem. The movement is fundamentally antihuman. That is what motivates it. This is a more widely occurring phenomenon than you might suppose. We know of serial killers, but every once in a while similar mentalities gain political power, as happened with the communists and the Nazis. There is a lot of hatred and hostility in many people that is just looking for something to attach itself to.

When the *Austrian Economic Newsletter* asked 'An attack on human life by another means?' Reisman (2001) replied: 'That is essentially what environmentalism amounts to. It is the political movement where the destructive impulse has parked itself today. First you have the hatred, then you have a cultural vehicle, such as a totalitarian political movement or an insane religion, that allows and encourages the hatred to be expressed. Intellectually, environmentalism is nothing more than the death rattle of socialism and should be much easier to overcome. Socialists used to masquerade as defenders of science and reason, and now they are openly anti-science and technology, as we see with environmentalism.'

Reisman (2001) then illustrated the quality of Austrian thought: 'their idea of success is thwarting human success. In their view, the environment is only destroyed by human beings. The caribou eat the vegetation, and that's okay. The wolves kill the caribou, and that's okay. Microbes are killing them both, and that's okay. The only thing that's not okay is if human beings attempt to do anything. Only then does the environment need protection, in their view. We can conclude from this that it is only human beings they are really after.' Also according to Reisman, the minimum-wage law is a 'good example of something that restricts the freedom of opportunity. In a free society, our fates are not determined.'

After the Austrian-promoted deregulation of the financial sector, the US taxpayers lost $9.26 billion bailing out General Motors, Chrysler, Ally Financial, Chrysler Financial and automotive suppliers through the federal Auto Industry Financing Program (Snaverly 2014). Along with

Ford and Chrysler, General Motors funded the American Enterprise Association, which in 1962 was renamed the American Enterprise Institute for Public Policy Research (Phillips-Fine 2009, 61–62). In 2001, there were 42,196 motor vehicle deaths on American roads. Reisman (2001) praised 'the automobile, which has eliminated the stench of horse manure and horse urine in the streets.' He also had other policy solutions: 'If we didn't have restrictions on strip mining and nuclear power, those are substitutes and they would further drive down the price by a reduction in the demand for oil.'

T. R. Reid (2017a, b), the author of *A Fine Mess, A Global Quest for a Simpler, Fairer, and More Efficient Tax System*, reported: 'There are hundreds and hundreds of giveaways in the tax code. Some of them only applied to one taxpayer, and they never list the name. They say a company organized in Delaware on October 13, 1916. That would be General Motors, but they never mention that in the bill. And they cost us hundreds of billions of dollars.'

In *Mises and Austrian Economics a Personal View*, three-time presidential candidate Congressman Ron Paul (2008, 37–38, 52)—proclaiming that 'Liberty is my first goal'—defined 'government partnership with business' as a 'euphemism for fascism.' General Motors funded the cartoon version of *The Road to Serfdom*,[24] which warned of the dangers of propaganda and insisted that government intervention in the economy was poison: the choice lay between firing squads or the right to fire employees.[25] In a 4 June 1945 campaign broadcast, Winston Churchill also took an emergency theme from *The Road to Serfdom* (Hayek 1944): a Labour Government wouldn't 'allow free, sharp or violently worded expressions of public discontent … They would have to fall back on some form of Gestapo, no doubt very humanely directed in the first instance. And this would nip opinion in the bud; it would stop criticism as it reared its head, and it would gather all the power to the supreme Party and the Party leaders, rising like stately pinnacles above their vast bureaucracies of Civil Servants, no longer servants and no longer civil. And where would the ordinary simple folk—the common people as they like to call them in America—where would they be once this mighty organism had got them in its grip?' Churchill added that socialism was 'inseparably interwoven with Totalitarianism and the abject worship of the State' (cited by Lane 2013, 52).

Keynes told John Davenport that Churchill was 'no Tory':

Like so many enlightened Conservatives, Churchill is inherently a traditionalist. His religion is the historical and traditional community of British life. For him the past holds an immense amount of value, and he says 'we mustn't play monkey tricks with it' … His great mission is to preserve 'the rich character of British life.'[26]

This led Churchill (1935) to wonder whether Hitler was 'Monster or Hero?' Mises (1985 [1927]) was less ambivalent.

Rothbard (1973) complained about 'the large majority' of Mises' 'eminent and formerly devoted students' who 'decided to bend with the new breeze.' The July 1945 British general election took place as evidence about the gas chambers emerged. One of the largest concentration camps, Mauthausen–Gusen, close to Hitler's Austrian childhood town, Linz, was liberated two days before Victory in Europe, VE Day: over a quarter of a million inmates failed to survive the war. Hayek (1994, 107) didn't 'regard it as impossible' that Churchill's 'Gestapo speech' and the resulting backlash against 'Professor Friedrich August von Hayek' may have cost the Conservatives the 1945 election. *The New York Times* reported that after Labour leader, Clement Attlee, referred to his Party political influence, Hayek complained: 'I am a teacher of economics, not a politician. I have no connection whatsoever with the Conservative Party.'[27] The evidence, however, reveals that *The Road to Serfdom*—with Hayek's permission—played an important role in Conservative Party election propaganda (Shearmur 2006, 310).

Hayek (1978), who had just returned from his American *Road to Serfdom* promotional tour, lunched at the Reform Club with John Wood and Stanley Denison the day after Churchill's broadcast and was 'evidently pleased that his ideas had been taken up with such gusto' (Cockett 1995, 95). Attlee described Churchill's 'Gestapo speech' as a 'second-hand version of the academic views of an Austrian professor, Friedrich August von Hayek' (cited by Lane 2013, 52). Hayek (1994, 106) complained that henceforth, he was 'officially in socialist terms, "Friedrich August von Hayek".' Presumably for tactical reasons, Hayek (1946) signed his *Economica* essay on 'The London School of Economics 1895–1945' 'FAH.'

As US Secretary of State (1853–1857), William L. Marcy (who is credited with the term, 'to the victor belong the spoils') directed US diplomats to eschew the 'court-dress' used by European aristocrats in favour of ordinary American attire. Austrians have 'seen the past and it works.'

6 THE 'FREE' MARKET 'EMERGENCY' DEMAND FOR 'FASCISM' 291

Shenoy (2003, 4)—who obtained lifetime tenure on the back of a recommendation from 'von' Hayek—was nostalgic for a cartoon version of the neo-feudal century which culminated in the 'Great' War: 'You had free trade, free movement of people, free movement of capital, a gold standard, falling prices in the latter part of the century, peaceful development, and no major wars between 1815 and 1914. The world's armies and navies did not know what to do.' Reisman (2001)—who presumably received a recommendation from 'von' Mises—was also nostalgic for the century which culminated in the French Revolution: 'Men from the eighteenth and nineteenth centuries rode around in carriages and some wore powdered wigs, but they were thinking the thoughts that created modern industrial civilization. Today's intellectuals fly around in jet planes, but they are thinking the thoughts that will destroy us. For good economics to prevail requires that individuals recognize the truth for themselves and fight to uphold it.'

Mises (1963, 282; 1966, 282) lobbied for the Warfare State: 'He who in our age opposes armaments and conscription is, perhaps unbeknown to himself, an abettor of those aiming at the enslavement of all.' In addition to the Cold War, the USA used conscription during the Civil War, the 'Great' War and World War II. Ebeling (2013) was nostalgic: 'The government did not control, order, or plan his life for him. He chose his own career; he earned his own way; he was responsible for caring for himself and his family; all of his associations and relationships with others, both inside and outside of the commercial arena of trade and exchange, were based on his voluntary agreement in mutual consent with others.' Rothbard was the first person Raico (2013) had met who defended 'a fully voluntary society—nudge, nudge.'

The 13th Amendment to the US Constitution ensured that 'neither slavery nor involuntary servitude… shall exist within the United States, or any place subject to their jurisdiction.' During Thomas Jefferson's administration (1801–1809), Congress had prohibited the importation of slaves (1808); but the 'free' market (smuggling) continued. Domestic slave trading remained 'free'—the Deep South bought more than one million slaves from the Upper South. Before 1865, there were four million slaves in the South.

The 'free' market is funded by the oil industry. John D. Rockefeller's Standard Oil dominated the international 'free' market through horizontal and vertical integration and predatory pricing (to destroy competitors). In 1911, the US Supreme Court ruled that it was an illegal monopoly. According to Heartland Institute's Ebeling (2013), the history of the USA from the:

> time of its founding in the late 18th century up to the early decades of the 20th century was a period during which virtually all market activities were free from government regulation, control or manipulation ... This was the essence of 'American Exceptionalism.' In America, society was made up of uniquely self-governing and sovereign individuals. In this exceptional American experience, government was limited to a relatively small number of explicitly enumerated functions and responsibilities. Outside of protecting each in his individual rights, every individual was self-governing and sovereign in guiding and directing his own life. His life was his own to plan and implement. There was no welfare state; there were, in general, no government guarantees or 'bailouts'; there were some special interest subsidies and various foreign trade protections at times in that earlier period of American history. But in comparison to the world before and the world since, the market place was practically left alone. Each individual 'ruled' over himself, his own 'sovereign,' as long as he respected and did not violate the equal rights of all others to their lives, liberty and honestly acquired property. This made America a most 'exceptional' country and society! That is, he is not the slave or sacrificial lamb for arbitrary monarchs or voting majorities.

According to Rockwell (2010, 289), 'Everyone, both proponents and opponents, knew exactly' what the 1964 Civil Rights Act was: 'a statist, centralizing measure that fundamentally attacked the rights of property and empowered the state as mind reader: to judge not only our actions, but our motives, and to criminalize them. The good folks who resisted the civil-rights juggernaut were not necessarily ideologically driven. Mostly they resented horrible intrusions into their communities, the media smears, and the attacks on their fundamental freedoms that civil rights represented.'

According to Ebeling (2013): 'America was a living reality of a society based on and respecting the individual's right to be free, and not the manipulated pawn in the hands of arbitrary monarchs or democratic majorities.' In 1970, another emergency emerged: Allende's democratically elected Socialist Party government.

Hayek and Hitler sought to create *irreversible* versions of the past. Hitler's method was to 'cleanse the nation of its enemies' (cited by Heiden 1944, 312); and the *Law, Legislation and Liberty* 'Model

6 THE 'FREE' MARKET 'EMERGENCY' DEMAND FOR 'FASCISM'   293

Constitution' that Hayek (2013 [1979], 483) sent to Pinochet 'would of course make all socialist measures for redistribution impossible'—and could, therefore, only be imposed when socialists were unable to effectively object. Hayek (1981) supported Pinochet, Videla and other 'transitional' dictators as 'a means of establishing a stable democracy and liberty, clean of impurities.' But after cleansing by Hitler, Pinochet and Videla, socialists won elections in Germany, Chile and Argentina. Clearly, the permanent (largely imaginary) threats faced by the 'free' market require the permanent credible threats of a 'free' market 'Fascist' coup.

In Pinochet's Chile, Hayek (1981) insisted that 'Democracy needs a "good cleaning" by strong government.' Reisman (2006)—who at age 15 had been recruited 'to hold out through the long libertarian winter of the 1960s and 1970s, thus enabling the breakthrough of Misesian ideas of the 1980s and 1990s' (Hülsmann 2007, 847–848, 896)—insists that Pinochet 'deserves to be remembered for having rescued his country from becoming the second Soviet satellite in the Western hemisphere … a totalitarian dictatorship.' But he 'is denounced again and again for the death or disappearance of over 3000 Chilean citizens and the alleged torture of thousands more … in a struggle to avoid the establishment of a Communist dictatorship, it is undoubtedly true that many or most of those who died or suffered were preparing to inflict a far greater number of deaths and a vastly larger scale of suffering on their fellow citizens. Their deaths and suffering should certainly not be mourned, any more than the deaths of Lenin, Stalin, and Hitler, and their helpers should be mourned.'

In August 1917, the Commander-in-Chief of the Russian Army, General Lavr Kornilov, launched an unsuccessful *Putsch* against Alexander Kerensky's Russian Provisional Government. According to Reisman (2006): 'Had there been a General Pinochet in Russia in 1918 or Germany in 1933, the people of those countries and of the rest of the world would have been incomparably better off, precisely by virtue of the death, disappearance, and attendant suffering of vast numbers of Communists and Nazis. Life and liberty are positively helped by the death and disappearance of such mortal enemies. Their absence from the scene means the absence of such things as concentration camps, and is thus ardently to be desired.'

Reisman (2006) rectified history: 'Pinochet voluntarily relinquished his dictatorship. He did so after both preventing a Communist takeover and imposing major pro-free-market reforms, inspired largely by Milton Friedman (who in large part was himself inspired by Ludwig von Mises).' He was thus one of the 'most extraordinary dictators in history, a dictator who stood for major limits on the power of the state, who imposed such limits, and who sought to maintain such limits after voluntarily giving up his dictatorship.'

Reisman (2006), who was horrified that Pinochet did not get away with human rights abuses, appeared to advocate permanent dictatorships. When Pinochet 'stepped down, he did so with a guarantee of immunity from prosecution for his actions while in power. However, the present and previous regime in Chile violated this agreement and sought to ensnare the General in a web of legal actions and law suits, making the last years of his life a period of turmoil. This was a clear violation of contract, comparable to the seizure of property in violation of contract. Not surprisingly the regimes in question were avowedly socialist. As a result of their breach, it is now considerably less likely that the world will soon see any other dictator voluntarily relinquish his power. The Chilean socialists will have taught him that to be secure, he must remain in power until he dies.'

Ebeling (2016) pretended to cite from Mises' (1951 [1932], 458) *Socialism: An Economic and Sociological Analysis*:

> Socialism is not in the least what is pretends to be. It is not the pioneer of a better and finer world, but the spoiler of what thousands of years of civilization have created. It does not build, it destroys. For destruction is the essence of it. It produces nothing, it only consumes what the social order based on private ownership in the means of production has created ... Each step leading towards Socialism must exhaust itself in the destruction of what already exists.

Mises (1951 [1932], 458) had been rectified by deleting a qualifying clause: 'Since a socialist order of society cannot exist, unless it be as a fragment of Socialism within an economic order resting otherwise on private property, each step leading towards Socialism must exhaust itself in the destruction of what already exists.'

Tax-funded education is the invisible ladder of social mobility. In a *Freeman* review of Rickenbacker's (1974) *The Twelve-Year Sentence Radical Views on Compulsory Education*, Chamberlain (1974) described the emergency of compulsory education:

The State has not yet outlawed the high school or college teaching of such things as free enterprise economics or a biology that tells the truth about individual variations, but there is a subtle presumption in our school lounges and on our campuses that political solutions must be sought for all our complex problems. We are becoming a standardized people, ready to accept 'controls' without bleating. When the ultimate inflationary blow-off comes, we will be doormats for our first dictator. It will be done by way of 'Welfarism'; our Fuhrer, taking a tip from the late Huey Long, will do as Fascists do but will call it Progressivism.

When the Senator from Vermont proposed that the taxpayer should fund a higher proportion of human capital formation, Ebeling (2015) declared an emergency: 'When voices are raised today calling for socialism in America, including by those attempting to win a major party candidacy to run for the presidency of the United States, it is important—no, it is crucial—that the history and reality of socialism-in-practice in those parts of the world in which it was most thoroughly imposed and implemented be remembered and fully understood. If we do not, well, history has its own ways of repeating itself.'

Notes

1. https://www.nationalww2museum.org/students-teachers/student-resources/research-starters/research-starters-worldwide-deaths-world-war.
2. This was deleted from the Chilean version of their essay (2015b).
3. Friedrich Hayek, interviewed by Jack High date unspecified 1978 (Centre for Oral History Research, University of California, Los Angeles, http://oralhistory.library.ucla.edu/).
4. https://www.montpelerin.org/statement-of-aims/.
5. MPS Archives Box 43.5.
6. Hayek Archives Box 109.7,
7. Friedrich Hayek, interviewed by James Buchanan 28 October 1978 (Centre for Oral History Research, University of California, Los Angeles, http://oralhistory.library.ucla.edu/).
8. Friedrich Hayek, interviewed by Thomas Hazlett 12 November 1978 (Centre for Oral History Research, University of California, Los Angeles, http://oralhistory.library.ucla.edu/).
9. https://mises.org/library/middle-road-policy-leads-socialism.
10. Davenport Archives Box 40.15.

11. MPS Archives Box 41.
12. MPS Archives Box 41.6.
13. https://mises.org/profile/morgan-o-reynolds-0.
14. MPS Archives Box 4.4.
15. MPS Archives Box 46.1.
16. http://www.vanityfair.com/news/2017/07/donald-trump-law-enforcement-speech-long-island-ms-13.
17. https://www.forbes.com/sites/davidmarotta/#5e7d87eb4c79. Accessed 30 June 2017.
18. Crozier (1993, 118) dated the editorial to 15 April 1976—which was after Callaghan's subsequent run-off victory.
19. CLS Archives Box 2.4.
20. To David Boaz of the Council for a Competitive Economy. Hayek Archives Box 16.43.
21. Hayek Archives Box 25.22.
22. Hayek Archives Box 154. Handwritten note.
23. To William Ballou (7 October 1979). Hayek Archives Box 11.19. The context of these remarks is not entirely clear from the correspondence.
24. https://fee.org/articles/the-essence-of-the-road-to-serfdom-in-cartoons/.
25. Mises (1950) asserted that 'The few books which tried to explain adequately the working of the free market economy were hardly noticed by the public. Their authors remained obscure, while such authors as Veblen, Commons, John Dewey and Laski were exuberantly praised.'
26. Davenport Archives Box 30.7.
27. Cited by Claude Robinson (6 June 1945) to Hayek. Hayek Archives Box 46.28.

REFERENCES

Archival Insights into the Evolution of Economics (and Related Projects)

Lane, M. (2013). The Genesis and Reception of The Road to Serfdom. In R. Leeson (Ed.), *Hayek: A Collaborative Biography Part I Influences from Mises to Bartley*. Basingstoke, UK: Palgrave Macmillan.

Leeson, R. (1997a). The Political Economy of the Inflation Unemployment Trade-Off. *History of Political Economy, 29*(1), 117–156.

Leeson, R. (1997b). The Eclipse of the Goal of Zero Inflation. *History of Political Economy, 29*(3), 445–496.

Leeson, R. (1998). The Origins of the Keynesian Discomfiture. *Journal of Post Keynesian Economics, 20*(4), 597–619.

Leeson, R. (2018a). *Hayek: A Collaborative Biography Part VIII: The Constitution of Liberty: 'Shooting in Cold Blood' Hayek's Plan for the Future of Democracy*. Basingstoke, UK: Palgrave Macmillan.

Leeson, R. (2018b). *Hayek: A Collaborative Biography Part XI: Orwellian Rectifiers, Mises' 'Evil Seed' of Christianity and the 'Free' Market Welfare State*. Basingstoke, UK: Palgrave Macmillan.

Teacher, D. (2018a). 'Neutral Academic Data' and the International Right. In R. Leeson (Ed.), *Hayek: A Collaborative Biography Part XIII 'Fascism' and Liberalism in the (Austrian) Classical Tradition*. Basingstoke, UK: Palgrave Macmillan.

Teacher, D. (2018b). Private Club and Secret Service Armageddon. In R. Leeson (Ed.), *Hayek: A Collaborative Biography Part XIII 'Fascism' and Liberalism in the (Austrian) Classical Tradition*. Basingstoke, UK: Palgrave Macmillan.

Other References

Ayau, M. (1984, November). Give Freedom Its Turn in Latin America. *Imprimis, 13* (11).

Baudin, L. (1956). Soviet Expansion in the under-developed world. Mimeo.

Bernstein, R. (1989, May 16). Magazine Dispute Reflects Rift on U.S. Right. *New York Times*. http://www.nytimes.com/1989/05/16/us/magazine-dispute-reflects-rift-on-us-right.html.

Blundell, J. (2014). IHS and the Rebirth of Austrian Economics: Some Reflections on 1974–1976. *Quarterly Journal of Austrian Economics, 17*(1), 92–107. https://mises.org/library/ihs-and-rebirth-austrian-economics-some-reflections-1974%E2%80%931976.

Boettke, P. J. (2001). *Calculation and Coordination: Essays on Socialism and Transitional Political Economy*. London: Routledge.

Boettke, P. J. (2011). Teaching Austrian Economics to Graduate Students. *Journal of Economics and Finance Education, 10*(2), 19–30. http://www.economics-finance.org/jefe/econ/special-issue/Special%20Issue%20AE%20003%20Boettke-Abstract.pdf.

Boettke, P. J. (2012). *Interview with Peter Boettke*. Rationality Unlimited. https://rationalityunlimited.wordpress.com/2012/04/02/interview-with-peter-boettke/.

Boettke, P. J. (2015, January 25). The Transformative Rise of Austrian Economics. *The Daily Bell*. http://www.thedailybell.com/exclusive-interviews/anthony-wile-peter-boettke-the-transformative-rise-of-austrian-economics/.

Buchanan, J. (1986, October 26). Why Governments 'Got Out of Hand.' *The New York Times*.

Buckley, W. F., Jr. (1995, February 6). Murray Rothbard RIP. *National Review*. http://notableandquotable.blogspot.com.au/2008/04/william-f-buckleys-obituary-of-murray.html.

Caldwell, B. (1995). Editorial Notes. In B. Caldwell (Ed.), *Contra Keynes and Cambridge. The Collected Works of F.A. Hayek*. Chicago: University of Chicago Press.

Caldwell, B., & Montes, L. (2014a, August). *Friedrich Hayek and His Visits to Chile* (CHOPE Working Paper No. 2014-12).

Caldwell, B., & Montes, L. (2014b). Friedrich Hayek and His Visits to Chile. *Review of Austrian Economics* (First Online: 26 September 2014).

Caldwell, B., & Montes, L. (2015a, September). Friedrich Hayek and His Visits to Chile. *Review of Austrian Economics, 28*(3), 261–309.

Caldwell, B., & Montes, L. (2015b). Friedrich Hayek y Sus Dos Visitas a Chile. *Estudios Públicos, 137*(Verano), 87–132. https://www.cepchile.cl/cep/site/artic/20160304/asocfile/20160304101209/rev137_BCaldwell-LMontes.pdf.

Chafuen, A. (1986). *Christians for Freedom: Late Scholastic Economics*. New York: Ignatius Press.

Chafuen, A. (2010). How I Became a Liberal. In W. Block (Ed.), *I Chose Liberty: Autobiographies of Contemporary Libertarians*. Auburn, AL: Ludwig von Mises Institute.

Champion, R. (2015). Hayek in Australia. In R. Leeson (Ed.), *Hayek: A Collaborative Biography: Part V Hayek's Great Society of Free Men*. Basingstoke, England: Palgrave Macmillan.

Chamberlain, J. (1974, August). The 12-Year Sentence. *The Freeman*, 501–504. http://www.unz.org/Pub/Freeman-1974aug-00501?View=PDF.

Chamberlain, J. (1987, March). Reason Interview with John Chamberlain. *Reason*. http://reason.com/archives/1987/03/01/reason-interview-with-john-cha/2.

Chozick, A. (2016, September 10). Hillary Clinton Calls Many Trump Backers 'Deplorables,' and G.O.P. Pounces. *New York Times*. https://www.nytimes.com/2016/09/11/us/politics/hillary-clinton-basket-of-deplorables.html.

Churchill, W. (1935, November). Hitler: Monster or Hero? *Strand Magazine*.

Cockett, R. (1995). *Thinking the Unthinkable Think Tanks and the Economic Counter-Revolution, 1931–1983*. London: HarperCollins.

Cubitt, C. (2006). *A Life of Friedrich August von Hayek*. Bedford, UK: Authors Online.

Davenport, J. (1949, March). Socialism by Default. *Fortune, XXXIX*(3).

Davenport, J. (1958, Spring). Arms and the Welfare State. *The Yale Review* (Davenport Archives Box 18.17).

Davenport, J. (1965). *The US Economy*. Chicago: H. Regnery Company.

Davenport, J. (1976, Summer). Civilization at Risk. *Modern Age*.

Davis, F. (1974, November). Federal Control Hurts Young Doctors the Most. *Private Practice*, 4.
Deaton, A. (2017, July 13). Without Governments, Would Countries Have More Inequality, or Less? *Economist*. https://www.economist.com/news/world-if/21724910-angus-deaton-nobel-prize-winning-economist-explores-question-intrigued-him-without.
Demick, B., & Lee, K. (2017, July 28). Trump Orders Officers and Immigration Officials to be 'Rough' on 'Animals' Terrorizing U.S. Neighborhoods. *Los Angeles Times*. http://www.latimes.com/nation/la-na-pol-trump-ms13-story.html.
Ebeling, R. M. (2013, June 15). Richard Ebeling on Higher Interest Rates, Collectivism and the Coming Collapse. *Daily Bell*. http://www.thedailybell.com/gold-silver/anthony-wile-richard-ebeling-on-higher-interest-rates-collectivism-and-the-coming-collapse/.
Ebeling, R. M. (2015, September 9). The Human Cost of Socialism in Power. *Future of Freedom Foundation*. https://www.fff.org/explore-freedom/article/the-human-cost-of-socialism-in-power/.
Enbeling, R. M. (2016, December 19). The 25th Anniversary of the End of the Soviet Union. *Foundation for Economic Freedom*. https://fee.org/articles/the-25th-anniversary-of-the-end-of-the-soviet-union/.
Frum, D. (2003, March 25). Unpatriotic Conservatives. *National Review*. http://www.nationalreview.com/article/391772/unpatriotic-conservatives-david-frum.
Glassman, J. K. (2011). Market-Based Man. *Philanthropy Roundtable (Fall)*. http://www.philanthropyroundtable.org/topic/excellence_in_philanthropy/market_based_man.
Gregory, T. E., von Hayek, F. A., Plant, A., & Robbins, L. (1932, October 19). Spending and Saving Public Works from Rates. *The Times*, 11.
Hamilius, J.-P. (1976). The Grave-Diggers of Western Freedom. In *Le Libéralisme De Karl Marx à Milton Friedman*. Paris: Congrés de la Société du Mont Pélerin (MPS Archives Box 19.2).
Hamowy, R. (2003). Memories of Rothbard and Hayek. *LewRockwell.com* http://www.lewrockwell.com/2003/07/murray-n-rothbard/memories-of-rothbard-and-hayek/.
Hayek, F. A. (1944). *The Road to Serfdom*. London: Routledge.
Hayek, F. A. (1946, February). The London School of Economics 1895–1945. *Economica, XIII*, 1–31 (New Series).
Hayek, F. A. (1962). Preface. In H. Schoeck (Ed.), *Financing Medical Care: An Appraisal of Foreign Programs*. London: Caxton.
Hayek, F. A. (1975a). *A Discussion with Friedrich von Hayek*. Washington:American Enterprise Institute. https://www.aei.org/wp-content/uploads/2017/03/Discussion-with-Friedrich-von-Hayek-text.pdf .

Hayek, F. A. (1975b). *Face the Press.* https://mises.org/library/hayek-meetspress-1975

Hayek, F. A. (1976a). Socialism and Science. Economic Society of Australia and New Zealand, Canberra Branch.

Hayek, F. A. (1976b, October 13). *The Inseparability of Economic and Political Freedom.* Foundation for Economic Education (Australia). Hayek Archives Box 109.7.

Hayek, F. A. (1977, September). An Interview with Friedrich Hayek, by Richard Ebeling. *Libertarian Review,* 10–18 (Hayek Archives Box 109.14).

Hayek, F. A. (1978). *Oral History Interviews.* Centre for Oral History Research, University of California, Los Angeles. http://oralhistory.library.ucla.edu/.

Hayek, F. A. (1981, April 12). Extracts from an Interview Friedrich von Hayek. *El Mercurio.* http://www.economicthought.net/blog/wp-content/uploads/2011/12/LibertyCleanOfImpuritiesInterviewWithFVonHayekChile1981.pdf.

Hayek, F. A. (1994). *Hayek on Hayek an Autobiographical Dialogue.* Supplement to *The Collected Works of F.A. Hayek* (S. Kresge & L. Wenar, Eds.). Chicago: University of Chicago Press.

Hayek, F. A. (1995). *Contra Keynes and Cambridge. The Collected Works of F.A. Hayek* (B. Caldwell, Ed.). Chicago: University of Chicago Press.

Hayek, F. A. (2013). *Law, Legislation and Liberty.* London: Routledge.

Heiden, K. (1944). *Der Fuehrer* (R. Manheim, Trans.). Boston: Houghton Mifflin.

Hülsmann, J. G. (2007). *Mises: The Last Knight of Liberalism.* Auburn, AL: Ludwig von Mises Institute.

Hülsmann, J. G. (2008). *Ethics of Money Production.* Auburn, AL: Ludwig von Mises Institute.

Koch, C. (1978, August). The Business Community: Resisting Regulation. *Libertarian Review,* 7(7), 30–34. https://www.libertarianism.org/lr/LR788.pdf.

Liggio, L. (2010). A Classical Liberal Life. In W. Block (Ed.), *I Chose Liberty: Autobiographies of Contemporary Libertarians.* Auburn, AL: Ludwig von Mises Institute.

Maier, K. F. (1949). *The Demand for Social Security.* New York: Mimeo.

Mises, L. (1950, May 4). Middle-of-the-Road Policy Leads to Socialism. *Commercial and Financial Chronicle.* https://mises.org/library/middle-road-policy-leads-socialism.

Mises, L. (1951 [1932]). *Socialism: An Economic and Sociological Analysis* (J. Kahane, Trans.). New Haven: Yale University Press.

Mises, L. (1961a, April). Liberty and its Antithesis. Review of Hayek's The Constitution of Liberty. *Christian Century.*

Mises, L. (1961b, August 1). Liberty and its Antithesis. Review of Hayek's The Constitution of Liberty. *Christian Economics*, 1, 3 (Hayek Archives Box 167).
Mises, L. (1963). *Human Action: A Treatise on Economics* (2nd ed.). New Haven: Yale University Press.
Mises, L. (1966). *Human Action : A Treatise on Economics* (3rd ed.). Chicago: Henry Regnery.
Mises, L. (1985 [1927]). *Liberalism in the Classical Tradition* (R. Raico, Trans.). Auburn, AL: Mises Institute.
Moss, R. (1973). *Chile's Marxist Experiment*. New York: Wiley.
North, G. K. (2002, January 21). *Mises on Money*. Lewrockwell.com. https://archive.lewrockwell.com/north/north83.html.
Paul, R. (2008). *Mises and Austrian Economics a Personal View*. Auburn, AL: Ludwig von Mises Institute.
Perkins, H. (1989). *The Rise of Professional Society: England Since 1880*. London: Routledge.
Peterson, W. H. (1996, July 1). A History of the Mont Pelerin Society. *The Freeman*. https://fee.org/articles/a-history-of-the-mont-pelerin-society/.
Polanyi, M. (1947). *The Present Political Crisis*. New York: Mimeo.
Phillips-Fine, K. (2009). Business Conservatives and the Mont Pèlerin Society. In P. Mirowski & D. Plehwe (Eds.), *The Road from Mont Pèlerin The Making of the Neoliberal Thought Collective*. Cambridge, MA: Harvard University Press.
Raico, R. (2013, February 20). *An Interview with Ralph Raico*. Mises Institute. https://mises.org/library/interview-ralph-raico-0.
Raico, R. (2014, October 16). *Leonard Liggio*. RIP lewrockwell.com. https://www.lewrockwell.com/lrc-blog/515224/.
Reid, T. R. (2017a). *A Fine Mess: A Global Quest for a Simpler, Fairer, and More Efficient Tax System*. New York: Penguin.
Reid, T. R. (2017b, April 13). Interview. PBS Newshour. http://www.pbs.org/newshour/bb/dreading-taxes-countries-show-us-theres-another-way/.
Reisman, G. (2001). Mises as Mentor an Interview with George Reisman. *Austrian Economics Newsletter*, 21(3). https://mises.org/system/tdf/aen21_3_1_0.pdf?file=1&type=document.
Reisman, G. (2005 [1990], October 3). The Toxicity of Environmentalism. *Mises Daily*. https://mises.org/library/toxicity-environmentalism.
Reisman, G. (2006, December 16). General Augusto Pinochet Is Dead. *Mises Wire*. https://mises.org/blog/general-augusto-pinochet-dead.
Reynolds, M. (2003). Labor and the Austrian School. *Austrian Economic Newsletter , (Summer)*. https://mises.org/library/labor-and-austrian-school.
Rickenbacker, W. F. (Ed.). (1974). *The Twelve-Year Sentence Radical Views on Compulsory Education*. LaSalle, IL: Open Court.

Robbins, J. (2010). The *Sine Qua Non* of Enduring Freedom. *The Trinity Review*, 295. http://www.trinityfoundation.org/PDF/The%20Trinity%20Review%2000295%20SineQuaNonEnduringFreedom.pdf.
Rockwell, L. H., Jr. (1974, November 21). Government Subsidy Means Government Control. *Private Practice*.
Rockwell, L. H., Jr. (1991, March 10). COLUMN RIGHT: It's Safe Streets Versus Urban Terror: In the '50s, Rampant Crime Didn't Exist Because Offenders Feared What the Police Would Do. *Los Angeles Times*.
Rockwell, L. H., Jr. (2010). Libertarianism and the Old Right. In W. Block (Ed.), *I Chose Liberty: Autobiographies of Contemporary Libertarians*. Auburn, AL: Ludwig von Mises Institute.
Röpke, W. (1949). *The Proletarianized Society*. New York: Mimeo.
Ross, J. (2015, December 21). Obama Revives His 'Cling to Guns or Religion' Analysis—For Donald Trump Supporters. *Washington Post*.
Rothbard, M. N. (1973, October 20). Ludwig von Mises 1881–1973. *Human Events*, 7.
Rothbard, M. N. (1992a, March). A Strategy for the Right. *Rothbard-Rockwell Report*, 3(3). https://mises.org/library/strategy-right.
Rothbard, M. N. (1992b, January). Right-Wing Populism: A Strategy for the Paleo Movement. *Rothbard Rockwell Report*, 5–14. http://rothbard.altervista.org/articles/right-wing-populism.pdf.
Rothbard, M. N. (1994a, July). Revolution in Italy! *Rothbard-Rockwell Report*, 5(7), 1–10. http://www.unz.org/Pub/RothbardRockwellReport-1994jul-00001.
Rothbard, M. N. (1994b, October). A New Strategy for Liberty. *Rothbard Rockwell Report*, 5(10). http://www.unz.org/Pub/RothbardRockwellReport-1994oct-00001.
Rothbard, M. N. (1994c, September). Invade the World. *Rothbard Rockwell Report*, 5(9). http://www.unz.org/Pub/RothbardRockwellReport-1994sep-00001.
Rothbard, M. N. (2007). *Betrayal of the American Right*. Auburn, AL: Ludwig von Mises Institute.
Rothbard, M. N. (2016). *The Rothbard Reader*. Auburn, AL: Ludwig von Mises Institute. https://mises.org/library/rothbard-reader/html/c/414.
Shearmur, J. (2006). Hayek, The Road to Serfdom, and the British Conservatives. *Journal of the History of Economic Thought*, 28, 309–314.
Shenfield, A. (1980, September). Hayek's Completed Trilogy. *The Freeman*, 30(9), 558–571. https://isistatic.org/journal-archive/ma/24_02/shenfield.pdf?width=640&height=700&iframe=true.
Shenoy, S. (2003, Winter). An Interview with Sudha Shenoy. *Austrian Economics Newsletter*, 1–8. http://mises.org/journals/aen/aen23_4_1.pdf.
Skousen, M. (2000, December). Dr. Jekyll and Mr. Robhard. *Inside Liberty*, 14(12), 52–53. http://mises.org/journals/liberty/Liberty_Magazine_December_2000.pdf.

Snaverly, B. (2014, December 30). Final Tally: Taxpayers Auto Bailout Loss $9.3B. *USA Today.* https://www.usatoday.com/story/money/cars/2014/12/30/auto-bailout-tarp-gm-chrysler/21061251/.

Steinacher, G. (2011). *Nazis on the Run: How Hitler's Henchmen Fled Justice.* Oxford: Oxford University Press.

Williams, R. (1995, July 7). 'Sunday Times' Pays Foot Damages over KGB Claim. *Independent.* http://www.independent.co.uk/news/sunday-times-pays-foot-damages-over-kgb-claim-1590325.html.

Wollstein, J. (1992a, October 1). Why We Spend Too Much on Health Care and Twenty Myths About National Health Insurance. *The Freeman.* https://fee.org/articles/why-we-spend-too-much-on-health-care-and-twenty-myths-about-national-health-insurance/.

Wollstein, J. (1992b, October 2). National Health Insurance: A Medical Disaster. *The Freeman.* https://fee.org/articles/national-health-insurance-a-medical-disaster/.

CHAPTER 7

'[Italian] Fascism'

SUMMARY

'Free' market economists embrace the form or pose of scholarship, while also promoting crude caricatures and outright fraud: National Public Radio is run by 'Nazis,' and externalities were invented by an underground Communist. Some of this 'knowledge' appears to have been inspired by the satirical BBC television series Monty Python's Flying Circus, and some has been derived from official government white supremacist propaganda (Rhodesia and Apartheid South Africa). 'Free' market funding is provided by the Gaddafi family, the Liechtenstein tax haven, the tobacco industry and the carbon lobby. And the best defence of 'economic liberalism' is, they believe, provided by political 'Fascists' and tax-evading billionaire populists. Mises' promotion of the Warfare State has been rectified by deletion; and his promotion of all 'Fascists,' 'German and Italian,' including 'Ludendorff and Hitler,' has been rectified by insertion: '[Italian].' This chapter examines these 'free' market rectifications.

Hitler's strategy was:

> a 'policy of catastrophe,' that is so to muddle things up that of chaos National Socialism would reap the advantage (Clark 1964 [1935], 323); the Nazi's behaviour was not dissimilar to that of the apocryphal (and not always so apocryphal) fireraiser who, as a member of the local volunteer fire brigade, fights the very fires he has started (Fischer 2002, 92); That is Hitler. The house must burn for the sake of this flame. (Heiden 1944, 419)

© The Author(s) 2018
R. Leeson, *Hayek: A Collaborative Biography*,
Archival Insights into the Evolution of Economics,
https://doi.org/10.1007/978-3-319-74509-1_7

Hayek and Mises promoted the deflation that facilitated Hitler's rise to power; and Hitler embraced Austrian business cycle theory to assist the burning (Leeson 2018). After being sworn-in as Chancellor, President Paul Hindenburg agreed to Hitler's request to dissolve the Reichstag, and new elections were scheduled for 5 March 1933. In his diary, Josef Goebbels (31 January 1933) described the interwar 'strategy of tension': 'In a conference with the Leader we establish the directives for the struggle against the red Terror. For the present we shall dispense with direct counter-measures. The Bolshevik attempt at revolution must first flare up. At the proper moment we shall then strike' (cited by Heiden 1944, 544). On 27 February 1933, Marinus van der Lubbe, a disturbed Dutch pyromaniac, was found in the smoking ruins of the Reichstag. *Cui bono?* No consensus has yet emerged about responsibility for the fire—but there is no doubt about the beneficiary. Shortly afterwards, von Hindenburg signed the Reichstag Fire Decree into law: civil liberties were suspended, and the Nazi dictatorship began.

For *The Collected Works of F. A. Hayek*, Caldwell chose a hagiographer, Hamowy, to edit *The Definitive Edition* of *The Constitution of Liberty*— in which one of Hayek's motives for writing the book (to market to dictators such as Salazar and later Pinochet) was rectified through deletion. And to edit *Hayek and the Austrian Economists: Correspondence and Related Documents*, Caldwell chose Ebeling. *Cui bono?*

MPS President James Buchanan (14 April 1986) blackballed Ebeling from receiving an Earhart Fellowship because he was a 'total fool.'[1] In 'Evaluating Information: The Cornerstone of Civic Online Reasoning,' the Stanford University History Study Group (2016) reported a 'stunning and dismaying consistency. Overall, young people's ability to reason about the information on the Internet can be summed up in one word: *bleak* [emphasis in original].' The 'fake news' that entraps them is fuelled by outrage; as is 'free' market 'scholarship.'

According to Rothbard (1994c), Hilary Clinton is the 'evil witch in the White House.' And according to the front page of the *Rothbard-Rockwell Report*, a 'female Secret Service agent is in big trouble: by mistake, she walked in on a scene of lesbian debauchery at the White House, and Hillary was one of the debauchees' (Barton 1994).[2] During the 2016 Presidential election, stories about Hillary Clinton and a paedophile ring attached to a Washington DC pizza restaurant circulated widely—Trump's National Security Adviser, Lt. Gen. Michael Flynn, was a prominent circulator of such 'knowledge' (Bender and Hanna 2016).

Too Good to Be True: The Colossal Book of Urban Legends and *The Truth Never Stands in the Way of a Good Story* recognises as a classic example the lipstick-messaging 'AIDS Mary' (Brunvand 1999, 2000). In 'The Plague Has Come At Last,' the Mises Institute Rothbard Medal of Freedom holder revealed one of his sources of his 'knowledge':

> It's a true story. It was reported a few weeks ago in Ft. Worth, Texas. A young married man was propositioned by a good looking woman. He hadn't been a swinger, but he decided to take advantage of a special situation. When he awoke the next morning, the girl was gone. On the mirror, she had written a message in lipstick: 'Welcome to the world of AIDS.' (North 1987)

Austrian 'knowledge' is a species of apodictic faith: 'It cannot be denied' (Mises 1985 [1927], 49, 51); 'If we take as premises some undisputed facts, which everybody accepts as facts of daily observation, we can logically deduce from them certain consequences, which permit only one answer to the problem. In other words, if we deduce certain consequences from admitted facts, by logically correct argument, the truth of our deductions has to be accepted' (Hayek 1975, 14).

According to the sixteen- or seventeen-year-old Tyler Cowen (1979, 3), at the 1979 Rutgers 'Conference on Inflation,' Axel Leijonhufvud criticised Gerald O'Driscoll's paper and made a 'sharp attack on the Mises-Hayek theory of the business cycle. Although the theory is analytically coherent, he argued that it is not relevant to recent, if any, actual experience, claiming that we have not seen any general pattern of excessive roundaboutness, an essential characteristic of Hayek's *Prices and Production* scenario.' Many of the Austrians attending the session were 'disappointed that O'Driscoll declined to respond in detail to Leijonhufvud's spirited challenge to the Mises-Hayek theory.'

Leland Yeager (1991) declared himself to be 'not a card-carrying Austrian. I don't like the way the business cycle theory gets repeated without any new evidence or logic … Divine inspiration is not as good as looking at the facts.' At the 'Rutgers Conference on Inflation,' Ebeling and Block provided a defence of their apodictic faith by speaking 'up in defense of Hayek. Block argued that the fact that we don't see over-investment in the capital goods industry doesn't mean it isn't there because we do not know what these industries would look like in the absence of inflation' (Cowen 1979, 3).

Austrians embrace the *form* or the pose of disinterested scholarship. For example,

> Calm analysis and willingness to admit that truth may occasionally reside in the other fellow's point of view is more likely to open discussion and gain a fair hearing than terse insistence upon 'revelation' and apodictic faith. (Ebeling 1978, 9)

Thirty-six years later, Ebeling (2014b) described the Austrian objective: 'It would be a world of sovereign individuals who respect each other, who treat each other with dignity and who view each other as an end in himself, rather than one of those pawns to be moved and sacrificed on that chessboard of society to serve the ends of another who presumes to impose coercive control over his fellow human beings. If we can do this, the collectivist counter-revolution can be defeated and the Classical Liberal revolutionary ideal of free men who form a great and good society through their associations on the basis of trade rather than tyranny can bring us liberty, peace and prosperity before the end of this new century.'

But with respect to the *substance* of scholarship: on the tax-exempt Heartland Institution website, Ebeling (2017)—who has named successive dogs after a card-carrying 'Fascist' ('Ludwig von Mises IV,' etc.)—describes National Public Radio journalists as Nazis: 'National Socialist Radio.'[3]

Hayek's (1994, 136–137) 'revelations' about Pigou were published in *The Collected Works of F.A. Hayek*. Immediately, Ebeling (1994) uncritically repeated Hayek's outrage: Pigou was both 'the father of modern welfare economics' and part of the:

> web of subversion ... an important and respected voice of academic reason and reflection calling for deliberate redistribution of wealth and a gradual transformation of the market economy into a socialist planned society ... a world-renowned scholar holding up the Soviet Union as a model of a good, caring society (at the very moment that Stalin's Great Purges were sending millions to their execution or to the slave-labor camps of the Gulag). What more legitimate advocate of socialism and the Soviet Union could be imagined? There was one major problem with Pigou's supposedly

disinterested analysis and policy prescriptions: he was a Soviet secret agent. In the interwar years, he served as a recruiter for the Soviet secret police; he would find potential candidates among the young men at Cambridge and bring them into contact with Soviet handlers, if they were found to be the right types.

According to Ebeling (1994), two 'Historians'—'Deacon' McCormick, the author of *The British Connection Russia's Manipulation of British Individuals and Institutions* (1979), and John Costello (1988), the author of *The Mask of Treachery: Spies, Lies, Buggery and Betrayal: The First Documented Dossier on Anthony Blunt's Cambridge Spy Ring*— 'present *the evidence* [emphasis added] for this, and one of the sources for their revelation about Pigou's Soviet activities is none other than Friedrich von Hayek.'

Like Ebeling, Costello (1988, 149, 176, 646–647, n. 13) uncritically repeated 'Deacon' McCormick's fraud:

> Although 'Roger' is now dead, Deacon considers that it would be inadvisable to reveal his identity.

'Roger'—who according to 'Deacon' McCormick's research assistant was an imaginary informant (West 2015)—was still alive in *The Greatest Treason* ('Deacon' McCormick 1990, 73): 'he is now very old indeed, but for his own safety his identity needs to be kept a secret.' In 'Boys of Rough Trade and Laddies of Leisure,' Costello stated that the 'left wing' Pigou 'enjoyed taking handsome undergraduates mountaineering' and had 'back channel dealings with Moscow.' Hayek was one of Costello's sources: 'Deacon also told me that corroboration for his contention that Pigou – who sponsored Keynes at the beginning of his career – was a longtime secret supporter of the Soviet Union came from the noted economist Professor F. A. von Hayek.' According to Ebeling (2014a): 'There can be little doubt that Friedrich A. Hayek was one of the most profound and important economists of the 20th century. In my humble opinion, I consider Mises and Hayek to be the two greatest economists of our time.'

Ebeling's fellow FEE President, Skousen, offers to:

> put you on the bullet train to financial freedom … **starting with how you can add an average of $8,774 in monthly income to your portfolio… That's more than $315,000 in just three years** (bold in original).[4]

In *Economics on Trial: Lies, Myths and Realities*, Skousen (1991, 12, 276, 287) declared: the 'teaching of economic science needs radical surgery ... This book is an all-out attack on bad economics.' And in *The Making of Modern Economics*, Skousen (2009, 338–339), a CIA 'intelligence' officer, uncritically repeats 'Deacon' McCormick's fraud:

> It's difficult to say at what point Pigou shifted views and became an underground supporter of revolutionary causes ... there is considerable evidence that he had been an underground agent for revolutionary causes much earlier in his career. According to British agent Richard Deacon (a pseudonym), in 1905 Pigou attended a clandestine meeting of the Russian Social Democrats in London and decided to become a secret agent, committed to developing a British spy network and arranging payments for arms shipments to Russia. He even kept a diary that year written entirely in code. (Deacon 1989, 44–45)

Buckley arranged for Skousen (2008) to become a Columbia University Professor; and:

> Dr. Richard M. Ebeling is the BB&T Distinguished Professor of Ethics and Free Enterprise Leadership at The Citadel. He conducts courses such as 'Leadership, Entrepreneurship, and Capitalist Ethics' as well as 'The Morality and Economics of Capitalist Society.'[5]

What sort of 'knowledge' is taught in what Skousen calls 'The Expanding Austrian Universe' where Austrians had 'taken hold': George Mason University, New York University, Auburn University, the University of Nevada at Las Vegas, Grove City College, the State University of California, Hayward/East Bay and the Citadel Military College? A 2006 'article' on the 'Murder of John Costello' reported that 'Costello died after complaining of stomach pain after eating shellfish at a Spanish restaurant. 36 hours later while aboard a British Airways flight to Miami, he was found slumped in his seat, and immediately certified as dead.' According to the author of this 'article,' the murderers could have been the British, the Americans, the Soviets or 'The Jews, to protect the real causes for the war.' The article appeared in the *Illuminati News* and was written by 'T. Stokes, Lecturer in Paranormal Studies.' His 'information' had been 'Collected from many sources over 40 years.'[6]

Ebeling (2014a) was outraged: 'It is not surprising that the advocates of government intervention and income redistribution focus their intellectual guns on the Austrians, since they offer many of the most insightful and powerful arguments on the workings of a competitive free market, and the inconsistencies, contradictions and negative consequences to be found in the more interventionist and redistributive approaches to economic policy. I often find that many of those who criticize the Austrian approach do so through the tactics of distortion, misrepresentation, or exaggeration, most especially in the popular press.'

Hayek—the University of Chicago's Professor of Social and Moral Sciences—promoted Pinochet's dictatorship. But according to Ebeling (2015), 'morality plays no role for dictators.' He was citing Dmitri Volkogonov (1991) who reflected: 'That's when I understood why my father was shot, why my mother died in exile, why millions of people died.'

According to Mises (1990 [1949/1950], 301–302): 'Between the philosophers and scholars who contrive new ideas and build up elaborate systems of thought and the narrow-minded dullards whose poor intellect cannot grasp but the simplest things there are many gradual transitions … Only a small elite has the ability to absorb more refined chains of thought. Most people are simply helpless when faced with the more subtle problems of implication or valid inference. … They cannot grasp but the primary propositions of reckoning; the avenue to mathematics is blocked to them. It is useless to try to make them familiar with thorny problems and with the theories thought out for their solution. They simplify and mend in a clumsy way what they hear or read. They garble and misrepresent propositions and conclusions. They transform every theory and doctrine in order to adapt it to their level of intelligence.' Ebeling's Austrian 'logic' is that:

- Volkogonov's 'knowledge' is axiomatically unimpeachable (presumably, because it fuels his outrage)
- 'Deacon' McCormick's 'knowledge' is axiomatically unimpeachable (also, presumably, because it fuels his outrage)

But two quantities of 'knowledge' that contradict each other cannot both be unimpeachable—quality must be examined: why are 'Deacon' McCormick's assertions about Pigou and Stalin not reproduced in Volkogonov's (1991) biography of Stalin?

According to 'James Burley, of Woodhouse near Sheffield,' in 1910, 'Josef Stalin used the Continental Café a lot. Josef Georgi, he called himself. He was a bombastic little man, not very big. But there was always an air of mystery about him ... The cafe was popular because it was only a short walk from the Communist Club in Charlotte Street.' A coded 16-item entry on 25 April 1905 in Pigou's diary was interpreted as 'Josef Georgi – Berne' which was 'certainly the name by which Stalin was known to the Bolsheviks in London.' Moreover,

> British police records show that the man known as 'Josef Georgi' was regarded as an agent of the Russian secret police at the time of the Sidney Street affair which seems fairly conclusive. ('Deacon' McCormick 1972, 162–163, 166; 1979, 6–7, 11, 263, n. 11; 1987, 106)[7]

This fiction was repeated in *The Presence of Evil* by Ian Moffitt (1983, 209), a former Murdoch employee.[8]

By his own account, Leube accompanied Hayek to his 1984 Reform Club lunch with 'Deacon' McCormick. 'Dr. Kurt Leube' (1984) is the author of the one-page 'Essay: Hayek, Orwell, and The Road to Serfdom' in:

> *Prometheus*, the Journal of the Libertarian Futurist Society ... founded in 1982 to recognize and promote libertarian science fiction. The LFS is a tax-exempt nonprofit group with an international membership of libertarians and freedom-loving science fiction fans who believe cultural change is as vital as political change in achieving freedom. After all, imagination is the first step in envisioning a free future – and the peace, prosperity and progress that can take humankind to the stars ... People come to libertarianism through fiction.[9]

In 'How I Became a Libertarian and an Austrian Economist,' Ebeling (2016) described his first encounter with 'liberty':

> When I was about seventeen, and living in Hollywood, I met two men who introduced me to the works of Ayn Rand. I ran into them at a restaurant called 'Hody's' that was at the corner of Hollywood and Vine. Drawing me into a conversation, they asked if I had ever heard of Ayn Rand. I replied that I had heard of the Rand Corporation, but was an 'Ayn'? They handed me a copy of Ayn Rand's Capitalism: the Unknown Ideal, and told me to read it and come back in three days. I did, and we met.

In 1968, Ebeling visited the *Goddess of the Market*: 'Ayn Rand was dressed in a red denim railway man's-like outfit with a train conductor's cap, and her husband, Frank O'Conner [sic], was in a Nehru suit with beads. I have no idea of the meaning or reason for either one.'

In December 1969, as 'Deacon' McCormick was seeking to spice-up his *History of the Russian Secret Service* (1972), the satirical BBC television series, Monty Python's Flying Circus, had included a sketch about Hitler living in England under the name 'Mr. Hilter' and conspiring in the 'Axis Café in Rosedale Road' (Chapman and Monty Python 1989 [1969], Episode 12). Before the Monty Python sketch, 'Deacon' McCormick's (1969, 129–131) *History of the British Secret Service* recycled verbatim London-based material about Jack the Ripper, Peter the Painter and the Siege of Sidney Street without the assertion that in 1910, Stalin frequented London cafes calling himself 'Josef Georgi.' 'Josef Georgi' was added to the London stories in 1972; Pigou was added to the Cambridge stories in 1979.

Boettke (2014), the President of Hayek's MPS, regards historians of economics as 'gullible'—they play 'ideological checkers' while he plays 'scholarly chess.' Ebeling (SHOE 22 May 2014) informed historians of thought that 'anyone familiar with Mises' writings knows that he opposed war.' After this was exposed as nonsense (SHOE 29 May 2014), Boettke (2016a) doubled down: 'Mises was a cosmopolitan liberal who argued forcefully against colonialism, protectionism, populism, migration restrictions, and totalitarianism left, right and center.' But the evidence contained in an Ebeling-edited volume reveals that Mises—like Hitler—promoted *Lebensraum* (Leeson 2018, Chapter 7).

Four years after the demise of the Habsburg Empire, Mises (1951 [1922], 234–235) found a replacement:

> The wars waged by England during the era of Liberalism to extend her colonial empire and to open up territories which refused to admit foreign trade, laid the foundations of the modern economy … In judging the English policy for opening up China, people constantly put in the foreground the fact that it was the opium trade which gave the direct, immediate occasion for the outbreak of war complications. But in the wars which the English and French waged against China between 1839 and 1860 the stake was the general freedom of trade and not only the freedom of the opium trade … It was not cant for English free traders to speak of England's vocation to elevate backward people to a state of civilisation.

England has shown by acts that she has regarded her possessions in India, in the Crown colonies, and in the Protectorates as a general mandatory of European civilisation.

According to Boettke (2016a), Mises:

> argued throughout his long career for the free flow of capital and labor internationally, and for peacefully social cooperation grounded in the Kantian aspirations that global citizens be 'Strangers Nowhere in this World.'

And according to Ebeling (SHOE 20 December 2015), Mises criticised 'countries like Australia that limited non-whites from migrating and settling there' and was a:

> strong proponent of free movement of people – that is, 'open immigration.'

According to Boettke (2016b), Ebeling is one of the 'most articulate spokesman for the Austrian school of economics – its history and its teachings.' Ebeling and Block (2000, 55) attended a '*Human Action* seminar, where we read and discussed this book chapter by chapter.' In *Human Action*, Mises (1998 [1949], 820–821) stated that there could be no 'question of appeasing the aggressors by removing migration barriers. As conditions are today, the Americas and Australia in admitting Germans, Italians, and Japanese immigrants would merely open their doors to vanguards of hostile armies.' According to Mises (in a volume edited by Ebeling), '*Combating Emigration*' was required to bolster the Austro-German Second Reich (Leeson 2018, Chapter 6).

Ebeling (1990, xxv–xxvi) reveals his attachment to disinterested scholarship:

> With the collapse of Keynesian supremacy and the initiation of a new battle of ideas among economists and policy-makers, the writings of Ludwig von Mises might once again be of assistance to the new generation of combatants who will be manning the intellectual trenches. It is with this idea in mind that this volume of essays on *Money, Method, and the Market Process* is offered to the public.

According to Hoppe (1992), Ebeling's *Money, Method, and the Market Process* would help Mises and his work 'receive their proper recognition in the academy as one of the great intellectual heroes of our time and the paradigm of a new age defined by a renaissance of economic reason.'

Hayek (1978a) described the origins of the threat to the spontaneous order: 'The beginning of it was 150 years ago. Before that, there was never any serious revolt against the market society, because every farmer knew he had to sell his grain.'[10] The year before his family's ennoblement, the Merchants' Petition to the House of Commons (14 February 1788) sought to protect the 'free' market in slaves: the 'enterprising spirit of the people' had 'enabled them to carry on the African Slave Trade with vigour.' The African Slave Trade has 'hitherto received the sanction of Parliament, and for a long series of years has constituted and still continues to form a very extensive branch of the commerce of Liverpool.' Its abolition 'must ruin the property of the English merchants in the West Indies, diminish the public revenue and impair the maritime strength of Great Britain.'[11]

Hayek (1997 [1949], 224) described the definitive qualification of a genuine scholar: 'experience of the working of the economic system which the administration of property gives.' Mises (1985 [1927], 19, 51) insisted that 'The victory of Fascism in a number of countries is only an episode in the long series of struggles over the problem of property.' For private consumption, Mises (2007 [1958]) also wrote to Rand from his rent-controlled three-bedroom New York apartment: 'You have the courage to tell the masses what no politician told them: you are inferior and all the improvements in your conditions which you simply take for granted you owe to the effort of men who are better than you. If this be arrogance, as some of your critics observed, it still is the truth that had to be said in this age of the Welfare State.'

According to Ebeling (1990, xxv), Mises' 'The Role of Doctrines in Human History' emphasises 'that the ultimate contest in politics and economics is not between nations and armies, but between the ideas that rule the actions of men.' In 'The Role of Doctrines in Human History,' Mises (1990 [1949/1950], 290, 291, 301) again expressed his 'thoroughly Hitlerian contempt for the democratic man': 'Why did not the Negroes of Africa discover means to fight the germs which menace their lives and health and why did European scholars discover efficient methods to fight these diseases?' Mises answered: 'Any attempt to study human conduct and historical changes has to make ample allowance for the fact of intellectual inequality of men ... As an animal, man has to adjust himself to the natural conditions of the earth or the part of the earth where he lives. But this adjustment is a work of the brain. The geographical interpretation of history failed to recognize this deciding point. The environment works only through the medium of human mind. On the same soil where the white settlers have developed modern American civilization the Indian aborigines did not succeed even in inventing wheels and carriages.'

According to Ebeling (1990, 289), the 'previously unpublished' 'Role of Doctrines in Human History' was 'probably written in either 1949 or 1950'—when America consisted of forty-eight states. Mises (1990 [1950 /1949], 299–300) must have been rectified: 'The people of the fifty American states live peacefully together because their doctrine teaches them that a peaceful cooperation suits better their objectives than warring does.'

When Hayek was asked what his:

> attitude to black people was ... he said that he did not like 'dancing Negroes.' He had watched a Nobel laureate doing so which had made him see the 'the animal beneath the facade of apparent civilisation.' (Cubitt 2006, 23)

In 1992, 'Ron Paul' stated in his fund-raising *Ron Paul Newsletters*: 'even in my little town of Lake Jackson, Texas, I've urged everyone in my family to know how to use a gun in self defense ... for the animals are coming.' It is widely suspected that in addition to Rothbard, two consummate Washington insiders, Rockwell (Paul's Chief-of-Staff) and North (one of Paul's staffers), co-authored the *Newsletters* (Leeson 2017). According to Julian Sanchez and David Weigel (2008), Rockwell was publicly named as Paul's ghostwriter as far back as a 1988 issue of the now-defunct movement monthly *American Libertarian*.

> 'This was based on my understanding at the time that Lew would write things that appeared in Ron's various newsletters,' former *AL* editor Mike Holmes told *reason*. 'Neither Ron nor Lew ever told me that, but other people close to them such as Murray Rothbard suggested that Lew was involved, and it was a common belief in libertarian circles.'

One recipient of the 1974 Nobel Prize for Economic Sciences wrote *An American Dilemma: The Negro Problem and Modern Democracy* (Myrdal 1944); the other, when confronted with the prospect of having to deal with African-Americans, informed Neil McLeod at the Liberty Fund that he wished to find an alternative to his 'gone negro' Chicago bank (Hayek 5 March 1975).[12] Hayek (1978a) defended the 'civilization' of Apartheid' from the American 'fashion' of 'human rights' (Chapter 1); and in *Assault on Private Enterprise: The Freeway to Communism*, the Hayek-nominated MPS member, Andreas Wassenaar (1977), described the Misean alternative to the Communist forces that were undermining South Africa.[13]

In addition to the tobacco industry and the carbon lobby, the 'free' market is funded by the Gaddafi family, the Liechtenstein tax haven and white supremacist regimes. 'Count' Max Thurn (30 April 1981) told MPS Treasurer, Ed Feulner, that in South Africa (from where he had just returned), *anyone* who is prepared to say 'something nice [Thurn's emphasis]' was welcome, particularly if 'he' is 'black and Libertarian or Conservative.' GMU's Walter Williams had been 'put' on a lecture tour and Thomas Sowell had also been invited.[14]

In *Up from the Projects*, Williams (2010, 43–44, 122, 125) described being a victim of American police brutality in his journey through the 'free' market to another form of neo-feudalism—Apartheid:

> our hosts treated us royally. We had no problem with apartheid because, as Leon Louw put it, the necessary paperwork was done to make us 'honorary white people.' That meant we stayed at such stately hotels as the Sunnyside Park and Carleton during shorter stays and enjoyed a lovely apartment in Johannesburg high-rise and a Mercedes-Benz during our 1980 three month stay. Just about every day we were wined, dined and entertained.

While serving in the US military in Fort Stewart, Georgia, Williams persuaded eight of his fellow non-whites to gatecrash a white's only dance:

> After one black soldier asked a white girl to dance, the event was cancelled ... The hostess called the MPs [Military Police] and they made an 'incident report.'

Williams was threatened with 'charges of inciting to riot' and told: 'You know how it is down here.'

What surprised Williams 'most was the friendliness of South Africans' who told him that:

> 'we seek to separate instead of exterminate.' In other words, they argued that Americans killed off much of their potential problems while South African whites tried to set up 'homelands' – separate living areas for their native population.

South African whites told Williams that Apartheid was light-touch regulation: 'They pointed to overt American racialism, brutality and lynching that was never a significant factor in South Africa. Afrikaners also cited what they saw as their general humaneness towards their native peoples, again as compared to the comparable Americans' situation.'

Rothbard was the first person ralph Raico (2013) had met who defended 'a fully voluntary society—nudge, nudge.' Like Emma Lazarus (1849–1887), Rothbard (1926–1995) and Raico (1936–2016) were New York Jews. Lazarus—who sought be assist Jews fleeing the Russian pogroms that followed the 1881 assassination of Tsar Alexander II—composed the poem that is engraved on the Statue of Liberty in New York harbour.

> 'Keep, ancient lands, your storied pomp!' cries she
> With silent lips. 'Give me your tired, your poor,
> Your huddled masses yearning to breathe free,
> The wretched refuse of your teeming shore.
> Send these, the homeless, tempest-tost to me,
> I lift my lamp beside the golden door!'

New York was a melting pot—and Harlem was the recipient of part of the 'Great Migration'—the 1916–1970 movement of 6 million African Americans out of the rural South to the urban Northeast, Midwest and West. During Rothbard's childhood, there was a cultural, social and artistic explosion in the 'underclass'—the Harlem Renaissance or 'New Negro Movement.'

In *Mein Kampf*, Hitler (1939 [1925], 334) complained that the press often reported that 'for the first time in that locality, a Negro had become a lawyer, a teacher, a pastor, even a grand opera tenor or something else of that kind ... the more cunning Jew sees in this fact a new proof to be utilized for the theory with which he wants to infect the public, namely that all men are equal ... it is an act of criminal insanity to train a being who is only an anthropoid [the pretense of a human] by birth until the pretense can be made that he has been turned into a lawyer.' Had Hayek's cousin and second wife been non-white, they would have been committing a crime in many parts of the USA. Miscegenation laws (which remained in force until 1967) required operational categories: in Arkansas, where Hayek obtained his divorce, whites were 'protected' from 'any person who has in his or her veins any negro blood whatsoever' (Lusane 2003, 98). Hitler didn't 'see much future for the Americans ... it's a decayed country. And they have their racial problem, and the problem of social inequalities ... My feelings against Americanism are feelings of hatred and deep repugnance ... Everything about the behaviour of American society reveals that it's half Judaised, and the other half Negrified. How can one expect a State like that to hold together – a country where everything is built on the dollar?' (cited by Shirer 1960, 1069).

Hayek (1978a) also had a visceral dislike of 'detestable' Indians and the 'fundamentally dishonest' 'people of the eastern Mediterranean,' including Jews: 'I don't have many strong dislikes. I admit that as a teacher–I have no racial prejudices in general–but there were certain types, and conspicuous among them the Near Eastern populations, which I still dislike because they are fundamentally dishonest. And I must say dishonesty is a thing I intensely dislike. It was a type which, *in my childhood in Austria* (emphasis added), was described as Levantine, typical of the people of the eastern Mediterranean. But I encountered it later, and I have a profound dislike for the typical Indian students at the London School of Economics, which I admit are all one type–Bengali moneylender sons. They are to me a detestable type, I admit, but not with any racial feeling. I have found a little of the same amongst the Egyptians–basically a lack of honesty in them.'[15]

One of Caldwell's picks to edit *The Collected Writings of F.A. Hayek* commented:

> But I must say, I understand what Hayek is saying. I came to notice this attitude frequently among a number of the Middle Eastern students; that establishing 'friendships' was supposedly the way to (I don't want to say, 'buy') 'influence' their situation in life ... As for cheating. My institution, [...] University, has an associative relationship with two Chinese universities, and a sizable number of Chinese students come to [...] as part of their final year of study. There is 'statistically significant' degree of attempted

group cheating among many of them. My step-daughter, who earned her [...] degree from [...] told me she observed the same thing when she studied there ... Those, like Hayek, who had grown up and then still worked in societies in which rule of law, 'fair play,' 'honesty is its own reward,' a sense of individual responsibility, etc., meant something would be shocked and bothered when they came into contact with people from cultures and institutional orders in which the 'rules of the game' were viewed as being very different. By the way, any such accusation that Hayek was racist is totally misplaced, just as was the accusation a few years ago that he was anti-Semitic. (Email to Leeson 29 August 2010)

Hitler arrived in Vienna without anti-Semitism—which he acquired from the proto-Nazi culture co-created by the von Hayeks. The hate-filled culture that Hitler (1941 [1925], 954) absorbed during Hayek's 'childhood' included contempt for 'adventurous Indian or Egyptian' students:

> Already in the year 1920-21, when the young National Socialist movement was slowly beginning to raise itself above the political horizon and here and there was pronounced the German national freedom movement, people came to the party from various quarters trying to establish some connection between it and the freedom movements of other countries. This was along the lines of the 'league of oppressed nations' propagated by many. There were involved chiefly representatives of individual Balkan States and, in addition, some from Egypt and India, who individually always impressed me as gabbling pomposities without any realistic background. Not a few Germans, however, especially in the nationalist camp, let themselves be confused by such inflated Orientals and immediately believed they had before them, in the person of some adventurous Indian or Egyptian student or other, a 'representative' of India or Egypt. These people were not at all clear that these were at most individuals behind whom stood nothing at all, who were, above all, authorized by nobody to conclude any agreement with anybody at all, so that the practical result of every relation with such elements was null, unless one particularly wants to record the loss of time as a deficit. I always guarded against such attempts.

Rothbard (1994b, 6) responded to the 'dopey reporter for the *New York Times*' who described Irene Pivetti as a 'Catholic fundamentalist':

> There ain't no such thing. 'Fundamentalists' are pre-millennial dispensationalist Protestants. Period. What he means is: *real* [Rothbard's emphasis] Catholic.

Mises (1990 [1949/1950], 301-302) asserted that 'All doctrines are taught and accepted at least in two different, nay, conflicting varieties ... Catholicism [for example] had a different meaning for Cardinal Newman and for the hosts of the credulous ... The same dualism can be stated with all social, economic, and political doctrines ... An unbridgeable gulf separates the esoteric teaching from the exoteric one ... Between the philosophers and scholars who contrive new ideas and build up elaborate systems of thought and the narrow-minded dullards whose poor intellect cannot grasp but the simplest things there are many gradual transitions.'

According to Reisman (2002, 26-27), Mises was distinguishing between the 'genuine,' 'esoteric'—'version, which is typically complicated and more or less difficult to understand' and the 'exoteric'—'far more simplified versions of the same doctrine ... suitable for or communicated to the general public.'

Those on either wing of the anti-democratic spectrum are hissing-cousins—and many flip from extreme to extreme. Before (apparently unsuccessfully) submitting an article to Rothbard's *Journal of Libertarian Studies*, Geoffrey Partington (2015) had been a Communist Party academic.[16] According to Hoppe (2014 [1995]), it is the 'pure theory aspect of the Austrian School that gives us a huge advantage. These days, probably only Marxism can compare with the Austrian School in its worldwide scope.' As a 'leftwinger myself,' Hoppe had 'became disillusioned by Marxian politics as a result of Böhm-Bawerk's critique. It convinced me that Marxism was untenable... What I had liked about Marxism is that it made the attempt to provide a rigorous, deductively derived system. Back then, unlike now, Marxists accepted standards of logic. I thought this approach was superior to having ad hoc opinions on various subjects. With deductive systems, it is easier to discover whether they deliver the promised goods or collapse. Of course, Marxism collapses.'

Rand and Rothbard saved Block (2014): 'In the fifties and sixties, I was just another commie living in Brooklyn. My economic views were conventionally socialistic. I believed that the free market would cause massive social divisions and financial calamities. In 1962, I remember hissing and booing Ayn Rand when she came to speak to my college. Later, though, I entered into a debate with Nathaniel Branden, who was her partner. He recommended Henry Hazlitt and Rand for me to read, and these books brought me around to a free enterprise position.' Later, Block was 'told' about Rothbard, and 'eventually met him. He was the sort my parents warned me about. I stayed up until six in the morning with him and his group. One of the occupational hazards of hanging around with Murray was that you would get stomach cramps from laughing. We did lots of that. Well, Murray brought me the full way to the anarchist position by using my own arguments against me. It was simply a matter of applying market logic to the institutions of police, armies, and courts. Anarcho-capitalism is nothing more than the conviction that market logic applies across the board.'

According to Rothbard (1994b, 8–9), the Mises Institute Academic Vice President: the 'good thing about Fascism' was that it 'saved' Italy from the 'terrible ravages' of Marxism and anarcho-syndicalism; the 'bad' thing was its economic statism and its foreign policy of imperialism—both features, according to where 'our enemies' (leftists, Mensheviks, neocons, Official Cons, etc.), are 'far closer to fascism than we paleos are.' Thus, the next time:

> some leftist or Menshevik hisses 'fascist!' at you, you would be fully justified in hissing back, and double in spades.

To justify Mises' (1985 [1927]) promotion of 'Fascists,' his translator, Raico (2012, 250, 274, 275), reported that in 1906, Vilfredo Pareto complained that the right to strike had turned into 'the freedom, for the strikers, to bash in the brains of workers who wish to continue to work and to set fire to the factories with impunity.' In one of his last essays, Pareto (1948–1923) again complained about the 'transformations' demanded by 'modernity' that facilitated 'the ascent of the proletariat': the right to strike included 'the ability to constrain others to do so and to punish strikebreakers.' The only ones left to defend the freedom to work were, Pareto ironically wrote, the supporters of laissez-faire: 'those abominable Manchesterians'

Raico (2012, 274, 275) explained that Pareto 'endorsed the Fascist takeover, and, a year before his death, permitted Mussolini to appoint him to the Senate.' One of Pareto's associates, Maffeo Pantaleoni (1857–1924), the neoclassical 'Marshall of Italy,' was engaged in 'intense work in support of fascism' and ran a 'vigorous anti-Semitic campaign' in the decade before his death (Michelini and Maccabelli 2015, 92, 93). Raico (2012, 273–274), who described Pantaleoni as among 'Fascism's earliest and most fervent supporters,' noted that Hayek had referred to Pantaleoni as the author of 'one of the most brilliant summaries of economic theory that has ever appeared.' Pantaleoni wrote: The 'public powers, which historically have already been most effective instruments of spoliation in the hands of the nobility, first, and then of the bourgeoisie, will now become the means of procuring bread and circuses for the people ... If it had not been for the intervention of Fascism, Italy would have suffered not merely an economic and political catastrophe, but rather a catastrophe of its very civilization, equal in its kind to that of Russia and Hungary.' Italy was saved from the 'destructive hurricane' of Bolshevism 'only by fascism and by the heroism of the fascists who died *pro libertate Patriae* in the struggle of civil war.' This, Raico explained, was a position 'similar to that of Mises.'

According to Raico (2012, 188, n. 16, 278, n. 37), A. de Viti de Marco wrote that Pantaleoni was 'enraged by the collectivist and interventionist features of post-War Italy,' including 'the demagoguery of taxation organized by the alliance of all the parasitic groups for the speedier spoliation of the well-to-do and the savers and the free [i.e., non-unionized] workers—that is of the *producers* (emphasis in original).' At the 1980 MPS meeting, 'Count Max Thurn' and Martino celebrated tax evasion—the only way to make law respected would be to make them 'respectable.' John Chamberlain (1980) reflected: 'It's a sobering thought that the best will be forced to do the worst as governments more and more take on the mortal lineaments of robbers.'

The tax-evading Hayek (1978a) 'believe[d] in democracy as a system of peaceful change of government; but that's all its whole advantage is, no other.'[17] For Rothbard (1994a; 1992, 8), the purpose of Austrian economics is to replace 'underclass rule' with a 'small, self-perpetuating oligarchy of the ablest and most interested'; and for Raico (2012, 278, 280, n. 38)—like Mises—Fascism and Classical Liberalism had common Continental (Italian-Austro-Lausanne) neoclassical objectives: Pantaleoni, who was a 'bitter opponent of universal suffrage precisely because of the immense vista it opens up for lower-class plunder of the economically successful,' was also 'happy' to report that Mussolini (in a speech, 8 November 1921) stated: 'In economic matters, we are liberals in the more classical sense of the word.'

In his 'Translator's Notes' of Mises (1932) *Sozialismus*, Kahane (1951, 14) stated that Mises had 'lent assistance at every stage' and had 'inserted certain additions' which are 'not to be found in the German edition.' In 1956, Raico began translating *Liberalismus* into English; and

Mises probably began working on a new edition of *Human Action* in 1962 (Hülsmann 2007, 897, n. 35, 1022).

Hayek's (1978a) 'determination to become a scholar was certainly affected by the unsatisfied ambition of my father to become a university professor ... So I grew up with the idea that there was nothing higher in life than becoming a university professor.'[18] Mises (2009 [1978 (1940)], 77) provided an implausible explanation for his inability to obtain academic employment: 'No other calling was as desirable to me as that of a university professor. As a liberal, I recognized early on that I would always be denied a full professorship at a German-speaking university.' Hayek (1978b [1976], 235) clarified:

> The term 'liberal' is of course used here ... in the classical English, not in the modern American, sense.

For Ebeling's benefit, Hayek (1977, 15) reiterated this point: 'I prefer the European usage because it is older and corresponds more to the original meaning of the original terms. In Europe you use the term liberal when you wish to speak about libertarianism. In America you have to describe what in Europe is liberal by the term conservative. What irritates me so much is that these conservatives allowed the American socialists and half-socialists to usurp the term liberal and are now using it themselves as a term of condemnation, and that seems to me almost irreversible. When I speak about American liberals I prefer to call them pseudoliberals. There are no liberals in my sense.'

Hayek (1984) told the *Cato Policy Report*:

> I no longer dare call myself a liberal in America because it is so completely misunderstood, and the new meaning is invading Europe. Even here, one has to explain what one means by liberal.

In 'The Mont Pelerin Society,' Hunold (1951) also clarified:

> Liberal is always used here in the classical sense and not in the sense in which it is used in America where it has become identical with 'left-wing.'

In the third and fourth editions of *Human Action*, Mises (1963, v; 1996 [1966], vii) also explained that he was using the term 'liberal in the sense attached to it everywhere in the nineteenth century and still today in the countries of continental Europe.' According to the Cato Institute's Richard L. Gordon (1994, 172), 'Mises was so concerned about the changing meaning of liberalism that the original title given the translation of *Liberalismus* [1927] was *The Free and Prosperous Commonwealth* [1962].'

Yet in his Preface, Mises (1985 [1962], xviii) asserted that he had 'not changed anything in the original text of the book and did not influence *in any way* [emphasis added] the translation made by Dr. Ralph Raico and the editing done by Mr. Arthur Goddard.' In a footnote, Raico (2012, 258, n. 7), a Mises Institute Senior Fellow, revealed that Mises was lying:

> When I undertook to translate *Liberalismus* into English in the late 1950s, Mises at one point suggested that I include a translator's note explaining the historical context of these and similar remarks on Italian [sic] Fascism. My reply, in retrospect mistaken, was that such a note was superfluous, since the grounds for the views he expressed in 1927 were obvious. The English translation appeared, unfortunately, without any such explanation. I had vastly underestimated the prevelance of historical cluelessness among Mises's socialist critics.

When Hitler came to power, the Jewish Herbert Marcuse escaped to the New York Institute of Social Research, where he published 'The Struggle Against Liberalism in the Totalitarian View of the State.' Liberalism, Marcuse (1968 [1934], 3, 11–12) argued, was a front for the 'total-authoritarian state ... In order to get behind the usual camouflage and distortion and arrive at a true image of the liberalist economic and social system, it suffices to turn to Von Mises' portrayal of liberalism.' Raico (2012, 260) accused Marcuse and other Marxist writers of 'outright dishonesty' and was outraged by their 'venomous' critique of Mises.

In his 'History of Economic Thought' presentation to the Mises Institute 'Austrian Economics Research Conference on 'Mises and the Struggle Against Italian Fascism in World War II,' Kaza (2013) sought to 'bury this false history' with 'revelations from the archives.' Marcuse 'supervised studies for the CIA, OK?' and there was only 'one paragraph' referring to Fascism in *Liberalism in the Classical Tradition*. Mises 'worked with US intelligence against Fascism' and helped 'in the struggle against Fascism' by writing unsigned editorial for the *New York Times* and by providing to US military intelligence the names of 11 'Austrian economists who did not yield to the Nazis.' This is 'compelling' evidence: 'he was an anti-fascist, OK?'

Rothbard (1994b, 7) objected to 'anti-fascists': under the Comintern's influence, World War II (fought against Hitler and Japan) became a 'crusade' against:

> 'international fascism,' with the noble 'antifascist' crusaders, of course, including Bolsheviks and Mensheviks alike. And now that Bolshevism has fallen apart, our neocon/Official Con/social democrats would like nothing better than to revive the 'anti-fascist coalition.'

Hülsmann (2007, 538) reported that 'Marxist socialists vociferously object to being classified [by Mises (2011 [1929])] under the same heading that includes Fascist Socialists and National Socialists. But as Mises showed, all distinctions between these groups are on the surface. Economically, they are united.' And in the Preface to the second English edition of *Socialism*, Mises (2009 [1950], 13) declared:

> Neither is there any substantive difference between the intensions of the self-styled 'progressives' and those of the Italian Fascists and the German Nazis.

Referring to Mises' endorsement of conscription, Hoppe (2014 [1995]) complained: 'This passage is very peculiar ... It comes out of the blue, and has no foundation in his overall thinking. To me, this addition appears completely ad hoc.' The 'Fascists' that Mises (1985 [1927], 49, 51,) praised included 'Germans and Italians,' 'Ludendorff and Hitler.' Caldwell's (2008) posthumous ventriloquism—'[Italian] Fascism'—came in a review of Hülsmann's (2007, 677, n. 149) *The Last Knight of Liberalism* which presented the archival evidence that revealed Mises to have been a card-carrying Austro-Fascist and member of the official Fascist social club. Caldwell was outraged that Hülsmann had not requested permission from him to cite from the Hayek Archives—and denigrated him as an 'amateur.'

Raico (2012, 258) also inserted '[Italian]': 'It cannot be denied that [Italian] Fascism and similar movements aiming at the establishment of dictatorships are full of the best intentions and that their intervention has, for the moment, saved European civilization.' David Gordon (2012, xxi), Mises Institute Senior Fellow and editor of *The Mises Review*, inserted 'Italian' twice:

Mises said this about Italian Fascism: 'It cannot be denied that [Italian] Fascism and similar movements aiming at the establishment of dictatorships are full of the best intentions and that their intervention has for the moment, saved European civilization.' (p. 166). Was Mises, the supposed champion of freedom, really a fascist? Raico's comment on this issue is simple and straightforward. Mises was of course not a fascist.

Almost a quarter of a century before the deregulated 'private sector' retook Washington (the Trump Administration), Rothbard (1994b, 1, 3) declared that there is 'hope, hope for America.' Just as the Italian Left prepared to 'romp to power, Fate stepped into save the day': Berlusconi was determined to keep the

> 'ex' Communists from coming to power in Italy.

Rothbard objected to Berlusconi being described as the Italian Ross Perot—in his ownership of three TV networks and publishing houses, he is 'closer' to Rupert Murdoch. The 'big' difference is that Berlusconi is a 'dedicated free-marketeer, far more principled than Murdoch, more consistent than Perot.'[19]

The 'free' market is promoted via neo-feudal patronage. Rothbard (1994b, 5) promoted the 'spoils system'—a term derived from William L. Macey's phrase, 'to the victor belongs the spoils,' which described the patronage available to Andrew Jackson after his 1828 Presidential election victory. In 2017, President Trump told a gathering at the CIA headquarters:

> When I was young, we were always winning things in this country. We'd win with trade. We'd win with wars. At a certain age, I remember hearing from one of my instructors, 'The United States has never lost a war.' And then, after that, it's like we haven't won anything. We don't win anymore. The old expression, 'to the victor belong the spoils' – you remember. I always used to say, keep the oil. I wasn't a fan of Iraq. I didn't want to go into Iraq. But I will tell you, when we were in, we got out wrong. And I always said, in addition to that, keep the oil. Now, I said it for economic reasons. But if you think about it, [Vice President] Mike [Pence], if we kept the oil you probably wouldn't have ISIS because that's where they made their money in the first place. So we should have kept the oil. But okay. (Laughter.) Maybe you'll have another chance. But the fact is, should have kept the oil.[20]

Less than nine months after taking power, Hitler's Foreign Minister, Konstantin Freiherr von Neurath (19 October 1933) announced that Nazi Germany was withdrawing from the League of Nations.[21] This was followed by a military build-up which culminating in the German conquest of Poland (1 September 1939) and World War II. In 1935, 'Fascist' Italy conquered Ethiopia; up to 20,000 members of the Ethiopian nobility and intelligentsia were massacred (Campbell 2017). The League of Nations voted for economic sanctions (which were not fully applied)—Italy ignored the sanctions and left the League. The crisis discredited the League and moved Italy closer to an alliance with Nazi Austro-Germany.

According to Rothbard (1994b, 9), the National Alliance 'idiotically' aspired to return to 'Roman imperial glory' by reconquering the parts of Slovenia and Croatia that Italy had taken as a result of being on the winning side in 1918 and had lost as a result of being on the losing side in 1945. While Rothbard took literally Berlusconi's 'free market' aspirations, he nonchalantly dismissed the National Alliance's stated policy objectives: he didn't think that 'anyone' need seriously concern themselves about this claims to Slovenia and Croatia.

Rothbard was expelled from the Rand cult because he 'refused their demand that he divorce his wife Joey, who had committed the unpardonable sin of being a Christian' (Gordon 2013). According to the atheist Rothbard (1994b, 6): in the Western media version of 'Alice-in-Wonderland, of course,' any Christian who regards all other religions as:

> false (i.e. all *genuine* (Rothbard's emphasis) Christians) is denounced *ipso facto* as 'anti-Semitic.'

Rothbard found Rand 'intellectually oppressive': 'A cobra-type personality – coiled and ready to strike. She had hypnotic eyes and fantastic energy ... She was a totalitarian personality' (cited by Sublett 1987). In the Rand cult, devotees were expected to listen to all-night monologues from the amphetamine-fuelled *Goddess of the Market* (Burns 2009)—her tobacco and amphetamine addiction may have been driven by body image issues: they allowed her to lose weight, but she died of lung cancer. Raico was a Jewish 'gay liberationist,' and Hamowy was known in Austrian circles as the 'gay dwarf.'[22] Rothbard hated nature and public health and sought (in effect) to turn obesity into a communicable disease. In the 1960s, he was a 'little fat man': when eating with Rothbard began to adversely affect Block's (1995, 21, 22) own weight, he was told:

> every calorie says 'yea' to life. What could I say?

Frequently marooned on Manhattan Island because of a travel phobia, Rothbard—who had been bullied as a child and was frightened of the dark, or at least unable to sleep outside daylight hours—was entertained by his comrades, who were 'all ardent movie fans ... we spent our evenings playing board games ... like Mille Borne, Monopoly, Scrabble, and, if we felt particularly adult, Diplomacy.' Their:

> favorite was Risk, which gave rise to Murray's perennial comment, which we were forever repeating: 'Harry him in the Congo!' (Hamowy 2003)

Rothbard's Jewish parents would most likely have perished in the Holocaust had they not migrated to the USA (from Poland and Russia, respectively). Rothbard (1994b, 7) sought to persuade his readers to move beyond such issues:

> Whenever the word 'neofascist' is uttered, or nostalgic devotion is accorded to the Fascist founder Mussolini, the Western media, once again, know and yell about only one thing: 'anti-Semitism.' What *else* [Rothbard's emphasis] is or was 'fascism?' Who knows? Who cares? In truth the fascists were never anti-Semitic; indeed, there were always many Jews high up in the Fascist party. In fact, anti-Semitism has never been a factor in Italy period. It was only with the approach and waging of World War II that pushed the Italians, with great reluctance, into an anti-Jewish policy.

Rothbard (1994b, 7) praised Italian 'Fascists' because only 15% of Italian Jews were sent to gas chambers. His source was a letter to the editor of the *New York Times* which he described as 'protesting' the 'usual nonsense' about Mussolini:

> as 'anti-Semitic, responsible for the deportation of thousands of Italian Jews to Nazi death camps.'

In this letter, Roland N. Stromberg (1994) wrote: 'The Italian government did not turn a single Jew over to the Germans despite great pressure, and 85% of the Italian Jews survived even though the Nazis took control of northern Italy in 1943.' Stromberg—described by Rothbard (1994b, 7) as 'the eminent historian'—had 'based this largely on Susan Zuccotti's *Italians and the Holocaust* (1987).'

In *Italians and the Holocaust*, Zuccotti (1987, xxv–xxvi) reported:

> in 1938, Italy became officially anti-Semitic and non-Jewish Italians were informed that Jews were their enemies and the cause of all evil. Furthermore, Italy became Hitler's willing ally in war in June 1940 and a full partner in the crusade that included, amongst other objectives, the goal of making Europe *Judenrein* – free of Jews. After the German occupation of Italy, Benito Mussolini's puppet regime continued to cooperate fully with the Nazis ... The Holocaust was executed in Italy with ferocious determination.

Notes

1. MPS Archives Box 82.
2. 'Barton' may be a pseudonym.
3. Under the Trump Administration, the budget of the Environmental Protection Agency would be 'cut by over 31%. The climate and land-use social engineers are being driven berserk by this one. That the swarm of regulatory locusts will be reined in or even stopped in some instances who plague the country with their wetland rules, their land-use restrictions, their market-hampering prohibitions and abridgements of private property rights, is being forecasted as meaning the end to an environmental-friendly planet Earth. The heavens will darken, the seas will rise, and the land will be barren. How can humanity survive without environmental central planning by the self-righteous regulatory elite meant to lead mankind into socially sensitive green pastures? And, oh, no, the National Endowment for the Arts, the National Endowment for the Humanities, the Institute for Museum and Library Services, and the Corporation for Public Broadcasting are targeted for a virtual 100 per cent cut. Oh, the horror! Those concerned with arts and the humanities may have to put more of their own private charitable money where their culturally sensitive mouths are. The thought that those who enjoy driving to and from work listening to those mushy, moralizing collectivist voices on National Socialist Radio—I mean, National Public Radio—may have to pay for it completely out of their own pockets with donations or

subscriptions, or from interruptions of their leftie listening pleasure from capitalist commercials (please, please, not that!) is just too, too much for their delicate group-think souls to bear.'

4. https://www.markskousen.com/offer/five-star-web/?source=5stdefsi. Accessed 13 November 2017.
5. https://www.heartland.org/about-us/who-we-are/richard-ebeling.
6. http://www.illuminati-news.com/091006b.htm.
7. 'Deacon' McCormick (1987, 106) also stated that 'It is known for *certain* [emphasis added] that [Stalin] was in Switzerland in 1909.' This also is not supported by the scholarly literature.
8. 'Mr Whittecombe' a fictional character, 'wasn't crazy, of course (although he had confessed to spending a week in a straight jacket after the execution of mutineers during World War I). His memory was astonishing: he had met (and disliked) Stalin as a lad in London in 1910. Stalin was strutting around Soho then as Josef Georgi, and Mr Wittacombe's father took him several times to the Continental Cafe in Little Newport Street where Stalin presided.'
9. http://www.lfs.org/index.htm.
10. Friedrich Hayek, interviewed by Leo Rosten 15 November 1978 (Centre for Oral History Research, University of California, Los Angeles, http://oralhistory.library.ucla.edu/).
11. http://www.liverpoolmuseums.org.uk/ism/slavery/europe/liverpool_petition.aspx.
12. Hayek Archives Box 34.17.
13. MPS Archives Box 74.
14. MPS Archives Box 136.
15. Friedrich Hayek, interviewed by Robert Chitester date unspecified 1978 (Centre for Oral History Research, University of California, Los Angeles, http://oralhistory.library.ucla.edu/).
16. CLS Archives Box 5.1.
17. Friedrich Hayek, interviewed by Leo Rosten 15 November 1978 (Centre for Oral History Research, University of California, Los Angeles, http://oralhistory.library.ucla.edu/).
18. Friedrich Hayek, interviewed by Robert Chitester date unspecified 1978 (Centre for Oral History Research, University of California, Los Angeles, http://oralhistory.library.ucla.edu/).
19. In the 1992 Presidential election, Perot won 18.9% of the popular vote.
20. http://www.politico.com/story/2017/01/full-text-trump-pence-remarks-cia-headquarters-233978.
21. https://www.wdl.org/en/item/11598/.
22. Or at least by Bartley (Cubitt 2006, 265).

References

Archival Insights into the Evolution of Economics (and Related Projects)

Leeson, R. (2017). *Hayek: A Collaborative Biography Part VII 'Market Free Play with an Audience': Hayek's Encounters with Fifty Knowledge Communities*. Basingstoke, UK: Palgrave Macmillan.

Leeson, R. (2018). *Hayek: A Collaborative Biography Part VIII: The Constitution of Liberty: 'Shooting in Cold Blood' Hayek's Plan for the Future of Democracy*. Basingstoke, UK: Palgrave Macmillan.

Other References

Barton, S. (1994). The Ear. *Rothbard-Rockwell Report, 5*(1). http://www.unz.org/Pub/RothbardRockwellReport-1994may-00001.

Bender, B., & Hanna, A. (2016, December 5). Flynn Under Fire for Fake News. *Politico*. http://www.politico.com/story/2016/12/michael-flynn-conspiracy-pizzeria-trump-232227.

Block, W. (1995). In L. H. Rockwell, Jr. (Ed.), *Murray Rothbard: In Memorandum*. Auburn, AL: Ludwig von Mises Institute.

Block, W. (2000). Libertarianism vs Objectivism; A Response to Peter Schwartz. *Reason Papers, 26*, 39–62. http://www.reasonpapers.com/pdf/26/rp_26_4.pdf.

Block, W. (2014). Radical Economics an Interview with Walter Block. *Austrian Economics Newsletter, 19*(2). https://mises.org/library/radical-economics-interview-walter-block.

Boettke, P. J. (2014, June 7). Robert Leeson, Hayek and the Underpants Gnome. *Coordination Problem*. http://www.coordinationproblem.org/2014/06/robert-leeson-hayek-and-the-underpants-gnomes.html.

Boettke, P. J. (2016a, October 17). Ludwig von Mises, the Academic. *The Freeman*. https://fee.org/articles/ludwig-von-mises-the-academic/.

Boettke, P. J. (2016b, September 1). Richard Ebeling and FFF's Austrian Economics Project. *Coordination Problem*. http://www.coordinationproblem.org/2016/09/richard-ebeling-and-fffs-austrian-economics-project.html.

Brunvand, J. H. (1999). *Too Good to Be True: The Colossal Book of Urban Legends*. New York: W. W. Norton.

Brunvand, J. H. (2000). *The Truth Never Stands in the Way of a Good Story*. Illinois: University of Illinois Press.

Buchanan, J. (1986, October 26). Why Governments 'Got Out of Hand.' *The New York Times*.

Burns, J. (2009). *Goddess of the Market Ayn Rand and the American Right*. New York: Oxford University Press.

Caldwell, B. (2008). Book Review: History in the Service of Ideology: A Review Essay of Jörg Guido Hülsmann, *Mises: The Last Knight of Liberalism*. *History of Economic Ideas*, *16*(3), 143–148.

Campbell, I. (2017). *The Addis Ababa Massacre: Italy's National Shame*. Oxford: Oxford University Press.

Chamberlain, J. (1980, November 28). Mont Pelerin Society: Robber Governments. *National Review* (MPS Archives Box 48.3).

Chapman, G., & Python, M. (1989). *The Complete Monty Python's Flying Circus: All the Words* (Vol. 1). London: Pantheon.

Clark, R. T. (1964). *The Fall of the German Republic a Political Study*. New York: Russell and Russell.

Costello, J. (1988). *The Mask of Treachery: Spies, Lies, Buggery and Betrayal: The First Documented Dossier on Anthony Blunt's Cambridge Spy Ring*. New York: William Morrow.

Cowen, T. (1979). The Rutgers Conference on Inflation. *Austrian Economics Newsletter*, *2*(2), 1–4. https://mises.org/system/tdf/aen%20v.%202%2C%20no.%202%20Fall%201979.pdf?file=1&type=document.

Cubitt, C. (2006). *A Life of August von Hayek*. Bedford, UK: Authors OnLine.

Deacon, R. (1989). *Super Spy: The Man Who Infiltrated the Kremlin and the Gestapo*. London: Macdonald.

Ebeling, R. M. (1978). Review: On the Manipulation of Money and Credit. *Austrian Economic Newsletter*, *1*(3), 8–9.

Ebeling, R. M. (1990). Introduction. In L. Mises (Ed.), *Money, Method and the Market Process* (Selected by Margit von Mises and Edited with an Introduction by Richard M. Ebeling). Auburn, AL: Ludwig von Mises Institute.

Ebeling, R. M. (1994). Review of Stephen Koch *Double Lives: Spies and Writers in the Secret Soviet War of Ideas Against the West*. New York: Free Press. Future of Freedom Foundation, July 1. http://fff.org/explore-freedom/article/book-review-double-lives/.

Ebeling, R. M. (2014a, February 16). EXCLUSIVE INTERVIEW, Gold & Silver. Richard Ebeling on Austrian Economics, Economic Freedom and the Trends of the Future. *Daily Bell*. http://www.thedailybell.com/gold-silver/anthony-wile-richard-ebeling-on-austrian-economics-economic-freedom-and-the-trends-of-the-future/.

Ebeling, R. M. (2014b, June 16). *The Rise and Fall of Classical Liberalism*. Free Market Liberalism. https://rebeling.liberty.me/the-rise-and-fall-of-classical-liberalism-by-richard-ebeling/.

Ebeling, R. M. (2015, March 25). *A World Without the Welfare State*. Future of Freedom Foundation. https://www.fff.org/explore-freedom/article/world-without-welfare-state/.

Ebeling, R. M. (2016, May 2). *How I Became a Libertarian and an Austrian Economist*. Future of Freedom Foundation. https://www.fff.org/explore-freedom/article/became-libertarian-austrian-economist/.
Ebeling, R. M. (2017, March 20). *Trump's Budgetary Blueprint Retains America's Welfare State*. Heartland Institute. https://www.heartland.org/news-opinion/news/trumps-budgetary-blueprint-retains-americas-welfare-state.
Fischer, C. (2002). *The Rise of the Nazis*. Manchester: Manchester University Press.
Gordon, R. L. (1994). *Regulation and Economic Analysis: A Critique Over Two Centuries*. Boston: Kluwer Academic Publishers.
Gordon, D. (2012). Preface. In Raico, R., *Classical Liberalism and the Austrian School*. Auburn, AL: Ludwig von Mises Institute.
Gordon, D. (2013, April 18). *The Kochtopus vs. Murray N. Rothbard*, Part II. https://www.lewrockwell.com/2013/04/david-gordon/explaining-beltway-libertarians/.
Hamowy, R. (2003). Memories of Rothbard and Hayek. *LewRockwell.com*. http://www.lewrockwell.com/2003/07/murray-n-rothbard/memories-of-rothbard-and-hayek/.
Hayek, F. A. (1949). The Intellectuals and Socialism. *University of Chicago Law Review*, *16*(3), 417–433.
Hayek, F. A. (1975). *A Discussion with Friedrich von Hayek*. Washington: American Enterprise Institute. https://www.aei.org/wp-content/uploads/2017/03/Discussion-with-Friedrich-von-Hayek-text.pdf.
Hayek, F. A. (1976a). *Law, Legislation and Liberty, Volume 2: The Mirage of Social Justice*. Chicago: University of Chicago Press.
Hayek, F. A. (1976b, February 23). Politicians Can't Be Trusted with Money. *American Institute for Economic Research Reports* (Hayek Archives Box 109.1).
Hayek, F. A. (1976c, March 18). Institutions May Fail, but Democracy Survives. *US News and World Report* (Hayek Archives Box 109.4).
Hayek, F. A. (1976d, October 13). *The Inseparability of Economic and Political Freedom*. Foundation for Economic Education (Australia) (Hayek Archives Box 109.7).
Hayek, F. A. (1976e). *Socialism and Science*. Economic Society of Australia and New Zealand, Canberra Branch.
Hayek, F. A. (1977, September). An Interview with Friedrich Hayek, by Richard Ebeling. *Libertarian Review*, 10–18 (Hayek Archives Box 109.14).
Hayek, F. A. (1978a). *Oral History Interviews*. Centre for Oral History Research, University of California, Los Angeles. http://oralhistory.library.ucla.edu/.
Hayek, F. A. (1978b). *New Studies in Philosophy, Politics, Economics and the History of Ideas*. London: Routledge & Kegan Paul.

Hayek, F. A. (1984). *The Essence of Hayek* (C. Nishiyama & K. R. Leube, Eds.). Stanford, CA: Hoover Institution Press.
Hayek, F. A. (1994). *Hayek on Hayek an Autobiographical Dialogue*. Supplement to *The Collected Works of F. A. Hayek* (S. Kresge & L. Wenar, Eds.). Chicago: University of Chicago Press.
Hayek, F. A. (1997). *Socialism and War: Essays, Documents, Reviews. The Collected Works of F. A. Hayek* (B. Caldwell, Ed.). Indianapolis: Liberty Fund.
Heiden, K. (1944). *Der Fuehrer* (R. Manheim, Trans.). Boston: Houghton Mifflin.
Hitler, A. (1939 [1925]). *Mein Kampf* (J. Murphy, Trans.). London: Hurst and Blackett.
Hitler, A. (1941 [1925]). *Mein Kampf*. New York: Raynal and Hitchcock.
Hoppe, H.-H. (1992). Review of R. M. Ebeling's *Money, Method, and the Market Process*. *Austrian Economic Newsletter*.
Hoppe, H.-H. (2014 [1995]). The Private Property Order: An Interview with Hans-Hermann Hoppe. *Austrian Economic Newsletter*, 18(1). https://mises.org/library/private-property-order-interview-hans-hermann-hoppe.
Hülsmann, J. G. (2007). *Mises: The Last Knight of Liberalism*. Auburn, AL: Ludwig von Mises Institute.
Hunold, A. (1951, Spring). The Mont Pelerin Society. *World Liberalism* (MPS Archives Box 4.12).
Kahane, J. (1951 [1932]). Translator's Notes. In L. Mises (Ed.), *Socialism: An Economic and Sociological Analysis* (J. Kahane, Trans.). New Haven: Yale University Press.
Kaza, G. (2013). Mises and the Struggle Against Italian Fascism in World War II. *Austrian Economics Research Conference*.
Leube, K. R. (1984, July). Essay: Hayek, Orwell, and The Road to Serfdom. *Prometheus*, 2(3). http://www.lfs.org/index.htm.
Lusane, C. (2003). *Hitler's Black Victims: The Historical Experiences of Afro-Germans, European Blacks, African and African Americans in the Nazi Era*. New York: Routledge.
Marcuse, H. (1968). *Negations Essays in Critical Theory*. Boston: Beacon.
McCormick, D. (pseudonym: Deacon, R.) (1969). *A History of the British Secret Service*. London: Frederick Muller.
McCormick, D. (pseudonym: Deacon, R.) (1972). *A History of the Russian Secret Service*. London: Frederick Muller.
McCormick, D. (pseudonym: Deacon, R.) (1979). *The British Connection Russia's Manipulation of British Individuals and Institutions*. London: Hamish Hamilton.
McCormick, D. (pseudonym: Deacon, R.) (1987). *Spyclopedia: The Comprehensive Handbook of Espionage*. New York: William Morrow.

McCormick, D. (pseudonym: Deacon, R.) (1990). *The Greatest Treason: The Bizarre Story of Hollis, Liddell and Mountbatten* (Rev. Ed.). London: Century.

Michelini, L., & Maccabelli, T. (2015). Economics and Anti-Semitism: The Case of Maffeo Pantaleoni. *History of Political Economy*, 47(1), 91–118.

Mises, L. (1932). *Die Gemeinwirtschaft: Untersuchungen über den Sozialismus* (2nd ed.). Jena: Gustav Fischer Verlag.

Mises, L. (1949). *Human Action: A Treatise on Economics* (1st ed.). New Haven: Yale University Press.

Mises, L. (1950, May 4). Middle-of-the-Road Policy Leads to Socialism. *Commercial and Financial Chronicle.* https://mises.org/library/middle-road-policy-leads-socialism.

Mises, L. (1951 [1932]). *Socialism: An Economic and Sociological Analysis* (J. Kahane, Trans.). New Haven: Yale University Press.

Mises, L. (1962). *The Ultimate Foundation of Economic Science An Essay on Method.* New York: Van Nostrand.

Mises, L. (1962). Preface. In Mises, L. 1985 [1927], *Liberalism in the Classical Tradition*, (R. Raico, Trans.). Auburn, AL: Mises Institute.

Mises, L. (1963). *Human Action: A Treatise on Economics* (2nd ed.). New Haven: Yale University Press.

Mises, L. (1985 [1927]). *Liberalism in the Classical Tradition*, (R. Raico, Trans.). Auburn, AL: Mises Institute.

Mises, L. (1990). *Money, Method and the Market Process.* Auburn, AL: The Ludwig von Mises Institute, Norwell, MA: Kluwer Academic Publishers. Selected by Margit von Mises and Edited with an Introduction by Richard M. Ebeling.

Mises, L. (1996 [1966]). *Human Action: A Treatise on Economics* (B. Greaves, Ed.). Indianapolis: Liberty Fund.

Mises, L. (1998 [1949]). *Human Action: A Treatise on Economics the Scholars Edition.* Auburn, AL: Ludwig von Mises Institute.

Mises, L. (2007 [1958]). Mises and Rothbard letters to Ayn Rand. *Journal of Libertarian Studies*, 21(4), 11–16.

Mises, L. 2009 ([1978 (1940)]). *Memoirs.* Auburn, AL: Ludwig von Mises Institute.

Mises, L. (2011 [1929]). *A Critique of Interventionism.* Auburn, AL: Ludwig von Mises Institute.

Moffitt, I. (1983). *The Presence of Evil.* New York: National Book Network.

Myrdal, G. (1944). *An American Dilemma: The Negro Problem and Modern Democracy.* New York: Harper and Brothers.

North, G. K. (1987). *The Plague Has Come at Last.* http://soamc.org/tfh/FILES/Abortion_Gays_and_AIDS.

Partington, G. (2015). *Party Days.* Xlibris.

Raico, R. (2012). *Classical Liberalism and the Austrian School.* Auburn, AL: Ludwig von Mises Institute.
Raico, R. (2013, February 20). *An Interview with Ralph Raico.* Mises Institute. https://mises.org/library/interview-ralph-raico-0.
Reisman, G. (2002). Eugen von Böhm-Bawerk's 'Value, Cost, and Marginal Utility.' Austrian Scholars' Conference of the Ludwig von Mises Institute, March 16, 2002, Auburn, AL. https://www.capitalism.net/articles/Reisman%20Full.pdf.
Rothbard, M. N. (1992, January). Right-wing Populism: A Strategy for the Paleo Movement. *Rothbard Rockwell Report,* 5–14. http://rothbard.altervista.org/articles/right-wing-populism.pdf.
Rothbard, M. N. (1994a). Nation by Consent. Decomposing the National State. *Journal of Libertarian Studies, 11*(1), 1–10. https://mises.org/library/uk-nation-consent.
Rothbard, M. N. (1994b, July). Revolution in Italy! *Rothbard-Rockwell Report, 5*(7), 1–10. http://www.unz.org/Pub/RothbardRockwellReport-1994jul-00001.
Rothbard, M. N. (1994c, December). Saint Hilary and the Religious Left. *Rothbard Rockwell Report.*
Sanchez, J., & Weigel, D. (2008, January 16). Who Wrote Ron Paul's Newsletters? Libertarian Movement Veterans, and a Paul Campaign Staffer, Say it was 'Paleolibertarian' Strategist Lew Rockwell. *Reason.* http://reason.com/archives/2008/01/16/who-wrote-ron-pauls-newsletter.
Shirer, W. L. (1960). *Rise and Fall of the Third Reich.* London: Secker and Warburg.
Skousen, M. (1991). *Economics on Trial: Lies, Myths and Realities.* Homewood, IL: Business One Irwin.
Skousen, M. (2008, February 28). Bill Buckley and Me a True Story. *Human Events Powerful Conservative Voices.* http://www.humanevents.com/2008/02/28/bill-buckley-and-me-a-true-story/.
Skousen, M. (2009). *The Making of Modern Economics: The Lives and Ideas of the Great Thinkers* (2nd ed.). London: M. E. Sharpe.
Stanford University History Study Group. (2016). *Evaluating Information: The Cornerstone of Civic Online Reasoning.* https://sheg.stanford.edu/upload/V3LessonPlans/Executive%20Summary%2011.21.16.pdf.
Stromberg, R. (1994, April 13). Mussolini's Italy Withheld Jews From the Nazis. *New York Times.* http://www.nytimes.com/1994/04/13/opinion/l-mussolini-s-italy-withheld-jews-from-the-nazis-770507.html.
Sublett, S. (1987, July 30). Libertarians' storied guru. *Washington Times* (MPS Archives Box 45.7).
Volkogonov, D. (1991). *Stalin: Triumph and tragedy.* London: Grove Weidenfeld.

Wassenaar, A. (1977). *Assault on Private Enterprise: The Freeway to Communism.* Cape Town: Tafelberg.

Williams, W. (2010). *Up from the Projects An Autobiography.* Stanford, CA: Hoover Press.

Yeager, L. (1991). An Interview with Leland B. Yeager. *Austrian Economics Newsletter,* 12(3). https://mises.org/library/interview-leland-b-yeager.

Zuccotti, S. (1987). *The Italians and the Holocaust: Persecution, Rescue, and Survival.* Nebraska: University of Nebraska Press.

CHAPTER 8

Austrian 'Instincts,' Serfdom, and Spanish and Portuguese 'Fascism'

SUMMARY

In Europe, 'Fascism,' as defined and praised by Mises, overthrew democracy in Italy (1922), Spain (1923), Portugal (1926), Germany (1933), Austrian (1934) and Spain (1936–1939); and in Latin America, similar outcomes occurred in the Operation Condor countries: Paraguay (1954), Brazil (1964), Bolivia (1971), Uruguay (1973), Chile (1973) and Argentina (1976). In 1940, Mises had not wished to leave neutral Switzerland when escaping the 'Fascists,' who, he had asserted, had 'saved European civilization': he apparently preferred 'Fascist' Portugal to the USA.

In 1960, Prime Minister, Dr. Hendrik Frensch Verwoerd, created the Republic of South African, refused to accept black ambassadors from Commonwealth states and blocked non-white sportsmen from representing 'their' country. In 1961, Verwoerd appointed Balthazar Johannes Vorster—who had been interned during World War II as a Nazi sympathiser—as Minister of Justice. In 1962, Hayek appeared to have considered Apartheid South Africa as his post-Chicago retirement home, while simultaneously trying to persuade Portugal's Dr. António de Oliveira Salazar, to supplement his 'God, Fatherland, and Family' 'Fascist' dictatorship with *The Constitution of Liberty*. And in 1977, Hayek sent General Pinochet a copy of his *Law, Legislation and Liberty* 'Model Constitution.' Hayek and Mises encountered 'instinctive' sycophancy, and Hayek described the defence of the neo-feudal 'spontaneous' order

© The Author(s) 2018
R. Leeson, *Hayek: A Collaborative Biography*,
Archival Insights into the Evolution of Economics,
https://doi.org/10.1007/978-3-319-74509-1_8

as a beautiful 'artistic creation.' This chapter examines what lies behind the 'slogan of liberty.'

In Europe, 'Fascism,' as defined and praised by Mises (1985 [1927]), overthrew democracy in Italy (1922), Spain (1923), Portugal (1926), Germany (1933), Austrian (1934) and Spain (1936–1939); and in Latin America, similar outcomes occurred in what became known as the Operation Condor countries: Paraguay (1954), Brazil (1964), Bolivia (1971), Uruguay (1973), Chile (1973) and Argentina (1976). When Hayek (1976a) praised Brazil's 'free-enterprise,' *US News and World Report* asked: 'What about military dictatorship of the Brazilian and Chilean type? Do you feel they are better placed than others?' Hayek appeared to conflate Hitler with Brazil and Pinochet's Chile: 'Dictatorships can exploit the situation to prepare secretly for a military conflict at a time that suits them best—when they have an initial advantage over their capitalist enemies'—adding that 'socialism has destroyed such a flourishing capitalist economy as Argentina.'[1] When asked about Brazil, Bolivia, Uruguay, Chile and Argentina, Hayek (1977) told the Argentine dictator-promoter, Alvaro Carlos Alsogaray (1913–2005): 'Inflation is the greatest threat to freedom' (see Filip 2018).[2]

Crozier (1967) wrote a 'sympathetic' biography of Franco—who liquidated about 200,000 'impurities' (Richards 1998; Preston 2012). Rothbard's (2002 [1982], xlv) devotion to 'liberty' 'began in childhood and has intensified ever since.' According to his obituary (published in the Holocaust-denying *Institute for Historical Review*), Rothbard recalled:

> In one family gathering featuring endless pledges of devotion to 'Loyalist' Spain during the Civil War. I piped up, at the age of 11 or 12, 'What's wrong with Franco, anyway? … My query was a conversation stopper, all right, but I never received an answer. (cited by Weber 1995)

In 'Socialism and Science,' Hayek (1976b, 96) told the Canberra branch of the Economic Society of Australia and New Zealand that the 'most idealistic among the socialists will be forced to destroy democracy to serve their idealistic socialist vision of the future,' leaving a population who 'will have to be subdued with the knout and the machine-gun: This too, by the very people who genuinely intended to grant all their wishes.'[3]

Had Mises and Hayek been genuine Classical Liberals, they would have objected to human rights abuses; had they been White Terror promoters masquerading as scholars, they would have been indifferent. Like Hayek, Mises (1985 [1927], 49, 54, 154) was indifferent: although in Soviet Russia, 'every free expression of opinion is suppressed,' this 'land of the knout and the prison-camp no longer poses a threat to the world today. With all their will to war and destruction, the Russians are no longer capable seriously of imperiling the peace of Europe. One may therefore safely let them alone.' The deflation that Hayek and Mises promoted had deepened the Great Depression, facilitated Hitler's rise to power and legitimised the expansion of the Soviet Empire into the heart of Europe.

In 'Setting the Record Straight: How Stalin Used Hitler To Start World War II,' Ebeling (2016) claimed to have exploded the 'Soviet Fairy Tale': 'in Stalin's mind, Hitler's drive for a Europe dominated by Nazi Germany was in fact a tool for him to use for advancing the global cause of communism.' Before the 1941 invasion of Russia, Hitler declared: 'I shall give a propagandist reason for starting the war, no matter whether it is plausible or not. The victor will not be asked afterwards, whether he told the truth or not. When starting and waging war it is not right that matters but victory. Close your hearts to pity. Act brutally, eighty million people must obtain what is their right. Their existence must be made secure. The strongest man is right' (cited by Snyder 1982, 329). Mises (1985 [1927], 48–49) described the Austrian Fairy Tale: 'Fascism will *never* (emphasis added) succeed as completely as Russian Bolshevism in freeing itself from the power of liberal ideas.' The 'deeds of the Fascists and of other parties corresponding to them were emotional reflex actions evoked by indignation at the deeds of the Bolsheviks and Communists. As soon as the first flush of anger had passed, their policy took a more moderate course and will probably become even more so with the passage of time. This moderation is the result of the fact that traditional liberal views still continue to have an unconscious influence on the Fascists.'

According to Charles Koch (1978, 31), 'Businessmen should realize that the more regulated an industry becomes, the less it can cope with changing conditions in the world.' Mises' intellectual world was intensely regulated—and bolstered by the 'demand' for 'sycophancy' (Buchanan 1992, 190). But instead of a Pact with the Austrian School of Economics, Hitler chose a Nazi-Soviet Pact (1939–1941). For Red Terrorists like Stalin, 'The Party' (which he controlled) is 'Always Right'; and for White Terror promoters like Mises, 'The Free Market' (which funded him) is 'Always Right.' According to Ebeling (2016), Stalin had miscalculated: 'the swift defeat and German occupation of France in June 1940 changed the configuration of forces and the likely length of the war.' In May 1940, the *Wehrmacht* overran Western Europe in a series of blitzkrieg attacks. The official Mises Institute biographer reported that Mises could 'hardly believe' what he read in the newspapers—'completely taken by surprise. He had not realized that conditions had once again changed profoundly.' According to *The Last Knight of Liberalism*, this was the 'only' time that Mises was 'ever' wrong in forecasting an 'important' political or economic event (Hülsmann 2007, 750–751). In reality, Mises apodictic truth (about 'Fascists,' the 'free' market, etc.) was self-evident only to himself and his disciples. Scientific knowledge, in contrast, embraces the 'certainty of uncertainty.'

When the *Austrian Economics Newsletter* suggested that Katsuichi Yamamoto 'seems somewhat like Mises's Japanese counterpart,' the Japanese Austrian, Hiroyuki Okon (1997), concurred: 'It seems tragedy had struck Austrians all over the world. At a time when Mises was struggling to get a job in the U.S., after having been forced to flee his homeland, Yamamoto was jailed by occupation forces in his own country.' The *Austrian Economics Newsletter* reinforced the parallel martyrdom: 'It appears that Yamamoto's life and intellectual interests parallel that of Mises's and Hayek's.'

According to an 'Adjunct Professor at Northwood University' who 'serves in the Michigan House of Representatives (42nd District),' the 'Nazis closed in on' Mises (Kaza 2013). Mises' (2009 [1978 (1940)], 55) motto was 'Do not give into evil, but proceed ever more boldly against it.' The panicked journey from neutral Switzerland to neutral America via neutral Portugal was unbearable for *The Last Knight of Liberalism*: Mises was in a 'terrible state of mind.' Beneath his 'calm and composed' aristocratic façade, he was not suited for 'adventures and uncertainties of this kind': Margit Mises (1984, 58) needed 'all' her 'courage' to help him overcome his 'desolation.'

Hayek (1992 [1977]) described the MPS achievement: a 'consistent doctrine and some international circles of communication.' According to MPS member Caldwell (1995, 70, n. 67), Hayek's (1995 [1929], 68) endorsement of Mises' 'ruthless consistency' in developing 'economic liberalism to its *ultimate* (emphasis added) consequences' is a reference to *Liberalism in the Classical Tradition*, in which Mises (1985 [1927], 19, 51) stated:

> The program of [Austrian] liberalism, therefore, if condensed into a single word, would have to read: *property* (Mises' emphasis) ... All the other demands of liberalism result from this fundamental demand ... The victory of Fascism in a number of countries is only an episode in the long series of struggles over the problem of property.

The previous year, 'Fascism'—as defined and praised by Mises—had overthrown democracy in Portugal (the *coup d'état* of 28 May 1926); António de Oliveira Salazar subsequently became Prime Minister of 'Fascist' Portugal (1932–1968). Hayek (1978a) informed James Buchanan that his constitutional proposal was 'received exceedingly friendly by the people whom I really respect, but that's a very small crowd. I've received higher praise, which I personally value, for *The Constitution of Liberty* [1960] but from a very small, select circle.'[4] In 1962, Hayek sent *The Constitution of Liberty* to Salazar with a covering note explaining that he hoped that it might assist him 'in his endeavour to design a constitution which is proof against the abuses of democracy' (cited by Farrant et al. 2012, 521). The end of Portuguese 'Fascism' (1974) and the death of the 'Fascist' dictator of Spain, General Franco (1975), were defining traumas for the 'International Right' (Teacher 2018a, b).

In *Taken for a Ride: The History of Cons and Con-men*, the Hayek-promoter, 'Deacon' McCormick (1976, 97, 124, 167), referred to the 'remarkable psychological insights which is the hall-mark of a true impostor ... a genius for organisation in his gigantic imposture ... the type of outrageous fiction which any critic would savagely reject on the grounds that it described the impossible.' Mises' (1985 [1927], 49, 51) insisted: '*It cannot be denied* (emphasis added) that Fascism and similar movements aiming at the establishment of dictatorships are full of the best intentions and that their intervention has, for the moment, saved European civilization.' Hayek (1978a) 'just learned he was usually right in his conclusions, but I was not completely satisfied with his argument. That, I think, followed me right through my life. I was always influenced by Mises's answers, but not fully satisfied by his arguments. It became very largely an attempt to improve the argument, which I realized led to correct conclusions. But the question of why it hadn't persuaded most other people became important to me; so I became anxious to put it in a more effective form.'[5]

Hayek (1975, 14) described the improved 'logic' which underpinned Austrian conclusions: 'If we take as premises some undisputed facts, which everybody accepts as facts of daily observation, we can logically deduce from them certain consequences, which permit only one answer to the problem. In other words, if we deduce certain consequences from admitted facts, by logically correct argument, the truth of our deductions *has to be accepted* (emphasis added).' Therefore,

- since it is an Austrian undisputed fact that externalities were invented by a gun-runner for Stalin (Pigou);
- those who fund the 'free' market (the carbon emission and tobacco industries) should not have full-cost pricing (regulations and externality taxes) imposed upon them; and
- there is 'no justification for government subsidisation of education on the grounds of beneficial externalities' because many teachers 'ridicule traditional religious and cultural values' (Skousen 1991, 155).

When Randal Holcombe (1998) stated: 'What's surprising is that the theory of public goods has survived despite its lack of theoretical or empirical merit,' the *Austrian Economics Newsletter* asked: 'Why has idea survived?' Holcombe replied:

> Why does most government propaganda survive? The people who have promoted public goods theory as a justification for government intervention are researchers with a vested interest in supporting the activities of government, either because they work in government schools and universities or heavily subsidized private ones. If you want to get a more compliant population, you can beat them into submission. But it would be easier and better to convince them that your way of thinking is right. That's the role of public education. Public educators even admit this. They say the main role of public schools is to socialize children, that is, propagandize them.

Also according to Holcombe (1998), 'liberty' had been hijacked by democracy: the Founders 'wanted popular government, but not for the people to determine public policy ... the House would choose the president.' The Electoral College had been designed 'to be a kind of search committee. They would be knowledgeable people, know the strengths and weaknesses of the possible candidates, and the electors would forward a slate of candidates to the House.' But, Holcombe lamented: 'As it happened, it didn't work out that way. A majority of electors usually agreed on one candidate. And by the 1820s, most states had already gone to popular election of electors. By 1828, political parties were out campaigning for presidents.'

Holcombe's nostalgia corresponded with Hayek's (1978a):

> the revolt against this is an affair of the last 150 years. Even in the nineteenth century, people accepted it all as a matter of course. An economic crisis, a loss of a job, a loss of a person, was as much an act of God as a flood or something else. It's certain developments of thinking, which happened since, which made people so completely dissatisfied with it. On the one hand, that they are no longer willing to accept certain ethical or moral traditions; on the other hand, that they have been explicitly told, 'Why should we obey any rules of conduct, the usefulness or reasonableness of which cannot be demonstrated to us?' Whether man can be made to behave decently, I would even say, so long as he insists that the rules of decency must be explained to him, I am very doubtful. It may not be possible.[6]

Like Jaime Guzmán in Pinochet's Chile (Cristi 2017), Hülsmann (2008, 189) objected to the State taking over functions (many of which had previously been provided by the Church):

> Today, the [non-Austrian] welfare state provides a great number of services that in former times have been provided by families (and which would, we may assume, still be provided to a large extent by families if the welfare state ceased to exist). Education of the young, care for the elderly and the sick, assistance in times of emergencies—all of these services are today effectively 'outsourced' to the state. The families have been degraded into small production units that share utility bills, cars, refrigerators, and of course the tax bill. The tax-financed welfare state then provides them with education and care.

Newsweek asked Hayek (1979) how he would respond to Paul Samuelson who 'once said if you had your way you would lead the world back to the nineteenth century days of limited Whig government,' Hayek replied: 'That is most certainly the case.' The Whigs in both

America (1833–1854) and Britain (1678–1859) had long gone—but in *The Constitution of Liberty*, Hayek (2011 [1960], Postscript) was chronologically more precise:

> The more I learn about the evolution of ideas, the more I have become aware that I am simply an unrepentant Old Whig—with the stress on the 'old.' To confess one's self an Old Whig does not mean, of course, that one wants to go back to where we were at the end of the seventeenth century.

Three years before the 1789 French Revolution (and the rise of Hayek's family into the nobility), Thomas Jefferson (1786) wrote from Paris to George Wythe about 'these countries where ignorance, superstition, poverty, & oppression of body & mind in every form, are so firmly settled on the mass of the people, that their redemption from them can never be hoped.' Jefferson concluded that 'by far the most important bill in our whole code is that for the diffusion of knowledge among the people. No other sure foundation can be devised, for the preservation of freedom and happiness. If anybody thinks that kings, nobles, or priests are good conservators of the public happiness send them here. It is the best school in the universe to cure them of that folly. They will see here with their own eyes that these descriptions of men are an abandoned confederacy against the happiness of the mass of the people. The omnipotence of their effect cannot be better proved than in this country particularly, where notwithstanding the finest soil upon earth, the finest climate under heaven, and a people of the most benevolent, the most gay and amiable character of which the human form is susceptible, where such a people I say, surrounded by so many blessings from nature, are yet loaded with misery by kings, nobles and priests, and by them alone.'

Jefferson (1786) sought to provide the foundations of the new American Republic: 'Preach, my dear Sir, a crusade against ignorance; establish & improve the law for educating the common people. Let our countrymen know that the people alone can protect us against these evils, and that the tax which will be paid for this purpose is not more than the thousandth part of what will be paid to kings, priests & nobles who will rise up among us if we leave the people in ignorance.'

The USA was founded by those who were apprehensive about inherited titles: this found expression in The Title of Nobility Clause—Article 1, Section 9, Clause 8 of the Constitution.[7] Thomas Paine's (2000

[1775]) 'Reflections on Titles' is part of *The Founders' Constitution* (Kurland and Lerner 2000). Paine approved of the title 'The Honorable Continental Congress'; but when reflecting on the 'pompous titles bestowed on unworthy men, I feel an indignity that instructs me to despise the absurdity ... The lustre of the *Star* and the title of *My Lord*, over-awe the superstitious vulgar, and forbid them to inquire into the character of the possessor: Nay more, they are, as it were, bewitched to admire in the great, the vices they would honestly condemn in themselves. This sacrifice of common sense is the certain badge which distinguishes slavery from freedom; for when men yield up the privilege of thinking, the last shadow of liberty quits the horizon (emphases in original).'[8] Paine's 'Reflections on Titles' is available on the Ludwig von Mises Institute website.[9]

Jefferson (1786) echoed Paine: 'The people of England, I think, are less oppressed than here [France]. But it needs but half an eye to see, when among them, that the foundation is laid in their dispositions for the establishment of a despotism. Nobility, wealth & pomp are the objects of their adoration.' In 1870, 20% of American 'whites' and 79.9% of 'blacks and others' were illiterate; by 1920, this had fallen to 6 and 20%, respectively.[10]

In 'many ways,' 'von' Mises was 'still attached to the old world: he had a color picture of the Emperor Franz Josef II hanging on the wall' of his New York rent-controlled apartment (Koether 2000, 5). The Habsburg Empire rested on 'tradition, on dynastic rights.' In 1918, the Habsburgs left a legacy of 85% illiteracy; the 'nationalist intellectuals had appealed to the masses; the masses answered by repudiating intellectual values' (Taylor 1964, 35, 41, 161). In India in 1947, the British left a legacy of 88% illiteracy (Nayaka and Nurullah 1974). Mises (1951 [1932], 234–235) asserted: 'Were England to lose India today, and were that great land, so richly endowed by nature, to sink into anarchy, so that it no longer offered a market for international trade—or no longer offered so large a market—it would be an economic catastrophy of the first order ... It was not cant for English free traders to speak of England's vocation to elevate backward people to a state of civilisation. England has shown by acts that she has regarded her possessions in India, in the Crown colonies, and in the Protectorates as a general mandatory of European civilisation.'

In an encyclopedia entry first published before his Nobel Prize, Hayek (1978b [1973], 142) defined a crucial ingredient of classical

'Liberalism': the 'chief instrument' of a 'progressive increase of vertical mobility' was the provision—where 'necessary' out of public funds—of a 'universal' system of education to enhance social mobility and allow the low born to 'rise in accordance with their abilities.' Providing such services to those 'not yet able to provide for themselves' was the vehicle through which 'many liberals' sought to reduce the social 'barriers' which 'tied individuals to the class into which they were born.'

For Chitester's benefit, 'von' Hayek (1978a) defended the 'civilisation' of Apartheid from the American 'fashion' of 'human rights' (Chapter 1); while questioning

> whether the too-rapid growth of civilization can be sustained–whether it will mean the revolt of our instincts against too much imposed restraints. This may destroy civilization and may be very counterproductive. But that man is capable of destroying the civilization which he has built up, by instincts and by rules which he feels to be restraints, is entirely a possibility.[11] Once you put it out that the market society does not satisfy our instincts, and once people become aware of this and are not *from childhood taught* (emphasis added) that these rules of the market are essential, of course we revolt against it.[12]

In *The Law of Power*, 'von' Wieser (1983 [1926], 38, 45) stated that 'traces of true leadership may be perceived only when the despot rallies the masses in order to have them *fight and work for himself* (emphasis added). When despotic leadership thus turns into *lordly leadership* (Wieser's emphasis), the function of leading the way is performed more efficaciously; compliance with the commands imposed by the lord on his subject is already genuine following ... Every truly active following by the masses must be borne by spiritual and moral forces—how else could a sense for law and ethics, true culture, and *a strong sense of liberty* (emphasis added) endure with the populace.'

After almost two-thirds of a century living as a common 'von' criminal, Hayek 'had the happiest day' of his life when Queen Elizabeth II gave him a 'decoration' (Leeson 2013, Chapter 9; Ebenstein 2003, 305). The defining trauma of Hayek's (1978a) life had been the 1919 abolition of his Second Estate entitlement programme by a 'republic of peasants and workers.'[13] Koestler (1950, 19) described some of the affected: 'Those who refused to admit that they had become déclassé, who clung to the empty shell of gentility, joined the Nazis and found comfort in blaming their fate on Versailles and the Jews.' At the University of Vienna, Othmar Spann—'The Philosopher of Fascism' (K. Polanyi 1934, 1935)—was the dominant influence over Hayek: in 1919, 'It's very curious; the man who drew my attention to Menger's [1871] book was Othmar Spann ... he drew my attention to Menger's book at a very early stage, and Menger's *Grundsetze*, probably more than any other book, influence me.'[14]

According to Hayek (1978a), this 'conception of the spontaneous generation of institutions is worked out more beautifully' in Menger's (1871) *Grundsetze* 'than in any other book I know.'[15] Wieser (1983 [1926], 293) described the 'spontaneous submission to the protection of the mighty one' (Chapter 2); and Hayek (1952 [1926], 555, 567) gushed about Wieser's (1983 [1926]) 'artistic creation':

> a fitting demonstration of the *general truth* (emphasis added) that a work which is carried by a great idea assumes the characteristics of a great piece of art. Having as its architect a sovereign master of science, it reaches a towering height above all indispensable detail and becomes related to artistic creation ... In him the civilization of old Austria had found its most perfect expression.

Like 'Deacon' McCormick, Hayek wrote in the language of 'faction'—a mixture of fact and fiction (or fraud). Yet economists don't *expect* to encounter beautiful, 'artistic creations' masquerading as scholarship. As 'an adult,' Hayek (1978a) 'went through the pleasure of learning to master a new language. And while my spoken English is not faultless, I pride myself– If I have time, I can write as good English as anyone. And to learn this and to see myself even in middle age constantly make progress in learning what is an art was a very enjoyable experience.'[16]

One of his disciples and Ph.D. students detected little or no interest in his students: Hayek was 'aristocratic,' seeking only to make 'money' from teaching (Raico 2013). For a 'long time,' Hayek's (1978a) 'ideal in the field, from whom I got my main general introduction to economics,' was Wieser, who 'floated high above the students as a sort of God.'[17] Armen Alchian (1978) told Hayek that the first time he heard him speak,

> you got up and gave a spontaneous lecture, and all I could say was, 'I don't know what he was saying, but how can he phrase that so beautifully, so elegantly?' You've always done that; that's a remarkable talent that

some have. How did you develop it, or was it just natural? Whatever natural may mean.

Hayek's *Sensory Order* is remembered by Richard Stern (the Helen A Regenstein Professor of English and American Literature at the University of Chicago): he 'looked unapproachable, haughty, as if he were sniffing something disagreeable in his mustache, although I didn't feel patronized by him' (cited by Ebenstein 2003, 180). Hayek's (1978a) 'present attempt is to say, yes, we rely on traditional instincts, but some of them mislead us and some not, and our great problem is how to select and how to restrain the bad ones.'[18] These 'instincts, of course, are the source of most of our pleasure in the whole field of art. There it's quite clear; but how you can *evoke this same sort of feeling* (emphasis added) by what comes essentially to these rules of conduct which are required to maintain this civilized society, I don't know.'[19]

The co-founder of the Ludwig von Mises Institute instinctively knows that 'Karl von Habsburg-Lothringen, Archduke of Austria, is the custodian of this civilization ... in European history, the Habsburg monarchy was a famed guardian of Western civilization. But even those of us devoted to the old [pre-1861?] American republic are aware of the warm and long relationship between the Austrian school and the House of Habsburg' (Rockwell cited by Palmer 1997).

At Brooklyn Polytechnic, Hayek's co-leader of the fourth-generation Austrian School

> occupied a small, grungy and windowless office that he had to share with a history professor. In Germany, even research assistants enjoyed more comfortable surroundings, not to speak of full professors ... my German National Science Foundation grant at the time - a Heisenberg scholarship - turned out to be considerably higher than Murray's university salary (something that I was too ashamed to reveal to him after I had discovered it). And Murray's apartment in Manhattan, large and filled to the ceiling with books, was dark and run-down. Certainly nothing like the penthouse that I had imagined him to occupy. (Hoppe 2017)

Murray Rothbard (1973) reported that:

> Mises's death takes away from us not only a deeply revered friend and mentor, but it tolls the bell for the end of an era: the last living mark of

that nobler, freer and far more civilized era of pre-1914 Europe. Mises's friends and students will know *instinctively* (emphasis added) what I mean: for when I think of Ludwig Mises I think first of all of those landmark occasions when I had the privilege of afternoon tea at the Mises's: in a small apartment that virtually breathed the atmosphere of a long lost and far more civilized era. The graciousness of Mises's devoted wife Margit; the precious volumes that were the remains of a superb home library destroyed by the Nazis; but above all Mises himself, spinning in his inimitable way anecdotes of Old Vienna, tales of scholars past and present, brilliant insights into economics, politics and social theory, and astute comments on the current scene.

Austrians promote high interest rates for deflationary purposes. They also blame high personal interest rates (time preferences) on personal deficiencies. But is poverty caused by high time preferences or should the causal sequence be reversed? Or some combination of the two?

'Free' market logic is that:

- If you offer a small boy one candy bar now or 10 tomorrow, he'll grab the one. That's because children have what economists call a 'high time preference.' They want it, and they want it now. The future is a haze. The punishing of children must take this into account. One good whack on the bottom can have an effect. A threat about no TV all next year will not ... street criminals, as economist Murray N. Rothbard points out, have the time preference of depraved infants. The prospect of a jail sentence 12 months from now has virtually no effect. (Rockwell 1991)

Therefore, the 'free' market requires an Austrian Police State with only notional controls on coercive power:

- Today's criminals know that they probably won't be convicted, and that if they are, they face a short sentence—someday ... Liberals talk about banning guns. As a libertarian, I can't agree. I am, however, beginning to wonder about video cameras. (Rockwell 1991)

Or as Rothbard (1992b) put it:
- **Take Back the Streets: Crush Criminals**. And by this I mean, of course, not 'white collar criminals' or 'inside traders' but violent

street criminals—robbers, muggers, rapists, murderers. Cops must be unleashed and allowed to administer instant punishment, subject of course to liability when they are in error. **Take Back the Streets: Get Rid of the Bums**. Again, unleash the cops to clear the streets of bums and vagrants. Where will they go? Who cares? Hopefully, they will disappear, that is, move from the ranks of the petted and cosseted bum class to the ranks of the productive members of society. (Rothbard's bold)

During a famine, the supply of pogroms increases (Anderson et al. 2017); and many of the starving will fall off the neoclassical demand curve for food. And in the 'free' market, many low-income parents would fall off the neoclassical demand curve for their children's education—allowing ascribed status to become intergenerational.

Mises (1985 [1927], 115) provided the intellectual foundations of *Liberalism in the [Austrian] Classical Liberalism*: 'There is, in fact, only one solution: the state, the government, the laws must not in any way concern themselves with schooling or education. Public funds must not be used for such purposes. The rearing and instruction of youth must be left entirely to parents and to private associations and institutions. It is better that a number of boys grow up without formal education than that they enjoy the benefit of schooling only to run the risk, once they have grown up, of being killed or maimed. A healthy illiterate is always better than a literate cripple.' Salazar provided the practical foundations: in the mid-twentieth century, half of Portuguese homes had running water and 30% had electricity. Illiteracy was widespread. Even after joining the European Union, Portugal failed to catch up with respect to human capital formation: according to figures from the Organisation for Economic Cooperation and Development, in 2009, only 30% of Portuguese adults had completed high school or its equivalent (Sayare 2012).

Margit Mises (1984, 58–59) sympathetically described the resulting neo-feudal spontaneous order: there was 'great poverty' in Lisbon (the most 'picturesque' city she had ever seen) and, in consequence, there were 'many, many children' trying to earn a living, 'often begging for money' and riding for free by hanging on to the boards of the tram—which Margit interpreted as a 'game.' The 'poorer' women—fish-venters—were either pregnant or carried a baby (none had prams) and were unbelievably 'modest,' and their 'needs were few.'

In his *Memoirs*, Mises (2009 [1978 (1940)], 116) rectified history: 'Because I could no longer bear living in a country that considered my presence a political burden and a threat to its security, I left the Institut in July of 1940.' When Hitler invaded the Netherlands (10 May 1940), Mises exclaimed in his notebook 'Belgium! Holland!' A month later, Mises exclaimed again: 'Paris!' (14 June) 'Armistice!' (17 June). Later, Mises reported that May 1940 was the 'most disastrous' month in European history (Hülsmann 2007, 750–751).

Margit (1984, 54) corrected Mises: on 10 May 1940, she 'really became frightened' and 'had to talk' to her husband. But Mises did 'not want to leave.' Margit 'begged him, I implored him to leave, to think of me, if he would not think of himself.' Finally, Mises 'gave in' and promised to make the necessary preparations to leave for the USA: 'In his heart, of course,' Mises was 'reluctant' to leave not only because the Graduate Institute of International Studies in Geneva was his only-ever full-time academic job but also because he 'feared' how he would be received in America, the home of 'young people, the paradise of youth.' Mises was 'afraid' of the language difference—the prospect of having to speak English meant more to him than it would to an 'average' citizen. Language was his most important tool, his essential mechanism for communicating his knowledge and his source of income.

The hearts of the first Pretenders, Charles I and Zita, are buried in the family crypt in Muri Abbey, near Basel, Switzerland. Zita's (1892–1989) body was allowed to be buried in the 'Imperial Crypt' in Vienna, while Charles's (1887–1922) body is buried on the Portuguese Island of Madeira. Mises (1881–1973) appeared to have become reconciled to staying in 'Fascist' Portugal: they had to wait for 13 days in Lisbon before obtaining a passage to America. Mises got 'so tired of this begging and asking, he refused to go any more.' Margit 'had to take over.' Yet Mises was acclimatising himself to the capital. When they went out, they took public transport and crisscrossed the town: the 'only' way to really get to know a place. While Margit continued to search for a passage to America, her husband made 'no further move.'[20]

In *The Anti-capitalist Mentality*, Mises (1956, 19–20) contrasted European 'society' with its American non-equivalent:

> Access to European society is open to everybody who has distinguished himself in any field. It may be easier to people of noble ancestry and great wealth than to commoners with modest incomes. But neither riches nor

titles can give to a member of this set the rank and prestige that is the reward of great personal distinction. The stars of the Parisian salons are not the millionaires, but the members of the *Académie Française*. The intellectuals prevail and the others feign at least a lively interest in intellectual concerns ... Society in this sense is foreign to the American scene. What is called 'society' in the United States almost exclusively consists of the richest families. There is little social intercourse between the successful businessmen and the nation's eminent authors, artists, and scientists. Those listed in the Social Register do not meet socially the molders of public opinion and the harbingers of the ideas that will determine the future of the nation. Most of the 'socialites' are not interested in books and ideas. When they meet and do not play cards, they gossip about persons and talk more about sports than about cultural matters. But even those who are not averse to reading, consider writers, scientists and artists as people with whom they do not want to consort. An almost unsurmountable gulf separates 'society' from the intellectuals.

Hayek (1978a) detected that in Britain, 'very sharp' class distinctions are 'not resented. [laughter] They're still accepted as part of the natural order.'[21] In 1923–1924, Hayek found America 'extremely stimulating and even knew I could have started on in an assistantship or something for an economic career, I didn't want to. I still was too much a European and didn't the least feel that I belonged to this society.'[22]

Four years before fleeing to America, Mises (January 1936) expressed his contempt for the New World—telling Machlup that he hoped that he would 'not become American over there.' Instead, Machlup should become a missionary: 'convert the Americans to liberalism and Austrianism. They need it indeed.' According to *The Last Knight of Liberalism*, the contemporary American intellectual world was 'deeply anti-capitalistic.' How could Mises 'integrate himself into such an environment'? (Hülsmann 2007, 699, 790). In 1940, the first year in New York was 'not a happy memory' for Margit (1984, 63): Mises' 'spirits were at a low point':

> Very often he would say: 'If it were not for you, I would not want to live any more.'

In New York, Mises (2009 [1978 (1940)]) wrote the *Memoirs* that he later denied having written (Rothbard 2005 [1978]). According to Hülsmann (2009, x–xi), they were a 'balance sheet' of his 'achievements in the Old World,' written in the style of a 'testament,' at the 'absolute low point' of his life. Margit Mises (1984, 10, 63) reported that the post-war inflation 'consumed' the value of all savings; and in New York in 1940, they had to live from Mises' savings, and to see his 'money dwindle is a sad sight for an economist.'

Post-war hyperinflation devastated Austria (October 1921–September 1922) and Germany (June 1921–January 1924). But then for a short period before the policy-induced deflation of the Great Depression (1929-), democracy appeared to be taking root.[23]

According to Ebeling (2006), in 'late 1922 and early 1923 the Great Austrian Inflation was brought to a halt.' But according to Mises (2009 [1978 (1940)], 64), Austria 'had to bear the destructive consequences of continuing inflation for many years' after inflation ended: 'Its banking, credit, and insurance systems had suffered wounds that could no longer heal, and no halt could be put to the consumption of capital. We met with too much resistance. Our victory had come too late. It had postponed the collapse by many years, but it could no longer save Austria.' Wilhelm 'Rosenberg and I suffered no illusions on this matter. We knew the truth surrounding the restoration. My friend succumbed to the pessimism borne of hopelessness, the lot of all enlightened Austrians. It was not only the grief of having lost his only son, but the knowledge of the futility of his toils in Vienna that drove him to his death.'

Mises (2003 [1969], 17), who appeared in his 1940-written *Memoirs* to be justifying his own planned suicide, projected his own depressive tendencies onto 'all sharp-sighted Austrians ... The tragic privilege attached to being Austrian was the opportunity it afforded to *recognize fate* (emphasis added).' For Mises, 'evidence' had to be rectified: he arrived in New York aged 58; Dr. Wilhelm Rosenberg, the Vice President of the Anglo-Austrian Bank, died on 3 April 1923, aged 53; and his son, Franz, had died on 17 January 1921 in Paris, Île-de-France, France.[24]

In Portugal, 'von' Mises and his wife were staying at a 'beautifully' located hotel on the coast. They frequently met the Habsburg 'Count' and President of the Paneuropean Union, Richard Coudenhove-Kalergi; another regular contact was Professor M. Bensabat Amzalek, the Portuguese Minister of Finance, who arranged for Mises to meet Salazar (Margit Mises 1984, 58, 60). According to the archival evidence uncovered by Antonio Louca (a Portuguese journalist and historian) and Isabelle Paccaud (a Swiss historian), Amzalek, the 'leader of the Jewish community in Portugal was a supporter of Nazi Germany, and the authorities of the Third Reich honored him with a medal of excellence.' Amzalak was a 'friend and supporter' of Salazar and 'like him … believed that the Nazis were defending Europe from communism. Amzalak had a newspaper, O Seculo, which gave the Nazis sympathetic coverage' (Segev 2007).

On 15 July 1940, a friend drove Mises and his wife to Cascais to show them the Devil's Mouth (a visually impressive gorge leading to the Atlantic Ocean) where the Duke of Windsor, the Duke of Luxembourg and President Salazar had their 'beautiful' houses with 'most luxurious' tropical gardens. Mises held a seminar at the statistical office and was permanently 'busy' (Margit Mises 1984, 60). The Windsors stayed in the villa of Ricardo do Espírito Santo Silva, a banker believed to have pro-Nazi sympathies. In post-'Fascist' Portugal, the bank was nationalised (under a Decree Law of 1975) and the Espírito Santo family was prevented from doing business in Portugal (Block 1984, Prologue).

The Duke of Luxembourg was Prince Félix of Luxembourg (1893–1970), the younger brother of Empress Zita of Austria, the wife of Charles I, and thus the Habsburg Pretender's uncle. Richard Nikolaus Eijiro, the Habsburg Count of Coudenhove-Kalergi (1894–1972), was the founding President of the Paneuropean Union of which Otto was Vice President (Teacher 2018a). The Duke of Windsor (1894–1972), the abdicated Edward VIII, famously encouraged the future Queen Elisabeth to give a Nazi salute and reportedly sought to be reinstated as King after the Austro-German conquest of Britain (Leeson 2018).

According to Michael Block's (1984, Chapter 11) *Operation Willi: The Plot to Kidnap the Duke of Windsor, July 1940*, the German Ambassador to Madrid (Eberhard von Stohrer), the German Minister to Lisbon (Baron Oswald von Hoyningen-Huene) and Hitler's Foreign Minister (Joachim von Ribbentrop) were involved in an SS plot to kidnap Edward as a possible prelude to his becoming King of Nazi-controlled Britain. Walter Monckton arrived in Cascais on 28 July 1940 to forestall the kidnap.

Those members of Rose Friedman's family who had not emigrated 'all died in the Holocaust. We have never learned where or how.' In 1950, while Milton worked on the Schuman Plan, Rose experienced trauma: it was very difficult for her to let their two children 'run freely as they were accustomed to do at home because always there was the nagging fear that they might suddenly disappear. Of course I knew that they would no Nazis in the park that somehow there was always in my subconsciousness those terrible stories about what happened to Jewish children during the

Nazi era. That trip to Germany haunted me for many years' (Friedman and Friedman 1998, 3, 180).

For some time after his arrival in the New World, even his closet associates addressed him with the 'deferential' 'Professor' Mises. And Mises and Hayek continued to refer to the pinnacle of their neo-feudal order as 'His Majesty, Kaiser Otto' and 'Imperial Highness' (Hülsmann 2007, 829, 818). The first Austrian School revivalist conference met in 1974 in Royalston, Vermont, where one of the highlights was the baiting of Milton and Rose Friedman—in person—with the accusation that their son, David, detected 'latent fascist tendencies' in his father (Ebeling 1974): 'Murray Rothbard made the whole affair fun' (Shenoy 2003).

'La Bastille,' in another Royalston, had a

> most famous guest, the aforementioned Empress Zita, the last Empress of Austria, the last Queen of Hungary and the last Queen of Bohemia … Zita and her brood were 'Europe's most distinguished refugees,' said *Life* magazine in December 1940. 'But up in Royalston, Massachusetts,' said the *South Amboy Citizen* newspaper that same month, 'only a low white fence of wooden palings separates the last of the great Habsburg families from the world.'[25]

Wallis Simpson (1956, 19, 14, 210) described her fairy tale rise from a 'proud southern family' with 'little money' to wife of the Duke of Windsor. Despite her limitations—'no one has ever accused me of being intellectual'—she was aware that 'Waltzes (even of Viennese perfection) and gypsy music (even of Hungarian wildness) can hardly be considered the sturdiest handmaidens of reality; rather they are the stuff dreams are made on and from which illusions spring.'

Vienna is the 'City of Dreams' (Leonard 2011), and opponents are *Dupes* of Moscow (Kengor 2010) to Hayek's (1978a) 'intellectuals.' Hayek explained that these 'secondhand dealers in ideas' were for 'some reason or other … are probably more subject to waves of fashion in ideas and more influential in the American sense than they are elsewhere.'[26] Hayek received an anonymous letter (23 July 1975) which explained that for participants in the second Austrian School revivalist conference (June 1975),

> spiritually and intellectually Vienna will always be our home: and we will always return to the charge against the forces of macro-darkness now threatening to overwhelm the world, carrying aloft the intellectual flag of Austria-Hungary … we still love you: and we feel that by continued

association with us, we may yet show you the light and truth of anarcho-Hayekianism ... And so, ladies and gentlemen, I give you two toasts to victory in the future, and to the best legacy of Vienna to the world, Professor Hayek (emphases in original).[27]

Referring to the author of these remarks, as the 'Joan Robinson of the Vienna School,' who had 'summed up' the 'sentiments of all participants,' Ebeling (1975, 7)—Caldwell's pick to edit the tax-exempt *Collected Works of F.A. Hayek: Hayek and the Austrian Economists: Correspondence and Related Documents*—quoted Shenoy's muddled Hegelianism: the new generation of Austrians 'shall do all that is in our power to ensure that the economic mind of the age does move with relentless logic, with consistent consistency to the priori conclusions of the Austrian system.' Ebeling then deleted Shenoy's promise about 'carrying aloft the intellectual flag of Austria-Hungary ... spiritually and intellectually Vienna will always be our home.' But the 1975 Hillsdale College MPS meeting, Roche III toasted the British monarch (Wheeler 1975); and the 1976 Austrian revivalist conference was held in St. George's House, Windsor Castle.[28]

Hayek's (1992 [1977]) 'only hope really is that some minor country or countries which for different reasons will have to construct a new constitution will do so along sensible lines and will be so successful that the others find it in their interest to imitate it. I do not think that countries that are rather proud of their constitutions will ever really need to experiment with changes in it. The reform may come from, say, Spain, which has to choose a new constitution. It might be prepared to adopt a sensible one. I don't think its really likely in Spain, but it's an example. And they may prove so successful that after all it is seen that there are better ways of organizing government than we have.'

After Hitler's suicide, 'Fascism' in Europe—as defined and praised by Mises—survived only in Spain and Portugal. For public consumption, Franco announced 'I PLAN DEMOCRACY, FREE PRESS, ELECTIONS' (*Sunday Chronicle* 17 June 1945).[29] But Otto revealed that Franco had invited him to 'resume' the Spanish Crown; Franco was a 'dictator of the South American type ... not totalitarian like Hitler or Stalin.' Shortly after the end of World War II, Somary informed Otto that 'Aristocracy has to begin somewhere,' and—pointing to some westward bound 'unkempt' train passengers (some presumably refugees)—added: 'These are going to be our overlords in the future.' But Otto had hope: 'There is an extraordinary revival of religion in France … I never would have thought one could dare to say in France what [Nikolas] Sarkozy is saying – that the separation of church and state in France is wrong.' To the Habsburg Pretender, political aristocrats, like the Kennedy and Bush dynasties, were acceptable: 'It isn't bad for a country to have people with a certain tradition, where the father gives the son the same outlook and training' (Watters 2005; Morgan 2011).

According to David Rockefeller (2002, 413), 'von' Habsburg remained an unabashed 'claimant to all the lands of the Austro-Hungarian empire.' Like Rockefeller, Otto was a prominent participant in the post-war 'International Right' (Teacher 2018a). After the fall of the Berlin Wall, 'many' of the 400-strong 'Von Habsburg clan have staked claims to properties previously confiscated by the Communists' (Watters 2005; Morgan 2011).[30]

Notes

1. Hayek's (1976a) full reply was: 'In peaceful economic competition, the totalitarian states—whether leftist or right-wing—simply cannot win. But there is a danger. Dictatorships can exploit the situation to prepare secretly for a military conflict at a time that suits them best—when they have an initial advantage over their capitalist enemies.' Before being reached-out to by Chilean Hayekians, was he implying that Pinochet's Chile was a totalitarian state?
2. '*La inflación es la mayor amenaza contra la libertad*.'
3. The President of the Canberra branch at the time was Chris Higgins, later Secretary of the Australian Treasury.
4. Friedrich Hayek, interviewed by James Buchanan 28 October 1978 (Centre for Oral History Research, University of California, Los Angeles, http://oralhistory.library.ucla.edu/).
5. Friedrich Hayek, interviewed by Earlene Craver date unspecified 1978 (Centre for Oral History Research, University of California, Los Angeles, http://oralhistory.library.ucla.edu/).
6. Friedrich Hayek, interviewed by Leo Rosten 15 November 1978 (Centre for Oral History Research, University of California, Los Angeles, http://oralhistory.library.ucla.edu/).
7. This states: 'No title of nobility shall be granted by the United States: and no person holding any office of profit or trust under them, shall, without the consent of the Congress, accept of any present, emolument, office, or title, of any kind whatever, from any king, prince, or foreign state.'

8. http://press-pubs.uchicago.edu/founders/documents/a1_9_8s2.html.
9. http://mises.org/books/paine2.pdf.
10. https://nces.ed.gov/naal/lit_history.asp.
11. Friedrich Hayek, interviewed by Robert Chitester date unspecified 1978 (Centre for Oral History Research, University of California, Los Angeles, http://oralhistory.library.ucla.edu/).
12. Friedrich Hayek, interviewed by Leo Rosten 15 November 1978 (Centre for Oral History Research, University of California, Los Angeles, http://oralhistory.library.ucla.edu/).
13. Friedrich Hayek, interviewed by Robert Chitester date unspecified 1978 (Centre for Oral History Research, University of California, Los Angeles, http://oralhistory.library.ucla.edu/).
14. Friedrich Hayek, interviewed by Armen Alchian 11 November 1978 (Centre for Oral History Research, University of California, Los Angeles, http://oralhistory.library.ucla.edu/).
15. Friedrich Hayek, interviewed by James Buchanan 28 October 1978 (Centre for Oral History Research, University of California, Los Angeles, http://oralhistory.library.ucla.edu/).
16. Friedrich Hayek, interviewed by Robert Chitester date unspecified 1978 (Centre for Oral History Research, University of California, Los Angeles, http://oralhistory.library.ucla.edu/).
17. Friedrich Hayek, interviewed by Earlene Craver date unspecified 1978 (Centre for Oral History Research, University of California, Los Angeles, http://oralhistory.library.ucla.edu/).
18. Friedrich Hayek, interviewed by James Buchanan 28 October 1978 (Centre for Oral History Research, University of California, Los Angeles, http://oralhistory.library.ucla.edu/).
19. Friedrich Hayek, interviewed by Robert Chitester date unspecified 1978 (Centre for Oral History Research, University of California, Los Angeles, http://oralhistory.library.ucla.edu/).
20. Mises may have been apprehensive about having to perjure himself by answering 'No' to US immigration questions such as 'Have you committed, ordered, incited, assisted, or otherwise participated in extrajudicial killings, political killings, or other acts of violence?'
21. Friedrich Hayek, interviewed by Leo Rosten 15 November 1978 (Centre for Oral History Research, University of California, Los Angeles, http://oralhistory.library.ucla.edu/).
22. Friedrich Hayek, interviewed by Earlene Craver date unspecified 1978 (Centre for Oral History Research, University of California, Los Angeles, http://oralhistory.library.ucla.edu/).

23. Friedrich Hayek, interviewed by Robert Chitester date unspecified 1978 (Centre for Oral History Research, University of California, Los Angeles, http://oralhistory.library.ucla.edu/).
24. https://www.geni.com/people/Dr-Wilhelm-Rosenberg/6000000013020100907.
25. http://www.nehomemag.com/article/all-calm.
26. Friedrich Hayek, interviewed by Robert Chitester date unspecified 1978 (Centre for Oral History Research, University of California, Los Angeles, http://oralhistory.library.ucla.edu/).
27. Hayek Archives Box 26.28.
28. Hayek Archives Box 163.5.
29. Hayek Archives Box 107.4.
30. Habsburg continued: Sarkozy 'points out that a state which subsidizes football clubs and refuses to do any economic favors to religions who want to build churches is absurd.'

REFERENCES

Archival Insights into the Evolution of Economics (and Related Projects)

Cristi, R. (2017). The Genealogy of Jaime Guzman's Subsidiary State. In R. Leeson (Ed.), *Hayek: A Collaborative Biography Part IX: The Divine Right of the 'Free' Market*. Basingstoke, UK: Palgrave Macmillan.

Filip, B. (2018). Hayek on Limited Democracy, Dictatorships and the Free-Market Economy: An Interview in Argentina in 1977. In R. Leeson (Ed.), *Hayek: A Collaborative Biography Part XIII: 'Fascism' and Liberalism in the (Austrian) Classical Tradition*. Basingstoke, UK: Palgrave Macmillan.

Leeson R. (Ed.). (2013). *Hayek: A Collaborative Biography Part I Influences From Mises to Bartley*. Basingstoke, UK: Palgrave Macmillan.

Leeson, R. (2018). *Hayek: A Collaborative Biography Part VIII: The Constitution of Liberty: 'Shooting in Cold Blood' Hayek's Plan for the Future of Democracy*. Basingstoke, UK: Palgrave Macmillan.

Teacher, D. (2018a). 'Neutral Academic Data' and the International Right. In R. Leeson (Ed.), *Hayek: A Collaborative Biography Part XIII 'Fascism' and Liberalism in the (Austrian) Classical Tradition*. Basingstoke, UK: Palgrave Macmillan.

Teacher, D. (2018b). Private Club and Secret Service Armageddon. In R. Leeson (Ed.), *Hayek: A Collaborative Biography Part XIII 'Fascism' and Liberalism in the (Austrian) Classical Tradition*. Basingstoke, UK: Palgrave Macmillan.

Other References

Alchian, A. (1978). In F. A. Hayek, *Oral History Interviews*. Centre for Oral History Research, University of California, Los Angeles. http://oralhistory.library.ucla.edu/.

Anderson, R. W., Johnson, N. D., & Koyama, N. (2017). Jewish Persecutions and Weather Shocks: 1100–1800. *Economic Journal, 127*(602), 924–958.

Block, M. (1984). *Operation Willi: The Plot to Kidnap the Duke of Windsor, July 1940*. London: Little, Brown.

Buchanan, J. (1992). I Did Not Call Him 'Fritz': Personal Recollections of Professor F. A. v. Hayek. *Constitutional Political Economy, 3*(2), 129–135.

Caldwell, B. (1995). Editorial Notes. In B. Caldwell (Ed.), *Contra Keynes and Cambridge. The Collected Works of F.A. Hayek*. Chicago: University of Chicago Press.

Crozier, B. (1967). *Franco*. London: Eyre and Spottiswoode.

Ebeling, R. M. (1974, October). Austrian Economics on the Rise. *Libertarian Forum*. http://mises.org/daily/4174.

Ebeling, R. M. (1975, July). The Second Austrian Conference. *Libertarian Forum*, Vol. VII, No. 7, pp. 4–8. http://rothbard.altervista.org/articles/libertarian-forum/lf-7-7.pdf.

Ebeling, R. M. (2006, April 1). *The Great Austrian Inflation*. Foundation for Economic Education. https://fee.org/articles/the-great-austrian-inflation/.

Ebeling, R. M. (2016, May 9). Setting the Record Straight: How Stalin Used Hitler To Start World War II. *Future of Freedom Foundation*. https://www.fff.org/explore-freedom/article/setting-record-straight-stalin-used-hitler-start-world-war-ii/.

Ebenstein, A. (2003). *Friedrich Hayek: A Biography*. Chicago: University of Chicago Press.

Farrant, A., McPhail, E., & Berger, S. (2012). Preventing the "Abuses" of Democracy: Hayek, the "Military Usurper" and Transitional Dictatorship in Chile? *American Journal of Economics and Sociology, 71*(3), 513–538.

Friedman, M. F., & Friedman, R. D. (1998). *Two Lucky People: Memoirs*. Chicago: University of Chicago Press.

Hayek, F. A. (1952 [1926]). Hayek on Wieser. In H. W. Spiegel (Ed.), *The Development of Economic Thought*. New York: Wiley.

Hayek, F. A. (1975). *A Discussion with Friedrich von Hayek*. Washington: American Enterprise Institute. https://www.aei.org/wp-content/uploads/2017/03/Discussion-with-Friedrich-von-Hayek-text.pdf.

Hayek, F. A. (1976a, March 18). Institutions May Fail, but Democracy Survives. *US News and World Report* (Hayek Archives Box 109.4).

Hayek, F. A. (1976b). *Socialism and Science*. Economic Society of Australia and New Zealand, Canberra Branch.

Hayek, F. A. (1977, November 25). La inflación es la mayor amenaza contra la libertad. *Somos* (Hayek Archives Box 109.17).
Hayek, F. A. (1978a). *Oral History Interviews*. Centre for Oral History Research, University of California, Los Angeles. http://oralhistory.library.ucla.edu/.
Hayek, F. A. (1978b). *New Studies in Philosophy, Politics, Economics and the History of Ideas*. London: Routledge & Kegan Paul.
Hayek, F. A. (1979, December 5). A Period of Muddle-Heads. *Newsweek*.
Hayek, F. A. (1992 [1977], July). The Road from Serfdom. *Reason*. http://reason.com/archives/1992/07/01/the-road-from-serfdom/5.
Hayek, F. A. (1995). *Contra Keynes and Cambridge. The Collected Works of F.A. Hayek* (B. Caldwell, Ed.). Chicago: University of Chicago Press.
Hayek, F. A. (2011 [1960]). *The Constitution of Liberty. The Definitive Edition. The Collected Works of F.A. Hayek* (R. Hamowy, Ed.). Chicago: University of Chicago Press.
Holcombe, R. (1998, Summer). Markets and the Quality of Life an Interview with Randall Holcombe. *Austrian Economics Newsletter*. https://mises.org/library/markets-and-quality-life-interview-randall-g-holcombe.
Hoppe, H.-H. (2017, October 7). *Coming of Age with Murray*. Mises Institute's 35th Anniversary Celebration in New York City. https://mises.org/library/coming-age-murray-0.
Hülsmann, J. G. (2007). *Mises: The Last Knight of Liberalism*. Auburn, AL: Ludwig von Mises Institute.
Hülsmann, J. G. (2008). *Ethics of Money Production*. Auburn, AL: Ludwig von Mises Institute.
Hülsmann, J. G. (2009). Preface. In L. Mises (Ed.), *Memoirs*. Auburn, AL: Ludwig von Mises Institute.
Jefferson, T. (1786, August 13). *Letter to George Wythe*. http://www.let.rug.nl/usa/presidents/thomas-jefferson/letters-of-thomas-jefferson/jefl47.php.
Kaza, G. (2013). Mises and the Struggle Against Italian Fascism in World War II. Austrian Economics Research Conference.
Kengor, P. (2010). *Dupes: How America's Adversaries Have Manipulated Progressives for a Century*. Intercollegiate Studies Institute.
Koch, C. (1978, August). The Business Community: Resisting Regulation. *Libertarian Review*, 7(7), 30–34. https://www.libertarianism.org/lr/LR788.pdf.
Koestler, A. (1950). Arthur Koestler. In R. Crossman (Ed.), *Communism: The God that Failed*. New York: Harper and Row.
Koether, G. (2000). A Life Among Austrians. *Austrian Economics Newsletter*, 20(3). https://mises.org/system/tdf/aen20_3_1_0.pdf?file=1&type=document.
Leonard, R. (2011). The Collapse of Interwar Vienna: Oskar Morgenstern's Community, 1925–50. *History of Political Economy*, 43(1), 83–130.

McCormick, D. (1976). *Taken for a Ride: The History of Cons and Con-men*. London: Hardwood Smart.

Menger, C. (1871). *Grundsätze der Volkswirtschaftslehre*. Wien: Erster allgemeiner Teil.

Mises, L. (1951 [1932]). *Socialism: An Economic and Sociological Analysis* (J. Kahane, Trans.). New Haven: Yale University Press.

Mises, L. (1956). *The Anti-capitalist Mentality*. Canada: D. Van Nostrand Company Inc.

Mises, L. (1985 [1927]). *Liberalism in the Classical Tradition* (R. Raico, Trans.) Auburn, AL: Mises Institute.

Mises, L. (2003 [1969]). *The Historical Setting of the Austrian School of Economics*. Auburn, AL: Ludwig von Mises Institute.

Mises, L. (2009 [1978 (1940)]). *Memoirs*. Auburn, AL: Ludwig von Mises Institute.

Mises, M. (1984). *My Years with Ludwig von Mises* (2nd ed.). Cedar Falls, IA: Center for Futures Education.

Morgan, L. (2011, July 18). End of a Royal Dynasty as Otto von Habsburg is Laid to Rest… with His Heart Buried in a Crypt 85 Miles Away. *MailOnline*.

Nayaka, J. P., & Nurullah, S. (1974). *A Students' History of Education in India (1800–1973)* (6th ed.). New York: Macmillan.

Okon, H. (1997). Austrian Economics in Japan: An Interview with Hiroyuki Okon. *Austrian Economic Newsletter, 17*(4). https://mises.org/library/austrian-economics-japan-interview-hiroyuki-okon.

Paine, T. (2000 [1775]). Reflections on Titles. In P. B. Kurland & R. Lerner (Eds.), *The Founders' Constitution*. Chicago: University of Chicago Press. http://press-pubs.uchicago.edu/founders/.

Palmer, T. (1997, September). Lew Rockwell's Vienna Waltz. *Liberty*. http://web.archive.org/web/20050318091128/http://www.libertysoft.com/liberty/features/61palmer.html.

Polanyi, K. (1934). Othmar Spann: The Philosopher of Fascism. *New Britain, 3*(53), 6–7.

Polanyi, K. (1935). The Essence of Fascism. In D. Lewis, K. Polanyi, & J. Kitchen (Eds.), *Christianity and the Social Revolution*. London: Gollancz.

Preston, P. (2012). *The Spanish Holocaust Inquisition and Extermination in Twentieth-Century Spain*. New York: W. W. Norton.

Raico, R. (2013, February 20). *An Interview with Ralph Raico*. Mises Institute. https://mises.org/library/interview-ralph-raico-0.

Richards, M. (1998). *A Time of Silence: Civil War and the Culture of Repression in Franco's Spain, 1936–1945*. Cambridge: Cambridge University Press.

Rockefeller, D. (2002). *Memoirs*. New York: Random House.

Rockwell, L. H., Jr. (1991, March 10). COLUMN RIGHT: It's Safe Streets Versus Urban Terror: In the '50s, Rampant Crime Didn't Exist Because Offenders Feared What the Police Would Do. *Los Angeles Times*.

Rothbard, M. N. (1973, October 20). Ludwig von Mises 1881–1973. *Human Events*, 7.
Rothbard, M. N. (1992, January). Right-Wing Populism: A Strategy for the Paleo Movement. *Rothbard Rockwell Report*, 5–14. http://rothbard.altervista.org/articles/right-wing-populism.pdf.
Rothbard, M. N. (2002 [1982]). *The Ethics of Liberty*. Auburn, AL: Ludwig von Mises Institute.
Rothbard, M. N. (2005 [1978]). *The Mises We Never Knew*. https://mises.org/library/mises-we-never-knew-0.
Sayare, S. (2012, June 7). Portuguese Just Shrug and Go on in the Face of Cuts and Job Losses. *New York Times*. http://www.nytimes.com/2012/06/08/world/europe/portugal-shrugs-at-austerity.html?pagewanted=all&_r=0.
Segev, T. (2007, November 29). How We Missed Out on the Swiss Option A last-minute Arab proposal in 1947/The Portuguese Jew Who Supported the Nazis/The Death of an Austrian Jew 90 Years Ago. *Haaretz*. http://www.haaretz.com/israel-news/how-we-missed-out-on-the-swiss-option-1.234249.
Shenoy, S. (2003, Winter). An Interview with Sudha Shenoy. *Austrian Economics Newsletter*, 1–8. http://mises.org/journals/aen/aen23_4_1.pdf.
Simpson, B. W. (1956). *The Heart Has Its Reasons the Memoirs of the Duchess of Windsor*. London: Michael Joseph.
Skousen, M. (1991). *Economics on Trial: Lies, Myths and Realities*. Homewood, IL: Business One Irwin.
Snyder, L. L. (Ed.). (1982). *Hitler's Third Reich: A Documentary History*. Chicago: Nelson-Hall.
Taylor, A. J. P. (1964). *The Habsburg Monarchy 1809–1918: A History of the Austrian Empire and Austria Hungary*. UK: Peregrine.
Watters, S. (2005, June 28). Von Habsburg on Presidents, Monarchs, Dictators. *Women's Wear Daily*. http://www.wwd.com/eye/people/von-habsburg-on-presidents-monarchs-dictators.
Weber, M. (1995, May–June). Murray Rothbard (1926–1995). *The Journal of Historical Review*, 15(3), 33–34.
Wheeler, T. (1975, September 26). Mont Pelerin Society: Microeconomics, Macrofellowship. *National Review*.
Wieser, F. (1983 [1926]). *The Law of Power*. Lincoln: University of Nebraska–Lincoln, Bureau of Business Research.

Bibliography

Archival Insights into the Evolution of Economics (and Related Projects)

Champion, R. (2015). Hayek in Australia. In R. Leeson (Ed.), *Hayek: A Collaborative Biography: Part V Hayek's Great Society of Free Men*. Basingstoke, UK: Palgrave Macmillan.

Cristi, R. (2017). The Genealogy of Jaime Guzman's Subsidiary State. In R. Leeson (Ed.), *Hayek: A Collaborative Biography Part IX: The Divine Right of the 'Free' Market*. Basingstoke, UK: Palgrave Macmillan.

Farrant, A., & McPhail, E. (2017). Hayek, Thatcher, and the Muddle of the Middle. In R. Leeson (Ed.), *Hayek: A Collaborative Biography Part IX: The Divine Right of the 'Free' Market*. Basingstoke, UK: Palgrave Macmillan.

Filip, B. (2018a). Hayek on Limited Democracy, Dictatorships and the Free-Market Economy: An Interview in Argentina in 1977. In R. Leeson (Ed.), *Hayek: A Collaborative Biography Part XIII: 'Fascism' and Liberalism in the (Austrian) Classical Tradition*. Basingstoke, UK: Palgrave Macmillan.

Filip, B. (2018b). Hayek and Popper on Piecemeal Engineering and Ordo-Liberalism. In R. Leeson (Ed.), *Hayek: A Collaborative Biography Part XIV: Liberalism in the Classical Tradition: Orwell, Popper, Humboldt and Polanyi*. Basingstoke, UK: Palgrave Macmillan.

Friedman, M. F. (2017 [1991]). Say 'No' to Intolerance. In R. Leeson & C. Palm (Eds.), *Milton Friedman on Freedom*. Stanford, CA: Hoover Press.

Goldschmidt, N., & Hesse, J.-O. (2013). Eucken, Hayek, and The Road to Serfdom. In R. Leeson (Ed.), *Hayek: A Collaborative Biography Part II Influences, from Mises to Bartley*. Basingstoke, UK: Palgrave Macmillan.

Haiduk, K. (2015). Hayek and Coase Travel East: Privatization and the Experience of Post-socialist Economic Transformation. In R. Leeson (Ed.), *Hayek: A Collaborative Biography Part VI Good Dictators, Sovereign Producers and Hayek's 'Ruthless Consistency'*. Basingstoke, UK: Palgrave Macmillan.

Jackson, B. (2015). Hayek, Hutt and the Trade Unions. In R. Leeson (Ed.), *Hayek: A Collaborative Biography: Part V Hayek's Great Society of Free Men*. Basingstoke, UK: Palgrave Macmillan.

Jenks, J. (2015). Authoritative Sources: The Information Research Department, Journalism and Publishing. In R. Leeson (Ed.), *Hayek: A Collaborative Biography Part III Fraud, Fascism and Free Market Religion*. Basingstoke, UK: Palgrave Macmillan.

Kimberley, H. (2015). 'Deacon' McCormick and the Madoc Myth. In R. Leeson (Ed.), *Hayek: A Collaborative Biography Part III Fraud, Fascism and Free Market Religion*. Basingstoke, UK: Palgrave Macmillan.

Lane, M. (2013). The Genesis and Reception of The Road to Serfdom. In R. Leeson (Ed.), *Hayek: A Collaborative Biography Part I Influences from Mises to Bartley*. Basingstoke, UK: Palgrave Macmillan.

Leeson, R. (1994a, May). A.W.H. Phillips, M.B.E. (Military Division). *Economic Journal, 104*(424), 605–618.

Leeson, R. (1994b, November). A.W.H. Phillips, Inflationary Expectations and the Operating Characteristics of the Macroeconomy. *Economic Journal, 104*(427), 1420–1421.

Leeson, R. (1997a, February). The Trade-Off Interpretation of Phillips' Dynamic Stabilisation Exercise. *Economica, 64*(253), 155–173.

Leeson, R. (1997b). The Political Economy of the Inflation Unemployment Trade-Off. *History of Political Economy, 29*(1), 117–156.

Leeson, R. (1997c). The Eclipse of the Goal of Zero Inflation. *History of Political Economy, 29*(3), 445–496.

Leeson, R. (1998). The Origins of the Keynesian Discomfiture. *Journal of Post Keynesian Economics, 20*(4), 597–619.

Leeson, R. (1999). Keynes and the Keynesian Phillips Curve. *History of Political Economy, 31*(3), 494–509.

Leeson, R. (2000). Inflation, Disinflation and the Natural Rate of Unemployment: A Dynamic Framework for Policy Analysis. *The Australian Economy in the 1990s* (pp. 124–175). Sydney: Reserve Bank of Australia.

Leeson, R. (2003). *Ideology and the International Economy: The Decline and Fall of Bretton Woods*. Basingstoke, UK: Palgrave Macmillan.

Leeson, R. (2005, August 19). Assessing the Effect of Taxes on the Economy: Deflate Housing Bubble with Targeted Taxes. *San Francisco Chronicle*. http://www.sfgate.com/default/article/Assessing-the-Effect-of-Taxes-on-the-Economy-2646541.php.

Leeson, R. (2011, December). The MONIAC Updated for the Era of Permanent Financial Crises. *Economia Politica*, 4(4), 103–130.

Leeson, R. (Ed.). (2013). *Hayek: A Collaborative Biography Part I Influences from Mises to Bartley*. Basingstoke, UK: Palgrave Macmillan.

Leeson, R. (Ed.). (2015a). *Hayek: A Collaborative Biography Part III Fraud, Fascism and Free Market Religion*. Basingstoke, UK: Palgrave Macmillan.

Leeson, R. (Ed.). (2015b). *Hayek: A Collaborative Biography Part II Austria, America and the Rise of Hitler, 1899–1933*. Basingstoke, UK: Palgrave Macmillan.

Leeson, R. (Ed.). (2015c). *Hayek: A Collaborative Biography Part IV England, The Ordinal Revolution and The Road to Serfdom, 1931–1950*. Basingstoke, UK: Palgrave Macmillan.

Leeson, R. (2017). *Hayek: A Collaborative Biography Part VII 'Market Free Play with an Audience': Hayek's Encounters with Fifty Knowledge Communities*. Basingstoke, UK: Palgrave Macmillan.

Leeson, R. (2018a). *Hayek: A Collaborative Biography Part VIII: The Constitution of Liberty: 'Shooting in Cold Blood' Hayek's Plan for the Future of Democracy*. Basingstoke, UK: Palgrave Macmillan.

Leeson, R. (2018b). *Hayek: A Collaborative Biography Part XI: Orwellian Rectifiers, Mises' 'Evil Seed' of Christianity and the 'Free' Market Welfare State*. Basingstoke, UK: Palgrave Macmillan.

Leeson, R. (2018c). *Hayek: A Collaborative Biography Part XV: Chicago and the 1974 Nobel Prize for Economic Sciences*. Basingstoke, UK: Palgrave Macmillan.

Leeson, R. (Ed.). (2018d). *Hayek: A Collaborative Biography Part IX: The Divine Right of the 'Free' Market*. Basingstoke, UK: Palgrave Macmillan.

Shearmur, J. (2015). The Other Path to Mont Pelerin. In R. Leeson (Ed.), *Hayek: A Collaborative Biography Part IV England, The Ordinal Revolution and the Road to Serfdom, 1931–1950*. Basingstoke, UK: Palgrave Macmillan.

Teacher, D. (2018a). 'Neutral Academic Data' and the International Right. In R. Leeson (Ed.), *Hayek: A Collaborative Biography Part XIII 'Fascism' and Liberalism in the (Austrian) Classical Tradition*. Basingstoke, UK: Palgrave Macmillan.

Teacher, D. (2018b). Private Club and Secret Service Armageddon. In R. Leeson (Ed.), *Hayek: A Collaborative Biography Part XIII 'Fascism' and Liberalism in the (Austrian) Classical Tradition*. Basingstoke, UK: Palgrave Macmillan.

Theroux, D. (2015). Hayek and Me. In R. Leeson (Ed.), *Hayek: A Collaborative Biography Part V Hayek's Great Society of Free Men*. Basingstoke, UK: Palgrave Macmillan.

Tietze, T. (2015). Anders Breivik, Fascism and the Neoliberal Inheritance. In R. Leeson (Ed.), *Hayek: A Collaborative Biography Part VI Good Dictators, Sovereign Producers and Hayek's 'Ruthless Consistency'*. Basingstoke, UK: Palgrave Macmillan.

Vanberg, V. (2013). Hayek in Freiburg. In R. Leeson (Ed.), *Hayek: A Collaborative Biography Part I Influences, from Mises to Bartley*. Basingstoke, UK: Palgrave Macmillan.
West, N. (2015). Insights from one of 'Deacon' McCormick's Research Assistant. In R. Leeson (Ed.), *Hayek: A Collaborative Biography Part III Fraud, Fascism and Free Market Religion*. Basingstoke, UK: Palgrave Macmillan.
Weinberg, G. L. (2015). The Hitler Diary Fraud. In R. Leeson (Ed.), *Hayek: A Collaborative Biography Part III Fraud, Fascism and Free Market Religion*. Basingstoke, UK: Palgrave Macmillan.

Other References

Alchian, A. (1978). In F. A. Hayek (Ed.), *Oral History Interviews*. Centre for Oral History Research, University of California, Los Angeles. http://oralhistory.library.ucla.edu/.
Alejandro, C. (2010). How I Became a Liberal. In W. Block (Ed.), *I Chose Liberty: Autobiographies of Contemporary Libertarians*. Auburn, AL: Ludwig von Mises Institute.
Allison, J. (2015). *The Leadership Crisis and the Free Market Cure*. New York: McGraw Hill.
Amery, J., Biggs-Davidson, J., Hastings, S., Soref, H., & Wall, P. (1976). *Rhodesia and the Threat to the West*. London: Monday Club.
Anderson, J. L. (1998, October 19). The Dictator. *The New Yorker*. http://www.newyorker.com/magazine/1998/10/19/the-dictator-2.
Anderson, R. W., Johnson, N. D., & Koyama, N. (2017). Jewish Persecutions and Weather Shocks: 1100–1800. *Economic Journal, 127*(602), 924–958.
Annan, N. (1991). *Our Age: The Generation That Made Post-war Britain*. London: Fontana.
Anson, D. (2010). *The Sad Old State of Cloud Cuckoo Land—British Jews, the Right, and Islamophobia*. http://daphneanson.blogspot.com.au/2010/12/sad-old-state-of-cloud-cuckoo-land.html.
Arblaster, A. (1984). *The Rise and Decline of Western Liberalism*. Oxford: Basil Blackwell.
Austrian Economics Newsletter. (1993). F.A. Hayek. *Memoriam, 14*(1), 1–2. https://mises.org/system/tdf/aen14_1_1_0.pdf?file=1&type=document.
Axelrod, A. (2007). *Encyclopedia of World War II* (Vol. 1). New York: Infobase.
Bark, D. L. (2007). *Americans and Europeans Dancing in the Dark on Our Differences and Affinities, Our Interests, and Our Habits of Life*. Stanford, CA: Hoover Institution Press.
Barros, R. (2004). *Constitutionalism and Dictatorship. Pinochet, the Junta, and the 1980 Constitution*. Cambridge: Cambridge University Press.

Bartley, W. W., III. (1989). Rehearsing a Revolution—Karl Popper: A Life. Mimeo.
Barton, S. (1994). The Ear. *Rothbard-Rockwell Report, 5,* 1. http://www.unz.org/Pub/RothbardRockwellReport-1994may-00001.
Baxendale, T. (2011, January 9). The Rediscovery of Hayek's Masterpieces. *Mises Daily.* https://mises.org/library/rediscovery-hayeks-masterpieces.
Bender, B., & Hanna, A. (2016, December 5). Flynn Under Fire for Fake News. *Politico.* http://www.politico.com/story/2016/12/michael-flynn-conspiracy-pizzeria-trump-232227.
Benham, F. (1932). *British Monetary Policy.* London: P.S. King & Son.
Bernstein, R. (1989, May 16). Magazine Dispute Reflects Rift on U.S. Right. *New York Times.* http://www.nytimes.com/1989/05/16/us/magazine-dispute-reflects-rift-on-us-right.html.
Beveridge, W. (1931). *Tariffs: The Case Examined.* London: Longmans, Green.
Beveridge, W. (1942). *The Report of the Inter-Departmental Committee on Social Insurance and Allied Services.* New York: Macmillan.
Beveridge, W. (1944). *Full Employment in a Free Society.* London: Allen & Unwin.
Beveridge, W. (1953). *Power and Influence.* London: Beechhurst.
Block, M. (1984). *Operation Willi: The Plot to Kidnap the Duke of Windsor, July 1940.* London: Little, Brown.
Block, W. (1995). In L. H. Rockwell, Jr. (Ed.), *Murray Rothbard: In Memorandum.* Auburn, AL: Ludwig von Mises Institute.
Block, W. (2000). Libertarianism vs Objectivism; A Response to Peter Schwartz. *Reason Papers, 26,* 39–62. http://www.reasonpapers.com/pdf/26/rp_26_4.pdf.
Block, W. (2014). Radical Economics an Interview with Walter Block. *Austrian Economics Newsletter, 19*(2). https://mises.org/library/radical-economics-interview-walter-block.
Blundell, J. (2008). *Margaret Thatcher: A Portrait of the Iron Lady.* New York: Algora.
Blundell, J. (2014). IHS and the Rebirth of Austrian Economics: Some Reflections on 1974–1976. *Quarterly Journal of Austrian Economics, 17*(1), 92–107. https://mises.org/library/ihs-and-rebirth-austrian-economics-some-reflections-1974%E2%80%931976.
Boettke, P. J. (2001). *Calculation and Coordination Essays on Socialism and Transitional Political Economy.* London: Routledge.
Boettke, P. J. (2009a, August 4). Setting the Record Straight. *Coordination Problem.* http://austrianeconomists.typepad.com/weblog/2009/08/setting-the-record-straight-on-austropunkism-and-the-sociology-of-the-austrian-school-of-economics.html.

Boettke, P. J. (2009b). *Human Action: The Treatise in Economics*. FEE, August 19. https://fee.org/articles/human-action-the-treatise-in-economics/.

Boettke, P. J. (2010a). Reflections on Becoming an Austrian Economist and Libertarian and Staying One. In W. Block (Ed.), *I Chose Liberty: Autobiographies of Contemporary Libertarians*. Auburn, AL: Ludwig von Mises Institute.

Boettke, P. J. (2010b, January 12). Charles Rowley on the State of Macroeconomics. *Coordination Problem*. http://www.coordinationproblem.org/2010/01/charles-rowley-on-the-state-of-macroeconomics.html.

Boettke, P. J. (2010c, December 12). EXCLUSIVE INTERVIEW Peter Boettke on the Rise of Austrian Economics, Its Academic Inroads and Why the Market Should Decide by Anthony Wile. *Daily Bell*. http://www.thedailybell.com/exclusive-interviews/anthony-wile-peter-boettke-on-the-rise-of-austrian-economics-its-academic-inroads-and-why-the-market-should-decide/.

Boettke, P. J. (2010d, October 3). EXCLUSIVE INTERVIEW Steve Horwitz on GMU, the Mises Controversy and the Promise of Austrian Economics in the 21st Century. By Anthony Wile. *Daily Bell*. http://www.thedailybell.com/exclusive-interviews/anthony-wile-steve-horwitz-on-gmu-the-mises-controversy-and-the-promise-of-austrian-economics-in-the-21st-century/.

Boettke, P. J. (2011). Teaching Austrian Economics to Graduate Students. *Journal of Economics and Finance Education*, *10*(2), 19–30. http://www.economics-finance.org/jefe/econ/special-issue/Special%20Issue%20AE%20003%20Boettke-Abstract.pdf.

Boettke, P. J. (2012). *Interview with Peter Boettke*. Rationality Unlimited. https://rationalityunlimited.wordpress.com/2012/04/02/interview-with-peter-boettke/.

Boettke, P. J. (2014, June 7). Robert Leeson, Hayek and the Underpants Gnome. *Coordination Problem*. http://www.coordinationproblem.org/2014/06/robert-leeson-hayek-and-the-underpants-gnomes.html.

Boettke, P. J. (2015, January 25). The Transformative Rise of Austrian Economics. *The Daily Bell*. http://www.thedailybell.com/exclusive-interviews/anthony-wile-peter-boettke-the-transformative-rise-of-austrian-economics/.

Boettke, P. J. (2016a, October 17). Ludwig von Mises, the Academic. *The Freeman*. https://fee.org/articles/ludwig-von-mises-the-academic/.

Boettke, P. J. (2016b, March 30). 'When A Man Like Walter Williams Calls You To Duty, You Report'—Fred Boettke. *Coordination Problem*. http://www.coordinationproblem.org/2016/03/31/.

Boettke, P. J. (2016c, September 1). Richard Ebeling and FFF's Austrian Economics Project. *Coordination Problem*. http://www.coordinationproblem.org/2016/09/richard-ebeling-and-fffs-austrian-economics-project.html.

Boettke, P. J. (2017, September 17). Hayek's Epistemic Liberalism. *Online Library of Liberty*. http://oll.libertyfund.org/pages/lm-hayek.

Boettke, P. J., & Haeffele-Balch, S. (2017, June 5). The Case for Ordinary Economics. *USA Today*. https://www.usnews.com/opinion/economic-intelligence/articles/2017-06-05/remember-3-basic-economic-principles-in-todays-chaotic-world.
Bogle, J., & Bogle, J. (1990). *A Heart for Europe: The Lives of Emperor Charles and Empress Zita of Austria Hungary*. London: Fowler Wright.
Böhm Bawerk, E. (1949 [1896]). *Karl Marx and the Close of His System*. New York: Augustus M. Kelley.
Böhm-Bawerk, E. (1959). *Capital and Interest* (3 Vols., H. Sennholz, Trans.). South Holland, IL: Libertarian Press.
Boller, P. F., & George, J. H. (1989). *They Never Said It: A Book of Fake Quotes, Misquotes, and Misleading Attributions*. Oxford: Oxford University Press.
Booth, C. (1889). *Life and Labour of the People of London* (Vol. 1). London: Macmillan.
Booth, C. (1891). *Life and Labour of the People of London* (Vol. 2). London: Macmillan.
Bostaph, S. (1989, Spring–Summer). Review of Hayek's The Fatal Conceit. *Austrian Economics Newsletter*, 13–16. https://mises.org/library/subjective-value-theory-and-government-intervention-labor-market-full-edition-vol-10-no-3.
Boyle, A. (1979). *The Fourth Man the Definitive Account of Kim Philby, Guy Burgess, and Who Recruited Them to Spy for Russia*. New York: Bantum.
Boyle, A. (1982). *The Climate of Treason* (2nd ed.). London: Hutchison.
Brittan, S. (1977). *The Economic Consequences of Democracy*. London: Temple Smith.
Brittan, S. (1995). *Capitalism with a Human Face*. Cambridge, MA: Harvard University Press.
Brittan, S. (2005). *Against the Flow Reflections of an Individualist*. London: Atlantic Books.
Brook-Shepherd, G. (2003). *Uncrowned Emperor: The Life and Times of Otto Von Habsburg*. London: Hambledon and London.
Brook-Shepherd, G. (2009). *The Austrians: A Thousand-Year Odyssey*. New York: HarperCollins.
Brooks, D. (2017, July 11). How We Are Ruining America. *New York Times*. https://www.nytimes.com/2017/07/11/opinion/how-we-are-ruining-america.html.
Brown, C., & Hastings, C. (2003, May 4). Fury as Dalyell Attacks Blair's 'Jewish Cabal.' *The Daily Telegraph*. http://web.archive.org/web/20071115200404/http://www.telegraph.co.uk/news/main.jhtml?xml=/news/2003/05/04/ndaly04.xml&sSheet=/portal/2003/05/04/ixportaltop.html.

Brunvand, J. H. (1999). *Too Good to Be True: The Colossal Book of Urban Legends*. New York: W. W. Norton.
Buchanan, J. (1965). An Economic Theory of Clubs. *Economica, 32*(125), 1–14 (New Series).
Buchanan, J. (1973). Prospects for America's Third Century. *Atlantic Economic Journal, 1*, 3–13. https://link.springer.com/article/10.1007/BF02299808.
Buchanan, J. (1986, October 26). Why Governments 'Got Out of Hand.' *The New York Times*.
Buchanan, J. (1987). An Interview with Laureate James Buchanan. *Austrian Economics Newsletter, 9*(1). http://mises.org/journals/aen/aen9_1_1.asp.
Buchanan, J. (1992). I Did Not Call Him 'Fritz': Personal Recollections of Professor F. A. v. Hayek. *Constitutional Political Economy, 3*(2), 129–135.
Buckley, W. F., Jr. (1995, February 6). Murray Rothbard RIP. *National Review*. http://notableandquotable.blogspot.com.au/2008/04/william-f-buckleys-obituary-of-murray.html.
Buckley, W. F., Jr., & Bozell, L. B. (1954). *McCarthy and His Enemies the Record and Its Meaning*. Chicago: Henry Regnery.
Bullock, A. (1991). *Hitler: A Study in Tyranny*. New York: Harper Perennial.
Bull, A. C. (2012). *Italian Neofascism: The Strategy of Tension and the Politics of Nonreconciliation*. Oxford: Berghahn.
Burke, E. (1790). *Reflections on the Revolution in France*. London: J. Dodsley.
Burlingham, R., & Billis, R. (2005). *Reformed Characters: The Reform Club in History and Literature*. London: Reform Club.
Caldwell, B. (1995). Editorial Notes. In B. Caldwell (Ed.),*Contra Keynes and Cambridge. The Collected Works of F.A. Hayek*. Chicago: University of Chicago Press.
Caldwell, B. (2004). *Hayek's Challenge: An Intellectual Biography of F.A. Hayek*. Chicago: University of Chicago Press.
Caldwell, B. (2005, January). Interview: Hayek for the 21st Century. *Reason*. http://public.econ.duke.edu/~bjc18/Publications_Frameset.htm.
Caldwell, B. (2006). Popper and Hayek: Who Influenced Whom? In I. Jarvie, K. Milford, & D. W. Miller (Eds.), *Karl Popper: A Centenary Assessment* (Vol. I, pp. 111–124). Burlington: Ashgate Publishing Company.
Caldwell, B. (2007). Introduction and Editorial Notes. In F. A. Hayek (Ed.), *The Road to Serfdom Texts and Documents: The Definitive Edition. The Collected Works of F.A. Hayek*. Chicago: University of Chicago Press.
Caldwell, B. (2008). Book Review: History in the Service of Ideology: A Review Essay of Jörg Guido Hülsmann, *Mises: The Last Knight of Liberalism. History of Economic Ideas, 16*(3), 143–148.
Caldwell, B. (2009). A Skirmish in the Popper Wars: Hutchison Versus Caldwell on Hayek, Popper, Mises, and Methodology. *Journal of Economic*

Methodology, *16*(3), 315–324. http://www.tandfonline.com/doi/pdf/10.1080/13501780903129306.

Caldwell, B. (2010a). The Secret Behind the Hot Sales of 'The Road to Serfdom' by Free-Market Economist F.A. Hayek. *The Washington Post*. http://voices.washingtonpost.com/shortstack/2010/02/the_secret_behind_the_hot_sale.html.

Caldwell, B. (2010b). Introduction. In F. A. Hayek (Ed.), *Studies on the Abuse and Decline of Reason. Texts and Documents. The Collected Works of F.A. Hayek*. London: Routledge.

Caldwell, B. (2010c, September). Review of P. Mirowski & D. Phehwe (Eds.), *The Road from Mont Pelerin: The Making of the Neoliberal Thought Collective*. EH.NET. http://eh.net/book_reviews/the-road-from-mont-plerin-the-making-of-the-neoliberal-thought-collective/.

Caldwell, B. (2016). Hayek's Nobel. In P. Boettke & V. Storr (Eds.), *Revisiting Hayek's Political Economy*. Bingley, UK: Emerald.

Caldwell, B., & Montes, L. (2014a, August). *Friedrich Hayek and His Visits to Chile* (CHOPE Working Paper No. 2014-12).

Caldwell, B., & Montes, L. (2014b). Friedrich Hayek and His Visits to Chile. *Review of Austrian Economics* (First Online: 26 September 2014).

Caldwell, B., & Montes, L. (2015a, September). Friedrich Hayek and His Visits to Chile. *Review of Austrian Economics, 28*(3), 261–309.

Caldwell, B., & Montes, L. (2015b). Friedrich Hayek y Sus Dos Visitas a Chile. *Estudios Públicos*, No. 137: 87–132. https://www.cepchile.cl/cep/site/artic/20160304/asocfile/20160304101209/rev137_BCaldwell-LMontes.pdf.

Campbell, I. (2017). *The Addis Ababa Massacre: Italy's National Shame*. Oxford: Oxford University Press.

Cannan, E. (1928). *An Economist's Protest*. London: P.S. King & Son.

Cassidy, J. (2000, June 30). The Hayek Century. *Hoover Digest*, No. 3. http://www.hoover.org/research/hayek-century.

Chafuen, A. (1986). *Christians for Freedom: Late Scholastic Economics*. New York: Ignatius Press.

Chafuen, A. (2010). How I Became a Liberal. In W. Block (Ed.), *I Chose Liberty: Autobiographies of Contemporary Libertarians*. Auburn, AL: Ludwig von Mises Institute.

Chaloner, W. H. (1962). In C. F. Charter (Ed.), The Birth of Modern Manchester. In *Manchester and its Region a Survey Prepared by the British Association*. Manchester: Manchester University Press.

Chamberlain, J. (1944). Foreword. In F. A. Hayek (Ed.), *The Road to Serfdom*. Chicago: University of Chicago Press.

Chamberlain, J. (1974a, September 28). May We Borrow the Crystal Ball? *Chicago Tribune.* http://archives.chicagotribune.com/1974/09/28/page/34/article/may-we-borrow-the-crystal-ball.
Chamberlain, J. (1974b, August). The 12-Year Sentence. *The Freeman,* 501–504. http://www.unz.org/Pub/Freeman-1974aug-00501?View=PDF.
Chamberlain, J. (1977, April 19). Africa: Why Not Peace. *New Haven Register* (Davenport Archives Box 9.5).
Chamberlain, J. (1980, November 28). Mont Pelerin Society: Robber Governments. *National Review* (MPS Archives Box 48.3).
Chamberlain, J. (1982). *A Life With the Printed Word.* Chicago: Regnery Gateway.
Chamberlain, J. (1987, March). Reason Interview with John Chamberlain. *Reason.* http://reason.com/archives/1987/03/01/reason-interview-with-john-cha/2.
Chapman, G., & Python, M. (1989). *The Complete Monty Python's Flying Circus: All the Words* (Vol. 1). London: Pantheon.
Chazan, D. (2014, August 16). French Politician Defends Plan for Crimean Theme Park. *Daily Telegraph.* http://www.telegraph.co.uk/news/worldnews/europe/france/11038730/French-politician-defends-plan-for-Crimean-theme-park.html.
Childers, E. (1903). *Riddle of the Sands.* London: Smith, Elders & Co.
Chozick, A. (2016, September 10). Hillary Clinton Calls Many Trump Backers 'Deplorables,' and G.O.P. Pounces. *New York Times.* https://www.nytimes.com/2016/09/11/us/politics/hillary-clinton-basket-of-deplorables.html.
Churchill, W. (1935, November). Hitler: Monster or Hero? *Strand Magazine.*
Clark, R. T. (1964). *The Fall of the German Republic a Political Study.* New York: Russell and Russell.
Cockett, R. (1995). *Thinking the Unthinkable Think Tanks and the Economic Counter-Revolution, 1931–1983.* London: Harper Collins.
Connolly, K. (2005, January 19). Hitler's Mentally Ill Cousin Killed in Nazi Gas Chamber. *Daily Telegraph.*
Cornwell, J. (1999). *Hitler's Pope the Secret History of Pius XII.* New York: Viking.
Cornwell, J. (2003, October 29). Hitler's Pope. Pope Pius XII Helped Hitler Destroy German Catholic Political Opposition. *Vanity Fair.* http://www.vanityfair.com/style/1999/10/pope-pius-xii-199910.
Costello, J. (1988). *The Mask of Treachery: Spies, Lies, Buggery and Betrayal: The First Documented Dossier on Anthony Blunt's Cambridge Spy Ring.* New York: William Morrow.
Cowell, A. (1994, May 12). Berlusconi and Cabinet with Neo-fascists Take Office in Italy. *New York Times.* http://www.nytimes.com/1994/05/12/world/berlusconi-and-cabinet-with-neo-fascists-take-office-in-italy.html.

Cowen, T. (1979). The Rutgers Conference on Inflation. *Austrian Economics Newsletter,* 2(2), 1–4. https://mises.org/system/tdf/aen%20v.%202%2C%20no.%202%20Fall%201979.pdf?file=1&type=document.
Crook, J. M. (1973). *The Reform.* London: The Reform Club.
Crozier, B. (1967). *Franco.* London: Eyre and Spottiswoode.
Crozier, B. (1979). *The Minimum State: Beyond Party Politics.* London: Hamish Hamilton.
Crozier, B. (1993). *Free Agent the Unseen War 1941–1991.* London: HarperCollins.
Cubitt, C. (2006). *A Life of August von Hayek.* Bedford, UK: Authors OnLine.
Dahrendorf, R. (1995). *LSE: A History of the London School of Economics and Political Science, 1895–1995.* Oxford: Oxford University Press.
Daily Express Obituary. (2012, September 1). Blunt Tory Rhodes Boyson Devoted to Education. *Daily Express.* http://www.express.co.uk/expressyourself/343295/Blunt-Tory-Rhodes-Boyson-devoted-to-education.
Daily Telegraph. (2010, March 2). *Winston Churchill.* http://www.telegraph.co.uk/news/obituaries/politics-obituaries/7352232/Winston-Churchill.html.
Dalin, D. (2005). *The Myth of Hitler's Pope: How Pope Pius XII Rescued Jews from the Nazis.* Washington, DC: Regnery.
Dalton, H. (1953). *Call Back Yesterday: Memoirs, 1887–1931.* London: Frederick Muller.
Dalton, H. (1986). *The Political Diaries of Hugh Dalton, 1918–1940, 1945–1960* (B. Pimlott, Ed.). London: Cape.
Davis, F. (1974, November). Federal Control Hurts Young Doctors the Most. *Private Practice,* 4.
Davenport, J. (1949, March). Socialism by Default. *Fortune, XXXIX*(3).
Davenport, J. (1958, Spring). Arms and the Welfare State. *The Yale Review* (Davenport Archives Box 18.17).
Davenport, J. (1965). *The US Economy.* Chicago: H. Regnery Company.
Davenport, J. (1976, Summer). Civilization at Risk. *Modern Age.*
Davenport, J. (1981, July). Reflections on Mont Pelerin. *The Mont Pelerin Society Newsletter.*
Davenport, J. (1985, August 1). The Anti-apartheid Threat. *The Freeman.* https://fee.org/articles/the-anti-apartheid-threat/.
Davidson, E. (1966). *The Trials of the Germans: An Account of the Twenty-Two Defendants Before the International Military Tribunal at Nuremberg.* London: Macmillan.
Davidson, A. (2012, August 21). Prime Time for Paul Ryan's Guru (The One Who's Not Ayn Rand). *New York Times.* http://www.nytimes.com/2012/08/26/magazine/prime-time-for-paul-ryans-guru-the-one-thats-not-ayn-rand.html.

Deaton, A. (2017, July 13). Without Governments, Would Countries Have More Inequality, or Less? *Economist*. https://www.economist.com/news/world-if/21724910-angus-deaton-nobel-prize-winning-economist-explores-question-intrigued-him-without.
Deist, J. (2017, February 17). Democracy, the God That's Failing. *Mises Wire*. https://mises.org/blog/democracy-god-thats-failing.
Demick, B., & Lee, K. (2017, July 28). Trump Orders Officers and Immigration Officials to be 'Rough' on 'Animals' Terrorizing U.S. Neighborhoods. *Los Angeles Times*. http://www.latimes.com/nation/la-na-pol-trump-ms13-story.html.
De Tocqueville, A. (1835–1840). *Democracy in America*. London: Saunders and Otley.
Disraeli, B. (1845). *Sybil the Two Nations* (3 Vols.). London: Henry Colburn.
Doherty, B. (2007). *Radicals for Capitalism: A Freewheeling History of the Modern. American Libertarian Movement*. New York: Public Affairs.
Doherty, B. (2010). In M. N. Rothbard (Ed.), *Strictly Confidential: The Private Volker Fund Memos of Murray N. Rothbard* (D. Gordon, Ed.). Auburn, AL: Ludwig von Mises Institute.
Dorey, P. (1995). *Conservative Party and the Trade Unions*. London: Routledge.
Driessen, P. (2005). *Eco-imperialism Green Power, Black Death*. New Delhi: Liberty Institute.
Dorril, S. (2006). *Black Shirt: Sir Oswald Mosley and British Fascism*. London: Viking.
Dudley Edwards, O. (1969, March). Review of *The Private Life of Mr. Gladstone*, by Richard Deacon. *Irish Historical Studies*, XVI(63), 389–392.
Dudley Edwards, R. (1995). *The Pursuit of Reason: The Economist 1843–1993*. London: Hamish Hamilton.
Duke of Edinburgh. (1978). Intellectual Dissent and the Reversal of Trends. In W. H. Chaloner (Ed.), *The Coming Confrontation: Will the Open Society Survive to 1989?*. London: Institute of Economic Affairs.
Dwyer, P. G. (2001). *Modern Prussian History, 1830–1947*. London: Longman.
Ebeling, R. M. (1974, October). Austrian Economics on the Rise. *Libertarian Forum*. http://mises.org/daily/4174.
Ebeling, R. M. (1975, July). The Second Austrian Conference. *Libertarian Forum*, Vol. VII, No. 7, pp. 4–8. http://rothbard.altervista.org/articles/libertarian-forum/lf-7-7.pdf.
Ebeling, R. M. (1978). Review: On the Manipulation of Money and Credit. *Austrian Economic Newsletter*, Vol. 1, No. 3.
Ebeling, R. M. (1990). Introduction. In L. Mises (Ed.), *Money, Method and the Market Process* (Selected by Margit von Mises and Edited with an Introduction by Richard M. Ebeling). Auburn, AL: Ludwig von Mises Institute.

Ebeling, R. M. (1994). Review of Stephen Koch *Double Lives: Spies and Writers in the Secret Soviet War of Ideas against the West* by Stephen Koch. New York: Free Press. Future of Freedom Foundation, July 1. http://fff.org/explore-freedom/article/book-review-double-lives/.

Ebeling, R. M. (1997, August). The Free Market and the Interventionist State. *Imprimus, 26*(8) (MPS Archives Box 122).

Ebeling, R. M. (2001). F.A. Hayek a Biography. Review of Friedrich Hayek: A Biography by Alan Ebenstein. *Mises Daily*.https://mises.org/daily/638/FA-Hayek-A-Biography.

Ebeling, R. M. (2006, April 1). *The Great Austrian Inflation*. Foundation for Economic Education. https://fee.org/articles/the-great-austrian-inflation/.

Ebeling, R. M. (2010a). *Political Economy, Public Policy and Monetary Economics: Ludwig Von Mises and the Austrian Tradition*. New York: Routledge.

Ebeling, R. M. (2010b, January 12). Charles Rowley on the State of Macroeconomics. *Coordination Problem*. http://www.coordinationproblem.org/2010/01/charles-rowley-on-the-state-of-macroeconomics.html.

Ebeling, R. M. (2013, June 15). Richard Ebeling on Higher Interest Rates, Collectivism and the Coming Collapse. *Daily Bell*. http://www.thedailybell.com/gold-silver/anthony-wile-richard-ebeling-on-higher-interest-rates-collectivism-and-the-coming-collapse/.

Ebeling, R. M. (2014a, February 16). EXCLUSIVE INTERVIEW, Gold & Silver. Richard Ebeling on Austrian Economics, Economic Freedom and the Trends of the Future. *Daily Bell*. http://www.thedailybell.com/gold-silver/anthony-wile-richard-ebeling-on-austrian-economics-economic-freedom-and-the-trends-of-the-future/.

Ebeling, R. M. (2014b, June 16). The Rise and Fall of Classical Liberalism. *Free Market Liberalism*. https://rebeling.liberty.me/the-rise-and-fall-of-classical-liberalism-by-richard-ebeling/.

Ebeling, R. M. (2015a, March 25). A World Without the Welfare State. *Future of Freedom Foundation*. https://www.fff.org/explore-freedom/article/world-without-welfare-state/.

Ebeling, R. M. (2015b, September 9). The Human Cost of Socialism in Power. *Future of Freedom Foundation*. https://www.fff.org/explore-freedom/article/the-human-cost-of-socialism-in-power/.

Ebeling, R. M. (2016a, May 2). How I Became a Libertarian and an Austrian Economist. *Future of Freedom Foundation*. https://www.fff.org/explore-freedom/article/became-libertarian-austrian-economist/.

Ebeling, R. M. (2016b, December 19). The 25th Anniversary of the End of the Soviet Union. *Foundation for Economic Freedom*. https://fee.org/articles/the-25th-anniversary-of-the-end-of-the-soviet-union/.

Ebeling, R. M. (2016c, May 9). Setting the Record Straight: How Stalin Used Hitler To Start World War II. *Future of Freedom Foundation.* https://www.fff.org/explore-freedom/article/setting-record-straight-stalin-used-hitler-start-world-war-ii/.

Ebeling, R. M. (2017, March 20). Trump's Budgetary Blueprint Retains America's Welfare State. *Heartland Institute.* https://www.heartland.org/news-opinion/news/trumps-budgetary-blueprint-retains-americas-welfare-state.

Ebenstein, A. (1997). *Edwin Cannan: Liberal Doyen.* London: Routledge (Foreword by Arthur Seldon).

Ebenstein, A. (2003). *Friedrich Hayek: A Biography.* Chicago: University of Chicago Press.

Eccleshall, R. (1990). *English Conservatism Since the Restoration: An Introduction and Anthology.* London: Unwin Hyman.

Edsall, N. (1986). *Richard Cobden Independent Radical.* Cambridge, MA: Harvard University Press.

Einzig, P. (1937). *World Finance, 1935–1937.* New York: Macmillan.

Elliott, N. (1993). *With My Little Eye: Observations Along the Way.* London: Michael Russell.

Engels, F. (1969 [1845]). *The Condition of the Working Class in England.* London: Panther.

Evans, A. (2010). The Parallels Between Sports Coaching and Graduate Teaching: Coach Boettke as Exemplar. *The Journal of Private Enterprise, 26*(1), 73–83.

Evans, H. (2007). *My Paper Chase: True Stories of Vanished Times: An Autobiography.* London: Little, Brown.

Evans, H. (2011). Preface. *Good Times Bad Times.* New York: Open Road (First edition 1984).

Evans, K. (2010, August 28). Spreading Hayek, Spurning Keynes. Professor Leads an Austrian Revival. *Wall Street Journal.*

Evans, R. J. (2002). *Telling Lies About Hitler: The Holocaust, History and the David Irving Trial.* London: Verso.

Faber, D. (2005). *Speaking for England: Leo, Julian and John Amery, the Tragedy of a Political Family.* London: Free Press.

Farrant, A., McPhail, E., & Berger, S. (2012). Preventing the "Abuses" of Democracy: Hayek, the "Military Usurper" and Transitional Dictatorship in Chile? *American Journal of Economics and Sociology, 71*(3), 513–538.

Farrell, J. (2017). *Richard Nixon: The Life.* New York: Doubleday.

Finer, H. (1945). *The Road to Reaction.* Chicago: Quadrangle Books.

Fink, R. (1996). From Ideas to Action: The Role of Universities, Think Tanks, and Activist Groups. *Philanthropy Magazine,* Vol. 10, No. 1. http://www.

learnliberty.org/wp-content/uploads/2014/08/CreatingYourPathToA PolicyCareer.pdf.
Fischer, C. (2002). *The Rise of the Nazis*. Manchester: Manchester University Press.
Foot, P. (1968). *The Politics of Harold Wilson*. London, UK: Penguin.
Francis, S. (1995). In L. H. Rockwell, Jr. (Ed.), *Murray Rothbard: In Memorandum*. Auburn, AL: Ludwig von Mises Institute.
Friedman, M. (1995). Interview with Alan Ebenstein. Mimeo.
Friedman, M. F., & Friedman, R. D. (1998). *Two Lucky People: Memoirs*. Chicago: University of Chicago Press.
Frum, D. (2003, March 25). Unpatriotic Conservatives. *National Review*. http://www.nationalreview.com/article/391772/unpatriotic-conservatives-david-frum.
Gadshiiev, K. (2004 [1996]). Totalitarianism as a Twentieth Century Phenomenon. In H. Maier (Ed.), *Totalitarianism and Political Religions*. London: Routledge.
Galbraith, J. K. (1952). *American Capitalism: The Concept of Countervailing Power*. Boston: Houghton Mifflin Harcourt.
Galbraith, J. K. (1981). *A Life in Our Time*. Boston: Houghton Mifflin Harcourt.
Galbraith, R. (2000). *Inside Out: The Biography of Tam Dalyell: The Man They Can't Gag*. New York: Mainstream.
Garrison, R. (2003). LSE'S First Hayek Visiting Fellow. *Austrian Economics Newsletter (Fall)*. https://mises.org/system/tdf/aen23_3_1_0.pdf?file=1&type=document.
Gash, N. (1972). *Sir Robert Peel: The Life of Sir Robert Peel After 1830*. Lanham, NJ: Rowman & Littlefield.
Giroux, S. S. (2010). *Between Race and Reason: Violence, Intellectual Responsibility, and the University to Come*. Stanford, CA: Stanford University Press.
Gladstone, W. E. (1990). *The Gladstone Diaries: Volume 10: January 1881–June 1883* (H. C. G. Mathew, Ed.). Oxford: Oxford University Press.
Glassman, J. K. (2011). Market-Based Man. *Philanthropy Roundtable (Fall)*. http://www.philanthropyroundtable.org/topic/excellence_in_philanthropy/market_based_man.
Goodwin, C. (1988). The Heterogeneity of the Economists' Discourse: Philosopher, Priest, and Hired Gun. In A. Klamer, D. N. McCloskey, & R. M. Solow (Eds.), *The Consequences of Economic Rhetoric*. Cambridge: Cambridge University Press.
Gordon, R. L. (1994). *Regulation and Economic Analysis: A Critique over Two Centuries*. Boston: Kluwer Academic Publishers.

Gordon, D. (2013, April 18). *The Kochtopus vs. Murray N. Rothbard, Part II*. https://www.lewrockwell.com/2013/04/david-gordon/explaining-beltway-libertarians/.

Grant, J. (1996). The Trouble with Prosperity: An Interview with James Grant. *Austrian Economics Newsletter, 16*(4).

Gray, R. (2017, February 10). Conflict over Trump Forces Out an Opinion Editor at *The Wall Street Journal*. *The Atlantic*. https://www.theatlantic.com/politics/archive/2017/02/conflict-over-trump-forces-out-an-opinion-editor-at-the-wall-street-journal/516318/.

Gregory, T. E., von Hayek, F. A., Plant, A., & Robbins, L. (1932, October 19). Spending and Saving Public Works from Rates. *The Times*, 11.

Greig, I. (1979). Iran and the Lengthening Soviet Shadow. *Atlantic Community Quarterly, 17*(1), 66–72.

Griffiths, R. (1983). *Fellow Travellers of the Right British Enthusiasts for Nazi Germany, 1933–39*. Oxford: Oxford University Press.

Grigg, J. (1973). *The Young Lloyd George*. Berkeley: University of California Press.

Grigg, J. (1978). *Lloyd George: The People's Champion*. London: Methuen.

Grigg, J. (1983). *Lloyd George: From Peace to War 1912–1916*. London: Eyre.

Grimond, J. (1980). *The Future of Liberalism: The Inaugural Eighty Club Lecture*. London: Association of Liberal Lawyers.

Gusejnova, D. (2012). Nobel Continent: German Speaking Nobles as Theorists of European Identity in the Inter-War Period. In M. Hewitson & M. D'Auria (Eds.), *Europe in Crisis: Intellectuals and the European Idea, 1917–1957*. New York, US: Berghahn.

Habsburg, O. (1986). Introduction. In F. Somary (Ed.), *The Raven of Zurich. The Memoirs of Felix Somary* (A. J. Sherman, Trans.). New York: St Martin's.

Hamilius, J.-P. (1976). The Grave-Diggers of Western Freedom. In *Le Libéralisme De Karl Marx à Milton Friedman*. Paris: Congrés de la Société du Mont Pélerin (MPS Archives Box 19.2).

Harberger, A. C. (1999, March). Interview with Arnold Harberger. An Interview with the Dean of the 'Chicago Boys.' *The Region*. The Federal Reserve Bank of Minneapolis. https://www.minneapolisfed.org/publications/the-region/interview-with-arnold-harberger.

Harberger, A. C. (2016). Sense and Economics: An Oral History with Arnold Harberger. Interviews Conducted by Paul Burnett in 2015 and 2016 Oral History Center, The Bancroft Library, University of California, Berkeley, California. http://digitalassets.lib.berkeley.edu/roho/ucb/text/harberger_arnold_2016.pdf.

Harris, R. (1986). *Selling Hitler*. London: Faber and Faber.

Hartwell, R. M. (1995). *A History of the Mont Pelerin Society*. Indianapolis: Liberty Fund.

Hayek, F. A. (1933, May). The Trend of Economic Thinking. *Economica*, 40, 121–137.
Hayek, F. A. (1935a). *Collectivist Economic Planning Critical Studies on the Possibilities of Socialism*. London: Routledge and Kegan Paul.
Hayek, F. A. (1935b, August). The Maintenance of Capital. *Economica*, 2, 241–276 (New Series).
Hayek, F. A. (1939 [1802]). Introduction. In H. Thornton (Ed.), *Enquiry into the Nature and Effects of the Paper Credit of Great Britain, 1802* (Edited with an introduction by F.A. Hayek). London: George Allen & Unwin. http://oll.libertyfund.org/titles/thornton-an-enquiry-into-the-nature-and-effects-of-the-paper-credit-of-great-britain.
Hayek, F. A. (1944). *The Road to Serfdom*. London: Routledge.
Hayek, F. A. (1945). The Use of Knowledge in Society. *American Economic Review, XXXV*(4), 519–530.
Hayek, F. A. (1946, February). The London School of Economics 1895–1945. *Economica, XIII*, 1–31 (New Series).
Hayek, F. A. (1948). *Individualism and Economic Order*. Chicago: University of Chicago Press.
Hayek, F. A. (1949). The Intellectuals and Socialism. *University of Chicago Law Review, 16*(3), 417–433.
Hayek, F. A. (1951). *John Stuart Mill and Harriet Taylor*. London: Routledge.
Hayek, F. A. (1952 [1926]). Hayek on Wieser. In H. W. Spiegel (Ed.), *The Development of Economic Thought*. New York: Wiley.
Hayek, F. A. (1960). *The Constitution of Liberty*. Chicago: University of Chicago Press.
Hayek, F. A. (1962). Preface. In H. Schoeck (Ed.), *Financing Medical Care: An Appraisal of Foreign Programs*. London: Caxton.
Hayek, F. A. (1973). *Law, Legislation and Liberty Volume 1. Rules and Order*. Chicago: University of Chicago Press.
Hayek, F. A. (1974). *The Pretence of Knowledge*. Nobel Lecture. https://www.nobelprize.org/nobel_prizes/economic-sciences/laureates/1974/hayek-lecture.html.
Hayek, F. A. (1975a). *A Discussion with Friedrich von Hayek*. Washington: American Enterprise Institute. https://www.aei.org/wp-content/uploads/2017/03/Discussion-with-Friedrich-von-Hayek-text.pdf.
Hayek, F. A. (1975b). *Face the Press*. https://mises.org/library/hayek-meets-press-1975.
Hayek, F. A. (1976a). *Law, Legislation and Liberty, Volume 2: The Mirage of Social Justice*. Chicago: University of Chicago Press.
Hayek, F. A. (1976b, February 23). Politicians Can't Be Trusted with Money. *American Institute for Economic Research Reports* (Hayek Archives Box 109.1).

Hayek, F. A. (1976c, March 18). Institutions May Fail, but Democracy Survives. *US News and World Report* (Hayek Archives Box 109.4).
Hayek, F. A. (1976d, October 13). *The Inseparability of Economic and Political Freedom*. Foundation for Economic Education (Australia) (Hayek Archives Box 109.7).
Hayek, F. A. (1976e). *Socialism and Science*. Economic Society of Australia and New Zealand, Canberra Branch.
Hayek, F. A. (1977a, September). An Interview with Friedrich Hayek, by Richard Ebeling. *Libertarian Review*, 10–18 (Hayek Archives Box 109.14).
Hayek, F. A. (1977b, November 25). La inflación es la mayor amenaza contra la libertad. *Somos* (Hayek Archives Box 109.17).
Hayek, F. A. (1978a). *Oral History Interviews*. Centre for Oral History Research, University of California, Los Angeles. http://oralhistory.library.ucla.edu/.
Hayek, F. A. (1978b). *New Studies in Philosophy, Politics, Economics and the History of Ideas*. London: Routledge & Kegan Paul.
Hayek, F. A. (1978c). Will the Democratic Ideal Prevail? In W. H. Chaloner (Ed.), *The Coming Confrontation: Will the Open Society Survive to 1989?* (pp. 61–73). London: Institute of Economic Affairs.
Hayek, F. A. (1979, December 5). A Period of Muddle-Heads. *Newsweek*.
Hayek, F. A. (1981, April 12). Extracts from an Interview Friedrich von Hayek. *El Mercurio*. http://www.economicthought.net/blog/wp-content/uploads/2011/12/LibertyCleanOfImpuritiesInterviewWithFVonHayekChile1981.pdf.
Hayek, F. A. (1983, February). Interview with F.A. Hayek. *Cato Policy Report*. http://www.cato.org/policy-report/february-1982/interview-fa-hayek.
Hayek, F. A. (1984a). *1980s Unemployment and the Unions: The Distortion of Relative Prices by Monopoly in the Labour Market. Essays on the Impotent Price Structure of Britain and Monopoly in the Labour Market*. London: Institute of Economic Affairs.
Hayek, F. A. (1984b). *The Essence of Hayek* (C. Nishiyama & K. R. Leube, Eds.). Stanford, CA: Hoover Institution Press.
Hayek, F. A. (1988). *The Fatal Conceit: The Errors of Socialism. The Collected Works of F.A. Hayek* (W. W. Bartley III, Ed.). Chicago: University of Chicago Press.
Hayek, F. A. (1992a). *The Fortunes of Liberalism Essays on Austrian Economics and the Ideal of Freedom. The Collected Works of F.A. Hayek* (P. Klein, Ed.). Chicago: University of Chicago Press.
Hayek, F. A. (1992b [1977], July). The Road from Serfdom. *Reason*. http://reason.com/archives/1992/07/01/the-road-from-serfdom/5.
Hayek, F. A. (1994). *Hayek on Hayek an Autobiographical Dialogue*. Supplement to *The Collected Works of F.A. Hayek* (S. Kresge & L. Wenar, Eds.). Chicago: University of Chicago Press.

Hayek, F. A. (1995). *Contra Keynes and Cambridge. The Collected Works of F.A. Hayek* (B. Caldwell, Ed.). Chicago: University of Chicago Press.
Hayek, F. A. (1997). *Socialism and War: Essays, Documents, Reviews. The Collected Works of F.A. Hayek* (B. Caldwell, Ed.). Indianapolis: Liberty Fund.
Hayek, F. A. (1999). *Good Money Part 1 the New World. The Collected Works of F.A. Hayek* (S. Kresge, Ed.). Chicago: University of Chicago Press.
Hayek, F. A. (2007 [1944]). *The Road to Serfdom: The Definitive Edition. The Collected Works of F.A. Hayek* (B. Caldwell, Ed.). Chicago: University of Chicago Press.
Hayek, F. A. (2009 [1979]). A Conversation with Professor Friedrich A. Hayek. In D. Pizano (Ed.), *Conversations with Great Economists*. Mexico: Jorge Pinto Books.
Hayek, F. A. (2011 [1960]). *The Constitution of Liberty. The Definitive Edition. The Collected Works of F.A. Hayek* (R. Hamowy, Ed.). Chicago: University of Chicago Press.
Hayek, F. A. (2012). *Business Cycles Part II. The Collected Works of F.A. Hayek* (H. Klausinger, Ed.). Chicago: University of Chicago Press.
Hayek, F. A. (2013). *Law, Legislation and Liberty*. London: Routledge.
Hayek, F. A. (Forthcoming). *Hayek and the Austrian Economists: Correspondence and Related Documents. The Collected Works of F. A. Hayek* (R. M. Ebeling, Ed.). Chicago: University of Chicago Press.
Heiden, K. (1944). *Der Fuehrer* (R. Manheim, Trans.). Boston: Houghton Mifflin Harcourt.
Heldman, D. C., Bennett, J. T., & Johnson, M. H. (1981). *Deregulating Labor Relations*. Dallas: Fisher Institute.
Hildebrandt, S. (2013, July). Wolfgang Bargmann (1906–1978) and Heinrich von Hayek (1900–1969): Careers in Anatomy Continuing Through German National Socialism to Postwar Leadership. *Annals of Anatomy Anatomischer Anzeiger, 195*(4), 283–295. http://www.sciencedirect.com/science/article/pii/S0940960213000782.
Hildebrand, S. (2016). *The Anatomy of Murder Ethical Transgressions and Anatomical Science During the Third Reich*. New York: Berghahn.
Hitler, A. (1939 [1925]). *Mein Kampf* (J. Murphy, Trans.). London: Hurst and Blackett.
Hitler, A. (1941 [1925]). *Mein Kampf*. New York: Raynal and Hitchcock.
Holcombe, R. (1998, Summer). Markets and the Quality of Life an Interview with Randall Holcombe. *Austrian Economics Newsletter*. https://mises.org/library/markets-and-quality-life-interview-randall-g-holcombe.
Hooper, J. (2012, April 6). Umberto Bossi Resigns as Leader of Northern League Amid Funding Scandal. *Guardian*. https://www.theguardian.com/world/2012/apr/05/umberto-bossi-resigns-northern-league.

Hoover, H. (1952). *The Memoirs of Herbert Hoover, Vol. 3: The Great Depression 1929–1941*. New York: Macmillan.
Hoppe, H.-H. (1992, Spring). Review of R.M. Ebeling's *Money, Method, and the Market Process*. Austrian Economic Newsletter.
Hoppe, H.-H. (1995). In L. H. Rockwell, Jr. (Ed.), *Murray Rothbard: In Memorandum*. Auburn, AL: Ludwig von Mises Institute.
Hoppe, H.-H. (2001). *Democracy the God that Failed: The Economics and Politics of Monarchy, Democracy and Natural Order*. New Brunswick: Transaction Publishers.
Hoppe, H.-H. (2014 [1995]). The Private Property Order: An Interview with Hans-Hermann Hoppe. *Austrian Economic Newsletter, 18*(1). https://mises.org/library/private-property-order-interview-hans-hermann-hoppe.
Hoppe, H.-H. (2017, October 7). *Coming of Age with Murray*. Mises Institute's 35th Anniversary Celebration in New York City. https://mises.org/library/coming-age-murray-0.
Horwitz, S. (2011, April 29). New Spanish Volume of Interviews with Austrians Steven Horwitz. *Coordination Problem*. http://www.coordinationproblem.org/2011/04/new-spanish-volume-of-interviews-with-austrians.html.
Horwitz, S. (2014, June 12). In Natural Disasters, Companies Operate Like Neighbours. *Wall Street Journal*. https://www.wsj.com/articles/in-natural-disasters-companies-operate-like-neighbors-1465338881. https://dailytimes.com.pk/76210/in-natural-disasters-companies-operate-like-neighbours/.
Hospers, J. (1978, April). Liberty's Heritage. *Libertarian Review*, 11–14. http://www.unz.org/Pub/LibertarianRev-1978apr-00011.
Howson, S. (2011). *Lionel Robbins*. Cambridge: Cambridge University Press.
Hülsmann, J. G. (2007). *Mises: The Last Knight of Liberalism*. Auburn, AL: Ludwig von Mises Institute.
Hülsmann, J. G. (2008a). *Deflation and Liberty*. Auburn, AL: Ludwig von Mises Institute.
Hülsmann, J. G. (2008b). *Ethics of Money Production*. Auburn, AL: Ludwig von Mises Institute.
Hülsmann, J. G. (2009). Preface. In L. Mises (Ed.), *Memoirs*. Auburn, AL: Ludwig von Mises Institute.
Hunold, A. (1951, Spring). The Mont Pelerin Society. *World Liberalism* (MPS Archives Box 4.12).
Hunt, T. (2010, July 10). Hugh Trevor-Roper the Biography Review. *Daily Telegraph*. http://www.telegraph.co.uk/culture/books/bookreviews/7879092/Hugh-Trevor-Roper-the-Biography-review.html.
Hutton, G. (1960). *All Capitalists Now*. London: Institute of Economic Affairs.
Ickes, H. L. (1953). *The Secret Diary of Harold L. Ickes: The First Thousand Days*. New York: Simon & Schuster.

Janner, G., & Taylor, D. (2008). *Jewish Parliamentarians*. London: Vallentine Mitchell.
Jefferson, T. (1786, August 13). *Letter to George Wythe*. http://www.let.rug.nl/usa/presidents/thomas-jefferson/letters-of-thomas-jefferson/jefl47.php.
Jenks, J. (2006). *British Propaganda and News Media in the Cold War*. Edinburgh: Edinburgh University Press.
Jenkins, S. (2006). *Thatcher and Sons: A Revolution in Three Acts*. London, UK: Penguin.
Jewkes, J. (1948). *Ordeal by Planning*. London: Macmillan.
Jones, A. G. (1985). *Star Wars: Suicide or Survival?*. London: Weidenfeld & Nicolson.
Johnson, H. G. (1960). A.C. Pigou 1877–1959. *Canadian Journal of Economics and Political Science, 26*, 150–155.
Johnson, I. (2014, May 11). Academic Claims that the Former Chancellor's Foundation Complained to His Employer. *Independent*. https://web.archive.org/web/20140511082724/http://www.independent.co.uk/environment/climate-change/nigel-lawsons-climatechange-denial-charity-intimidated-environmental-expert-9350069.html.
Johnson, P. (2009). *Churchill*. New York: Viking.
Kahane, J. (1951 [1932]). Translator's Notes. In L. Mises (Ed.), *Socialism: An Economic and Sociological Analysis* (J. Kahane, Trans.). New Haven: Yale University Press.
Kahn, R. F. (1974). On Re-reading Keynes. In *Proceedings of the British Academy* (pp. 361–391).
Kahn, R. F. (1984). *The Making of Keynes' General Theory*. Cambridge: Cambridge University Press.
Kamen, A. (2009, March 16). On Warming, a Cold Splash From Across the Pond. *Washington Post*. http://www.washingtonpost.com/wp-dyn/content/article/2009/03/15/AR2009031501855.html.
Kass, J. (2017, September 12). Durbin, Democrats Reveal Their Bigotry in Questioning of Judicial Nominee From Notre Dame. *Chicago Tribune*. http://www.chicagotribune.com/news/columnists/kass/ct-federal-judge-catholic-kass-met-0913-20170912-column.html.
Kaza, G. (2013). Mises and the Struggle Against Italian Fascism in World War II. Austrian Economics Research Conference.
Kengor, P. (2010). *Dupes: How America's Adversaries Have Manipulated Progressives for a Century*. Intercollegiate Studies Institute.
Keynes, J. M. (1936). *The General Theory of Employment, Interest and Money*. London: Macmillan.
Keynes, J. M. (1973–1989). *The Collected Writings of John Maynard Keynes*. London: Macmillan.

Kirk, T. (1996). *Nazism and the Working Class in Austria: Industrial Unrest and Political Dissent in the National Community.* Cambridge: Cambridge University Press.

Kirzner, I. (1978). *Competition and Entrepreneurship.* Chicago: University of Chicago Press.

Klausinger, H. (2006). From Mises to Morgenstern: Austrian Economics During the Ständestaat. *Quarterly Journal of Austrian Economics, 9*(3), 25–43.

Klausinger, H. (2010). Hayek on Practical Business Cycle Research: A Note. In H. Hagemann, T. Nishizawa, & Y. Ikeda (Eds.), *Austrian Economics in Transition: From Carl Menger to Friedrich Hayek* (pp. 218–234). Basingstoke, UK: Palgrave Macmillan.

Klausinger, H. (2012). Editorial Notes. In F. A. Hayek (Ed.), *Business Cycles. The Collected Works of F.A. Hayek.* Chicago: University of Chicago Press.

Klausinger, H. (2014). Academic Anti-semitism and the Austrian School: Vienna 1918–1945. *Atlantic Economic Journal, 42,* 191–204.

Klausinger, H. (2015, June). Hans Mayer, Last Knight of the Austrian School, Vienna Branch. *History of Political Economy, 47*(2), 271–305.

Klein, L. (1986). Lawrence R. Klein. In W. Breit & R. W. Spencer (Eds.), *Lives of the Laureates Seven Nobel Laureates.* Cambridge, MA: MIT Press.

Klor, E. F., Saiegh, S., & Satyanath, S. (2017). Cronyism in State Violence: Evidence from Labor Repression During Argentina's Last Dictatorship. Mimeo. http://pages.ucsd.edu/~ssaiegh/paper_KSS.pdf.

Koch, C. (1978, August). The Business Community: Resisting Regulation. *Libertarian Review, 7*(7), 30–34. https://www.libertarianism.org/lr/LR788.pdf.

Koestler, A. (1950). Arthur Koestler. In R. Crossman (Ed.), *Communism: The God that Failed.* New York: Harper and Row.

Koether, G. (2000). A Life Among Austrians. *Austrian Economics Newsletter, 20*(3). https://mises.org/system/tdf/aen20_3_1_0.pdf?file=1&type=document.

Konner, M. (2017, July 1). In Tough Times, Religion Can Offer a Sturdy Shelter. *Wall Street Journal.* https://www.wsj.com/articles/in-tough-times-religion-can-offer-a-sturdy-shelter-1498829765.

Kresge, S. (1994). Introduction. In F. A. Hayek (Ed.), *Hayek on Hayek an Autobiographical Dialogue.* Supplement to *The Collected Works of F.A. Hayek* (S. Kresge & L. Wenar, Eds.). Chicago: University of Chicago Press.

Kuehnelt-Leddihn, E. (n.d.). *The Cultural Background of Ludwig von Mises.* http://www.mises.org/pdf/asc/essays/kuehneltLeddihn.pdf.

Kuehnelt-Leddihn, E. (pseudonym Campbell, F. S.) (1978 [1943]). *The Menace of the Herd: Or, Procrustes at Large (Studies in Conservative Philosophy).* New York: Gordon Press.

Kuehnelt-Leddihn, E. R. (1992). The Road from Serfdom. *National Review,* 44(8), 32.
Kummer, F. (1932). German Trade-Unions and Their 1931 Congress. *Monthly Labor Review,* 34(1).
Lackman, L. (1978). An Interview with Ludwig Lackman. *Austrian Economic Newsletter,* 1(3). https://mises.org/library/interview-ludwig-lachmann.
Lancet Commission on Pollution and Health. (2017, October 19). *The Lancet.* http://www.thelancet.com/commissions/pollution-and-health.
Landman, A., & Glanz, S. A. (2009, January). Tobacco Industry Efforts to Undermine Policy-Relevant Research. *American Journal of Public Health,* 99(1), 45–58.
Lake, R. (2005, February 5). Lecture Causes Dispute. *Los Vegan Review Journal.* https://web.archive.org/web/20050209040615/http://www.reviewjournal.com/lvrj_home/2005/Feb-05-Sat-2005/news/25808494.html.
Lal, D. (2009). *The Mont Pelerin Society: A MANDATE RENEWED.* MPS Presidential Address. http://www.econ.ucla.edu/lal/MPS%20Presidential%20Address%203.5.09.pdf.
Lamis, A. P. (1990). *The Two-Party South.* Oxford: Oxford University Press.
Lange, O. (1938). *On the Economic Theory of Socialism* (B. Lippincott, Ed.). Minneapolis: University of Minnesota Press.
Lashmar, P., & Oliver, J. (1998). *Britain's Secret Propaganda War.* Stroud: Sutton Publishing Company.
Lashmar, P., Mullins, A. (1998, August 24). Churchill Protected Scottish Peer Suspected of Spying for Japan Second World War: Government Papers Show Prominent Aristocrat was Believed to be Leaking Naval Secrets to Tokyo. *The Independent.* http://www.independent.co.uk/news/churchill-protected-scottish-peer-suspected-of-spying-for-japan-1173730.html.
László, P., & Rady, M. (Eds.) (2004). *British–Hungarian Relations Since 1848.* London: Hungarian Cultural Centre, School of Slavonic and East European Studies, University of London.
Law, R. (1950). *Return from Utopia.* London: Faber & Faber.
Lawson, D. (2011, September 24). Ridley Was Right It May Have Cost Him His Job, but He Was Correct to be Concerned About Our Loss of Sovereignty. *The Spectator.* http://www.spectator.co.uk/features/7256363/ridley-was-right/.
Lawson, N. (1992). *The View From No. 11. Memoirs of a Tory Radical.* London: Bantam.
Leonhardt, D. (2016, December 8). The American Dream, Quantified at Last. *New York Times.* https://www.nytimes.com/2016/12/08/opinion/the-american-dream-quantified-at-last.html.
Leonard, R. (2010). *Von Neumann, Morgenstern, and the Creation of Game Theory: From Chess to the Social Sciences.* Cambridge: Cambridge University Press.

Leonard, R. (2011). The Collapse of Interwar Vienna: Oskar Morgenstern's Community, 1925–50. *History of Political Economy, 43*(1), 83–130.

Liggio, L. (2010). A Classical Liberal Life. In W. Block (Ed.), *I Chose Liberty: Autobiographies of Contemporary Libertarians*. Auburn, AL: Ludwig von Mises Institute.

Louw, L. (2011, November 20). Leon Louw on Sinking South Africa—And How Free-Market Thinking Can Help Recover Prosperity. *Daily Bell*. http://www.thedailybell.com/exclusive-interviews/anthony-wile-leon-louw-on-sinking-south-africa-and-how-free-market-thinking-can-help-recover-prosperity/.

Le Queux, W. T. (1874). *The Great War in England in 1897*. London: Tower.

Le Queux, W. T. (1906). *The Invasion of 1910 with an Account of the Siege of London*. London: E. Nash.

Leube, K. R. (1984, July). Essay: Hayek, Orwell, and The Road to Serfdom. *Prometheus, 2*(3). http://www.lfs.org/index.htm.

Leube, K. R. (2004). *Friedrich A. Hayek: His Life and Work*. February 10. Auditorio Friedrich A. Hayek, Universidad Francisco Marroquín, Guatemala. http://www.newmedia.ufm.edu/gsm/index.php/Leubehayek.

Liggio, L. (1979). *Mont Pelerin: 1947–1978, the Road to Libertarianism*. Libertarianism.org. https://www.libertarianism.org/publications/essays/mont-pelerin-1947-1978-road-libertarianism.

Lusane, C. (2003). *Hitler's Black Victims: The Historical Experiences of Afro-Germans, European Blacks, African and African Americans in the Nazi Era*. New York: Routledge.

Macaulay, T. B. (1853). *The History of England From the Accession of James II*. Philadelphia: Porter and Coates.

Machlup, F. (1974, December). Hayek's Contribution to Economics. *Swedish Journal of Economics, 76*, 498–531.

Machlup, F. (1980). An Interview with Fritz Machlup. *Austrian Economics Newsletter, 3*(1). https://mises.org/library/interview-fritz-machlup.

Maier, H. (2004). *Totalitarianism and Political Religions Volume 1: Concepts for the Comparison of Dictatorships*. London: Routledge.

Manne, H. G. (1993). *An Intellectual History of the George Mason University School of Law*. GMU Law and Economics Center. https://www.law.gmu.edu/about/history.

Marcuse, H. (1968). *Negations Essays in Critical Theory*. Boston: Beacon.

Marsh, P. T. (1994). *Joseph Chamberlain: Entrepreneur in Politics*. New Haven: Yale University Press.

Mayer, J. (2010, August 30). Covert Operations: The Billionaire Brothers Who Are Waging a War Against Obama. *New Yorker*. https://www.newyorker.com/magazine/2010/08/30/covert-operations.

Mayer, J. (2016). *Dark Money: The Hidden History of the Billionaires Behind the Rise of the Radical Right*. New York: Penguin.

McCord, N., & Purdue, W. A. (2011). *British History 1815–1914.* Oxford: Oxford University Press.
McCormick, D. (1960). *The Wicked Village.* London: Jarrolds.
McCormick, D. (1962). *Temple of Love.* London: Jarrolds.
McCormick, D. (1963). *The Mask of Merlin: A Critical Biography of David Lloyd George.* London: Mcdonald.
McCormick, D. (1965). *The Private Life of Mr. Gladstone.* London: Frederick Muller.
McCormick, D. (1967). *Madoc and the Discovery of America: Some New Light on an Old Controversy.* London: Frederick Muller.
McCormick, D. (1968). *John Dee: Scientist, Geographer, Astrologer and Secret Agent to Elizabeth I.* London: Frederick Muller.
McCormick, D. (pseudonym: Deacon, R.). (1969). *A History of the British Secret Service.* London: Frederick Muller.
McCormick, D. (1970a). *The Identity of Jack the Ripper* (2nd ed.). London: John Long.
McCormick, D. (1970b). *Murder by Perfection: Maundy Gregory, the Man Behind Two Unsolved Mysteries.* London: John Long.
McCormick, D. (pseudonym: Deacon, R.) (1972). *A History of the Russian Secret Service.* London: Frederick Muller.
McCormick, D. (pseudonym: Deacon, R.) (1973). *The Master Book of Spies: The World of Espionage, Master Spies, Tortures, Interrogations, Spy Equipment, Escapes, Codes & How You Can Become a Spy.* London: Hodder Causton.
McCormick, D. (1975). *The Hell-Fire Club: The Story of the Amorous Knights of Wycombe.* London: Sphere.
McCormick, D. (1976a). *Taken for a Ride: The History of Cons and Con-Men.* London: Hardwood Smart.
McCormick, D. (1976b). *A Biography of William Caxton: The First English Editor, Printer, Merchant, and Translator.* London: Frederick Mueller.
McCormick, D. (1977). *Who's Who in Spy Fiction.* London: Hamish Hamilton.
McCormick, D. (pseudonym: Deacon, R.) (1978). *The Silent War: A History of Western Naval Intelligence.* London: David & Charles.
McCormick, D. (pseudonym: Deacon, R.) (1979). *The British Connection Russia's Manipulation of British Individuals and Institutions.* London: Hamish Hamilton.
McCormick, D. (pseudonym: Deacon, R.) (1980a). *Approaching 1984.* London: David & Charles.
McCormick, D. (1980b). *Love in Code, or, How to Keep Your Secrets.* London: Eyre Metheun.
McCormick, D. (pseudonym: Deacon, R.) (1982). *With My Little Eye: The Memoirs of a Spy-Hunter.* London: Frederick Muller.

McCormick, D. (pseudonym: Deacon, R.) (1985). *The Cambridge Apostles: A History of Cambridge University's Elite Intellectual Secret Society.* London: Royce.
McCormick, D. (pseudonym: Deacon, R.) (1987). *Spyclopedia: The Comprehensive Handbook of Espionage.* New York: William Morrow.
McCormick, D. (pseudonym: Deacon, R.) (1990). *The Greatest Treason: The Bizarre Story of Hollis, Liddell and Mountbatten* (Rev. Ed.). London: Century.
McCormick, D. (1993). *17F—The Life of Ian Fleming.* London: Peter Owen.
McGurn, W. (2017, October 2). The Morality of Charles Koch. *Wall Street Journal.* https://www.wsj.com/articles/the-morality-of-charles-koch-1506983981.
McMaken, R. (2014, April 24). Our Oligarchs Can Thank James Madison. *Mises Daily.* https://mises.org/library/our-oligarchs-can-thank-james-madison.
McLean, J. J. (1974). *Campbell-Bannerman: The New Imperialism and the Struggle for Leadership within the Liberal Party, 1892–1906.* Ann Arbor, MI: University Microfilms International.
McLellan, D. (1976). *Karl Marx His Life and Thought.* St. Albans, UK: Granada.
McGreal, C. (2006, February 7). Brothers in Arms—Israel's Secret Pact with Pretoria. *Guardian.* https://www.theguardian.com/world/2006/feb/07/southafrica.israel.
McManus, D. (1987, June 15). Reagan Impeachment Held Possible: It's Likely if He Knew of Profits Diversion, Hamilton Says. *Los Angeles Times.* http://articles.latimes.com/1987-06-15/news/mn-4220_1_president-reagan.
Menger, C. (1871). *Grundsätze der Volkswirtschaftslehre.* Wien: Erster allgemeiner Teil.
Michelini, L., & Maccabelli, T. (2015). Economics and Anti-semitism: The Case of Maffeo Pantaleoni. *History of Political Economy, 47*(1), 91–118.
Mises, L. (1912). *Theorie des Geldes und der Umlaufsmittel.* Munich: Duncker and Humblot.
Mises, L. (1922). *Die Gemeinwirtschaft: Untersuchungen über den Sozialismus.* Jena: Gustav Fischer Verlag. http://docs.mises.de/Mises/Mises_Gemeinwirtschaft.pdf.
Mises, L. (1932). *Die Gemeinwirtschaft: Untersuchungen über den Sozialismus* (2nd ed.). Jena: Gustav Fischer Verlag.
Mises, L. (1944). *Bureaucracy.* New Haven: Yale University Press.
Mises, L. (1949). *Human Action: A Treatise on Economics* (1st ed.). New Haven: Yale University Press.
Mises, L. (1950, May 4). Middle-of-the-Road Policy Leads to Socialism. *Commercial and Financial Chronicle.* https://mises.org/library/middle-road-policy-leads-socialism.
Mises, L. (1951 [1932]). *Socialism: An Economic and Sociological Analysis* (J. Kahane, Trans.). New Haven: Yale University Press.

Mises, L. (1956). *The Anti-capitalist Mentality.* Canada: D. Van Nostrand Company Inc.

Mises, L. (1960). *Planning for Freedom and Twelve Other Essays and Addresses.* South Holland, IL: Libertarian Press.

Mises, L. (1961a, April). Liberty and its Antithesis. Review of Hayek's The Constitution of Liberty. *Christian Century.*

Mises, L. (1961b, August 1). Liberty and its Antithesis. Review of Hayek's The Constitution of Liberty. *Christian Economics, 1,* 3 (Hayek Archives Box 167).

Mises, L. (1962). *The Ultimate Foundation of Economic Science an Essay on Method.* New York: Van Nostrand.

Mises, L. (1963). *Human Action: A Treatise on Economics* (2nd ed.). New Haven: Yale University Press.

Mises, L. (1964, February 4). Deception of Government Intervention. *Christian Economics.* https://history.fee.org/publications/deception-of-government-intervention/.

Mises, L. (1966). *Human Action: A Treatise on Economics* (3rd ed.). Chicago: Henry Regnery.

Mises, L. (1985 [1927]). *Liberalism in the Classical Tradition* (R. Raico, Trans.). Auburn, AL: Ludwig von Mises Institute.

Mises, L. (1990). *Money, Method and the Market Process.* Auburn, AL: Ludwig von Mises Institute; Norwell, MA: Kluwer Academic Publishers. Selected by Margit von Mises and Edited with an Introduction by Richard M. Ebeling.

Mises, L. (1993 [1964]). Indefatigable Leader. Remarks by Ludwig von Mises on the occasion of Henry Hazlitt's 70th birthday, on November 28, 1964. In Sennholz, H. (Ed.), *The Wisdom of Henry Hazlitt.* New York: The Foundation for Economic Education, Inc. http://www.mises.ch/library/Hazlitt_Wisdom_of_HH.pdf.

Mises, L. (1996 [1966]). *Human Action: A Treatise on Economics* (B. Greaves, Ed.). Indianapolis: Liberty Fund. http://oll.libertyfund.org/titles/mises-human-action-a-treatise-on-economics-vol-1-lf-ed.

Mises, L. (1998 [1949]). *Human Action: A Treatise on Economics the Scholars Edition.* Auburn, AL: Ludwig von Mises Institute.

Mises, L. 2000. *Selected Writings of Ludwig von Mises, Vol. 3: The Political Economy of International Reform and Reconstruction.* Indianapolis: Liberty Fund. http://oll.libertyfund.org/titles/mises-selected-writings-of-ludwig-von-mises-vol-3-the-political-economy-of-international-reform-and-reconstruction.

Mises, L. (2003 [1969]). *The Historical Setting of the Austrian School of Economics.* Auburn, AL: Ludwig von Mises Institute.

Mises. L. (2006). *The Causes of the Economic Crisis and Other Essays Before and After the Great Depression* (P. Greaves, Ed.). Auburn, AL: Ludwig von Mises Institute.

Mises, L. (2007a [1958]). Mises and Rothbard Letters to Ayn Rand. *Journal of Libertarian Studies, 21*(4), 11–16.

Mises, L. (2007b [1957]). *Theory and History an Interpretation of Social and Economic Evolution.* Auburn, AL: Ludwig von Mises Institute.

Mises, L. (2009 [1978 (1940)]). *Memoirs.* Auburn, AL: Ludwig von Mises Institute.

Mises, L. (2011 [1929]). *A Critique of Interventionism.* Auburn, AL: Ludwig von Mises Institute.

Mises, M. (1976). *My Years with Ludwig von Mises.* New York: Arlington House.

Mises, M. (1984). *My Years with Ludwig von Mises* (2nd ed.). Cedar Falls, IA: Center for Futures Education.

Moffitt, I. (1983). *The Presence of Evil.* New York: National Book Network.

Montes, L. (2015). *Friedman's Two Visits to Chile in Context.* http://jepson.richmond.edu/conferences/summer-institute/papers2015/LMontesSIPaper.pdf.

Montgomery Hyde, H. (1991). *Walter Monckton.* London: Sinclair-Stevenson.

Monypenny, W. F. (1912). *The Life of Benjamin Disraeli, Earl of Beaconsfield Volume II 1837–1846.* London: The Times Publishing Company.

Morgan, L. (2011, July 18). End of a Royal Dynasty as Otto von Habsburg is Laid to Rest... with His Heart Buried in a Crypt 85 Miles Away. *MailOnline.*

Mosley, D., & Le Vien, J. (1981). *The Duchess of Windsor.* London: Stein and Day.

Morgan, K. O. (2001). *Britain Since 1945: The People's Peace.* Oxford: Oxford University Press.

Morton, A. (2015). *17 Carnations: The Windsors, the Nazis and the Cover-Up.* London: Michael O'Mara.

Moss, R. (1973). *Chile's Marxist Experiment.* New York: Wiley.

Moss, R. (1978, Summer). On Standing Up to the Russians in Africa. *Policy Review,* 97–116. http://www.unz.org/Pub/PolicyRev-1978q3-00097.

Muggeridge, M. (1982). *Like it was: The Diaries of Malcolm Muggeridge.* New York: William Morrow. Selected and edited by J. Bright-Holmes.

Mummery, A. F., & Hobson, J. A. (1889). *The Physiology of Industry: Being an Exposure of Certain Fallacies in Existing Theories of Economics.* London: John Murray.

Murdoch, R. (1990). The War on Technology. *City Journal* Manhattan Institute Third Annual Walter B. Wriston Lecture in Public Policy. http://www.city-journal.org/article01.php?aid=1631.

Myers, D. B. (2007, January 24). Recording of Reagan's Fair Speech Found. *Neshoba Democrat.* http://www.neshobademocrat.com/Content/NEWS/News/Article/Recording-of-Reagan-s-Fair-speech-found/2/297/13920.

Myrdal, G. (1944). *An American Dilemma: The Negro Problem and Modern Democracy.* New York: Harper and Brothers.

Najarjuly, N. (2017, July 20). India Picks Ram Nath Kovind, of Caste Once Called 'Untouchables,' as President. *New York Times.*
Nasar, S. (1992, March 24). Friedrich von Hayek Dies at 92; An Early Free-Market Economist. *New York Times.* http://www.nytimes.com/1992/03/24/world/friedrich-von-hayek-dies-at-92-an-early-free-market-economist.html.
Nayaka, J. P., & Nurullah, S. (1974). *A Students' History of Education in India (1800–1973)* (6th ed.). New York: Macmillan.
North, G. K. (1987). *The Plague Has Come at Last.* http://soamc.org/tfh/FILES/Abortion_Gays_and_AIDS.
North, G. K. (2002, January 21). *Mises on Money.* Lewrockwell.com. https://archive.lewrockwell.com/north/north83.html.
North, G. K. (2010). It All Began with Fred Schwartz. In W. Block (Ed.), *I Chose Liberty: Autobiographies of Contemporary Libertarians.* Auburn, AL: Ludwig von Mises Institute.
Norton-Taylor, R. (2005, April 1). Months Before War, Rothermere Said Hitler's Work was Superhuman. *Guardian.* http://www.theguardian.com/media/2005/apr/01/pressandpublishing.secondworldwar.
Odehnal, B. (2014, June 3). Gipfeltreffen mit Putins fünfter Kolonne. *Tages-Anzeiger.*http://www.tagesanzeiger.ch/ausland/europa/Gipfeltreffen-mit-Putins-fuenfter-Kolonne/story/30542701.
Okon, H. (1997). Austrian Economics in Japan: An Interview with Hiroyuki Okon. *Austrian Economic Newsletter, 17*(4). https://mises.org/library/austrian-economics-japan-interview-hiroyuki-okon.
Olson, W. (1998, November). Reasonable Doubts: Invitation to a Stoning Getting Cozy with Theocrats. *Reason.* http://reason.com/archives/1998/11/01/invitation-to-a-stoning.
Paine, T. (2000 [1775]). Reflections on Titles. In P. B. Kurland & R. Lerner (Eds.), *The Founders' Constitution.* Chicago: University of Chicago Press. http://press-pubs.uchicago.edu/founders/.
Palmer, T. (1997, September). Lew Rockwell's Vienna Waltz. *Liberty.* http://web.archive.org/web/20050318091128/http://www.libertysoft.com/liberty/features/61palmer.html.
Panton, J. (2011). *Historical Dictionary of the British Monarchy.* Plymouth, UK: Scarecrow.
Partington, G. (2015). *Party Days.* Xlibris.
Paul, R. (2008). *Mises and Austrian Economics a Personal View.* Auburn, AL: Ludwig von Mises Institute.
Penrose, B., & Freedman, S. (1987). *Conspiracy of Silence: The Secret Life of Anthony Blunt.* London: Vintage.
Perkins, H. (1989). *The Rise of Professional Society: England Since 1880.* London: Routledge.

Peterson, W. H. (1996, July 1). A History of the Mont Pelerin Society. *The Freeman.* https://fee.org/articles/a-history-of-the-mont-pelerin-society/.
Peterson, W. H. (2009). *Mises in America.* Auburn, AL: Ludwig von Mises Institute.
Phillips, K. (1974). *Mediacracy: American Parties and Politics in the Communications Age.* New York: Doubleday.
Phillips-Fine, K. (2009). Business Conservatives and the Mont Pèlerin Society. In P. Mirowski & D. Plehwe (Eds.), *The Road From Mont Pèlerin the Making of the Neoliberal Thought Collective.* Cambridge, MA: Harvard University Press.
Pigou, A. C. (1905). *Principles and Methods of Industrial Peace.* London: Macmillan.
Pigou, A. C. (1906). *Protective Preferential Import Duties.* London: Macmillan.
Pigou, A. C. (1912). *Wealth and Welfare.* London: Macmillan.
Pigou, A. C. (1921). Review of Keynes' *Treatise on Probability. Economic Journal, 31,* 507–512.
Pigou, A. C. (1935). *Economics in Practice: Six Lectures on Current Issues.* London: Macmillan.
Pigou, A. C. (1939). Presidential Address. *Economic Journal, XLIV*(194), 215–221.
Pigou, A. C. (1942). Night Life on High Hills. *Alpine Journal, 53*(264), 246–255.
Pigou, A. C. (1944). Review *Road to Serfdom. Economic Journal, 54,* 217–219.
Pigou, A. C. (1950). *Keynes's 'General Theory': A Retrospective View.* London: Macmillan.
Pigou, A. C. (1954, February). Beveridge. Power and Influence (Book Review). *Economica, 21*(81), 73–76 (New Series).
Pimlott, B. (1985). *Hugh Dalton A Life.* London: Cape.
Pincher, C. (1981). *Their Trade is Treachery.* London: Sidgwick & Jackson.
Plumptre, A. (1947). Keynes in Cambridge. *Canadian Journal of Economics, XIII,* 366–371.
Polanyi, K. (1934). Othmar Spann: The Philosopher of Fascism. *New Britain, 3*(53), 6–7.
Polanyi, K. (1935). The Essence of Fascism. In D. Lewis, K. Polanyi, & J. Kitchen (Eds.), *Christianity and the Social Revolution.* London: Gollancz.
Popkin, S. (2012). *The Candidate: What it Takes to Win—And Hold—The White House.* Oxford: Oxford University Press.
Ponting, C. (1998). *Progress and Barbarism: The World in the Twentieth Century.* New York: Random House.
Preston, P. (2012). *The Spanish Holocaust Inquisition and Extermination in Twentieth-Century Spain.* New York: W. W. Norton.

Prowse, M. (2014 [1996]). Austrian Economics and the Public Mind. *Austrian Economics Newsletter,* 16(1). https://mises.org/library/austrian-economics-and-public-mind.

Pugh, M. (2005). *Hurrah For The Blackshirts!: Fascists and Fascism in Britain Between the Wars.* London: Pimlico.

Raico, R. (2012). *Classical Liberalism and the Austrian School.* Auburn, AL: Ludwig von Mises Institute.

Raico, R. (2013, February 20). *An Interview with Ralph Raico.* Mises Institute. https://mises.org/library/interview-ralph-raico-0.

Raico, R. (2014, October 16). Leonard Liggio, RIP. lewrockwell.com. https://www.lewrockwell.com/lrc-blog/515224/.

Raimondo, J. (2000). *An Enemy of the State: The Life of Murray N. Rothbard.* New York: Prometheus Books.

Raina, P. (2001). *George Macaulay Trevelyan: A Portrait in Letters.* Edinburgh: Pentland.

Ranelagh, J. (1991). *Thatcher's People.* London: Harper Collins.

Rapoport, R. (2000). *Hillsdale: Greek Tragedy in America's Heartland.* Oakland, CA: RDR Books.

Rathkolb, O. (2009). The *Anschluss* in the Rear View Mirror, 1938–2008: Historical Memories Between Debate and Transformation. In G. Bischof, F. Plasser, & B. Stelzl-Marx (Eds.), *New Perspectives on Austrian and World War II.* Contemporary Austrian Studies, Volume 17. New Brunswick: Transaction.

Reagan, R. (1984). In M. Mises (Ed.), *My Years with Ludwig von Mises* (2nd ed.). Cedar Falls, IA: Center for Futures Education.

Rees, G. (1972). *Chapter of Accidents.* New York: The Library Press.

Rees, J. (2000). *Looking for Mr. Nobody: The Secret Life of Goronwy Rees.* Piscataway, NJ: Transaction.

Regnery, A. S. (2008). *Upstream: The Ascendance of American Conservatism.* New York: Threshold.

Repp, K. (2000). *Reformers, Critics, and the Paths of German Modernity: Antipolitics and the Search for Alternatives, 1890–1914.* Cambridge, MA: Harvard University Press.

Readfearn, G. (2011, May 6). *Australia Prepares to Swallow Monckton Yet Again.* ABC. http://www.abc.net.au/unleashed/1816194.html.

Reid, T. R. (2017a). *A Fine Mess: A Global Quest for a Simpler, Fairer, and More Efficient Tax System.* New York: Penguin.

Reid, T. R. (2017b, April 13). Interview. PBS Newshour. http://www.pbs.org/newshour/bb/dreading-taxes-countries-show-us-theres-another-way/.

Reisman, G. (2001). Mises as Mentor an Interview with George Reisman. *Austrian Economics Newsletter,* 21(3). https://mises.org/system/tdf/aen21_3_1_0.pdf?file=1&type=document.

Reisman, G. (2002). Eugen von Böhm-Bawerk's 'Value, Cost, and Marginal Utility.' Austrian Scholars' Conference of the Ludwig von Mises Institute, March 16, 2002, Auburn, AL. https://www.capitalism.net/articles/Reisman%20Full.pdf.
Reisman, G. (2005 [1990], October 3). The Toxicity of Environmentalism. *Mises Daily*. https://mises.org/library/toxicity-environmentalism.
Reisman, G. (2006, December 16). General Augusto Pinochet Is Dead. *Mises Wire*. https://mises.org/blog/general-augusto-pinochet-dead.
Revere, R. H. (1959). *Senator Joe McCarthy*. London: Methuen.
Reynolds, M. (2003, Summer). Labor and the Austrian School. *Austrian Economic Newsletter*. https://mises.org/library/labor-and-austrian-school.
Richards, M. (1998). *A Time of Silence: Civil War and the Culture of Repression in Franco's Spain, 1936–1945*. Cambridge: Cambridge University Press.
Rickenbacker, W. F. (Ed.). (1974). *The Twelve-Year Sentence Radical Views on Compulsory Education*. LaSalle, IL: Open Court.
Ridley, J. (2012). *Bertie: A Life of Edward VII*. London: Chatto and Windus.
Ridley, M. W. (2006). Government is the Problem Not the Solution. *Edge The World Question Centre*. http://edge.org/q2006/q06_11.html.
Ridley, M. W. (2010). *The Rational Optimist: How Prosperity Evolves*. New York: HarperCollins.
Ridley, M. W. (2011). *Hayek Award Acceptance Speech*. Manhattan Institute. http://www.manhattan-institute.org/video/index.htm?c=092611MI.
Ridley, M. W. (2014, March 27). Climate Forecast: Muting the Alarm Even While It Exaggerates the Amount of Warming, the IPCC is Becoming More Cautious About Its Effects. *Wall Street Journal*. http://online.wsj.com/news/articles/SB10001424052702303725404579460973643962840.
Ridley, N. (1991). *My Style of Government: The Thatcher Years*. London: Hutchinson.
Rifkind, H. (2006, June 2). People: Monday Club Still on Reich Track. *The Times*.
Robbins, L. (1961, February). Hayek on Liberty. *Economica, 28*(109), 66–81.
Robbins, L. (1971). *Autobiography of an Economist*. London: Macmillan.
Robbins, L. (2012 [1931]). Foreword. In F. A. Hayek (Ed.), *Business Cycles Part I. The Collected Works of F.A. Hayek* (H. Klausinger, Ed.). Chicago: University of Chicago Press.
Robbins, J. (2010). The *Sine Qua Non* of Enduring Freedom. *The Trinity Review*, 295. http://www.trinityfoundation.org/PDF/The%20Trinity%20Review%2000295%20SineQuaNonEnduringFreedom.pdf.
Roberts, T. (2017, October 11). Koch, Turkson Speak at Catholic University's 'Good Profit' Conference. *National Catholic Reporter*. https://www.ncronline.org/news/people/koch-turkson-speak-catholic-universitys-good-profit-conference.

Robinson, J. (1962). *Economic Philosophy*. Chicago: Aldine.
Robinson, J. (1972). The Second Crisis of Economic Theory. *American Economic Review*, 62(1), 1–10.
Rockefeller, D. (2002). *Memoirs*. New York: Random House.
Rockwell, L. H., Jr. (1974, November 21). Government Subsidy Means Government Control. *Private Practice*.
Rockwell, L. H., Jr. (1991, March 10). COLUMN RIGHT: It's Safe Streets Versus Urban Terror: In the '50s, Rampant Crime Didn't Exist Because Offenders Feared What the Police Would Do. *Los Angeles Times*.
Rockwell, L. H. (1994, December). The Cognitive State. *Rothbard Rockwell Report*, 18–19. http://www.unz.org/Pub/RothbardRockwellReport-1994dec-00018.
Rockwell, L. H., Jr. (1997). The Future of Liberty Lets Not Give Into Evil. *Vital Speeches of the Day*, 64(3), 88–91. https://www.econbiz.de/Record/the-future-of-liberty-lets-not-give-into-evil-llewelyn-h-rockwell-jr-founder-and-president-of-the-ludwig-von-mises-institute/10005980503.
Rockwell, L. H., Jr. (2010a). Libertarianism and the Old Right. In W. Block (Ed.), *I Chose Liberty: Autobiographies of Contemporary Libertarians*. Auburn, AL: Ludwig von Mises Institute.
Rockwell, L. H., Jr. (2010b, February 21). EXCLUSIVE INTERVIEW Lew Rockwell on von Mises, Ron Paul, Free Markets and the Future of Freedom by Anthony Wile. *Daily Bell*.
Rockwell, L. H., Jr. (2016). A Message from Lew Rockwell, December 21. https://mises.org/blog/message-lew-rockwell.
Ross, J. (2015, December 21). Obama Revives His 'Cling to Guns or Religion' Analysis—For Donald Trump Supporters. *Washington Post*.
Rothbard, M. N. (1973, October 20). Ludwig von Mises 1881–1973. *Human Events*, 7.
Rothbard, M. N. (1992a, March). A Strategy for the Right. *Rothbard-Rockwell Report*, 3(3). https://mises.org/library/strategy-right.
Rothbard, M. N. (1992b, January). Right-Wing Populism: A Strategy for the Paleo Movement. *Rothbard Rockwell Report*, 5–14. http://rothbard.altervista.org/articles/right-wing-populism.pdf.
Rothbard, M. N. (1993, August). Who Are the Terrorists? *Rothbard Rockwell Report*, 4(8). http://www.unz.org/Pub/RothbardRockwellReport-1993aug-00001.
Rothbard, M. N. (1994a). Nation by Consent. Decomposing the National State. *Journal of Libertarian Studies*, 11(1), 1–10. https://mises.org/library/uk-nation-consent.
Rothbard, M. N. (1994b, July). Revolution in Italy! *Rothbard-Rockwell Report*, 5(7), 1–10. http://www.unz.org/Pub/RothbardRockwellReport-1994jul-00001.

Rothbard, M. N. (1994c, October). A New Strategy for Liberty. *Rothbard Rockwell Report,* 5(10). http://www.unz.org/Pub/RothbardRockwellReport-1994oct-00001.

Rothbard, M. N. (1994d, September). Invade the World. *Rothbard Rockwell Report,* 5(9). http://www.unz.org/Pub/RothbardRockwellReport-1994sep-00001.

Rothbard, M. N. (1994e, December). Saint Hilary and the Religious Left. *Rothbard Rockwell Report.*

Rothbard, M. N. (2001 [1962]). *Man, Economy and State, with Power and Market: Scholars' Edition.* Auburn, AL: Ludwig von Mises Institute.

Rothbard, M. N. (2002 [1982]). *The Ethics of Liberty.* Auburn, AL: Ludwig von Mises Institute.

Rothbard, M. N. (2005 [1978]). *The Mises We Never Knew.* https://mises.org/library/mises-we-never-knew-0.

Rothbard, M. N. (2007). *Betrayal of the American Right.* Auburn, AL: Ludwig von Mises Institute.

Rothbard, M. N. (2010). *Strictly Confidential: The Private Volker Fund Memos of Murray N. Rothbard* (D. Gordon, Ed.). Auburn, AL: Ludwig von Mises Institute.

Rothbard, M. N. (2016). *The Rothbard Reader.* Auburn, AL: Ludwig von Mises Institute. https://mises.org/library/rothbard-reader/html/c/414.

Russell, B. (1935). Some Psychological Difficulties of Pacifism in Wartime. In J. Bell (Ed.), *We Did Not Fight 1914–1918 Experiences of War Resisters.* London: Cobden-Sanderson.

Russell, B. (1985). *Autobiography.* London: Unwin.

Russell, S. (1975). In Memoriam Sir Claude Elliott 1888–1973. *Alpine Journal,* 295–298. https://www.alpinejournal.org.uk/Contents/Contents_1975_files/AJ%201975%20294-304%20In%20Memoriam.pdf.

Sachar, H. M. (2015). *The Assassination of Europe, 1918–1942: A Political History.* Toronto: University of Toronto Press.

Sanders, M. L. (1975). Wellington House and British Propaganda During the First World War. *The Historical Journal, 18,* 119–146.

Sayare, S. (2012, June 7). Portuguese Just Shrug and Go on in the Face of Cuts and Job Losses. *New York Times.* http://www.nytimes.com/2012/06/08/world/europe/portugal-shrugs-at-austerity.html?pagewanted=all&_r=0.

Saltmarsh, J., & Wilkinson, L. P. (1960). *Arthur Cecil Pigou 1877–1959. A Memoir Prepared by the Direction of the Council of King's College Cambridge.* Cambridge: University Press Printed for King's College.

Sampson, A. (1962). *Anatomy of Britain.* London: Hodder & Stoughton.

Samuelson, P. A. (2009). A Few Remembrances of Friedrich von Hayek (1899–1992). *Journal of Economic Behavior and Organization, 69,* 1–4.

Sanchez, J., & Weigel, D. (2008, January 16). Who Wrote Ron Paul's Newsletters? Libertarian Movement Veterans, and a Paul Campaign Staffer, Say it was 'Paleolibertarian' Strategist Lew Rockwell. *Reason.* http://reason.com/archives/2008/01/16/who-wrote-ron-pauls-newsletter.

Schlesinger, A. M. (1960). *The Politics of Upheaval.* Boston: Houghton Mifflin Harcourt.

Schmelzer, M. (2010). *Freiheit für Wechselkurse und Kapital: Die Ursprünge neoliberaler Währungspolitik und die Mont Pélerin Society.* Marburg, Germany: Metropolitis.

Schulak, E. M., & Unterköfler, H. (2011). *The Austrian School of Economics. A History of Its Ideas, Ambassadors, and Institutions* (A. Oost-Zinner, Trans.). Auburn, AL: Ludwig von Mises Institute.

Schumpeter, J. (1946, June). Review: F. A. Hayek, The Road to Serfdom. *Journal of Political Economy, 54,* 269–270.

Segev, T. (2007, November 29). How We Missed Out on the Swiss Option a Last-Minute Arab Proposal in 1947/The Portuguese Jew Who Supported the Nazis/The Death of an Austrian Jew 90 Years Ago. *Haaretz.* http://www.haaretz.com/israel-news/how-we-missed-out-on-the-swiss-option-1.234249.

Sereny, G. (1985, May 9). The Sage of the Free Thinking World. *The Times.*

Sereny, G. (2001). *The Healing Wound Experiences and Reflection on Germany, 1938–2000.* London: Allen Lane/Penguin.

Seaman, L. C. B. (1966). *Post-Victorian Britain 1902–1951.* London: Methuen & Co.

Shearmur, J. (2006). Hayek, The Road to Serfdom, and the British Conservatives. *Journal of the History of Economic Thought, 28,* 309–314.

Shearmur, J. (2010). How I Became Almost a Libertarian. In W. Block (Ed.), *I Chose Liberty: Autobiographies of Contemporary Libertarians.* Auburn, AL: Ludwig von Mises Institute.

Shepley, N. (2013). *Hitler, Chamberlain and Munich: The End of the Twenty Year Truce.* Luton, UK: Andrews.

Shirer, W. L. (1960). *Rise and Fall of the Third Reich.* London: Secker & Warburg.

Shehadi, N. (1991). The London School of Economics and the Stockholm School in the 1930s. In L. Jonung (Ed.), *The Stockholm School of Economics Revisited.* Cambridge: Cambridge University Press.

Shenfield, A. (1980, September). Hayek's Completed Trilogy. *The Freeman, 30*(9), 558–571. https://isistatic.org/journal-archive/ma/24_02/shenfield.pdf?width=640&height=700&iframe=true.

Shenfield, A. (1988 [1968]). *On the State of Bad Economics.* London: Libertarian Alliance. http://www.libertarian.co.uk/lapubs/econn/econn012.pdf.

Shenk, T. (2013). *Maurice Dobb: Political Economist.* New York: Palgrave Macmillan.

Shenoy, S. (2003, Winter). An Interview with Sudha Shenoy. *Austrian Economics Newsletter*, 1–8. http://mises.org/journals/aen/aen23_4_1.pdf.

Simpson, B. W. (1956). *The Heart Has Its Reasons the Memoirs of the Duchess of Windsor*. London: Michael Joseph.

Silverman, P. (1984). Law and Economics in Interwar Vienna Kelsen, Mises and the Regeneration of Austrian Liberalism. University of Chicago PhD, Department of History, Faculty of the Division of the Social Sciences.

Skidelsky, R. (1975). *Oswald Mosley*. London: Macmillan.

Skousen, M. (1991). *Economics on Trial: Lies, Myths and Realities*. Homewood, IL: Business One Irwin.

Skousen, M. (2000, December). Dr. Jekyll and Mr. Robhard. *Inside Liberty*, 14(12), 52–53. http://mises.org/journals/liberty/Liberty_Magazine_December_2000.pdf.

Skousen, M. (2008, February 28). Bill Buckley and Me a True Story. *Human Events Powerful Conservative Voices*. http://www.humanevents.com/2008/02/28/bill-buckley-and-me-a-true-story/.

Skousen, M. (2009). *The Making of Modern Economics: The Lives and Ideas of the Great Thinkers* (2nd ed.). London: M. E. Sharpe.

Simon, E., Simon, S., Robson, W. A., & Jewkes, J. (2015 [1937]). *Moscow in the Making*. London: Routledge.

Simon, H. (1991). *Models of My Life*. New York: Basic Books, Sloan Foundation Series.

Smith, A. (1986). *The Essential Adam Smith* (R. Heilbroner, Ed.). New York: W. W. Norton.

Smith, J. (1980). *The Coming Currency Collapse and What You Can Do About It*. San José, Costa Rica: Griffin Publishing Company.

Snaverly, B. (2014, December 30). Final Tally: Taxpayers Auto Bailout Loss $9.3B. *USA Today*. https://www.usatoday.com/story/money/cars/2014/12/30/auto-bailout-tarp-gm-chrysler/21061251/.

Snyder, L. L. (Ed.). (1982). *Hitler's Third Reich: A Documentary History*. Chicago: Nelson-Hall.

Sobran, M. J., Jr. (1975). Hayek and the Angels. *National Review* (Hayek Archives Box 167).

Socker, K. (1990). The State of Economics Today in Austria an Interview with Karl Socker. *Austrian Economics Newsletter*, 1–4. https://mises.org/library/state-economics-austria-today-interview-karl-socher.

Soref, H. (1979, September). Disgrace Abounding. Review of *The British Connection*. *Tory Challenge*, 9–10.

Stanford University History Study Group. (2016). Evaluating Information: The Cornerstone of Civic Online Reasoning. https://sheg.stanford.edu/upload/V3LessonPlans/Executive%20Summary%2011.21.16.pdf.

Stedman Jones, G. (1983). *Languages of Class: Studies in English Working Class History 1832–1982.* Cambridge: Cambridge University Press.
Steele, D. R. (2000, November). 'Monstrous!' Review of Justin Raimondo—*An Enemy of the State: The Life of Murray N. Rothbard. Liberty.* http://againstpolitics.com/an-enemy-of-the-state/.
Steers, E. (2007). *Lincoln Legends: Myths, Hoaxes, and Confabulations Associated with Our Greatest President.* Lexington: University of Kentucky Press.
Stephen, L. (1871). *The Playground of Europe.* London: Longman, Green.
Stocks, M. D. (1963). *Ernest Simon of Manchester.* Manchester: University of Manchester Press.
Steinacher, G. (2011). *Nazis on the Run: How Hitler's Henchmen Fled Justice.* Oxford: Oxford University Press.
Stigler, G. J. (1978). Why Have the Socialists Been Winning? Mont Pelerin Society 1978 General Meeting, Hong Kong, September 3–9.
Stigler, G. J. (1988). *Memoirs of an Unregulated Economist.* New York: Basic Books.
Stromberg, R. (1994, April 13). Mussolini's Italy Withheld Jews from the Nazis. *New York Times.* http://www.nytimes.com/1994/04/13/opinion/l-mussolini-s-italy-withheld-jews-from-the-nazis-770507.html.
Stolper, G. (1967). *The German Economy from 1870 to the Present Day.* New York: Harcourt, Brace & World.
Swedberg, R. (1992). *Schumpeter: A Biography.* Princeton: Princeton University Press.
Talmon, J. L. (1960). *The Origins of Totalitarian Democracy.* Britain: Secker & Warburg.
Tambini, D. (2001). *Nationalism in Italian Politics: The Stories of the Northern League, 1980–2000.* London: Routledge.
Tanaka, S. (1974, May 17). What Will Happen to the World as Keynesian Economic Theories are Disproved? Views of Professor Hayek, a World-Famous Authority on Inflation Sought. *Shuukan Post* (Hayek Archives Box 52.28).
Targetti, F. (1992). *Nicholas Kaldor: The Economics and Politics of Capitalism as a Dynamic System.* Oxford: Clarendon Press.
Taylor, A. (2014, December 12). Brazil's Torture Report Brings President Dilma Rousseff to Tears. *Sydney Morning Herald.* http://www.smh.com.au/world/brazils-torture-report-brings-president-dilma-rousseff-to-tears-20141211-125fzz.html.
Taylor, A. J. P. (1955). *Bismarck the Man and the Statesman.* London: Hamish Hamilton.
Taylor, A. J. P. (1964). *The Habsburg Monarchy 1809–1918: A History of the Austrian Empire and Austria Hungary.* UK: Peregrine.

Taylor, A. J. P. (1974). *The First World War: An Illustrated History.* London, UK: Penguin.
Taylor, A. J. P. (1979, July 22). Reds Under Beds. *Observer.*
Taylor, B. (1976, August 28). The Pit of State Control. *St Andrew's Citizen* (MPS Archives Box 48.4).
Taylor, P. M. (1999). *British Propaganda in the 20th Century.* Edinburgh: Edinburgh University Press.
Teles, S. M. (2008). *The Rise of the Conservative Legal Movement: The Battle for Control of the Law.* Princeton: Princeton University Press.
Thirlwall, A. (1987). *Nicholas Kaldor.* Brighton: Wheatsheaf Press.
Thompson, D. W. (2012). Widening Participation from an Historical Perspective: Increasing our Understanding of Higher Education and Social Justice. In T. N. Basit & S. Tomlinson (Eds.), *Social Inclusion and Higher Education.* Bristol: Policy Press.
Titcomb, J. (2015, January 7). How the Bank of England Abandoned the Gold Standard. *Daily Telegraph.* http://www.telegraph.co.uk/finance/commodities/11330611/How-the-Bank-of-England-abandoned-the-gold-standard.html.
Tollison, R., & Wagner, R. E. (1988). *Smoking and the State.* Lexington, MA: DC Health.
Tollison, R., & Wagner, R. E. (1992). *The Economics of Smoking.* Boston: Kluwer Academic Publishing.
Trevor-Roper, H. (1947). *The Last Days of Hitler.* New York: Macmillan.
Trevor-Roper, H. (1976). *A Hidden Life: The Enigma of Sir Roger Backhouse.* London: Macmillan.
Thomas, B. (1991). Comment. In L. Jonung (Ed.), *The Stockholm School of Economics Revisited.* Cambridge: Cambridge University Press.
Thurlow, R. C. (2006). *Fascism in Britain: From Oswald Mosley's Blackshirts to the National Front.* London: I.B. Tauris.
Tugwell, R. (1972). *In Search of Roosevelt.* Cambridge, MA: Harvard University Press.
Turner, H. A. (1985). *German Big Business and the Rise of Hitler.* New York: Oxford University Press.
Turner, J. (2000). *The Tories and Europe.* Manchester: Manchester University Press.
Tweedy, N., & Day, P. (2005, March 1). When Rothermere Urged Hitler to Invade Romania. *Telegraph.* http://www.telegraph.co.uk/news/uknews/1484647/When-Rothermere-urged-Hitler-to-invade-Romania.html.
Twigge, S., Hampshire, E., & Macklin, G. (2008). *British Intelligence: Secrets, Spies and Sources.* National Archives: Richmond, Surrey.
Tyrmand, L. (1981, January 20). The Conservative Ideas in Reagan's Victory. *The Wall Street Journal.*

Vedder, R. (1999). A Passion for Economics: An Interview with Richard K. Vedder. *Austrian Economics Newsletter, 19*(1). https://mises.org/library/passion-economics-interview-richard-k-vedder.

Walsh, M. C. (1968). *Prologue A Documentary History of Europe 1848–1960*. Melbourne, Australia: Cassell.

Watters, S. (2005, June 28). Von Habsburg on Presidents, Monarchs, Dictators. *Women's Wear Daily*. http://www.wwd.com/eye/people/von-habsburg-on-presidents-monarchs-dictators.

Ward, B. (2010, June 22). Thatcher Becomes Latest Recruit in Monckton's Climate Sceptic Campaign Monckton's Use of Britain's Former PM Illustrates that Climate Denialism is About Politics, Not Science. *Guardian*. http://www.theguardian.com/environment/2010/jun/22/thatcher-climate-sceptic-monckton.

Wassenaar, A. (1977). *Assault on Private Enterprise: The Freeway to Communism*. Cape Town: Tafelberg.

Weber, M. (1995). Murray Rothbard (1926–1995). *The Journal of Historical Review, 15*(3), 33–34.

Weyr, T. (2005). *The Setting of the Pearl: Vienna Under Hitler*. Oxford: Oxford University Press.

Wheeler, B. (2006, March 9). Wilson 'Plot': The Secret Tapes. *BBC News*. http://news.bbc.co.uk/2/hi/uk_news/politics/4789060.stm.

Wheeler, T. (1975, September 26). Mont Pelerin Society: Microeconomics, Macrofellowship. *National Review*.

White, L. H. (2008). Did Hayek and Robbins Deepen the Great Depression? *Journal of Money, Credit and Banking, 40*, 751–768.

Wieser, F. (1927 [1914]). *Social Economics* (A. Ford Hinrichs, Trans., with a preface by Wesley Clair Mitchell). London: George Allen and Unwin.

Wieser, F. (1983 [1926]). *The Law of Power*. Lincoln: University of Nebraska–Lincoln, Bureau of Business Research.

Williams, R. (1995, July 7). 'Sunday Times' Pays Foot Damages over KGB Claim. *Independent*. http://www.independent.co.uk/news/sunday-times-pays-foot-damages-over-kgb-claim-1590325.html.

Wistrich, R. S. (2012). *Who's Who in Nazi Germany*. New York: Routledge.

Wood, G. (2006, January). 364 Economists on Economic Policy. *Econ Journal Watch, 3*(1), 137–147.

Woodbridge, G. (1978). *The Reform Club 1836–1978. A History from the Club's Records*. Privately Printed for Members of the Reform Club in Association with Clearwater Publishing Company, New York.

Wollstein, J. (1992a, October 1). Why We Spend Too Much on Health Care and Twenty Myths About National Health Insurance. *The Freeman*. https://fee.org/articles/why-we-spend-too-much-on-health-care-and-twenty-myths-about-national-health-insurance/.

Wollstein, J. (1992b, October 2). National Health Insurance: A Medical Disaster. *The Freeman.* https://fee.org/articles/national-health-insurance-a-medical-disaster/.

Wright, T. C., & Oñate, R. (2005). Chilean Diaspora. In C. R. Ember, M. Ember, & I. Skoggard (Eds.), *Encyclopedia of Diasporas: Immigrant and Refugee Cultures Around the World* (Vol. II, pp. 57–65). New York: Springer. https://mises.org/system/tdf/qjae5_3_4.pdf?file=1&type=document.

Wyatt, W. (1956). *The Peril in Our Midst.* London: Phoenix House.

Yeager, L. (1991). An Interview with Leland B. Yeager. *Austrian Economics Newsletter,* 12(3). https://mises.org/library/interview-leland-b-yeager.

Young, G. W. (1953). *The Grace of Forgetting.* London: Country Life.

Young, H. (1898). *One of Us.* London: Macmillan.

Zuccotti, S. (1987). *The Italians and the Holocaust: Persecution, Rescue, and Survival.* Nebraska: University of Nebraska Press.

INDEX

A
Addison, Paul, 117
Al-Qaeda, viii, 26, 66, 286
American Renaissance organisation, 279
Archival Insights in the Evolution of Economics (AIEE), 4, 40, 48
Aristocratic influence, Hayek and clubs, 103–111
  early reform club history, 115–118
  entitlement history, 111–115
  intersecting clubs, 128–129
  later reform club history, 118–127
  Nobel Prize, 138–143
  overview, 103
  road to divorce, 129–138
Austrian School fourth generation, 12–14, 26

B
Bartley, William Warren III, 25
Beck, Glenn, 5, 204
Becker, Gary, 128
Beveridge, William, 49, 67, 70, 86, 122–124, 141, 145n38, 157, 162, 229
Blunt, Anthony, 105, 107, 109, 125, 159–160, 175–176, 309
Boettke, Peter
  "Charles Rowley on the State of Macroeconomics", 36
  on free market, 274
  GMU professorship, 66–67, 207, 222, 225, 277
  on Hayek, 36
  on HES, 5
  influences on, 10, 24, 36–39, 70, 83, 313–314
  Koch brothers and, 35–37, 277
  on markets, 40–41
  Mises and, 313–314
Böhm-Bawerk, Eugen, 9, 112, 167, 321
British Union of Fascists, 198, 215
Brittan, Samuel, 49, 195, 232, 241, 243, 285
Brown, Gordon, 237

Buchanan, James, 8, 13, 15–16, 21, 24, 29, 38, 40, 42, 68, 79, 81, 91, 93, 128, 168, 170, 225, 270, 306, 343
Buchanan, Pat, 208, 212, 279
Buckley, William Jr., 42, 278, 310
Bush, George H.W., 26, 104, 221, 359
Bush, George W., 280, 359
Byrd, William, 174

C

Caldwell, Bruce
  anti-semitism and, 11
  Austrian fascism and, 4–5
  Chile and, 11, 65
  Collected Works of F. A. Hayek, 306, 319, 358
  "emergency" call for fascism and, 267–268, 284
  "free market" economics and, 5
  Hayek and, 10, 114, 134, 142, 160, 343
  Italian fascism and, 320, 327
  market failure and, 180
  Mises and, 199
  persuasion of intellectuals, 65, 67, 80, 90
Casey, William, 240
Cecil family, 106, 110, 123, 125, 163
CFACT lobby, x, xi, 65, 246
"Charles Rowley on the State of Macroeconomics" (Boettke), 36
Civil War (US), 20, 113, 168, 279, 291
Classical Liberalism and, 167
Clinton, Bill, 280
Clinton, Hillary, 280, 307
Clinton, Hillary and, 306
Cold War, 119, 174, 214, 244, 246, 277, 291
Competition and Entrepreneurship, 66
Confederate States of America, 20, 168, 279
Confederation of British Industry, 217, 237
Corn Laws, 113, 115
Crozier, Brian, 217, 231, 281, 340

D

D'Amato, Alphonse, 26
D'Souza, Dinesh, 265
Davis, Francis A., 275
Davis, Jefferson, 168
De-Nazification laws, 26
Deacon, Richard. *See McCormick, Donald*
Deedes, William "Bill", 175
Deflation
  economy and, 84–85
  Great Depression and, 341, 355
  Hayek, Friedrich von on, 229–230
  Hitler's rise to power and, 9, 20, 43, 48, 80, 156, 199, 230, 284, 306
  Hoover, Herbert and, 81
  interest rates and, 351
  labour unions and, 68, 77
  socialism and, 68
  unemployment and, 77, 230
  Weimar Republic and, 80, 126, 159
  Welfare State and, 81, 84
Dirty War (Argentina), 43, 283
Duke, David, 169, 207, 280

E

Ebeling, Richard
  on Austrian fascism, 355, 358
  Cowen and, 33
  "emergency" call for fascism and, 291–295

Hayek and, 133
"How I Became a Libertarian and an Austrian Economist", 30
Italian fascism and, 306, 308–311, 313–316, 324
Keynes and, 39
Liggio and, 167
Mises and, 71, 74
persuasion of intellectuals and, 71, 73, 81–84, 93
Pigou and, 46
Rand and, 31
"Setting the Record Straight", 341
on Stalin, 341–342
white supremacism and, 197, 206, 228, 291–295
"Emergency" demand for fascism
Caldwell and, 267–268, 284
democracy and, 266–295
overview, 265
European Union, 218, 220, 352

F

Falkland Islands, 44–45
Ferdinand, Franz, 130
Fleming, Ian, 108, 110
Fleming, Thomas, 279
Forbes-Sempill, William, 106
Foundation of Economic Education (FEE), 5, 30–31, 73, 225, 272, 277–278, 309
Fox News, xi, 5, 204, 265, 278, 286
Fox, Vicente, 93
Friedman, Milton
Buchanan, James and, 15, 128
Coase and, 157
global warming argument and, 241
Hayek and, 111, 160, 223
Heritage Foundation and, 241, 282
influence on theorists, 285, 294
Keynes and, 227–228
Mises and, 74
MPS and, 233
Nutter and, 180
Robbins and, 142
Welfare State and, 17, 83
WWII and, 356–357

G

Gladstone, William Ewart, 104, 115–116, 119, 123, 125, 238
Global Warming Policy Foundation, 241, 246
Gordon, David, 326
Gordon, Richard L., 325

H

Hayek, Friedrich von
Caldwell and, 10, 114, 134, 142, 160, 343
deflation and, 229–230
Ebeling and, 133
Friedman and, 111, 160, 223
Keynes and, 69, 111, 129, 139, 141, 203, 227–228, 229, 234
Mont Pelerin Society (MPS) and, 47
Thatcher and, 111, 127, 134, 160, 164, 240, 244, 285–286
Hindenburg, Paul, 306
Hitler, Adolf
aristocratic influence and, 107, 117–118, 120, 131, 134
Chamberlain and, 107, 197
Ebeling and, 39
'emergency demand for fascism' and, 265, 269, 283, 290, 293, 294
fake diaries, 177
fourth-generation Austrian thought and, 20, 24–25
Hayek and, 67, 71, 205, 340–342

international right and, 202–203, 215, 218, 220, 225, 230, 239, 242
Italian fascism and, 305, 313, 315, 319–320, 325–326, 328, 330
market failure and, 157–158, 165, 198
Mises and, 32, 353
persuasion of intellectuals and, 67, 71, 76–78, 80, 83, 85–86, 90
rise to power, 43–45, 48, 156–157, 201–202
Selling Hitler, 177, 202
suicide, 358
third-generation Austrian thought and, 9–12
Wieser and, 7–8
Hoover Institution, 285, 287
Hoover, Herbert, 81, 95n28, 200, 204, 235
"How I Became a Libertarian and an Austrian Economist" (Ebeling), 30

I
Intergenerational entitlements, 4, 39, 47, 89, 181
Italian fascism, 21, 305–330

J
Jackdaw Network, 48, 103–104, 233
Jackson, Andrew, 327
Jefferson, Thomas, 213, 291, 346–347
Johnson, Boris, 109
Johnson, Harry, 167
Johnson, Lyndon B., 161, 240
Johnson, Paul, 164
Jones, Michael, 205

K
Kemp, Jack, 212
Kennedy, John F., 213, 359
Keynes, John Maynard
  Boettke and, 40
  construction of economic theory, 34, 49, 126
  Davenport and, 209
  Ebeling and, 39
  gold standard and, 209
  Great Depression and, 157–158, 161
  Hayek and, 111, 139, 141, 203, 229, 234
  Hoppe and, 34
  McCormick and, 166
  Myrdal and, 129
  Pigou and, 173, 176, 179, 236, 309
  Prowse and, 236
  Robbins and, 141
Keynesianism
  Baxendale and, 235
  Davenport and, 210–211, 289
  Hayek and, 69–70, 129, 227–228
  Koch brothers and, 276–277
  Mises and, 69, 276, 315
  Rothbard and, 20
  WWI and, 67
Koch brothers, 5, 28, 35–38, 40, 43, 195, 200–202, 205, 275–276, 341
Kohl, Helmut, 26
Ku Klux Klan, 20, 23, 169, 207, 239, 280

L
Labour unions, 44, 68, 77–80, 85–88, 125, 158–160, 181, 223, 240, 244, 270, 323
Laffer, Arthur, ix, 65
Law & Economics Center, 206

Law of Power, The (Wieser), 6, 348
Law on the Abolition of Nobility, 8, 12
Law, Legislation, and Liberty (Hayek), 16, 42, 51, 68, 198, 292, 339
Law, Richard, 223
Lawson, Dominic, 220
Lawson, Nigel, ix, 49, 195, 214, 231–233, 241–242, 246
Leube, Kurt, ix, 25, 31–32, 65, 167, 170, 312
Liggio, Leonard, ix, 29, 40, 50, 88, 91, 167, 271
Limbaugh, Rush, 5, 41
Lincoln, Abraham, 220
Louw, Leon, x–xi, 49, 65, 195, 221, 246, 317

M
Macey, William L., 290–291, 327
Marxism, 24, 45, 67, 113, 120, 123, 160, 171–172, 203, 247, 270, 283, 285, 286, 321–322, 326
Mayer, Hans, 10–11, 40
McCarthy, Joseph, 200–201
McCormick, Donald (aka Richard Deacon)
  aristocratic influence and, 103–105, 108–111, 116–118, 120–122
  background, viii
  British Connection, 166, 214
  Dalyell and, 221
  Duke of Edinburgh and, 165
  Ebeling and, x, 309
  Elliott and, 108–109
  externalities and, xi
  Fleming and, 110
  Hayek and, viii, 47–48, 166–167, 233, 244, 312, 349
  History of the Russian Secret Service, 313
  Jackdaw Network and, 48, 103
  Madoc and the Discovery of America, 110
  McCarthy and, 201
  Mises and, 311
  Pigou and, 163–164, 171–180
  Private Life of Mr. Gladstone, 116
  Reform Club and, 105, 312
  Skousen and, x, 310
  Soref and, viii, 214
  With My Little Eye, 108
McGurn, William, 200
Mellon, Andrew, 81, 235
Menger, Carl, 6, 10, 113, 176, 349
Mises, Ludwig von
  aristocratic influence, 113, 126, 134, 137, 143
  Austrian thought and fascism, 3, 6–13, 17, 19–25, 27–29, 31–34, 38–40, 44, 49–51
  Boettke and, 313–314
  Caldwell and, 198
  Ebeling and, 71, 73
  "emergency" demand for fascism, 265–268, 270, 273–274, 276–278, 280, 282–284, 286–294
  Friedman and, 74
  international fascism and, 195, 197–199, 202–203, 225–227, 229, 231, 236–237, 245–247
  Italian fascism and, 305–308, 309, 311, 313–316, 321–327
  Keynesianism and, 69, 276, 314
  persuasion of intellectuals, 67, 69–78, 81, 83, 85–93
  Pigou and, 167, 172, 181
  spread of European fascism and, 339–344, 347, 350–358
Monckton, Christopher, xi, 49, 65, 195, 220, 241–242, 245–248
Monckton, Walter, 131, 180, 356
Monday Club, 214
Mont Pelerin Society (MPS)

aristocratic influence, 127–129,
    138–139, 143
Austrian fascism and, 358
Buchanan and, 81
deflation and, 85
"emergency" demand for fascism,
    265, 269, 274, 279, 282–285,
    287
Hayek and, 47
Hitler's rise to power and, 20
international right and, 204–207,
    210–211, 214, 221–230, 233,
    241
Italian fascism and, 313, 317, 323
Leoni and, 4
persuasion of intellectuals to join,
    81, 89, 93, 114
prominent members, 32–33, 36,
    41–42, 81, 89, 93
Spanish fascism and, 342
stagflation and, 126
Stigler and, 14
Murdoch, Rupert, 5, 47, 49, 177,
    195, 197, 202, 204, 240, 242,
    278, 286, 312, 327
Mussolini, Benito, 7, 11, 78, 147n65,
    215, 282, 322–324, 329–330

N
National Public Radio (NPR), xi, 50,
    305, 308, 330n3
New Deal, 200, 210, 278
North Atlantic Treaty Organization
    (NATO), 214
North, Gary, ix, 33, 41, 169, 209,
    266, 307, 316
Northern Ireland Civil Rights
    Association, 218
Northern League, 273, 278
Northern Rock, xi, 239
Nutter, Warren, 180

O
Obama, Barack, 200, 280

P
Paine, Thomas, 346–347
Paneuropean Union, 218, 355–356
Patton, William A., 12
Paul, Ron, 169, 289, 316
Persuasion of intellectuals
    Caldwell and, 65, 67, 80, 90
    Ebeling and, 71, 73, 80–84, 93
    Hitler and, 67, 71, 76–78, 80, 83,
        85–86, 90
    Mises and, 66, 69–78, 81, 82,
        85–93
    MPS and, 81, 89, 93, 114
Peterloo Massacre, 12, 114
Pigou, A. C., 17, 28, 46, 48, 109,
    111, 120, 129, 141, 209, 214,
    222, 244, 287, 308–309, 312,
    313, 344
Pigouvian market failure
    free trade and the Reform Club,
        160–164
    Hayek and British government,
        164–182
    London and Cambridge "opinion",
        155–160
    overview, 155
Pinochet, Augusto, 15, 26, 43–46,
    50–51, 76, 88–90, 127, 203–204,
    216, 230, 265, 282, 284, 286,
    293–294, 306, 311, 340, 345
Pope John Paul II, 167
Portuguese fascism, 46, 50–51,
    209, 339–340, 342–343, 352,
    355–356, 358
Proudfoot, William, 114

R
Raico and, 21, 318

Raico, Ralph, 9, 21, 29, 67, 78, 167, 208, 271, 291, 318, 322–323, 325–327, 328, 349
Rand, Ayn, 29–31, 36, 68, 70, 181, 229, 246–247, 312–313, 315, 321, 328
Reagan, Ronald, 26, 127, 160, 169, 208, 212, 220, 229–230, 233, 239–240, 280, 285–287
Rees-Mogg, William, 197, 209, 244
Reid, T. R., 289
Review of Austrian Economics, 11, 39, 66
Rickenbacker, William, 211–212, 274, 294
Ridley Report, 220
Ridley, Adam, 219
Ridley, Matthew White, xi, 49, 195, 220–222, 239, 241–242
Ridley, Nicholas, 221
Ripper, William, 166
Road to Serfdom (Hayek), 5, 13, 43, 69, 74, 113, 134, 136, 138, 164–165, 170, 172, 179–181, 203–204, 223, 230, 269, 289–290, 312
Roche, Lissa Jackson, 5
Rockefeller, David, 359
Rockefeller, John D., 291
Rockford Institute, 279
Rockwell, Llewelyn Jr., x, 13, 24, 27, 43, 169, 274, 281, 292, 316, 350–351
Roosevelt, Franklin D., 108, 204
Rothbard, Murray
  "emergency" call for fascism and, 265–266, 271–273, 276, 278–279, 281
  "free market" thought and, 14, 17, 21, 43, 49–50, 181
  "Outreach to the Redneck", 169
  "Ron Paul" newsletter, 169, 316
Ryan, Paul, 205

S
Samuelson, Paul, 25, 345
Scaife, Richard Mellon, 81
Schumpeter, Joseph, viii, 10
Sennholz, Hans, 9, 30, 38, 83, 284
"Setting the Record Straight" (Ebeling), 341
Seven Years' War, 113
Shenoy, Sudha, ix, 10, 25, 33, 47, 65, 166–167, 209, 291, 357–358
Skousen, Mark, x, 46, 196, 271, 310, 344
Slavery, 291
Smith-Stanley, Edward, 115
Smith, Adam, 80–81, 121, 142, 239
Smith, F. E., 34
Smith, Ian, 212, 219
Smith, Vernon, 128
Smith, W. H., 121
Soref, Harold, viii, 46, 120, 196–198, 214–215
Soviet Union, 7, 80, 176, 180, 212, 276, 287, 309
Spanish fascism, 7–8, 46, 50, 283–284, 339–340, 343, 358
Spann, Othmar, 10, 24, 171, 349
Stagflation, 126, 239, 233
Straw, Jack, 221

T
Thatcher, Margaret
  Blunt and, 107, 159
  Churchill and, 217–218
  electoral appeal, 126
  faith-based deregulation, 232
  fall of communism and, 26
  Fourth Man and, 107, 159–160
  Hayek and, 111, 127, 134, 160, 164, 240, 244, 285–286
  Lawson and, 232
  Monckton and, 246–248
  Reagan and, 26, 229

Reform Club and, 107, 109
Ridley and, 219–221
rise to power, 205, 220
Trevor-Roper and, 178
War on Technology, 240
Trump, Donald, ix, 200–202, 242, 281–282, 307, 327–328, 330n1

W

War on Technology, 240
Warfare State, 17, 50, 66, 291, 305
Warhanek, Hans, 132, 133
"We want externalities" chants, 17, 49–50, 81, 195, 244, 278
White supremacism
  American Renaissance organisation, 279
  Caldwell and, 198, 204–205, 215, 223, 229
  Ebeling and, 196, 205, 228, 291–295
  'free' market and, 21, 50, 195, 243, 280, 317
  Italy and, 214–215, 305
  Monday Club, 214
  propaganda, 50, 305
  South Africa and, 195, 214
White supremacism, 195–248
Wieser, Friedrich Freiherr von, 6–8, 10–11, 75, 92–93, 112, 348–349
William Volker Charities Fund, 135
Williams, Thomas Charles, 118
Williams, Walter E., 40–42, 207, 317–318
Wilson, Harold, 123, 127, 227
Wilson, Horace, 107
Wilson, Woodrow, 278
Wolfowitz, Paul, 221
World War I, 6–8, 67, 82, 88, 112, 137, 167, 181, 226, 231, 291
World War II, 3, 50, 122, 207, 210, 227, 235, 266, 291, 326, 328, 329, 339, 341, 358
  Friedman and, 356–357
  See also Hitler, Adolf

Y

Yeager, Leland, 223, 307

CPSIA information can be obtained
at www.ICGtesting.com
Printed in the USA
LVHW01*1213130518
577031LV00012B/585/P